SCOTT FORESMAN · ADDISON WESLEY

Mathematics

Authors

Randall I. Charles

Janet H. Caldwell
Mary Cavanagh
Dinah Chancellor
Alma B. Ramirez

Warren Crown

Jeanne F. Ramos
Kay Sammons
Jane F. Schielack

Francis (Skip) Fennell

William Tate
Mary Thompson
John A. Van de Walle

Consulting Mathematicians

Edward J. Barbeau
Professor of Mathematics
University of Toronto
Toronto, Ontario, Canada

David M. Bressoud
DeWitt Wallace Professor of
   Mathematics
Macalester College
Saint Paul, Minnesota

Gary Lippman
Professor of Mathematics
   and Computer Science
California State University
   Hayward
Hayward, California

PEARSON

Scott
Foresman

Editorial Offices: Glenview, Illinois • Parsippany, New Jersey • New York, New York

Sales Offices: Parsippany, New Jersey • Duluth, Georgia • Glenview, Illinois
Coppell, Texas • Ontario, California • Mesa, Arizona

Reading Consultants

Peter Afflerbach
Professor and Director of The Reading Center
University of Maryland
College Park, Maryland

Donald J. Leu
John and Maria Neag
  Endowed Chair in Literacy and Technology
University of Connecticut
Storrs, Connecticut

Reviewers

Mary Bacon
Mathematics Specialist
East Baton Rouge Parish School
  System
Baton Rouge, Louisiana

Cheryl Baker
Mathematics Teacher
Norton Middle School
Norton, Ohio

Marcelline A. Barron
Curriculum Leader Math and
  Science, K–5
Fairfield Public Schools
Fairfield, Connecticut

Mary Connery-Simmons
Mathematics Specialist
Springfield Public Schools
Springfield, Massachusetts

Anthony C. Dentino
Supervisor of Curriculum
Brick Township Schools
Brick, New Jersey

Dawn Evans
Mathematics Teacher
Bret Harte Elementary School
Chicago, Illinois

Sam Hanson
Teacher
Totem Falls Elementary
Snohomish, Washington

Allison Harris
Professional Development
  School Coach
Seattle Public Schools
Seattle, Washington

Pamela Renee Hill
Teacher
Durham Public Schools
Durham, North Carolina

Catherine Kuhns
Teacher
Country Hills Elementary
Coral Springs, Florida

Madeleine A. Madsen
District Curriculum Resource
Community Consolidated
  School District 59
Arlington Heights, Illinois

Lynda M. Penry
Teacher
Wright Elementary
Ft. Walton Beach, Florida

Deanna P. Rigdon
District Math Curriculum
  Specialist, Grades 3–4
Granite School District
Salt Lake City, Utah

Thomas Romero
Principal
Adams Elementary
Wapato, Washington

Wendy Siegel
Mathematics Coordinator, K–12
Orchard Park Middle School
Orchard Park, New York

Sandra Smith
Teacher
Cheat Lake Elementary
Morgantown, West Virginia

Rochelle A. Solomon
Mathematics Resource Teacher
Cleveland Municipal School
  District
Cleveland, Ohio

Frank L. Sparks
Curriculum Design and Support
  Specialist, Secondary
  Mathematics
New Orleans Public Schools
New Orleans, Louisiana

Beth L. Spivey
Lead Teacher, Elementary
  Mathematics
Wake County Public
  School System
Raleigh, North Carolina

Paula Spomer
Teacher
Chisholm Elementary
Edmond, Oklahoma

Robert Trammel
Math Consultant
Fort Wayne Community Schools
Fort Wayne, Indiana

Annemarie Tuffner
Mathematics Lead Teacher,
  K–12
Neshaminy School District
Langhorne, Pennsylvania

Judy L. Wright
Curriculum and Staff
  Development Specialist
Columbus Public Schools
Columbus, Ohio

Theresa Zieles
Teacher
Indianapolis Public School 88
Indianapolis, Indiana

CHAPTER

1

Numbers, Expressions, and Equations

Instant Check System
- Diagnosing Readiness, 2
- Warm Up, daily
- Talk About It, daily
- Check, daily
- Diagnostic Checkpoint, 23, 39, 57

Test Prep
- Mixed Review and Test Prep, daily
- Test Talk, daily, 58
- Cumulative Review and Test Prep, 64

Reading For Math Success

Reading Helps!
- Reading Helps, 20, 36, 52
- Key Vocabulary and Concept Review, 60

Writing in Math
- Writing in Math exercises, daily

 Problem-Solving Applications, 54

 Discovery SCHOOL Discover Math in Your World, 35

Additional Resources
- Learning with Technology, 43
- Practice Game, 11
- Enrichment, 7, 27, 47, 51
- Chapter 1 Test, 62
- Reteaching, 66
- More Practice, 70

iii

2 Decimals

Instant Check System
- Diagnosing Readiness, 74
- Warm Up, daily
- Talk About It, daily
- Check, daily
- Diagnostic Checkpoint, 85, 105, 123

Test Prep
- Mixed Review and Test Prep, daily
- Test Talk, daily, 124
- Cumulative Review and Test Prep, 130

Reading For Math Success
Reading Helps!
- Reading for Math Success, 114
- Reading Helps, 98, 116
- Key Vocabulary and Concept Review, 126

Writing in Math
- Writing in Math exercises, daily

Problem-Solving Applications, 120

Discover Math in Your World, 103

Additional Resources
- Learning with Technology, 109
- Practice Game, 93
- Enrichment, 89, 97
- Chapter 2 Test, 128
- Reteaching, 132
- More Practice, 136

3 Number Theory and Fraction Concepts

Instant Check System
- Diagnosing Readiness, 140
- Warm Up, daily
- Talk About It, daily
- Check, daily
- Diagnostic Checkpoint, 159, 185

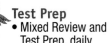

Test Prep
- Mixed Review and Test Prep, daily
- Test Talk, daily, 186
- Cumulative Review and Test Prep, 192

Reading For Math Success
Reading Helps!
- Reading for Math Success, 154
- Reading Helps, 156, 180
- Key Vocabulary and Concept Review, 188

Writing in Math
- Writing in Math exercises, daily

 Problem-Solving Applications, 182

 Discover Math in Your World, 175

Additional Resources
- Learning with Technology, 163, 167
- Enrichment, 145, 149, 179
- Chapter 3 Test, 190
- Reteaching, 194
- More Practice, 198

Adding and Subtracting Fractions

5

Multiplying and Dividing Fractions

Instant Check System
- Diagnosing Readiness, 246
- Warm Up, daily
- Talk About It, daily
- Check, daily
- Diagnostic Checkpoint, 261, 273, 283

Test Prep
- Mixed Review and Test Prep, daily
- Test Talk, daily, 284
- Cumulative Review and Test Prep, 290

Reading Helps!
- Reading for Math Success, 262
- Reading Helps, 264, 278
- Key Vocabulary and Concept Review, 286

Writing in Math
- Writing in Math exercises, daily
- Writing to Explain, 278

Problem-Solving Applications, 280

 Discover Math in Your World, 269

Additional Resources
- Learning with Technology, 255
- Practice Game, 255
- Enrichment, 251
- Chapter 5 Test, 288
- Reteaching, 292
- More Practice, 295

Ratio, Rates, and Proportion

Percent

8 Algebra: Integers and Rational Numbers

Instant Check System
- Diagnosing Readiness, 406
- Warm Up, daily
- Talk About It, daily
- Check, daily
- Diagnostic Checkpoint, 417, 439, 453

Test Prep
- Mixed Review and Test Prep, daily
- Test Talk, daily, 454
- Cumulative Review and Test Prep, 460

Reading For Math Success

Reading Helps!
- Reading for Math Success, 432
- Reading Helps, 414, 434
- Key Vocabulary and Concept Review, 456

Writing in Math
- Writing in Math exercises, daily

 Problem-Solving Applications, 450

 Discover Math in Your World, 421

Additional Resources
- Learning with Technology, 425
- Practice Game, 443
- Chapter 8 Test, 458
- Reteaching, 462
- More Practice, 466

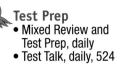
Geometry

Instant Check System
- Diagnosing Readiness, 470
- Warm Up, daily
- Talk About It, daily
- Check, daily
- Diagnostic Checkpoint, 493, 505, 523

Test Prep
- Mixed Review and Test Prep, daily
- Test Talk, daily, 524
- Cumulative Review and Test Prep, 530

Reading For Math Success
Reading Helps!
- Reading for Math Success, 488
- Reading Helps, 490, 512
- Key Vocabulary and Concept Review, 526

Writing in Math
- Writing in Math exercises, daily
- Writing to Compare, 512

 Problem-Solving Applications, 520

Discovery SCHOOL Discover Math in Your World, 479

Additional Resources
- Learning with Technology, 499, 519
- Enrichment, 475, 483, 487, 509
- Chapter 9 Test, 528
- Reteaching, 532
- More Practice, 536

10 Measurement

11

Data, Graphs, and Probability

Algebra: Inequalities, Equations, and Graphs

Instant Check System
- Diagnosing Readiness, 696
- Warm Up, daily
- Talk About It, daily
- Check, daily
- Diagnostic Checkpoint, 709, 727

Test Prep
- Mixed Review and Test Prep, daily
- Test Talk, daily, 728
- Cumulative Review and Test Prep, 734

Reading For Math Success
Reading Helps!
- Reading for Math Success, 704
- Reading Helps, 706, 710
- Key Vocabulary and Concept Review, 730

Writing in Math
- Writing in Math exercises, daily

 Problem-Solving Applications, 724

 Discover Math in Your World, 721

Additional Resources
- Practice Game, 715
- Enrichment, 703
- Chapter 12 Test, 732
- Reteaching, 736
- More Practice, 739

What can help you get higher test scores?
Turn the page to find out.

Test-Taking Strategies

Remember these six test-taking strategies that will help you do well on tests. These strategies are also taught in the Test Talk before each chapter test.

Understand the Question

- **Look for important words.**
- **Turn the question into a statement: "I need to find out..."**

1. Which figure is NOT a parallelogram?

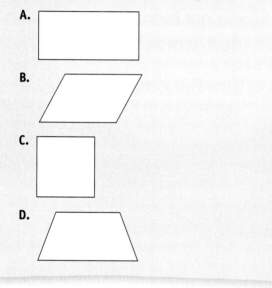

A.

B.

C.

D.

1. What are some important words in the problem that tell you what the problem is about?

2. What important word in the problem is highlighted using capital letters?

3. Turn the question into a statement that begins with "I need to find out . . .."

Get Information for the Answers

- **Get information from text.**
- **Get information from pictures, maps, diagrams, tables, graphs.**

2. Abby is buying a T-shirt from The T-Shirt Shop. She needs to tell the clerk which color and which size she wants. How many color-size combinations does she have to choose from? Explain.

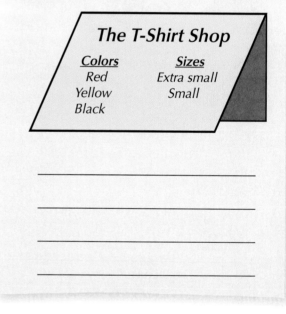

The T-Shirt Shop

Colors	Sizes
Red	Extra small
Yellow	Small
Black	

4. What information from the picture is needed to solve the problem?

5. What information in the text is needed to solve the problem?

Most strategies can be used with any type of test item.

Use the strategy below with multiple-choice test items.

Plan How to Find the Answer

- **Think about problem-solving skills and strategies.**
- **Choose computation methods.**

3. Enya visits her aunt 3 times a week. She lives 2 miles from her aunt's apartment. How many feet is this? (Remember, there are 5,280 feet in a mile.)

A. 1,760 feet

B. 2,640 feet

C. 10,560 feet

D. 15,840 feet

6. Tell how you would use the following problem-solving skills and strategies as you solve the problem.

- Identify extra or missing information.
- Choose an operation.
- Draw a picture.

7. Which of the following computation methods would you use to solve this problem?

- Mental math
- Paper and pencil
- Calculator

Make Smart Choices

- **Eliminate wrong answers.**
- **Try working backward from an answer.**
- **Check answers for reasonableness; estimate.**

4. Mrs. Lawrence bought 12 blank video tapes for a total price of $24.04, which included sales tax of $1.36. What was the price of one tape before tax?

A. $0.11

B. $1.89

C. $2.00

D. $272.16

8. Which answer choices can you eliminate because you are sure they are wrong answers? Explain.

9. How could you work backward from an answer to see if it is correct?

10. How could you estimate the answer? Is the correct answer close to the estimate?

Use these two strategies when you have to write an answer.

Use Writing in Math

- Make your answer brief but complete.
- Use words from the problem and use math terms accurately.
- Describe steps in order.
- Draw pictures if they help you to explain your thinking.

5. The measures of two angles of a triangle are 42° and 87°. Find the measure of the third angle. Explain how you found your answer.

Work space

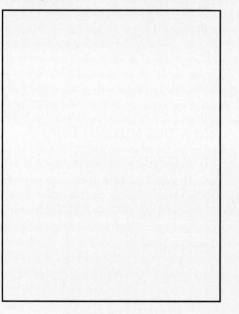

11. What words from the problem will you use in your response?

12. What steps could you describe in your response?

13. How can drawing a picture help you explain your thinking?

Improve Written Answers

- Check if your answer is complete.
- Check if your answer is clear and easy to follow.
- Check if your answer makes sense.

6. The school band is selling cheesecakes to raise money for a trip. The director made a table to show how much money the band makes for selling a certain number of cases of cheesecakes. Teresa sold 5 cases of cheesecakes. How much money did she raise for the band? Explain how you found your answer.

Number of cases	1	2	3	4	5
Money raised	$21.50	$43.00	$64.50	$86.00	

Teresa raised $107.50 for the band.

First I found a pattern in the table. Then I added.

14. Is the answer that is given worth 4 points, using the rubric that is shown on the next page? Explain.

15. If the answer is not worth 4 points, tell how to improve the answer.

Scoring Rubric

4 points

Full credit: 4 points

The answer is correct. A full explanation is given as to how the answer is found.

3 points

Partial credit: 3 points

The answer is correct, but the explanation does not fully explain how the answer was found.

2 points

Partial credit: 2 points

The answer is correct or the explanation is correct, but not both.

1 point

Partial credit: 1 point

A solution is attempted, but the answer is incorrect. The explanation is unclear.

0 points

No credit: 0 points

The solution is completely incorrect or missing.

For more on Test-Taking Strategies, see the following Test Talk pages.

Test-Taking Strategies

Test Prep

As you use your book, look for these features that help you prepare for tests.

Test Talk before each chapter test teaches Test-Taking Strategies.

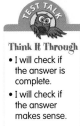

Think It Through
• I will check if the answer is complete.
• I will check if the answer makes sense.

Test Talk: Think It Through within lessons helps you do the kind of thinking you need to do when you take a test.

Mixed Review and Test Prep

Mixed Review and Test Prep at the end of lessons gives you practice with the kind of items on tests.

Take It to the NET Test Prep
www.scottforesman.com

Take It to the Net: Test Prep at the end of lessons offers online test prep.

Cumulative Review and Test Prep

Cumulative Review and Test Prep at the end of chapters helps you remember content you'll need to know when you take tests.

CHAPTER 1

Numbers, Expressions and Equations

DIAGNOSING READINESS

A Vocabulary
(Grade 5)

Choose the best term from the box.

1. __?__ is the multiple of ten telling how much a digit represents.

2. Numbers you add are __?__.

3. The answer to a division problem is the __?__.

4. __?__ are numbers that are multiplied to give a product.

Vocabulary

- addends
- place value
- divisor
- factors
- quotient

B Place Value
(Grade 5)

Write the place of the 5 in each number.

5. 453 **6.** 2,509 **7.** 51,893

8. 1,975 **9.** 95,002 **10.** 583,099

Write the value of each underlined digit.

11. 3,<u>7</u>21 **12.** 65,4<u>0</u>9 **13.** 22,<u>0</u>08

14. 171,03<u>8</u> **15.** <u>1</u>6,000 **16.** <u>9</u>80,320

17. Explain the difference between the two 6s in the number 636,459.

18. How long would it take you to spend a million dollars if you spent $1,000 each day?

Do You Know...

What is the total number of refrigerators, tires, and washing machines that are produced in the world each day?

You will find out in Lesson 1-17.

THE WORLD IN ONE DAY

Every day ... 7 million pizzas are eaten in America ... one human heart pumps enough blood to fill 170 bathtubs ... lightning strikes Earth 8 million times ...

By RUSSELL ASH, *author of* INCREDIBLE COMPARISONS

C Comparing and Ordering Whole Numbers *(Grade 5)*

Use < or > to compare.

19. 32   40   **20.** 18   8

21. 120   98   **22.** 201   102

Order the numbers from least to greatest.

23. 843, 556, 792, 1,038

24. 126, 99, 871, 817

25. 31,521; 31,251; 13,521

26. Melinda had bowling scores of 133, 141, 162, and 128. Order her scores from greatest to least.

D Estimation *(Grade 5)*

Round each number to the place of the first digit. Then estimate each answer.

27. 568 + 932   **28.** 403 − 279

29. 350 + 688 + 421

30. 68 × 9   **31.** 49 × 22

32. 83 ÷ 4   **33.** 611 ÷ 34

34. Explain how you would round 498 to the nearest ten.

35. One month Damien earned $488 and the next month he earned $605. Estimate the difference in the amounts Damien earned.

Key Idea
Our place-value number system is based on 10. Each place is 10 times the place to its right.

Vocabulary
• expanded form

Place Value

LEARN

How can you find the place and value of a digit in a number?

WARM UP
1. 7 × 100
2. 6 × 1,000
3. 9 × 10,000
4. 3 × 1,000,000

Example A

A *light-year* is the distance light travels in one year, or 5,878,000,000,000 miles. Use the place value chart below to identify the place and value of the 7 in 5,878,000,000,000.

Each group of three numbers is called a **period.**

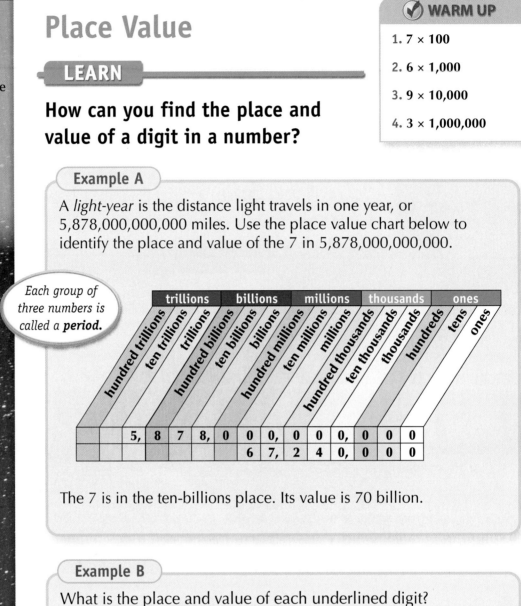

The 7 is in the ten-billions place. Its value is 70 billion.

Example B

What is the place and value of each underlined digit?

26,701,583,460,905

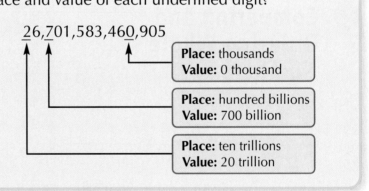

Place: thousands
Value: 0 thousand

Place: hundred billions
Value: 700 billion

Place: ten trillions
Value: 20 trillion

✓ **Talk About It**

1. Find the place and value of the 6 and 4 in the second number in the place-value chart above.

What are some ways to read and write a number?

Example C

Venus is 67,240,000 miles from the sun. The chart on page 4 can help you write this number in different forms.

Standard form: 67,240,000

Word form: sixty-seven million, two hundred forty thousand

Short-word form: 67 million, 240 thousand

Expanded form: $60,000,000 + 7,000,000 + 200,000 + 40,000$
or
$(6 \times 10,000,000) + (7 \times 1,000,000) + (2 \times 100,000) + (4 \times 10,000)$

Example D

Write $(5 \times 10,000,000) + (3 \times 100,000) + (6 \times 10,000) + (2 \times 1,000) + (9 \times 1)$ in standard form.

$50,000,000 + 300,000 + 60,000 + 2,000 + 9$

Standard form: 50,362,009

✔ Talk About It

2. Explain how commas help you read and write numbers.

CHECK ✔

For another example, see Set 1-1 on p. 66.

1. Write the place and value for each underlined digit: 4,536,021,985

Write each number in short-word form and in expanded form.

2. 6,354,000,120,000

3. 77,537,000,320

Write each number in word form and in standard form.

4. $20,000 + 5,000 + 60 + 2$

5. 15 trillion, 450 billion, 89 million, 34

6. Number Sense What does the zero in 62,778,304,525 represent?

A Skills and Understanding

Write the place and value for each underlined digit.

7. 1,36<u>4</u>   **8.** 3<u>5</u>,000,991   **9.** <u>6</u>8,475,325,995,211   **10.** 7,<u>3</u>31,797

Write each number in short-word form.

11. 45,840,331   **12.** 96,000,000,000   **13.** 63,000,121,762,001

Write each number in expanded form in two ways.

14. 206,790,455   **15.** 8,400,000,000   **16.** 92,300,005,600,007

For 17-20, write each number in word form and in standard form.

17. 38 million, 607 thousand, 49   **18.** 110 billion, 6 million

19. (6 × 1,000,000,000) + (3 × 10,000) + (5 × 100)

20. 8,000,000,000,000 + 20,000,000 + 200,000 + 6,000 + 10 + 5

21. Number Sense Explain why the value of each digit in a number depends on its place.

B Reasoning and Problem Solving

Math and Social Studies

22. Which is the first year that shows the population in the billions?

23. Write the value of the 5 in the populations for the years 1600, 1800, and 2000.

24.  **Writing in Math** Is the explanation given below correct? If not, explain.

> Write the place and value of the underlined digit in 678,2<u>5</u>8,400.
>
> The underlined digit is in the thousands place. Its value is 50,000.

Data File

Year	Estimated World Population
1600	579,000,000
1700	679,000,000
1800	954,000,000
1900	1,633,000,000
2000	6,135,000,000

TEST TALK

Think It Through
I know the **value of the digit depends on its place** in the number.

C Extensions

25. Write a number that is between 20 trillion and 21 trillion.

26. Write a number that is greater than 3 trillion and has a 7 in the hundred-billions place, thousands place, and tens place. Do not write a 7 in any of the other places.

Mixed Review and Test Prep

Take It to the NET
Test Prep
www.scottforesman.com

27. Mental Math Find $57 \times 10,000$.   **28. Mental Math** Find $350 \div 70$.

29. $34 + 23$ **30.** $41 + 37$ **31.** $302 + 17$ **32.** $60 + 812$

33. After 8 weeks, Gretchen had saved $36. If she deposited the same amount each week, how much did Gretchen save each week?

   A. $4.00   **B.** $4.50   **C.** $6.50   **D.** $9.00

Enrichment

Roman Numerals

The ancient Romans used letters to represent numbers. The Roman-numeral system is based on addition and subtraction.

ROMAN NUMERALS	I	V	X	L	C	D	M
DECIMAL VALUE	1	5	10	50	100	500	1000

If the value of a letter is greater than or equal to the value of the letter to its right, add.

Write VI and LXII as decimal numbers.

V I
↓ ↓
$5 + 1 = 6$

L X II
↓ ↓ ↓
$50 + 10 + 2 = 62$

If the value of a letter is less than the value of the letter to its right, subtract.

Write IX and CD as decimal numbers.

I X
$10 - 1 = 9$

C D
$500 - 100 = 400$

Many numbers, such as MCMXCVIII, require both adding and subtracting.

M   C M   X C   V III
   1,000 – 100   100 – 10   5 + 3
1,000 +   900   +   90   +   8   = 1,998

Write each Roman numeral as a decimal number.

1. XLIX   **2.** MMDCCXXIII   **3.** XCVIII   **4.** CCCLXXXIX

5. CCXIX   **6.** MCMIII   **7.** DCLV   **8.** LVIII

Write each number as a Roman numeral.

9. 84   **10.** 254   **11.** 2,114   **12.** 99   **13.** 2,007   **14.** 831

Algebra

Key Idea
Exponents are used to show the number of times a factor is repeated.

Vocabulary
- exponential form
- base
- exponent
- power
- expanded form (p. 4)
- squared
- cubed
- expanded form using exponents

Exponents

LEARN

Activity

What is the pattern?

a. Copy the table below.

b. Fold a sheet of paper in half and record the number of sections you see when unfolded. Continue folding the paper in half 5 more times. Record the number of sections each time.

Number of Folds	Number of Sections	Number of 2s
1	2	1
2	$2 \times 2 = 4$	2
3	$2 \times 2 \times 2 = 8$	3
4	$\times \quad \times \quad \times \quad = ?$	
5		
6		

c. How many sections will there be after 7 folds? 8 folds?

d. Describe any patterns you see in the table.

After 3 folds there are $2 \times 2 \times 2$ sections. You can write $2 \times 2 \times 2$ in **exponential form** as 2^3. The **base** is the repeated factor. The **exponent** or **power** tells how many times the base is used as a factor.

$$\underbrace{2 \times 2 \times 2}_{3 \text{ factors}} = 2^{\overset{\text{exponent}}{3}} \quad \underset{\text{base}}{\uparrow}$$

2^3 is the third power of 2.

You can write the product of repeated factors in three ways.

Expanded form using factors: $2 \times 2 \times 2 \times 2 \times 2$ or $2 \cdot 2 \cdot 2 \cdot 2 \cdot 2$

> A raised dot ($\cdot$) has the same meaning as the symbol $\times$.

Exponential form: 2^5

Standard form: 32

✔ Talk About It

1. Number Sense Write $5 \cdot 5 \cdot 5$ in exponential form and standard form.

How do you read and evaluate numbers in exponential form?

Example A

How do you read 7^2 and 5^3?

7^2 is read "seven to the second power" or "seven **squared**."

5^3 is read "five to the third power" or "five **cubed**."

Example B

Evaluate 8^2.

One Way
$8^2 = 8 \times 8 = 64$.

Another Way
Use a calculator.

Press: 8 $\boxed{y^x}$ 2 $\boxed{=}$

Display: $\boxed{64}$

✔ **Talk About It**

2. **Reasoning** What is the standard form of 8^1? Of any number to the first power?

How can you write a number in expanded form using exponents?

Example C

Write 78,045 in expanded form using exponents.

Expanded form: $(7 \times 10,000) + (8 \times 1,000) + (4 \times 10) + 5$

Expanded form using exponents: $(7 \times 10^4) + (8 \times 10^3) + (4 \times 10^1) + (5 \times 10^0)$

Notice the patterns with the powers of 10 in Example C.
Any nonzero number raised to the zero power is 1.

✔ **Talk About It**

3. How many zeros are in 10^9 when it is in standard form?

Take It to the NET
More Examples
www.scottforesman.com

CHECK ✔   *For another example, see Set 1-2 on p. 66.*

1. What are two ways to read 6^3?

2. Write 6^3 as a product and then evaluate.

3. Write $15 \times 15 \times 15 \times 15 \times 15 \times 15$ in exponential form.

4. Write 35,402 in expanded form using exponents.

5. **Number Sense** Are 2^5 and 5^2 equal? Explain why or why not.

A Skills and Understanding

6. What are two ways to read 30^2?

Write each power as a product and then evaluate.

7. 7^3 **8.** 5^4 **9.** 10^6 **10.** 12^2 **11.** 8^3 **12.** 11^2

Write each expression in exponential form.

13. $2 \times 2 \times 2 \times 2$ **14.** 4×4 **15.** $5 \times 5 \times 5 \times 5$

16. $8 \times 8 \times 8$ **17.** $10 \times 10 \times 10 \times 10$ **18.** $7 \times 7 \times 7 \times 7 \times 7$

19. $6 \times 6 \times 6 \times 6 \times 6$ **20.** $9 \cdot 9 \cdot 9 \cdot 9 \cdot 9 \cdot 9 \cdot 9$ **21.** $23 \times 23 \times 23 \times 23$

22. $12 \times 12 \times 12 \times 12 \times 12$ **23.** 87 squared   **24.** fifteen cubed

25. the fourth power of 6   **26.** the sixth power of 4

Write each number in expanded form using exponents.

27. 78,552   **28.** 481,366   **29.** 12,224,394

30. Is 3^4 equal to 9^2? Explain why or why not.

31. Reasoning What is the value of 1^{102}? What is the value of 1 raised to any power?

B Reasoning and Problem Solving

Math and Science

32. Under certain conditions, an *E. coli* cell will divide every 20 minutes to make 2 cells. How many *E. coli* cells will there be after 4 hours?

33. Certain skin cells quadruple each hour. Start with one cell. Write in exponential form the number of cells that could exist after 10 hours.

34. Humans can distinguish up to 18,400,000 individual dots called pixels on a typical computer display. Can a human distinguish pixels on a same-sized HDTV with 2×10^6 pixels? Explain.

E. coli bacteria cell

35. **Writing in Math** Is the answer below correct? If not, tell why and write a correct response.

> Write 60,528 in expanded form using exponents.
> $(6 \times 10^3) + (5 \times 10^2) + (2 \times 10^1) + (8 \times 10^0)$

C Extensions

Calculator Use a calculator to evaluate.

36. 27^2 **37.** 12^3 **38.** 6^5 **39.** 2^{10} **40.** 10^7 **41.** 90^4

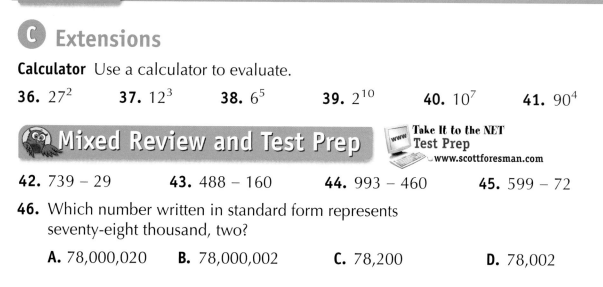

Mixed Review and Test Prep

Take It to the NET
Test Prep
www.scottforesman.com

42. $739 - 29$ **43.** $488 - 160$ **44.** $993 - 460$ **45.** $599 - 72$

46. Which number written in standard form represents seventy-eight thousand, two?

A. 78,000,020 **B.** 78,000,002 **C.** 78,200 **D.** 78,002

Practice Game

Billionaire

Players: 2

Materials: 2 number cubes, place-value chart

1. Each player needs a place-value chart like the one shown above.

2. Players take turns tossing 2 number cubes and writing the tossed numbers in any of the empty place-value cells of their chart.

3. Players read their numbers aloud and compare them.

4. The player with the greater number wins the round. The first player to win 5 rounds wins the game.

Variation: The player with the lesser number wins the round.

The place-value chart reads: billions (hundred billions, ten billions, billions), millions (hundred millions, ten millions, millions), thousands (hundred thousands, ten thousands, thousands), ones (hundreds, tens, ones).

 All text pages available online and on CD-ROM.

Key Idea
Place value is used to compare and order numbers.

Comparing and Ordering Whole Numbers

LEARN

How can you compare and order numbers?

Example A

Compare the height of Lhotse to the height of Makalu.

STEP 1	Write the numbers, lining up places. Begin at the left and compare.	**27,920** 27,790
STEP 2	Find the first place where the digits are different and compare.	27,**9**20 27,**7**90

Since 9 > 7, 27,920 > 27,790.

The height of Lhotse is greater than the height of Makalu.

Data File

Himalayan Mountain	Height (ft)
Dhaulagiri I	26,810
Everest	29,035
Kanchenjunga	28,208
Lhotse	27,920
Makalu	27,790

TEST TALK

Think It Through
I can compare two numbers with the same number of digits **by starting at the left and moving right** until I come to a pair of digits that **do not have the same value.**

Example B

Order the heights of the first three mountains in the Data File from least to greatest.

STEP 1	Write the numbers, lining up places. Compare.	26,810 29,035 ← greatest 28,208
STEP 2	Write the remaining numbers, lining up places. Compare.	26,810 28,208 ← greater
STEP 3	Write the numbers from least to greatest.	26,810 28,208 29,035

In order from least to greatest, the heights are 26,810, 28,208, and 29,035.

✓ Talk About It

1. Explain how to compare two whole numbers that do not have the same number of digits.

Use < or > to compare.

1. 5,532   5,523   **2.** 62,889   104,772   **3.** 76,501   76,498

4. Order 35,002,010; 35,001,950; and 35,001,999 from least to greatest.

5. Number Sense Is any 4-digit whole number greater than any 3-digit whole number? Explain.

PRACTICE

For more practice, see Set 1-3 on p. 70.

Ⓐ Skills and Understanding

Use < or > to compare.

6. 783   2,001   **7.** 201,053   200,855   **8.** 4,619   4,618

9. 5,856   5,860   **10.** 1,211   1,121   **11.** 569,120   596,120

For 12–15, order the numbers from least to greatest.

12. 7,800; 778; 8,878; 7,798   **13.** 97,580; 96,850; 97,500; 69,900

14. 3,120,000; 3,101,001; 3,099,999   **15.** 2 billion, 300; 290 thousand; 10 million

16. Number Sense Write three numbers that are between 23,455,700 and 23,455,789.

Ⓑ Reasoning and Problem Solving

For 17–19, use the Data File.

17. Which populations were greater than 20 million in 2000?

18. For which cities did the population increase more than 5 million from 1990 to 2000?

19. **Writing in Math** Explain how you can tell which city's population increased the least from 1990 to 2000.

Data File

Populations of World's Largest Urban Areas		
City	1990	2000
Tokyo/Yokohama	27,250,000	29,970,000
Mexico City	20,900,000	27,870,000
Sao Paulo	18,700,000	25,350,000
Seoul	16,800,000	21,980,000
New York	14,600,000	14,650,000

Mixed Review and Test Prep

Take It to the NET
Test Prep
www.scottforesman.com

Evaluate each expression.

20. 11^2 **21.** $5 \times 5 \times 5 \times 5$ **22.** 10^7 **23.** six cubed

24. Give the standard form for 50 million, 3 thousand, 8.

     A. 50,030,080   **B.** 50,003,008   **C.** 50,003,800   **D.** 50,003,080

Key Idea
There are times when an exact amount is not needed.

Vocabulary
• round

Materials
• number lines

Rounding Whole Numbers

---**LEARN**---

How do you round a number?

On November 25, 2001, a website said the U. S. population was 285,610,627 and the world population was 6,185,538,778.

Example A

Draw a number line that shows how to round 285,610,627 to the nearest ten thousand.

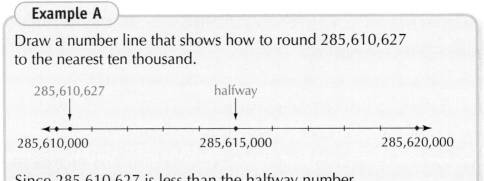

Since 285,610,627 is less than the halfway number, it rounds to 285,610,000.

Example B

Round 285,610,627 to the nearest ten million and nearest ten thousand.

Use these four steps to **round** numbers.	To the nearest **10,000,000**	To the nearest **10,000**
STEP 1 Find the rounding place.	2<u>8</u>5,610,627	285,6<u>1</u>0,627
STEP 2 Look at the digit to the right of this place.	28 <u>5</u> ,610,627	285,61 <u>0</u> ,627
STEP 3 If this digit is 5 or greater, add 1 to the rounding digit. If the digit is less than 5, leave the rounding digit alone.	Since the digit is 5, add 1 to 8. The number is "rounded up."	Since the digit is 0, leave 1 alone. The number is "rounded down."
STEP 4 Change all digits to the right of the rounding digit to zeros.	290,000,000	285,610,000

✔ **Talk About It**

1. Round the world's population on November 25, 2001, to the nearest billion and nearest million.

Round each number to the underlined place.

1. 3,101,9<u>2</u>2   **2.** 45,6<u>9</u>9,825   **3.** 895,7<u>7</u>4   **4.** 6,49<u>8</u>,555

5. Number Sense Write three numbers that round to 5,600 when rounded to the nearest *hundred*.

PRACTICE

For more practice, see Set 1-4 on p. 70.

Ⓐ Skills and Understanding

Round each number to the underlined place.

6. <u>6</u>,808,386   **7.** 5<u>2</u>,799,335   **8.** 195,<u>8</u>21   **9.** <u>9</u>,443,647

10. 7,00<u>9</u>,765,345   **11.** 1,<u>5</u>28   **12.** 7<u>1</u>,635,231   **13.** 1,072,<u>4</u>00

14. 9<u>6</u>,875   **15.** 52,147,0<u>2</u>3   **16.** <u>9</u>36   **17.** <u>2</u>27,849

18. Number Sense Write three numbers that round to 75,700,000 when rounded to the nearest ten thousand.

Ⓑ Reasoning and Problem Solving

In 2000, the number of arrivals and departures at O'Hare Airport was reported as 72,000,000 and as 72,136,000.

19. Write three numbers that would round to 72,000,000 when rounded to the nearest million.

20. Draw a number line that shows how to round 72,136,000 to the nearest million.

21. Round each number in the table to the nearest thousand.

22. Round the enrollment number of elementary students to the nearest hundred thousand.

23. **Writing in Math** Describe a situation in which it would be better to round to the greater number rather than to the lesser number.

Data File

Chicago Public Schools, 2001
Enrollment of Students

Preschool	19,067
Kindergarten	33,733
Elementary	283,755
High School	96,189

🦉 Mixed Review and Test Prep

Take It to the NET
Test Prep
www.scottforesman.com

24. Order 9,781; 9,178; 917; 9,187 and 8,971 from least to greatest.

25. Which of the following is NOT true?

A. $1^3 = 1 \times 1 \times 1$ **B.** $5^2 = 5 \times 2$ **C.** $3^3 = 27$ **D.** Three squared is 9.

Key Idea
You can estimate the sums and differences of whole numbers in a variety of ways.

Vocabulary
- estimate
- round (p. 14)
- clustering
- front-end estimation
- front-end estimation with adjusting

Think It Through

I **remember** that the symbol "≈" means "is approximately equal to" or "is about."

Estimating Sums and Differences

LEARN

How can you estimate sums and differences of whole numbers?

✔ **WARM UP**

Round 634,998,050 to the indicated place.

1. hundreds

2. 10-thousands

3. 100-thousands

4. 100-millions

Example A

Estimate 5,824 − 298.

The numbers do not have the same number of digits. So **round** each number to the greatest place of the lesser number.

5,824 − 298
   ↓   ↓
5,800 − 300 = 5,500

So, 5,824 − 298 ≈ 5,500.

Example B

Estimate 412 + 398 + 385 + 409.

You can use **clustering** to estimate when the numbers are close to the same number.

The numbers below are all close to 400.

412 + 398 + 385 + 409
 ↓   ↓   ↓   ↓
400 + 400 + 400 + 400 = 1,600

So, 412 + 398 + 385 + 409 ≈ 1,600.

Example C

Estimate 6,829 + 3,401.

You can use **front-end estimation** to get a rough estimate. Add only the first digits that have the same place value.

6,829 + 3,401
 ↓   ↓
6,000 + 3,000 = 9,000

6,829 + 3,401 ≈ 9,000 using front-end estimation.

You can use **front-end estimation with adjusting** to get a better estimate.

829 + 401   After adding the front-end
 ↓   ↓   digits, add the hundreds.
800 + 400 = 1,200

9,000 + 1,200 = 10,200   Adjust the front-end estimate by adding 1,200.

6,829 + 3,401 ≈ 10,200.

✔ Talk About It

1. Estimate the answer to Example C by rounding. Which estimate is more accurate? Explain.

Estimate each answer. Tell which method you used.

1. 668 + 4,329   **2.** 5,092 − 847   **3.** 774 + 802 + 815 + 785 + 798

4. 919 − 56   **5.** 4,632 − 4,018   **6.** 578 + 389 + 402 + 83

7. Reasoning Estimate 67,076 − 5,821 by rounding. Explain why both numbers should be rounded to the nearest thousand.

PRACTICE

For more practice, see Set 1-5 on p. 71.

Ⓐ Skills and Understanding

Estimate each answer. Tell which method you used.

8. 382 + 2,109   **9.** 781 − 37   **10.** 38,249 + 22,943

11. 38 + 43 + 37 + 44 + 36   **12.** 804 − 311   **13.** 486 + 22

14. 73,487 − 38,932   **15.** 734 − 482   **16.** 27,364 − 8,936

17. 678 − 323   **18.** 706 + 698 + 712   **19.** 99,743 − 11,236

20. Reasoning An estimate for 389 + 345 + 397 is 900. Is the estimate high or low? Explain.

Ⓑ Reasoning and Problem Solving

The table shows weekly U.S. ticket sales for some films.

21. Estimate the difference in weekly U.S. ticket sales for films C and D.

22. Estimate the sum of the two films that had the greatest weekly ticket sales.

23. Estimate the total ticket sales for all films.

24. **Writing in Math** Explain how you would use front-end estimation with adjusting to estimate 5,892 + 3,204 + 338 + 1,116.

Data File

Film	Weekly U.S. Ticket Sales
A	$11,863,363
B	$2,804,539
C	$9,620,254
D	$4,098,007
E	$13,352,905
F	$10,780,865

Mixed Review and Test Prep

Take It to the NET
Test Prep
www.scottforesman.com

Round each number to the underlined place.

25. 9̲8,036   **26.** 4̲32,128,973   **27.** 1,25̲7   **28.** 5̲0,319

29. Write 5 × 5 × 5 × 5 × 5 in exponential form.

    A. 25   **B.** 5 × 5   **C.** 5^5 **D.** 125

Key Idea
You can estimate
the products
and quotients
of whole numbers
in a variety of ways.

Vocabulary
• compatible
  numbers
• range

Estimating Products and Quotients

| LEARN |

How can you estimate products and quotients?

You can estimate either a product or a quotient by first rounding each number to its greatest place value and then computing.

Example A	Example B
Estimate 8,659 × 122.	Estimate 588 ÷ 29.
8,659 × 122	**588 ÷ 29**
↓ ↓	↓ ↓
9,000 × 100	600 ÷ 30
900,000	20
So, 8,659 × 122 ≈ 900,000.	So, 588 ÷ 29 ≈ 20.

You can estimate by using **compatible numbers,** which are close to the actual numbers, but are easier to compute with.

Example C	Example D
Estimate 24 × 41.	Estimate 362 ÷ 48.
24 × 41 24 is close to 25.	**362 ÷ 48** 362 is close to 350.
↓ ↓ 41 is close to 40.	↓ ↓ 48 is close to 50.
25 × 40	350 ÷ 50
1,000	7
So, 24 × 41 ≈ 1,000.	So, 362 ÷ 48 ≈ 7.

You can estimate by finding a **range**. When you find a range, the exact answer is between two estimates.

Example E

Estimate 342 × 687.

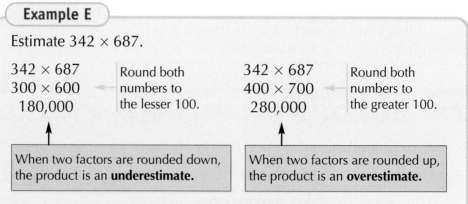

342 × 687   Round both numbers to the lesser 100.
300 × 600
  180,000

342 × 687   Round both numbers to the greater 100.
400 × 700
  280,000

When two factors are rounded down, the product is an **underestimate.**

When two factors are rounded up, the product is an **overestimate.**

So, the product 342 × 687 is between 180,000 and 280,000.

✔ Talk About It

1. Estimate the quotient in Example D by rounding the divisor and dividend. Which estimate is more accurate? Why?

For another example, see Set 1-6 on p. 67.

Estimate each answer. Tell which method you used.

1. $562 \times 9,031$ **2.** $638 \div 72$ **3.** $5,893 \div 301$ **4.** $489 \times 2,970$

5. Number Sense Give an example of an overestimate and an underestimate for $186 \times 4,900$. Which is closer to the actual product?

PRACTICE

For more practice, see Set 1-6 on p. 71.

Ⓐ Skills and Understanding

Estimate each answer. Tell which method you used.

6. $6,238 \div 76$ **7.** $4,892 \times 436$ **8.** $24,387 \div 6,751$ **9.** $26,437 \div 786$

10. 912×82 **11.** $351 \div 38$ **12.** $798 \div 87$ **13.** 684×52

14. 456×723 **15.** $5,473 \times 407$ **16.** $3,736 \times 6,337$ **17.** $46,932 \div 7,498$

18. Number Sense Give an example of an overestimate and an underestimate for $6,832 \times 934$. Which is closer to the actual product?

Ⓑ Reasoning and Problem Solving

The table lists some famous bridges with the lengths of their main spans.

19. Which bridge's length is about three times that of the Brooklyn Bridge?

20. Estimate the difference in lengths of the two New York bridges.

21. **Writing in Math** Ann used compatible numbers to find that $285 \div 8$ is between 30 and 40. Explain what she did.

Data File

Bridge	Length (m)
George Washington Bridge, NY	1,067
Golden Gate Bridge, CA	1,280
Brooklyn Bridge, NY	486
Delaware Memorial, DE	655

🦉 Mixed Review and Test Prep

Take It to the NET Test Prep
www.scottforesman.com

22. Write 682,403 in expanded notation using exponents.

23. Evaluate 6^4.

24. Which is the best estimate for $58 + 63 + 59 + 60$?

A. 400 **B.** 240 **C.** 200 **D.** 180

All text pages available online and on CD-ROM.

Problem-Solving Skill

Reading Helps!

Identifying steps in a process

can help you with...

the *Read and Understand* phase of the problem-solving process.

Key Idea
Read and Understand is the first phase of the problem-solving process

Read and Understand

LEARN

What steps can help you get started with solving a problem?

Dogs, Cats, and their Owners
About how many more cats than dogs were there in the year 2000?

Number of Dogs, Cats, and their Owners in the United States, 2000	
Dogs	59,000,000
Dog Owners	38,000,000
Cats	75,000,000
Cat Owners	35,000,000
Both Dog and Cat Owners	16,000,000

Actual figures have been rounded to the nearest million.

Read and Understand

Step 1: What do you know?

- Tell what you know about the problem in your own words.

- Identify key facts and details.

Compare the number of cats to the number of dogs in the year 2000.

- Number of cats: 75,000,000
- Number of dogs: 59,000,000

Step 2: What are you trying to find?

- Tell what the question is asking.

- Show the main idea.

Find how many more cats than dogs there were in 2000.

75,000,000 cats	
59,000,000 dogs	?

Use subtraction to compare.

Number of cats → | Number of dogs → | Difference →

$75,000,000 - 59,000,000 = 16,000,000$

✔ Talk About It

1. Give the answer to the problem, Dogs, Cats, and their Owners, in a complete sentence.

For another example, see Set 1-7 on p. 67.

CHECK ✓

For Problems 1–3, use the Cats and their Owners problem.

1. **Step 1:** What do you know?

   a. Tell what you know about the problem in your own words.

   b. Identify key facts and details.

2. **Step 2:** What are you trying to find?

   a. Tell what the question is asking.

   b. Show the main idea.

3. Use estimation to solve the problem.

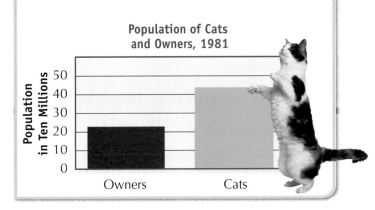

Cats and their Owners In 1981, there were about 22,688,000 cat owners and 44,579,000 cats. About how many cats did each cat owner have?

Population of Cats and Owners, 1981

PRACTICE

For more practice, see Set 1-7 on p. 71.

For Problems 4–6, use the Cats and Dogs problem.

4. **Step 1:** What do you know?

   a. Tell what you know about the problem in your own words.

   b. Identify key facts and details.

5. **Step 2:** What are you trying to find?

   a. Tell what the question is asking.

   b. Show the main idea.

6. Solve the problem and write your answer in a complete sentence.

Cats and Dogs From 1996 to 2000, did the number of dogs or the number of cats increase more? How much more was the increase for one than the other?

Cats and Dogs in U.S. Households, to Nearest Million

Year	1996	1997	1998	1999	2000
Cats	68	70	71	73	75
Dogs	56	56	58	58	59

7. How many bags of Chewy Morsels could fit in a bag of Chewy Chunks?

8. Libby eats Cat's Meow food, which comes in 3-ounce cans. If Libby eats 1 can of Cat's Meow a day, how many ounces does she eat in 30 days?

9. Dr. Terry sees about 120 pets per week. Estimate the number of pets he sees in a year (52 weeks).

Chewy Chunks
48 oz.

Chewy Morsels
4 oz.

All text pages available online and on CD-ROM.

Do You Know How?

Do You Understand?

Place Value (1-1)

Write the place and value for each underlined digit.

1. 76,30$\underline{7}$,195

2. $\underline{1}$2,375,403,275

3. Write 34,003,931 in expanded form.

A Tell how you found the value of the 7 in Exercise 1.

B Explain how you write a number containing zeros in expanded form.

Exponents (1-2)

Write as a product and then evaluate.

4. 6^3 5. 15^2 6. $7 \cdot 7 \cdot 7$

C Tell how you evaluated 6^3.

Comparing and Ordering Whole Numbers (1-3)

Use < or > to compare.

7. 3,472 ⬤ 3,481

8. Order 4,950,000; 4,951,000, and 4,949,999 from least to greatest.

D In Exercise 7, tell which digit helped you find the greater number and why.

E Tell how you ordered the numbers in Exercise 8.

Rounding Whole Numbers (1-4)

In 9–10, round to the underlined place.

9. $\underline{4}$8,956   10. 1,2$\underline{0}$3,349

F Tell how you rounded the number in Exercise 9.

Estimating Sums and Differences of (1-5) Estimating Products and Quotients (1-6)

Estimate. Tell which method you used.

11. 5,913 − 3,135   12. 58 × 382

13. 4,320 ÷ 72   14. 2,142 + 3,906

G Use another method for Exercise 14. Which method gives a better estimate?

Problem-Solving Skill: Read and Understand (1-7)

Solve the problem.

15. The Taubner family buys 3 gallons of milk every week. How many gallons of milk does the family buy in a year?

H Tell what you know about the problem. Identify key facts and details.

I Tell what the question is asking.

MULTIPLE CHOICE

1. Which shows 274,956 rounded to the nearest thousand? (1-4)

A. 300,000   **B.** 275,000   **C.** 274,000   **D.** 270,000

2. Which number sentence is NOT true? (1-3)

A. 2,304 < 2,340   **B.** 587 > 578   **C.** 1,001 > 1,010   **D.** 199 > 190

FREE RESPONSE

Write the place and value for each underlined digit. (1-1)

3. 2<u>7</u>4,963   **4.** 25<u>8</u>   **5.** 1,<u>2</u>03,547,386

Write in exponential form and then evaluate. (1-2)

6. $6 \times 6 \times 6 \times 6$ **7.** 8 squared   **8.** four to the fourth power

9. Write 35,092 in expanded form using exponents. (1-2)

Write the numbers in order from least to greatest. (1-3)

10. 2,507; 563; 2,499; 2,057   **11.** 359, 387, 298, 342

Round each number to the underlined place. (1-4)

12. 58,<u>6</u>83   **13.** 7<u>8</u>1   **14.** 12,3<u>6</u>3,192   **15.** 4,<u>9</u>97

Estimate each answer. Tell which method you used. (1-5, 1-6)

16. 5,721 + 6,398   **17.** 2,812 ÷ 38   **18.** 42 × 287   **19.** 78,158 − 6,842

For Problems 20–22, use the U.S. Waterfalls problem. (1-7)

U.S. Waterfalls Estimate the difference between the height of Ribbon Falls, which is 1,612 feet and Widows' Tears, which is 1,170 feet.

TEST TALK

Think It Through
I should **reread a problem to make sure I answer the right question.**

20. What do you know? What are you trying to find?

21. What is the main idea?

22. Solve the problem.

Writing in Math

23. Explain how to use front-end estimation to estimate 21,325 + 5,687. (1-5)

24. Explain why 5^3 does not equal 3^5. (1-2)

Order of Operations

LEARN

Which operation should you perform first?

Scientific and nonscientific calculators can give different answers for **numerical expressions** such as $10 + 5 \times 3$.

Jared used a nonscientific calculator.

$10 \boxed{+} 5 \boxed{\times} 3 \boxed{\text{ENTER} =}$ **45**

Alanna used a scientific calculator.

$10 \boxed{+} 5 \boxed{\times} 3 \boxed{=}$ **25**

The nonscientific calculator that Jared used added first and then multiplied. The scientific calculator that Alanna used multiplied first and then added.

To make sure everyone gets the same answer to a problem, mathematicians use a set of rules called **order of operations.** Scientific calculators follow these steps.

Order of Operations

1. Compute inside parentheses first.

2. Evaluate terms with exponents.

3. Multiply and divide from left to right.

4. Add and subtract from left to right.

When you follow the order of operations to evaluate $10 + 5 \times 3$, you first multiply the 5 and 3 and then add 10.

Example A

Evaluate $15 + (16 - 7) \div 3$.

One Way

$15 + (16 - 7) \div 3$ ← Compute inside parentheses first.
$15 + \quad 9 \quad \div 3$
$15 \quad + \quad 3$ ← Next, divide.
$\quad\quad 18$ ← Then add.

Another Way

With a scientific calculator:

Press: 15 ⊞ ⬚(16 ⊟ 7 ⬚) ⊞÷ 3 ⊟=

Display: 18

Example B

Evaluate $36 - 8 \times 4 + 3^3$.

One Way

$36 - 8 \times 4 + 3^3$
$36 - 8 \times 4 + 27$ ← Simplify exponents first.
$36 - \quad 32 \quad + 27$ ← Then multiply.
$\quad\quad\quad 4 + 27$ ← Next, subtract.
$\quad\quad\quad\quad 31$ ← Then add.

Another Way

With a scientific calculator:

Press: 36 ⊟ 8 ×⬚ 4 ⊞ 3 y^x 3 ⊟=

Display: 31

Example C

Where would you insert parentheses to make $36 \div 9 \times 4 + 1 = 2$ a true sentence?

Divide first. Then compute from left to right.	Add first. Then compute from left to right.	Multiply first. Then compute from left to right.
$(36 \div 9) \times 4 + 1$	$36 \div 9 \times (4 + 1)$	$36 \div (9 \times 4) + 1$
$4 \quad \times 4 + 1$	$36 \div 9 \times \quad 5$	$36 \div \quad 36 \quad + 1$
$16 \ + 1$	$4 \quad \times \quad 5$	$1 \quad\quad + 1$
17	20	$2 \quad$ It works!

✔ Talk About It

1. Use parentheses to make $18 - 2 \times 3 - 3 = 18$ a true sentence.

2. Reasoning Explain why $5 \times 3 + 4^2$ does not equal 95.

Take It to the NET
More Examples
www.scottforesman.com

CHECK ✔

For another example, see Set 1-8 on p. 67.

Evaluate each expression.

1. $4 + 9 \times 6 - 3$ **2.** $(72 \div 8) \times 2 + 7$ **3.** $62 - (5 \times 4) \div 2$

Use parentheses to make each sentence true.

4. $9 \times 3 + 4 = 63$ **5.** $5 - 1 \times 8 \div 4 = 8$ **6.** $200 \div 4 \times 5 = 10$

7. Number Sense Wendy entered $16 + 3 \times 8 - 4$ into her calculator. The display showed 36. In what order did the calculator compute?

For more practice, see Set 1-8 on p. 71.

Ⓐ Skills and Understanding

Evaluate each expression.

8. $4^2 - 3 \times 2$

9. $(3^2 + 4) \times 5$

10. $5 \times 3 - 3 + 1$

11. $2 + 9 \div 3 \times 2$

12. $64 \div (3 + 5) \times 9$

13. $19 - 5 \times 3 - 2$

14. $(14 + 6) \times 4 \times 5$

15. $5 \times (3 - 3) + 1$

16. $57 - 6 \times (48 \div 12)$

17. $9 - 2^3 + 4$

18. $7 - 3 \times 2 + 9$

19. $6^2 \times (4 \div 2)$

20. $8 + 6 - 2 \times 2 - 3^2$

21. $27 \div (7 + 2) \times (2 + 3)$

22. $14 - 4 \cdot 3 - 2$

Use parentheses to make each sentence true.

23. $4 - 3 \times 7 = 7$

24. $7 \times 0 + 8 = 56$

25. $3^2 - 6 \times 3 = 9$

26. $16 + 2^2 - 5 + 3 = 12$

27. $8^2 + 5 \times 4 \div 2^2 = 69$

28. $7 \times 4 - 2 + 1 = 21$

29. Reasoning Do you need to use order of operations to decide what to compute first in the expression $12 + 8 + 34$? Explain.

Ⓑ Reasoning and Problem Solving

30. Karissa bought 3 pairs of gloves and used a $2 coupon toward the total. Tax on the purchase was $1. Her father paid half the total cost. Write an expression to show the amount Karissa paid.

31. Number Sense Use the symbols $+, -, \times, \div$ to make the number sentence true.

$8 \quad 3 \quad (6 \quad 5) = 4$

32. <u>Writing in Math</u> Is C.J.'s explanation below correct? If not, tell why and write a correct explanation.

> Evaluate $24 \div 4 \times 2$.
>
> I multiplied 4 by 2 and got 8.
> Then I divided 24 by 8 and got 3.
> So, $24 \div 4 \times 2 = 3$.

Think It Through
I should **use order of operations** to evaluate the expression.

Ⓒ Extensions

33. The number 12 can be computed using exactly five 2s: $2 \times 2 \times 2 + 2 \times 2$. Use exactly five 2s to write numerical expressions for the numbers 1 through 10.

Mixed Review and Test Prep

Take It to the NET
www **Test Prep**
www.scottforesman.com

For 34–35, use the Savings problem.

Savings Mario had a certain amount of money in his savings account on Monday. Tuesday he withdrew $45 and was left with $96 in the account. How much was in Mario's account on Monday?

34. Identify key facts and details.　　**35.** Solve the problem.

36. Which number shows 28,375,936 rounded to the nearest million?

　　A. 30,000,000　　**B.** 29,000,000　　**C.** 28,000,000　　**D.** 20,000,000

Enrichment

Binary Numbers

Because computers are internally limited to using two digits, 0 and 1, they use the **binary** number system. In the binary system, each place is 2 times the place to its right.

		Powers of 2				
		2^4	2^3	2^2	2^1	2^0
Base 10 Number	Binary Number	16	8	4	2	1
1	1_{two}					1×2^0
2	10_{two}				1×2^1	0×2^0
3	11_{two}				1×2^1	1×2^0
4	100_{two}			1×2^2	0×2^1	0×2^0
5	101_{two}			1×2^2	0×2^1	1×2^0

This table shows you how to write whole numbers 1 through 5 as binary numbers. A binary number is written with a subscripted "two" to distinguish it from a decimal number.

$$1101_{two} = (1 \times 2^3) + (1 \times 2^2) + (0 \times 2^1) + (1 \times 2^0)$$
$$= (1 \times 8) + (1 \times 4) + (0 \times 2) + (1 \times 1)$$
$$= 8 + 4 + 0 + 1$$
$$= 13$$

To write a binary number as a decimal number, first write the binary number in expanded notation. Then write the standard form.

Write the decimal number for each binary number and the binary number for each decimal number.

1. 11111_{two} 　　　　**2.** 101110_{two} 　　　　**3.** 1100101_{two}

4. 9 　　　　**5.** 28 　　　　**6.** 50

You can create other number systems by changing the place-value pattern. Making each place five times the value of the place to its right will allow you to write numbers in the base 5 system.

7. Write 239 in base 5.　　**8.** What does 4444_{five} equal in base 10?

Algebra

Key Idea
Properties of operations can help you simplify computations.

Vocabulary
- Commutative Properties
- Associative Properties
- Identity Properties
- Multiplication Property of Zero

Properties of Operations

LEARN

How can properties of operations be used to rewrite expressions?

✓ WARM UP

True or false

1. $28 + 678 = 678 + 28$

2. $24 \div 4 = 4 \div 24$

3. $(18 - 6) + 12 = 18 - (6 + 12)$

Properties of Addition and Multiplication

	Addition	**Multiplication**
Commutative Properties	The order in which numbers are added does not affect the sum. $9 + 15 = 15 + 9$	The order in which numbers are multiplied does not affect the product. $4 \times 12 = 12 \times 4$
Associative Properties	The way in which numbers are grouped does not affect the sum. $4 + (5 + 6) = (4 + 5) + 6$	The way in which numbers are grouped does not affect the product. $(3 \times 2) \times 4 = 3 \times (2 \times 4)$
Identity Properties	The sum of any number and zero is that number. $567 + 0 = 567$	The product of any number and 1 is that number. $422 \times 1 = 422$
Multiplication Property of Zero	This property is a property of multiplication.	The product of any number and zero is zero. $389 \times 0 = 0$

Example

Name the property or properties shown by each number sentence.

a. $(3 \times 4) \times 5 = 3 \times (4 \times 5)$ Associative Property of Multiplication

b. $6 + (5 + 4) = 6 + (4 + 5)$ Commutative Property of Addition

c. $(5 \times 1) \times 7 = 5 \times 7$ Identity Property of Multiplication

d. $12 \times 45 \times 23 \times 0 = 0$ Multiplication Property of Zero

e. $(8 + 29) + 2 = (2 + 8) + 29$ Commutative and Associative Properties of Addition

✓ Talk About It

1. In number sentence **e** in the Example above, explain how the Commutative and Associative Properties are used.

For another example, see Set 1-9 on p. 68.

CHECK ✓

Find each missing number. Tell what property or properties are shown.

1. 15 + (48 + 5) = 15 + (☐ + 48)

2. (78 + 29) + ☐ = 78 + 29

3. 84 ÷ 12 = 84 ÷ 12 × ☐

4. (26 × ☐) × 30 = 30 × (26 × 4)

5. Number Sense Show two different ways to compute 5 × 6 × 3. Do you get the same answer each time?

PRACTICE

For more practice, see Set 1-9 on p. 72.

Ⓐ Skills and Understanding

Find each missing number. Tell what property or properties are shown.

6. ☐ × (3 × 9) = (2 × 3) × 9

7. 1,588 + ☐ = 72 + 1,588

8. 12 = ☐ + 12

9. 8 + 7 + ☐ = 8 + 2 + 7

10. 6 × (8 × 5) = (☐ × 8) × 5

11. ☐ × 85 = 85

12. (8 × 6) × ☐ = 8 × (6 × 5)

13. 1 + (☐ + 2) = (1 + 7) + 2

14. ☐ × 85 = 0

15. (6 × 12) × 3 = 6 × (☐ × 3)

16. (7 × 8) × 15 = (☐ × 7) × 15

17. (3 + 9) + 7 = (3 + 7) + ☐

18. 3 + (☐ + 18) = (3 + 5) + 18

Ⓑ Reasoning and Problem Solving

19. Mia biked the 9-mile trail and then the 15-mile trail. Josef biked the 15-mile trail and then the 9-mile trail. Using one of the properties, write a number sentence to show that each traveled the same distance.

20. Reserved seating in a theater includes 5 sections. Each section has 9 rows. Each row seats 8 people. Using one of the properties write a number sentence that shows two different ways of finding the number of reserved seats.

21. **Writing in Math** Can you use the Associative Property with subtraction and division? Use (18 − 12) − 6 and 40 ÷ (10 ÷ 2) to explain.

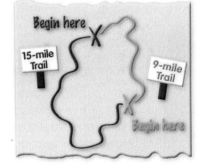

🦉 Mixed Review and Test Prep

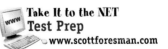
Take It to the NET
Test Prep
www.scottforesman.com

Evaluate each expression.

22. 7 + 2 × 3 − 4

23. (5 − 2) ÷ 3 + 4 × 2

24. 36 ÷ 6 × 2 + 4³

25. Which is the standard form for 35 million, 28 thousand, 4?

A. 35,284   **B.** 35,028,004   **C.** 35,280,004   **D.** 35,280,400

All text pages available online and on CD-ROM.

Algebra

Key Idea
You can use the Distributive Property to compute products mentally.

Vocabulary
• Distributive Property
• break apart

Mental Math: Using the Distributive Property

LEARN

What is the Distributive Property?

The **Distributive Property** says that multiplying a sum by a number is the same as multiplying each addend by the number and then adding the products.

Show two ways to find 8 × (20 + 4).

8 × (20 + 4)
(8 × 20) + (8 × 4)
160   +   32
192

I used pencil and paper.
8 × (20 + 4)
8 ×   24
192

Sheila used the Distributive Property to find the answer mentally.

Gene added first and then multiplied.

Therefore, 8 × (20 + 4) = (8 × 20) + (8 × 4).

Think It Through
Another way to write (40 + 7) × 6 is (40 + 7)6.

Example A

Find 47 × 6 using mental math.

47 × 6   **40   7**
(40 + 7)6   **Break apart** 47.

40(6) + 7(6)   Use the Distributive
240 + 42   Property.
282

Example B

Find (9)45 + (9)5 using mental math.

(**9**)45 + (**9**)5   Each product has a 9 as one of its factors.

9(45 + 5)   Use the Distributive
(**9**)50   Property.
450

✔ **Talk About It**

1. How is Sheila's method easier than Gene's?

2. In Example A, why does (40 + 7)6 = 6(40 + 7)?

For another example, see Set 1-10 on p. 68.

Find each missing number.

1. 5(8 + 12) = 5(8) + ☐(12)   **2.** 9(☐ + 7) = 9(80) + 9(7)

Use the Distributive Property to multiply mentally.

3. (35 + 7)2   **4.** 7(150)   **5.** 15(40 + 4)

6. Number Sense Does the Distributive Property work with subtraction?
Try it with 9(50 − 1) and (20 − 4)5.

PRACTICE

For more practice, see Set 1-10 on p. 72.

Ⓐ Skills and Understanding

Find each missing number.

7. 8(40 + 2) = 8(☐) + 8(2)   **8.** ☐(7) + ☐(6) = 9(7 + 6)   **9.** (10 + 6)20 = 10(20) + 6(☐)

Use the Distributive Property to multiply mentally.

10. (40 + 3)30   **11.** 8(60 + 2)   **12.** 6(45) + 6(5)   **13.** 9(8) + 9(2)

14. 25(12)   **15.** 9(28)   **16.** 20(59)   **17.** (82)7

18. Number Sense Does the Distributive Property always work
with division? Try it with 24 ÷ (6 + 2) and (32 + 8) ÷ 4.

Ⓑ Reasoning and Problem Solving

A florist sells a variety of
flower arrangements. For
19–21, use the Data File to
find the total number of
carnations needed for
each type of arrangement.

| Number of Carnations for Arrangement | | | | | |
Carnation Arrangement	Red	White	Blue	Yellow	Green
Patriotic	3	3	3		
Colorful	4		4	4	4
Anniversary		8	5	5	

19. 9 Patriotic
arrangements

20. 12 Colorful
arrangements

21. 15 Anniversary
arrangements

22. **Writing in Math** Explain how you can find 83 × 7 using
the Distributive Property.

🦉 Mixed Review and Test Prep

Take It to the NET
Test Prep
www.scottforesman.com

23. Which is 387,436 rounded to the nearest ten-thousand?

   A. 380,000   **B.** 387,000   **C.** 390,000   **D.** 400,000

24. Find the missing number in 8 + 5 + 2 = ☐ + 8 + 2. What property is shown?

Key Idea
You can use the properties of operations to help you learn mental math strategies.

Vocabulary
• break apart (p. 30)
• compatible numbers (p. 18)
• compensation
• equal additions

Mental Math Strategies

LEARN

How can you use the properties of operations to compute mentally?

Example A

When the gift shop at the science museum first opened, there were 38 different items to choose from. Later, 77 new items were added. How many different items can be purchased at the shop now?

Find 38 + 77 using mental math.

What You **Think**	Why It **Works**	
Break apart the numbers into tens and ones. Add the tens: 30 + 70 = 100 Add the ones: 8 + 7 = 15 Add the sums: 100 + 15 = 115 So, 38 + 77 = 115.	$38 + 77$ $(30 + 8) + (70 + 7)$ $(30 + 70) + (8 + 7)$ $100 + 15$ 115	Commutative and Associative Properties of Addition

There are 115 items that can be purchased.

Example B

Find 57 + 28 + 3 using mental math.

What You **Think**	Why It **Works**	
First, look for **compatible numbers** that are easy to add in your head. **57 + 3 = 60** Then, add the other number. **60 + 28 = 88** So, 57 + 3 + 28 = 88.	$(57 + 28) + 3$ $(57 + 3) + 28$ $60 + 28$ 88	Commutative and Associative Properties of Addition

Example C

Find 4 × 9 × 50 using mental math.

What You **Think**	Why It **Works**	
First look for numbers whose product is a multiple of 10 or 100. **4 × 50 = 200** Then multiply by the other number. **200 × 9 = 1,800** So, 4 × 50 × 9 = 1,800.	$(4 \times 9) \times 50$ $(4 \times 50) \times 9$ 200×9 $1,800$	Commutative and Associative Properties of Multiplication

✔ Talk About It

1. **Number Sense** Explain how the Commutative and Associative Properties of Addition were used in Example A.

How can you use compensation and equal additions to compute mentally?

Compensation can be used to find the sum of two numbers mentally.

> **Example D**
>
> Find 39 + 88 using mental math.
>
> **One Way**
> Add an amount to one number and subtract the same amount from the sum.
>
> 39 + 88
> ↓
> 39 + **1**   Add 1 to 39.
> ↓
> 40 + 88 = 128
>
> 128 − **1** = 127   Subtract 1 from the answer to compensate.
>
> **Another Way**
> Add an amount to one number and subtract the same amount from the other number.
>
> 39   +   88
> ↓   ↓
> 39 + **1** +   88 − **1**   Add 1 to 39, then subtract 1 from 88 to compensate.
> ↓   ↓
> 40   +   87
>
>   127

> **Example E**
>
> Find 742 − 295 using mental math.
>
> 742 − 295
>   ↓
>   295 + **5**   Add 5 to 295.
>   ↓
> 742 − 300 = 442
>
> 442 + **5** = 447   Since you subtracted 5 more than you should have, you must add 5 to 442 to compensate.

> **Example F**
>
> **Equal additions** can be used to find the difference of two numbers mentally.
>
>   742 − 295
> (742 + 5) − (295 + 5)   Adding 5 to both numbers does not affect the difference.
>   747 − 300
>
>   447

✔ Talk About It

2. In Example D, explain how you can find 39 + 88 by adding 2 first.

3. In Example F, explain how equal additions were used.

4. Find 83 − 48 using equal additions.

Compute mentally.

1. $20 \times 39 \times 5$ **2.** $973 - 645$ **3.** $159 + 328$

4. $4 \times 23 \times 250$ **5.** $87 + 78$ **6.** $870 - 358$

7. Reasoning Explain the steps you can use to find $794 - 439$ mentally.

A Skills and Understanding

Compute mentally.

8. $47 + 68$ **9.** $893 - 457$ **10.** $5 + 9 + 12 + 115$ **11.** $2,000 - 472$

12. $2 \times 125 \times 5$ **13.** $467 - 96$ **14.** $18 + 36 + 22 + 14$ **15.** $58 + 75$

16. $900 - 398$ **17.** $2,896 + 426$ **18.** $754 - 292$ **19.** $6 \times 7 \times 50$

20. Reasoning Explain the steps you can use to find $40 \times 7 \times 25$ mentally.

B Reasoning and Problem Solving

Math and Science

The science museum gift shop sells a wide variety of items, some of which are shown at the right.

For 21–25, use the prices at the right. Compute mentally.

21. Find the cost of one pair of binoculars and a microscope.

22. How much more does a digital camera cost than a rocks and minerals kit?

23. How much less does a microscope cost than a telescope?

24. Find the total cost for 6 binoculars.

25. Find the total cost of 9 rocks and minerals kits and 2 microscopes.

Digital Camera $352

Rocks & Minerals Kit $53

Microscope $179

Refracting Telescope $379

Binoculars $68

26. **Writing in Math** Is Toby's explanation of the steps he used for mental math correct? If not, give the correct answer and explanation.

Find 565 + 302.

565 + 5 = 570   I added 5 to 565.
570 + 302 = 872
872 + 5 = 877   Then I added 5 to
                 the answer.

C Extensions

Algebra Evaluate each expression using order of operations and mental math.

27. $12 + 58(36 \div 4 \div 9)$

28. $26(42 \div 7 - 6) + 88$

29. Copy and complete the table. Describe a mental-math strategy to use when a number is multiplied by 5.

30. Describe a mental-math strategy that could be used when multiplying a number by 15.

Number	× 10	× 5
2		
4		
5		
31		

 **Mixed Review and Test Prep**

Take It to the NET
Test Prep
www.scottforesman.com

Find each missing number. Tell what property or properties are shown.

31. $10 + (12 + 3) = 10 + (3 +)$

32. $(9 \times 41) \times = (5 \times 9) \times 41$

33. Evaluate $12^2 - 2(42 + 6) \div 4^2$

A. 3   B. 18   C. 66   D. 138

Discovery
CHANNEL
SCHOOL™

Discover Math in Your World

Take It to the NET
Video and Activities
www.scottforesman.com

Beyond Bottles and Bags

PET is a plastic resin used to make bottles and containers. About 379,000 tons of PET bottles are recycled into fiber used in polyester T-shirts, carpets, and car bumpers.

1. Find the number of pounds of PET bottles that are recycled into fiber. (1 ton = 2,000 pounds).

2. The average household generates about 34 pounds of PET waste per year. Find the amount generated by 30 households per year.

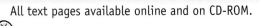

Problem-Solving Skill

Key Idea
Plan and Solve is the second phase of the problem-solving process.

Plan and Solve

LEARN

How can you make a plan to solve a problem?

Stamp Collection One month a friend gave Kayla 15 international stamps. Every month thereafter, Kayla decided to buy 20 new stamps. During which month will she have at least 100 stamps?

Plan and Solve

Step 1: Choose a strategy.
Think about which strategy or strategies might work.

A table shows the total number of stamps Kayla will have each month.

Month	New Stamps	Total
1	15	15
2	20	35
3	20	55
4	20	75
5	20	95
6	20	115

STRATEGIES

- **Show What You Know**
  Draw a Picture
  Make an Organized List
  Make a Table
  Make a Graph
  Act It Out or Use Objects
- **Look for a Pattern**
- **Try, Check, and Revise**
- **Write an Equation**
- **Use Logical Reasoning**
- **Solve a Simpler Problem**
- **Work Backward**

Choose a tool

Mental Math

Step 2: Stuck? Don't give up.
Try the tips at the right when you get stuck.

Step 3: Answer the question.
Kayla will have at least 100 stamps during the 6th month.

TEST TALK

Think It Through
- Reread the problem.
- Tell what you know.
- Identify key facts and details.
- Tell the problem in your own words.
- Show the main idea.
- Try a different strategy.
- Retrace your steps.

✔ Talk About It

1. What strategy was used to solve this problem?

Choir Members Ms. Liu is forming a 24-member choir. She wants to have twice as many girls as boys. How many girls and how many boys should she pick?

1. Name the strategy Barry used to solve the Choir Members problem.

2. Give the answer to the problem in a complete sentence.

Barry's Solution

Try 9 boys. Then there will be 15 girls.
9 + 15 = 24, 2 × 9 = 18; too many boys.
Try 7 boys. Then there will be 17 girls.
7 + 17 = 24, 2 × 7 = 14; too few boys.
Try 8 boys. Then there will be 16 girls.
8 + 16 = 24, 2 × 8 = 16; that's it!

PRACTICE

For more practice, see Set 1-12 on p. 72.

Pansey's Age In 1998, the Northfield Zoo adopted Pansey, a 5-year-old chimpanzee. How old will Pansey be in the year 2010?

3. Name the strategy Rosa used to solve the Pansey's Age problem.

4. Give the answer to the problem in a complete sentence.

Rosa's Solution

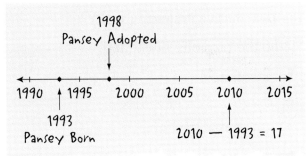

1998
Pansey Adopted

1990   1995   2000   2005   2010   2015

1993
Pansey Born

2010 — 1993 = 17

Coin Combinations Jamie has coins with a total value of 40¢. None of the coins are pennies. How many combinations of coins might Jamie have?

5. Name the strategy Jon used to solve the Coin Combinations problem.

6. Give the answer to the problem in a complete sentence.

Jon's Solution

Quarters	1	1	0	0	0	0	0
Dimes	1	0	4	3	2	1	0
Nickels	1	3	0	2	4	6	8
Totals	40¢	40¢	40¢	40¢	40¢	40¢	40¢

There are 7 different combinations.

Entertainment Darnel is having a party. It will last 5 hours. About how many CDs can he play if each lasts about 53 minutes?

7. Name the strategy Tamara used to solve the Entertainment problem.

8. Give the answer to the problem in a complete sentence.

9. Refer to the steps of Read and Understand at the right. Answer the questions for the Entertainment problem.

Tamara's Solution

300 minutes = 5 hours					
50	50	50	50	50	50

About 6 complete CDs can be played.

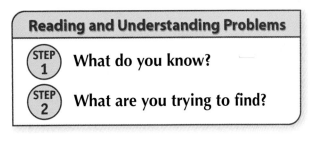

Reading and Understanding Problems

STEP 1 What do you know?

STEP 2 What are you trying to find?

Do You Know How?

Do You Understand?

Order of Operations (1-8)

Use order of operations to evaluate.

1. $6 \times 3 - (3 + 1)$ **2.** $19 - 5 \times 3 - 2$

3. $50 + 36 \div 9$ **4.** $(12 \div 3) - 3 + 2^2$

A Tell the order of operations for evaluating a numerical expression.

B In Exercise 2, which operation would you perform first? Tell why.

Properties of Operations (1-9)
The Distributive Property (1-10)

Name the property illustrated.

5. $3 + (4 + 7) = 3 + (7 + 4)$

6. $4 \times (5 \times 3) = (4 \times 5) \times 3$

7. $5(6 + 3) = (5 \times 6) + (5 \times 3)$

8. $(4 \times 9) + (7 \times 9) = (4 + 7)9$

C Tell how you determined which property was illustrated in each exercise.

D Explain why $4(8 + 7)$ is equal to $(4 \times 8) + (4 \times 7)$.

Mental Math Strategies (1-11)

Compute mentally.

9. $25 \times 32 \times 4$ **10.** $487 + 98$

11. $98 - 36$ **12.** $5 \times 18 \times 2$

13. $13 + 38 + 27$ **14.** $359 - 227$

E For Exercise 13, tell which mental-math strategy you used and why you chose it.

F Describe two ways to find $250 \times 3 \times 4$. Which is easier?

Problem-Solving Skill: Plan and Solve (1-12)

Pictures Steve wanted to take a picture of Debbie, Karen, and Wendy. In how many ways could he arrange the girls for the picture?

Steve's Solution

D K W, D W K,

K D W, K W D,

W D K, W K D

15. Give the answer to the Pictures problem.

G What strategy did Steve use to solve the problem?

H Can you think of another strategy to solve this problem? Explain.

Chapter 1 Section B
Diagnostic Checkpoint

TEST TALK

Think It Through

I need to **read each answer choice carefully.**

MULTIPLE CHOICE

1. Which property is illustrated in the sentence? (1-9)
   $(9 \times 8) \times 5 = 9 \times (8 \times 5)$

   A. Identity Property of Multiplication

   B. Associative Property of Multiplication

   C. Distributive Property

   D. Commutative Property of Multiplication

2. Which operation should be performed first in $54 + 24 \div (12 - 2^3)$? (1-8)

   A. $54 + 24$ **B.** $24 \div 12$ **C.** $12 - 2$ **D.** 2^3

FREE RESPONSE

Evaluate each expression. (1-8)

3. $(6^2 - 32) \div 4$ 4. $36 \div 9 + 4 \times 5 - 3$ 5. $5^2 - 9 \div 3$

6. $16 - 7 \times 2$ 7. $6^2 \div 6 \div 2$ 8. $8 + 6 - 2 \times 2 - 3^2$

Tell which property is shown. (1-9, 1-10)

9. $8 \times 9 \times 0 = 0$ 10. $(8 + 9) \times 3 = (8 \times 3) + (9 \times 3)$

11. $(7 \times 8) \times 5 = 7 \times (8 \times 5)$ 12. $15(9 + 2) = 15(2 + 9)$

Compute mentally. (1-10, 1-11)

13. $3(20 + 7)$ 14. $8 \cdot 9 \cdot 5$ 15. $12 + 9 + 7 + 8$ 16. $9(47)$

17. $778 - 396$ 18. $48 + 63$ 19. 8×43 20. $6 + 38 + 44$

A company makes semi-trailers with 8 wheels and 16 wheels. If the company used 112 wheels for 10 trailers, how many trailers of each type were made? (1-12)

21. What strategy was used to solve the problem?

22. What is the answer to the problem?

8-Wheel Trailers	16-Wheel Trailers	Total Number of Wheels
1	9	152
2	8	144
3	7	136
4	6	128
5	5	120
6	4	112

Writing in Math

23. When Michael evaluated $2 + 3 \times 4 + 5$, his answer was 25. Was his answer correct? Explain why or why not. (1-8)

Find each answer mentally. Explain the method you used.

24. 6×74 (1-10)   25. $49 + 68 + 25$ (1-11)

Algebra

Key Idea
Relationships among quantities can be written using algebra.

Vocabulary
• variable
• evaluate

Variables and Expressions

LEARN

How can you write an algebraic expression?

Example A

Nita bought some candles costing $4 each. How can you represent their total cost?

Make a table to show the cost for different quantities of candles. Use a letter such as *n* to represent the number of candles. Because *n* represents a quantity whose value can vary, it is called a **variable.**

The total cost of the candles is represented by $4 \times n$ or $4n$.

Number of Candles	Total Cost ($)
1	4×1
2	4×2
3	4×3
4	4×4
⋮	⋮
n	$4 \times n$

An **algebraic expression** is a mathematical expression containing variables, numbers, and operation symbols. Before you write an algebraic expression, identify the operation. The table below shows how two or more word phrases can refer to an operation.

Word Phrase	Operation	Algebraic Expression
the **sum** of 9 and a number *n* a number *m* **increased** by 8 six **more than** a number *t* **add** eighteen to a number *h*	Addition	$9 + n$ $m + 8$ $t + 6$ $h + 18$
the **difference** of 12 and a number *n* seven **less than** a number *y* ten **decreased** by a number *p*	Subtraction	$12 - n$ $y - 7$ $10 - p$
the **product** of 4 and a number *k* fifteen **times** a number *t* two **multiplied** by a number *m*	Multiplication	$4k$ $15t$ $2m$
the **quotient** of a number divided by five twenty-five **divided** by a number *m*	Division	$\dfrac{a}{5}$ $\dfrac{25}{m}$

> ### Example B
>
> Sam had x dollars. Later he doubled his money. Then his father gave him $5 more. Write an algebraic expression that represents how much Sam has now.
>
> Sam has $2x + 5$ dollars.

✔ Talk About It

1. In the algebraic expression $\frac{25}{m}$, what number can m never be? Explain.

2. In Example B, is $5 + 2x$ also correct? Explain.

How can you evaluate an algebraic expression?

To **evaluate** an algebraic expression, substitute a number for the variable and simplify. **Substitution** is the same as replacing the variable with a number.

> ### Example C
>
> Evaluate $18 - x$ for $x = 12$.
> $18 - x$
> $18 - 12$
> 6

> ### Example D
>
> Evaluate $28 + r$ for $r = 2$.
> $28 + r$
> $28 + 2$
> 30

> ### Example E
>
> Evaluate $4n$ for $n = 20$.
> $4n$
> $4(20)$
> 80

> ### Example F
>
> Use order of operations to evaluate each expression.
>
> | | | |
> |---|---|---|
> | $3x + 1$ for $x = 7$ | $m^2 + 1$ for $m = 3$ | $4(a - 8)$ for $a = 18$ |
> | $3x + 1$ | $m^2 + 1$ | $4(a - 8)$ |
> | $3(7) + 1$ Multiply. | $3^2 + 1$ Evaluate exponents. | $4(18 - 8)$ Compute inside |
> | $21 + 1$ Then add. | $9 + 1$ Then add. | $4(10)$ parentheses. |
> | 22 | 10 | 40 Then multiply. |

✔ Talk About It

Take It to the NET
www More Examples
www.scottforesman.com

3. Explain how to evaluate $\frac{n}{4} + 7$ when n is 20.

CHECK ✔

For another example, see Set 1-13 on p. 69.

Write each word phrase as an algebraic expression.

1. 5 less than k
2. n increased by 7
3. twice b divided by 9

Evaluate each expression for $x = 5$.

4. $\frac{45}{x}$
5. $20x - 1$
6. $x^2 - 19$

7. **Number Sense** Write two different word phrases for $5 - m$.

A Skills and Understanding

Write each word phrase as an algebraic expression.

8. p increased by 3

9. a squared minus 7

10. the quotient of x and 3

11. 3 times w

12. 5 less than $4e$

13. the product of r and 12

14. x divided by 23

15. m decreased by 11

16. the sum of 20 and w

Copy and complete each table by evaluating the algebraic expression.

17.

n	0	5	10	20	40	50
$\frac{n}{5}$						

18.

a	0	2	5	8	12	20
$20 - a$						

For 19–28, evaluate each expression for $x = 2$, 6, and 10.

19. $7x$

20. $5x + 8$

21. $\frac{60}{x}$

22. $x \times 0$

23. $1x$

24. $\frac{x}{2}$

25. $x - 2$

26. $10x - 1$

27. x^2

28. $\frac{x}{x}$

29. Number Sense Write a word phrase for $5 + 3k$.

B Reasoning and Problem Solving

Math and Social Studies

30. If a country makes n cars each year, write an expression for the average number of cars made each month. Then write an expression for the number of cars made in a 3-year period.

31. In 2000, about 517,000 German cars and k domestic cars were sold. Write an expression for the approximate number of German and domestic cars that were sold in the U.S. in 2000.

32. Writing in Math Paulo was asked to write an expression for the distance around the square shown at the right. Is his expression correct? If not, write the correct expression and explain.

> I can find the distance around the square by adding the lengths of the sides. There are 4 sides, so the total distance is $s + 4$.

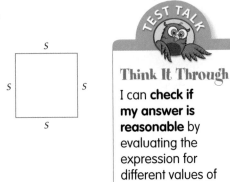

Think It Through
I can **check if my answer is reasonable** by evaluating the expression for different values of the variable.

C Extensions

Write an expression for each word phrase.

33. 4 times the sum of a number *n* and 7

34. 2 times the square of a number *n*

35. Meg is 3 years younger than Rudy. Andrew is twice as old as Meg. Let *r* stand for Rudy's age. Write an expression to represent Meg's age. Using *r*, write an expression for Andrew's age.

Mixed Review and Test Prep

Take It to the NET
www **Test Prep**
www.scottforesman.com

Compute mentally.

36. $398 - 252$ **37.** $6(86)$ **38.** $48 + 16 + 22 + 34$ **39.** $\frac{264}{24}$

40. Which of the following is NOT a problem-solving strategy?

A. Use Objects

C. Make an Organized List

B. Write the Solution in Words

D. Draw a Picture

Learning with Technology

Spreadsheet/Data/Grapher eTool

The spreadsheet below calculates the weight ranges for an Irish Wolfhound.

	A	B	C	D
1	Age	Minimum	Maximum	Weight
2		Weight (lbs)	Weight (lbs)	Range
3	Birth	1.00	1.50	= C3 – B3
4	12 weeks	25.00	40.00	
5	6 months	80.00	100.00	
6	18 months	105.00	120.00	
7				

For a simple calculation, type = followed by the formula. The formula in D3 calculates the weight range at birth. Copy the formula from D3 to cells D4, D5, and D6.

1. Select D4. What formula appears? How does the formula in D4 differ from the formula in D3? How are the formulas the same?

2. Replace the data in column B and C with made-up weights. What happens to the numbers in column D?

Algebra

Key Idea
Properties of equality are used to keep equations balanced.

Vocabulary
• equation
• properties of equality
• inverse operations

Properties of Equality

LEARN

How can you keep an equation balanced?

An **equation** is a sentence stating that two expressions are equal.

You can think of a pan balance as a model of an equation. To keep the pans balanced, you do the same thing to both sides. To keep an equation balanced, you do the same operation to both sides by using **properties of equality.**

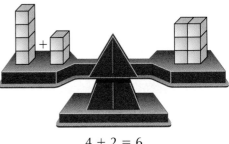

$4 + 2 = 6$

Properties of Equality

Addition Property of Equality Adding the same number to both sides of an equation does not change the equality.	You know: $9 + 8 = 17.$ Therefore: $9 + 8 + 3 = 17 + 3.$
Subtraction Property of Equality Subtracting the same number from both sides of an equation does not change the equality.	You know: $10 + 7 = 17.$ Therefore: $10 + 7 - 5 = 17 - 5.$
Multiplication Property of Equality Multiplying both sides of an equation by the same nonzero number does not change the equality.	You know: $4 \times 3 = 12.$ Therefore: $4 \times 3 \times 2 = 12 \times 2.$
Division Property of Equality Dividing both sides of an equation by the same nonzero number does not change the equality.	You know: $12 + 8 = 20.$ Therefore: $(12 + 8) \div 4 = 20 \div 4.$

Properties of equality can be used with numerical equations.

Example A

You know $11 + 12 = 23.$
Does $11 + 12 + 8 = 23 + 8$?
Why or why not?

Yes; the same number, 8, was added to both sides of the equation.

Both $11 + 12 + 8$ and $23 + 8$ equal 31.

Example B

You know $10 \times 3 = 30.$
Does $10 \times 3 - 5 = 10 \times 3 \div 5$?
Why or why not?

No; 5 was subtracted from the left side of the equation, but the right side was divided by 5.

$10 \times 3 - 5 = 25,$ but
$10 \times 3 \div 5 = 6.$

Properties of equality can be used with equations that contain variables.

Example C	Example D
You know $3x = 15$. Does $3x \div 3 = 15 \div 3$? Why or why not? Yes; both sides of the equation were divided by the same number, 3.	You know $n + 6 = 8$. Does $n + 6 - 6 = 8 - 6$? Why or why not? Yes; the same number, 6, was subtracted from both sides of the equation.

☑ **Talk About It**

1. **Number Sense** What could be done to the equation in Example B to keep the sides equal to each other?

How can you get the variable alone in an equation?

You can get the variable alone by using **inverse operations** to "undo" the operation applied to the variable. Addition and subtraction are inverse operations, as are multiplication and division.

Example E	Example F
Explain how to get the variable alone.	Explain how to get the variable alone.
$x - 12 = 19$ — The operation is subtraction.	$\frac{n}{15} = 45$ — The operation is division.
$x - 12 + 12 = 19 + 12$ — Add 12 to both sides to get x alone and to keep the equation balanced.	$\frac{n}{15} \times 15 = 45 \times 15$ — Multiply both sides by 15 to get n alone.

☑ **Talk About It**

2. In Example E, why was 12 added to *both* sides of the equation?

CHECK ☑

For another example, see Set 1-14 on p. 69.

1. You know $35 + 22 = 57$.
   Does $35 + 22 + 63 = 57 + 63$?
   Why or why not?

2. You know $10m = 120$.
   Does $10m - 18 = 120 - 18$?
   Why or why not?

Explain how to get the variable alone in each equation.

3. $k - 13 = 25$

4. $\frac{y}{7} = 14$

5. $8n = 64$

6. **Number Sense** A balanced scale shows $8 + 6 = 14$. If 5 weights are removed from one side, what needs to be done to the other side to keep the scale balanced?

Ⓐ Skills and Understanding

7. You know $20 \times 4 = 80$.
Does $20 \times 4 + 6 = 80 + 6$?
Why or why not?

8. You know $5n = 350$.
Does $\frac{5n}{5} = \frac{350}{5}$?
Why or why not?

9. You know $\frac{c}{12} = 11$. Does $\frac{c}{12} + 14 = 11 + 4$? Explain.

10. You know $25 = a + 13$. Does $25 - 13 = a + 13 - 13$? Explain.

Explain how to get the variable alone in each equation.

11. $k - 13 = 29$ **12.** $\frac{w}{15} = 45$ **13.** $6n = 42$ **14.** $\frac{y}{14} = 7$

15. $21 + m = 32$ **16.** $a - 48 = 0$ **17.** $\frac{d}{10} = 17$ **18.** $5c = 65$

19. $72 = 9y$ **20.** $b + 43 = 60$ **21.** $63 = 12 + t$ **22.** $30 = x - 14$

23. Reasoning A level pan balance shows $4a = 20$. Explain why you should divide to get the variable alone.

Ⓑ Reasoning and Problem Solving

Math and Art

24. Keisha has 125 pieces of glass to make windows. Each window requires 5 pieces. Let w be the number of windows she can make. Then $5w = 125$ represents the situation. How can you get the variable alone?

25. The production cost per window is $140, the profit is p, and the selling price of $225. The equation $140 + p = 225$ represents this situation. How can you get the variable alone?

26. The cost to insure and ship one window is $8. Since Keisha uses part of her profit to pay the shipping cost, the equation $p - 8 = 85$ represents this situation. How can you get the variable alone?

27. <u>Writing in Math</u> Is the answer below correct? If not, tell why and write the correct expression.

Think It Through
I should **check if my answer is reasonable.**

> A level pan balance shows $b - 3 = 13$. Explain how to get the variable alone.
>
> I would take 3 away from both sides of the balance.

C Extensions

Evaluate each expression for $x = 12$ and $y = 3$.

28. $2y^2$　　　　**29.** $\frac{x}{y}$　　　　**30.** xy　　　　**31.** $x - y$

Mixed Review and Test Prep

Take It to the NET
Test Prep
www.scottforesman.com

Write each word phrase as an algebraic expression.

32. 23 less than a number m　　　　**33.** a number s divided by 8

Evaluate each expression for $x = 3$, 5, and 8.

34. $8x - 5$　　　**35.** $x - 3$　　　**36.** $15 + x$　　　**37.** $x^2 + 3$

38. Which is the *best* estimate for 39×24?

　　A. 600　　　　**B.** 800　　　　**C.** 1,000　　　　**D.** 1,200

Enrichment

The Reflexive, Symmetric, and Transitive Properties

The equality properties are the rules you use when solving equations.
Here are three more properties that are used.

Property	Statement	Meaning	Example
Reflexive	$a = a$	A number is equal to itself.	$8 = 8$
Symmetric	If $a = b$, then $b = a$.	If numbers are equal, they will remain equal if their order is changed.	If $x = 5$, then $5 = x$
Transitive	If $a = b$ and $b = c$, then $a = c$.	If numbers are equal to the same number, they are equal to each other.	If $9 - 3 = 6$, and $6 = 4 + 2$, then $9 - 3 = 4 + 2$

For 1–3, name the property shown.

1. $x + 4 = y$ and $y = 7$, then $x + 4 = 7$　　　　**2.** $4g = 4g$　　　　**3.** $x + 11 = 11 + x$

In 4–6, name a property that describes each situation.

4. Kyle is the same height as Derek, so Derek is the same height as Kyle.

5. Ana is the same age as Emilio, and Emilio is the same age as Eva.
So, Ana and Eva are the same age.

6. One million equals one million.

Algebra

Key Idea
You can use inverse operations and the properties of equality to solve equations.

Vocabulary
• equation (p. 44)
• inverse operations (p. 45)
• properties of equality (p. 44)

Solving Equations with Whole Numbers

LEARN

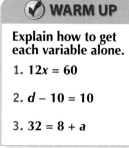
WARM UP

Explain how to get each variable alone.

1. $12x = 60$

2. $d - 10 = 10$

3. $32 = 8 + a$

How can you solve an equation?

When you **solve** an equation, you find the value of the variable that makes the equation true.

Example A

Wynn sold 6 sketches, each for the same amount, and made $180 in sales. How much did he charge for each sketch?

Let s equal the amount for each sketch.

Then the equation is $6s = 180$.

What You Write	Balancing the Pans	
$6s = 180$		The pans are balanced.
$6s \div 6 = 180 \div 6$		180 has been separated into 6 equal parts.
$s = 30$		Each ⑤ equals ㉚.

Wynn charged $30 for each sketch.

✔ Talk About It

1. Why was each side of the equation in Example A divided by 6?

How can you check your answer?

To check your answer, substitute it for the variable in the original equation. In Example A, substitute 30 for s in $6s = 180$.

Check: $6s = 180$
$6(30) = 180$
$180 = 180$ When both sides of the equation can be simplified to the same number, the value of the variable is correct.

Wynn had *x* pastel pencils. After he purchased 14 new ones, he had 29 pencils. How many pencils did Wynn begin with? Solve $x + 14 = 29$.

What You Write	**Balancing the Pans**
$x + 14 = 29$	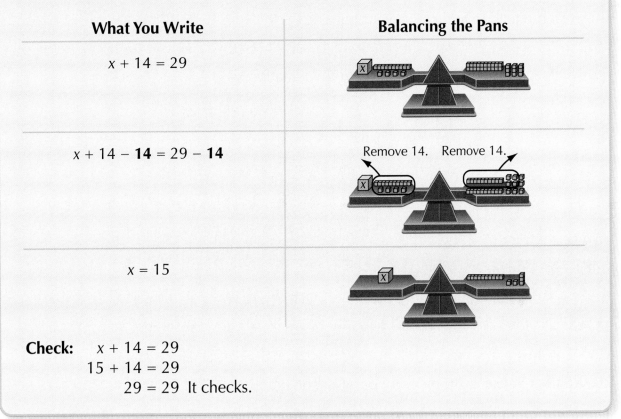
$x + 14 - \mathbf{14} = 29 - \mathbf{14}$	Remove 14. Remove 14.
$x = 15$	

Check: $x + 14 = 29$
     $15 + 14 = 29$
         $29 = 29$ It checks.

Example C

Solve $15 = y - 12$.

     $15 = y - 12$
$15 + \mathbf{12} = y - 12 + \mathbf{12}$
     $27 = y$

Check:
  $15 = y - 12$
  $15 = 27 - 12$
  $15 = 15$ It checks.

Example D

Solve $\frac{m}{5} = 24$.

     $\frac{m}{5} = 24$

$\frac{m}{5} \times \mathbf{5} = 24 \times \mathbf{5}$

     $m = 120$

Check:
  $\frac{m}{5} = 24$

  $\frac{120}{5} = 24$

  $24 = 24$ It checks.

TEST TALK

Think It Through
I can **use the properties of equality** to keep an equation balanced.

✔ Talk About It

2. What was done to both sides of the equation in each of the examples?

Take It to the NET
www **More Examples**
www.scottforesman.com

Explain how to get the variable alone in each equation.

1. $43 + x = 72$ **2.** $y - 17 = 45$ **3.** $3n = 72$ **4.** $15 = \frac{c}{5}$

Solve each equation and check your answer.

5. $x - 24 = 13$ **6.** $16 = 9 + y$ **7.** $\frac{a}{5} = 10$ **8.** $10s = 120$

9. Number Sense Is 24 the solution of the equation $x - 12 = 12$? Explain.

PRACTICE

For more practice, see Set 1-15 on p. 73.

A Skills and Understanding

Explain how to get the variable alone in each equation.

10. $23 = a + 15$ **11.** $n - 37 = 42$ **12.** $18r = 72$ **13.** $\frac{m}{12} = 24$

Solve each equation and check your answer.

14. $k - 12 = 36$ **15.** $\frac{w}{3} = 9$ **16.** $5n = 40$ **17.** $b + 14 = 26$

18. $\frac{y}{53} = 2$ **19.** $0 = a - 49$ **20.** $\frac{d}{5} = 7$ **21.** $8c = 0$

22. $42 = 42y$ **23.** $50 + m = 170$ **24.** $18 = 9 + t$ **25.** $x - 28 = 10$

26. Number Sense Is 80 the solution of the equation $4n = 20$? Explain.

B Reasoning and Problem Solving

Math and Art

27. At an art fair, Pera received $270 for her sketches. This amount was $60 more than the amount, r, for her paintings. Solve the equation $r + 60 = 270$ to find the amount Pera received for her paintings.

28. Maleko bought m feet of the wooden molding to make 7 frames. Solve the equation $\frac{m}{14} = 7$ to determine how many feet of molding Maleko bought.

Each frame requires 14 feet of molding.

29. <u>Writing in Math</u> Kaiko said, "I am thinking of a number. If I subtract 15 from it, I will get 25. What is my number?" Dru's solution is shown below. Is she correct? Why or why not?

> I let n be Kaiko's number.
> I wrote and solved the equation n − 15 = 25.
> Since n = 40, her number is 40.

C Extensions

Decide if the solution is correct.

30. $\frac{m}{4} + 2 = 9$; $m = 28$

31. $6y - 3 = 117$; $y = 21$

32. $3x - 5 = 6x - 14$; $x = 3$

33. $12n - 5 = 4n + 35$; $n = 4$

34. $2(t + 7) = 5t - 7$; $t = 7$

35. $n^3 = 12$; $n = 4$

Mixed Review and Test Prep

Take It to the NET
Test Prep
www.scottforesman.com

36. Which property of equality allows you to get the variable alone in the equation $18x = 216$?

37. Evaluate $3^2 + 24 \div 3 + 5$.

A. 41   **B.** 22   **C.** 16   **D.** 12

Enrichment

Figurate Numbers

Triangular, square, and rectangular numbers are examples of figurate numbers.

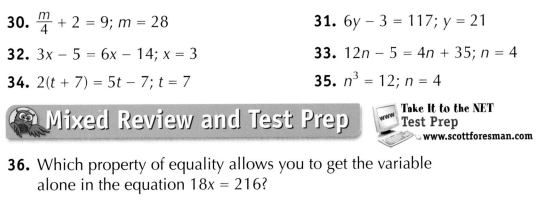

The Pythagoreans discovered relationships among triangular, square, and rectangular numbers, and so can you. Complete the table below.

Number of Dots in Array

	1st	2nd	3rd	4th	5th	6th	7th	8th	9th	10th
Triangular Number	1	3	6	10						
Square Number	1	4	9	16						
Rectangular Number	2	6	12	20						

1. Describe the patterns you used to complete the table.

2. What do you notice about the sum of a rectangular number and the corresponding square number?

3. What do you notice about the sum of two consecutive triangular numbers?

Problem-Solving Skill

Reading Helps!

Identifying steps in a process **can help you with...**

the *Look Back and Check* phase of the problem-solving process.

Key Idea
Look back and check is the final phase of the problem-solving process.

Look Back and Check

LEARN

What are the last steps in solving a problem?

Trading Cards A company makes a profit of $25 per box for hobby cards and $33 per box for archive cards. If 800 boxes of archive cards and twice as many boxes of hobby cards were sold, what was the total profit?

Gina's Solution

Profit on boxes of hobby cards:
1,600 x $25 = $40,000

Profit on boxes of archive cards:
800 x $33 = $26,400

Total profit: $40,000 + $26,400 = $66,400

Check: Profit per box is about $30.
Boxes of cards sold is 2,400.
Total profit is about 2,400 x $30 = $72,000.
My answer is reasonable.

Look Back and Check

Step 1: Have you checked your answer?

- Check that you answered the right question.

  Gina found the total profit. She answered the right question.

- Use estimation and reasoning to decide if your answer makes sense.

  Gina used estimation to check. Her answer and estimate are fairly close.

Step 2: Have you checked your work?

- Look back at your work and compare it against the information in the problem.

  Gina found the total profit for each type of card and added the totals. Her work matches the information in the problem.

- Check that you used the correct operation or procedure.

  Gina multiplied the profit for each box by the number of boxes sold. She then added to find the total profit.
  She used the correct operations.

✔ **Talk About It**

1. Why do you think Gina used $30 in her estimate?

For Problems 1–4, use the Parking problem.

1. Has the right question been answered?

2. Does Janelle's work match the information in the problem?

3. Are operations correctly used? Are all calculations correct?

4. Is Janelle's answer reasonable? Explain.

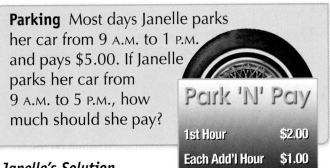

Parking Most days Janelle parks her car from 9 A.M. to 1 P.M. and pays $5.00. If Janelle parks her car from 9 A.M. to 5 P.M., how much should she pay?

Park 'N' Pay

1st Hour	$2.00
Each Add'l Hour	$1.00

Janelle's Solution

For 4 hours of parking, I pay $5. So, for 8 hours of parking, I should pay twice as much.
2 × $5 = $10
Eight hours of parking will cost $10.

PRACTICE

For more practice, see Set 1-16 on p. 73.

For Problems 5–8, use the Summer Job problem.

5. Has the right question been answered?

6. Does the work below match the information in the problem?

> 8 + 7 + 9 + 9 + 7 = 40
> 40 × $9 = $360
> Marco made $360 for the week.

7. Are operations correctly used? Are all calculations correct?

8. Is the student's answer reasonable? Explain.

Use the Point Problem for 9–10.

9. Solve the Point Problem.

10. After solving the Point Problem, answer the four questions in the steps for Look Back and Check on page 52.

Summer Job Marco makes $9 an hour at his summer job. How much did he make for the week shown in the graph below?

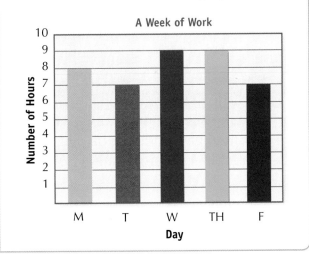

A Week of Work

Point Problem In a basketball game, Sonya scored five 2-point field goals in the first half. In the second half, she scored four 3-point field goals and two free throws, each worth 1 point. The manager recorded 23 points for Sonya. Was the manager correct? Explain.

DK Problem-Solving Applications

Production Each day, the world's factories produce an enormous quantity of goods. If all these goods were put into different piles, the landscape would be dominated by huge mountains of products the size of ski slopes!

Trivia Each day, six billion cubic meters of natural gas are produced. This is enough gas to fill about 2,600,000 hot-air balloons.

① Japan, Germany, United States, and France manufacture the greatest number of vehicles each day. Each country's production is shown below. Write these numbers in order from least to greatest.

② Together, France and another country produce 15,914 cars each day. Let c represent the number of cars the other country produces. Write an equation to find c. What is the other country?

③ Using the information from Trivia, write the average number of cubic meters of natural gas produced daily as a number in standard form.

Using Key Facts

④ Use mental math to find the combined number of refrigerators, tires, and washing machines that are produced each day.

Key Facts
Worldwide Daily Production

•Refrigerators	137,000
•Washing machines	101,000
•Tires	2,300,000
•Soap powder	59,000 tons
•Steel	3,300,000 tons

Vehicle Production (vehicles per day)

United States: 32,836   Germany: 12,787   United Kingdom: 4,836

Japan: 27,933   Canada: 6,662

France: 9,520   South Korea: 6,922   Spain: 6,394

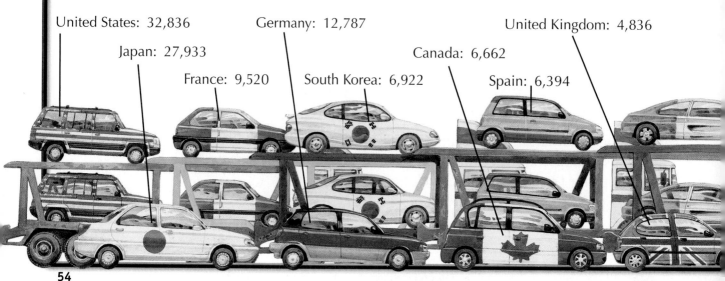

5 Enough trees are cut each day to manufacture about 150 million planks, which could be used to build a tower that would reach outer space! Write 150,000,000 in expanded form using exponents.

6 **Decision Making** If the world's daily harvest of around 11,000 tons of jute, sisal, and mulberry were made into one string, it would stretch 6.5×10^6 kilometers. Which method of estimation would you use to get the closest approximation of the number of times this string would stretch the 384,000-kilometer-distance between Earth and the moon?

7 **Writing in Math** The world's banks send money to each other 24 hours a day. During this time, over 1,500,000 electronic messages are transmitted. An average of about 2 trillion dollars is transferred electronically around the globe each day. Explain how you can find the average amount of money transferred each month.

Good News/Bad News Seven tons of gold are mined per day, but because gold is so dense, all of it could fit inside a refrigerator! Unfortunately, 330 pounds of gold (much of it recycled) is used for dental fillings every day.

Italy: 4,568

Brazil: 3,737

Do You Know How?

Do You Understand?

Variables and Expressions (1-13)

For 1–2, write an algebraic expression.

1. Three times a number x

2. The quotient of a number c divided by a 27

Evaluate each expression for $x = 3$.

3. $15 - x$ **4.** $8x + 2$ **5.** x^2

Ⓐ Tell how you decided which operation to use for Exercises 1–2.

Ⓑ How do you evaluate algebraic expressions?

Properties of Equality (1-14)

Explain how to get the variable alone.

6. $m - 8 = 1$ **7.** $3b = 45$

Ⓒ How do the Properties of Equality help you solve equations?

Solving Equations with Whole Numbers (1-15)

Solve and check each equation.

8. $17 + x = 28$ **9.** $m - 3 = 16$

10. $18 = \frac{z}{2}$ **11.** $5y = 30$

12. $\frac{d}{3} = 7$ **13.** $42 = 6p$

Ⓓ For Exercises 8 and 10, tell which property of equality you used to solve the equation.

Ⓔ How can you tell if your solution to an equation is correct?

Problem-Solving Skill: Look Back and Check (1-16)

14. At field day, teams earn 3 points for 1st place and 2 points for 2nd place. If Randy's team took 1st place five times and ended the day with 27 points, how many times did his team take 2nd place?

Randy's Solution

> $27 - (5 \times 3)$
> $27 - \quad 15$
> $\qquad 12$
> $12 \div 2 = 6$ The team took second place 6 times.

Ⓕ How do you know if the right question has been answered?

Ⓖ How do you check that the operations and calculations are correct?

Ⓗ Is Randy's answer reasonable? Explain.

MULTIPLE CHOICE

1. Solve the equation $\frac{m}{6} = 6$. (1-15)

   A. $m = 0$ **B.** $m = 1$ **C.** $m = 6$ **D.** $m = 36$

2. Evaluate $5x$ for $x = 12$. (1-13)

   A. 7   **B.** 17   **C.** 45   **D.** 60

FREE RESPONSE

Write each word phrase as an algebraic expression. (1-13, 1-17)

3. six less than a number n **4.** 14 times a number x

Evaluate each expression for $a = 2$ and 5. (1-13)

5. $7a$ **6.** $\frac{40}{a}$ **7.** $5 - a$ **8.** $3a + 6$

Explain how to get the variable alone in each equation. (1-14)

9. $5 + p = 30$ **10.** $8 = w - 9$ **11.** $16p = 64$ **12.** $\frac{m}{3} = 9$

Solve each equation. Check your answer. (1-15, 1-17)

13. $12 = m - 1$ **14.** $3e = 0$ **15.** $b + 4 = 18$ **16.** $\frac{h}{3} = 2$

17. $6 + n = 18$ **18.** $40 = 4q$ **19.** $c - 5 = 5$ **20.** $7 = \frac{v}{5}$

For Problems 21–24, use the Paint Service problem. (1-16)

21. Has the right question been answered?

22. Does Ari's work match the wording and the information in the problem?

23. Are operations and calculations correct?

24. Is Ari's answer reasonable? Explain.

> **Paint Service** Ari paints part-time on the weekends. He earned $84 for painting 14 shutters. He wants to know how much he would earn for painting 22 shutters.

Ari's Solution

> $84 ÷ 14 = $6
> 22 × $6 = $132
> I'd earn $132 for painting 22 shutters.

Writing in Math

25. Explain how to use inverse operations to solve $3 + m = 8$. (1-15)

26. Explain how to use a pan balance to model solving the equation $4x = 24$. (1-14)

TEST TALK

Think It Through

My writing should be **brief but complete.**

Test-Taking Strategies

| Understand the question. |
| Get information for the answer. |
| Plan how to find the answer. |
| Make smart choices. |
| Use writing in math. |
| Improve written answers. |

Understand the Question

Before you can answer a test question, you have to understand it. You can use the tips below to help you understand what the question is asking.

1. Casandra made a table showing the distance of each planet from the sun.

Planet	Distance from Sun (in kilometers)
Earth	149,600,000
Jupiter	778,600,000
Mars	227,900,000
Mercury	57,900,000
Neptune	4,495,100,000
Pluto	5,869,700,000
Saturn	1,433,500,000
Uranus	2,872,500,000
Venus	108,200,000

Write a sentence to **compare** the numbers that show the distances of Venus and Mars from the sun. Use the symbol for **greater than** (>).

Understand the question.

• Look for important words (words that tell what the problem is about and highlighted words).

• Use important words from the problem in a sentence that begins "I need to ...."

*The words **compare** and **greater than** are in bold. So, I am to compare numbers, giving the greater number first.*

I need to write a sentence using > that compares the distances of Venus and Mars from the sun.

2. A **rectangular** section of a park is being made into a picnic area and a play area.

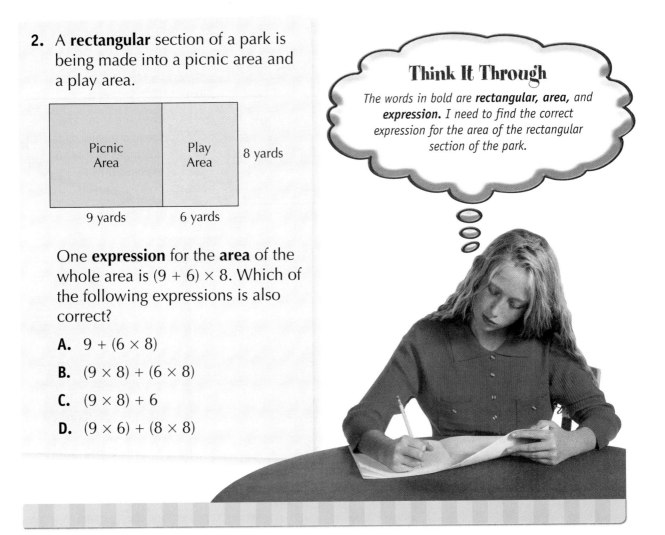

| Picnic Area | Play Area | 8 yards |
| 9 yards | 6 yards | |

One **expression** for the **area** of the whole area is $(9 + 6) \times 8$. Which of the following expressions is also correct?

A. $9 + (6 \times 8)$

B. $(9 \times 8) + (6 \times 8)$

C. $(9 \times 8) + 6$

D. $(9 \times 6) + (8 \times 8)$

Think It Through

*The words in bold are **rectangular, area,** and **expression.** I need to find the correct expression for the area of the rectangular section of the park.*

Now it's your turn.

For each problem, identify important words. Finish the statement "I need to find ... ."

3. The amount of United States currency in circulation worldwide as of July, 2000, was over five hundred thirty-nine trillion, eight hundred ninety million dollars.

Write this number in standard form.

4. Which of the following expressions is NOT another way to find the product 5×27?

A. $(5 \times 20) + (5 \times 7)$

B. 27×5

C. $5 \times 20 + 7$

D. $5 \times (20 + 7)$

Self Check

The base of a floor lamp is the lower part of it. The **base** of a number is the lower part and the upper number is called the **exponent**. (8-9)

Numbers can be written different ways. (Lessons 1-1, 1-2, 1-3, 1-4, 1-5, 1-6)

125^2 is written in **exponential form.**

exponent

Write 125^2 in words.

one hundred twenty-five to the second **power** OR
one hundred twenty-five **squared**

Find the value of 125^2.

$125 \times 125 = 15{,}625$

Write this in **word form** and **short-word form.**

fifteen thousand, six hundred twenty-five   15 thousand, 625

Write this in **expanded form.**

$10{,}000 + 5{,}000 + 600 + 20 + 5$ OR
$(1 \times 10{,}000) + (5 \times 1{,}000) + (6 \times 100) + (2 \times 10) + (5 \times 1)$

1. Write 4^3 and sixteen thousand, seventeen in standard form.

Equality contains the word "equal." The properties of equality state that if any operation is performed on both sides of the equation, the equality is not changed. (p. 44)

Self Check

Properties and the order of operations can help you find the value of numerical expressions. (Lessons 1-8, 1-9, 1-10, 1-11)

Find $9 \times (10 + 6) - 15 - 3^2$.

Use the **order of operations** to evaluate.

$9 \times \mathbf{(10 + 6)} - 15 - 3^2 =$	compute inside parentheses
$9 \times (16) - 15 - \mathbf{3^2} =$	simplify exponents
$\mathbf{9 \times (16)} - 15 - 9 =$	multiply and divide from left to right
$\mathbf{144} - 15 - 9 =$	add and subtract from left to right
120	

2. Evaluate $8^2 \div (10 - 6) + 2$ and $18 - 2^3 + 6 \div 3$.

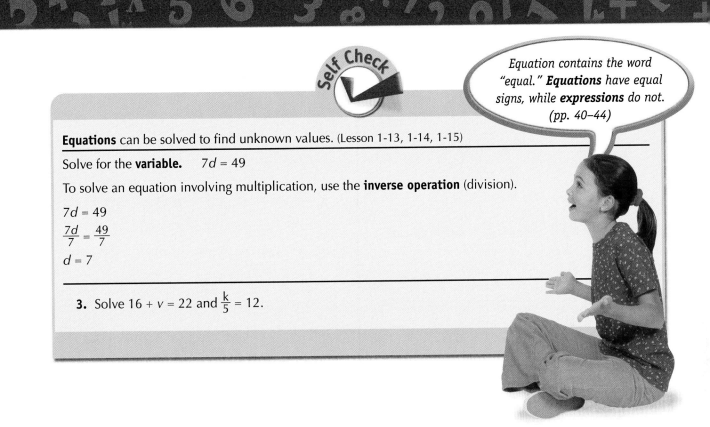

Equation contains the word "equal." **Equations** have equal signs, while **expressions** do not. (pp. 40–44)

Equations can be solved to find unknown values. (Lesson 1-13, 1-14, 1-15)

Solve for the **variable.** $7d = 49$

To solve an equation involving multiplication, use the **inverse operation** (division).

$7d = 49$

$\dfrac{7d}{7} = \dfrac{49}{7}$

$d = 7$

3. Solve $16 + v = 22$ and $\dfrac{k}{5} = 12$.

Read and Understand and Plan and Solve to **solve problems.** Then Look Back and Check. (Lesson 1-7, 1-12, 1-16)

To read and understand, look for key words. Tell what the question is asking.

Nicholas has 6 gallons of milk. How many 1-pint containers can he fill?

"How many" asks for the total. Find how many pints are in 6 gallons.

To plan and solve, think of a strategy that would help. Then solve.

Make a table to find the answer.

Gallons	1	2	3	4	5	6
Pints	8	16	24	32	40	48

Nicholas can fill 48 1-pint containers

To look back and check, check that you answered the right question. Decide if the answer is reasonable. The question was answered. The answer is reasonable.

---

4. A gardener has a rectangular plot of land that measures 25 ft by 11 ft. The gardener wants to plant rose bushes around the perimeter of the plot of land. Each rose bush will be 6 feet along the perimeter from any other rose bush. How many rose bushes does the gardener need?

1. 64 and 16,017 2. 18 and 12 3. $v = 6$ and $k = 60$ 4. 12 rose bushes

MULTIPLE CHOICE

Choose the correct letter for each answer.

1. Which is the standard form for $8 \times 100{,}000 + 3 \times 1{,}000 + 4 \times 10 + 6$?

A. 8,346   **C.** 803,046

B. 80,346   **D.** 803,406

2. Which is 10^6 written in standard form?

A. 100,000   **C.** 10,000,000

B. 1,000,000   **D.** 100,000,000

3. Which list shows numbers in order from least to greatest?

A. 5,789; 5,879; 5,987; 5,897

B. 5,789; 5,879; 5,897; 5,987

C. 5,987; 5,897; 5,879; 5,789

D. 5,789; 5,897; 5,879; 5,987

4. Which is 4,080,499 rounded to the nearest thousand?

A. 4,000,000   **C.** 4,081,000

B. 4,080,000   **D.** 4,100,000

5. Estimate $382 + 1{,}206 + 243$ by rounding to the nearest hundred.

A. 1,000   **C.** 1,800

B. 1,500   **D.** 1,900

6. Which is the best estimate for 251×202?

A. 90,000   **C.** 50,000

B. 75,000   **D.** 40,000

7. Calculate the value of $4^2 \div (2 + 2) \times 3$.

A. 30   **C.** 12

B. 14   **D.** 2

8. The sentence $5 \times (9 + 1) = (9 + 1) \times 5$ illustrates which property?

A. Distributive Property

B. Identity Property of Addition

C. Associative Property of Multiplication

D. Commutative Property of Multiplication

9. Which algebraic expression represents 18 less than twice a number m?

A. $18 - 2m$ **C.** $18 + 2m$

B. $2m - 18$ **D.** $m - 2(18)$

10. How can you get the variable alone in the equation $12x = 12$?

A. Multiply both sides by 12.

B. Multiply both sides by 1.

C. Divide both sides by 1.

D. Divide both sides by 12.

11. Which equation does NOT have the solution $a = 24$?

A. $29 - a = 5$

B. $\frac{a}{2} = 12$

C. $2a = 48$

D. $\frac{a}{2} = 48$

Think It Through

• I should **watch for words like NOT and except.**

• I can **eliminate wrong answers.**

FREE RESPONSE

For 12–13, write the place and the value of each underlined digit.

12. 568,9<u>02</u>,874

13. 43<u>2</u>,668,000,000

14. Write the short-word form and the expanded form for 20,588,639.

For 15–16, write as a product and evaluate.

15. 7^3

16. nine squared

17. Find $56 + 38 + 14$ using mental math.

18. Use the Distributive Property to find $(25 + 8)4$.

Estimate each answer.

19. $6,892 - 5,309$

20. $512 \div 72$

21. $4,093 \times 52$

22. $28 + 31 + 32 + 29 + 27$

23. For Exercise 22, tell what method you used.

Evaluate each expression for $c = 4$ and 6.

24. $\dfrac{36}{c}$ **25.** $2c - 8$

Solve each equation. Check your answer.

26. $15 + n = 25$

27. $m - 12 = 8$

28. $9y = 72$

29. $\dfrac{x}{3} = 6$

30. For Exercise 29, explain how to get x alone.

31. State the Multiplication Property of Zero in your own words.

32. Evaluate $4 + 16 \div (10 - 8)$

Writing in Math

For 33–35, use the Mystery Numbers problem.

Mystery Numbers Aaron says he is thinking of two numbers. Their sum is 26. Their product is 165. What two numbers is Aaron thinking of?

33. Write what you are trying to find.

34. Solve the problem and write your answer in a complete sentence. What strategy did you use to complete the problem?

35. Check your answer. Did you answer the right question? Using an example, show that there are other numbers with a product greater than 165 but whose sum is still 26.

Think It Through

When writing my answer I need to **use math terms accurately.**

Number and Operation

MULTIPLE CHOICE

1. Which is the best estimate for $2,479 \times 43$?

   A. 90,000   **C.** 120,000

   B. 100,000   **D.** 150,000

2. The equator of Earth measures 24,902 miles. Round this number to the nearest thousand miles.

   A. 20,000 mi   **C.** 25,000 mi

   B. 24,900 mi   **D.** 25,900 mi

FREE RESPONSE

3. Rosita multiplied her age by 2, subtracted 5, and divided by 3. The result was 11. How old is she?

4. The equatorial diameters of Mercury, Venus, Earth, and Mars are 4,880 km, 12,100 km, 12,756 km, and 6,794 km, respectively. List the diameters from least to greatest.

5. Write the number 5,309 in expanded notation using exponents.

6. Write 85 billon, 73 thousand in standard form.

Writing in Math

7. Explain a mental-math strategy you would use to find the difference $2,000 - 795$.

8. Write each expression in words.
   $5m - 8$
   $5(m - 8)$
   Are they equal to each other? Explain.

Geometry and Measurement

MULTIPLE CHOICE

9. An angle that measures 60° is

   A. a straight angle.

   B. a right angle.

   C. an obtuse angle.

   D. an acute angle.

10. Reanna needs 108 inches of binding for a quilt she is making. How many yards of binding should she buy?

    A. 324 yards   **C.** 9 yards

    B. 12 yards   **D.** 3 yards

FREE RESPONSE

11. A cement company has 2,700 pounds of sand on its lot. A supplier delivers 4 tons of sand. How many pounds of sand are now on the lot? (1 ton = 2,000 pounds)

12. Draw a polygon that is similar but not congruent to the figure shown.

    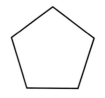

Writing in Math

13. What unit of customary measurement should be used to determine the amount of water in a swimming pool? Explain your choice.

14. Two sides of a triangle measure 8 inches and 9 inches. Can the third side measure 18 inches? Explain.

Data Analysis and Probability

MULTIPLE CHOICE

15. A restaurant serves peach or apple pie with a choice of milk, tea, or coffee. How many different dessert and drink combinations are there?

A. 4   **C.** 6

B. 5   **D.** 7

16. The key in a pictograph shows that each ◯ = 10 people. How many ◯s would represent 75 people?

A. 7   **C.** 8

B. $7\frac{1}{2}$ **D.** $8\frac{1}{2}$

FREE RESPONSE

In 17–18 use the bar graph.

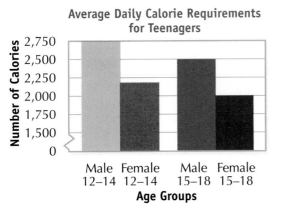

Average Daily Calorie Requirements for Teenagers

17. Which age group requires the greatest number of calories?

18. About how many more calories does a 13-year-old male need than a 17-year-old male?

Writing in Math

19. Gerald said the chances for rain on Tuesday are "50/50." What did he mean?

Algebra

MULTIPLE CHOICE

20. Which equation does NOT have the solution of $x = 12$?

Think It Through

I should **read the problem carefully.** I'll **watch for tricky words** like NOT.

A. $x - 3 = 9$

B. $\frac{x}{2} = 4$

C. $2x = 24$

D. $x + 2 = 14$

21. Evaluate $4 \times 3 + 8 \div 4 - 5$.

A. 3   **C.** 12

B. 9   **D.** 14

22. Solve $\frac{n}{5} = 10$.

A. $n = 2$ **C.** $n = 20$

B. $n = 5$ **D.** $n = 50$

FREE RESPONSE

23. Eight less than a number n is 15. Find the number.

24. Meg had 17 silver dollars before she received some as a gift. Now she has 30. How many silver dollars did she receive as a gift?

Writing in Math

25. Explain how you would get the variable alone in the equation $3x = 24$.

26. Explain the difference between a numerical and algebraic expression. Use an example to support your answer.

Set 1-1 (pages 4–7)

Write the place and value for the underlined digit in 2̲7,856,415.

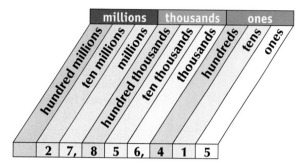

millions			thousands			ones		
2	7,	8	5	6,	4	1	5

The 7 is in the millions place.
Its value is $7 \times 1,000,000 = 7,000,000$.

Remember to start at the right when finding the place and value of a digit in a whole number.

1. 3,7̲52,983   **2.** 2̲53

3. 11̲,286,432,017   **4.** 3̲,000,702

5. 2,83̲6   **6.** 328,8̲94

7. 5̲78,241   **8.** 3,2̲90

Set 1-2 (pages 8–11)

Write $2 \times 2 \times 2 \times 2 \times 2 \times 2$ in exponential form and evaluate.

Two is used as a factor 6 times. Two is the base and 6 is the exponent.

$2 \times 2 \times 2 \times 2 \times 2 \times 2 = 2^6 = 64$

Remember, "squared" means the exponent is 2 and "cubed" means the exponent is 3.

1. 4 cubed   **2.** $5 \times 5 \times 5$

3. $8 \times 8 \times 8 \times 8$ **4.** 13 squared

Set 1-3 (pages 12–13)

Compare. Use >, <, or = for ⬤.

27,836 ⬤ 27,941

Compare the digits in each place.

27,836
27,941

The ten thousands digits and thousands digits are the same, and $8 < 9$.

$27,836 < 27,941$

Remember, when you compare two whole numbers with an unequal number of digits, the one with more digits is greater.

1. 77,892 ⬤ 77,298

2. 5,380,905 ⬤ 5,830,905

3. 2 million ⬤ 500,948

4. 4,757,841,258 ⬤ 4,577,841,258

Set 1-4 (pages 14–15)

Round 28,3̲75,432 to the underlined place.

If the digit to the right of the rounding digit is 5 or greater, round up. If it is less than 5, leave the rounding digit alone.

$7 > 5$, so round up.

28,375,432 → 28,400,000

Remember to change all the digits to the right of the rounding digit to zeros.

1. 2̲,486   **2.** 3̲6,453,987

3. 4,3̲75,983   **4.** 28,3̲64

5. 50̲3,475,892   **6.** 9̲68

Estimate the answer.

7,638 − 549

$$\begin{array}{r} 7,638 \rightarrow 7,600 \\ -\ 549 \rightarrow -\ 500 \\ \hline 7,100 \end{array}$$

Round each number to the greatest place of the lesser number. Then subtract.

Remember you can also use front-end estimation and clustering to estimate.

1. 23 + 18 + 22   **2.** 27,365 − 9,321

3. 48,932 − 31,241

4. 27,341 + 15,936

5. 1,431 + 988   **6.** 5,602 − 4,786

7. 7,253 + 5,700 + 3,102 + 4,301

Estimate the answer.

4,376 ÷ 585

$$\downarrow \qquad \downarrow$$

4,200 ÷ 600 = 7

Use compatible numbers. 42 ÷ 6 is easy to compute mentally.

Remember you can find a range to estimate.

1. 5,393 ÷ 923   **2.** 4,756 × 873

3. 475 × 563   **4.** 15,236 ÷ 47

5. 249 × 4,015   **6.** 8,941 ÷ 315

There are steps to help you read and understand a problem.

Step 1: What do you know?
Tell what you know about the problem in your own words. Identify key facts and details.

Step 2: What are you trying to find out?
Tell what the question is asking. Show the main idea.

Remember to read the problem carefully before you try to solve it.

Write (a) what you know; and (b) what you are trying to find out. Then solve.

1. Mario bought notebooks for $2 each. He bought 3 notebooks yesterday and 4 notebooks today. Excluding tax, how much did Mario spend on notebooks in all?

Find $3^2 \times (4 - 2) + 8 \div 2$

Use the Order of Operations.

$3^2 \times (\mathbf{4 - 2}) + 8 \div 2 =$ Compute inside parentheses first.

$\mathbf{3^2} \times 2 + 8 \div 2 =$ Simplify exponents.

$\mathbf{9 \times 2} + 8 \div 2 =$ Multiply and divide from left to right.

$\mathbf{18 + 4} =$ Add and subtract from left to right.

$\mathbf{22}$

Remember to follow the order of operations whenever an expression has more than one operation.

1. 2 + 3 × 4 − 1

2. $4^2 \div (4 \times 2) + 3 \times 2$

3. 9 + 12 ÷ 1 − 1

4. $12 \div 2^2 \times 3 - 2$

Set 1-9 (pages 28–29)

Find the missing number.

(5 + 7) + 3 = ☐ + (7 + 3)

The Associative Property states that the way in which numbers are grouped does not affect the sum.

The missing number is 5.

Remember that the properties of operations can help you write numeric expressions.

1. 25 × (4 × 6) = (25 × 4) × ☐

2. 359 = ☐ × 359

3. 87 × 0 = ☐

4. (6 × 7) × 50 = 50 × (6 × ☐)

Set 1-10 (pages 30–31)

Compute the expression mentally.

50 (20 + 8) =

(50 × 20) + (50 × 8) =

1,000 + 400 =

1,400

1. Multiply each addend by the factor.
2. Add the products.

Remember that the Distributive Property states that the product of a factor and a sum equals the sum of the products of the factor and the addends.

1. (9 × 17) + (9 × 3) **2.** (12 × 5) + (8 × 5)

3. 10 × (9 + 8) **4.** (18 × 4) + (2 × 4)

5. (14 + 6) 20 **6.** 7 (10 + 5)

Set 1-11 (pages 32–35)

Compute mentally.

56 + 79

79 + 1 = 80

56 + 80 = 136

136 − 1 = 135

1. Use compensation. Add 1 to 79 to get 80.
2. Subtract 1 from the answer.

Remember that you can also use compatible numbers to compute mentally.

1. 48 + 37 **2.** 456 − 97

3. 7 + 26 + 43 + 4 **4.** 20 × 87 × 5

5. 580 − 468 **6.** (4 × 36) × 25

Set 1-12 (pages 36–37)

There are strategies you can use to solve problems.

Draw a Picture
Make an Organized list
Make a Table or Chart
Make a Graph
Use Objects
Look for a Pattern

Try, Check, and Revise
Write an Equation
Use Logical Reasoning
Solve a Simpler
    Problem
Work Backward

Remember to try a different strategy if you get stuck.

1. Square tables in a café can seat one person on a side. If five tables are arranged end-to-end to form a rectangle, how many people can be seated?

Write an algebraic expression for the word phrase.

12 less than n

The word less means subtraction.

$n - 12$

Remember that when evaluating an expression, substitute given values for the variable and then simplify.

1. 5 multiplied by x

2. 15 more than w

Evaluate each expression for $x = 2, 3,$ and 5.

3. $\frac{30}{x}$

4. $6 - x$

Use an inverse operation and the properties of equality to get the variable alone.

$n - 13 = 28$

$n - 13 + \mathbf{13} = 28 + \mathbf{13}$

$n = 28 + 13$

Thirteen has been subtracted from n, so add 13 to both sides of the equation.

Remember that an equation stays balanced if the same operation is performed on both sides of the equation.

1. $w + 7 = 18$

2. $\frac{b}{16} = 4$

3. $18 = 2c$

4. $q - 32 = 44$

Solve the equation.

$6a = 42$

$6a \div \mathbf{6} = 42 \div \mathbf{6}$

$a = 7$

Use division to undo multiplication.

Remember to check your answer by substituting for the variable and simplifying.

1. $x - 19 = 11$

2. $y + 32 = 46$

3. $5x = 45$

4. $\frac{y}{3} = 1$

When you look back and check a problem, follow these steps.

Step 1: Have you checked your answer? Check that you answered the right question. Use estimation and reasoning to decide if your answer makes sense.

Step 2: Have you checked your work? Look back at your work and compare it to the information in the problem. Check that you used the correct operation.

Remember to look back and check your answers.

1. Manuel earns $7 an hour for regular hours and $9 an hour for overtime hours. How much will he earn if he works 30 hours regular time and 7 hours overtime? Check the solution below and explain why it is or is not reasonable.

30 × $7 = $210 and 7 × $9 = $63, so Manuel will earn $210 + $63 = $273.

Chapter 1
More Practice

Set 1-1 (pages 1–7)

Write the place and value of each underlined digit.

1. 12,256,789 **2.** 2,458 **3.** 681 **4.** 697,542,105

Write each number in short-word form and expanded form.

5. 26,589,136 **6.** 8,642 **7.** 756 **8.** 489,634

9. The population of Illinois in the year 2000 was 12,419,293. Write this number in word form.

Set 1-2 (pages 8–11)

Write each power as a product and then evaluate.

1. 5^3 **2.** 6 squared **3.** 2^4 **4.** 10^5

5. 33^0 **6.** 20 cubed **7.** 15^2 **8.** 1^{10}

Write each number in expanded form using exponents.

9. 6,782 **10.** 82,901 **11.** 5,603,992 **12.** 4,300,081,200

13. There are 10^3 safety pins in a box. How many safety pins are in the box?

Set 1-3 (pages 12–13)

Compare. Use >, <, or = for ●.

1. 2,567 ● 2,657 **2.** 3 thousand ● 3 hundred **3.** 12,365 ● 21,365

4. 27,003 ● 27,030 **5.** 700,000 ● 7×10^5 **6.** 489,173 ● 489,168

Order from least to greatest.

7. 62 thousand; 6 million; 6; sixty

8. 5,257; 5,527; 5,275

9. 89,314; 809,003; 98,431

10. The Georgia Dome in Atlanta can seat 65,352 people. Ericsson Stadium in Charlotte can seat 73,250. Use > or < to compare these numbers.

Set 1-4 (pages 14–15)

Round each number to the underlined place.

1. 36,272,349 **2.** 3,489 **3.** 7,899 **4.** 283,472

5. 9,874,315 **6.** 10,983 **7.** 14,098,499 **8.** 43,027

9. Write three numbers that would round to 230,000,000 when rounded to the nearest ten million.

Set 1-5 (pages 16–17)

Estimate each answer.

1. 6,346 − 238   **2.** 56,936 + 22,148   **3.** 568 − 329

4. 128,936 − 64,387   **5.** 74 + 67 + 72 + 66   **6.** 2,364 + 587

7. 2,798 + 3,257 + 2,903 + 2,899 + 3,075

8. Jupiter is about 483,880,000 miles from the sun, while Mars is about 141,710,000 miles from the sun. Estimate the difference in the two planets' distances from the sun.

Set 1-6 (pages 18–19)

Estimate each answer.

1. $3{,}493 \times 82$ **2.** 564×738 **3.** $44{,}864 \div 375$ **4.** $2{,}528 \div 43$

5. $35{,}047 \div 543$ **6.** $4{,}312 \div 68$ **7.** $3{,}502 \div 723$ **8.** $827 \times 9{,}003$

9. $6{,}780 \div 84$ **10.** 196×318 **11.** $875 \times 4{,}972$ **12.** $55{,}499 \div 113$

13. Roberto has $125 and he wants to buy 16 used CDs that sell for $8 each, including tax. Does he have enough money? Explain.

Set 1-7 (pages 20–21)

Use the Sandy's Books problem.

Sandy's Books Sandy has four books to read this quarter. She wants to read the books in order by their number of pages, starting with the longest. In what order should she read her books?

Book	Number of Pages
Ali's Visit to Mars	360
Stars All Around	548
Joseph and the Dragon	472
Sixteen Years	316

1. Identify the key facts and details.

2. Tell what the question is asking.

3. Answer the question using a complete sentence.

Set 1-8 (pages 24–27)

Evaluate each expression.

1. $(8 - 4) \div 2 \times 5$ **2.** $4^2 \times 4 + 3 \div 3$ **3.** $8 \div 4 - 2 + 5$

4. $2^4 \div (6 \div 3)$ **5.** $7 - 3 \times 2 + 9$ **6.** $8 \div 4 + 2 \times 3$

7. $63 \div (7 + 2) - 2^3 \div 4$ **8.** $72 \div (3 + 5) \times 9$ **9.** $(3 + 2)^2 \times 4$

10. June had $45. She bought 3 toys for $4 each, including tax, and 2 games for $9 each, including tax. How much money did she have left?

Set 1-9 (pages 28–29)

Find each missing number. Tell what property or properties are shown.

1. 7 + ▢ = 7

2. (6 × 12) × 4 = ▢ × (12 × 4)

3. 18 + (7 + ▢) = (7 + 8) + 18

4. 22 + 36 = ▢ + 22

5. Jerome has saved $4. He earned four times that amount on Friday, and six times that amount on Saturday. How much did Jerome have after he was paid Saturday?

Set 1-10 (pages 30–31)

Find each missing number.

1. 5(17 + ▢) = (5 × 17) + (5 × 3)

2. 65(10 + 20) = (10 + ▢)65

3. (12 + 8)15 = 15(12) + ▢(8)

4. 42(35 + 5) = (▢ × 35) + (▢ × 5)

Use the Distributive Property to multiply mentally.

5. 8(70 + 3)

6. (75 × 3) + (75 × 7)

7. (10 + 8)40

8. (9 × 6) + (9 × 4)

9. (50 + 6)30

10. (4 × 55) + (4 × 5)

11. Mr. Muñoz sold 6 DVD players at $105 each, including tax. How much money did he make in all?

Set 1-11 (pages 32–35)

Compute mentally.

1. 78 + 64

2. 463 − 97

3. 20 × 87 × 5

4. 8 × 9 × 50

5. 699 × 338

6. 684 − 298

7. 25 × 31 × 4

8. 188 + 46

9. 11 × 23

10. 168 + 75

11. 462 − 398

12. 19 × 4

13. Explain how to use compensation to find 498 + 615.

Set 1-12 (pages 36–37)

Kevin decides to save spare change for 10 days and begins the first day by saving 1¢. Each day after, he will save twice the amount as the day before. How much will he have saved after 10 days?

Andrew's Solution

Day	1	2	3	4	5	6	7	8	9	10
Amount	1¢	2¢	4¢	8¢	16¢	32¢	64¢	$1.28	$2.56	$5.12

1. Name the strategy used to solve this problem. Give the answer in a complete sentence.

Take It to the NET
More Practice
www.scottforesman.com

Set 1-13 (pages 40–43)

Write each word phrase as an algebraic expression.

1. b increased by 3

2. The product of p and 3

3. 4 less than w

4. A number n divided by 25

5. 18 more than t

6. twice k

Evaluate each expression for $x = 3$, 6, and 9.

7. $8x$

8. $\dfrac{36}{x}$

9. $x - 3$

10. x^2

11. Raul had n CDs. He gave 5 CDs away. Write an expression to describe the situation. Then evaluate that expression for $n = 14$.

12. Lottie bought x bracelets on sale for \$2 each. Write an expression to describe the price of the bracelets. Then evaluate that expression for $x = 5$.

Set 1-14 (pages 44–47)

Explain how to get the variable alone in each equation.

1. $x + 7 = 64$

2. $y - 35 = 16$

3. $3t = 12$

4. $\dfrac{p}{4} = 5$

5. $18 = q - 4$

6. $7 = \dfrac{n}{3}$

7. $6 + z = 17$

8. $20 = 10a$

9. Geno shared some baseball cards equally among five friends. Each friend received 13 cards. The equation $\dfrac{c}{5} = 13$ represents the situation. Explain how you would get the variable alone.

Set 1-15 (pages 48–51)

Solve each equation and check your answer.

1. $e - 15 = 2$

2. $36 = a + 12$

3. $24c = 240$

4. $\dfrac{w}{2} = 22$

5. $28 = 4k$

6. $g - 42 = 1$

7. $m + 17 = 17$

8. $\dfrac{t}{5} = 30$

9. In an 800-meter relay, each of four runners runs the same distance. Solve the equation $4d = 800$ to find the distance for each runner.

10. Janelle is eighteen years old. She is six years older than her sister Karen. Solve the equation $k + 6 = 18$ to find Karen's age.

Set 1-16 (pages 52–53)

Leo earns \$6 an hour plus tips. If he worked for 8 hours and earned \$60, how much did he make in tips?

1. Does the work match the problem?

2. Are operations and calculations correct?

3. Is the answer reasonable? Explain.

Solution:
8 × \$6 = \$48;
\$60 − \$48 = \$12.
Leo made \$12 in tips.

Decimals

DIAGNOSING READINESS

A Vocabulary
(pages 8, 18, 44)

Choose the best term from the box.

1. A mathematical sentence stating two expressions are equal is an __?__.

2. An __?__ tells how many times a number is used as a factor.

3. Equations can be solved using __?__.

4. You can often use __?__ when computing mentally.

Vocabulary

- **base** *(p. 8)*
- **compatible numbers** *(p. 18)*
- **exponent** *(p. 8)*
- **inverse operations** *(p. 44)*
- **equation** *(p. 44)*

B Comparing and Ordering
(pages 12–13)

Use < or > to compare.

5. 389 ⬤ 398   6. 1,802 ⬤ 1,798

7. 5,623 ⬤ 5,632   8. 102,002 ⬤ 10,202

Write the numbers from least to greatest.

9. 56,887; 56,878; 56,877

10. The table below shows the point totals for Summer Olympics heptathlon gold medalists. Write the points in order from greatest to least.

Year	Athlete	Points
1984	Glynis Nunn, Australia	6,390
1988	Jackie Joyner-Kersee, U.S.A.	7,291
1992	Jackie Joyner-Kersee, U.S.A.	7,044
1996	Ghada Shouaa, Syria	6,780
2000	Denise Lewis, Britain	6,584

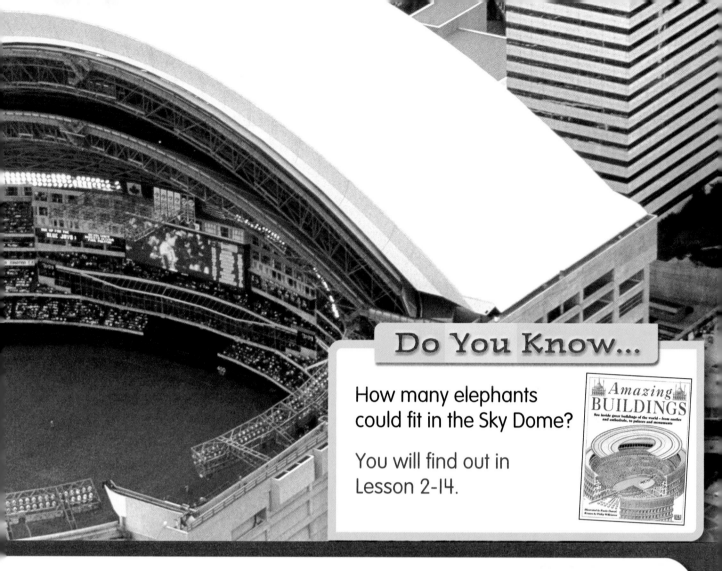

Do You Know...

How many elephants could fit in the Sky Dome?

You will find out in Lesson 2-14.

Amazing **BUILDINGS**
See inside great buildings of the world – from castles and cathedrals, to palaces and monuments

 C **Estimating**
(pages 16–19)

Estimate each answer.

11. $502 + 889$

12. 250×41

13. $462 - 39$

14. $610 \div 31$

15. 867×52

16. $8{,}658 - 7{,}302$

17. $725 \div 79$

18. $942 + 3{,}559$

19. 295×491

20. $301 - 13$

21. $887 \div 72$

22. $1{,}418 + 272$

23. An auditorium has 3 sections with 22 rows in each section. Each row has 18 seats. Estimate the total number of seats.

24. There are 5,280 feet in a mile and 12 inches in a foot. Estimate the number of inches in a mile.

D **Solving Equations**
(pages 48–51)

Solve each equation and check your answer.

25. $a + 14 = 1{,}869$

26. $n - 125 = 398$

27. $8y = 184$

28. $\frac{c}{2} = 93$

29. $29 = 12 + x$

30. $30 = m + 30$

31. $25s = 25$

32. $91 = \frac{b}{91}$

33. $41 + h = 107$

34. $\frac{w}{24} = 17$

35. The distance around a square garden is 240 feet. Use the equation $4s = 240$ to find the length of one side of the garden.

36. Walking at a rate of 550 ft per hour, it took Ari 3 hours to complete a hiking trail. Use the equation $d = 550(3)$ to find the length of the trail.

Vocabulary
• decimal
• expanded form (p. 4)

Materials
• place-value chart or  tools

Think It Through
Since **I know** that the places to the left of a decimal point are *ones, tens, hundreds, thousands. . . ,* **I can remember** the places to the right of a decimal point as *tenths, hundredths, thousandths, . . .*

Understanding Decimals

LEARN

What are some ways to read and write decimals?

A **decimal** is a number that uses a decimal point.

A decimal has one or more digits to the right of a decimal point.

The atomic mass of the metal gold is 196.9655 units.

Give the place and value of the 6s in 196.9655.

The 6 to the left of the decimal point is in the ones place and its value is 6 ones, or 6.

The 6 to the right of the decimal point is in the hundredths place and its value is 6 hundredths, or 0.06.

You can use a place-value chart to help you read and write decimals.

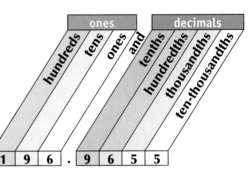

✓ WARM UP

Identify the place and value of the underlined digit.

1. 3,003,158

2. 47,890,256

3. 5,017,903

4. 79,522,008

Example

How do you read and write 1.00797?

Standard form: 1.00797

Word form: One and seven hundred ninety-seven hundred-thousandths

Short-word form: 1 and 797 hundred-thousandths

Expanded form: $(1 \times 1) + (0 \times 0.1) + (0 \times 0.01) + (7 \times 0.001) + (9 \times 0.0001) + (7 \times 0.00001) =$
$1 + 0.007 + 0.0009 + 0.00007$

✓ Talk About It

1. Use a place-value chart to find the place and value of each digit in the decimal 0.53482.

2. **Number Sense** One way to read a decimal is to say it as you would a fraction or mixed number. How would you write 55.847 as a mixed number?

For another example, see Set 2-1 on p. 132.

CHECK ✓

Give the place and value of the 7 in each number.

1. 34.789   **2.** 0.07964   **3.** 45.62173

Copy and complete the table.

	Standard Form	Short-Word Form	Expanded Form
4.	0.5402		
5.		3 and 897 hundred-thousandths	

6. Number Sense Express $\frac{7}{10}$, $\frac{70}{100}$, and $\frac{700}{1,000}$ as decimal numbers.

PRACTICE

For more practice, see Set 2-1 on p. 136.

Skills and Understanding

Give the place and value of the 4 in each number.

7. 0.34861   **8.** 1.97642   **9.** 24.365

Copy and complete the table.

	Standard Form	Short-Word Form	Expanded Form
10.	1.3506		1 + 0.3 + 0.05 + 0.0006
11.		204 thousandths	

12. Number Sense How many hundredths are in one tenth? in ten thousandths?

Reasoning and Problem Solving

Write the atomic mass of each element in expanded form.

13. Helium   **14.** Iron   **15.** Uranium   **16.** Oxygen

17. <u>Writing in Math</u> Explain how you know eight hundredths is less than 1.

Data File

Element	Atomic Mass
Gold	196.9665
Helium	4.0026
Iron	55.847
Mercury	200.59
Oxygen	15.9994
Uranium	238.029

🦉 Mixed Review and Test Prep

Take It to the NET
Test Prep
www.scottforesman.com

Mona plans to work her regular 40-hour week plus 4 overtime hours. She is paid $8 an hour for regular hours and $12 an hour for overtime. How much will she earn?

18. Did Mona use the correct information and operations?

19. Estimate to check if Mona's answer is reasonable.

20. Solve $8x = 24$.

   A. $x = 3$ **B.** $x = 30$ **C.** $x = 32$ **D.** $x = 4$

Mona's Solution

$(40 \times \$8) + (4 \times \$12)$
$\$320 + \$48$
$\$368$

Comparing and Ordering Decimals

LEARN

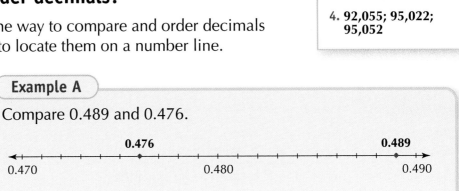
How can you compare and order decimals?

One way to compare and order decimals is to locate them on a number line.

Example A

Compare 0.489 and 0.476.

```
                    0.476                                    0.489
◄─┼──┼──┼──┼──┼──●──┼──┼──┼──┼──┼──┼──┼──┼──┼──●──►
 0.470                        0.480                         0.490
```

Since 0.489 is to the right of 0.476, 0.489 > 0.476.

Another way to compare and order decimals is to align the digits by place value. Annexing zeros can help you do this. When you annex zeros to the right of a decimal, you do not change its value.

Think It Through

I can **use a number line** to order and compare numbers.

Example B

Compare 2.34 and 2.3.

2.34 Write the numbers, lining
2.3**0** up the decimal points.
Annex zeros so that place
values are aligned.

2 . 3 4 Start at the left and
2 . 3 0 compare digits in the
same place values.

The ones and tenths digits are the same.

The hundredths digits differ.
Since 4 hundredths > 0 hundredths,

2.34 > 2.3

Example C

Order 5.36, 4.98, 5.52, and 5.5 from least to greatest.

Start at the left and compare digits in the same place value. Order the digits by place value.

Order ones.	Order tenths.	Order hundredths.
5.36	4.98	4.98
4.98	5.36	5.36
5.52	5.50	5.52
5.50	5.52	5.50

4.98 < 5.36 < 5.50 < 5.52

✔ Talk About It

1. If 35 is greater than 4, why is 0.4 greater than 0.35?

2. **Reasoning** Is it true that a decimal with 5 digits is always greater than a decimal with 4 digits? Use an example to support your answer.

For another example, see Set 2-2 on p. 132.

Use >, <, or = to compare each pair of numbers.

1. 0.0567　0.0499　　**2.** 1.45　1.3942　　**3.** 17.003　17.030

4. 32.84　32.8400　　**5.** 4.882　5.01　　**6.** 0.001　0.0019

Order from least to greatest.

7. 1.58, 0.99, 1.4　　**8.** 3.066, 3.0666, 3.66　　**9.** 1.6, 2.251, 2.32, 1.85, 0.9

10. Number Sense Faris said that 8.56 is greater than 8.9 because 56 is greater than 9. Is he correct? Explain.

PRACTICE

For more practice, see Set 2-2 on p. 136.

Ⓐ Skills and Understanding

Use >, <, or = to compare each pair of numbers.

11. 0.0237　0.237　　**12.** 56.78945　54.98　　**13.** 87.314　87.3138

14. 7.32256　7.32356　　**15.** 5.6　5.06　　**16.** 0.00495　0.04095

Order from least to greatest.

17. 0.0387, 0.0378, 0.0873　**18.** 1.001, 1.01, 10.1　**19.** 13.23, 13.235, 13.240, 13.2351

20. Number Sense Name 4 decimals that are between 0.9 and 1.

Ⓑ Reasoning and Problem Solving

The table at the right lists the sizes of the planets in our solar system relative to the size of Earth's diameter.

Data File	
Planet	**Relative Size**
Earth	1.0
Jupiter	11.209
Mars	0.5328
Mercury	0.3825
Neptune	3.883
Pluto	0.18
Saturn	9.449
Uranus	4.007
Venus	0.9488

21. Which planets are smaller than Venus?

22. How many planets are larger than Earth?

23. Order the planets from largest to smallest.

24. **Writing in Math** Explain how to write a number between 3.4 and 3.5.

🦉 Mixed Review and Test Prep

Take It to the NET
Test Prep
www.scottforesman.com

Write each number in short-word and expanded form.

25. 1.023　　　**26.** 0.65　　　**27.** 6.325　　　**28.** 12.006

29. Algebra Which property is illustrated by (3 + 8) + 2 = 3 + (8 + 2)?

A. Commutative Property of Addition　　**C.** Distributive Property

B. Associative Property of Addition　　**D.** Multiplication Property of Zero

Vocabulary
• round (p. 14)

Think It Through

I can **use a number line** to show the position of a number in relation to the halfway point.

Rounding Decimals

LEARN

How can you round decimals?

A stage micrometer is a microscope slide with a scale that allows you to estimate lengths to the nearest hundredth of a centimeter. The head of a Costa Rican Azteca ant ranges in width from 0.105 cm to 0.142 cm.

You can **round** decimals when you want to estimate an answer, or when you don't need as precise a measurement as the one you are given.

Example A	
Round 0.105 to the nearest hundredth.	
Find the rounding place.	0.1<u>0</u>5
Look at the digit to the right of this place.	0.10 5
If this digit is 5 or greater, add 1 to the rounding digit.	5 = 5
Drop the digits to the right of the rounding digit.	0.11
0.105 rounds to 0.11.	

Example B	
Round 0.142 to the nearest hundredth.	
Find the rounding place.	0.1<u>4</u>2
Look at the digit to the right of this place.	0.14 2
If this digit is less than 5, leave the rounding digit alone.	2 < 5
Drop the digits to the right of the rounding digit.	0.14
0.142 rounds to 0.14.	

On a number line, 0.142 is between 0.140 and 0.150. Since it is to the left of the halfway number 0.145, 0.142 rounds to 0.14.

```
          0.142
  ←—+——+——+—●——+——+——+——+——+——+——+——+—→
  0.140              0.145              0.150
```

✔ Talk About It

1. **Number Sense** What is the halfway number between 0.10 and 0.11?

2. Which place do you look at when rounding to the nearest whole number?

3. Round 56.94715 to the nearest hundredth, to the nearest thousandth, and to the nearest ten-thousandth.

Take It to the NET
More Examples
www.scottforesman.com

Round to the underlined place.

1. 35.9<u>9</u>2

2. 56.0<u>0</u>4

3. 8,04<u>7</u>.99

4. 0.0<u>3</u>41

5. Number Sense Samuel rounded 8.49 to 9 and Nuela rounded 8.49 to 8. Who is correct? Explain.

PRACTICE

For more practice, see Set 2-3 on p. 136.

A Skills and Understanding

Round to the underlined place.

6. 1<u>2</u>.5987

7. 0.00<u>2</u>56

8. 1.<u>5</u>273

9. 2,609.<u>0</u>78

10. 125.64<u>7</u>9

11. 7.<u>8</u>7642

12. 22.263<u>4</u>8

13. 36<u>5</u>.4

14. 0.10<u>0</u>1

15. 7.3<u>0</u>06

16. 56.<u>0</u>98

17. 11.<u>9</u>9

18. Number Sense A number rounds to 2.250. List 3 possibilities for the number.

B Reasoning and Problem Solving

Packages of paper towels are on sale. The price per package appears in the table at the right.

19. Calculate the price per roll for each brand of paper towel.

20. Which is the best buy? Explain how you know.

21. Number Sense Name 2 decimals that will round to 4.05.

22. <u>Writing in Math</u> Explain how 0.8, 0.85, and 0.847 can all be rounded forms of 0.8468.

Paper Towels on Sale!

Brand	Package	Price
Wet No More	12 rolls	$3.79
Clean 'n' Dry	6 rolls	$1.89
Quick Draw	24 rolls	$7.49

Press: 7.49 ÷ 24 =

Display: 0.3120833

Mixed Review and Test Prep

Take It to the NET
Test Prep
www.scottforesman.com

Use >, <, or = to compare each pair of numbers.

23. 256.002 ● 256.020

24. 12.567 ● 1.2567

25. 0.258 ● 0.2580

Write each in exponential form.

26. $4 \times 4 \times 4 \times 4 \times 4$

27. 2 cubed

28. 10 to the sixth power

29. Algebra Which is the expression for "four fewer than twice a number."

A. $4 - 2x$

B. $2(4 - 2x)$

C. $2(x - 4)$

D. $2x - 4$

Key Idea
You can estimate with decimals using the same methods you used to estimate with whole numbers.

Think It Through

I can **use the symbol** ≈ to show an estimate. I know that it means **"is approximately equal to."**

Estimating with Decimals

LEARN

How can you estimate sums and differences of decimals?

Example A

Callie ordered 1 small veggie pizza, 1 medium mushroom pizza, and 1 large cheese pizza. Estimate the total cost.

Primo Pizzeria

	Small	Medium	Large
Cheese	$6.75	$9.45	$11.35
Mushroom	$7.75	$10.85	$13.00
Veggie	$7.25	$10.00	$12.00
The Works	$9.25	$12.95	$15.50

$7.25 → $7.00   Round each number to
$10.85 → $11.00   the nearest dollar.
+ $11.35 → $11.00   Add.
_____
$29.00

So, the total cost for the 3 pizzas is about $29.00.

✓ **Talk About It**

1. Estimate the difference between the cost of a medium mushroom pizza and a medium "The Works."

How can you estimate products and quotients of decimals?

Example B

Estimate the cost of 22 medium cheese pizzas.

$9.45 × 22   Round each factor.

$9 × 20 = $180

$9.45 × 22 ≈ $180

Example C

Estimate the number of small cheese pizzas you can buy with $50.

$50 ÷ $6.75   Use compatible numbers.

$49 ÷ $7 = 7

You can buy about 7 small cheese pizzas for $50.

✓ **Talk About It**

2. Use compatible numbers and the Distributive Property to estimate the cost of 9 small mushroom pizzas.

CHECK ✓

Estimate each answer.

1. $95.89 + $12.02   **2.** 70.508 ÷ 8.4   **3.** 48.52 × 3.9   **4.** 75.370 − 29.499

5. Number Sense Is 6 or 7 a better estimate for the quotient 35.8 ÷ 5.6? Explain.

PRACTICE

For more practice, see Set 2-4 on p. 137.

A Skills and Understanding

Estimate each answer.

6. $22.78 − $15.18   **7.** 75.6 + 52.39   **8.** $48.52 + $63.97   **9.** 87.015 − 3.6

10. 64.32 × 1.78   **11.** 28.7 ÷ 8.9   **12.** 3.7 × 7.8   **13.** 23.6 ÷ 5.68

14. $6.27 × 28   **15.** 12.098 − 5.7   **16.** $232.57 ÷ 11   **17.** 1,268.17 + 934.3

18. 5.76 + 3.19   **19.** 26.53 − 8.47   **20.** 35.8 ÷ 8.7   **21.** 4.448 × 13.603

22. Number Sense To estimate 25.6 × 2.7, would you round or use compatible numbers? Explain.

B Reasoning and Problem Solving

23. Kelly has $10 to buy 3 of the same item. Which items can she buy?

24. Reasoning Azi has $10. Can he buy 2 deli sandwiches? Why or why not?

25. Reasoning You bought 4 CDs at the same price. Based on rounding, your estimate of the total cost was $60 before tax. If you rounded to the nearest cent, what is the maximum price per CD?

26. Writing in Math Describe two everyday situations in which you would want your estimate to be less than the exact answer.

Regina's CAFE

Soup of the Day	$2.79
Tuna Sandwich	$3.58
Deli Sandwich	$5.23
Café Salad	$4.53
Deluxe Salad	$6.99
Bottled Water	$1.45
Fresh Fruit Slices	$1.19

Mixed Review and Test Prep

Take It to the NET
Test Prep
www.scottforesman.com

Round to the underlined place value.

27. 26.1<u>8</u>64   **28.** 0.003<u>4</u>81   **29.** 1<u>2</u>.11362   **30.** 32.9<u>5</u>28

31. Algebra Solve $\frac{n}{5} = 5$
   A. $n = 25$ **B.** $n = 10$ **C.** $n = 1$ **D.** $n = 0$

32. Algebra Evaluate the expression $12x - 5$ for $x = 9$.
   A. $x = 25$ **B.** $x = 103$ **C.** $x = 1$ **D.** $x = 0$

All text pages available online and on CD-ROM.

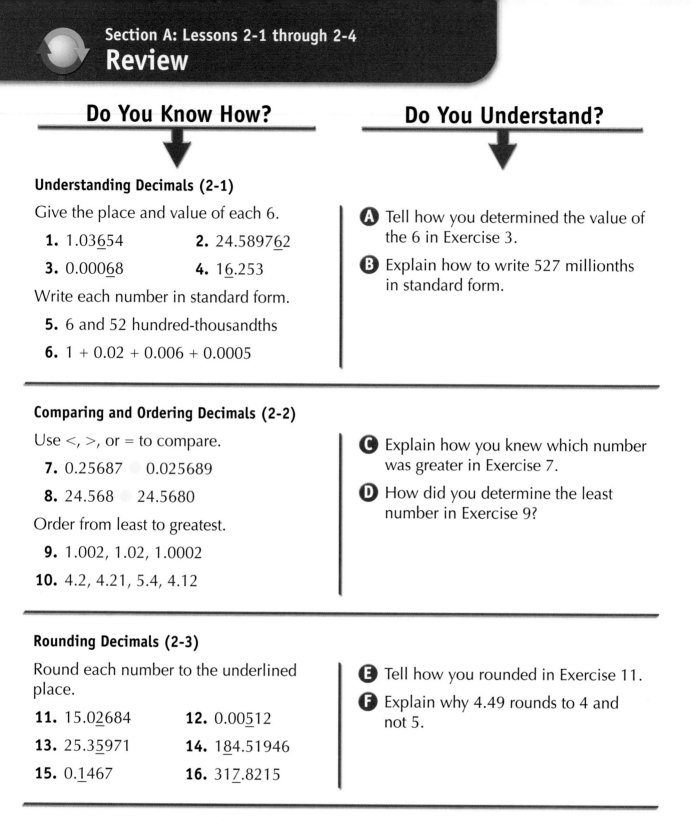

Do You Know How?

Do You Understand?

Understanding Decimals (2-1)

Give the place and value of each 6.

1. 1.03654

2. 24.589762

3. 0.00068

4. 16.253

Write each number in standard form.

5. 6 and 52 hundred-thousandths

6. 1 + 0.02 + 0.006 + 0.0005

Ⓐ Tell how you determined the value of the 6 in Exercise 3.

Ⓑ Explain how to write 527 millionths in standard form.

Comparing and Ordering Decimals (2-2)

Use <, >, or = to compare.

7. 0.25687 ⬤ 0.025689

8. 24.568 ⬤ 24.5680

Order from least to greatest.

9. 1.002, 1.02, 1.0002

10. 4.2, 4.21, 5.4, 4.12

Ⓒ Explain how you knew which number was greater in Exercise 7.

Ⓓ How did you determine the least number in Exercise 9?

Rounding Decimals (2-3)

Round each number to the underlined place.

11. 15.02684

12. 0.00512

13. 25.35971

14. 184.51946

15. 0.1467

16. 317.8215

Ⓔ Tell how you rounded in Exercise 11.

Ⓕ Explain why 4.49 rounds to 4 and not 5.

Estimating with Decimals (2-4)

Estimate each answer.

17. 36 × $8.95

18. $8.35 + $12.95

19. 49.95 ÷ 7.68

20. 78.56 − 39.18

21. 2.6 × 48.1

22. 17.3 + 2.5 + 9.8

23. 197.16 ÷ 8.3

24. 54.35 − 11.49

Ⓖ Describe the method you used to estimate in Exercise 22.

Ⓗ Explain what compatible numbers are and how you can use them in Exercise 21.

MULTIPLE CHOICE

1. Which is 12.056874 rounded to the nearest thousandth? (2-3)

    A. 12.1   **B.** 12.06   **C.** 12.057   **D.** 12.0569

2. Which is the standard form for 25 hundred-thousandths? (2-1)

    A. 0.0025   **B.** 0.00025   **C.** 0.025   **D.** 0.000025

FREE RESPONSE

Give the place and value of the 8 in each number. (2-1)

3. 12.8679   **4.** 16.258   **5.** 1.02968   **6.** 385.62

Write each in standard form. (2-1)

7. $1 + 0.03 + 0.005 + 0.0006$ **8.** 47 hundredths

Use $<$, $>$, or $=$ to compare. (2-2)

9. 1.365   13.65   **10.** 1.02   1.020   **11.** 1.658   1.568

Order from least to greatest. (2-2)

12. 1.02, 1.2, 1.12, 1.32   **13.** 36.52, 3.652, 3.562, 35.62

Think It Through

I should **align the numbers** first before comparing them.

Round each number to the underlined place. (2-3)

14. 27.56<u>4</u>92   **15.** 0.03<u>5</u>198   **16.** 76.<u>5</u>367   **17.** <u>0</u>.9842

Estimate each answer. (2-4)

18. $95.86 \div 15.7$ **19.** $18.23 − $5.98

20. 2.8×3.122 **21.** $36 + 58.4$

22. $4.5 + 2.78 + 30.0138$ **23.** $78.234 − 12.005666$

24. 74.89×103.305 **25.** $13.3666 \div 6.89$

26. Use the table of Leroy's batting averages at the right. List the batting averages from least to greatest. (2-2)

Leroy's Batting Averages

Year	Average
1	0.351
2	0.339
3	0.329
4	0.357

Writing in Math

27. Which compatible numbers could you use to estimate the quotient $57.9 \div 6.2$. Explain your choice. (2-4)

28. Explain how you know that 7.2 is greater than 7.08. (2-2)

Key Idea
Adding and
subtracting
decimals is similar
to adding and
subtracting whole
numbers.

Think It Through

I **remember** that
annexing zeros
does not change
the decimal's value.

Adding and Subtracting Whole Numbers and Decimals

LEARN

How can you add decimals?

When the starting gun is fired, relay runners can lose
0.2 second in reaction time, and another 1.8 seconds to
go from a standing start to running speed. About how
many seconds pass before running speed is reached?

✓ **WARM UP**

Estimate.

1. 80.6 + 501 + 102.4

2. 6,289.867 − 284.499

3. 8.592 − 4.635

4. 0.198 + 1.18

Example A

Find 0.2 + 1.8.
Estimate: 0 + 2 = 2

	What You **Think**	What You **Write**

STEP 1 Write the numbers,
lining up decimal
points.

$$\begin{array}{r} 0.2 \\ + 1.8 \\ \hline \end{array}$$

STEP 2 Add the tenths.
Regroup if necessary.
Write the decimal
point in your answer.

$$\begin{array}{r} 0.2 \\ + 1.8 \\ \hline 2.0 \end{array}$$

The answer and estimate match, so the answer is reasonable.

Example B

Find 5.6 + 2.973.
Estimate: 6 + 3 = 9

$$\begin{array}{r} 5.600 \\ + 2.973 \\ \hline 8.573 \end{array}$$

Write the numbers,
lining up the decimal
points. Add thousandths,
hundredths, tenths.
Regroup if necessary.
Write the decimal point
in your answer.

Since 8.573 is close to 9, the
answer is reasonable.

Example C

Use a calculator to find
338.09 + 517.3.

Estimate: 300 + 500 = 800

Press: 338.09 ⊞ 517.3 [ENTER =]

Display: ┌──────────┐
│ *855.39* │
└──────────┘

Since 855.39 is close to 800,
the answer in the display is
reasonable.

✔ Talk About It

1. Why do you line up decimal points when you add decimals?

2. Is it necessary to annex zeros when adding decimals? Explain.

How can you subtract decimals?

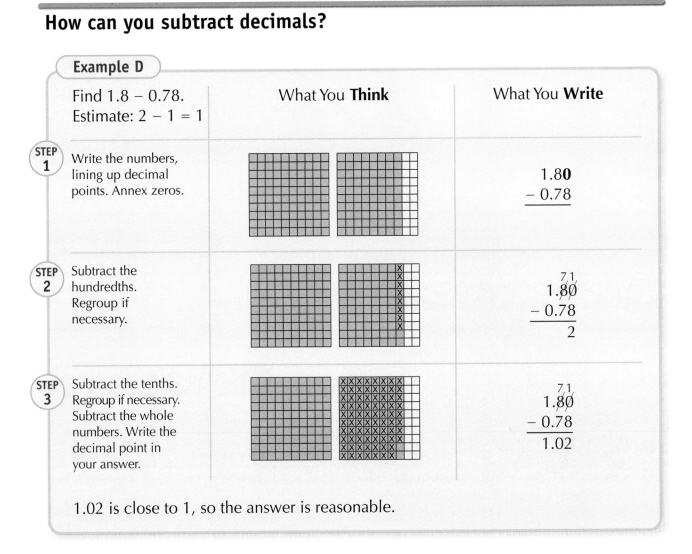

Example D

Find 1.8 – 0.78. Estimate: 2 – 1 = 1	What You **Think**	What You **Write**
STEP 1 Write the numbers, lining up decimal points. Annex zeros.		1.**80** – 0.78
STEP 2 Subtract the hundredths. Regroup if necessary.		7 1 1.8̶0̶ – 0.78 2
STEP 3 Subtract the tenths. Regroup if necessary. Subtract the whole numbers. Write the decimal point in your answer.		7 1 1.8̶0̶ – 0.78 1.02

1.02 is close to 1, so the answer is reasonable.

✔ Talk About It

3. Comparing your answer to an estimate is one way to check your subtraction. What other method can you use to check your answer?

4. Find 12 – 8.62. Explain how you found your answer.

5. Where would you place the decimal point in the number 3,321?

CHECK ✔

For another example, see Set 2-5 on p. 133.

Find each sum or difference.

1. 16.4 – 3.85   **2.** 5.83 + 6.025 + 13.7   **3.** 3.6 – 2.973   **4.** 2 – 0.25

5. Number Sense Using each of the digits 3, 6, 2, and 8 exactly once, make 2 decimals whose sum is between 14 and 15.

A Skills and Understanding

Find each sum or difference.

6. 36 − 17.23   **7.** 1.235 + 3.56   **8.** 5.628 − 0.785   **9.** 0.35 + 0.87

10. 28.3 − 17.25   **11.** 6.234 + 0.582   **12.** 62.987 − 54.3   **13.** 6.23 + 15.6

14. 2,368 + 569   **15.** 0.364 + 26   **16.** 0.55 − 0.364   **17.** 7,659.3 − 578.62

18. 23,491 − 2,678   **19.** 56.1 − 31.08   **20.** 479.92 + 0.832   **21.** 32 − 16.23

22. $5.26 + $3.12 + $9.56   **23.** 8.6 + 40 + 23.7888   **24.** 304,562 + 431 + 990.21

25. How many times greater is 3 than 0.3? than 0.03?

26. Number Sense Using each of the digits 9, 5, 3, 2, 1, and 0 exactly once, make 2 decimals whose difference is between 40 and 42.

B Reasoning and Problem Solving

Math and Social Studies

27. Find the total cost for a baseball glove, ball, and bat in 1933. Calculate the cost for the same items given with 2003 prices.

For 28–30, find the difference in price from 1933 to 2003.

28. bicycle   **29.** football   **30.** ice skates

31. Use estimation to find the item price that increased the most over 70 years. Which item price increased the least?

For 32–37, use mental math to find each sum or difference.

Toy	1933	2003
Baseball	$0.19	$3.49
Baseball bat	$0.59	$12.98
Baseball glove	$2.89	$9.99
Bicycle	$29.95	$139.95
Board game	$1.59	$19.95
Electric train	$8.79	$259.95
Football	$0.98	$14.95
Ice skates	$4.69	$34.95

32. 5.62 + 3.25   **33.** 8.7 + 2.05

34. 9.56 − 3.24   **35.** 2 − 1.6

36. 16.82 + 19.18   **37.** 62.04 − 59.99

38. Writing in Math Is the way Leah subtracted correct? If not, tell why and provide the correct answer.

Leah's Solution

Find 34.7 - 23.083

```
  34.7
- 23.083
  11.783
```

C Extensions

39. Solve for *y*.
$y - 4.5 = 8.6$

40. Solve for *n*.
$n + 0.7 = 19.2$

41. Reasoning Use the Associative and Commutative Properties of Addition to mentally compute the sum $0.8 + 0.3 + 0.7 + 4.6 + 0.2$.

Mixed Review and Test Prep

Take It to the NET
Test Prep
www.scottforesman.com

Estimate each answer.

42. $25.79 \div 3.6$

43. $32.698 - 21.065$

44. 62.4×2.85

45. Find $24.3 - 15.28$.

A. 9.18 **B.** 8.18 **C.** 9.02 **D.** 9.12

Enrichment

Venn diagram and Sets

A **set** is a collection of objects or numbers. Sets are described by the objects they contain. For example, the set *quadrilaterals* contains all 4-sided polygons. The set *parallelograms* contains 4-sided polygons having opposite sides the same length and parallel. The set *parallelograms* is a **subset** of the set *quadrilaterals* because every parallelogram is a 4-sided polygon. *Squares* is a subset of *rectangles* and *rhombuses*.

A **Venn diagram** can be used to show how certain sets and subsets are related.

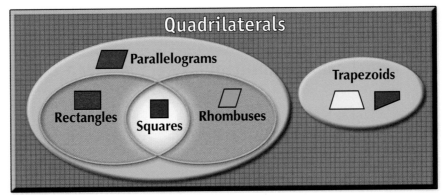

1. Is the set *rhombuses* a subset of *parallelograms*? How do you know?

2. Is a square always a rectangle? Why or why not?

3. Is the set *trapezoids* a subset of *quadrilaterals*? of *parallelograms*? Explain.

The set that contains no members is called **the empty set.**

4. The set of all 2-sided polygons is the empty set. Why?

Materials
- 10-by-10 decimal grids or
  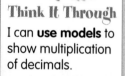 **tools**

- colored pencils or markers

Think It Through
I can **use models** to show multiplication of decimals.

Multiplying Whole Numbers and Decimals

LEARN

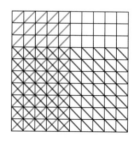
✔ **WARM UP**

Estimate.

1. 5.88 × 3.03

2. 725 × 4

3. 172 × 9.9

How can you multiply a whole number by a decimal?

You can use the same methods for multiplying decimals as you use for multiplying whole numbers.

Activity

a. To find 3 × 0.64, shade the tenths for the decimal number on a grid. Do this 3 times, using a different color each time.

b. Using the same 3 colors, shade three groups of the hundredths for the decimal number.

3 × 0.64 = 192 hundredths = 1.92

c. Count all of the shaded hundredths.

d. Use grids to find 1.2 × 2 and 2 × 0.18.

How can you multiply a decimal by a decimal?

Activity

a. To find 0.5 × 0.7, shade 5 columns using the same color to show 5 tenths.

b. Shade 7 rows in another color to show 7 tenths.

c. Count the hundredths in the overlapping shaded area.

0.5 × 0.7 = 35 hundredths = 0.35

d. Use grids to find 0.4 × 0.7 and 1.6 × 0.3.

Where is the decimal point placed in a product?

TEST TALK

Think It Through

It is **reasonable** that the product of two numbers less than 1 is less than 1.

Example A

Find 52.3×2.6.
Estimate: $50 \times 3 = 150$

$$
\begin{array}{r}
\overset{1\ 1}{52.3} \leftarrow \text{1 decimal place} \\
\times\ \ 2.6 \leftarrow \text{1 decimal place} \\
\hline
3138 \\
+\ 10460 \\
\hline
135.98 \leftarrow \text{2 decimal places from the right}
\end{array}
$$

Count the decimal places in each factor. Add the number of decimal places. Start at the right of the product and move left the total number of decimal places.

The answer is reasonable because 135.98 is close to 150.

Example B

Find 0.42×0.09.

$$
\begin{array}{r}
\overset{1}{0.42} \leftarrow \text{2 decimal places} \\
\times\ 0.09 \leftarrow \text{2 decimal places} \\
\hline
0.0378 \leftarrow \text{4 decimal places from the right}
\end{array}
$$

Sometimes you have to annex zeros to the left of a product in order to place the decimal point correctly.

Use a calculator to check your answer.

Press: 0.42 [×] 0.09 [=]

Display: | 0.0378 |

✔ Talk About It

1. Estimate the product in Example B. How does your estimate help you place the decimal point in the product?

2. The product of tenths times tenths is hundredths. How does this relate to moving 2 decimal places in the answer for Example A?

3. When you multiply two numbers, each of which is less than 1, is the product always less than either of the factors? Explain using at least 2 examples.

CHECK ✓

For another example, see Set 2-6 on p. 133.

Place the decimal point in each product.

1. $5 \times 0.403 = 2015$ **2.** $93.3 \times 0.03 = 2799$ **3.** $6.7 \times 8.42 = 56414$

Find each product.

4. 15×0.8 **5.** 6.8×2.3 **6.** 0.4×0.18 **7.** 0.007×0.33

8. 52.4×2.8 **9.** 210×0.001 **10.** $8.3 \times 100 \times 0.1$ **11.** $10 \times 0.4 \times 0.02$

12. Reasoning Explain why $0.8 \times 0.6 \neq 4.8$.

A Skills and Understanding

Place the decimal point in each product.

13. 6 × 0.216 = 1296   **14.** 4 × 58.2 = 2328   **15.** 0.6 × 2.56 = 1536

Find each product.

16. 2,365 × 28   **17.** 268 × 587   **18.** 0.36 × 100   **19.** 1.236 × 2.6

20. 22.6 × 1.3   **21.** 68.54 × 10   **22.** 0.6 × 0.7   **23.** 2.65 × 0.36

24. 1.2 × 2.3 × 12.6   **25.** 32.4 × 0.3 × 100   **26.** 89.7 × 0.1 × 2.6

27. Explain why multiplying numbers by 100 moves the decimal point to the right, and multiplying by 0.01 moves the decimal point to the left.

28. Reasoning Find the product 5.04 × 3. How can you check your answer by using addition?

B Reasoning and Problem Solving

Math and Science

The bar graph gives the mean amounts of rainfall for several U.S. cities.

29. Which city has 3 times the rainfall that Albuquerque has?

30. The mean rainfall for April in New Orleans is 2.5 times greater than that of Denver. Calculate the April mean rainfall for New Orleans, LA.

31.  Is the explanation below correct? If not, explain why.

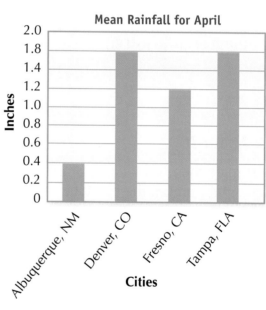

Mean Rainfall for April

Explain where to place the decimal point in the product 2.6 × 5.5.

```
   5.5
 × 2.6
  330
+1100
 14.30
```

The decimal point belongs between the 4 and the 3. I counted the number of decimal places in the factors and counted that many places from the right to place the decimal into the product.

Think It Through
If I **estimate** a product **I can tell if my answer is reasonable.**

C Extensions

Algebra Evaluate each expression.

32. $3.4 + 5.2 \times 1.2$ **33.** $8.5 - 4.5 \times 0.2$ **34.** $0.9 + 7.1 \times 2.3$

Algebra Evaluate each expression for $n = 0.7$ and 0.07.

35. n^2 **36.** $4n$ **37.** $1.7n + 8.21$

To multiply two decimals mentally, sometimes it helps to halve one factor and double the other factor.

$$24 \times 1.5 = (24 \div 2) \times (1.5 \times 2) = 12 \times 3 = 36$$

For 38–40, use halving and doubling to find each product mentally.

38. 18×4.5 **39.** 0.25×40 **40.** 32×1.25

Mixed Review and Test Prep

**Take It to the NET
Test Prep**
www.scottforesman.com

Find each sum or difference.

41. $23.6 - 18.05$ **42.** $\$659.25 + \$1,362.18$ **43.** $2.3 + 5.689$

44. 12.38456 rounded to the nearest thousandth is

    A. 12.38   **B.** 12.39   **C.** 12.384   **D.** 12.385

45. 374.0153 rounded to the nearest hundredth is

    A. 374.00   **B.** 374.01   **C.** 374.02   **D.** 400

Practice Game

Powerful Ten

Players: 2   **Materials:** 2 number cubes, labeled 1–6

1. Players take turns tossing 2 number cubes.

2. Players choose a number on one cube as a power of 10, and use the other number as a factor. A player tossing a 3 and a 5 can write 3×10^5 or 5×10^3.

3. Players express their numbers in standard form.

4. After 3 rounds, players add their numbers.

5. The player with the greater sum is the winner.

Variation: The player with the lesser sum wins.

Materials
• calculator

Think It Through

To divide, **I can think about equal parts.**

Dividing by a Whole Number

LEARN

How can you write a quotient?

WARM UP

Estimate.

1. $832 \div 41$
2. $15.9 \div 8$
3. $6.39 \div 2.2$
4. $100.5 \div 10.8$

Example A

Find $8,954 \div 44$.

STEP 1

Estimate. Use compatible numbers. Since $8,000 \div 40 = 200$, start dividing in the hundreds place.

$$\begin{array}{r} 2 \\ 44\overline{)8,954} \\ -88 \\ \hline 1 \end{array}$$

Divide.
Multiply.
Subtract.
Compare: $1 < 44$

STEP 2

Divide the tens.

$$\begin{array}{r} 20 \\ 44\overline{)8,954} \\ -88\downarrow \\ \hline 15 \\ -0 \\ \hline 15 \end{array}$$

Bring down.
Divide.
Multiply.
Subtract.
Compare: $15 < 44$

STEP 3

Divide the ones.

$$\begin{array}{r} 203 \\ 44\overline{)8,954} \\ -88\downarrow \\ \hline 15 \\ -0\downarrow \\ \hline 154 \\ -132 \\ \hline 22 \end{array}$$

Bring down.
Divide.
Multiply.
Subtract.
Compare: $22 < 44$
Write the remainder.

$8,954 \div 44 = 203$ R22

Example B

Find $8,954 \div 44$.

STEP 1

Divide as usual.

$$\begin{array}{r} 203 \\ 44\overline{)8,954} \\ -88 \\ \hline 15 \\ -0 \\ \hline 154 \\ -132 \\ \hline 22 \end{array}$$

Bring down.
Divide.
Multiply.
Subtract.
Compare: $22 < 44$

STEP 2

Place the decimal point. Annex a zero in the dividend and bring it down.

$$\begin{array}{r} 203. \\ 44\overline{)8,954.0} \\ -88\downarrow\downarrow \\ \hline 15 \\ -0\downarrow \\ \hline 154 \\ -132\downarrow \\ \hline 22\ 0 \end{array}$$

STEP 3

$$\begin{array}{r} 203.5 \\ 44\overline{)8,954.0} \\ -88\downarrow\downarrow \\ \hline 15 \\ -0\downarrow \\ \hline 154 \\ -132\downarrow \\ \hline 22\ 0 \\ -22\ 0 \\ \hline 0 \end{array}$$

Divide.
Multiply.
Subtract.
Continue until there is no remainder.

$8,954 \div 44 = 203.5$

✔ Talk About It

1. Explain why a remainder of 22 in Example A is the same as 0.5 in Example B.

2. Explain how to check a division problem.

Take It to the NET
More Examples
www.scottforesman.com

What can the divisor and dividend tell you about place values in the quotient?

Example C

Divisor is less than dividend

Find 113.76 ÷ 48.

Estimate: 100 ÷ 50 = 2

Place the decimal point in the quotient above the decimal point in the dividend. Divide as usual.

```
       2.37
48)113.76
  - 96
    17 7
  - 14 4
     3 36
   - 3 36
        0
```

113.76 ÷ 48 = 2.37

Example D

Divisor is greater than dividend

Find 7.65 ÷ 9.

Estimate: 7 ÷ 7 = 1,
        so 7 ÷ 9 < 1.

Since the quotient is less than 1, put a zero in the ones place. Place the decimal point in the quotient above the decimal point in the dividend. Divide as usual.

```
      0.85
9)7.65
 - 7 2
    45
  - 45
     0
```

7.65 ÷ 9 = 0.85

Example E

Dividing money

Find $114 ÷ 48.

Estimate: $100 ÷ 50 = $2

Place the decimal point and divide as usual.

```
      2.375
48)114.000    Since it is a
  - 96        money amount,
    18 0      you need to
  - 14 4      annex 3 zeros
    3 60      in the dividend
  - 3 36      so you can
     240      round the
   - 240      quotient to
       0      hundredths.
```

$114 ÷ 48 = $2.38

✔ Talk About It

3. In Example C, how do you know to place the first digit of the quotient in the ones place?

4. Why do you need to round the quotient in Example E to hundredths?

CHECK ✔

For another example, see Set 2-7 on p. 133.

Copy and complete.

1.
```
       .9
56)278.88
 -  2
    5
  - 5 0 4
      4
    -
        0
```

2.
```
    0.   1
6)3.006
 -
         6
 -
```

3.
```
       .8
45)622.8
  -    0
      72
   - 135
       8
   - 360
      18
    -  8
       0
```

Find each quotient. Round to the nearest hundredth.

4. 62 ÷ 5   5. 5.68 ÷ 8   6. 90 ÷ 9,000   7. $4.73 ÷ 11

8. **Number Sense** Give the quotient to 15 ÷ 8 to the nearest hundredth. Explain how you computed the quotient.

A Skills and Understanding

Find each quotient. Round to the nearest hundredth if necessary.

9. $2{,}244 \div 17$ **10.** $1.36 \div 10$ **11.** $2.16 \div 12$ **12.** $441 \div 98$

13. $1.694 \div 14$ **14.** $8 \div 8{,}000$ **15.** $\$94.56 \div 5$ **16.** $54.30 \div 15$

17. $2.7 \div 9$ **18.** $6.03 \div 9$ **19.** $\$23.10 \div 11$ **20.** $100 \div 1{,}000$

21. Calculator Use your calculator to find $2.7 \div 2{,}000{,}000$ and $5.4 \div 4{,}000{,}000$. How do the answers compare? Explain.

22. Number Sense Without using a calculator or paper and pencil, decide which is greater, $23.8 \div 4$ or $23.8 \div 40$.

B Reasoning and Problem Solving

Math and Everyday Life

Many shoppers decide which products to buy by comparing the unit cost or price per item, pound, ounce, etc.

For 23–25, find the price per ounce or pound of each item in the table to the nearest cent.

	Item	Name Brand	Price per oz or lb	Generic	Price per oz or lb
23.	Dish Detergent	14 oz, $1.25		32 oz, $2.29	
24.	Beans	2 lb, $1.25		1 lb, $0.59	
25.	Rice	10 lb, $4.99		5 lb, $2.25	

Which is the most economical size and brand for each item?

26. dish detergent

27. rice

28. Reasoning Is the name brand or generic brand always the most economical? Can you think of a reason why or why not?

29. Writing in Math Is Jon's work below correct? If not, explain why and give a correct response.

Find $0.04 \div 20$. Explain how you found your answer.

$$\begin{array}{r} 0.2 \\ 20\overline{)0.040} \\ -\ 40 \\ \hline 0 \end{array}$$

I put the decimal point in the quotient above the decimal point in the dividend. Then I divided 2 into 4 and got 2.

C Extensions

Study the examples below. Use a calculator to find a pattern.

$16 \div 40 = 0.4$	$60 \div 600 = 0.1$	$30 \div 6{,}000 = 0.005$
$1.6 \div 40 = 0.04$	$6 \div 600 = 0.01$	$3 \div 6{,}000 = 0.0005$
$0.16 \div 40 = 0.004$	$0.6 \div 600 = 0.001$	$0.3 \div 6{,}000 = 0.00005$

Think It Through
- I can **look for patterns** of zeros and patterns in the decimal point placement to find a rule.
- I can **use basic facts** to help.

30. Describe the patterns that you see in the examples above.

31. Explain why all the quotients are less than 1.

Mixed Review and Test Prep

Take It to the NET
Test Prep
www.scottforesman.com

Find each product.

32. 23.5×0.23

33. 0.63×100

34. 12.6×2.1

35. Algebra What is the solution of $3x = 39$?

    A. $x = 13$ **B.** $x = 35$ **C.** $x = 42$ **D.** $x = 117$

36. What is the greatest possible remainder when you divide by 12?

    A. 0   **B.** 6   **C.** 11   **D.** 12

Enrichment

Gauss' Sum

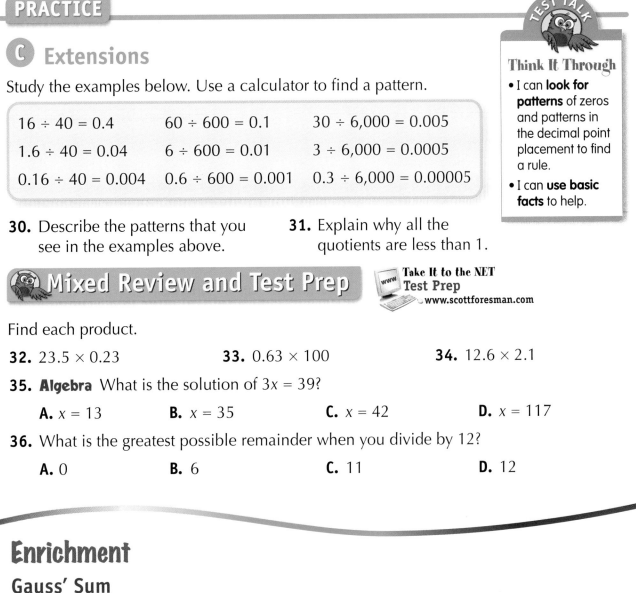

$1 + 2 + 3 + 4 + 5 + \ldots + 95 + 96 + 97 + 98 + 99 + 100$

When the mathematician Carl Friedrich Gauss was a student, his teacher gave him the assignment to add up all the numbers from 1 to 100. Carl used the pattern above to find the sum within minutes.

1. Gauss paired addends and noticed that the sum of each pair was the same. What is this common sum?

2. How many pairs of addends could Gauss make?

3. What multiplication sentence gives the sum of all the numbers 1 to 100? 1 to 10? 1 to 20?

Carl Friedrich Gauss

Problem-Solving Skill

Reading Helps!

Creating graphic organizers
can help you with...
interpreting remainders.

Key Idea
The real-world situation tells how to interpret the remainder.

Think It Through

I can **use the information** in the problem to help me interpret the remainder.

Interpreting Remainders

LEARN

How is the remainder important when giving the answer to a problem?

When you solve a word problem using division, the real-world situation tells how to make sense of the answer.

Hiking The John Muir Trail is a path through the Sierra Nevada Mountains in California. Your group plans to cover 210 miles of the trail by hiking 12 miles each day.

Daily Schedule

6 AM – 6:45 AM	Breakfast	1 PM – 4 PM	Hike
7 AM – 10 AM	Hike	4 PM – 6 PM	Free Time
10 AM – 12 PM	Free Time	6 PM – 6:45 PM	Dinner
12 PM – 12:45 PM	Lunch	7 PM – 10 PM	Free Time

Example A	Example B	Example C
Read and Understand		
How many days will your group hike exactly 12 miles?	How many days will it take to hike 210 miles of the trail?	Of the scheduled 6 hours of hiking time, how many hours will you be hiking on the last day?
Plan and Solve		
$210 \div 12 = 17$ R6 The group will hike exactly 12 miles each day for 17 days.	$210 \div 12 = 17$ R6 Since the remainder is $\frac{1}{2}$ the divisor, only $\frac{1}{2}$ an extra day is needed.	$210 \div 12 = 17$ R6 $= 17.5$ You will be hiking about 0.5 days beyond 17. 0.5×6 hours $= 3$ hours You will hike 3 hours on the last day.
Look Back and Check		
Because 17R6 is greater than 17, you know more than 17 days are needed.	$17.5 \times 12 =$ 210 miles	$(17 \text{ days} \times 6 \text{ hours}) + 3$ $= 105$ hours $= 17.5$ days.

✔ Talk About It

1. What is the answer to each of the three questions above?

2. How much of the trail was left to hike at the end of the 17th day?

3. Number Sense If your group plans to hike 10 miles per day, how many days would it take to cover the 210-mile path? Use mental math.

CHECK ✓

For another example, see Set 2-8 on p. 134.

Trail Supplies There are 18 hikers in your group. The supplies are divided so that each hiker will carry the same amount.

1. There are 60 packages of granola. How many whole packages of granola will each hiker carry?

2. What does the remainder or decimal part of your answer represent?

3. How many packages of granola are left over?

4. The cost for 60 packages of granola was $76. Find the cost per package.

PRACTICE

For more practice, see Set 2-8 on p. 138.

Miles Hiked Because of the trail's steep terrain, it took your group 6 hours to hike 7 miles.

5. How many whole miles did the group cover each hour?

6. What does the remainder or decimal part of your answer represent?

7. How many hours will it take your group to cover 12 miles?

Getting to the Trail The group of 18 hikers drove to the beginning of the trail in mini-vans. Each vehicle could hold up to 7 hikers.

8. If two mini-vans were filled to capacity, how many hikers were left over?

9. How many mini-vans were needed to transport the hikers?

10. The total cost for mini-van rentals and driver fees was $201. What was each hiker's share of the cost?

11. **Writing in Math** After finishing the hike, you and 2 friends went to a deli for dinner. You split 2 large submarine sandwiches and 2 large bottled waters, sharing the cost equally. How much did each person pay? Explain how you found your answer and interpreted the remainder.

Trail's End Deli	SMALL	LARGE
SANDWICHES		
Submarine	$2.99	$5.19
Tuna Melt	$1.89	$3.75
SALAD		
Chef's Salad	$1.99	$3.50
Caesar Salad	$2.49	$4.89
BEVERAGES		
Fruit juice	$1.29	$2.25
Bottled Water	$1.85	$2.89

 All text pages available online and on CD-ROM.

Materials
• decimal models
  or  tools

Think It Through
I can **use models** to show division by decimals.

Dividing by a Decimal

LEARN

How can you divide by a decimal?

Nihad and his friends divide the cost of a $2.70 bag of nuts. Each person contributes $0.90. How many people will share the nuts?

Activity

You can use the same methods for dividing decimals as you use for dividing whole numbers.

a. Find $2.7 \div 0.9$.

b. Circle groups of 0.9.

c. Count the circled groups.

d. Use decimal models to find $3.0 \div 0.3$ and $2.5 \div 0.5$.

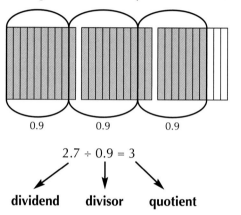

$2.7 \div 0.9 = 3$

dividend   divisor   quotient

How can you change a decimal divisor into a whole number divisor without changing the quotient?

Activity

a. Study the patterns below. Compare the first and second columns.

Pattern 1	
$80 \div 0.4 = 200$	$800 \div 4 = 200$
$8 \div 0.4 = 20$	$80 \div 4 = 20$
$0.8 \div 0.4 = 2$	$8 \div 4 = 2$
$0.08 \div 0.4 = 0.2$	$0.8 \div 4 = 0.2$

Pattern 2	
$80 \div 0.04 = 2,000$	$8,000 \div 4 = 2,000$
$8 \div 0.04 = 200$	$800 \div 4 = 200$
$0.8 \div 0.04 = 20$	$80 \div 4 = 20$
$0.08 \div 0.04 = 2$	$8 \div 4 = 2$

b. For Pattern 1, what happens to the quotient when you multiply the dividend and divisor by 10?

c. What number were the dividend and divisor multiplied by in Pattern 2?

d. Complete the table at the right.

Dividend	Divisor	Multiply Dividend and Divisor by:	Quotient
5.2	0.013	1,000	
5.2	0.13		40
5.2	1.3		

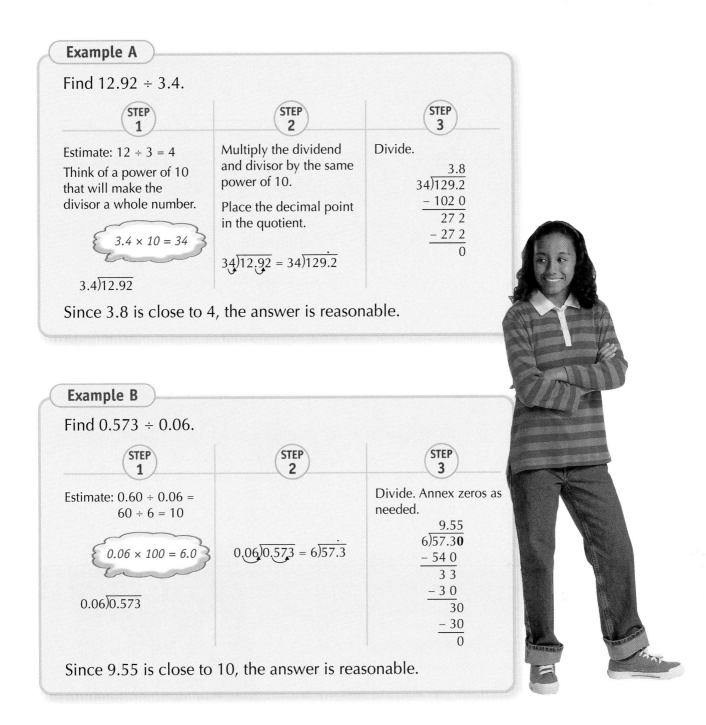

Example A

Find 12.92 ÷ 3.4.

STEP 1

Estimate: 12 ÷ 3 = 4

Think of a power of 10 that will make the divisor a whole number.

3.4 × 10 = 34

3.4)‾12.92‾

STEP 2

Multiply the dividend and divisor by the same power of 10.

Place the decimal point in the quotient.

34)‾12.92‾ = 34)‾129.2‾

STEP 3

Divide.

```
      3.8
34)129.2
   -102 0
     27 2
   - 27 2
        0
```

Since 3.8 is close to 4, the answer is reasonable.

Example B

Find 0.573 ÷ 0.06.

STEP 1

Estimate: 0.60 ÷ 0.06 = 60 ÷ 6 = 10

0.06 × 100 = 6.0

0.06)‾0.573‾

STEP 2

0.06)‾0.573‾ = 6)‾57.3‾

STEP 3

Divide. Annex zeros as needed.

```
      9.55
6)57.30
  - 54 0
     3 3
   - 3 0
       30
     - 30
        0
```

Since 9.55 is close to 10, the answer is reasonable.

✔ Talk About It

1. Why is it necessary to multiply the dividend and divisor by the same power of 10?
2. A number is divided by a decimal less than 1. Is the quotient greater than the dividend?

Take It to the NET
More Examples
www.scottforesman.com

CHECK ✓

For another example, see Set 2-9 on p. 134.

Find each quotient.

1. 21 ÷ 0.4   **2.** 0.02 ÷ 0.5   **3.** 2.7 ÷ 5.4   **4.** 64.97 ÷ 8.9

5. Number Sense 4 ÷ 1.2 ≈ 4. Is the actual quotient greater than 4? Explain.

Ⓐ Skills and Understanding

Find each quotient.

6. $6.39 \div 0.9$ **7.** $15.75 \div 2.5$ **8.** $10.755 \div 0.1$ **9.** $4.788 \div 0.42$

10. $96.1 \div 0.1$ **11.** $53.30 \div 8.2$ **12.** $0.3567 \div 8.7$ **13.** $26 \div 0.5$

14. $3.2 \div 0.8$ **15.** $22.8 \div 0.4$ **16.** $24.06 \div 0.01$ **17.** $24.2 \div 55$

18. Reasoning An estimate for $41.9 \div 8$ is about 5. Is the actual quotient greater than or less than 5? Explain.

19. Mental Math Compute the quotients $4.5 \div 0.9$ and $2.4 \div 0.8$ mentally.

Ⓑ Reasoning and Problem Solving

Math and Social Studies

The table at the right shows bushel prices paid to U.S. farmers for grain crops. For 20–22, find how many times as great the 2000 price was compared to the 1940 price. Round your answer to the nearest whole number.

Data File

Crop	1940($)	2000($)
Corn	0.62	1.85
Oats	0.30	1.05
Soybeans	0.89	4.54
Wheat	0.67	2.65

20. oats   **21.** soybeans   **22.** wheat

23. Which crop showed the greatest increase? Give a possible reason for the increase.

24. Writing in Math In *Polar the Titanic Bear,* Polar was purchased with German currency known as Deutsche marks. Suppose Polar cost 25 Deutsche marks and 1 United States dollar is worth about 1.94 Deutsche marks. What would Polar's purchase price be in dollars?

Ⓒ Extensions

25. Calculator Use a calculator to find 0.868×0.007.
Press: 0.868 [×] 0.007 [ENTER =]

26. Calculator Use a calculator to find $0.868 \div 0.007$.
Press: 0.868 [÷] 0.007 [ENTER =]

27. Calculator Copy and complete the table at the right. Use your calculator to find each product and quotient. Round each answer to the nearest hundredth. Use your completed table to answer Exercises 28–30.

Product	Quotient
$13.698 \times 0.82 = $ ____	$13.698 \div 0.82 = $ ____
$41.037 \times 0.95 = $ ____	$41.037 \div 0.95 = $ ____
$24.316 \times 1.02 = $ ____	$24.316 \div 1.02 = $ ____

28. What happens to a number when you multiply it by a decimal less than 1? greater than 1?

29. What happens to a number when you divide it by a decimal less than 1? greater than 1?

30. Which do you think is greater, 79.63 × 0.484 or 79.63 ÷ 0.482? Use your calculator to check your answer.

31. On Tuesday, a sports announcer mentioned that the baseball season would open in 60 days. Kimiko can go to the opening game only if it is on a Saturday or Sunday. Explain how to interpret the remainder to decide if Kimiko will be able to go to the game.

 **Mixed Review and Test Prep**

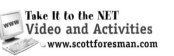 **Take It to the NET**
Test Prep
www.scottforesman.com

Find each answer.

32. 3.16 × 7.5   **33.** 0.206 × 0.14   **34.** 12 − 9.58   **35.** 22.1 + 3.68

36. Algebra Choose the correct answer for $2(13 − 8)^2 − 2 × 8$.

   A. 384   **B.** 368   **C.** 34   **D.** 25

37. The Renner's rented a large truck for $49.95 plus $0.60 per mile. Before returning the truck they filled the gas tank, which cost $9.00. The total cost for renting the truck, including gasoline, was $93.23. Find the number of miles the truck was driven to the nearest mile.

   A. 20 mi   **B.** 57 mi   **C.** 72 mi   **D.** 155 mi

DISCOVERY CHANNEL SCHOOL

Discover Math in Your World

Take It to the NET
Video and Activities
www.scottforesman.com

Tilting Toward Toppling

In 1990, the Leaning Tower of Pisa was closed to the public for fear it would topple over. At the time of its closure, the tower leaned 17 feet from vertical.

1. If 2.7 feet represents one degree of tilt, estimate the degree of tilt in 1990.

2. In 1999, engineers used dozen of drills to remove soil from underneath one side of the tower. This process straightened the tower by about 2 degrees of tilt. What was the tilt in feet after soil extraction?

Do You Know How?

Do You Understand?

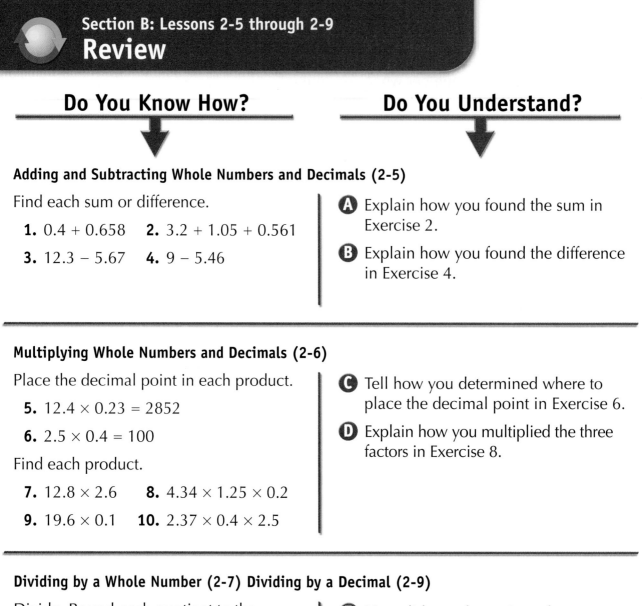

Adding and Subtracting Whole Numbers and Decimals (2-5)

Find each sum or difference.

1. 0.4 + 0.658   **2.** 3.2 + 1.05 + 0.561

3. 12.3 − 5.67   **4.** 9 − 5.46

A Explain how you found the sum in Exercise 2.

B Explain how you found the difference in Exercise 4.

Multiplying Whole Numbers and Decimals (2-6)

Place the decimal point in each product.

5. 12.4 × 0.23 = 2852

6. 2.5 × 0.4 = 100

Find each product.

7. 12.8 × 2.6   **8.** 4.34 × 1.25 × 0.2

9. 19.6 × 0.1   **10.** 2.37 × 0.4 × 2.5

C Tell how you determined where to place the decimal point in Exercise 6.

D Explain how you multiplied the three factors in Exercise 8.

Dividing by a Whole Number (2-7) Dividing by a Decimal (2-9)

Divide. Round each quotient to the nearest hundredth if necessary.

11. 7 ÷ 9   **12.** 38.4 ÷ 4

13. 12 ÷ 25   **14.** 42.8 ÷ 5.4

15. 46.75 ÷ 0.025   **16.** 100 ÷ 7.5

E How did you determine where to place the decimal point in the quotient for Exercise 16.

F Explain how to divide a whole number by a larger whole number.

Problem-Solving Skill: Interpreting Remainders (2-8)

Buttons and Bows Denise makes pillows to sell at her home-decor shop.

17. Denise has 32 yards of ribbon to decorate 12 pillows. How much ribbon can she use for each pillow?

18. Denise needs 108 buttons. If buttons come on cards of 8, how many cards will she need?

G How was the remainder used to determine the answer to Problem 17? to Problem 18?

H For Problem 18, suppose buttons come on cards of 5. How many whole cards of buttons will Denise use?

MULTIPLE CHOICE

1. Which is the quotient for 36.45 ÷ 0.5? (2-9)

A. 7.29   **B.** 72.9   **C.** 0.729   **D.** 729

2. Which is the product for 12.4 × 0.1? (2-6)

A. 0.124   **B.** 1.24   **C.** 12.4   **D.** 0.0124

FREE RESPONSE

Find each sum or difference. (2-5)

3. 12.4 + 3.068   **4.** 18 − 15.94   **5.** 36.089 + 15.34

6. 12.05 + 3.64 + 0.0059   **7.** 17.65 − 14.068   **8.** 0.9517 − 0.3576

Find each product. (2-6)

9. 25.8 × 2.3   **10.** 3.6 × 0.4   **11.** 42.3 × 1.9   **12.** 0.19 × 0.9

13. 3.54 × 0.1   **14.** 0.06 × 0.7   **15.** 0.5 × 3.6 × 27   **16.** 2.5 × 8 × 7.8

Find each quotient. (2-7, 2-9)

17. 52.98 ÷ 100   **18.** 5.11 ÷ 14   **19.** 6 ÷ 15   **20.** 36.87 ÷ 0.03

21. 37.95 ÷ 5   **22.** 9.54 ÷ 1,000   **23.** 0.768 ÷ 0.4   **24.** 11.7652 ÷ 8.78

25. Mrs. Aimi plans to serve 100 barbecue sandwiches at the company picnic. How many packages of barbecue buns will she need if buns come in packages of 8? In packages of 12? (2-8)

26. Mrs. Aimi will put one bowl of potato salad on each of 8 tables. If she makes 30 pounds of potato salad, how many pounds should she put in each bowl? (2-8)

Think It Through
I should **reread the problem to make sure I answered the right question.**

Writing in Math

27. Explain how to add 0.488 + 94.0362. (2-5)

28. Explain why it is sometimes necessary to annex a zero onto the dividend to find the quotient. (2-2)

29. Explain how to determine where to place the decimal in the product 12.5 × 0.244. (2-6)

30. Write a problem that involves division with a remainder. Explain how the remainder determines the answer. (2-8)

Key Idea
Multiplying and dividing by powers of ten is easy to do mentally.

Vocabulary
• exponent (p. 8)
• negative power of ten

Multiplying and Dividing by Powers of Ten

LEARN

What are positive and negative powers of ten?

Some circuit boards have holes with diameters as small as 10^{-2} or 0.01 of an inch. The table at the right shows values for powers of ten. The **positive powers of ten** shown in the table range in value from 1 to 100,000. The **negative powers of ten** range in value from 0.1 to 0.00001. Notice that 10^0 is equal to 1.

Exponential Form	Standard Form	Word Form
10^5	100,000	1 hundred-thousand
10^4	10,000	1 ten-thousand
10^3	1,000	1 thousand
10^2	100	1 hundred
10^1	10	1 ten
10^0	1	one
10^{-1}	0.1	1 tenth
10^{-2}	0.01	1 hundredth
10^{-3}	0.001	1 thousandth
10^{-4}	0.0001	1 ten-thousandth
10^{-5}	0.00001	1 hundred-thousandth

✔ **Talk About It**

1. **Reasoning** What is the relationship between the **exponents** and the number of zeros in the positive powers of ten?

2. **Reasoning** Describe the pattern you see with the number of digits after the decimal point and negative powers of ten.

How can you multiply and divide by positive powers of ten?

Example A

Find 3.45×10^5.

$3.45 \times 10^5 =$

$3.45000. =$

345,000

Move the decimal point the same number of places to the **right** as the exponent.

Annex zeros if necessary.

$3.45 \times 10^5 = 345,000$

Why it Works

Since $10^5 = 100,000$, multiply by 100,000.

$$\begin{array}{r} 100,000 \\ \times \quad 3.45 \\ \hline 345,000 \end{array}$$

TEST TALK

Think It Through
I can use **another method** to prove my answer is the same.

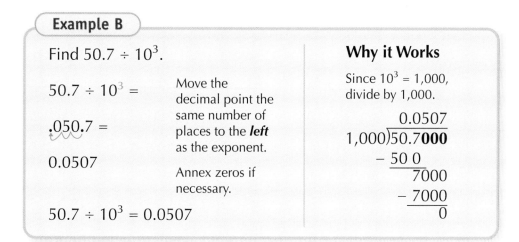

Example B

Find $50.7 \div 10^3$.

$50.7 \div 10^3 =$

$.050.7 =$

0.0507

Move the decimal point the same number of places to the **left** as the exponent.

Annex zeros if necessary.

$50.7 \div 10^3 = 0.0507$

Why it Works

Since $10^3 = 1,000$, divide by 1,000.

$$\begin{array}{r} 0.0507 \\ 1,000\overline{)50.7\mathbf{000}} \\ -\ 50\ 0 \\ \hline 7000 \\ -\ 7000 \\ \hline 0 \end{array}$$

✔ Talk About It

3. Explain why the decimal point moved to the right in Example A and to the left in Example B.

How can you multiply and divide by negative powers of ten?

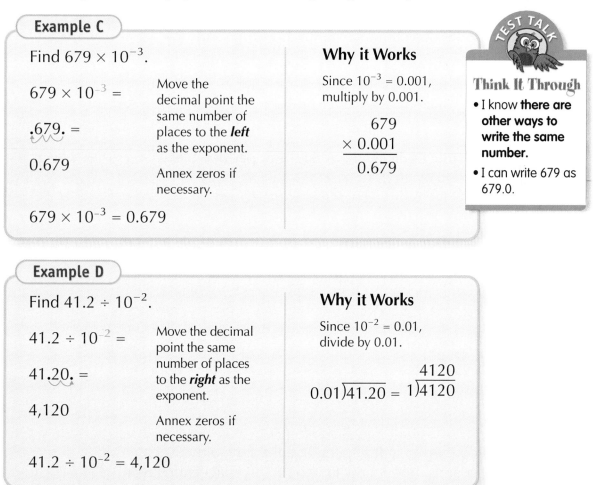

Example C

Find 679×10^{-3}.

$679 \times 10^{-3} =$

$.679. =$

0.679

Move the decimal point the same number of places to the **left** as the exponent.

Annex zeros if necessary.

$679 \times 10^{-3} = 0.679$

Why it Works

Since $10^{-3} = 0.001$, multiply by 0.001.

$$\begin{array}{r} 679 \\ \times\ 0.001 \\ \hline 0.679 \end{array}$$

Think It Through

- I know **there are other ways to write the same number.**
- I can write 679 as 679.0.

Example D

Find $41.2 \div 10^{-2}$.

$41.2 \div 10^{-2} =$

$41.20. =$

$4,120$

Move the decimal point the same number of places to the **right** as the exponent.

Annex zeros if necessary.

$41.2 \div 10^{-2} = 4,120$

Why it Works

Since $10^{-2} = 0.01$, divide by 0.01.

$$0.01\overline{)41.20} = 1\overline{)4120}$$
$$4120$$

✔ Talk About It

4. In Examples A, B, and D, why was it necessary to annex zeros to the product or the quotient?

Take It to the NET
More Examples
www.scottforesman.com

Find each product or quotient.

1. 302.7×10^{-3} **2.** 0.0389×10^{5} **3.** $1{,}549 \times 10^{-2}$

4. $4.87 \div 10^{4}$ **5.** $15{,}781 \div 10^{7}$ **6.** $0.802 \div 10^{-4}$

7. Number Sense Is 70.5×10^{2} equal to $70.5 \div 10^{-2}$?

PRACTICE

For more practice, see Set 2-10 on p. 138.

Ⓐ Skills and Understanding

Find each product or quotient.

8. 2.18×10^{4} **9.** $106.9 \div 10^{-2}$ **10.** 53.98×10^{-4} **11.** 0.236×10^{5}

12. $325 \div 10^{-5}$ **13.** $1{,}258 \div 10^{3}$ **14.** 0.023897×10^{7} **15.** 123.874×10^{4}

16. $0.349 \div 10^{-4}$ **17.** $62.3 \div 10^{-2}$ **18.** $22{,}136.5 \times 10^{-3}$ **19.** $0.001 \div 10^{6}$

20. 27.6×10^{2} **21.** $3.009 \div 10^{2}$ **22.** 52.8×10^{-3} **23.** $0.506 \div 10^{-4}$

24. Number Sense What do you notice about the word forms for 10^{1} and 10^{-1}? 10^{2} and 10^{-2}?

25. Reasoning Why is the product 77×10^{-1} less than 77?

Ⓑ Reasoning and Problem Solving

26. In 1967, a 30-second commercial during the Super Bowl cost 42 thousand dollars. In the year 2002, the cost was 1.9 million dollars. Write these costs in standard form.

Math and Science

27. The unit used to measure computer time is the *nanosecond,* which is 0.000000001 second. Write this number as a power of ten.

> A *googol* and a *googolplex* are defined as follows:
>
> 10^{100} = one googol 10^{googol} = one googolplex

28. How many zeros are in the standard form of a *googol,* which is 10^{100}?

29. One googolplex is 1 followed by how many zeros?

30. If a spacecraft could travel at the speed of light, it would travel almost 10^{6} miles in 5 seconds. About how far would this spacecraft travel in 50 seconds? Write your answer as a power of ten.

31. The speed of light is about 3×10^{10} centimeters per second. A light-year is the distance that light travels in one year. About how many centimeters are in a light-year?

32. <u>Writing in Math</u> Is the explanation below correct? If not, tell why and write a correct response.

> Explain how to find $815.59 \div 10^{-3}$ mentally.

> Because I was dividing by 10^{-3}, I counted over 3 places to the left of the decimal point in 815.59 and wrote 0.81559.

Think It Through

I can **use reasoning** to decide if my answer makes sense.

C Extensions

Negative powers of ten can also be used to write numbers in expanded form. In expanded form, 7.34 is written as follows:

$$7.34 = (7 \times 1.0) + (3 \times 0.1) + (4 \times 0.01) = (7 \times 10^0) + (3 \times 10^{-1}) + (4 \times 10^{-2})$$

Write each number in expanded form using negative powers of ten.

33. 0.582   **34.** 0.0144   **35.** 6.0078   **36.** 52.439

Mixed Review and Test Prep

Take It to the NET
Test Prep
www.scottforesman.com

Find each quotient. If necessary, round to the nearest tenth.

37. $27.8 \div 0.2$ **38.** $126 \div 1.2$ **39.** $39.65 \div 1.5$ **40.** $2.75 \div 9.5$

41. Which expression is equal to zero?

     A. $2^4 \div (8 \times 2)$ **B.** $2^4 \div 8 \times 2$ **C.** $2^4 - 8 \times 2$ **D.** $(2^4 - 8) \times 2$

Learning with Technology

Multiplying by Powers of 10

You can use your calculator to compute numbers that are multiplied by a power of ten. To find 3.2×10^5,

Press: 3.2 $\boxed{\times}$ 10 $\boxed{\wedge}$ 5 $\boxed{\text{ENTER}}$

Display: $\boxed{320000}$

Use your calculator to find each product.

   1. $(2.4 \times 10^2) \times (3.0 \times 10^4)$ **2.** $(4 \times 10^3) \times (2.3 \times 10^3)$ **3.** $(3.2 \times 10^2) \times (2 \times 10^5)$

   4. Compare the power of 10 in each factor above to the power of 10 in each product. Use any pattern you see to predict the power of 10 in the product $(1.5 \times 10^9) \times (4 \times 10^6)$.

Key Idea
Scientific notation is another way to express very large and very small numbers.

Vocabulary
• scientific notation

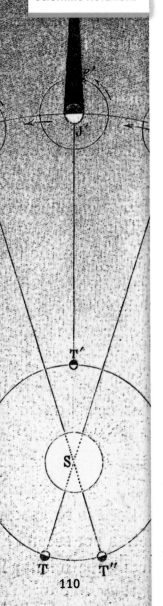

Think It Through
I can use **what I know about multiplying and dividing by powers of ten to write numbers in scientific notation.**

Scientific Notation

LEARN

What is scientific notation?

Over the last 500 years, there have been many methods and devices used to calculate the speed of light. A scientist named Jean Bernard Léon Foucault measured the different angles at which light hit mirrors. Another scientist named Olaus Roemer observed the frequent eclipses of Jupiter's moon, Io.

Light travels about 670,600,000 miles per hour. Scientific notation is used to write large and small numbers more easily. A number written in **scientific notation** is expressed as a number that is greater than or equal to 1, but less than 10, multiplied by a power of ten.

		Example A	Example B
		Write 670,600,000 in scientific notation.	Write 0.000597 in scientific notation.
STEP 1	Move the decimal point to make a number that is greater than or equal to 1, but less than 10.	6.70,600,000.	0.0005.97
STEP 2	Count the places and notice the direction you move the decimal point.	8 places to the left	4 places to the right
STEP 3	Write the number times a power of 10. The power is determined by the direction and number of places you move the decimal point.	6.706×10^8	5.97×10^{-4}

✓ Talk About It

1. In Example A, what does 10^8 equal? Multiply it by 6.706. What is the product?

2. In Example B, what does 10^{-4} equal? Multiply it by 5.97. What is the product?

Give each missing power of ten.

1. $352{,}090{,}000 = 3.5209 \times$ ▯ **2.** $0.006488 = 6.488 \times$ ▯

Write each number in scientific notation.

3. 786,002   **4.** 998,652,000   **5.** 0.00561   **6.** 0.0000225

7. Number Sense How can you tell if a number written in scientific notation is greater than one?

PRACTICE *For more practice, see Set 2-11 on p. 139.*

A Skills and Understanding

Give each missing power of ten.

8. $845{,}623 = 8.45623 \times$ ▯ **9.** $0.0000739 = 7.39 \times$ ▯ **10.** $0.0005 = 5.0 \times$ ▯

Write each number in scientific notation.

11. 268,200   **12.** 169,254,700,125 **13.** 0.023841   **14.** 0.0006987

15. 728   **16.** 0.06753   **17.** 2,056,105   **18.** 0.00940051

19. 25,698   **20.** 0.0019   **21.** 846,000   **22.** 0.000506

23. Number Sense How can you tell if a number written in scientific notation is less than 1?

B Reasoning and Problem Solving

In 24–26, write each number in standard form.

24. The mass of Earth: about 5.972×10^{21} metric tons

25. The wavelength of an X-ray: 1×10^{-11} m

26. The temperature of the sun's core: 2.7×10^{7} °F

27. Writing in Math Explain why negative exponents must be used to write numbers that are very small.

Mixed Review and Test Prep

Take It to the NET
Test Prep
www.scottforesman.com

Find each product or quotient.

28. $9{,}526 \times 10^{2}$ **29.** 0.258×10^{-3} **30.** $0.0036 \div 10^{-4}$ **31.** $562{,}021 \div 10^{6}$

32. Which is the product 27.36×1.2?

    A. 3.2832   **B.** 32.832   **C.** 328.32   **D.** 3,283.2

33. Find the quotient $98.64 \div 10^{0}$.

    A. 0.9864   **B.** 9.864   **C.** 98.64   **D.** 986.4

Algebra

Key Idea
You can solve equations with decimals using inverse operations, just as with whole numbers.

Vocabulary
• inverse operations (p. 44)
• properties of equality (p. 44)

Think It Through
I need to **check my answer to make sure it is reasonable.**

Solving Equations with Decimals

LEARN

How can you solve decimal equations?

Just as with whole number equations, decimal equations can be solved by using **inverse operations** and the **properties of equality.**

Example A

Solve $x + 4.7 = 10.2$.

$$x + 4.7 = 10.2$$
$$x + 4.7 - \mathbf{4.7} = 10.2 - \mathbf{4.7}$$
$$x = 5.5$$

Check: $x + 4.7 = 10.2$
$$5.5 + 4.7 = 10.2$$
$$10.2 = 10.2$$

Example B

Solve $n - 3.8 = 5.21$.

$$n - 3.8 = 5.21$$
$$n - 3.8 + \mathbf{3.8} = 5.21 + \mathbf{3.8}$$
$$n = 9.01$$

Check: $n - 3.8 = 5.21$
$$9.01 - 3.8 = 5.21$$
$$5.21 = 5.21$$

Example C

Solve $2.5y = 4$.

$$2.5y = 4$$
$$\frac{2.5y}{\mathbf{2.5}} = \frac{4}{\mathbf{2.5}}$$
$$y = 1.6$$

Check: $2.5y = 4$
$$2.5(1.6) = 4$$
$$4 = 4$$

Example D

Solve $\frac{a}{7} = 2.8$.

$$\frac{a}{7} = 2.8$$
$$\frac{a}{7}(\mathbf{7}) = 2.8(\mathbf{7})$$
$$a = 19.6$$

Check: $\frac{a}{7} = 2.8$
$$\frac{19.6}{7} = 2.8$$
$$2.8 = 2.8$$

✔ Talk About It

1. Explain how inverse operations and properties of equality were used to solve the equation in Example C.

2. What is another way to write $\frac{a}{7}$?

3. What would be a reasonable solution for the equation $31.5t = 598.5$?

Solve each equation and check your answer.

1. $c + 0.17 = 3$ **2.** $t - 1.8 = 3.4$ **3.** $0.03n = 21$ **4.** $\frac{r}{1.5} = 6$

5. Number Sense How can you solve $4a = 32.8$ using mental math?

PRACTICE   *For more practice, see Set 2-12 on p. 139.*

A Skills and Understanding

Solve each equation and check your answer.

6. $2.3m = 32.2$ **7.** $72.6 = k - 32.65$ **8.** $w + 0.023 = 12.38$ **9.** $0.06g = 21.6$

10. $\frac{z}{4.5} = 6.26$ **11.** $a - 7.98 = 74.2$ **12.** $129 = \frac{t}{0.27}$ **13.** $\frac{y}{1.5} = 4.62$

14. $9 = 3.6x$ **15.** $c - 2.6 = 5.87$ **16.** $p + 56.036 = 143$ **17.** $46 = a + 22.7$

18. Number Sense How can you solve $x + 8.2 = 16.8$ using mental math?

B Reasoning and Problem Solving

19. Michael Johnson set two world records in the 1996 Olympics, one for the 200-m run and the other for the 400-m run. His record time of 43.49 seconds for the 400-m run was 0.35 seconds less than his winning time for the same event in 2000. Use the equation $t - 0.35 = 43.49$ to find that time.

20. In 2002, adult admission to ride the Ferris wheel at Chicago's Navy Pier was 8 times the amount of admission to the Ferris wheel at the 1893 Chicago World's Fair. Use the equation $8a = \$4.00$ to find the cost to ride the Ferris wheel at the World's Fair.

21. **Writing in Math** Write a word problem for the equation $2.2 + 2.2 + 3.1 + x = 10.6$. Include a solution.

🦉 Mixed Review and Test Prep

Take It to the NET
www **Test Prep**
www.scottforesman.com

Write each number in scientific notation.

22. 245,200   **23.** 0.00365   **24.** 894   **25.** 0.00071

26. Which is the standard form for 5.38 billion?

A. 538,000   **B.** 5,800,000   **C.** 5,380,000,000   **D.** 538,000,000,000

27. Choose the best estimate for 5.89×2.9.

A. 18   **B.** 15   **C.** 1.8   **D.** 1.5

Identify the Main Idea

Identifying the main idea when you read in math can help you use the **problem-solving strategy, *Write an Equation,*** in the next lesson.

In reading, identifying the main idea helps you understand what the story is about. In math, the main idea for many story problems is **part-part-whole** or **equal groups** with something unknown.

A book costs $6.95. Ed has $4.25. How much more does he need to buy the book?

$6.95	
$4.25	**?**

Let m = the additional money Ed needs.

Part	Part	Whole
$4.25	+ m =	$6.95

The main idea here is part-part-whole with one part unknown.

Yvette worked 4 hours and earned $95.48. How much did she earn per hour?

Let s = the amount Yvette earned per hour.

Number of groups	Amount per group	Total amount
4	× s =	$95.48

The main idea here is equal groups with the amount per group unknown.

1. Write a different equation for the first problem.

2. For each problem above, tell how you can solve the equation.

For 3–5, use the problem below.

Ronnie bought the same shirt in three different colors. He paid a total of $45.66 for the shirts, excluding tax. How much did each shirt cost?

3. Identify the main idea.

4. Draw a picture to show the main idea.

5. Write an equation for the problem.

6. **Writing in Math** Tell how you can solve the equation.

For 7–10, use the problem below and the sign at the right.

Ming has hiked 3.8 km along Vista Hiking Trail. How much of the trail does she have left to hike?

7. Identify the main idea.

8. Draw a picture to show the main idea.

9. Write an equation for the problem.

10. **Writing in Math** Tell how you can solve the equation.

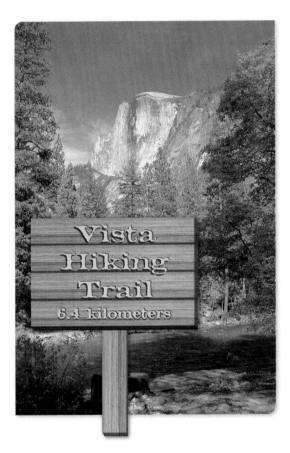

Vista Hiking Trail
6.4 kilometers

For 11–14, use the problem below and the sign at the right.

Tina spent $16.40 on trail mix. How many pounds did she buy?

11. Identify the main idea.

12. Draw a picture to show the main idea.

13. Write an equation for the problem.

14. **Writing in Math** Write a part-part-whole problem using data from the sign.

Popcorn- $1.88/bag
Peanuts- $3.35/can
Trail Mix- $4.10/bag
Pretzles- $2.50/bag

Problem-Solving Strategy

Reading Helps!

Identifying the main idea

can help you with...

the problem-solving strategy, *Write an Equation.*

Algebra

Key Idea
Learning how and when to write an equation can help you solve problems.

Write an Equation

LEARN

How can you write an equation to solve a problem?

Food Festival Maria paid a total of $6.90 for 6 jalapeño pepper plants. How much did she pay for each plant?

Read and Understand

What do you know?

Maria paid $6.90 for 6 plants. Each plant was the same price.

What are you trying to find?

Find the price for each plant.

Plan and Solve

What strategy will you use?

Step 1 Show the main idea in the problem.

Strategy: Write an Equation

$6.90

TEST TALK

Think It Through
The **most important idea** is the price per plant when the number of plants and total price is given, so I should write a multiplication equation.

Step 2 Decide which operation is indicated by the main idea.

Step 3 Use a variable to show what you are trying to find. Write an equation that describes the main idea.

Step 4 Solve the equation.

Use multiplication since the total price is the number of plants multiplied by the price for one plant.

Let p = the price per plant.

Number of plants × Price per plant = Total price

$$6 \quad \times \quad p \quad = \quad \$6.90$$

$$6p = 6.90$$
$$\frac{6p}{6} = \frac{6.90}{6}$$

$$p = 1.15$$

Each plant costs $1.15.

Look Back and Check

Is your answer reasonable?

Yes, because 6 × 1.15 = 6(1 + 0.15) = 6 + 0.90 = $6.90.

✔ Talk About It

1. In Step 1, what was the total paid? How many plants are there?

2. What equation was used to solve the problem?

When might you write an equation?

Chili Bowls You buy a large and small bowl of chili. A large bowl of chili costs $3.50. You pay $5.25 for both. What is the cost for the small bowl of chili?

Show the main idea:

$5.25	
$3.50	?

Let c = the cost for a small bowl of chili. Write an equation that describes the main idea.

$$c + \$3.50 = \$5.25$$

When to Write an Equation

Think about writing an equation when:
The story has an unknown quantity.
• The cost for a small bowl of chili
The relationship between the quantities involves one or more operations.
• The cost for a large and small bowl of chili combined

✔ Talk About It

3. Solve the equation in the Chili Bowls problem.

4. How can you check that your answer is reasonable?

CHECK ✓

For another example, see Set 2-13 on p. 135.

Write an equation to solve each problem. Give the answer in a complete sentence. Check that your answer is reasonable.

1. The number of tomato plants at the nursery is twice the number of broccoli plants. If there are 106 tomato plants, how many broccoli plants are there? Use the picture below to help you write an equation.

? ☐ Broccoli plants

106 ■ ■ Tomato plants

2. The Fairview Park District planted gladiolus bulbs at the entrance of the city. Fifteen rows with 8 bulbs in each row were planted. How many bulbs were planted in all? Draw a picture to help you write an equation.

Ⓐ Using the Strategy

Writing an Equation to Solve a Problem Write an equation to solve each problem. Give the answer in a complete sentence. Check to see that your answer is reasonable.

3. Maria found onion sets at the Food Festival for $4.49 a bag. This price was $1.50 more than the price at the Garden Shop. What was the price for onion sets at the Garden Shop? Draw a picture to help you write the equation.

4. Ramon grows onion and garlic plants. The area he uses for planting onions is 600 square feet. This is 4 times the area he uses for planting garlic. What is the area Ramon uses for growing his garlic plants?

5. After planting 13 bags of onion sets, Ramon still has 9 left. How many bags did he start with?

6. One box of strawberry fertilizer treats 250 square feet. How many boxes should Ramon purchase for his 1,500-square-foot strawberry patch?

Onion Sets

$4.49
each bag of
75 plants

 Math and Music

Pythagoras, an ancient Greek mathematician and philosopher, discovered that the tone of a vibrating string is related to the length of the string. For instance, the length of a string producing C, an octave lower than middle C, is twice the length of the middle-C string. Some other relationships are given in the table at the right.

Note in Relation to Middle C	String Length Factor
C Above	0.5
F Above	0.75
Middle C	1.0
A Below	1.2
G Below	1.5
E Below	1.4
C Below	2.0

7. If a middle-C string is 75 cm long, how long is the string for C below the middle-C string?

8. If the string for C above middle C is 24 cm long, how long is the middle-C string?

9. If the string for G below middle C is 24 in. long, how long is the middle-C string?

10. If the string for F above middle C is 18 in. long, how long is the middle-C string?

11. A string for E below middle C is 56 cm long. Write and solve an equation to find the length of the middle-C string.

B Mixed Strategy Practice

Solve each problem. Write the answer in a complete sentence.

12. Martina's grandmother's sewing circle sold 36 more quilts in November than they did in October. They sold one more quilt in December than they sold in November. In December, they sold 55 quilts. How many did the sewing club sell in the three months?

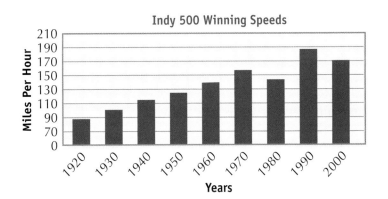

Indy 500 Winning Speeds

13. **Writing in Math** The first Indianapolis 500 auto race was won with an average speed of about 75 mph. Approximate speeds for the race in the decade years are graphed above. Predict the winning speed in the year 2010. Explain how you made this prediction.

STRATEGIES

- **Show What You Know**
  Draw a Picture
  Make an Organized List
  Make a Table
  Make a Graph
  Act It Out or Use Objects
- **Look for a Pattern**
- **Try, Check, and Revise**
- **Write an Equation**
- **Use Logical Reasoning**
- **Solve a Simpler Problem**
- **Work Backward**

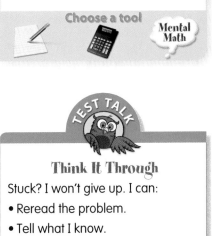

Choose a tool

Mental Math

Think It Through

Stuck? I won't give up. I can:
- Reread the problem.
- Tell what I know.
- Identify key facts and details.
- Tell the problem in my own words.
- Show the main idea.
- Try a different strategy.
- Retrace my steps.

Mixed Review and Test Prep

Take It to the NET
Test Prep
www.scottforesman.com

Solve and check each equation.

14. $1.8n = 72$ **15.** $5 = m + 4.7$ **16.** $c - 3.2 = 6.8$ **17.** $\frac{x}{0.4} = 16$

Write each number in expanded form.

18. 235,001 **19.** 7,004 **20.** 0.0088 **21.** 50.32

22. Evaluate $6^2 \div 3^2 - 3 + 1$

23. Which quotient is greater, $208.4 \div 0.1$ or $208.4 \div 0.01$? Explain.

24. Evaluate $5^2 + 73.8 \div 10^1 - 4 \times 2.655$

25. Which is a reasonable estimate for $618 \div 3.29$?

    A. 2,000 **B.** 250 **C.** 200 **D.** 20

DK Problem-Solving Applications

Toronto SkyDome The SkyDome is a very adaptable building. During sunny weather, the roof can open to provide the outdoor experience that sports fans enjoy. When the weather becomes uncomfortable, the roof can close. Sections of seats can be rotated to accommodate many types of entertainment.

Trivia The SkyDome's field has enough space to fit about 743 elephants or the whole ancient Roman Colosseum!

1 Read the trivia. By using other available exhibition floor space, the SkyDome could fit about 1.94 times as many elephants as when using just the field. How many elephants could fit in the SkyDome?

2 A ticket to an event costs $37.36 plus taxes of $6.64. What is the total cost?

Using Key Facts

3 The field is covered by artificial turf that is joined together with zippers. It can take 12 hours to unzip the turf. At this rate, how many rolls of turf are unzipped each hour? Round your answer to the hundredth.

4 The largest audience in the SkyDome had over 67,600 people. Write this number in scientific notation.

Key Facts
Toronto SkyDome

- Roof weighs 11,000 tons.
- 76 motors move the roof.
- Field is covered by 106 rolls of artificial turf.
- 8 miles of zippers hold turf together.

5 **Decision Making** You and 3 friends are going to see a baseball game. Hotdogs cost $0.99 each. First-row infield tickets cost $37.36, first-row outfield seats are $19.40, and upper-level infield tickets are $13.42. Where would you like to sit? How much will it cost altogether if each person buys a ticket and 2 hotdogs?

6 **Writing in Math** Write your own word problem that involves the information in this lesson. Solve it and write the answer in a complete sentence.

Good News/Bad News *Having a moveable roof enables the baseball players to play even if it is raining. Unfortunately, it takes 20 minutes to close the roof, so they have to plan ahead!*

Do You Know How?

Do You Understand?

Multiplying and Dividing by Powers of 10 (2-10)

Find each product or quotient.

1. 0.658×10^5 **2.** $235.7 \div 10^3$

3. $0.0045 \div 10^{-5}$ **4.** $5{,}163 \times 10^{-4}$

Ⓐ Tell how you found the quotient in Exercise 2.

Ⓑ Explain the difference between multiplying by a positive power of 10 and a negative power of 10.

Scientific Notation (2-11)

Write each number in scientific notation.

5. 125,360,000   **6.** 0.0000235

7. 0.0007052   **8.** 8,500,000,000

9. 397.52   **10.** 0.027489

Ⓒ Tell how you determined the power of 10 in Exercises 5 and 6.

Ⓓ How did you find the number you multiplied by a power of 10 in Exercises 7 and 8?

Solving Equations with Decimals (2-12)

Solve and check each equation.

11. $2.4m = 48$ **12.** $\frac{d}{1.3} = 4.2$

13. $k + 22.8 = 56$ **14.** $p - 52.4 = 9.023$

15. $125 = 0.1g$ **16.** $22.98 = w - 18$

Ⓔ Explain how to get the variable alone in Exercise 11.

Ⓕ Explain how to show a check for Exercise 16.

Problem-Solving Strategy: Write an Equation (2-13)

Write an equation to solve each problem.

17. There are 24 girls in Ms. Finn's sixth-grade chorus. This number is 8 more than the number of boys in the chorus. How many boys are in the chorus?

18. There are 8 soccer teams in a league with the same number of players on each team. The league has a total of 184 players. How many players are on each team?

Ⓖ Draw a picture to show the main idea in Problem 17.

Ⓗ How did you decide which operation to use in your equation for Problem 18?

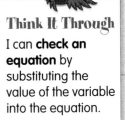

MULTIPLE CHOICE

1. Solve the equation $m - 3.6 = 7.8$. (2-12)

    A. $m = 3.2$ **C.** $m = 10.4$

    B. $m = 4.2$ **D.** $m = 11.4$

2. Find the product for 2.3×10^{-2}. (2-10)

    A. 230   **C.** 23

    B. 0.023   **D.** 0.23

FREE RESPONSE

Find each product or quotient. (2-10)

    3. $5.2 \div 10^{-3}$ **4.** 52.6×10^4 **5.** 0.2364×10^3 **6.** $0.6505 \div 10^{-5}$

Write each number in scientific notation. (2-11, 2-14)

    7. 0.0056   **8.** 13,500,000   **9.** 12.56   **10.** 48.0009

Solve and check each equation. (2-12, 2-14)

    11. $2.3m = 6.9$ **12.** $\frac{r}{1.8} = 5.4$ **13.** $k + 4.8 = 9$ **14.** $w - 15.89 = 27.5$

Write an equation to solve each problem. Give each answer in a complete sentence. (2-13)

15. Darci's hourly wage of $13.26 per hour is 1.3 times as great as her hourly wage last year. What was Darci's hourly wage last year?

16. How many hours must Darci work at $13.50 per hour to earn $472.50?

17. Roberto worked a total of 12.4 hours over the weekend. If he worked 8 hours on Saturday, how many hours did he work on Sunday?

Writing in Math

18. Tell how to find the product for 2.56×10^{-3}. (2-10)

19. Explain what scientific notation is used for and how to change a very small number into a number written in scientific notation. (2-11)

20. Write an equation that involves multiplication with decimals. Explain how you would solve the equation. (2-12, 2-14)

21. Describe the difference between dividing by a positive power of 10 and dividing by a negative power of 10. (2-10)

Test-Taking Strategies

Understand the question.

Get information for the answer.

Plan how to find the answer.

Make smart choices.

Use writing in math.

Improve written answers.

Get Information for the Answer.

After you understand a test question, you need to get information for the answer. Some test questions do not contain all the information you need in the text. You may need to look for more information in a picture, map, diagram, table, or graph.

1. Amanda bought 2.5 pounds of smoked turkey on sale at the Delicious Deli.

> **Delicious Deli Specials**
> Honey Baked Ham: $1.89 per pound
> Swiss Cheese: $0.99 per pound
> Smoked Turkey: $1.62 per pound

If sales tax for Amanda's purchase was $0.21, **how much** did she pay for the smoked turkey?

A. $1.62

B. $1.83

C. $4.05

D. $4.26

Understand the question.

*I need to find **how much** Amanda **paid**, including sales tax, for the turkey.*

Get information for the answer.

- Look for important information in the text.

- Look for important information in pictures, maps, diagrams, tables, or graphs.

The text tells me that Amanda bought 2.5 pounds of turkey and paid $0.21 in sales tax for the purchase.

The deli sign shows me that the turkey costs $1.62 per pound.

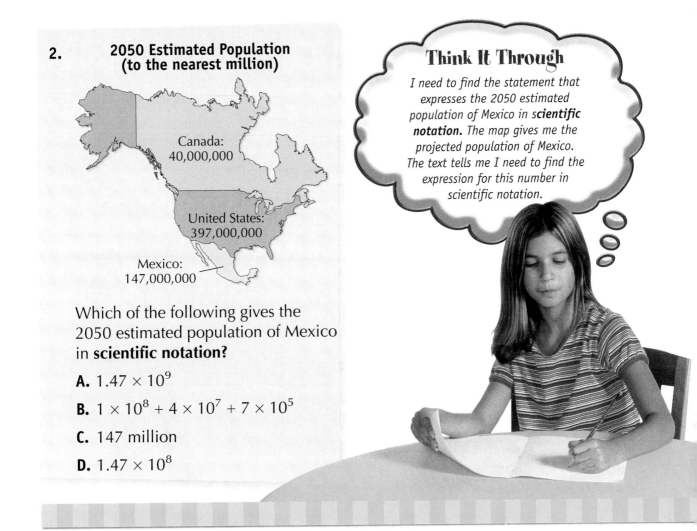

2.

2050 Estimated Population
(to the nearest million)

Canada:
40,000,000

United States:
397,000,000

Mexico:
147,000,000

Which of the following gives the
2050 estimated population of Mexico
in **scientific notation?**

A. 1.47×10^9

B. $1 \times 10^8 + 4 \times 10^7 + 7 \times 10^5$

C. 147 million

D. 1.47×10^8

Think It Through

*I need to find the statement that
expresses the 2050 estimated
population of Mexico in **scientific
notation.** The map gives me the
projected population of Mexico.
The text tells me I need to find the
expression for this number in
scientific notation.*

Now it's your turn.

For each problem, tell what information is needed to solve the problem.

3. A taxi service charges a flat rate
plus additional charges based on
miles traveled and the number of
passengers.

EACH TRIP

Flat rate: $3.00

Add'l charges: $1.25 per mile
$1.00 each additional passenger

What is the cost of an 8-mile
taxicab ride for 2 people?

A. $13.25

B. $14.00

C. $14.75

D. $20.20

4. The table gives the areas of the
largest bodies of water in the
world to the nearest hundred
thousand square kilometers.

Body of Water	Area (in sq km)
Arctic Ocean	1.4×10^7
Atlantic Ocean	8.2×10^7
Indian Ocean	7.3×10^7
Pacific Ocean	1.65×10^8

Which of the following also gives
the area of the Pacific Ocean?

A. 165,000 sq km

B. 16,500,000 sq km

C. 165,000,000 sq km

D. 16,500,000,000 sq km

Self Check

Decimals are numbers that use decimal points to show tenths, hundredths, and so on. (p. 76)

Decimals can be compared and rounded like whole numbers. (Lessons 2-1, 2-2, 2-3)

List 1.256, 1.652, 1.0652, and 1.562 in order from least to greatest.

Line up the decimal points to compare each digit.

1.**2**56
1.**6**52   All four decimals have a 1 in the ones place. Each decimal
1.**0**652   has a different number in the tenths place. Use this digit to
1.**5**62   order from least to greatest.

1.0652, 1.256, 1.562, 1.652

1. Round 34.577, 2.895, and 1,458.2617 to the nearest hundredth.

I write amounts of money using decimals because cents are part of a dollar.

Self Check

Pay special attention to decimal places when adding, subtracting, multiplying, and dividing decimals. (Lesson 2-4, 2-5, 2-6, 2-7, 2-9)

Find 56.3 × 17.5.

Estimate the product by rounding each decimal to the nearest whole number.

56.3 → 56   56
17.5 → 18   × 18
                      ‾‾‾‾
                      448
                   + 56
                   ‾‾‾‾
                   1,008

Multiply. Count the decimal places in each factor before placing the decimal point in the product.

          56.3   ← 1 decimal place
       × 17.5   ← 1 decimal place
       ‾‾‾‾‾‾
          2815
          3941
       + 563
       ‾‾‾‾‾‾
       985.25   ← 2 decimal places

2. Find 562 + 19.47, 422.3 – 18.502, and 7.8 ÷ 2.5.

On a number line, negative numbers are on the left. When 10 has a negative exponent, move the decimal to the left. $10^{-2} = \dfrac{1}{10 \times 10} = \dfrac{1}{100} = 0.01$. (p. 106)

Decimals can be used to write **scientific notation.** (Lesson 2-10, 2-11)

Write 56,302 in scientific notation.

Move the decimal point so the number is less than 10 but greater than or equal to 1.

$56,302 \rightarrow 5.6302$ (4 decimal places)

$56,302 = 5.6302 \times 10^4$

Write 4.523×10^{-2} in standard form.

The **exponent is negative,** so move the decimal point to the left.

$4.523 \rightarrow 0.4523$ (2 decimal places)

$4.523 \times 10^{-2} = 0.04523$

3. Write 260,000; 845.23; and 0.00714 in scientific notation.

You can interpret the remainder or write an equation to **solve problems.**
(Lesson 2-8, 2-12, 2-13)

To interpret the remainder, understand what the problem is asking.

Each box holds 16 books. How may boxes will 132 books fill?

132 books will fill 8 boxes. There will be 4 books left over.

To write an equation, decide which operation is indicated by the main idea.

Marcus earns $15 for each hour he paints. How long did Marcus paint if he made $105?

h = number of hours Marcus painted

$15h = 105$

$\dfrac{15h}{15} = \dfrac{105}{15}$

$h = 7$

Marcus painted for 7 hours.

4. Jeff is 3 times as old as Mary. If Mary is 5 years old, how old is Jeff?

1. 34.58; 2.90; 1,458.26; 2. 581.47; 403.798; 3.12; 3. 2.6×10^5; 8.4523×10^2; 7.14×10^{-3}; 4. 15 years old

MULTIPLE CHOICE

Choose the correct letter for each answer.

1. Find $8 - 2.64$.

   A. 5.36   **C.** 6.36

   B. 5.64   **D.** 6.64

2. Find $12.4 \div 0.4$.

   A. 310   **C.** 3.1

   B. 31   **D.** 0.31

3. Find 2.5×0.6.

   A. 0.15   **C.** 15

   B. 1.5   **D.** 150

4. Find $27.3 + 56.089$.

   A. 58.819   **C.** 83.389

   B. 83.092   **D.** 84.19

5. Find $43.68 \div 12$.

   A. 364   **C.** 3.64

   B. 36.4   **D.** 0.364

6. What symbol will make the statement below true?

$$0.235 \underline{} 0.253$$

   A. $>$ **C.** $=$

   B. $<$ **D.** $\cong$

7. Which is the best estimate of $23.56 + 4.98$?

   A. 29   **C.** 27

   B. 27.6   **D.** 25

8. Round 2.568 to the nearest hundredth.

   A. 2.56   **C.** 2.6

   B. 2.57   **D.** 3

For 9–10, use the following information: Maria ran 2.4 miles each day.

9. In about how many days would Maria have run a total of 10 miles?

   A. about 2 days   **C.** about 4 days

   B. about 3 days   **D.** about 5 days

10. About how many miles would she run in 8 days?

   A. about 24 miles   **C.** about 15 miles

   B. about 20 miles   **D.** about 14 miles

11. Fencing is sold in two-foot lengths. How many lengths will Shawn have to buy to fence the perimeter of his yard?

6.9 ft

12.9 ft

   A. 18 lengths   **C.** 20 lengths

   B. 19 lengths   **D.** 21 lengths

12. Which is the standard form of 408 hundred-thousandths?

   A. 408,000

   B. 0.408

   C. 0.0408

   D. 0.00408

TEST TALK

Think It Through

- I should pay attention to where I **place decimal points.**
- I can **eliminate** unreasonable answers.

FREE RESPONSE

Simplify.

13. 2.36×10^3

14. $0.0056 \div 10^{-5}$

Solve each equation.

15. $\frac{m}{4.3} = 2.5$

16. $2.36 + b = 8.47$

17. $0.6z = 4.53$

18. $k - 2.6 = 5$

Estimate each answer.

19. $56.98 + 44.37$

20. $77.2 - 8.95$

21. $247.65 \div 8.064$

22. 5.66×6.982

Write each number in scientific notation.

23. 0.0035

24. 78,500

Solve.

25. Jack deposited $52.36 into his savings account. His new balance was $143.94. Write and solve an equation to determine how much he had in the account before his deposit.

26. In Ms. Sing's English class, the students were put into groups. If there were 28 students in the class and each group had five members, how many groups were there?

Writing in Math

27. Explain how to subtract a decimal number from a whole number using the example below.

$$85 - 3.98$$

28. Tell how you know which inverse operation to use when solving the equation $\frac{x}{5.5} = 18$

Think It Through
- Identifying the main idea can help me **interpret the remainder.**
- I need to make sure **I explain my thinking** if I am asked to.

29. Andy solved the word problem below. Did he interpret the remainder correctly? Explain why or why not.

Each van holds 7 students. There are 38 students going on the trip. How many vans are needed?

$38 \div 7 \approx 5.4$
6 vans are needed.

Number and Operation

MULTIPLE CHOICE

1. What is 14.57 + 2.9?

    A. 1.747   **C.** 17.47

    B. 14.86   **D.** 174.7

2. Which is the best estimate of 46.7 ÷ 7.6?

    A. 8   **C.** 6

    B. 7   **D.** 5

FREE RESPONSE

3. Margo earned $27.15 each day over the 3-day weekend. What was the total amount Margo earned for 3 days?

TEST TALK

Think It Through
I can use the distributive property to find a product.

4. Use mental math to find 23 × 7.

5. Find 13.86 ÷ 1.4.

6. Find $0.382 \div 10^{-3}$.

Writing in Math

7. Explain how you would find 2.5 × 3.9.

8. Mark describes his method for finding the LCD of two or more fractions below. Do you agree with his method? Explain.

To find the LCD of two or more fractions, multiply the denominators.
$\frac{2}{9}$ and $\frac{1}{3}$
Because 9 × 3 = 27, the LCD of $\frac{2}{9}$ and $\frac{1}{3}$ is 27.

Geometry and Measurement

MULTIPLE CHOICE

9. The perimeter of an equilateral triangle is 7.2 feet. What is the length of one side?

    A. 1.8 ft   **C.** 2.4 ft

    B. 2 ft   **D.** 0.24 ft

10. How many inches are in $2\frac{1}{2}$ feet?

    A. 90 in.   **C.** 25 in.

    B. 30 in.   **D.** 7 in.

FREE RESPONSE

11. While training for a 5-mile run, Aurora ran 5.8 miles each day. About how many miles did she run in 9 days of training?

12. In the long jump, Lia jumped 5.6 m and Sam jumped 4.8 m. Who jumped farther? How much farther?

13. A square has an area of 81 ft². Find the length of its sides.

14. A rectangle has a length of 10.7 m and a width of 6.8 m. Find the area of this rectangle.

Writing in Math

15. Use the models below to describe the difference between congruent and similar figures.

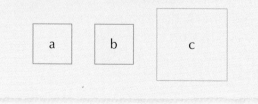

Data Analysis and Probability

MULTIPLE CHOICE

Use the spinner for Exercises 16–17.

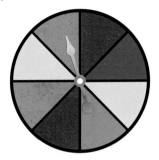

16. What is the probability of the spinner landing on a green space?

A. $\frac{1}{8}$ **C.** $\frac{3}{8}$

B. $\frac{1}{4}$ **D.** $\frac{2}{5}$

17. What is the probability of landing on a space that is NOT yellow?

A. $\frac{7}{8}$ **C.** $\frac{5}{8}$

B. $\frac{3}{4}$ **D.** $\frac{1}{4}$

FREE RESPONSE

Use the graph for Exercises 18–19.

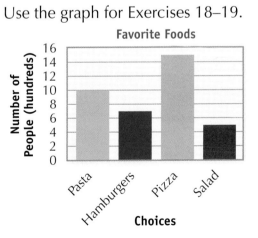

18. Which food got the most votes?

Writing in Math

19. How many more people chose pizza than hamburgers as their favorite food? Explain how you know.

Algebra

MULTIPLE CHOICE

20. Solve $\frac{x}{7.3} = 23.8$.

A. 1.7374   **C.** 173.74

B. 17.374   **D.** 1,737.4

21. Solve $p - 7.56 = 12$.

A. 19.56   **C.** 76.8

B. 8.76   **D.** 87.6

22. Which expression represents 6.8 more than twice a number?

A. $2y + 6.8$ **C.** $6.8 - 2y$

B. $2y \times 6.8$ **D.** $6.8y + 2$

FREE RESPONSE

23. Solve $m + 2.8 = 5$. Show your work.

24. Write a rule for the table below.

In	2	3	4	5
Out	5.5	6.5	7.5	8.5

25. A wagon weighs 165.3 kg. Carrying riders, the wagon weighs 465 kg. Use the equation $165.3 + x = 465$ to find the weight of the riders.

26. A chemist took a package of sodium chloride and split the contents into 9 equal groups, each having a mass of 0.08 kg. Use the equation $\frac{p}{9} = 0.08$ to find the mass of the original package.

Writing in Math

27. Write an equation that involves two operations and has an answer of 5.6.

28. Explain how to isolate the variable in the equation $2x - 5 = 7$.

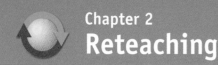

Chapter 2
Reteaching

Set 2-1 (pages 76–77)

Write 4 and 345 hundred thousandths in standard form.

Use a place value chart.

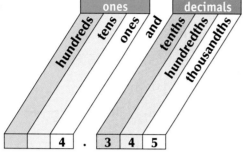

Remember to pay attention to zeros and decimals when determining place value.

Give the place and value of the 3 in each number.

1. 12.0365
2. 13.568
3. 0.0004583
4. 0.045381
5. 2.36
6. 32.894
7. 10,348.96
8. 767.1439

Set 2-2 (pages 78–79)

Compare 22.058 and 22.085

Write the numbers lining up the decimal points. Start at the left and compare digits in the same place

22.058
22.085

The hundredths digits differ.
Since 8 hundredths > 5 hundredths,

22.058 < 22.085

Remember to compare digits in the same place value when ordering numbers. Order from least to greatest.

1. 12.0235, 1.20235, 1.30225, 1.0325
2. 0.5614, 0.5641, 0.4165, 0.6154
3. 7.5842, 7.5824, 75.842, 5.8724
4. 1.002, 1.0019, 1.0021, 1.00201
5. 0.003, 0.3, 3.003, 3.3

Set 2-3 (pages 80–81)

Round the number to the underlined place.

67.05742	Find the rounding place.
67.05742	Look at the digit to the right of this place.
7 > 5	If this digit is 5 or greater, add 1 to the rounding digit.
67.06	

Remember to drop the digits to the right of the rounded digit.

1. 12.561
2. 4.5618
3. 0.56897
4. 589.3554
5. 12.9693
6. 3.102423
7. 98.607
8. 0.6304

Set 2-4 (pages 82–83)

Estimate the product.

4.2 × 5.8

4 × 6 = 24   Round each factor to the nearest whole number

4.2 × 5.8 ≈ 24

Remember that you can also use compatible numbers to estimate answers.

1. $57.98 − $35.02
2. 23.57 ÷ 3.87
3. 25.3 × 41
4. 31.3 × 6.25
5. $42.95 + $3.90
6. 71.89 ÷ 7.91

Find 19.4 − 8.28.

$$\begin{array}{r} \overset{3\,10}{19.4\cancel{0}} \\ -\ 8.28 \\ \hline 11.12 \end{array}$$

Line up the decimal points and annex zeros.

Subtract, regroup if necessary.

Write the decimal point in your answer.

Remember to compare your estimate and answer to check for reasonableness.

1. 35.6 + 239   **2.** 250 − 1.29

3. 12.698 + 55.2   **4.** 28 − 15.74

5. 87.3 + 648   **6.** 3.5 − 1.682

7. 1.005 − 0.062   **8.** 2.357 − 0.759

Find 5.62 × 2.3.

Estimate: 6 × 2 = 12

$$\begin{array}{r} \overset{1}{\overset{1}{5.62}} \\ \times\ 2.3 \\ \hline 1686 \\ +\ 1124 \\ \hline 12.926 \end{array}$$

⟵ 2 decimal places

⟵ 1 decimal place

Add the number of decimal places. Start at the right and move left the total number of decimal places.

Remember that you can use your estimate to help with placing the decimal point in the product.

1. 256 × 5.371   **2.** 2.6 × 6.8

3. 12.9 × 0.6   **4.** 0.003 × 0.05

5. 58.6 × 4.3   **6.** 0.8 × 0.7

7. 1.3 × 1.3   **8.** 4.8 × 5.3

Find 2.56 ÷ 16.

Estimate: 2 ÷ 2 = 1,
So 2 ÷ 16 < 1.

$$\begin{array}{r} 0.16 \\ 16\overline{)2.56} \\ -1\,6 \\ \hline 96 \\ -\ 96 \\ \hline 0 \end{array}$$

Since the quotient is less than 1, put a zero is in the ones place.

Place the decimal point in the quotient above the decimal point in the dividend. Divide as usual.

Remember you need to annex zeros when dividing money.

1. 4.2 ÷ 14   **2.** 94.56 ÷ 6

3. $14\overline{)1.694}$ **4.** $9\overline{)29.61}$

5. 16.3 ÷ 5   **6.** 33.58 ÷ 73

7. $6\overline{)104.4}$ **8.** $53\overline{)6.201}$

9. \$258.24 ÷ 32   **10.** 28.7 ÷ 41

11. $73\overline{)0.6205}$ **12.** $49\overline{)19.6}$

13. 264.6 ÷ 84   **14.** \$240 ÷ 89

Set 2-8 (pages 98–99)

Solve.

Jules and his classmates need to travel to a competition 450 miles away. If they plan to travel 120 miles each day, how many days will it take them to get there?

$$
\begin{array}{r}
3.75 \\
120\overline{)450.00} \\
-360 \\
\hline
900 \\
-840 \\
\hline
600 \\
-600 \\
\hline
0
\end{array}
$$

Since the quotient is 3.75, it will take 3 days plus 0.75 of the fourth day.

They should plan on it taking 4 days to get there.

Remember you need to look at the question being asked to interpret the remainder.

The soccer team has a game across town. There are 26 members on the team.

1. If there are 4 vans, how many team members will fit in each van?

2. If there needs to be one chaperone for every 10 members, how many chaperones are needed?

3. There are 48 pencils in each box. How many boxes should be ordered if 600 pencils are needed?

Set 2-9 (pages 100–103)

Find $4.42 \div 1.3$.

Estimate: $4 \div 1 = 4$

$$
\begin{array}{r}
3.4 \\
13\overline{)44.2} \\
-39 \\
\hline
52 \\
-52 \\
\hline
0
\end{array}
$$

To make the divisor a whole number, multiply the dividend and the divisor by the same power of 10.

Remember to place the decimal point in the quotient above the decimal point in the dividend.

1. $109.5 \div 0.05$ 2. $131.58 \div 8.6$

3. $0.0483 \div 2.1$ 4. $3.15 \div 0.07$

5. $1.1\overline{)1.21}$ 6. $0.3\overline{)0.48}$

7. $0.735 \div 0.14$ 8. $2.964 \div 0.13$

9. $0.0258 \div 0.086$ 10. $0.441 \div 0.63$

Set 2-10 (pages 106–109)

Find 22.563×10^{-2}.

22.563×10^{-2}

$.22.563$

0.22563

Move the decimal point the same number of places to the left as the exponent.

Find $0.598 \div 10^{-4}$.

$0.598 \div 10^{-4}$

$0.5980.$

$5,980$

Move the decimal point the same number of places to the right as the exponent.

Remember that multiplying by a positive power of ten moves the decimal point to the right and dividing by a positive power of ten moves the decimal point to the left.

1. 12.65×100 2. $0.658 \div 10^{-3}$

3. 6.983×10^{4} 4. $12.65 \div 1,000$

5. 0.56×10^{-3} 6. $58.375 \div 10^{2}$

7. $0.0567 \div 10^{-5}$ 8. 0.897×10^{3}

Write 12,360,000 in scientific notation.

$12,360,000 = 1.236 \times 10^7$

1.2,360,000.

Move the decimal point 7 places to the left to make a number that is less than ten, but greater than or equal to 1.

1.236×10^7

Remember that moving the decimal point to the right when writing a number in scientific notation will produce a negative exponent.

Write each number in scientific notation.

1. 36,400   **2.** 0.00589

3. 279   **4.** 0.034

Write each number in standard form.

5. 2.36×10^{-5} **6.** 3.95×10^{-6}

7. 9.876×10^6 **8.** 1.2×10^{-2}

Solve $\frac{b}{1.3} = 4.2$

$\frac{b}{1.3}(1.3) = 4.2\,(1.3)$

$b = 5.46$

Use inverse operations and properties of equality to solve.

Check: $\frac{b}{1.3} = 4.2$

$\frac{5.46}{1.3} = 4.2$

$4.2 = 4.2$

Remember check your answers by substituting for the variable.

1. $2.65 + m = 8$ **2.** $1.2d = 1.44$

3. $\frac{x}{2.6} = 15.4$ **4.** $y - 4.23 = 5.67$

5. $4 = a + 1.87$ **6.** $p - 4.9 = 587$

7. $24.8 = \frac{c}{1.5}$ **8.** $1.3g = 8.32$

Write an equation to solve the problem.

Louise buys four oranges and an apple. If the oranges are 4 for $2.40 and she pays $3.15 in all, how much does the apple cost?

Let a = cost of one apple

$a + 2.40 = 3.15$

$a + 2.40 - 2.40 = 3.15 - 2.40$

$a = 0.75$

Use a variable to represent the cost of the apple.

The apple costs $0.75.

Remember to look back and check to make sure your answer makes sense.

1. There are 16 players on each volleyball team. If there are 400 total players at the tournament, how many teams are there?

2. CDs cost $17.99 and tapes cost $9.99. If Juan bought one CD and some tapes, and his total, not including tax was $37.97, how many tapes did he buy?

Chapter 2
More Practice

Set 2-1 (pages 76–77)

Give the place and value of each underlined digit.

1. 2.06<u>5</u>8   **2.** 2.4<u>5</u>8   **3.** 0.003<u>6</u>89   **4.** 6.208<u>1</u>

5. 0.0365<u>4</u>8   **6.** 16<u>8</u>.103   **7.** <u>2</u>6.057   **8.** 9.5<u>6</u>7

Write each number in standard form.

9. 1 and 27 ten-thousandths   **10.** 13 hundredths

11. 2 + 0.02 + 0.006 + 0.0008   **12.** 0.1 + 0.06 + 0.009 + 0.000008

Write each number in expanded form.

13. 200.106   **14.** 1.7659

15. The wavelength of red light is approximately 0.00000065 meters. What value does the 6 have in this measurement?

Set 2-2 (pages 78–79)

Compare. Use >, <, or = to compare each pair of numbers.

1. 0.2356 ⬤ 0.23560   **2.** 12.35664 ⬤ 1.23564   **3.** 0.8756 ⬤ 0.8765

4. 23.4305 ⬤ 24.3503   **5.** 1.056 ⬤ 1.560   **6.** 2.7534 ⬤ 2.7354

Order from least to greatest.

7. 0.12, 0.21, 1.20, 12.1   **8.** 12.56, 1.256, 12.654, 1.562

9. 4.125, 0.4125, 4.215, 4.512   **10.** 0.01, 0.1, 0.001, 1.000

11. 2.364, 23.47, 276.4, 2.437, 0.2003   **12.** 45.928, 45.2895, 45.82, 45.2

13. Lia claims that 1.0005 is less than 1.0050. Is she correct? Explain.

Set 2-3 (pages 80–81)

Round each number to the underlined place.

1. 12.00<u>6</u>781   **2.** 0.6<u>1</u>4972   **3.** 5<u>2</u>.40036   **4.** 3.134<u>2</u>3

5. <u>0</u>.987587   **6.** 6.519<u>8</u>423   **7.** 1<u>2</u>.91   **8.** 0.64<u>2</u>847

Round each number to the nearest ten.

9. 56.0998   **10.** 39.92   **11.** 360.051   **12.** 445.5

Round each number to the nearest hundredth.

13. 13.0681   **14.** 5.231   **15.** 0.00875   **16.** 2.3109

Round 0.03846 to the nearest

17. hundredth.   **18.** tenth.   **19.** thousandth.   **20.** ten-thousandth.

21. List three numbers that round to 2.35.

Take It to the NET
More Practice
www.scottforesman.com

Set 2-4 (pages 82–83)

Estimate each answer.

1. $27.59 × 4.8   **2.** 2.0356 + 3.24   **3.** 18.064 − 11.96   **4.** 3.55 ÷ 1.16

5. 2.8 × 5.2   **6.** $18.07 − $15.97   **7.** $5.06 + $1.89   **8.** 25.86 ÷ 8.78

9. 12.43 + 3.98   **10.** $25.49 × 2.3   **11.** 62.18 ÷ 6.76   **12.** 17.5 − 3.7

13. Katherine wants to buy 30 snack cakes for her class. Each snack cake costs $1.72. Katherine has $45. Does she have enough money? Why or why not?

Set 2-5 (pages 86–89)

Find each sum or difference.

1. 2,387 − 1,895   **2.** 8,452 + 2,647   **3.** 12 − 8.56   **4.** 2.0065 + 6.254

5. 15.674 + 3.62   **6.** 1.0653 + 3.57   **7.** 0.26 + 0.635   **8.** $5.68 − $3.89

9. 0.56 + 0.369   **10.** 17 − 5.47   **11.** 0.89 − 0.51   **12.** 16.35 + 1.0982

13. 66.008 − 40.8   **14.** 5.07 + 3.98   **15.** 8.31 − 2.27   **16.** 42.7 + 4.036 + 8.1

17. Leo gave the cashier $60 for a CD set priced at $52.98. How much change did Leo receive?

Set 2-6 (pages 90–93)

Find each product.

1. 215 × 37   **2.** 541 × 304   **3.** 0.49 × 100   **4.** 1.54 × 2.5

5. 18.6 × 1.4   **6.** 15.24 × 10   **7.** 0.8 × 0.4   **8.** 6.054 × 1,000

9. 55.8 × 0.04   **10.** 0.0012 × 75   **11.** 32.7 × 4.9   **12.** 0.051 × 0.0033

13. 3.89 × 5.9   **14.** 0.38 × 5.2   **15.** 4.68 × 0.67   **16.** 9.42 × 0.13

17. Ground beef sells for $2.59 per pound. Find the price for 4.5 pounds of ground beef.

Set 2-7 (pages 94–97)

Find each quotient. Round to the nearest hundredth if necessary.

1. 2,622 ÷ 23   **2.** $26.80 ÷ 5   **3.** 37 ÷ 4   **4.** 7.65 ÷ 9

5. 68.467 ÷ 10   **6.** 3.0278 ÷ 36   **7.** $12.20 ÷ 5   **8.** 2,658 ÷ 100

9. 3.654 ÷ 18   **10.** 0.054 ÷ 9   **11.** 182 ÷ 26   **12.** 62.3 ÷ 7

13. Ramiro and his seven friends paid a total of $60.72. If they divided the bill evenly, how much was each person's share?

Set 2-8 (pages 98–99)

Solve each problem. Tell how to use the remainder in each problem to make sense of the answer.

1. How many $48 theatre tickets can you buy for $300?

2. Each section at a theatre seats 48 people. How many sections will be needed to seat 300 people?

3. The costumes for 48 dancers used 300 yards of material. How many yards of material were used for each costume?

4. There are 3,598 books for the library of an elementary school. Approximately 24 books fit on a shelf. How many shelves are needed?

Set 2-9 (pages 100–103)

Place the decimal point correctly in each quotient.

1. $0.4)\overline{0.92}$ quotient 23

2. $1.67)\overline{13.36}$ quotient 8

3. $0.86)\overline{68.8}$ quotient 80

4. $0.59)\overline{0.0649}$ quotient 11

Find each quotient. Round to the nearest hundredth if necessary.

5. $533 \div 8.2$

6. $12.92 \div 3.4$

7. $1.56 \div 0.01$

8. $10.755 \div 4.5$

9. $54.3 \div 1.2$

10. $13.2 \div 1.65$

11. $26.89 \div 0.1$

12. $3,402 \div 0.81$

13. $32.848 \div 0.8$

14. $15 \div 0.3$

15. $20.8 \div 0.65$

16. $0.658 \div 0.001$

17. $47.25 \div 2.5$

18. $36.8 \div 2.3$

19. $24.8 \div 1.6$

20. $19.92 \div 3.25$

21. Sylvester has saved $99.60 by saving $12.45 each month. How many months has Sylvester been saving?

22. It takes about 2,500 blossoms to make 0.5 ounce of saffron, the world's most expensive spice. About how many blossoms would make 6 ounces of saffron?

Set 2-10 (pages 106–109)

Place the decimal point in each answer.

1. $0.63 \times 10^1 = 0630$

2. $10.35 \times 10^{-4} = 00010350$

3. $3.06 \times 10^3 = 030600$

Find each product or quotient.

4. 5.45×10^3

5. $1,257.9 \div 10^4$

6. $5,721 \times 10^{-4}$

7. 0.462×10^4

8. $1.68 \div 10^{-5}$

9. $846 \div 10^{-4}$

10. 0.05614×10^6

11. 35.854×10^2

12. $2.159 \div 10^{-3}$

13. $84.7 \div 10^{-2}$

14. 346.5×10^{-3}

15. $1.0065 \div 10^6$

16. 13.5×10^{-3}

17. $4,125 \div 10^3$

18. 75.68×10^{-3}

19. $0.487 \div 10^{-3}$

20. The atomic mass of oxygen is 265×10^{-25} grams. Write this number in standard form.

Take It to the NET
www More Practice
www.scottforesman.com

Set 2-11 (pages 110–111)

Give each missing power of ten.

1. $9{,}370{,}000{,}000 = 9.37 \times$ **2.** $0.000439 = 4.39 \times$ **3.** $0.083 = 8.3 \times$

Write each number in scientific notation.

4. 0.00256   **5.** 13,250,000   **6.** 0.005   **7.** 256

8. 0.0000065   **9.** 1,658,000,000   **10.** 1,500   **11.** 0.0901

12. 56.88   **13.** 17.5874   **14.** 38,900,000   **15.** 0.00000879

16. The average distance of Jupiter's moon Callisto from Jupiter is 1,880,000 km. Write this distance in scientific notation.

17. The house spider weighs 0.00012 kilograms. Write this weight in scientific notation.

Set 2-12 (pages 112–113)

Solve each equation.

1. $\dfrac{p}{4.2} = 1.3$ **2.** $j - 2.56 = 18.3$ **3.** $s + 12.76 = 15$

4. $4.5b = 56.25$ **5.** $22.8 = \dfrac{z}{2.8}$ **6.** $1.44y = 72$

7. $8.04 = w - 5.19$ **8.** $9 = d + 4.85$ **9.** $11.2x = 89.6$

10. $f - 36.5 = 18$ **11.** $a + 14.68 = 25.1$ **12.** $\dfrac{b}{4.8} = 3.7$

13. $3.72 + c = 8$ **14.** $3.6 = 0.18x$ **15.** $\dfrac{a}{5.6} = 5$

16. Patricia McCormick of the United States won four gold medals in the 1952 and 1956 Summer Olympics diving competitions. Her winning score in 1956 for the high-diving event was 84.85 points, which was 5.48 points higher than her 1952 score in the same event. What was her 1952 score? Use the equation $p + 5.48 = 84.85$.

Set 2-13 (pages 116–119)

Write and solve an equation for each problem. Give each answer in a complete sentence.

At the Movies Popcorn is sold in three sizes: small, medium, and large. The medium sells for $3.50 and the small sells for $2.95.

1. Miguel bought a large popcorn and a medium popcorn and paid a non-tax total of $7.95. How much was the large popcorn?

2. Next week, extra large popcorn will be offered. It will sell for $2.65 more than the medium. How much will the extra large popcorn cost?

3. Ling bought 4 large sodas. She paid $11.80. How much was each soda?

Number Theory and Fraction Concepts

 DIAGNOSING READINESS

A Vocabulary

(pages 8, 95, 101)

Choose the best term from the box.

1. The ___?___ tells how many times the base is used as a factor.

2. In the example $6\overline{)36}$, the ___?___ is 36.

3. A number that is written as a product of repeated factors is in ___?___.

Vocabulary

- **exponent** *(p. 8)*   • **base** *(p. 8)*
- **exponential form** *(p. 8)*
- **dividend** *(pp. 95, 101)*

B Exponents

(pages 8–11)

Write each product using exponents.

4. $5 \times 5 \times 5$

5. $4 \cdot 4 \cdot 4 \cdot 4$

6. $2 \times 2 \times 2 \times 2 \times 2$

7. $5 \times 5 \times 3 \times 3$

8. $2 \cdot 2 \cdot 3 \cdot 2 \cdot 3$

9. $5 \times 5 \times 5 \times 2 \times 2$

10. A gross of pencils is 12 dozen. Write this number using exponents.

Do You Know...

What fraction of the Earth's land is used for cultivation and pasture?

You will find out in Lesson 3-13.

RUSSELL ASH
INCREDIBLE COMPARISONS

C Dividing by a Whole Number
(pages 94–97)

Divide. Write each quotient as a decimal.

11. $12 \div 5$ **12.** $7 \div 2$

13. $5 \div 4$ **14.** $76.2 \div 6$

15. $37.5 \div 3$ **16.** $29 \div 4$

17. Pointy Pens are 6 for $1.08. Find the price of one pen.

18. Last week, the museum gift shop sold 84 model dinosaurs for $662.76. If all the models were the same price, how much did each model cost?

D Comparing and Ordering Decimals
(pages 78–79)

Compare the numbers using $<$, $>$, or $=$.

19. 3.506 ● 3.51   **20.** 4.68 ● 3.99

21. 8.255 ● 8.525   **22.** 7.33 ● 7.330

Order from least to greatest.

23. 4.655, 4.598, 4.663, 4.589

24. 2.061, 2.06, 2.61, 2.601

25. Cathy's dog weighs 8.94 kg and Erik's dog weighs 8.49 kg. Which dog weighs more?

141

Vocabulary
• divisible
• multiple
• factor
• divisor

Think It Through

I can **make a table** to list all the possibilities.

Factors, Multiples, and Divisibility

LEARN

Activity

What is divisibility?

There are 48 students in a marching band. What are the ways all the band members can be arranged in rows with the same number of students in each row?

$48 \div 2 = 24$, so the band members can be arranged in 24 rows with 2 members in each row, or 2 rows with 24 members in each row.

Copy and complete the table to show all the ways the members can be arranged in equal rows.

Number of Band Members: 48						
Number of members in each row	1	2	3			
Number of rows	48	24				

a. Explain the method you used to complete the table.

b. Make tables like the one above to show all the ways the following bands can be arranged in equal rows: 45 members, 64 members, 100 members.

How are the numbers related?

You know that $3 \times 5 = 15$. Mathematical terms can be used to describe the relationship between the numbers 3, 5, and 15.

	Examples
A **multiple** of a given number is the product of that number and a whole number greater than 0.	15 is a multiple of 3. 15 is a multiple of 5.
A whole number is **divisible** by another whole number when the quotient is a whole number and the remainder is 0.	15 is divisible by 3. 15 is divisible by 5.
When a number is divided by any of its **factors**, or **divisors**, the remainder is 0.	3 and 5 are factors of 15. 3 and 5 are divisors of 15.

✔ Talk About It

1. Use the vocabulary terms introduced on page 142 to describe the relationship between 2, 24, and 48.

2. List all of the factors of 48.

What are divisibility rules?

For some numbers, you can use patterns to help you decide whether a number is divisible by another number.

Divisibility Rules	
A whole number is divisible by	**Examples**
2 if the ones digit is 0, 2, 4, 6, or 8.	2, 4, 6, 92, 168, 700
3 if the sum of the digits of the number is divisible by 3.	3, 6, 12, 135, 339, 723
4 if the last two digits of the number are divisible by 4.	4, 16, 24, 44, 104, 1,852
5 if the ones digit is 0 or 5.	5, 10, 15, 105, 380, 925
6 if the number is divisible by both 2 and 3.	6, 12, 24, 360, 612
9 if the sum of the digits of the number is divisible by 9.	9, 18, 36, 189, 963, 981
10 if the ones digit is 0.	10, 20, 80, 500, 810

> **Example**
>
> Tell whether 135 is divisible by 2, 3, 4, 5, 6, 9, or 10.
>
> 2: Is the ones digit even? **No**
>
> 3: Is the sum of the digits divisible by 3?
> $1 + 3 + 5 = 9$ Nine is divisible by 3. **Yes**
>
> 4: Are the last two digits divisible by 4? **No**
>
> 5: Is the ones digit a 0 or a 5? **Yes**
>
> 6: Is the number divisible by both 2 and 3? **No**
>
> 9: Is the sum of the digits divisible by 9?
> $1 + 3 + 5 = 9$ Nine is divisible by 9. **Yes**
>
> 10: Is the ones digit a 0? **No**
>
> So, 135 is divisible by 3, 5, and 9.

✔ Talk About It

3. How can you tell if 168 is divisible by 2? by 3? by 6?

4. The sum of the digits of a number is 18. What does the sum tell you about the divisibility of the number?

5. Reasoning Name a whole number that is divisible by both 2 and 5. Is the same number divisible by 10? Is this true of other numbers that are divisible by both 2 and 5?

Tell whether each number is divisible by 2, 3, 4, 5, 6, 9, or 10.

1. 75   **2.** 162   **3.** 236

Tell whether the first number is a multiple of the second.

4. 6,005; 5   **5.** 8,235; 9   **6.** 734; 6

7. Reasoning Which number has more factors, 17 or 18? Explain.

PRACTICE   *For more practice, see Set 3-1 on p. 198.*

A Skills and Understanding

Tell whether each number is divisible by 2, 3, 4, 5, 6, 9, or 10.

8. 1,125   **9.** 813   **10.** 468   **11.** 45   **12.** 253

13. 471   **14.** 555   **15.** 96   **16.** 1,264   **17.** 954

Tell whether the first number is a multiple of the second.

18. 54; 3   **19.** 108; 6   **20.** 3,001; 5   **21.** 2,618; 9   **22.** 1,090; 10

23. Number Sense Name 4 factors of 60 that are greater than 1 and less than 60.

B Reasoning and Problem Solving

Math and Social Studies

Contra dancing, such as the Virginia Reel, uses groups with an even number of dancers, usually six or more. Round dancing is done in pairs. The data file at the right shows the number of participants at a dance convention.

24. In which ballrooms can the dancers be divided into equal groups of 2, 6, or 10?

25. Square dancing is done in "squares" of eight people. If the dancers in Ballroom F are divided into groups for square dancing, how many people would not be in a group?

26. If the dancers in Ballroom C and Ballroom E are combined, is the total a multiple of 6?

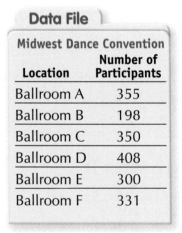

Data File

Midwest Dance Convention

Location	Number of Participants
Ballroom A	355
Ballroom B	198
Ballroom C	350
Ballroom D	408
Ballroom E	300
Ballroom F	331

27. <u>Writing in Math</u> Does Hugh's rule below work? If not, tell why and give an example.

> 36, 69, and 93 are all divisible by 3. So, if the ones digit of a number is 3, 6, or 9, the number is always divisible by 3.

Think It Through
If I can **find one number where the rule does not work,** then the rule is not a rule.

C Extensions

The divisibility rule for 8 states that if the number formed by the last three digits of the number is divisible by 8, then the entire number is divisible by 8. For example, 5,240 is divisible by 8 because 240 is divisible by 8. Tell whether the following numbers are divisible by 8.

28. 2,016   **29.** 538   **30.** 608   **31.** 1,776   **32.** 444

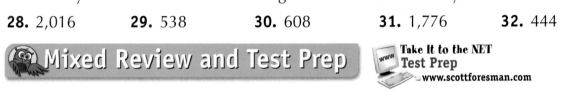

Mixed Review and Test Prep

Take It to the NET
www Test Prep
www.scottforesman.com

Write an equation to solve the problem.

33. Keira bought a clock radio that was $12 less than the regular price. If she paid $38 for the clock radio, what was the regular price?

34. Which is the solution for $t - 12.3 = 8.8$?

    A. $t = 3.5$ **B.** $t = 20.11$ **C.** $t = 21.1$ **D.** $t = 21.3$

Enrichment

Divisibility by 7

Here is a rule to test divisibility by 7.

Is 3,416 divisible by 7?

Isolate the digit in the ones place and multiply it by 2.
(6 × 2 = 12)

$$3,41|6$$
$$-12|$$
$$\overline{32|9}$$

Subtract the product from the remaining digits.

Repeat these steps until you get a multiple of 7 or zero.

$$-18|$$
$$\overline{14}$$

If the result is zero or another multiple of 7, then the original number is divisible by 7.

Since 14 is divisible by 7, you know that 3,416 is also divisible by 7.

For 1–4, use the pattern above to test for divisibility by 7.

    1. 686   **2.** 5,523   **3.** 2,754   **4.** 17,276

Prime and Composite Numbers

LEARN

Activity

How many factors are there?

You can use grid paper or square tiles to construct rectangles with different dimensions.

a. Copy and complete the table below. For each number of squares from 1 to 20, show the different rectangles that can be made. Two rectangles are the same if one can be turned to look like the other. Use the dimensions of the rectangles to list the factors of that number.

Number of Squares	Drawings	Dimensions	Factors
1	▪	1 × 1	1
2	▭	1 × 2	1, 2
3	▭	1 × 3	1, 3
4	▭▭	1 × 4	
	▦	2 × 2	1, 2, 4

b. For which numbers could you draw only one rectangle? How many factors do these numbers have?

c. For which numbers could you make more than one rectangle? How many factors do these numbers have?

d. Name a number between 20 and 30 that has only two factors. How many rectangles can you make with that number of squares?

e. For which of these numbers would you be able to draw only one rectangle? You may use a calculator to help decide.

91   47   119   143

What are prime and composite numbers?

Every whole number greater than 1 is either a prime number or a composite number.

A **prime number** is a whole number that is greater than 1 and has exactly two factors, 1 and itself.

Examples: 2, 3, 5, 7, 11, 13, 17, and 19 are prime numbers.

A **composite number** is a whole number that is greater than 1 and has more than two factors.

Examples: 4, 6, 8, 9, 10, 12, 14, 15, 16, 18, and 20 are composite numbers.

How can you find the prime factorization of a number?

Every composite number can be written in exactly one way as the product of prime numbers. This is known as the **prime factorization** of the number. The prime factorization of a prime number is just that number. For example, the prime factorization of 11 is 11.

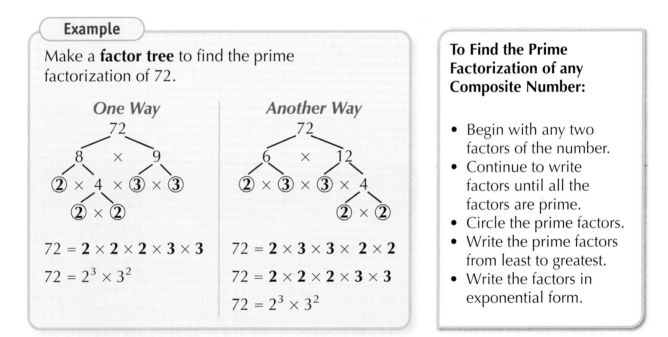

Example

Make a **factor tree** to find the prime factorization of 72.

One Way

$72 = 2 \times 2 \times 2 \times 3 \times 3$
$72 = 2^3 \times 3^2$

Another Way

$72 = 2 \times 3 \times 3 \times 2 \times 2$
$72 = 2 \times 2 \times 2 \times 3 \times 3$
$72 = 2^3 \times 3^2$

To Find the Prime Factorization of any Composite Number:

- Begin with any two factors of the number.
- Continue to write factors until all the factors are prime.
- Circle the prime factors.
- Write the prime factors from least to greatest.
- Write the factors in exponential form.

✔ Talk About It

1. In the first factor tree, why is 2 × 4 written under the 8?

2. How can you check that $2^3 \times 3^2$ is the correct answer?

3. The number 2 is an even prime number. Are there other even prime numbers? Why or why not?

4. **Reasoning** Maria said, "My factor tree for 72 begins with 3 and 24, so my prime factors will be different." Is Maria correct? Explain.

Tell whether each number is prime or composite.

1. 75 **2.** 87 **3.** 41 **4.** 51 **5.** 64

Write the prime factorization of each number.

6. 21 **7.** 33 **8.** 36 **9.** 61 **10.** 63

11. Reasoning How can divisibility rules help you find the prime factorization of a number?

Ⓐ Skills and Understanding

Tell whether each number is prime or composite.

12. 68 **13.** 93 **14.** 101 **15.** 61 **16.** 292 **17.** 147

Write the prime factorization of each number.

18. 27 **19.** 120 **20.** 56 **21.** 65 **22.** 57 **23.** 99

24. 201 **25.** 43 **26.** 85 **27.** 38 **28.** 300 **29.** 115

30. Number Sense Explain why the prime factorization of 90 is NOT $2 \times 5 \times 9$. How should the prime factorization be written?

Ⓑ Reasoning and Problem Solving

31. Multiples of what number are represented by the rectangles at the right?

32. If you continued the pattern, what would be the dimensions of the next three rectangles?

33. If you made a similar pattern of rectangles for multiples of 8, what would be the dimensions of the first five rectangles?

Math and Social Studies

In 1742, a Russian mathematician named Christian Goldbach conjectured (guessed) that every even number greater than 2 could be written as the sum of two prime numbers. Three examples of this conjecture are shown. Write each of the following numbers as a sum of two prime numbers. Primes may be repeated in the sum.

34. 20 **35.** 26 **36.** 48

37. 22 **38.** 68 **39.** 110

Goldbach's Conjecture	
Even Number	Sum
10	5 + 5
16	11 + 5
24	13 + 11

40. **Writing in Math** LaToya says, "To check whether a number is prime or composite, I just use the divisibility rules for 2, 3, 4, 5, 6, 8, 9, and 10. If none of them work, then I know the number is prime." Does LaToya's method work for all numbers? Give an example to support your explanation.

Think It Through
I should **try, check, and revise** numbers having lesser values first and then test numbers with greater values.

Ⓒ Extensions

41. Two prime numbers that differ by 2, such as 3 and 5, are called **twin primes.** Find the 8 pairs of twin primes that are less than 100.

Mixed Review and Test Prep

Take It to the NET
Test Prep
www.scottforesman.com

Tell whether each number is divisible by 2, 3, 4, 5, 6, 9 or 10.

42. 66   **43.** 75   **44.** 2,145   **45.** 101

46. Which is the product for 3.42×16?

   A. 5,472   **B.** 547.2   **C.** 54.72   **D.** 5.472

Enrichment

Sieve of Eratosthenes

About 230 B.C., the Greek mathematician Eratosthenes developed a method for identifying prime numbers. The method is called the **Sieve of Eratosthenes.**

Follow the steps to identify the prime numbers from 1 to 100.

Step 1 Copy the table at the right.

Step 2 Cross out 1 because it is neither prime nor composite.

Step 3 Circle 2. Then, cross out all other multiples of 2.

Step 4 Go to the first number that is not crossed out. Circle it and cross out its other multiples.

Step 5 Repeat Step 4 until all numbers in the table are either crossed out or circled. The circled numbers are prime.

1	2	3	4	5	6	7	8	9	10
11	12	13	14	15	16	17	18	19	20
21	22	23	24	25	26	27	28	29	30
31	32	33	34	35	36	37	38	39	40
41	42	43	44	45	46	47	48	49	50
51	52	53	54	55	56	57	58	59	60
61	62	63	64	65	66	67	68	69	70
71	72	73	74	75	76	77	78	79	80
81	82	83	84	85	86	87	88	89	90
91	92	93	94	95	96	97	98	99	100

1. List the prime numbers from 1 to 100.

2. Explain why some numbers could be crossed out more than once.

Key Idea

There are different ways to find the factors that are common to two or more numbers.

Vocabulary

- common factor
- greatest common factor (GCF)
- prime factorization (p. 147)

Think It Through

- I can **use factors** to identify equal groups for sharing.
- I can **make an organized list** to find the common factors and GCF.

Greatest Common Factor

■ LEARN

How can you use factors?

Janelle is making snack packs for a group hike. Each pack should have the same number of bags of trail mix and the same number of bottles of water. What is the greatest number of snack packs that she can make with no refreshments left over?

To solve this problem, you need to find the numbers that are factors of both 60 and 90. These are the **common factors** of 60 and 90. The **greatest common factor (GCF)** is the *greatest* number that is a factor of both 60 and 90.

✓ WARM UP

List the factors of each number.

1. 12   2. 31

3. 54   4. 100

Hike
Refresments
60 bags of trail mix
90 bottles of water

Example

Find the GCF of 60 and 90.

One Way

List the factors of each number.

60: 1, 2, 3, 4, 5, 6, 10, 12, 15, 20, 30, 60
90: 1, 2, 3, 5, 6, 9, 10, 15, 18, 30, 45, 90

Circle pairs of common factors. Select the greatest one.

60: 1, 2, 3, 4, 5, 6, 10, 12, 15, 20, 30, 60
90: 1, 2, 3, 5, 6, 9, 10, 15, 18, 30, 45, 90

The GCF is 30.

Another Way

Use prime factorization.

$60 = 2 \times 2 \times 3 \times 5$
$90 = 2 \times 3 \times 3 \times 5$

Find the product of the common prime factors. If there are no common prime factors, the GCF is 1.

$60 = 2 \times 2 \times 3 \times 5$
$90 = 2 \times 3 \times 3 \times 5$ $2 \times 3 \times 5 = 30$

The GCF is 30.

The greatest number of snack packs she can make is 30.

✔ Talk About It

1. In the second method, why is 2 used only once as a factor of the GCF?

2. In each of the 30 snack packs, how many bags of trail mix and how many bottles of water will there be?

3. **Reasoning** Find the GCF of 48 and 120. Which method did you use? Why?

Take It to the NET
More Examples
www.scottforesman.com

Find the GCF for each set of numbers.

1. 12, 21   **2.** 30, 45   **3.** 8, 13   **4.** 18, 72   **5.** 27, 42, 48

6. Number Sense The GCF of 6 and 24 is 6. Find two other pairs of numbers in which the first number in each pair is the GCF.

PRACTICE

For more practice, see Set 3-3 on p. 198.

Ⓐ Skills and Understanding

Find the GCF for each set of numbers.

7. 14, 35   **8.** 32, 80   **9.** 50, 75   **10.** 25, 90   **11.** 15, 36

12. 20, 25   **13.** 11, 15   **14.** 100, 200   **15.** 99, 121   **16.** 12, 49

17. 9, 18, 24   **18.** 13, 23   **19.** 54, 117   **20.** 20, 32, 44   **21.** 45, 36, 72

22. Number Sense Name two numbers for which the GCF is 1.

Ⓑ Reasoning and Problem Solving

23. Chris wants to buy storage boxes that are all the same height and can be stacked on 24-inch or 30-inch shelves with no spare space above or below. What is the tallest box that will work?

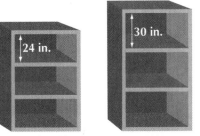

24. **Writing in Math** Explain how you use prime factors to find the GCF of 45 and 75.

Ⓒ Extensions

The **Venn diagram** at the right shows the common factors and the GCF of 30 and 42.

25. What do the shaded and non-shaded portions of both circles show?

26. Use a Venn diagram to show the common factors of 48 and 72. What is the GCF?

Factors of 30	Factors of 42
5 1	7
10 2	14
15 3	21
30 6	42

 Mixed Review and Test Prep

Take It to the NET
Test Prep
www.scottforesman.com

27. Is 2,529 a multiple of 9? Explain.

28. Is 78,423 divisible by 6? Explain.

29. Which is the prime factorization of 64?

     A. 4×16 **B.** 2×32 **C.** 8^2 **D.** 2^6

 All text pages available online and on CD-ROM.

Key Idea
There are different ways to find multiples that are common to two or more numbers.

Vocabulary
- common multiple
- least common multiple (LCM)
- prime factorization (p. 147)

Least Common Multiple

LEARN

How can you use multiples?

Fiona is planning a picnic. She wants to buy as many hot dogs as buns, and she wants to buy as few of each as possible. How many packages of each should she buy?

To solve this problem, you need to find multiples of both 8 and 10. These are the **common multiples** of 8 and 10.

The **least common multiple (LCM)** of 8 and 10 is the common multiple with the *least* value.

How can you find the LCM of two numbers?

Example

Find the LCM of 8 and 10.

One Way
List multiples of each number.

8: 8, 16, 24, 32, **40**, 48, 56, 64, 72, **80**, 88, 96, . . .

10: 10, 20, 30, **40**, 50, 60, 70, **80**, 90, 100, . . .

The least multiple that appears in both lists is 40.

The LCM of 8 and 10 is 40.

Another Way
Use prime factorization.

8 = 2 × 2 × 2
10 = 2 × 5

Circle the greater number of times each different factor appears. Then find the product of those factors.

8 = (2 × 2 × 2)
10 = 2 × (5)   2 × 2 × 2 × 5 = 40

The LCM of 8 and 10 is 40.

Fiona should buy 40 hot dogs and 40 buns. This is the same as 4 packages of hot dogs and 5 packages of buns.

✔ **Talk About It**

1. Name 3 common multiples of 8 and 10 that are NOT the LCM of 8 and 10.

2. **Reasoning** Brittany thinks that the LCM of two numbers is the least number that each divides into without a remainder. Is she right? Explain.

Find the LCM of each set of numbers.

1. 4, 6 **2.** 3, 13 **3.** 15, 30 **4.** 6, 27 **5.** 5, 9, 15

6. Number Sense Find the LCM of 5 and 7, the LCM of 4 and 9, and the LCM of 3 and 10. What is special about these LCMs?

PRACTICE

For more practice, see Set 3-4 on p. 199.

Ⓐ Skills and Understanding

Find the LCM of each set of numbers.

7. 6, 14 **8.** 3, 7 **9.** 10, 12 **10.** 18, 72 **11.** 20, 25 **12.** 6, 12, 30

13. 5, 12 **14.** 4, 22 **15.** 5, 6, 15 **16.** 8, 16, 24 **17.** 20, 30 **18.** 14, 21

19. Number Sense Find the LCM of 5 and 10, the LCM of 4 and 12, and the LCM of 3 and 15. What is special about these LCMs?

Ⓑ Reasoning and Problem Solving

20. Mr. Peterson plays golf only on Saturday. He jogs every fourth day. If Mr. Peterson plays golf and jogs on Saturday, how many days will it be before he golfs and jogs again on the same day?

21. Short films are shown continuously at the state fair. If the three films start together at 9:00 A.M., what time will it be when they all start at the same time again?

22. If one number is the multiple of another, what is the GCF? What is the LCM? (Hint: Test different pairs such as 5 and 20 or 8 and 16.)

23. **Writing in Math** Ira thinks the least common multiple of 8 and 10 contains both 8 and 10 as factors. Is he right? Explain.

FILM SCHEDULE

Feature	Length
Cartoons	24 minutes
Travelogue	60 minutes
Comedy	48 minutes

Mixed Review and Test Prep

Take It to the NET
Test Prep
www.scottforesman.com

Round each decimal to the nearest hundredth.

24. 20.9574 **25.** 16.002 **26.** 3,452.631

27. Write the prime factorization of 204.

28. What is the GCF of 24 and 72?

A. 36 **B.** 24 **C.** 12 **D.** 8

Understand Graphic Sources: Tables and Charts

Understanding graphic sources such as tables and charts when you read in math can help you use the **problem-solving strategy, *Make a Table,*** in the next lesson.

In reading, understanding tables can help you understand what you read. In math, understanding tables can help you solve problems.

This title tells you the table is about U.S. international trade in 2001.

The entry $126 is in the column for Japan and the row for imports. So, the U.S. imported $126 billion in goods from Japan in 2001.

*Read the title of the **table** or **chart** to find out in general what it is about.*

UNITED STATES INTERNATIONAL TRADE, 2001				
Country	Canada	Mexico	Japan	China
Total imports (in billions)	$216	$131	$126	$102
Total exports (in billions)	$163	$101	$57	$19

*The other information in the **table** are the entries. Each entry is a specific piece of information.*

These headings tell you that the data is about the total imports from and the total exports to certain countries.

*The headings describe the different types of data in the **table.** Sometimes the headings go across, and sometimes they go down.*

1. What was the value of the goods the United States imported from China in 2001?

2. Tell all the information about Canada given in the table.

For 3–6, use the Highest Waterfalls table at the right.

3. What is the table about? How do you know?

4. What type of data is in the table?

5. What is the height of Venezuela's Angel Falls?

6. <u>Writing in Math</u> What information about the Tugela waterfall is given in the table?

Highest Waterfalls	
Waterfall, Country	**Height (ft)**
Angel Falls, Venezuela	3,212
Utigord, Norway	2,625
Monge, Norway	2,540
Mutarazi, Zimbabwe	2,499
Yosemite, U.S.	2,425
Tugela, South Africa	2,014

For 7–9, use the United States Coins chart at the right.

7. How thick is a U.S. dime?

8. How much does a U.S. quarter weigh?

9. Write the names of the coins in order from the greatest diameter to the least diameter.

United States Coins				
Weight (g)	2.5	5	2.3	5.7
Thickness (mm)	1.55	1.95	1.35	1.75
Diameter (mm)	19.05	21.21	17.91	24.26

For 10–14, use the Train #671 Weekend Schedule below.

10. Why do two columns in this chart have the same heading?

11. How is the * symbol used?

12. Where in Pennsylvania does the train stop?

13. How long is the ride from Baltimore to Washington, D.C.?

14. <u>Writing in Math</u> Suppose you are planning to ride from Newark to Baltimore. What information is given in the schedule about your trip?

Train #671 Weekend Schedule

Depart	Time	Arrive	Time
New York, NY	1:05 P.M.	Newark, NJ	1:18 P.M.
Newark, NJ	1:23 P.M.	Philadelphia, PA	2:13 P.M.
Philadelphia, PA	2:20 P.M.	Wilmington, DE	2:40 P.M.
Wilmington, DE	2:45 P.M.	Baltimore, MD	3:15 P.M.
Baltimore, MD	3:22 P.M.	Washington, D.C.*	4:05 P.M.

* Free bus shuttle to and from airport

Problem-Solving Strategy

Reading Helps!

Understanding graphic sources such as tables and charts

can help you with...

the problem-solving strategy, *Make a Table.*

Key Idea

Learning how and when to make a table can help you solve problems.

Make a Table

LEARN

How can you make and use a table to solve a problem?

Babysitting Carrie is offered an afternoon babysitting job that will last 10 days. The parents who want to hire her offer two plans for payment. Which payment should Carrie accept?

Plan I: A single $100 payment for the 10 days worked

Plan II: Pay for the first day would be $0.25. Then each day thereafter, the total amount of pay would double.

Read and Understand

What do you know?   There are two different plans.

What are you trying to find?   Find the total pay for 10 days under Plan II.

Plan and Solve

What strategy will you use?   **Strategy:** Make a Table

Days			
Amount			

Days	1	2	3
Amount	$0.25	$0.50	$1

Days	1	2	3	4	5	6	7	8	9	10
Amount	$0.25	$0.50	$1	$2	$4	$8	$16	$32	$64	$128

Days	1	2	3	4	5	6	7	8	9	10
Amount	$0.25	$0.50	$1	$2	$4	$8	$16	$32	$64	$128

Answer: Carrie should accept Plan II which pays $128.

How to Make a Table

Step 1 Set up the table with the correct labels.

Step 2 Enter known data into the table.

Step 3 Look for a pattern. Extend the table.

Step 4 Find the answer in the table.

Look Back and Check

Is your answer reasonable?

Yes, the answer should be an even number because the amounts in the table were doubled.

✔ Talk About It

1. How did the table help to answer the question in the problem?

For another example, see Set 3-5 on p. 195.

CHECK ✔

Make a table to solve the problem. Write the answer in a complete sentence.

1. Savings The Skinner family has a savings account for their vacation. They will deposit $175 the first week and continue to deposit money into the account on a weekly basis. Each week they will deposit $15 more than the previous week. How much money will be deposited on the fifth week? What will be the total amount deposited after 5 weeks?

PRACTICE

For more practice, see Set 3-5 on p. 199.

Make a table to solve each problem. Write each answer in a complete sentence.

2. Kelsey started a club for helping senior citizens use computers. On the first day, she was the only member. On the second day, a friend joined. Each day after that, one more member joined than had joined on the previous day. What was the membership of the club on the 15th day?

3. Ramir makes his own pottery vases. It costs him $2.25 in materials for each vase. He sells them for $10 each. How many vases does he need to sell in order to make a profit of $93?

4. For every 3 items you buy at the school store you earn 25 points toward the purchase of other items. How many items would you need to buy in order to earn enough points for a backpack worth 175 points?

5. Grant notices that a long-distance company is advertising a new calling plan. The company charges $0.75 for the first minute and $0.04 for each additional minute. The rates for a plan Grant currently uses is shown at the right. Which plan is less expensive if Grant intends to make a long-distance call that lasts for 8 minutes?

6. <u>Writing in Math</u> Write a word problem that could be solved by using the table shown at the right. Provide the answer to the problem.

STRATEGIES

- **Show What You Know**
  Draw a Picture
  Make an Organized List
  Make a Table
  Make a Graph
  Act It Out or Use Objects
- **Look for a Pattern**
- **Try, Check, and Revise**
- **Write an Equation**
- **Use Logical Reasoning**
- **Solve a Simpler Problem**
- **Work Backward**

Choose a tool
Mental Math

Calling Plan

$0.50 first minute

$0.07 each additional minute

Omar's Work Schedule	
Week	**Hours Worked**
1	6
2	8.5
3	11
4	13.5
5	16

All text pages available online and on CD-ROM.

Do You Know How?

Do You Understand?

Factors, Multiples, and Divisibility (3-1)

Tell whether each number is divisible by 2, 3, 4, 5, 6, 9, or 10.

1. 121   **2.** 972   **3.** 125

4. 90   **5.** 81   **6.** 48

A Explain how you tested for divisibility of 972.

B How could you be sure that your answer to Exercise 1 is correct?

Prime and Composite Numbers (3-2)

Tell whether each number is prime or composite. If composite, use exponents to write the prime factorization.

7. 29   **8.** 144   **9.** 81

10. 84   **11.** 43   **12.** 112

C Explain how to determine whether or not a number is prime or composite.

D When you find the prime factorization of 36, does it matter which factors you start with? Explain.

Greatest Common Factor (3-3), Least Common Multiple (3-4)

Find the GCF of each set of numbers.

13. 36, 48   **14.** 25, 50   **15.** 27, 45, 63

16. 45, 68   **17.** 54, 99   **18.** 16, 24, 72

Find the LCM of each set of numbers.

19. 8, 15   **20.** 12, 48   **21.** 8, 16, 24

22. 42, 36   **23.** 36, 45   **24.** 4, 5, 21

E Which method did you use to find the GCF in Exercise 13?

F Which method did you use to find the LCM in Exercise 21?

Problem-Solving Strategy: Make a Table (3-5)

25. At an assembly checkpoint, safety engineers inspected the seat belt latches for every 18th car and the trunk release latch for every 15th car. If the first car at the checkpoint is car 1, what will be the number of the first car to be checked for both problems? Make a table to solve the problem. Write the answer in a complete sentence.

G Without using the table, how could you determine the number of the first car to be checked for both problems?

MULTIPLE CHOICE

TEST TALK

1. Which number is divisible by 2, 3, and 5? (3-1)

   A. 45   **B.** 66   **C.** 70   **D.** 90

2. Which number is the LCM of 6, 9, and 10? (3-4)

   A. 60   **B.** 90   **C.** 120   **D.** 180

Think It Through
First, I should **eliminate any unreasonable answers.**

FREE RESPONSE

Tell whether each number is divisible by 2, 3, 4, 5, 6, 9, or 10. (3-1)

3. 28   **4.** 45   **5.** 120   **6.** 96   **7.** 51   **8.** 40

Tell whether each number is prime or composite. If composite, use exponents to write the prime factorization. (3-2)

9. 32   **10.** 47   **11.** 45   **12.** 120   **13.** 53   **14.** 96

Find the GCF of each pair of numbers. (3-3)

15. 5, 14   **16.** 12, 18   **17.** 15, 45   **18.** 48, 64   **19.** 60, 100

Find the LCM of each set of numbers. (3-4)

20. 5, 14   **21.** 12, 18   **22.** 15, 45   **23.** 4, 6, 9   **24.** 5, 6, 12

25. Gary has 24 football cards, 18 basketball cards, and 30 baseball cards. He wants the same number of just one kind of card on each page of his album. What is the greatest number of cards he can have on each page? (3-3)

26. In a school kitchen during lunch, the timer for pizza buzzes every 14 minutes; the timer for hamburger buns buzzes every 6 minutes. The two timers just buzzed together. In how many minutes will they buzz together again? (3-4)

Make a table to answer Problems 27–28. (3-5)

Two shipping companies charge different amounts to mail packages. Company A charges an initial $5 fee, and each pound shipped is an additional $1. Company B charges an initial $3 fee, and $1.50 for each pound shipped.

27. At what weight will the two companies have the same charge?

28. Which company charges less for a 6-lb package? How much will you save?

Writing in Math

29. What does it mean if 18 is a GCF? What does it mean if 18 is an LCM? (3-3, 3-4)

Key Idea
Fractions are used to name a part of a whole, a part of a set, a location on a number line, or a division of whole numbers.

Vocabulary
• fraction
• denominator
• numerator

Materials
• scissors
• paper
  or **tools**

Think It Through
I need to be able to **understand and use mathematical terms** correctly.

Understanding Fractions

LEARN

How are fractions used?

A **fraction** is a number that can be used to describe a part of a set or a part of a whole. The **denominator** gives the total number of objects in the set or the number of equal parts in the whole. The **numerator** gives the number of objects or equal parts being considered.

When a fraction is used to describe part of a set, the items in the set do not have to be the same.

Example A

Baseballs make up $\frac{3}{7}$ of the sports equipment.

number of baseballs ⟶ $\underset{}{3}$ ← numerator
total pieces of equipment ⟶ $\overline{7}$ ← denominator

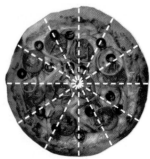

When a fraction describes part of a whole, the whole must be divided into equal parts.

Example B

The bolt is $\frac{7}{8}$ inch long.

```
0              1
INCHES
```

Example C

Joe and Dan ate $\frac{5}{6}$ of the pizza.

number of pieces eaten ⟶ $\dfrac{5}{6}$
number of pieces in all ⟶

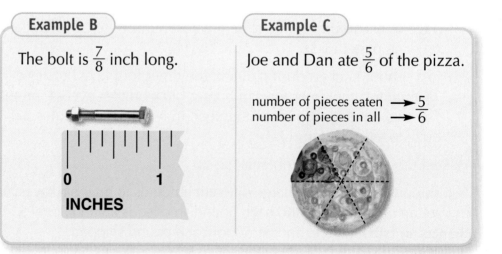

✔ Talk About It

1. In Example B, what is the "whole" on the ruler. Into how many equal parts is the whole divided?

2. **Number Sense** What fraction describes the whole pizza on the right? What fraction describes the pizza after all the pieces have been eaten?

WARM UP
Write the number for the word name given.

1. one half
2. five eighths
3. two thirds
4. six sevenths

How are fractions related to division?

Activity

Think It Through
- I can **act it out** to find equal shares.
- I can **look for a pattern** in the table.

At a scout meeting, 5 cakes are divided evenly among 8 families. How much does each family get?

You need to find 5 ÷ 8. Modeling this situation will help find the answer.

a. Use 5 sheets of paper to represent the 5 cakes. Since there are 8 families, divide each sheet into 8 equal parts. You can use paper folding to do this.

b. Fold and cut the first "cake" into 8 equal "pieces." Act out sharing the pieces among 8 families. What *fraction* of a cake does each family get? Copy the table and record your answer.

c. Cut and share the pieces from the second cake. Altogether, what fraction of a cake does each family get? Record your answer.

Number of cakes	Number of families	Division expression	Fraction of a cake
1	8	1 ÷ 8	$\frac{1}{8}$
2	8	2 ÷ 8	
3	8	3 ÷ 8	

d. Repeat Step c for the third, fourth, and fifth cakes.

e. What relationship do you notice between each division expression and the numerator and denominator of the fraction?

In general, you can think of a fraction as division.

$$\frac{7}{8} = 7 \div 8 = 8\overline{)7}$$

Take It to the NET
More Examples
www.scottforesman.com

CHECK ✔

For another example, see Set 3-6 on p. 195.

Write a fraction for the blue shaded portion of each picture.

1.

2.

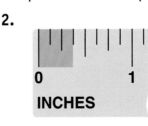

0   1
INCHES

3.

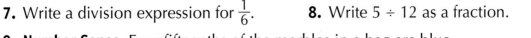

Draw a picture to show each fraction.

4. $\frac{1}{9}$ as part of a set   **5.** $\frac{3}{4}$ as a measure   **6.** $\frac{9}{10}$ as part of a whole

7. Write a division expression for $\frac{1}{6}$.   **8.** Write 5 ÷ 12 as a fraction.

9. Number Sense Four fifteenths of the marbles in a bag are blue. What fraction of the marbles are *not* blue?

A Skills and Understanding

Write a fraction for the blue shaded portion of each picture.

10.

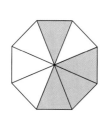

11.

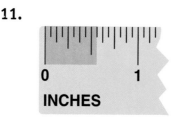

INCHES

12.

Draw a picture to show each fraction.

13. $\frac{7}{12}$ as part of a whole   **14.** $\frac{5}{8}$ as a measure   **15.** $\frac{10}{11}$ as part of a set

16. Write a division expression for $\frac{5}{9}$.   **17.** Write $1 \div 15$ as a fraction.

18. Number Sense Seven twelfths of a dozen eggs in a carton are brown. If one brown egg is removed, what fraction of the eggs left in the carton are brown?

B Reasoning and Problem Solving

Number Sense Tell what fraction should be written at each point on the number line.

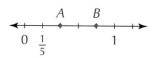

19. Point *A*   **20.** Point *B*

21. Point *C*   **22.** Point *E*

Math and Social Studies

The data at the right shows the populations for the 12 countries having the greatest populations in 2001.

23. What fraction of these countries have populations over 100 million?

24. What fraction of these countries have populations over one billion?

25. Writing in Math A small pizza was cut into 4 equal slices. Janie cut one of the pieces in half and ate it. She claimed that $\frac{4}{5}$ of the pizza was left. Is she correct? Explain.

Data File

Top 12 Greatest Populations, 2001	
Country	**Population**
China	1,273,111,290
India	1,029,991,145
United States	278,058,881
Indonesia	228,437,870
Brazil	174,468,575
Russia	145,470,197
Pakistan	144,616,639
Bangladesh	131,269,860
Japan	126,771,662
Nigeria	126,635,626
Mexico	101,879,171
Germany	83,029,536

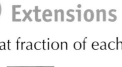

PRACTICE

C Extensions

What fraction of each square is shaded? How do you know?

26.    **27.**   **28.**   **29.**

30. Draw a square. Show a different way to divide it into fourths.

31. Here's a bigger challenge. Trace the trapezoid. Show how to divide it into fourths.

 **Mixed Review and Test Prep**

Take It to the NET
Test Prep
www.scottforesman.com

32. On a school field trip, there are 3 chaperones for every 16 students. Make a table that shows the number of chaperones needed for 80 students.

33. Which pair of numbers has 60 as their LCM?

A. 6, 10   **B.** 10, 12   **C.** 6, 8   **D.** 2, 30

Learning with Technology

Spreadsheet/Data/Grapher eTool: Generating a Sequence

Almost 800 years ago, an Italian mathematician named Leonardo Fibonacci discovered this sequence of numbers: 1, 1, 2, 3, 5, 8, 13, 21, 34, 55, 89, 144, 233, 377, 610,…

Beginning with the number 1, each number in the sequence is the sum of the previous two numbers.
$1 + 1 = 2$, $1 + 2 = 3$, $2 + 3 = 5$, $3 + 5 = 8$, $5 + 8 = 13$,
$8 + 13 = 21$, $13 + 21 = 34$, and so on.

Create a spreadsheet that will generate the first 32 terms of the Fibonacci sequence. Copy the formula in A5 to cells A6–A35, and B6 to cells B7–B35.

1. Do you think there is an infinite number of terms in the sequence? Explain.

2. Change the number in cell C2 to 3. What happens to the numbers in column B? How does the sequence depend on the numbers in cells B2 and C2?

Leonardo Fibonacci

	A	B	C
1	The Fibonacci Sequence	1st Number	2nd Number
2		1	1
3	Term	Fibonacci Number	
4	1	=B2	
5	=A4+1	=C2	
6		=B4+B5	

All text pages available online and on CD-ROM.

Section B Lesson 3-6   **163**

Key Idea
A part of a whole or of a set can be named by equivalent fractions.

Vocabulary
• equivalent fractions
• common factor (p. 150)
• least common denominator (LCD)
• greatest common factor (GCF) (p. 150)
• simplest form

Materials
• fraction strips or 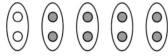 tools

Equivalent Fractions

LEARN

Activity

What are equivalent fractions?

Fractions that name the same amount are called **equivalent fractions**.

a. Use fraction strips to identify one or more fractions equivalent to each fraction below.

$$\frac{3}{4} \quad \frac{8}{12} \quad \frac{6}{10} \quad \frac{5}{6}$$

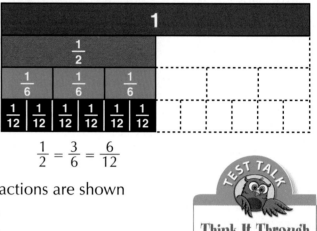

$$\frac{1}{2} = \frac{3}{6} = \frac{6}{12}$$

b. What two equivalent fractions are shown by this model? Explain.

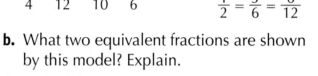

WARM UP
Find the common factors for each pair of numbers.

1. 6, 9   2. 10, 15

3. 4, 12   4. 24, 36

TEST TALK

Think It Through
I can **use objects** to help me identify equivalent fractions.

How can you find equivalent fractions?

Example A

Find two fractions that are equivalent to $\frac{18}{24}$.

One Way
Use multiplication.

Multiply both the numerator and denominator by the same nonzero number.

The number 2 is easy to use, so multiply the numerator and denominator by 2.

$$\frac{18}{24} = \frac{18 \times 2}{24 \times 2} = \frac{36}{48}$$

Another Way
Use division.

Divide both the numerator and denominator by the same nonzero number.

The number 3 is a common factor, so divide the numerator and denominator by 3.

$$\frac{18}{24} = \frac{18 \div 3}{24 \div 3} = \frac{6}{8}$$

So, $\frac{18}{24}$, $\frac{36}{48}$, and $\frac{6}{8}$ are all equivalent fractions.

Example B

Rewrite $\frac{5}{6}$ and $\frac{3}{8}$ as fractions with the same denominator.

STEP 1 Find a common multiple of the denominators. It is usually easier to work with the least common multiple. This is also called the **least common denominator (LCD).**

6: 6, 12, 18, **24**, 30, …   8: 8, 16, **24**, 32, 40, …

STEP 2 Multiply both the numerator and denominator by the same nonzero number to give equivalent fractions with a least common denominator.

$$\frac{5}{6} = \frac{5 \times 4}{6 \times 4} = \frac{20}{24}$$ $$\frac{3}{8} = \frac{3 \times 3}{8 \times 3} = \frac{9}{24}$$

$6 \times 4 = 24$ $8 \times 3 = 24$

Think It Through

I can also **use prime factorization** to find the least common denominator.

✔ Talk About It

1. In Examples A and B, why must the numerator and denominator of each fraction be multiplied or divided by the same nonzero number?

How can you write fractions in simplest form?

A fraction is in **simplest form** if 1 is the only common factor of both the numerator and the denominator.

Example C

Write $\frac{18}{24}$ in simplest form.

One Way
Use divisibility rules.

Divide the numerator and the denominator by a common factor. Repeat until 1 is the only common factor.

$$\frac{18 \div 3}{24 \div 3} = \frac{6 \div 2}{8 \div 2} = \frac{3}{4}$$

18 and 24 are divisible by 3.   *6 and 8 are divisible by 2.*

Another Way
Divide by the GCF.

Divide the numerator and the denominator by their **greatest common factor (GCF).**

$$\frac{18 \div 6}{24 \div 6} = \frac{3}{4}$$

The GCF of 18 and 24 is 6.

✔ Talk About It

2. Is $\frac{5}{12}$ written in simplest form? How can you tell?

3. **Reasoning** Name two equivalent fractions illustrated by the model at the right. Which fraction is in simplest form?

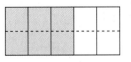

Find two fractions equivalent to each fraction.

1. $\frac{3}{4}$ **2.** $\frac{24}{48}$ **3.** $\frac{14}{42}$

Rewrite each pair of fractions with a common denominator.

4. $\frac{3}{5}, \frac{1}{2}$ **5.** $\frac{4}{9}, \frac{1}{6}$ **6.** $\frac{5}{8}, \frac{9}{16}$

Write each fraction in simplest form.

7. $\frac{8}{16}$ **8.** $\frac{15}{24}$ **9.** $\frac{10}{35}$ **10.** $\frac{12}{12}$ **11.** $\frac{5}{9}$ **12.** $\frac{25}{30}$

13. Number Sense Explain why $\frac{1}{6}$ and $\frac{6}{1}$ are not equivalent fractions.

PRACTICE

For more practice, see Set 3-7 on p. 200.

A **Skills and Understanding**

Find two fractions equivalent to each fraction.

14. $\frac{1}{4}$ **15.** $\frac{3}{8}$ **16.** $\frac{5}{10}$ **17.** $\frac{6}{9}$ **18.** $\frac{10}{11}$ **19.** $\frac{35}{56}$

Rewrite each pair of fractions with a common denominator.

20. $\frac{1}{3}, \frac{7}{9}$ **21.** $\frac{7}{8}, \frac{1}{12}$ **22.** $\frac{3}{4}, \frac{1}{3}$ **23.** $\frac{1}{10}, \frac{1}{2}$ **24.** $\frac{8}{9}, \frac{1}{4}$ **25.** $\frac{1}{5}, \frac{1}{8}$

Write each fraction in simplest form.

26. $\frac{3}{21}$ **27.** $\frac{9}{24}$ **28.** $\frac{42}{72}$ **29.** $\frac{14}{28}$ **30.** $\frac{18}{60}$ **31.** $\frac{17}{17}$

32. $\frac{8}{36}$ **33.** $\frac{7}{49}$ **34.** $\frac{30}{90}$ **35.** $\frac{17}{20}$ **36.** $\frac{32}{64}$ **37.** $\frac{55}{88}$

38. $\frac{42}{189}$ **39.** $\frac{31}{52}$ **40.** $\frac{16}{44}$ **41.** $\frac{30}{105}$ **42.** $\frac{19}{20}$ **43.** $\frac{108}{180}$

44. Number Sense How do you know that $\frac{7}{7} = \frac{12}{12}$?

B **Reasoning and Problem Solving**

45. Write $\frac{8}{9}, \frac{3}{4},$ and $\frac{5}{12}$ with a least common denominator.

46. Algebra Find the value of x so that $\frac{5}{7} = \frac{x}{42}$ are equivalent. Tell how you decided.

47. Algebra What is the GCF of 1 and x? Explain.

48. Some people say that a fraction in simplest form is in **lowest terms.** Why is *lowest terms* a good description?

49. Explain why fractions whose numerators are one less than their denominators are in simplest form.

50. Can the LCM and the GCF of two numbers ever be equal? Explain.

Math and Social Studies

Locations for the 34 State Parks in the state of Virginia are given here. For 51–52, write the fractions in simplest form.

51. What fraction of the parks are located in the Blue Ridge Highlands?

52. What fraction of the parks are in the Shenandoah and Central Regions combined?

53. **Writing in Math** Donald claims that $\frac{5}{10}$ and $\frac{3}{6}$ are not equivalent fractions because there is not a whole number he can divide 5 and 10 by to get 3 and 6. Is he correct? Explain.

> **Data File**
>
> **Virginia State Parks**
>
> • Blue Ridge Highlands: 8
> • Shenandoah Region: 3
> • Central Region: 11
> • Northern Region: 4
> • Tidewater, Eastern Shore Regions: 8

C Extensions

54. Sammy's method of simplifying fractions is shown at the right. Does his method always work? Explain.

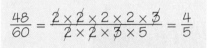

$$\frac{48}{60} = \frac{\cancel{2} \times \cancel{2} \times 2 \times 2 \times \cancel{3}}{\cancel{2} \times \cancel{2} \times \cancel{3} \times 5} = \frac{4}{5}$$

Mixed Review and Test Prep

Take It to the NET
Test Prep
www.scottforesman.com

55. Round 23,405 to the nearest 10,000, 1,000, 100, and 10.

56. Which of the following fractions represents the shaded part of the figure at the right?

A. $\frac{3}{4}$　　**B.** $\frac{2}{3}$　　**C.** $\frac{3}{5}$　　**D.** $\frac{2}{5}$

Learning with Technology

Using a Calculator to Find Equivalent Fractions

The  key allows you to change between fractions and decimals. To find an equivalent fraction for $\frac{3}{4}$, press 3 ☐ 4 [FⅭD]. You will see the decimal equivalent of $\frac{3}{4}$. Press [FⅭD] again to get a fraction equivalent to 0.75. Pressing [Simp] [=] until $\frac{N}{D} \rightarrow \frac{n}{d}$ disappears from the display, will give some equivalent fractions for $\frac{3}{4}$.

For 1–4, use your calculator to find two equivalent fractions.

1. $\frac{5}{8}$　　**2.** $\frac{14}{35}$　　**3.** $\frac{17}{25}$　　**4.** $\frac{19}{40}$

Vocabulary
• proper fraction
• improper fraction
• mixed number

Think It Through
I can **use different representations** for fractions that are greater than 1.

Improper Fractions and Mixed Numbers

✓ **WARM UP**
1. 9 ÷ 2   2. 14 ÷ 3
3. 28 ÷ 5   4. 20 ÷ 8

LEARN

How can you convert between improper fractions and mixed numbers?

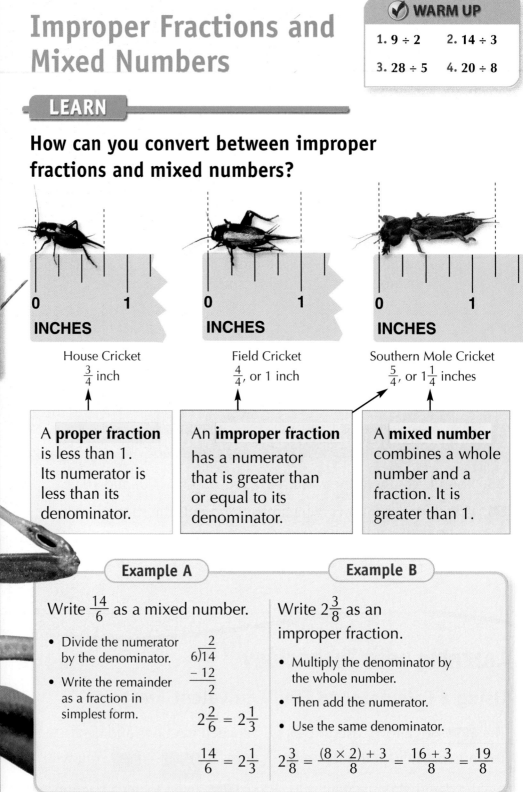

House Cricket
$\frac{3}{4}$ inch

Field Cricket
$\frac{4}{4}$, or 1 inch

Southern Mole Cricket
$\frac{5}{4}$, or $1\frac{1}{4}$ inches

A **proper fraction** is less than 1. Its numerator is less than its denominator.

An **improper fraction** has a numerator that is greater than or equal to its denominator.

A **mixed number** combines a whole number and a fraction. It is greater than 1.

Example A

Write $\frac{14}{6}$ as a mixed number.

• Divide the numerator by the denominator.

$$6\overline{)14}$$
$$\underline{-12}$$
$$2$$

with quotient 2

• Write the remainder as a fraction in simplest form.

$$2\frac{2}{6} = 2\frac{1}{3}$$

$$\frac{14}{6} = 2\frac{1}{3}$$

Example B

Write $2\frac{3}{8}$ as an improper fraction.

• Multiply the denominator by the whole number.

• Then add the numerator.

• Use the same denominator.

$$2\frac{3}{8} = \frac{(8 \times 2) + 3}{8} = \frac{16 + 3}{8} = \frac{19}{8}$$

✔ **Talk About It**

1. Can $\frac{12}{12}$ be expressed as a mixed number or a whole number? How do you know?

2. What method could you use to write a whole number, such as 5, as an improper fraction?

Take It to the NET
More Examples
www.scottforesman.com

1. Draw a picture to show $1\frac{5}{6}$.   **2.** Draw a picture to show $\frac{10}{3}$.

Write each improper fraction as a whole number or mixed number in simplest form. Write each mixed number as an improper fraction.

3. $\frac{19}{4}$ **4.** $\frac{24}{8}$ **5.** $2\frac{3}{5}$ **6.** $1\frac{5}{9}$

7. Reasoning Write 3 as an improper fraction with a denominator of 5.

PRACTICE

For more practice, see Set 3-8 on p. 200.

A Skills and Understanding

8. Draw a picture to show $\frac{8}{5}$.   **9.** Draw a picture to show $2\frac{2}{3}$.

Write each improper fraction as a whole number or mixed number in simplest form.

10. $\frac{15}{6}$ **11.** $\frac{37}{11}$ **12.** $\frac{21}{4}$ **13.** $\frac{30}{9}$ **14.** $\frac{66}{7}$ **15.** $\frac{19}{3}$

Write each mixed number as an improper fraction.

16. $4\frac{3}{8}$ **17.** $5\frac{5}{7}$ **18.** $3\frac{1}{2}$ **19.** $20\frac{2}{3}$ **20.** $7\frac{1}{4}$ **21.** $12\frac{4}{5}$

22. Reasoning Write 5 as an improper fraction with a denominator of 10.

B Reasoning and Problem Solving

Which letter on the number line corresponds to each number?

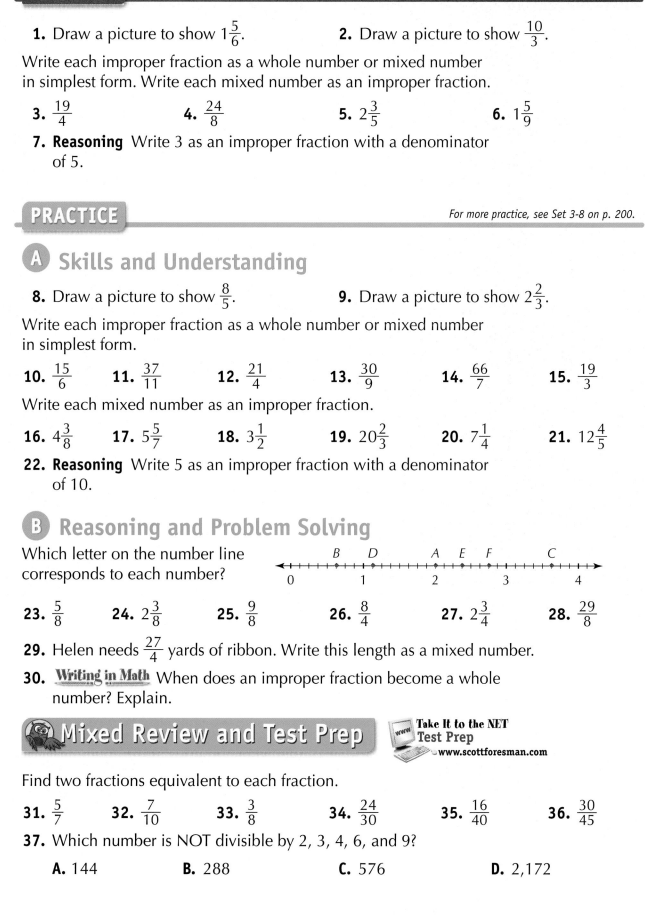

23. $\frac{5}{8}$ **24.** $2\frac{3}{8}$ **25.** $\frac{9}{8}$ **26.** $\frac{8}{4}$ **27.** $2\frac{3}{4}$ **28.** $\frac{29}{8}$

29. Helen needs $\frac{27}{4}$ yards of ribbon. Write this length as a mixed number.

30. **Writing in Math** When does an improper fraction become a whole number? Explain.

🦉 Mixed Review and Test Prep

Take It to the NET
Test Prep
www.scottforesman.com

Find two fractions equivalent to each fraction.

31. $\frac{5}{7}$ **32.** $\frac{7}{10}$ **33.** $\frac{3}{8}$ **34.** $\frac{24}{30}$ **35.** $\frac{16}{40}$ **36.** $\frac{30}{45}$

37. Which number is NOT divisible by 2, 3, 4, 6, and 9?

A. 144   **B.** 288   **C.** 576   **D.** 2,172

Vocabulary
• benchmark fraction

Think It Through
I need to **visualize** the benchmark fractions to help me estimate.

$\frac{1}{4}$

$\frac{1}{3}$

$\frac{1}{2}$

$\frac{2}{3}$

$\frac{3}{4}$

Estimating Fractional Amounts

LEARN

How can you estimate fractional amounts?

To estimate a fractional amount, use a **benchmark fraction** that is close to the actual amount. Some benchmark fractions are $\frac{1}{4}$, $\frac{1}{3}$, $\frac{1}{2}$, $\frac{2}{3}$, and $\frac{3}{4}$.

Example A

About what fraction of the day do sixth graders spend on leisure activities?

Typical Day of a Sixth Grader

Leisure Activities

Sleeping

School

Homework

Eating

The area for leisure activities is a little less than $\frac{1}{4}$ of the circle graph.

So, sixth graders spend about $\frac{1}{4}$ of their day doing leisure activities.

Example B

About what fraction of the sixth graders who were surveyed chose soccer as their favorite sport?

Favorite Sport

120 sixth-grade students surveyed	
Football	21
Basketball	62
Soccer	37

Soccer was chosen by $\frac{37}{120}$ of the students. Since $\frac{37}{120}$ is close to $\frac{40}{120}$, and $\frac{40}{120} = \frac{1}{3}$, $\frac{37}{120}$ is about $\frac{1}{3}$.

So, about $\frac{1}{3}$ of the sixth graders chose soccer as their favorite sport.

✓ **Talk About It**

1. What is the benchmark fraction in Example A? in Example B?

2. **Number Sense** About what fraction of a sixth grader's day is spent sleeping?

3. **Number Sense** About what fraction of the sixth graders surveyed chose basketball as their favorite sport?

Take It to the NET
More Examples
www.scottforesman.com

For another example, see Set 3-9 on p. 196.

CHECK ✓

Estimate the shaded part of each picture.

1.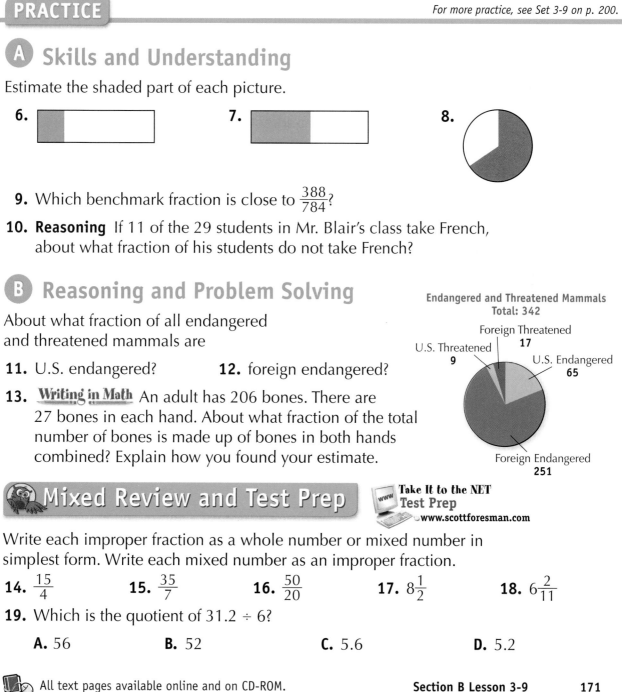

2.

3.

4. Which benchmark fraction is close to $\frac{304}{416}$?

5. **Reasoning** Do both squares have about the same fractional part shaded? Explain.

PRACTICE

For more practice, see Set 3-9 on p. 200.

A Skills and Understanding

Estimate the shaded part of each picture.

6.

7.

8.

9. Which benchmark fraction is close to $\frac{388}{784}$?

10. **Reasoning** If 11 of the 29 students in Mr. Blair's class take French, about what fraction of his students do not take French?

B Reasoning and Problem Solving

About what fraction of all endangered and threatened mammals are

11. U.S. endangered?

12. foreign endangered?

13. **Writing in Math** An adult has 206 bones. There are 27 bones in each hand. About what fraction of the total number of bones is made up of bones in both hands combined? Explain how you found your estimate.

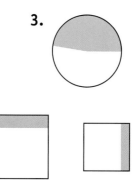

Endangered and Threatened Mammals Total: 342

Foreign Threatened 17

U.S. Threatened 9

U.S. Endangered 65

Foreign Endangered 251

Mixed Review and Test Prep

Take It to the NET
www Test Prep
www.scottforesman.com

Write each improper fraction as a whole number or mixed number in simplest form. Write each mixed number as an improper fraction.

14. $\frac{15}{4}$　　15. $\frac{35}{7}$　　16. $\frac{50}{20}$　　17. $8\frac{1}{2}$　　18. $6\frac{2}{11}$

19. Which is the quotient of $31.2 \div 6$?

    A. 56　　　　**B.** 52　　　　**C.** 5.6　　　　**D.** 5.2

Key Idea
A fraction and a decimal can be used to represent the same value.

Vocabulary
• terminating decimal
• repeating decimal

Materials
• decimal models or **e tools**

TEST TALK

Think It Through
I can **use objects** to represent fractions and decimals.

Connecting Fractions and Decimals

LEARN

WARM UP
Write each as a decimal.

1. one tenth
2. one hundredth
3. one and forty-seven hundredths
4. five and sixteen thousandths

Activity

How are fractions and decimals related?

Wholes divided into tenths or hundredths can be written using a fraction or a decimal.

a. Shade tenths grids or hundredths grids to show each fraction. Then give a decimal for the number modeled in the grid.

$$\frac{7}{10} \qquad \frac{47}{100} \qquad \frac{85}{100}$$

$$\frac{3}{10} = 0.3$$

b. Shade tenths grids or hundredths grids to show each decimal. Then give a fraction for the number modeled in the grid.

$$0.9 \qquad 0.41 \qquad 0.25$$

$$\frac{12}{100} = 0.12$$

How can you convert decimals to fractions?

Carpenters who measure wood in inches convert decimals to fractions and fractions to decimals.

To convert decimals to fractions, write the decimal as a fraction with a denominator of tenths, hundredths, or thousandths. Then write the fraction in simplest form.

Example A

Write 0.75 as a fraction.

$$0.75 = 75 \text{ hundredths} = \frac{75}{100}$$

$$\frac{75}{100} = \frac{3}{4}$$

So, $0.75 = \frac{3}{4}$.

Example B

Write 2.125 as a mixed number.

$$2.125 = 2 + 0.125$$

$$0.125 = 125 \text{ thousandths} = \frac{125}{1,000}$$

$$\frac{125}{1,000} = \frac{1}{8}$$

So, $2.125 = 2 + \frac{1}{8} = 2\frac{1}{8}$.

✔ Talk About It

1. In Example B, how can you tell that $\frac{125}{1,000}$ is not in simplest form?

2. Number Sense Are 0.5 and 0.50 equivalent to the same fraction? Explain.

How can you convert fractions to decimals?

Recall that a fraction can represent division. So to rewrite a fraction as a decimal, divide the numerator by the denominator.

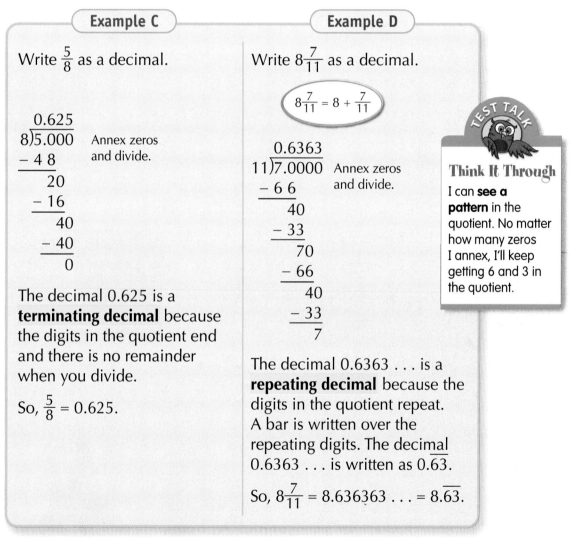

Example C

Write $\frac{5}{8}$ as a decimal.

$$\begin{array}{r} 0.625 \\ 8\overline{)5.000} \\ -\,4\,8 \\ \hline 20 \\ -\,16 \\ \hline 40 \\ -\,40 \\ \hline 0 \end{array}$$

Annex zeros and divide.

The decimal 0.625 is a **terminating decimal** because the digits in the quotient end and there is no remainder when you divide.

So, $\frac{5}{8} = 0.625$.

Example D

Write $8\frac{7}{11}$ as a decimal.

$$8\frac{7}{11} = 8 + \frac{7}{11}$$

$$\begin{array}{r} 0.6363 \\ 11\overline{)7.0000} \\ -\,6\,6 \\ \hline 40 \\ -\,33 \\ \hline 70 \\ -\,66 \\ \hline 40 \\ -\,33 \\ \hline 7 \end{array}$$

Annex zeros and divide.

The decimal 0.6363 . . . is a **repeating decimal** because the digits in the quotient repeat. A bar is written over the repeating digits. The decimal 0.6363 . . . is written as $0.\overline{63}$.

So, $8\frac{7}{11} = 8.636363 \ldots = 8.\overline{63}$.

Think It Through

I can **see a pattern** in the quotient. No matter how many zeros I annex, I'll keep getting 6 and 3 in the quotient.

✔ Talk About It

3. In Example C, how do you know the division ends with the quotient 0.625?

4. Describe the decimal indicated by $0.\overline{724}$.

5. How can you use the decimal form of $\frac{7}{11}$ in Example D to find the decimal form of $\frac{1}{11}$? Will it also be a repeating decimal? Explain.

Take It to the NET
More Examples
www.scottforesman.com

Write a decimal and a fraction in simplest form for each shaded portion.

1.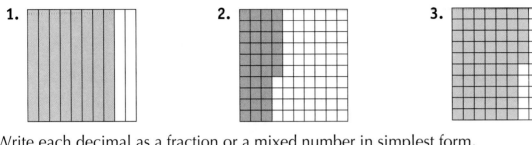

2.

3.

Write each decimal as a fraction or a mixed number in simplest form,
and each fraction or mixed number as a decimal.

4. 0.08　　**5.** 9.15　　**6.** 2.225　　**7.** $\frac{3}{10}$　　**8.** $4\frac{1}{6}$　　**9.** $3\frac{7}{8}$

10. Number Sense How can you show $\frac{6}{20}$ on a tenths grid? What decimal
does the model show?

PRACTICE

For more practice, see Set 3-10 on p. 201.

Ⓐ Skills and Understanding

Write a decimal and a fraction in simplest form for each shaded portion.

11.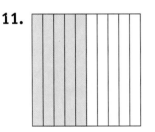

12.

13.

Write each decimal as a fraction or a mixed number in simplest form.

14. 0.6　　**15.** 0.16　　**16.** 2.45　　**17.** 0.375　　**18.** 0.04

19. 28.2　　**20.** 0.91　　**21.** 0.76　　**22.** 1.128　　**23.** 95.032

24. 0.245　　**25.** 7.95　　**26.** 0.125　　**27.** 12.005　　**28.** 13.975

Write each fraction or mixed number as a decimal.

29. $\frac{13}{100}$　　**30.** $\frac{3}{5}$　　**31.** $\frac{26}{50}$　　**32.** $\frac{1}{3}$

33. $\frac{13}{20}$　　**34.** $5\frac{2}{11}$　　**35.** $\frac{4}{9}$　　**36.** $\frac{17}{17}$

37. $\frac{2}{3}$　　**38.** $\frac{19}{38}$　　**39.** $\frac{9}{10}$　　**40.** $6\frac{9}{15}$

41. $4\frac{3}{5}$　　**42.** $\frac{1}{33}$　　**43.** $8\frac{4}{25}$　　**44.** $\frac{1}{15}$

45. Number Sense How can you show $\frac{1}{4}$ on a hundredths grid?
What decimal does the model show?

Think It Through
I need to remember
to **write a bar over
the repeating digits**
of a repeating
decimal.

B Reasoning and Problem Solving

Math and Social Studies

46. Africa, the second largest continent, makes up about one fifth of the world's total land mass. Write this number as a fraction and as a decimal.

47. **Writing in Math** Shondra thinks that 0.66, 0.660, and $0.\overline{66}$ all name the same number. Is she right? Explain.

C Extensions

48. **Mental Math** Memorize the decimal equivalents for these common fractions: $\frac{1}{4}$, $\frac{1}{3}$, $\frac{1}{2}$, $\frac{2}{3}$, and $\frac{3}{4}$. Have a friend test you.

Mixed Review and Test Prep

Take It to the NET
www **Test Prep**
www.scottforesman.com

49. If ▯▯▯▯ is a model for $\frac{3}{5}$, draw models for $\frac{6}{5}$, $\frac{5}{5}$, and $\frac{1}{5}$.

50. Which mixed number equals $\frac{19}{5}$?

A. $3\frac{3}{5}$　　　　**B.** $3\frac{4}{5}$　　　　**C.** $4\frac{3}{5}$　　　　**D.** $4\frac{4}{5}$

Discovery CHANNEL SCHOOL

Discover Math in Your World

Take It to the NET
www **Video and Activities**
www.scottforesman.com

Drag Free

The Hubble Space Telescope is a Low Earth Orbiting (LEO) satellite. To stay free of atmospheric drag, the Hubble maintains an altitude of approximately 600 km and an orbital velocity of about 27,200 kilometers per hour (kph).

1. Our moon has an altitude of about 384,400 km and an orbital velocity of about 3,700 kph. About what fraction of the Hubble's velocity is the velocity of our moon?

2. When the Hubble, the moon, and Earth are lined up, what is the distance from the Hubble to the moon?

Lesson 3-11

Key Idea
There are different ways to compare and order fractions and decimals.

Think It Through
I can **list common multiples** or use **prime factorization** to find a common denominator.

Comparing and Ordering Fractions and Decimals

✓ **WARM UP**

Write each fraction as a decimal.

1. $\frac{3}{4}$ 2. $\frac{6}{9}$

3. $\frac{7}{8}$ 4. $\frac{5}{12}$

LEARN

How can you compare and order fractions?

Joel raises sea monkeys to feed to his seahorses. His biggest sea monkey is $\frac{3}{4}$ in. long. His smallest seahorse is $\frac{9}{16}$ in. long. Which is longer?

Example A

Compare $\frac{3}{4}$ and $\frac{9}{16}$.

One Way
Write the fractions with a common denominator.

$\frac{3}{4} = \frac{3 \times 4}{4 \times 4} = \frac{12}{16}$ *The LCD is 16.*

$\frac{9}{16} = \frac{9 \times 1}{16 \times 1} = \frac{9}{16}$

Compare the numerators.

$\frac{9}{16} < \frac{12}{16}$, so $\frac{9}{16} < \frac{3}{4}$.

Another Way
Use a number line.

Divide the distance from 0 to 1 into sixteenths and fourths. Then place $\frac{9}{16}$ and $\frac{3}{4}$ on the number line.

$$\begin{array}{ccccccc} & & & & & \frac{9}{16} & & & & \\ 0 & & \frac{1}{4} & & \frac{1}{2} & & \frac{3}{4} & & 1 \end{array}$$

$\frac{9}{16}$ is to the left of $\frac{3}{4}$, so $\frac{9}{16} < \frac{3}{4}$.

The sea monkey is longer.

Example B

Order $\frac{1}{2}$, $\frac{3}{8}$, and $\frac{2}{5}$ from greatest to least.

$\frac{1}{2} = \frac{1 \times 20}{2 \times 20} = \frac{20}{40}$

$\frac{3}{8} = \frac{3 \times 5}{8 \times 5} = \frac{15}{40}$ Write the fractions with a common denominator. Then compare the numerators.

$\frac{2}{5} = \frac{2 \times 8}{5 \times 8} = \frac{16}{40}$

$\frac{20}{40} > \frac{16}{40}$ and $\frac{16}{40} > \frac{15}{40}$, so the order from greatest to least is $\frac{1}{2}$, $\frac{2}{5}$, $\frac{3}{8}$.

✓ **Talk About It**

1. Use the results from Example A to compare $2\frac{9}{16}$ and $2\frac{3}{4}$.

2. Use the results from Example B to tell which of these mixed numbers is between the other two: $5\frac{1}{2}$, $5\frac{3}{8}$, $5\frac{2}{5}$.

How can you compare and order fractions and decimals?

Example C

Compare $\frac{2}{3}$ and 0.6.

Write $\frac{2}{3}$ as a decimal. Then compare the decimals.

$\frac{2}{3} = 0.6666... = 0.\overline{6}$

$0.\overline{6} > 0.6$, so $\frac{2}{3} > 0.6$.

Example D

Order $\frac{2}{5}$, 0.48, and $\frac{1}{3}$ from least to greatest.

$$\frac{2}{5} \qquad 0.48 \qquad \frac{1}{3}$$
$$\downarrow \qquad \downarrow \qquad \downarrow$$
$$0.4 \qquad 0.48 \qquad 0.\overline{3}$$

Write the fractions as decimals. Then compare.

$0.\overline{3} < 0.4$ and $0.4 < 0.48$, so the order from least to greatest is $\frac{1}{3}$, $\frac{2}{5}$, 0.48.

Example E

Compare $\frac{37}{9}$ and 4.1.

$\frac{37}{9} = 4.1111... = 4.\overline{1}$

$4.\overline{1} > 4.1$, so $\frac{37}{9} > 4.1$.

Example F

Order $2\frac{1}{2}$, 2.4, and $\frac{8}{3}$ from least to greatest.

$$2\frac{1}{2} \qquad 2.4 \qquad \frac{8}{3}$$
$$\downarrow \qquad \downarrow \qquad \downarrow$$
$$2.5 \qquad 2.4 \qquad 2.\overline{6}$$

$2.4 < 2.5$ and $2.5 < 2.\overline{6}$, so the order from least to greatest is 2.4, $2\frac{1}{2}$, $\frac{8}{3}$.

✔ Talk About It

3. In Example C, compare $\frac{2}{3}$ and 0.6 using fractions. Which way do you think is easier? Explain.

4. In Example D, what benchmark fraction could you use for 0.48?

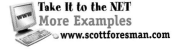
Take It to the NET
More Examples
www.scottforesman.com

5. Explain how to order $4\frac{2}{5}$, $\frac{17}{4}$, and 4.5 from least to greatest.

CHECK ✓

For another example, see Set 3-11 on p. 197.

1. Use a number line to compare $\frac{3}{5}$ and $\frac{7}{8}$.

Use <, >, or = to compare.

2. $\frac{1}{2}$ ⬤ $\frac{4}{9}$

3. 0.625 ⬤ $\frac{5}{8}$

4. $2\frac{3}{8}$ ⬤ $2\frac{5}{12}$

Order from least to greatest.

5. $\frac{3}{4}$, 0.9, $\frac{4}{5}$

6. $\frac{7}{9}$, $\frac{9}{12}$, $\frac{2}{3}$

7. $1\frac{1}{3}$, 1.5, $\frac{7}{6}$

8. **Number Sense** If the numerators of two fractions are the same, which fraction is greater? (Hint: Compare $\frac{1}{4}$ to $\frac{1}{5}$ and $\frac{5}{6}$ to $\frac{5}{8}$.)

A Skills and Understanding

9. Use a number line to compare 0.7 and $\frac{5}{6}$.

Use <, >, or = to compare.

10. $\frac{3}{10}$ ● $\frac{2}{5}$ **11.** $\frac{21}{12}$ ● $\frac{7}{4}$ **12.** $\frac{5}{100}$ ● 0.2   **13.** $12\frac{5}{18}$ ● 12.5   **14.** 1.38 ● $1\frac{1}{3}$

15. $\frac{2}{5}$ ● $\frac{2}{7}$ **16.** $\frac{1}{7}$ ● 0.22   **17.** 0.7 ● $\frac{7}{9}$ **18.** $43\frac{7}{8}$ ● $43\frac{4}{5}$ **19.** 0.22 ● $\frac{3}{16}$

Order from least to greatest.

20. $\frac{4}{5}, \frac{9}{10}, \frac{5}{6}$ **21.** 5.75, $5\frac{5}{18}, \frac{17}{3}$ **22.** $\frac{4}{8}, \frac{2}{5}$, 0.6, 0.58   **23.** $\frac{3}{4}$, 0.35, $\frac{2}{3}$, $0.\overline{5}$

24. Number Sense How could you use a benchmark fraction to decide which is greater, $\frac{2}{5}$ or $\frac{7}{12}$?

B Reasoning and Problem Solving

25. A potato salad recipe calls for $2\frac{1}{2}$ pounds of potatoes. Are 2.48 pounds of potatoes enough? Explain.

26. A backyard fence needs repair and requires $5\frac{3}{8}$ yards of chicken wire. Steven has 5.25 yards of chicken wire. Is this enough? Explain.

Math and Science

Some of the Earth's greatest ocean depths are listed at the right.

27. List the depths in order from shallowest to deepest.

28. What benchmark fraction could you use for the fractional amount of each trench depth?

29. The Kuril Trench, located in the north western Pacific Ocean near Japan, is the same depth as the Philippine Trench. Is the Kuril trench deeper or shallower than the Tonga Trench?

30. Writing in Math Explain the method you used to compare the depths of the Kuril and Tonga trenches in Problem 29.

Data File

Ocean Depths

Location	Depth (miles)
Tonga Trench	$6\frac{61}{100}$
Philippine Trench	$6\frac{11}{20}$
Kermadec Trench	6.21

31. <u>**Writing in Math**</u> Is Julie's method below correct? If not, explain why.

> Compare 0.75 and $\frac{3}{5}$. Explain your answer.
>
> $0.75 = \frac{3}{4}$
>
> The numerators are the same and since 4 is less
>
> than 5, $\frac{3}{4} < \frac{3}{5}$.

C Extensions

Copy the number line below. Mark a point for each number on the number line and label the point with the given letter.

```
0        1        2        3
```

32. 2.38, A   **33.** $\frac{3}{8}$, B   **34.** $1\frac{3}{5}$, C   **35.** 0.83, D   **36.** 2.875, E

Mixed Review and Test Prep

Take It to the NET
Test Prep
www.scottforesman.com

Algebra Solve and check each equation.

37. $5.1 = 0.3n$ **38.** $2.7 + p = 3.4$ **39.** $\frac{m}{3} = 0.9$ **40.** $11.8 = a - 1.8$

41. Which decimal is equivalent to $\frac{8}{25}$?

   A. 0.825   **B.** 0.34   **C.** 0.32   **D.** 0.28

Enrichment

To Terminate or Repeat

As you know, the decimal forms for some fractions terminate while others repeat. For example, the decimal forms of $\frac{1}{2}$, $\frac{3}{16}$, and $\frac{7}{25}$ terminate, but those of $\frac{1}{3}$, $\frac{5}{6}$, and $\frac{11}{15}$ do not.

For 1–5, use a calculator to find the decimal form of each fraction.

   1. $\frac{1}{4}$ **2.** $\frac{1}{9}$ **3.** $\frac{7}{200}$ **4.** $\frac{7}{30}$ **5.** $\frac{5}{12}$

Find the prime factors of the denominator of each fraction in the examples and exercises above.

   6. Find a rule that will tell you whether a decimal form of a fraction terminates or repeats.

Problem-Solving Skill

Key Idea
Identifying hidden questions helps you solve multiple-step problems.

Think It Through
To find hidden questions, I should figure out **what happened first, then next,** and so on.

Multiple-Step Problems

LEARN

How can you find hidden questions in multiple-step problems?

Some word problems have hidden questions. To solve these problems, you must first find and answer the hidden questions.

Collect Calls Phylicia calls collect from college to her parents' home each week, except on holidays. Each call she makes lasts about 15 min. How much money can she save if she calls on the weekend rather than during the week?

Day and Evening Collect-Calling Rates		
Days	First 3 Minutes	Each Additional Minute
Mon. – Fri.	$1.45	$0.35
Sat. – Sun.	$1.25	$0.15
Holidays	$1.00	$0.10

Read and Understand

Identify key facts and details and tell what the problem is asking.

Phylicia talks for about 15 minutes each time she calls home. The rates for collect calls are given. The problem asks for the amount that can be saved if calls are made on the weekend.

Plan and Solve

Identify and solve the hidden questions.

Hidden Question 1: How much does a 15-minute call cost during the week?

First 3 minutes   Next 12 minutes
↓   ↓
$1.45   +   (12 × $0.35)
$1.45   + $4.20
$5.65

Hidden Question 2: How much does a 15-minute call cost on the weekend?

↓   ↓
$1.25   +   (12 × $0.15)
$1.25   + $1.80
$3.05

✔ Talk About It

1. What is the answer to the Collect Calls problem?

1. Answer the hidden questions in the problem and then solve the problem.

Extra Options A car dealership pays $18,800 for the LX 450 Convertible. All of the extra options cost the car dealership an additional $1,851. How much profit does the dealership make if a customer purchases the car and all the extra options at the prices listed at the right?

Prices for LX 450 Convertible	
Base List Price:	$20,560

Extra Options	List Price
Air Conditioning	$845
Cruise Control	$275
AM/FM CD Stereo	$956
Power Windows	$225

Hidden Question 1: What is the total amount the dealership pays for the car with all of the extra options?

Hidden Question 2: What is the total amount the customer pays for the car with all of the extra options?

PRACTICE

For more practice, see Set 3-12 on p. 201.

Write and answer the hidden question or questions in each problem and then solve the problem.

2. The school cafeteria sold 611 lunches during the first 4 days of a week. The same number of lunches were sold on Monday and Tuesday. On Wednesday, 158 lunches were sold, and on Thursday, 149 lunches. How many lunches were sold on Tuesday?

3. Stan wants to buy 30 apples. If he wants to pay the lowest price, where should he purchase them? How much will they cost?

Paul's Fruit Stand
APPLES
3 for $0.72

Hogan's Market
APPLES
10 for $2.10

4. There are sixteen 8-oz cups of sports drink in a gallon. Will 10 gallons be enough for 47 hikers if each hiker drinks one cup every 3 miles of a 9-mile hike?

5. A radio station broadcasts a jazz show for 1.25 hours each weekday. On Saturday and Sunday, the jazz show is twice as long. How many hours of jazz does the radio station broadcast during a 4-week period?

6. **Writing in Math** Maggy ordered 12 standard-size reprints last week and 14 more this week. If she had brought in her reprint order all on the same day, how much could she have saved? Explain what hidden problem(s) you need to solve. Then explain how you would find the answer to the original problem.

Reprint charges

Size of Print	Cost per Reprint	Special Price
Standard	$0.58 per print	20 prints for $10.20
5 in. x 7 in.	$0.75 per print	20 prints for $12.60

Problem-Solving Applications

Earth's Surface Each region of the world contains a wide variety of people and lands. The sizes of the regions and the types of lands they contain have played an important role in shaping the cultures and histories of their people. Over time, the people themselves have also had an impact on the lands.

Trivia The largest island, Greenland, covers over 840,000 square miles. It is about $\frac{1}{4}$ the size of the smallest continent, Australia.

Oceania: 3,480,000 sq mi
Europe: 3,860,000 sq mi
Antarctica: 5,410,000 sq mi
South America: 6,950,000 sq mi
North America: 9,270,000 sq mi
Africa: 11,580,000 sq mi
Asia: 16,990,000 sq mi

1 Name the two regions whose combined areas come closest to the area of Asia.

2 What region is closest to $\frac{1}{2}$ the size of South America? of Africa?

3 About $\frac{3}{10}$ Earth's surface is land. Estimate the fraction of Earth's surface that is covered by water.

4 **Decision Making** The Pacific Ocean measures about 11,000 miles across at its widest point. Choose a method of travel from the list below. How many hours would it take you to cross the ocean at this widest point using your choice of transportation? How many days would your trip take to the nearest whole day?

Craft	Typical Speed
Jumbo jet	560 mph
Sail boat	8 mph
Cruise ship	30 mph
Submarine	18 mph

Good News/Bad News Technology and techniques now exist that combat desertification – the turning of good land into deserts. Unfortunately, desertification still affects millions of people around the globe.

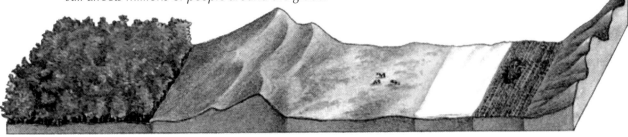

Forest   Desert   Pasture   Icecap   Cultivated   Other

Key Facts
Earth's Land Surface

Surface	Approximate Area
•Forest	15,000,000 sq mi
•Desert	14,000,000 sq mi
•Pasture	13,000,000 sq mi
•Icecap	6,000,000 sq mi
•Cultivated	6,000,000 sq mi
•Other	4,000,000 sq mi

Using Key Facts

5 What benchmark fraction of the Earth's total land area is used for cultivation and pastures combined? for deserts and forests combined?

6 Look at the areas of Borneo and Greenland in the picture at the right. Name a benchmark fraction that describes the portion of Greenland that could be covered by the area of Borneo.

7 **Writing in Math** Use the information in this lesson to write your own word problem that involves fractions. Write the answer to your problem in a complete sentence.

Honshu, Japan: 89,000 sq mi

Borneo: 287,000 sq mi

Greenland: 840,000 sq mi

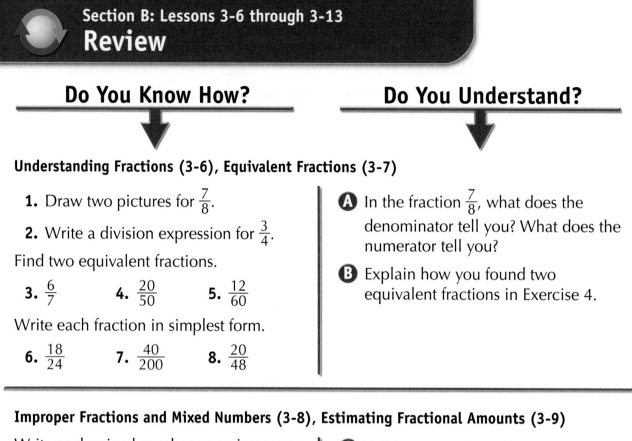

Do You Know How?

Do You Understand?

Understanding Fractions (3-6), Equivalent Fractions (3-7)

1. Draw two pictures for $\frac{7}{8}$.

2. Write a division expression for $\frac{3}{4}$.

Find two equivalent fractions.

3. $\frac{6}{7}$ **4.** $\frac{20}{50}$ **5.** $\frac{12}{60}$

Write each fraction in simplest form.

6. $\frac{18}{24}$ **7.** $\frac{40}{200}$ **8.** $\frac{20}{48}$

Ⓐ In the fraction $\frac{7}{8}$, what does the denominator tell you? What does the numerator tell you?

Ⓑ Explain how you found two equivalent fractions in Exercise 4.

Improper Fractions and Mixed Numbers (3-8), Estimating Fractional Amounts (3-9)

Write each mixed number as an improper fraction and each improper fraction as a mixed number in simplest form.

9. $5\frac{3}{5}$ **10.** $\frac{18}{12}$ **11.** $1\frac{5}{6}$

12. Ninety-two out of 148 students chose red and white for the colors of the school's new flag. About what fraction of the students chose red and white?

Ⓒ Tell how to write an improper fraction as a mixed number and a mixed number as an improper fraction.

Ⓓ Why are benchmark fractions used to estimate fractional amounts?

Connecting Fractions and Decimals (3-10), Comparing and Ordering Fractions and Decimals (3-11), Problem-Solving Skill: Multiple-Step Problems (3-12)

Write each fraction or mixed number as a decimal. Write each decimal as a fraction or mixed number in simplest form.

13. $\frac{13}{25}$ **14.** $1\frac{1}{8}$ **15.** 3.64

Order from least to greatest.

16. $\frac{3}{10}, \frac{1}{3}, \frac{2}{5}$ **17.** $\frac{4}{5}, \frac{3}{4}, 0.9, 0.7$

18. Tameka bought 3 shirts for $12 each and 3 pairs of jeans for $22 each. If she spent $100 or more she can use a coupon worth $20 off her total purchase. How much did she spend altogether?

Ⓔ Explain how to write a decimal as a fraction and a fraction as a decimal.

Ⓕ Write a rule for comparing unlike fractions with the same numerator.

Ⓖ What are the hidden questions in Problem 18?

✓ Diagnostic Checkpoint

MULTIPLE CHOICE

1. Which fraction is NOT equivalent to $\frac{16}{24}$? (3-7)

A. $\frac{2}{3}$ **B.** $\frac{4}{6}$ **C.** $\frac{32}{42}$ **D.** $\frac{48}{72}$

2. Which benchmark fraction is close to $\frac{596}{893}$? (3-9)

A. $\frac{1}{4}$ **B.** $\frac{1}{2}$ **C.** $\frac{2}{3}$ **D.** $\frac{3}{4}$

FREE RESPONSE

Write a fraction or mixed number in simplest form, and a decimal for the blue shaded portion of each model. (3-6, 3-8, 3-10)

3. **4.** **5.**

Write each mixed number as an improper fraction and each improper fraction as a mixed number in simplest form. (3-8)

6. $\frac{24}{10}$ **7.** $5\frac{2}{3}$ **8.** $\frac{28}{20}$ **9.** $4\frac{3}{8}$ **10.** $6\frac{6}{6}$

Write each decimal as a fraction or mixed number in simplest form. Write each fraction as a decimal. (3-10, 3-13)

11. 0.8 **12.** $\frac{3}{8}$ **13.** 1.25 **14.** $\frac{9}{20}$ **15.** $3\frac{30}{1000}$

Compare using <, >, or =. (3-11, 3-13)

16. $\frac{3}{4}$ ⬤ $\frac{3}{8}$ **17.** 3.2 ⬤ $3\frac{1}{5}$ **18.** $\frac{7}{8}$ ⬤ 0.78 **19.** 1.09 ⬤ $1\frac{9}{10}$

Answer the hidden question or questions in the problem and then solve the problem. Use the table to solve Exercise 20. (3-12, 3-13)

20. Nan's phone company is VROOM. Last month she made calls that totaled 30 weekend minutes. Could she have saved money using one of the other two companies? If so, how much?

Long Distance Calling Rates	
COMPANY	**RATE**
Dash	$2.95/month + $0.06/min anytime
Pulse	No monthly charge—$0.15/min M–F, $0.10/min on weekends
VROOM	No monthly charge—$0.13/min anytime

Writing in Math

21. Explain how to write 9 as an improper fraction with a denominator of 4. (3-8)

22. Explain the steps that you use to write $\frac{2}{11}$ as a decimal. (3-10)

Test-Taking Strategies

Understand the question.

Get information for the answer.

Plan how to find the answer.

Make smart choices.

Use writing in math.

Improve written answers.

Plan How to Find the Answer

After you understand a test question and get needed information, you need to plan how to find the answer. Think about problem-solving skills and strategies and computation methods you know.

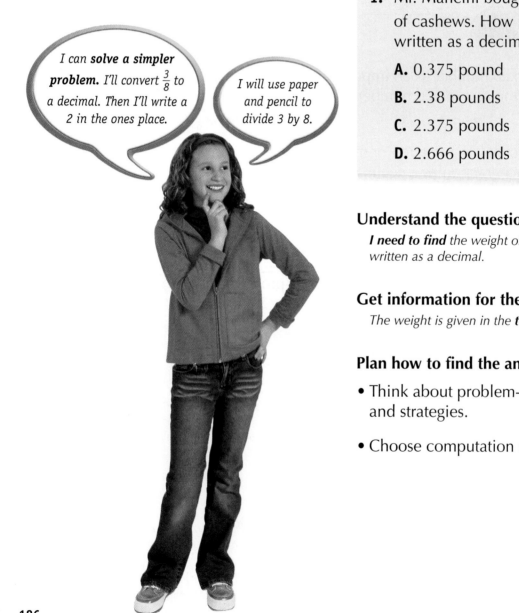

1. Mr. Mancini bought $2\frac{3}{8}$ pounds of cashews. How is this weight written as a decimal?

   A. 0.375 pound

   B. 2.38 pounds

   C. 2.375 pounds

   D. 2.666 pounds

*I can **solve a simpler problem.** I'll convert $\frac{3}{8}$ to a decimal. Then I'll write a 2 in the ones place.*

I will use paper and pencil to divide 3 by 8.

Understand the question.

I need to find the weight of the cashews written as a decimal.

Get information for the answer.

*The weight is given in the **text**.*

Plan how to find the answer.

- Think about problem-solving skills and strategies.

- Choose computation methods.

2. The sign below gives the length of each hiking trail at Deep Waters Recreation Area.

Crestview Trail	2¹/₂ Miles
Lake Trail	2²/₃ Miles
Bluff Trail	2⁵/₈ Miles
North Trail	2¹/₄ Miles

Which hiking trail is the longest?

A. Crestview Trail

B. Lake Trail

C. Bluff Trail

D. North Trail

Think It Through

I need to find the longest trail at the recreation area. The lengths I need to compare are given in the picture. I should order the fractions from least to greatest. I'll use paper and pencil to write them all with the same denominator, and then I'll compare the numerators.

Now it's your turn.

For each problem, describe a plan for finding the answer.

3. Lennie ran $5\frac{3}{4}$ miles in a marathon. How is the distance written as a decimal?

A. 0.75 mile

B. 5.33 miles

C. 5.34 miles

D. 5.75 miles

4. Donna is making costumes for 4 friends. The list shows how much fabric she needs for each.

Carl	$4\frac{1}{4}$ yards
Doris	$4\frac{7}{8}$ yards
Frank	$4\frac{2}{3}$ yards
Eduardo	$4\frac{1}{2}$ yards

Which student's costume requires the least amount of fabric?

A. Carl   **C.** Doris

B. Frank   **D.** Eduardo

Key Vocabulary and Concept Review

A musical composition is made by putting notes together.

A **composite number** is made by multiplying numbers together. (p. 146)

Self Check

Use **factors** and **multiples** to describe numbers. (Lessons 3-1, 3-2, 3-3, 3-4)

Find the LCM and GCF for 4 and 6.

Multiples of 4: 4, 8, **12**, …

Multiples of 6: 6, **12**, …

The **least common multiple** is 12.

Factors of 4: 1, **2**, 4

Factors of 6: 1, **2**, 3, 6

The **greatest common factor** is 2.

Write the **prime factorization** for the **composite number** 12.

Make a factor tree until all the **factors** are **prime.** Then use exponents.

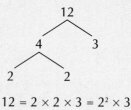

$12 = 2 \times 2 \times 3 = 2^2 \times 3$

1. Find the LCM and GCF of 8 and 10.

Self Check

To terminate means to end.

A **terminating decimal** ends with no remainder. (p. 173)

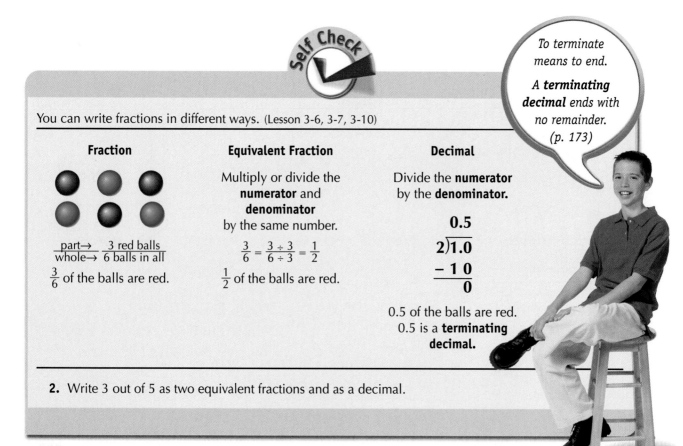

You can write fractions in different ways. (Lesson 3-6, 3-7, 3-10)

Fraction	**Equivalent Fraction**	**Decimal**

Equivalent Fraction: Multiply or divide the **numerator** and **denominator** by the same number.

Decimal: Divide the **numerator** by the **denominator.**

part→ 3 red balls
whole→ 6 balls in all

$\frac{3}{6}$ of the balls are red.

$\frac{3}{6} = \frac{3 \div 3}{6 \div 3} = \frac{1}{2}$

$\frac{1}{2}$ of the balls are red.

0.5

$2\overline{)1.0}$
$-\ 1\ 0$
$\overline{\quad\ 0}$

0.5 of the balls are red.
0.5 is a **terminating decimal.**

2. Write 3 out of 5 as two equivalent fractions and as a decimal.

When I cook, I mix, or combine ingredients. A **mixed number** is a combination of a whole number and a fraction. *(p. 168)*

You can write **mixed numbers** in different ways. (Lessons 3-7, 3-8, 3-10)

Mixed Number	**Improper Fraction**	**Decimal**

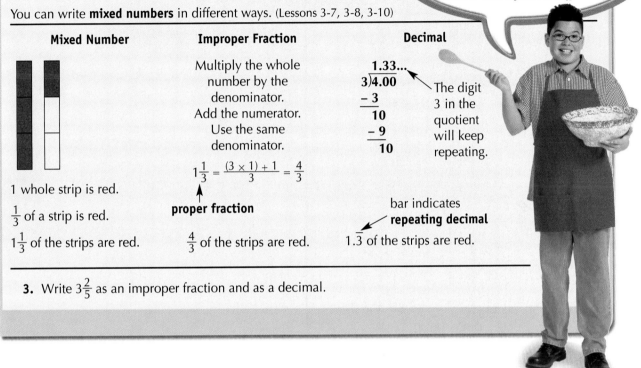

Mixed Number

1 whole strip is red.

$\frac{1}{3}$ of a strip is red.

$1\frac{1}{3}$ of the strips are red.

Improper Fraction

Multiply the whole number by the denominator.
Add the numerator.
Use the same denominator.

$$1\frac{1}{3} = \frac{(3 \times 1) + 1}{3} = \frac{4}{3}$$

↑ **proper fraction**

$\frac{4}{3}$ of the strips are red.

Decimal

$$\begin{array}{r} 1.33... \\ 3\overline{)4.00} \\ -3 \\ \hline 10 \\ -9 \\ \hline 10 \end{array}$$

The digit 3 in the quotient will keep repeating.

bar indicates
repeating decimal

$1.\overline{3}$ of the strips are red.

3. Write $3\frac{2}{5}$ as an improper fraction and as a decimal.

Make **tables** or follow **steps** in order when **solving problems.** (Lessons 3-5, 3-9, 3-11, 3-12)

Make a table when quantities change using a pattern.

Bill saved $115 in May. For each month after May, he saved $25 more than the previous month. How much did he save in the fourth month?

Month	1	2	3	4
Saving	$115	$140	$165	$190

He saved $190.

Plant A is $\frac{4}{5}$ in. tall, and Plant B is 0.45 in. tall. Which plant is taller?

Write 0.45 as a fraction: $\frac{45}{100} = \frac{9}{20}$

Compare both to a **benchmark,** or familiar, **fraction.**

$\frac{9}{20} < \frac{1}{2}$ and $\frac{4}{5} > \frac{1}{2}$

So, $\frac{9}{20} < \frac{4}{5}$.

Plant A is taller.

4. A pizza costs $12.75, and each topping costs $0.55. How much will a pizza with 6 toppings cost?

1. LCM = 40 and GCF = 2; 2. $\frac{3}{5}$, $\frac{6}{10}$, and 0.6; 3. $\frac{17}{5}$ and 3.4; 4. The pizza costs $16.05.

MULTIPLE CHOICE

Choose the correct letter for each answer.

1. Which number is divisible by 3?

    A. 86   **C.** 523

    B. 414   **D.** 902

2. Which number is a multiple of 6?

    A. 712   **C.** 2,638

    B. 1,055   **D.** 2,994

3. Which of the following is a prime number?

    A. 31   **C.** 121

    B. 81   **D.** 272

4. What is the prime factorization of 120?

    A. $3 \times 3 \times 4 \times 10$

    B. 5×24

    C. $2^3 \times 3 \times 5$

    D. $2^3 \times 15$

5. Find the GCF for 27 and 45.

    A. 3   **C.** 9

    B. 5   **D.** 15

6. Find the LCM for 2, 6, and 7.

    A. 14   **C.** 28

    B. 24   **D.** 42

7. Which fraction has a decimal equivalent of $0.1\overline{6}$?

    A. $\frac{16}{1,000}$ **C.** $\frac{1}{6}$

    B. $\frac{1}{8}$ **D.** $\frac{1}{5}$

8. What fraction does the shaded part of this figure represent?

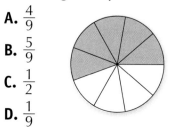

    A. $\frac{4}{9}$

    B. $\frac{5}{9}$

    C. $\frac{1}{2}$

    D. $\frac{1}{9}$

9. Which fraction is NOT equivalent to $\frac{3}{4}$?

    A. $\frac{22}{28}$ **C.** $\frac{9}{12}$

    B. $\frac{6}{8}$ **D.** $\frac{18}{24}$

10. What is $2\frac{3}{5}$ written as an improper fraction?

    A. $\frac{6}{5}$

    B. $\frac{10}{5}$

    C. $\frac{5}{5}$

    D. $\frac{13}{5}$

11. Which of the following is the best estimate for $\frac{576}{800}$?

    A. $\frac{1}{3}$ **C.** $\frac{5}{8}$

    B. $\frac{1}{2}$ **D.** $\frac{3}{4}$

12. Write 0.8 as a fraction in simplest form.

    A. $\frac{8}{10}$

    B. $\frac{4}{5}$

    C. $\frac{2}{5}$

    D. $\frac{1}{8}$

Think It Through

I need to **read each answer choice carefully**.

FREE RESPONSE

Compare using >, <, or =.

13. $\dfrac{5}{6}$ $\dfrac{3}{4}$

14. $\dfrac{2}{3}$ $\dfrac{3}{8}$

15. $\dfrac{9}{15}$ $\dfrac{3}{5}$

16. $\dfrac{9}{10}$ $\dfrac{7}{8}$

Order from least to greatest.

17. $1\dfrac{3}{4}$, 1.5, $\dfrac{5}{4}$

18. $\dfrac{9}{12}$, 0.3, $\dfrac{1}{5}$, 0.25

Find the LCM and GCF for each pair of numbers.

19. 4 and 9

20. 30 and 40

Write each fraction in simplest form.

21. $\dfrac{7}{3}$ **22.** $\dfrac{8}{28}$ **23.** $\dfrac{25}{60}$

24. There are 123 people going on the school field trip. The teacher wants to divide them all into groups of 2, 3, or 6 students. Which group size can she use?

25. Four friends ordered a pizza together. Who ate the most pizza if Lydia ate $\dfrac{5}{12}$ of it, Pam ate $\dfrac{1}{12}$ of it, Charles ate $\dfrac{1}{3}$ of it, and Devon ate $\dfrac{1}{6}$ of it?

26. Which letter on the number line below corresponds to $2\dfrac{3}{4}$?

27. Make a table to solve this problem.

Anita has her own greeting-card business. It costs her $2.50 to make 10 cards. Then she sells each package of 10 for $8. How many cards does she need to sell to make a profit of $27.50?

Writing in Math

28. Explain how to write eight twentieths as a simplified fraction and as a decimal.

29. Without dividing, explain how you can tell whether 524 flowers can be grouped into 9 arrangements with the same number of flowers in each arrangement.

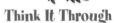

Think It Through
- I need to **find and answer hidden questions** to solve multistep problems.
- I can **make tables** to solve problems.

30. Identify and answer any hidden questions in the problem. Then solve the problem.

A package of 16 paper plates costs $2, and a package of 20 paper cups costs $3. Kyle bought the least number of each package possible to have equal amounts of plates and cups. How much money did he spend altogether?

Number and Operation

MULTIPLE CHOICE

1. What is seven million, four hundred sixty thousand, nine hundred twenty-eight written in standard form?

- **A.** 746,928
- **B.** 7,460,928
- **C.** 7,469,028
- **D.** 7,469,280

2. Which number is divisible by 6?

- **A.** 646
- **B.** 812
- **C.** 1,025
- **D.** 2,184

3. Which of the following is NOT equivalent to $\frac{4}{6}$?

- **A.** $\frac{2}{3}$
- **C.** $\frac{8}{12}$
- **B.** $\frac{14}{16}$
- **D.** $\frac{12}{18}$

FREE RESPONSE

4. Write these decimals in order from least to greatest.

2.709   2.079   2.970   2.907

5. Kim is 5.6 feet tall. Bill is $5\frac{2}{3}$ feet tall, and Mei is $5\frac{3}{4}$ feet tall. Who is the tallest?

Writing in Math

6. Explain how to find the GCF for 12 and 20.

Think It Through

I can **make organized lists** to solve problems.

Geometry and Measurement

MULTIPLE CHOICE

7. What is the surface area of the figure below?

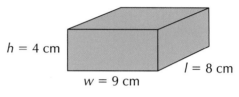

$h = 4$ cm

$w = 9$ cm

$l = 8$ cm

- **A.** 126 cm^2
- **B.** 140 cm^2
- **C.** 280 cm^2
- **D.** 288 cm^2

8. What is the perimeter of a regular hexagon with sides measuring 3 feet?

- **A.** 9 ft^2
- **C.** 18 ft
- **B.** 12 ft
- **D.** 18 ft^2

9. Which of the following is NOT a parallelogram?

- **A.** square
- **C.** rhombus
- **B.** trapezoid
- **D.** rectangle

FREE RESPONSE

10. If a concert started at 11:45 A.M. and ended at 1:20 P.M., how long was the concert?

11. A park has a width of 100 yards and a length of $162\frac{1}{2}$ yards. Find the perimeter of the park.

Writing in Math

12. Explain how the circumference and diameter of a circle are related.

Data Analysis and Probability

MULTIPLE CHOICE

13. You spin the spinner below twice. How many different ways could you get a sum of 7?

A. 1 way

B. 3 ways

C. 6 ways

D. 9 ways

14. You spin the spinner above once. On which of the following is it most likely to land?

A. an even number

B. an odd number

C. a number divisible by 3

D. a prime number

FREE RESPONSE

Use the stem-and-leaf plot for Items 15–17.

Math Test Scores

Stem	Leaf
9	0 1 5 7
8	2 4 8 8
7	0 1 2 5 6 9
6	7 7 9

15. What is the mode of the test scores?

16. What is the range of the test scores?

17. What is the median of the test scores?

Writing in Math

18. Explain how to use the stem-and-leaf plot to find the median of the test scores.

Algebra

MULTIPLE CHOICE

19. Evaluate the expression $15m$ for $m = 6$.

A. 9   **C.** 60

B. 21   **D.** 90

20. Solve $14n = 4{,}704$.

A. $n = 25$ **C.** $n = 336$

B. $n = 250$ **D.** $n = 364$

21. Bryant earned \$875 last month. After he paid his rent, he had \$525 left. Which equation models this situation?

A. $875 - n = 525$

B. $n - 875 = 525$

C. $875 + n = 525$

D. $875 + 525 = n$

FREE RESPONSE

22. What is the rule for this table?

In	1	2	3	4
Out	0.5	1	1.5	2

23. A bacteria cell splits in half when it reaches a certain size. After the first split, there are 2 cells. After the second split, there are 4 cells. How many cells will there be after the fifth split?

TEST TALK

Think It Through
I need to **read the problem carefully** and **look for patterns.**

Writing in Math

24. Explain how to find the value of the variable. Show each step.

$$\frac{b}{4} = 17$$

Set 3-1 (pages 142–145)

Tell whether 642 is divisible by
2, 3, 4, 5, 6, 9, or 10.

2: Yes, because the ones digit is 2.

3: Yes, because the sum of the digits of the number is divisible by 3.

4: No, because 42 is not divisible by 4.

5: No, because the ones digit is not 0 or 5.

6: Yes, because the number is divisible by both 2 and 3.

9: No, because the sum of the digits is not divisible by 9.

10: No, because the ones digit is not zero.

642 is divisible by 2, 3, and 6.

Remember if a number is divisible by 2, 3, and 6, it is not always divisible by 9.

1. 44	**2.** 110
3. 981	**4.** 312
5. 30	**6.** 55
7. 1,002	**8.** 610
9. 2,223	**10.** 3,431
11. 3,516	**12.** 4,316,280,948
13. 6,678	**14.** 4,938,219

Set 3-2 (pages 146–149)

Tell whether 15 is a prime or composite.

A composite number is greater than 1 and has more than 2 factors.

The number 15 is composite because it has 4 factors—1, 3, 5, and 15.

Remember that a prime number is greater than 1. Its only factors are 1 and the number itself.

1. 42	**2.** 103	**3.** 62
4. 57	**5.** 91	**6.** 17

Set 3-3 (pages 150–151)

Find the GCF for 24 and 42.

One Way
List the factors of 24 and 42.

24 : 1, 2, 3, 4, 6, 8, 12, 24
42 : 1, 2, 3, 6, 7, 14, 21, 42

Circle pairs of common factors. Select the greatest one.

The GCF is 6.

Another Way
Use prime factorization.

24 = 2 × 2 × 2 × 3
42 = 2 × 3 × 7

The greatest common factor is the product of the common factors: 2 × 3 = 6.

The GCF is 6.

Remember you can use divisibility rules to help you find the factors of a number.

1. 16, 32	**2.** 8, 18
3. 11, 77	**4.** 14, 56
5. 30, 85	**6.** 34, 51
7. 20, 60	**8.** 54, 72
9. 19, 38	**10.** 46, 115
11. 20, 26	**12.** 78, 91
13. 432, 378	**14.** 405, 486

Find the LCM for 9 and 15.

Use prime factorization.

9 = (3 × 3)   Circle the greater number of
              times each factor appears.
15 = 3 ×(5)   The LCM is the product of the
              circled factors: 3 × 3 × 5 = 45.

The LCM is 45.

Remember that a multiple of a number is the product of that number and a whole number greater than 0.

1. 10, 12   **2.** 6, 14

3. 5, 8   **4.** 2, 5

5. 8, 9   **6.** 9, 12

7. 15, 20   **8.** 5, 11

9. 6, 20   **10.** 14, 24

A table can organize data and show a pattern to help you answer a question.

In the first hour of collection, Team A collected 3 bags of litter. The number of collected bags doubled every hour after that. Team B collected 2 bags in the first hour and tripled the number of collected bags every hour. For which hour did the teams collect the same number of bags?

Remember to look for a pattern as you extend a table.

Make a table to solve the problem. Write your answer in a complete sentence.

1. Dial Rate has an anytime calling plan in which the first minute is $1 and each additional minute is $0.14. Phone Now has an anytime plan where the first minute is $1.05 and each additional minute is $0.12. Which plan is less expensive for a 4-minute call?

Bags of Litter Collected				
Team	1st Hour	2nd Hour	3rd Hour	4th Hour
A	3	6	12	24
B	2	6	18	54

Both teams collected 6 bags in the 2nd hour.

What fraction does the blue shaded portion of each picture represent?

There are 10 circles in the set and 7 are shaded. So, $\frac{7}{10}$ of the circles are shaded.

The rectangle is divided into 10 equal parts and 7 are shaded. So, $\frac{7}{10}$ of the rectangle is shaded.

Remember to write a fraction of a whole, the whole must be divided into equal parts.

1.   **2.**

3.   **4.**

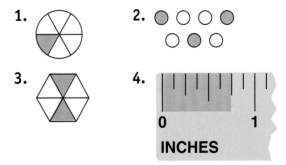

INCHES

Set 3-7 (pages 164–167)

Name an equivalent fraction for $\frac{4}{10}$.

$\frac{4 \times 2}{10 \times 2} = \frac{8}{20}$ Multiply or divide the numerator and denominator by the same
$\frac{4 \div 2}{10 \div 2} = \frac{2}{5}$ nonzero number.

Write $\frac{45}{60}$ in simplest form.

$\frac{45 \div 15}{60 \div 15} = \frac{3}{4}$ Divide the numerator and denominator by their GCF.

Remember that if you divide to simplify a fraction, use the greatest common factor.

For each fraction, name two equivalent fractions.

1. $\frac{7}{8}$ **2.** $\frac{5}{12}$ **3.** $\frac{40}{65}$

Write each fraction in simplest form.

4. $\frac{4}{32}$ **5.** $\frac{16}{18}$ **6.** $\frac{12}{60}$

7. $\frac{15}{55}$ **8.** $\frac{12}{36}$ **9.** $\frac{8}{40}$

10. $\frac{25}{125}$ **11.** $\frac{14}{16}$ **12.** $\frac{63}{108}$

Set 3-8 (pages 168–169)

Write $\frac{15}{8}$ as a mixed number.

$\frac{15}{8} = 15 \div 8$ Divide the numerator by the denominator to write the whole number. Write the remainder as
$\frac{15}{8} = 1\frac{7}{8}$ the numerator of the fraction. The divisor is the denominator.

Write $7\frac{3}{7}$ as an improper fraction.

$7\frac{3}{7} = \frac{(7 \times 7) + 3}{7}$ Multiply the denominator by the whole number and
$= \frac{52}{7}$ then add the numerator. Use the same denominator.

Remember that the denominator stays the same when you write the new mixed number or improper fraction.

Write each improper fraction as a mixed number.

1. $\frac{14}{5}$ **2.** $\frac{35}{9}$ **3.** $\frac{10}{7}$

4. $\frac{19}{6}$ **5.** $\frac{69}{14}$ **6.** $\frac{75}{8}$

Write each mixed number as an improper fraction.

7. $3\frac{1}{7}$ **8.** $9\frac{1}{9}$ **9.** $1\frac{11}{12}$

10. $10\frac{4}{5}$ **11.** $32\frac{3}{5}$ **12.** $23\frac{4}{9}$

Set 3-9 (pages 170–171)

Eleven out of 30 students chose *The View from Saturday* for their novel study. About what fraction of the students chose this novel?

Use a benchmark fraction to estimate.
$\frac{11}{30}$ is close to $\frac{10}{30}$, which equals the benchmark fraction $\frac{1}{3}$. So, about $\frac{1}{3}$ of the students chose *The View from Saturday*.

Remember that $\frac{1}{4}, \frac{1}{3}, \frac{1}{2}, \frac{2}{3}$, and $\frac{3}{4}$ are benchmark fractions.

1. There are 15 out of 58 divers on the swim team who can successfully execute a back flip. Use a benchmark fraction to estimate the number of divers who can perform the back flip.

Write 0.38 as a fraction in simplest form.

$0.38 = \dfrac{38}{100} = \dfrac{19}{50}$

Write $\dfrac{8}{22}$ as a decimal.

$$\begin{array}{r} 0.3636 \\ 22\overline{)8.0000} \\ -6\,6 \\ \hline 1\,40 \\ -1\,32 \\ \hline 80 \end{array}$$

Divide the numerator by the denominator.

So, $\dfrac{8}{22} = 0.\overline{36}$.

Remember that to write a decimal as a fraction, use the power of 10 as the denominator.

Write each decimal as a fraction in simplest form.

1. 0.09 **2.** 0.36 **3.** 2.25

4. 0.7 **5.** 0.325 **6.** 0.108

Write each fraction or mixed number as a decimal.

7. $\dfrac{3}{15}$ **8.** $1\dfrac{3}{5}$ **9.** $\dfrac{10}{18}$

10. $\dfrac{7}{7}$ **11.** $3\dfrac{12}{48}$ **12.** $7\dfrac{22}{25}$

Order $\dfrac{7}{10}$, $\dfrac{14}{15}$, and $\dfrac{2}{5}$ from least to greatest.

$\dfrac{7}{10} = \dfrac{21}{30}$
$\dfrac{14}{15} = \dfrac{28}{30}$
$\dfrac{2}{5} = \dfrac{12}{30}$

Write the fractions with the same denominator and compare.

The order from least to greatest is $\dfrac{2}{5}$, $\dfrac{7}{10}$, $\dfrac{14}{15}$.

Remember when comparing fractions, you can use the least common multiple of the denominators as a common denominator.

1. $\dfrac{3}{4}$, $\dfrac{5}{6}$, $\dfrac{6}{12}$ **2.** 5.25, $5\dfrac{4}{9}$, $5\dfrac{9}{10}$

3. $\dfrac{2}{3}$, $\dfrac{8}{9}$, 0.6 **4.** $4\dfrac{5}{7}$, $4\dfrac{8}{14}$, $4\dfrac{5}{6}$

5. $\dfrac{1}{5}$, 0.179, $\dfrac{1}{8}$ **6.** $3\dfrac{1}{3}$, 3.31, $3\dfrac{13}{40}$

To solve some word problems, you must first find and answer hidden questions.

Last week, Terry spent 45 minutes each weeknight reading a novel. On Saturday and Sunday, he read for an hour and 30 minutes each day. How much time did Terry spend reading his novel last week?

Hidden Question 1: How much time did Terry spend reading Monday through Friday?
45 min × 5 = 225 min = 3 hours 45 min

Hidden Question 2: How much time did Terry spend reading his novel during the weekend?
2 × (1 hour 30 min) = 2 hours 60 min = 3 hours

Question from the word problem: How much time did Terry spend reading his novel last week?

3 hours 45 minutes + 3 hours = 6 hours 45 minutes; Terry spent 6 hours 45 minutes reading his novel.

Remember that some word problems contain hidden questions.

Write and answer any hidden question(s). Then solve the word problem.

1. Margaret spent some time volunteering at the food pantry last month. During the first week, she spent 6 hours. During each of the last three weeks of the month, she spent 4 times the amount of time she spent during the first week. How much time did Margaret spend volunteering at the pantry last month?

Set 3-1 (pages 142–145)

Tell whether each number is divisible by 2, 3, 4, 5, 6, 9, or 10.

1. 370   **2.** 297   **3.** 425   **4.** 28   **5.** 78   **6.** 109

Tell whether the first number is a multiple of the second number.

7. 96, 5   **8.** 42, 2   **9.** 129, 3   **10.** 58, 6   **11.** 89, 9   **12.** 123, 3

13. 954, 4   **14.** 345, 10   **15.** 897, 6   **16.** 549, 9   **17.** 748, 4

18. There are 159 vases to be painted at an art studio. Can 3 students share the painting of an equal number of vases?

Set 3-2 (pages 146–149)

Tell whether each number is prime or composite.

1. 9   **2.** 48   **3.** 31   **4.** 51   **5.** 91   **6.** 27

Write the prime factorization of each number.

7. 28   **8.** 34   **9.** 95   **10.** 46   **11.** 400   **12.** 49

13. 19   **14.** 378   **15.** 464   **16.** 900   **17.** 625

18. Explain why the prime factorization of 24 is NOT $2 \times 3 \times 4$. What is the correct prime factorization?

Set 3-3 (pages 150–151)

Find the GCF for each pair of numbers.

1. 15, 40   **2.** 10, 25   **3.** 5, 8   **4.** 17, 51   **5.** 12, 32   **6.** 18, 24

7. 34, 85   **8.** 24, 32   **9.** 12, 60   **10.** 42, 64   **11.** 19, 27   **12.** 45, 72

13. Gina found the common factors of 18 and 60 to be 1, 2, 3, 4, and 5. Which factors in her list are incorrect? Is she missing any factors? If so, which ones?

14. The common factors of 42 and 96 are displayed in the Venn diagram below. What is the GCF of 42 and 96?

Factors of 42   **Factors of 96**

7   1   4 8
14   2   24
21   3   12 32
42   6   16 96
48

Take It to the NET
www More Practice
www.scottforesman.com

Set 3-4 (pages 152–153)

List the first 5 multiples for each number.

1. 7 **2.** 26 **3.** 12 **4.** 30 **5.** 14 **6.** 17

Find the LCM for each pair of numbers.

7. 5, 12 **8.** 8, 22 **9.** 8, 32 **10.** 12, 30 **11.** 12, 15 **12.** 16, 24

13. You are looking for the LCM of 4 and 14. How many multiples of 4 will you need to list?

Set 3-5 (pages 156–157)

Make a table to solve the problem. Write your answer in a complete sentence.

1. Lexi is starting her coin collection with 13 coins. Each year, she is planning to add to her collection twice the number of coins as she had the previous year. How many coins will Lexi have in her collection by the end of 5 years?

2. William has one school week to finish reading a novel for his book report. He plans to read for 20 minutes on Monday and then double his reading time each day through Thursday. How many hours and minutes will he have spent reading in all by Friday, when he will write his report?

Set 3-6 (pages 160–163)

Write a fraction for the blue shaded portion of each picture.

1. **2.** **3.** **4.**

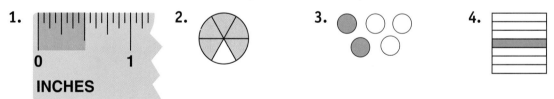

For 5–7, draw a picture to show each fraction.

5. $\frac{2}{9}$ as part of a set **6.** $\frac{7}{8}$ as a measure **7.** $\frac{5}{5}$ as part of a whole

Tell what fraction should be written at each point on the number line.

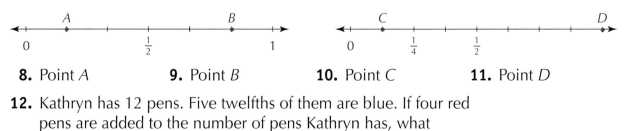

8. Point A **9.** Point B **10.** Point C **11.** Point D

12. Kathryn has 12 pens. Five twelfths of them are blue. If four red pens are added to the number of pens Kathryn has, what fraction of her pens are blue?

Set 3-7 (pages 164–167)

Find two fractions equivalent to each fraction.

1. $\frac{7}{35}$ **2.** $\frac{1}{5}$ **3.** $\frac{3}{10}$ **4.** $\frac{4}{9}$ **5.** $\frac{8}{11}$ **6.** $\frac{2}{8}$

Rewrite each pair of fractions with a common denominator.

7. $\frac{1}{6}, \frac{1}{10}$ **8.** $\frac{6}{7}, \frac{1}{9}$ **9.** $\frac{2}{15}, \frac{1}{20}$ **10.** $\frac{1}{12}, \frac{3}{8}$

Write each fraction in simplest form.

11. $\frac{17}{51}$ **12.** $\frac{9}{24}$ **13.** $\frac{12}{16}$ **14.** $\frac{15}{55}$ **15.** $\frac{14}{46}$ **16.** $\frac{10}{18}$

17. Rydell wants to simplify $\frac{18}{42}$. He divides the numerator and denominator by 6. Has Rydell simplified this fraction? How do you know?

Set 3-8 (pages 168–169)

Write each mixed number as an improper fraction.

1. $1\frac{3}{7}$ **2.** $4\frac{5}{8}$ **3.** $6\frac{1}{9}$ **4.** $1\frac{3}{10}$ **5.** $12\frac{3}{5}$ **6.** $5\frac{8}{20}$

Write each improper fraction as a mixed number in simplest form.

7. $\frac{35}{17}$ **8.** $\frac{18}{7}$ **9.** $\frac{49}{23}$ **10.** $\frac{70}{40}$ **11.** $\frac{26}{8}$ **12.** $\frac{13}{5}$

13. Caesar built a fort with a ceiling that was $\frac{21}{4}$ ft high. Douglas is $5\frac{3}{4}$ ft tall. Can Douglas stand up straight in Caesar's fort? Explain.

Set 3-9 (pages 170–171)

For 1–2, use the circle graph of a family's monthly expenses.

1. Name a benchmark fraction to estimate the monthly expenses needed for housing and clothing.

2. Name a benchmark fraction to estimate the monthly expenses needed for food.

3. Mr. Wilson notices that 39 out of the 50 compositions he collected from his students are 2 pages in length. Which benchmark fraction could be used to represent the number of 2-page compositions?

4. Keisha spent $11 of her $20 allowance. Which benchmark fraction could be used to represent the amount that Keisha spent of her allowance?

Monthly Expenses

Set 3-10 (pages 172–175)

Write each decimal as a fraction or mixed number in simplest form.

1. 0.34 **2.** 0.8 **3.** 4.58 **4.** 1.3 **5.** 0.19 **6.** 3.62

Write each fraction or mixed number as a decimal.

7. $\frac{3}{5}$ **8.** $\frac{4}{22}$ **9.** $\frac{7}{9}$ **10.** $1\frac{9}{12}$ **11.** $\frac{5}{50}$ **12.** $2\frac{6}{44}$

13. An example of a repeating decimal is 0.7676767676... Explain how and why bar notation should be used to write this decimal.

Set 3-11 (pages 176–179)

Compare using >, <, or =.

1. $\frac{5}{8}$ ⬤ $\frac{3}{8}$ **2.** $\frac{1}{4}$ ⬤ $\frac{1}{3}$ **3.** $3\frac{5}{8}$ ⬤ $3\frac{15}{24}$ **4.** $\frac{7}{7}$ ⬤ $\frac{10}{9}$ **5.** 6.25 ⬤ $6\frac{3}{10}$

Order from least to greatest.

6. $\frac{4}{5}, \frac{1}{10}, \frac{50}{100}$ **7.** $5\frac{2}{3}, 5\frac{1}{6}, 5\frac{2}{9}$ **8.** $\frac{4}{7}, \frac{7}{14}, \frac{11}{21}$ **9.** $0.25, \frac{4}{6}, \frac{5}{18}$ **10.** $\frac{1}{4}, \frac{1}{5}, 0.3$

11. One pattern of floor tile is $2\frac{3}{4}$ inches long. Another pattern of tile is $2\frac{7}{16}$ inches long. Which tile is longer?

Set 3-12 (pages 180–181)

Write and answer any hidden questions. Then solve the problem. Write your answer in a complete sentence.

1. Each layer of a box will hold 18 golf balls. If each box has 3 layers, will 4 boxes be enough to hold 200 golf balls?

2. Erin wants to spend the least amount of money on 6 balloons for a party. At Balloon Barn, each balloon costs $1.65. For every 5 balloons you buy, you get 1 free. Fun-Time Balloons sells 3 balloons for $4.50. From which store should Erin buy her balloons? How much money will she save?

3. The 18 members of the Science Club want to raise money for a field trip to a science museum. If admission is $7 per person and the bus fare is $2.60 per person each way, how much money do they need to raise?

4. Patrick uses hollow metal pipe to make wind chimes. Each wind chime requires 80 inches of pipe. How many chimes can Patrick make if he buys five 8-foot lengths of pipe?

5. Concert tickets for a group of 25 students cost $225. An individual student ticket costs $13. How much is saved by each person who attends with a group of 25?

CHAPTER 4

Adding and Subtracting Fractions

DIAGNOSING READINESS

A Vocabulary
(pages 146, 164, 168)

Choose the best term from the box.

1. Numbers which contain a whole number and a fraction are called __?__.

2. __?__ have numerators greater than or equal to denominators.

3. Fractions that name the same part of a whole or a set are __?__.

4. A fraction in __?__ has a numerator and denominator with no common factor.

Vocabulary
- **improper fractions** *(p. 168)*
- **equivalent fractions** *(p. 164)*
- **simplest form** *(p. 164)*
- **mixed numbers** *(p. 168)*
- **prime number** *(p. 146)*

B Finding a Least Common Multiple
(pages 152–153)

Find the least common multiple for each set of numbers.

5. 7, 21   6. 8, 12

7. 3, 9   8. 4, 10, 12

9. 12, 18   10. 16, 32, 48

11. 7, 5   12. 12, 20, 36

13. Rita wants to give her nieces her silver dollar collection. She plans to give Nicole $\frac{2}{5}$ the coins, Karen $\frac{1}{3}$ the coins, and Wendy $\frac{1}{4}$ the coins. What is the least number of silver dollars Rita could have in her collection for each niece to get the allotted share?

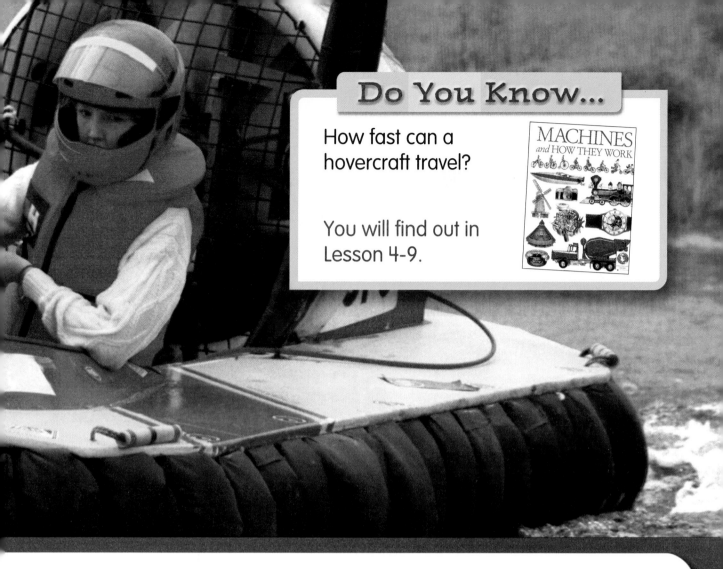

Do You Know...

How fast can a hovercraft travel?

You will find out in Lesson 4-9.

MACHINES
and HOW THEY WORK

C Relating Fractions and Mixed Numbers

(pages 168–169)

Find each missing number.

14. $\dfrac{18}{5} = 3\dfrac{5}{5}$ **15.** $8 = 7\dfrac{5}{}$

16. $\dfrac{29}{6} = 4\dfrac{5}{}$ **17.** $\dfrac{7}{3} = \dfrac{1}{3}$

18. $9 = \dfrac{8}{8}$ **19.** $\dfrac{10}{5} = $

20. $5\dfrac{4}{9} = \dfrac{}{9}$ **21.** $\dfrac{23}{4} = \dfrac{3}{4}$

22. Cathy buys 18 inches of ribbon. How many feet is this?

23. You have 5 oranges cut into thirds. How many friends could each be given 2 pieces if you save 1 piece for yourself?

D Adding and Subtracting Decimals

(pages 86–89)

Estimate each answer. Then find each answer.

24. $5.63 + 17.89$ **25.** $40.89 + 7.27$

26. $56 - 42.52$ **27.** $23.5 - 5.88$

28. $9.15 + 0.352$ **29.** $10.66 - 9.6$

30. $15 - 14.38$ **31.** $62.5 + 3.89$

32. Dean bought a paintbrush for $7.98, a gallon of paint for $34.95, and a paint scraper for $2.49. What was the total of his bill, not including tax?

33. Cedric lives 1.87 miles from school and Sam lives 2.14 miles from school. How much farther does Sam live from school than Cedric?

Key Idea
Fractions with like denominators are easy to add and subtract because the denominators represent pieces of the same size.

Vocabulary
• like denominators
• common denominator

Think It Through
I can **use a picture** to help me find the answer.

Adding and Subtracting Fractions with Like Denominators

✔ **WARM UP**
Simplify.
1. $\frac{9}{12}$ 2. $\frac{12}{16}$
3. $\frac{12}{8}$ 4. $\frac{15}{9}$

LEARN

How can you find sums and differences of fractions?

Example A

Darla's hockey team ordered different pizzas that were the same size and cut into 16 equal pieces. Darla ate $\frac{3}{16}$ of a veggie pizza, and $\frac{1}{16}$ of a cheese pizza. What fraction of a whole pizza did she eat in all?

Find $\frac{3}{16} + \frac{1}{16}$.	What You **Think**	What You **Write**
STEP 1 The fractions have **like denominators.** Add the numerators. Write the sum over the **common denominator.**		$\frac{3}{16} + \frac{1}{16} = \frac{4}{16}$
STEP 2 Simplify if possible.	The GCF of 4 and 16 is 4. $\frac{4 \div 4}{16 \div 4} = \frac{1}{4}$	$\frac{3}{16} + \frac{1}{16} = \frac{4}{16} = \frac{1}{4}$

Darla ate $\frac{1}{4}$ of a whole pizza.

Example B

Find $\frac{8}{16} - \frac{6}{16}$.	What You **Think**	What You **Write**
STEP 1 The fractions have like denominators. Subtract the numerators. Write the difference over the common denominator.		$\frac{8}{16} - \frac{6}{16} = \frac{2}{16}$
STEP 2 Simplify if possible.	The GCF of 2 and 16 is 2. $\frac{2 \div 2}{16 \div 2} = \frac{1}{8}$	$\frac{8}{16} - \frac{6}{16} = \frac{2}{16} = \frac{1}{8}$

✔ **Talk About It**

1. Give 3 different values for x that make the equation $\frac{3}{x} + \frac{5}{x} = \frac{8}{x}$ true.

Find each sum or difference. Simplify your answer.

1. $\frac{6}{15} + \frac{3}{15}$
2. $\frac{10}{14} - \frac{3}{14}$
3. $\frac{11}{20} - \frac{3}{20}$
4. $\frac{5}{8} + \frac{1}{8}$
5. $\frac{5}{12} + \frac{11}{12} + \frac{1}{12}$

6. **Number Sense** Is $\frac{4}{5} + \frac{3}{5}$ less than, equal to, or greater than 1? Without computing, how can you tell?

PRACTICE

For more practice, see Set 4-1 on p. 243.

A Skills and Understanding

Find each sum or difference. Simplify your answer.

7. $\frac{2}{15} + \frac{4}{15}$
8. $\frac{3}{9} + \frac{5}{9}$
9. $\frac{7}{16} - \frac{3}{16}$
10. $\frac{7}{12} + \frac{11}{12}$
11. $\frac{5}{3} - \frac{2}{3}$

12. $\frac{9}{10} - \frac{3}{10}$
13. $\frac{9}{20} + \frac{6}{20}$
14. $\frac{12}{18} - \frac{9}{18}$
15. $\frac{7}{9} - \frac{4}{9}$
16. $\frac{3}{16} + \frac{9}{16} + \frac{11}{16}$

17. **Number Sense** Give 2 fractions with like denominators whose sum is greater than 1.

B Reasoning and Problem Solving

18. What is the total amount of garlic powder, dry mustard, and paprika?

19. How much olive oil and sugar would you need to make 8 servings?

20. **Writing in Math** Malcolm says, "Adding fractions is easier if you just add the numerators and then the denominators." Use an example to explain why Malcolm's idea doesn't work.

Recipe for Salad Dressing

$\frac{3}{4}$ cup olive oil	$\frac{1}{2}$ tsp. garlic powder
$\frac{1}{4}$ cup vinegar	$\frac{1}{2}$ tsp. dry mustard
$\frac{3}{4}$ tsp. salt	$\frac{1}{2}$ tsp. paprika
$\frac{1}{4}$ tsp. sugar	

Put all ingredients into a pint jar and shake well. Refrigerate. Makes 4 servings.

Mixed Review and Test Prep

Take It to the NET
Test Prep
www.scottforesman.com

Copy and complete the following table.

21.

Fraction			$\frac{2}{3}$		$\frac{5}{6}$
Decimal	4.6	0.9		0.3	

22. Order from least to greatest. 0.4, 1.6, $\frac{1}{5}$, $\frac{9}{15}$

A. $\frac{9}{15}$, 0.4, 1.6, $\frac{1}{5}$
B. $\frac{1}{5}$, $\frac{9}{15}$, 0.4, 1.6
C. $\frac{9}{15}$, $\frac{1}{5}$, 1.6, 0.4
D. $\frac{1}{5}$, 0.4, $\frac{9}{15}$, 1.6

Adding and Subtracting Fractions with Unlike Denominators

Vocabulary
• unlike denominators
• least common multiple (LCM) (p. 152)
• least common denominator (LCD) (p. 164)

Materials
• fraction strips or  tools

WARM UP
Find the least common multiple for each set of numbers.

1. 12 and 4   2. 9 and 2

3. 10 and 5   4. 8 and 6

5. 6 and 5   6. 3, 4 and 6

LEARN

Activity

How can you use fraction strips to add?

Find $\frac{1}{2} + \frac{1}{3}$.

Step 1 Use fraction strips to show both fractions.

| $\frac{1}{2}$ | $\frac{1}{3}$ |

Step 2 Find a common denominator.

The least common denominator (LCD) of 2 and 3 is 6.

Step 3 Use fraction strips with the common denominator to represent each fraction.

Step 4 Write the sum.

$\frac{3}{6} + \frac{2}{6} = \frac{5}{6}$

Use fraction strips to find each sum.

a. $\frac{1}{4} + \frac{2}{3}$ **b.** $\frac{2}{5} + \frac{3}{10}$ **c.** $\frac{5}{8} + \frac{3}{4}$ **d.** $\frac{1}{6} + \frac{1}{2}$

TEST TALK

Think It Through
I can **use objects** to solve a simpler problem.

Activity

How can you use fraction strips to subtract?

Find $\frac{1}{2} - \frac{1}{3}$.

Step 1 Use fraction strips to show both fractions.

Step 2 Find a common denominator.

The LCD of 2 and 3 is 6.

Step 3 Find fraction strips with the common denominator to show the difference.

Step 4 Write the difference.

$\frac{1}{2} - \frac{1}{3} = \frac{1}{6}$

Use fraction strips to find each difference.

a. $\frac{2}{3} - \frac{1}{4}$ **b.** $\frac{9}{10} - \frac{2}{5}$ **c.** $\frac{7}{8} - \frac{1}{4}$ **d.** $\frac{5}{6} - \frac{1}{4}$

How can you find sums and differences of fractions with unlike denominators?

In order to add or subtract fractions that have different or **unlike denominators,** write them with the same denominator. That is, you need to find equivalent fractions.

		Example A	Example B
		Find $\frac{1}{2} + \frac{1}{5}$.	Find $\frac{5}{6} - \frac{1}{3}$.
STEP 1	Use the **least common multiple (LCM)** to find the **least common denominator.**	Since the LCM of 2 and 5 is 10, the **least common denominator (LCD)** is 10.	The LCD of 6 and 3 is 6.
STEP 2	Write equivalent fractions.	$\begin{array}{r} \frac{1}{2} = \frac{5}{10} \\ + \frac{1}{5} = + \frac{2}{10} \\ \hline \end{array}$	$\begin{array}{r} \frac{5}{6} = \frac{5}{6} \\ - \frac{1}{3} = - \frac{2}{6} \\ \hline \end{array}$
STEP 3	Add or subtract. Simplify if possible.	$\begin{array}{r} \frac{1}{2} = \frac{5}{10} \\ + \frac{1}{5} = + \frac{2}{10} \\ \hline \frac{7}{10} \end{array}$	$\begin{array}{r} \frac{5}{6} = \frac{5}{6} \\ - \frac{1}{3} = - \frac{2}{6} \\ \hline \frac{3}{6} = \frac{1}{2} \end{array}$

Think It Through
I'll try to **make a simpler problem.** I will write equivalent fractions with like denominators.

✔ Talk About It

1. In Example A, explain how to find the equivalent fractions for $\frac{1}{2}$ and $\frac{1}{5}$.

2. **Reasoning** In Example B, would 18 have worked just as well as a common denominator? Explain.

3. **Reasoning** Why would you use the least common denominator when adding or subtracting fractions with unlike denominators?

Take It to the NET
More Examples
www.scottforesman.com

CHECK ✔

For another example, see Set 4-2 on p. 240.

Find each sum or difference. Simplify your answer.

1. $\frac{5}{6} - \frac{1}{2}$ 2. $\frac{3}{4} + \frac{3}{5}$ 3. $\frac{7}{8} + \frac{1}{6}$ 4. $\frac{11}{12} + \frac{3}{4}$ 5. $\frac{4}{15} - \frac{1}{10}$

6. **Number Sense** Why is it necessary for fractions to have common denominators before you add or subtract them?

A Skills and Understanding

Find each sum or difference. Simplify your answer.

7. $\frac{2}{5} + \frac{3}{8}$ **8.** $\frac{5}{6} - \frac{1}{9}$ **9.** $\frac{9}{10} + \frac{3}{5}$ **10.** $\frac{5}{8} - \frac{1}{3}$ **11.** $\frac{7}{8} - \frac{5}{12}$

12. $\frac{7}{12} + \frac{2}{3}$ **13.** $\frac{4}{5} + \frac{11}{15}$ **14.** $\frac{2}{3} - \frac{5}{8}$ **15.** $\frac{6}{7} + \frac{11}{14}$ **16.** $\frac{9}{10} - \frac{1}{4} + \frac{3}{8}$

17. Convert the fractions in Exercises 7, 9, and 16 to decimals and find each answer. Does your decimal answer agree with your original answer?

18. Number Sense Is $\frac{15}{16} - \frac{4}{5}$ less than, equal to, or greater than $\frac{1}{2}$? How do you know without computing?

B Reasoning and Problem Solving

Math and Social Studies

One page of the *Lydia Lake Reporter* newspaper has advertisements covering $\frac{1}{3}$ of the page and a photo covering $\frac{1}{4}$ of the page. The rest of the page is a news story.

19. What fraction of the page contains ads and the photo?

20. How much more of the page is covered by ads than by the photo?

21. Reasoning What fraction of the page is a news story? Explain.

22. Suppose Wanda studied $\frac{3}{4}$ hour for the math quiz and Shantal studied $\frac{5}{6}$ hour. Who studied longer? How much longer?

23. Writing in Math Whose method do you prefer for finding $\frac{3}{8} + \frac{5}{6}$? Why?

June
I use the product of the denominators as my common denominator. It saves time and work.

Ramon
I find the least common denominator. It keeps me from making mistakes when I simplify my answer.

TEST TALK

Think It Through
I can **check how the denominators are related.** If they have common factors, their product will NOT be the least common denominator.

C Extensions

24. Write two fractions with unlike denominators whose difference is $\frac{1}{2}$.

25. Name 2 fractions with unlike denominators whose sum is greater than $1\frac{1}{2}$.

Add each pair of fractions. Describe any pattern you see.

26. $\frac{1}{2} + \frac{1}{4}$

27. $\frac{3}{4} + \frac{1}{8}$

28. $\frac{7}{8} + \frac{1}{16}$

Mixed Review and Test Prep

Take It to the NET
Test Prep
www.scottforesman.com

Find each answer.

29. $\frac{3}{5} + \frac{2}{5}$

30. $\frac{11}{12} + \frac{5}{12}$

31. $\frac{5}{6} - \frac{2}{6}$

32. $\frac{7}{8} - \frac{1}{8}$

33. Which is the decimal equivalent for $\frac{1}{50}$?

    A. 0.0150   **B.** 0.02   **C.** 0.15   **D.** 0.2

Learning with Technology

Fractions eTool: Strips and Wedges

You can use the Strips workspace to find sums of fractions. You can represent fractions by selecting pieces from the toolbar. You can also select a denominator to divide the strip into parts.

For 1–3, use the Strips workspace to find each sum.

1. $\frac{1}{8} + \frac{1}{3}$ **2.** $\frac{3}{5} + \frac{4}{16}$ **3.** $\frac{2}{3} + \frac{1}{12} + \frac{1}{16}$

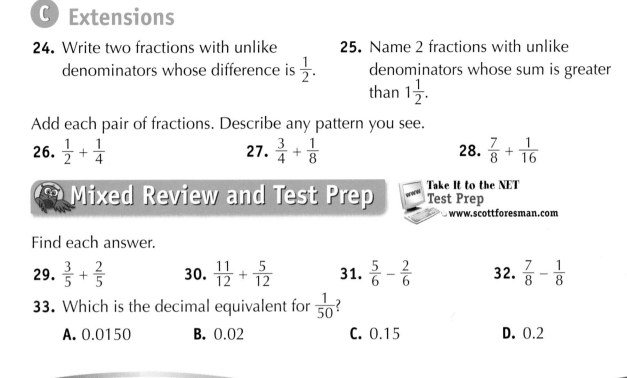

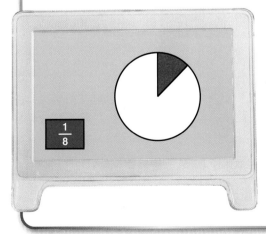

Use the Wedges workspace to find differences of fractions. Select pieces from the toolbar. To find $\frac{3}{4} - \frac{1}{8}$, select a $\frac{1}{8}$ wedge. Add other pieces until $\frac{3}{4}$ of the circle is filled.

For 4–6, use the wedges feature to find each difference.

4. $\frac{7}{8} - \frac{1}{2}$ **5.** $\frac{1}{2} - \frac{5}{12}$ **6.** $\frac{2}{3} - \frac{1}{12}$

Predict and Generalize

Predicting and generalizing when you read in math can help you use the **problem-solving strategy,** *Look for a Pattern,* in the next lesson.

Now look for a pattern in the differences.

In reading, predicting and generalizing can help you figure out what comes next in a story. In math, predicting and generalizing can help you figure out what comes next in a pattern.

Give the missing numbers.
Describe the pattern.

14, 15, 18, 23, 30, 39, 50, ___, ___

14, 15, 18, 23, 30, 39, 50, ___, ___

V V V V V V
1 3 5 7 9 11

One way to begin is to look at the difference from one number to the next number.

Generalize to describe the pattern: the difference from one number to the next increases by 2. Then predict the missing numbers:

50 + 13 = **63**   63 + 15 = **78**

1. Predict the next number in the pattern after 78.

2. If the pattern stayed the same, but the first number was 8, what would the fourth number be?

For 3–6, use the number pattern at the right.

3. What is the difference between the first number and the second? between the second and the third? Find the rest of the differences.

4. Generalize by describing the pattern.

5. Predict the next number.

6. **Writing in Math** How is this pattern different from the number pattern on page 210?

> 2.5, 5, 7.5, 10, 12.5, 15

For 7–9, use the picture below.

$6 $9 $15 $24 $36 $51

7. What is the difference between the amount of money in the first purse starting at the left and the second purse? between the second and the third? Find the rest of the differences.

8. Generalize by describing the pattern.

9. Predict the amount of money in the next purse.

For 10–13, use the picture at the right.

10. List the differences between consecutive pairs of locker numbers, starting at the left.

11. Generalize by describing the pattern.

12. If the pattern stayed the same, but the first locker number was 3, what would the fourth locker number be?

13. **Writing in Math** Predict the next locker number. Explain how you made your prediction.

8   10   14   22   38   70

Problem-Solving Strategy

Predicting and generalizing

can help you with...

the problem-solving strategy, *Look for a Pattern.*

Key Idea

Learning how and when to look for a pattern can help you solve problems.

Look for a Pattern

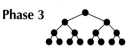 **LEARN**

What is the pattern?

Emergency Plan The president of Best Idea has a 5-phase emergency plan.

Phase 1 The president emails her 2 vice presidents.

Phase 2 Each vice president forwards the email to 2 employees.

Phase 3 Each employee who receives the email sends it to 2 employees. How many employees work for the company if everyone knows about the emergency in 5 phases?

Read and Understand

What do you know? Three employees know in Phase 1.
In Phase 2, seven employees know.
Fifteen employees know in Phase 3.

What are you trying to find? Find the number of employees in the company.

Plan and Solve

What strategy will you use?

Strategy: Look for a Pattern

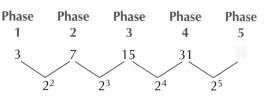

Phase 1	Phase 2	Phase 3	Phase 4	Phase 5
3	7	15	31	

$2^2 \quad 2^3 \quad 2^4 \quad 2^5$

Answer: There are 63 employees in the company.

Look Back and Check

Is your answer reasonable? Yes, the difference from one phase to the next doubles.

TEST TALK

Think It Through

Looking at how numbers or figures in a pattern compare can help you find the rule that creates the pattern.

✔ **Talk About It**

1. Do you see a relationship between the phase number and the exponent? Explain.

For another example, see Set 4-3 on p. 240.

Name the missing numbers or draw the next three figures.
Describe each pattern.

1. 0, 1, 3, 6, 10, ▒, ▒,

2.

3.

x	y	z
4	8	12
7	14	21
10	20	30
		39
	32	

4. 2, 3, 5, 8, 12, ▒, ▒,

5. Number Sense Write an expression that you can use to find the number of right angles in the diagram below. Find the number of right angles.

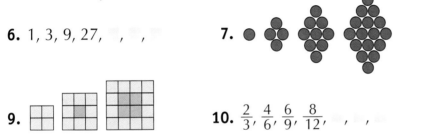

For more practice, see Set 4-3 on p. 243.

Name the missing numbers or draw the next three figures.
Describe each pattern.

6. 1, 3, 9, 27, ▒, ▒,

7.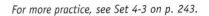

8.

a	b	c
12	48	96
18	72	144
		192
	120	

9.

10. $\frac{2}{3}, \frac{4}{6}, \frac{6}{9}, \frac{8}{12},$ ▒, ▒,

11. Number Sense Use the table below. Write an expression that you can use to find the total cost for 10 items. Find the total cost for 10 items.

Number of items	1	2	3	4	5	6
Total cost	$1.38	$2.76	$4.14	$5.52	$6.90	$8.28

Look for a pattern in each chart. Copy and write the missing numbers.

12.

$$1 \times 8 + 1 = 9$$
$$12 \times 8 + 2 = 98$$
$$123 \times 8 + 3 = 987$$
$$1{,}234 \times 8 + 4 = 9{,}876$$
$$12{,}345 \times 8 + 5 = ?$$
$$? \times 8 + 6 = ?$$

13.

$$\frac{1}{9} = 0.11111\ldots \qquad \frac{1}{11} = 0.090909\ldots$$
$$\frac{2}{9} = 0.22222\ldots \qquad \frac{2}{11} = 0.181818\ldots$$
$$\frac{3}{9} = 0.33333\ldots \qquad \frac{3}{11} = 0.272727\ldots$$
$$\frac{4}{9} = ? \qquad \frac{4}{11} = ?$$
$$\frac{5}{9} = ? \qquad \frac{5}{11} = ?$$

14. <u>Writing in Math</u> There are pairs of numbers that when squared, make an interesting pattern. One pair is 12^2 and 21^2; $12^2 = 144$ and $21^2 = 441$. Explain whether this pattern is the same for the pairs 13^2, 31^2 and 112^2, 211^2.

All text pages available online and on CD-ROM.

Do You Know How?

Do You Understand?

Adding and Subtracting Fractions with Like Denominators (4-1)

Find each sum or difference. Simplify if possible.

1. $\frac{2}{3} + \frac{2}{3}$

2. $\frac{7}{10} + \frac{1}{10}$

3. $\frac{5}{12} + \frac{11}{12}$

4. $\frac{9}{10} - \frac{4}{10}$

5. $\frac{7}{8} - \frac{1}{8}$

6. $\frac{8}{9} - \frac{2}{9}$

7. $\frac{8}{6} - \frac{3}{6}$

8. $\frac{9}{16} + \frac{7}{16}$

Ⓐ Explain how you found each sum or difference.

Ⓑ Explain why you should add or subtract only numerators and not denominators.

Adding and Subtracting Fractions with Unlike Denominators (4-2)

Find each sum or difference. Simplify if possible.

9. $\frac{3}{4} + \frac{1}{5}$

10. $\frac{5}{6} + \frac{7}{8}$

11. $\frac{9}{10} + \frac{1}{2}$

12. $\frac{11}{12} - \frac{3}{4}$

13. $\frac{2}{5} - \frac{1}{6}$

14. $\frac{7}{10} - \frac{1}{4}$

15. $\frac{7}{12} - \frac{3}{8}$

16. $\frac{3}{10} + \frac{3}{5}$

Ⓒ Explain how you found the difference in Exercise 13.

Ⓓ Redo Exercises 11 and 12 using a different common denominator. Are your answers the same as your original ones?

Problem Solving Strategy: Look for a Pattern (4-3)

17. The first three *rectangular numbers* are shown below. Look for a pattern to find the number of dots needed to represent the eighth rectangular number.

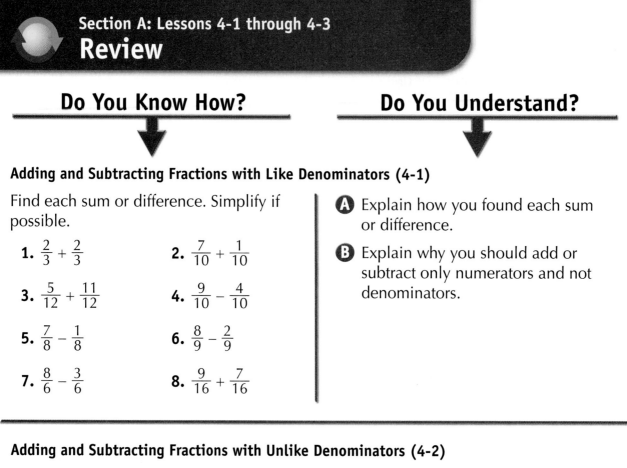

| 1st | 2nd | 3rd |

Ⓔ Explain how you found the pattern for the rectangular numbers.

Ⓕ Which method do you think is easier for solving this problem, drawing a picture or making a table? Explain.

Name the missing numbers.

18. 2, 4, 12, 48,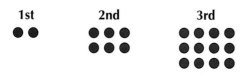

Diagnostic Checkpoint

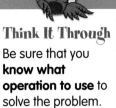

Think It Through
Be sure that you
**know what
operation to use** to
solve the problem.

MULTIPLE CHOICE

1. Juan bought $\frac{3}{4}$ pound of Delicious apples and $\frac{3}{4}$ pound of Granny Smith apples. How many pounds of apples did he buy in all? (4-1)

   A. $\frac{3}{8}$ pounds   **B.** $\frac{6}{8}$ pounds   **C.** $1\frac{1}{2}$ pounds   **D.** 3 pounds

2. Ms. Chan had $\frac{1}{3}$ yard of red felt and $\frac{1}{2}$ yard of blue felt. How much more blue felt than red felt did she have? (4-2)

   A. 2 yards   **B.** $\frac{5}{6}$ yard   **C.** $\frac{2}{5}$ yard   **D.** $\frac{1}{6}$ yard

FREE RESPONSE

Find each sum or difference. Simplify if possible. (4-1, 4-2)

3. $\frac{5}{8} + \frac{5}{8}$

4. $\frac{4}{5} - \frac{3}{10}$

5. $\frac{11}{12} + \frac{5}{12}$

6. $\frac{3}{4} + \frac{3}{6}$

7. $\frac{3}{8} + \frac{3}{5}$

8. $\frac{2}{3} - \frac{1}{6}$

9. $\frac{7}{15} - \frac{2}{15}$

10. $\frac{7}{8} + \frac{5}{12}$

11. $\frac{4}{5} - \frac{1}{3}$

12. $\frac{1}{6} + \frac{5}{9}$

13. $\frac{5}{8} - \frac{1}{6}$

14. $\frac{4}{21} + \frac{5}{7}$

George is to arrange oranges in a square pyramid in the produce section of his uncle's store. Use the information in the table at the right for Exercises 15–17. (4-3)

Oranges in Pyramid	
Layer	**Number**
Bottom	81
Second from bottom	64
Third from bottom	49
Fourth from bottom	36

15. How many oranges will be in the fifth layer from the bottom?

16. For which layer will George have 1 orange?

17. How many oranges will George use in all?

18. A recipe for muffins calls for $\frac{2}{3}$ cup granulated sugar and $\frac{3}{4}$ cup brown sugar. How much more brown sugar than granulated sugar is there in the muffins? (4-2)

Writing in Math

19. Explain how to find $\frac{3}{8} + \frac{7}{8}$. (4-1)

20. Explain how to find $\frac{5}{6} - \frac{1}{4}$. (4-2)

21. Show how to find $\frac{3}{4} + \frac{1}{6}$ using 3 different common denominators. Are your answers the same? (4-2)

Key Idea
Estimating sums and differences of fractions and mixed numbers is similar to estimating with whole numbers, decimals, and benchmark fractions.

Vocabulary
• round (p. 14)

Think It Through
I need **data from the problem** and **data from the table.**

Estimating Sums and Differences of Fractions and Mixed Numbers

✔ **WARM UP**
Estimate.
1. 3.55 + 7.3
2. 5 + 3.66
3. 0.8 – 0.25
4. 3 – 2.45

LEARN

Do you need an exact answer or is an estimate enough?

Ms. Patel wants to make a size 14 dress and a matching jacket. She has $4\frac{1}{2}$ yards of 45-inch wide fabric. Does she have enough to make the dress and jacket?

To decide if she has enough material, estimate $2\frac{7}{8} + 2\frac{1}{4}$.

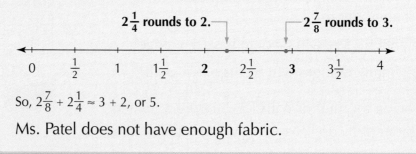

		Fabric Required (in yards)		
	Bolt Width	Size 10	Size 12	Size 14
Dress	45 in.	$2\frac{1}{4}$	$2\frac{1}{2}$	$2\frac{7}{8}$
	60 in.	$1\frac{5}{8}$	$1\frac{7}{8}$	$1\frac{7}{8}$
Jacket	45 in.	$1\frac{7}{8}$	2	$2\frac{1}{4}$
	60 in.	$1\frac{1}{2}$	$1\frac{5}{8}$	$1\frac{5}{8}$

What are some ways to estimate?

Example A

Estimate $2\frac{7}{8} + 2\frac{1}{4}$.

You can use a number line to **round** fractions and mixed numbers to the nearest whole number.

$2\frac{1}{4}$ rounds to 2.　　$2\frac{7}{8}$ rounds to 3.

$$0 \quad \frac{1}{2} \quad 1 \quad 1\frac{1}{2} \quad 2 \quad 2\frac{1}{2} \quad 3 \quad 3\frac{1}{2} \quad 4$$

So, $2\frac{7}{8} + 2\frac{1}{4} \approx 3 + 2$, or 5.

Ms. Patel does not have enough fabric.

Example B

Estimate $5\frac{2}{3} - 2\frac{3}{8}$ by rounding to the nearest whole number.

$5\frac{2}{3} - 2\frac{3}{8} \approx 4$

Since $\frac{2}{3}$ is greater than $\frac{1}{2}$, $5\frac{2}{3}$ rounds to 6. Since $\frac{3}{8}$ is less than $\frac{1}{2}$, $2\frac{3}{8}$ rounds to 2. 6 – 2 = 4.

✔ **Talk About It**

1. How would you round $5\frac{1}{2}$?

www **Take It to the NET**
More Examples
www.scottforesman.com

For another example, see Set 4-4 on p. 241.

Round to the nearest whole number.

1. $5\frac{2}{7}$ **2.** $4\frac{5}{8}$ **3.** $2\frac{9}{16}$ **4.** $4\frac{9}{11}$ **5.** $8\frac{1}{8}$

Estimate each sum or difference.

6. $5\frac{2}{7} + 6\frac{8}{15}$ **7.** $4\frac{5}{8} - 3\frac{1}{3}$ **8.** $8\frac{6}{10} + 2\frac{1}{2}$ **9.** $7 - 5\frac{2}{3}$ **10.** $8\frac{2}{3} - 1\frac{4}{9}$

11. Number Sense The difference of two numbers is about 3. One of the numbers is $7\frac{9}{16}$. What might the other number be? Explain.

PRACTICE

For more practice, see Set 4-4 on p. 244.

Ⓐ Skills and Understanding

Round to the nearest whole number.

12. $12\frac{1}{5}$ **13.** $6\frac{3}{5}$ **14.** $7\frac{4}{9}$ **15.** $71\frac{2}{96}$ **16.** $13\frac{61}{100}$

Estimate each sum or difference.

17. $10\frac{11}{20} - 3\frac{6}{25}$ **18.** $11\frac{5}{6} - 5\frac{12}{13}$ **19.** $10\frac{3}{5} + 2\frac{87}{100}$ **20.** $9 - 5\frac{3}{8}$ **21.** $3\frac{1}{5} + 6\frac{4}{7} + 5\frac{5}{9}$

22. Number Sense The sum of two numbers is about 5. One of the numbers is $3\frac{3}{7}$. What might the other number be? Explain.

Ⓑ Reasoning and Problem Solving

For 23–24, use the table on page 216.

Elena wants to make a size 10 dress and matching jacket from 60-inch wide fabric.

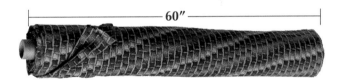

— 60″ —

23. About how much fabric will Elena need altogether?

24. <u>Writing in Math</u> Will Elena need more fabric if she uses 45-inch wide fabric? Explain.

🦉 Mixed Review and Test Prep

Take It to the NET
Test Prep
www.scottforesman.com

Find each answer.

25. $\frac{7}{10} + \frac{9}{10}$ **26.** $\frac{11}{16} - \frac{7}{16}$ **27.** $\frac{5}{12} + \frac{7}{8}$ **28.** $\frac{13}{15} - \frac{2}{5}$

29. Algebra In the equation $7\frac{1}{4} + x = 10\frac{1}{5}$, estimate the value of x.

30. What are the next 3 items in this pattern: 1, 5, 12, 22, 35, 51, ▢, ▢, ▢?

A. 68, 86, 105 **B.** 70, 92, 117 **C.** 71, 94, 120 **D.** 83, 174, 275

✏️ All text pages available online and on CD-ROM.

Key Idea
To add mixed numbers, you can add the fraction parts to the whole number parts, and simplify.

Vocabulary
• mixed number (p. 168)

Think It Through
I should **estimate** the sum before working the problem.

Adding Mixed Numbers

LEARN

How can you find the sum of mixed numbers?

✓ **WARM UP**
Write as mixed numbers.

1. $\frac{38}{3}$ 2. $\frac{41}{9}$

3. $\frac{50}{7}$ 4. $\frac{805}{8}$

Example A

Rossita measured the amount of precipitation over a 2-month period. It rained $2\frac{3}{10}$ inches in June and $2\frac{1}{2}$ inches in July. What was the total precipitation for June and July?

Find $2\frac{3}{10} + 2\frac{1}{2}$.   Estimate: $2 + 3 = 5$

STEP 1

Write equivalent fractions with the LCD.

$$2\frac{3}{10} = 2\frac{3}{10}$$
$$+ 2\frac{1}{2} = + 2\frac{5}{10}$$

STEP 2

Add the whole numbers. Add the fractions. Simplify if possible.

$$2\frac{3}{10} = 2\frac{3}{10}$$
$$+ 2\frac{1}{2} = + 2\frac{5}{10}$$
$$\overline{4\frac{8}{10}} = 4\frac{4}{5}$$

Example B

Find $7\frac{9}{10} + 3\frac{3}{5}$.   Estimate: $8 + 4 = 12$

STEP 1

Write equivalent fractions with the LCD.

$$7\frac{9}{10} = 7\frac{9}{10}$$
$$+ 3\frac{3}{5} = + 3\frac{6}{10}$$

STEP 2

Add the whole numbers. Add the fractions. Rename improper fractions as **mixed numbers.** Simplify.

$$7\frac{9}{10} = 7\frac{9}{10} = 7\frac{9}{10}$$
$$+ 3\frac{3}{5} = + 3\frac{6}{10} = + 3\frac{6}{10}$$
$$\overline{10\frac{15}{10}} = 11\frac{1}{2}$$

$$\frac{15}{10} = 1\frac{5}{10} = 1\frac{1}{2}$$

✓ **Talk About It**

1. Does it matter whether you add the fractions first or the whole numbers first?

For another example, see Set 4-5 on p. 241.

CHECK ✓

Find each sum. Simplify your answer.

1. $4\frac{3}{8} + 5\frac{5}{12}$ **2.** $1\frac{1}{4} + 3\frac{3}{5}$ **3.** $3\frac{5}{6} + 7\frac{8}{9}$ **4.** $2\frac{3}{4} + 6\frac{7}{8}$

5. Reasoning Before you add, how can you tell whether the fraction part of the sum will be an improper fraction?

PRACTICE

For more practice, see Set 4-5 on p. 244.

A Skills and Understanding

Find each sum. Simplify your answer.

6. $8 + 7\frac{2}{5}$ **7.** $8\frac{2}{9} + 1\frac{7}{12}$ **8.** $4\frac{1}{12} + 3\frac{5}{12}$ **9.** $\frac{8}{15} + 2\frac{11}{15}$ **10.** $8\frac{1}{6} + \frac{10}{12}$

11. $12\frac{1}{2} + 9$ **12.** $3\frac{3}{4} + 8\frac{7}{8}$ **13.** $8\frac{9}{10} + 2\frac{3}{4}$ **14.** $2\frac{2}{5} + 8\frac{7}{10} + 4\frac{1}{6}$ **15.** $\frac{5}{6} + 3\frac{5}{12} + 9\frac{3}{4}$

16. Number Sense Is the sum of two mixed numbers always a mixed number? Explain.

B Reasoning and Problem Solving

17. Find the annual average precipitation for Boise and Phoenix.

18. By how many inches do the two annual sums differ?

19.  Explain how to find $5\frac{7}{10} + 6\frac{11}{15}$.

Data File

Average Annual Precipitation (in inches)

City	Jan. to March	April to June	July to Aug.	Sept. to Dec.
Boise, ID	$3\frac{7}{10}$	$3\frac{2}{5}$	$1\frac{3}{10}$	$3\frac{2}{5}$
Phoenix, AZ	$2\frac{1}{10}$	$\frac{3}{5}$	$2\frac{3}{10}$	$1\frac{9}{10}$

C Extensions

20. Mental Math Explain how you could find $5\frac{5}{8} + 3\frac{3}{4} + 2\frac{1}{4} + 8\frac{3}{8}$ mentally.

21. Number Sense Without computing, tell which is greater, $2\frac{7}{8} + 3\frac{1}{4}$ or $2\frac{5}{6} + 3\frac{1}{4}$.

🦉 Mixed Review and Test Prep

Take It to the NET
Test Prep
www.scottforesman.com

Estimate each sum or difference.

22. $11\frac{5}{16} - 7\frac{7}{8}$ **23.** $5\frac{7}{8} + 3\frac{1}{3}$ **24.** $12\frac{1}{10} - 10\frac{8}{9}$ **25.** $3\frac{2}{3} + 5\frac{1}{5} + 9\frac{7}{10}$

26. Which property of numbers is illustrated by $15 + (5 \times 5) = (5 \times 5) + 15$?

     A. Commutative Property of Multiplication   **C.** Associative Property
     B. Distributive Property   **D.** Commutative Property of Addition

All text pages available online and on CD-ROM.

Think It Through
I can **use a model** to solve the problem.

Subtracting Mixed Numbers

LEARN

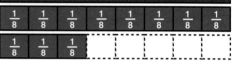
✓ **WARM UP**
Simplify.
1. $2\frac{3}{4} + \frac{5}{6}$ 2. $\frac{11}{12} - \frac{3}{4}$
3. $\frac{12}{10} - \frac{7}{10}$ 4. $7\frac{3}{5} + 2\frac{1}{2}$

How can you model the difference of mixed numbers?

Activity

Find $2\frac{3}{8} - 1\frac{7}{8}$.

Step 1   Use fraction strips to show $2\frac{3}{8}$.

Step 2   Rename $2\frac{3}{8}$ to show more eighths by exchanging a 1 strip for eight $\frac{1}{8}$-strips.

Step 3   Remove $1\frac{7}{8}$. Write the difference. Simplify if necessary.

$$2\frac{3}{8} - 1\frac{7}{8} = \frac{4}{8} = \frac{1}{2}$$

Use fraction strips to find each difference.

a. $5\frac{1}{4} - 3\frac{3}{4}$ **b.** $19\frac{1}{7} - 15\frac{5}{7}$ **c.** $10\frac{3}{8} - 7\frac{7}{8}$ **d.** $6\frac{1}{5} - 4\frac{4}{5}$

How can you find the difference of mixed numbers?

Example A

Find $4\frac{1}{4} - 2\frac{5}{6}$.   Estimate: $4 - 3 = 1$

STEP 1	STEP 2	STEP 3
Write equivalent fractions with the LCD.	To subtract, rename $4\frac{3}{12}$ to show more twelfths.	Subtract. Simplify if possible.
$4\frac{1}{4} = \quad 4\frac{3}{12}$ $-2\frac{5}{6} = -2\frac{10}{12}$	$4\frac{3}{12} = 3 + \frac{12}{12} + \frac{3}{12} = 3\frac{15}{12}$ $-2\frac{10}{12} =$	$3\frac{15}{12}$ $-2\frac{10}{12}$ $\overline{\quad 1\frac{5}{12}}$

Example B

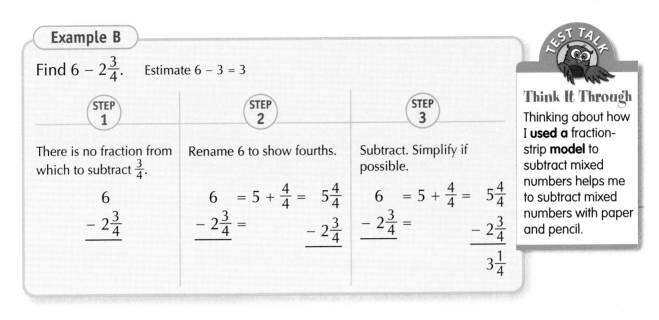

Find $6 - 2\frac{3}{4}$.   Estimate $6 - 3 = 3$

STEP 1	STEP 2	STEP 3
There is no fraction from which to subtract $\frac{3}{4}$.	Rename 6 to show fourths.	Subtract. Simplify if possible.
$\begin{array}{r} 6 \\ -2\frac{3}{4} \\ \hline \end{array}$	$\begin{array}{r} 6 = 5 + \frac{4}{4} = 5\frac{4}{4} \\ -2\frac{3}{4} = \\ \hline \qquad -2\frac{3}{4} \\ \hline \end{array}$	$\begin{array}{r} 6 = 5 + \frac{4}{4} = 5\frac{4}{4} \\ -2\frac{3}{4} = \qquad -2\frac{3}{4} \\ \hline \qquad 3\frac{1}{4} \end{array}$

Think It Through

Thinking about how I **used a** fraction-strip **model** to subtract mixed numbers helps me to subtract mixed numbers with paper and pencil.

✔ **Talk About It**

1. In Example B, explain why 6 was renamed $5 + \frac{4}{4}$.

2. Number Sense How is subtracting $2\frac{3}{4}$ from 6 like subtracting 3.9 from 5?

Do you always have to rename both mixed numbers before subtracting?

Example C

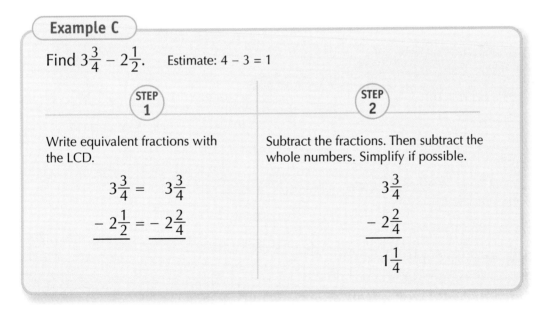

Find $3\frac{3}{4} - 2\frac{1}{2}$.   Estimate: $4 - 3 = 1$

STEP 1	STEP 2
Write equivalent fractions with the LCD.	Subtract the fractions. Then subtract the whole numbers. Simplify if possible.
$\begin{array}{r} 3\frac{3}{4} = \quad 3\frac{3}{4} \\ -2\frac{1}{2} = -2\frac{2}{4} \\ \hline \end{array}$	$\begin{array}{r} 3\frac{3}{4} \\ -2\frac{2}{4} \\ \hline 1\frac{1}{4} \end{array}$

✔ **Talk About It**

3. In Example C, why was $2\frac{1}{2}$ renamed as $2\frac{2}{4}$?

4. Number Sense Is the difference of two mixed numbers always a mixed number? Explain.

Take It to the NET
More Examples
www.scottforesman.com

Find each difference. Simplify if possible.

1. $8\frac{5}{6} - 3\frac{8}{9}$ **2.** $5\frac{1}{4} - 2\frac{7}{10}$ **3.** $11\frac{1}{2} - \frac{3}{4}$ **4.** $3 - \frac{5}{8}$ **5.** $8\frac{9}{10} - 7\frac{3}{10}$

6. Number Sense If you rewrite the numbers in Exercise 2 as decimals, will you need to do any renaming before subtracting? Explain.

PRACTICE

For more practice, see Set 4-6 on p. 244.

Ⓐ Skills and Understanding

Find each difference. Simplify if possible.

7. $3\frac{5}{16} - 2\frac{1}{8}$ **8.** $8\frac{7}{12} - 4\frac{5}{6}$ **9.** $2\frac{5}{6} - \frac{3}{8}$ **10.** $7 - 3\frac{2}{3}$ **11.** $10\frac{3}{4} - 10\frac{1}{8}$

12. $4\frac{1}{6} - 3\frac{8}{9}$ **13.** $3\frac{7}{8} - 2\frac{3}{8}$ **14.** $15\frac{9}{10} - 8\frac{1}{6}$ **15.** $4\frac{1}{5} - 3\frac{3}{5}$ **16.** $4\frac{2}{3} - 3$

17. $8\frac{2}{5} - 8$ **18.** $6 - 5\frac{3}{4}$ **19.** $2\frac{2}{5} - \frac{9}{10}$ **20.** $2\frac{1}{3} - 1\frac{3}{4}$ **21.** $1\frac{5}{12} - \frac{9}{16}$

22. Which of the exercises above could you compute mentally?

23. Number Sense Which of the numbers in Exercises 7–16 can be written as terminating decimals?

Ⓑ Reasoning and Problem Solving

Math and Science

Ladybug beetle

Stag beetle

Use the data file to find the difference in length for each pair of beetles.

24. Goliath and water scavenger

25. Stag and unicorn

26. Rhinoceros and ladybug

27. Ladybug and golden tortoise

28. **Writing in Math** Keanu's explanation for renaming mixed numbers is shown below. Is his method correct? Why or why not?

$$9\frac{1}{6} = \overset{8}{\cancel{9}}\frac{\overset{1}{1}}{6}$$
$$-2\frac{5}{6} = 2\frac{5}{6}$$
$$\overline{\hphantom{xxx}}$$
$$6\frac{6}{6} = 7$$

Data File

Type of Beetle	Length (in inches)
Goliath	$5\frac{1}{2}$
Stag	$2\frac{4}{5}$
Unicorn	$1\frac{7}{8}$
Water scavenger	$1\frac{3}{10}$
Caterpillar hunter	$1\frac{1}{5}$
Rhinoceros	1
Ladybug	$\frac{3}{10}$
Golden tortoise	$\frac{1}{4}$

Goliath beetle

C Extensions

Patterns Write the next three numbers in each pattern. Then give the rule.

29. $15\frac{1}{8}, 13\frac{3}{4}, 12\frac{3}{8}, \ldots$

30. $4\frac{4}{5}, 5\frac{1}{2}, 6\frac{1}{5}, \ldots$

 **Mixed Review and Test Prep**

Take It to the NET
Test Prep
www.scottforesman.com

Estimate each sum or difference.

31. $\frac{5}{6} + \frac{3}{5}$

32. $4\frac{1}{3} - 2\frac{7}{8}$

33. $6\frac{3}{4} + 6\frac{1}{8} + 10\frac{3}{10}$

Find each sum. Simplify if possible.

34. $3\frac{4}{5} + 8\frac{3}{4}$

35. $5\frac{5}{6} + \frac{7}{12}$

36. $\frac{7}{12} + 4\frac{1}{6} + 2\frac{1}{4}$

37. Algebra Evaluate the expression $4 \times 4 \div 2^2 - (2 + 2)$.

   A. 64   **C.** 4

   B. 8   **D.** 0

38. Algebra Evaluate the expression $30 \div (5 \times 3) + 4 \times 2$.

   A. 32   **C.** 14

   B. 20   **D.** 10

Discovery CHANNEL SCHOOL

Discover Math in Your World

A Braking Event

Perception time $\approx \frac{3}{4}$ second
Perception time is the average amount of time it takes a driver to perceive a braking event.

Reaction time $\approx \frac{3}{4}$ second
Reaction time is the time it takes the driver to move his or her foot from the gas pedal to the brake pedal.

1. What is the total time for perception and reaction?

2. A car going 60 mph covers 88 feet per second. How many feet would the car travel during the total time for perception and reaction?

Take It to the NET
Video and Activities
www.scottforesman.com

Key Idea
When computing, you can use mental math, paper and pencil, or a calculator, depending on the numbers involved.

Materials
• calculator

Choose a Computation Method

LEARN

What computation method should you use?

Mr. Womack's class made origami frogs and had a frog-jumping contest. Results appear in the table at the right.

✔ **WARM UP**

Use mental math if possible.

1. $3\frac{3}{8} - \frac{1}{8}$

2. $4\frac{5}{12} + 3\frac{1}{4}$

3. $2\frac{7}{10} + 11\frac{3}{10}$

4. $8\frac{5}{6} - 3\frac{1}{2}$

Origami Frog-Jumping Contest		
Student	Trial 1	Trial 2
Ali	$4\frac{5}{8}$ in.	$9\frac{1}{4}$ in.
Rosa	$7\frac{3}{4}$ in.	$2\frac{1}{4}$ in.
Kenji	$7\frac{5}{16}$ in.	$11\frac{1}{16}$ in.
Darrell	$4\frac{3}{4}$ in.	8 in.

Example A

Find the total distance Rosa's frog jumped.

Find $7\frac{3}{4} + 2\frac{1}{4}$.

This is easy to do using **mental math**.

$\frac{3}{4} + \frac{1}{4} = 1$;

$7 + 2 = 9$;

$9 + 1 = 10$.

So, $7\frac{3}{4} + 2\frac{1}{4} = 10$.

Example B

For Trial 1, how much farther did Kenji's frog jump than Darrell's frog?

Find $7\frac{5}{16} - 4\frac{3}{4}$.

There are two fractions, and it's easy to find a common denominator, so I'll use **paper and pencil**.

$$7\frac{5}{16} = 7\frac{5}{16} = 6\frac{21}{16}$$
$$- 4\frac{3}{4} = 4\frac{12}{16} = 4\frac{12}{16}$$
$$2\frac{9}{16}$$

Kenji's frog jumped $2\frac{9}{16}$ inches farther than Darrell's frog.

Example C

Find the average length of the jumps in Trial 1.

Find $(4\frac{5}{8} + 7\frac{3}{4} + 7\frac{5}{16} + 4\frac{3}{4}) \div 4$.

There are 4 fractions to add and they have different denominators. The sum needs to be divided by 4. I'll use a **calculator**.

Press: 4 [Unit] 5 [/] 8 [+] 7 [Unit]

3 [/] 4 [+] 7 [Unit] 5 [/]

16 [+] 4 [Unit] 3 [/] 4 [=]

[÷] 4 [=] [Ab/c]

Display: `6u 7/64`

TEST TALK

Think It Through

Sometimes using **mental math** or **paper and pencil** is faster than using a **calculator**.

✔ **Talk About It**

1. **Number Sense** Name some other numbers from the data table above that can easily be added using mental math.

Find each sum or difference. Tell what computation method you used.

1. $9\frac{1}{4} + 8$ **2.** $3\frac{1}{6} - \frac{2}{3}$ **3.** $4\frac{3}{4} + 5\frac{5}{6}$ **4.** $2\frac{5}{8} + 4\frac{5}{12} + 1\frac{17}{18}$

5. Number Sense Evan used paper and pencil to find $2\frac{1}{2} + \frac{3}{4}$. Could he have found the answer more quickly by using mental math? Explain.

PRACTICE   *For more practice, see Set 4-7 on p. 245.*

Ⓐ Skills and Understanding

Find each sum or difference. Tell what computation method you used.

6. $11\frac{5}{6} - 4\frac{3}{8}$ **7.** $7\frac{7}{9} + 4\frac{2}{9}$ **8.** $12\frac{1}{4} + 20\frac{3}{4}$ **9.** $4\frac{5}{16} - 3\frac{11}{12}$ **10.** $12 - 4\frac{5}{7}$

11. $14\frac{7}{8} + 5\frac{2}{15}$ **12.** $5\frac{3}{4} - 4\frac{5}{6}$ **13.** $8\frac{1}{5} + 3\frac{2}{5}$ **14.** $8\frac{1}{4} - 2\frac{2}{3}$ **15.** $23 + 17\frac{2}{3}$

16. $18\frac{9}{10} - 9\frac{3}{10}$ **17.** $6\frac{5}{8} - 2\frac{7}{10}$ **18.** $7\frac{1}{12} + 2\frac{1}{3}$ **19.** $5\frac{5}{6} - 5\frac{5}{8}$ **20.** $7\frac{3}{5} + 8\frac{1}{6}$

21. Number Sense Why is using a calculator NOT an efficient method for finding $3\frac{1}{4} + \frac{5}{8}$?

Ⓑ Reasoning and Problem Solving

22. How much higher was Blake's pole vault than his high jump?

23. Blake's triple jump was $29\frac{1}{4}$ feet more than his long jump. How long was his triple jump?

24. Writing in Math Would it make more sense to use mental math to find $13\frac{5}{6} + 8\frac{1}{2}$ or to find $5\frac{3}{4} + 2\frac{3}{8}$? Explain your reasoning.

Blake's Jumps
High jump: $7\frac{2}{3}$ ft
Pole vault: $18\frac{1}{2}$ ft
Long jump: $28\frac{1}{2}$ ft

🦉 Mixed Review and Test Prep

Take It to the NET
Test Prep
www.scottforesman.com

Find each difference. Estimate first.

25. $7\frac{3}{8} - 2\frac{5}{6}$ **26.** $10 - 4\frac{4}{15}$ **27.** $8\frac{1}{10} - 7\frac{6}{10}$ **28.** $5\frac{1}{3} - \frac{11}{12}$

Algebra Solve each equation.

29. $\frac{n}{0.3} = 6.6$ **30.** $36 = 3y$ **31.** $3.9 + m = 7.2$ **32.** $x - 15 = 15$

33. Which of the following is NOT a solution of $d + 3\frac{2}{3} = 5\frac{1}{6}$?

A. $\frac{3}{2}$ **B.** $\frac{9}{6}$ **C.** $1\frac{1}{2}$ **D.** $1\frac{2}{3}$

Problem-Solving Skill

Key Idea
Sometimes you need an exact answer to solve a problem, and sometimes an estimate is enough.

Exact Answer or Estimate

LEARN

Do you always need an exact answer to a word problem?

Look for phrases in the problem that suggest whether an exact answer or estimate is needed. If an estimate is all that's needed, you can often estimate using mental math.

Example A

On a map, Kim used a ruler to measure three line segments between cities. She measured $3\frac{1}{8}$, $2\frac{1}{2}$, and $2\frac{3}{16}$ inches. What was the total distance Kim measured?

Read and Understand

Step 1: What do you know?

The three distances are $3\frac{1}{8}$, $2\frac{1}{2}$ and $2\frac{3}{16}$.

Step 2: What are you trying to find?

The problem asks for the total distance. An exact answer is needed.

Example B

In 2002, each of 28 soccer teams had 21 players. Was this more or less than the 500 players who played in 2001?

Read and Understand

Step 1: What do you know?

In 2002, there were 28 teams with 21 players each.

In 2001, there were 500 players.

Step 2: What are you trying to find?

You need to know if the total is "more or less than 500," so an estimate is all that is needed.

✔ **Talk About It**

1. Would you use mental math or paper and pencil to solve Example A? Example B?

2. What is the answer to Example A? Example B?

3. Why was an exact answer needed in Example A, and an estimate needed in Example B?

Tell whether an exact answer or an estimate is needed. Then solve.

1. An advertisement is to have 8 lines of printing. The letters are to be $1\frac{1}{2}$ inches high with $\frac{1}{4}$ inch between lines. How much vertical space is needed for the printing?

2. Flight 719 carries 54 passengers, each with 2 suitcases. Each suitcase has an average weight of 36 pounds. If the airplane was built to carry 5,000 pounds of luggage, is the flight over or under its limit?

PRACTICE

For more practice, see Set 4-8 on p. 245.

Tell whether an exact answer or an estimate is needed. Then solve.

3. Jess is making 3 recipes that each require flour. One recipe calls for $\frac{2}{3}$ cup flour, another calls for $\frac{7}{8}$ cup, and the third requires $\frac{3}{4}$ cup. How much flour will Jess need?

4. To get the most for her money, should Alissha's grandmother buy 60 vitamins for $8.82 or 90 of the same vitamins for $10.85?

5. It is recommended that you tip a good waiter about $0.20 for each dollar of the meal's total cost. If your bill is $14.80, how much of a tip should you leave?

The map of Yolanda's neighborhood park is pictured at the right.

6. How much greater is the length of the park than the width?

7. When she walks, Yolanda covers $\frac{1}{10}$ mile every 2 minutes. Can she walk from the clubhouse to the pool in 8 minutes?

8. **Reasonableness** Yolanda has a goal to walk 3 miles each day. She decides that everyday she will walk the perimeter of the park twice. Will she meet or exceed her goal? Explain.

9. Using the map of the park above, describe an alternate walking route that Yolanda could take to reach her 3-mile-a-day goal.

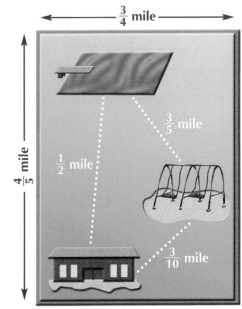

10. The coach of a baseball team has $500 with which to buy equipment. Including tax, a shirt costs $18.95, a cap costs $14.95, and a bat costs $28.95. Can the coach buy a shirt and a cap for each of the 15 players?

All text pages available online and on CD-ROM.

Problem-Solving Applications

Hovercraft A hovercraft can move faster than conventional boats because it floats above the water on a cushion of air. This cushion is created by large fans and it is contained by an inflatable skirt running around the bottom of the boat. Usually, large propellers are used to move the craft forward.

Trivia To make his first working model, the inventor of the hovercraft placed an empty cat food can inside an empty coffee can.

1 Two of the *Swift's* sister ships were stretched so that they could carry up to 424 passengers. If only 80 passengers traveled on these stretched hovercrafts, what fraction of the passenger cabin was filled? What fraction was empty?

2 It takes a conventional ferryboat more than 1 hour and 15 minutes to cross the English Channel. The *Swift* could cross the English channel in about 25 minutes. What fraction of a conventional ferryboat's time is this?

Using Key Facts

3 The length of the passenger cabin was about 0.63 times the total length of the *Swift*. What was the length of the passenger cabin?

4 During initial sea-trials, the *Swift* reached a record-breaking speed that was about 1.66 times faster than its cruising speed. How fast could this hovercraft travel? Write an equation that would help you solve this question.

Key Facts
Swift Hovercraft

- Weight when fully loaded = 200 tons
- Cruising speed = 60 knots
- Length = 40 meters
- Width = 23 meters
- Propeller diameter = 21 feet
- Maximum number of passengers = 254
- Maximum number of vehicles = 30

5 If only 24 cars were transported on a trip, what fraction of the car deck was filled? What fraction was empty?

6 **Writing in Math** Write your own fraction problem using any of the facts mentioned on these pages. Write the answer in a complete sentence.

Good News/ Bad News
Hovercraft can provide smooth, fast rides on calm waters, but they cannot handle large waves as well as conventional ships.

Paint Set	Number of Colors	Cost
Metallic	4	$3.80
Fluorescent	6	$5.46
Glossy	3	$2.58

7 **Decision Making** Racing radio-controlled model hovercrafts is a popular hobby in some areas. Suppose you needed to purchase one paint set for a small model. Which set of paints from the table above would you buy? How much would that paint cost per color? Is your choice of paint the most economical?

Review

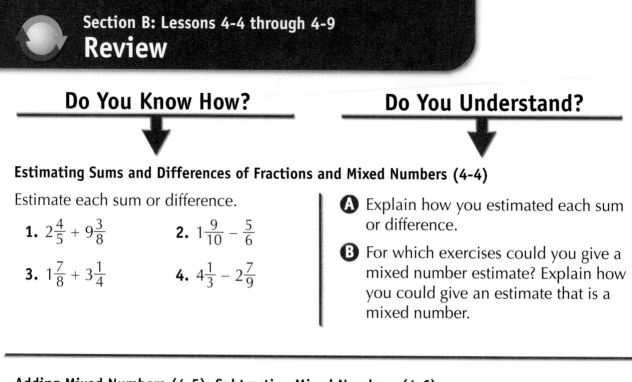

Do You Know How?

Do You Understand?

Estimating Sums and Differences of Fractions and Mixed Numbers (4-4)

Estimate each sum or difference.

1. $2\frac{4}{5} + 9\frac{3}{8}$

2. $1\frac{9}{10} - \frac{5}{6}$

3. $1\frac{7}{8} + 3\frac{1}{4}$

4. $4\frac{1}{3} - 2\frac{7}{9}$

A Explain how you estimated each sum or difference.

B For which exercises could you give a mixed number estimate? Explain how you could give an estimate that is a mixed number.

Adding Mixed Numbers (4-5); Subtracting Mixed Numbers (4-6)

Find each sum or difference. Simplify if possible.

5. $5\frac{3}{10} + 2\frac{9}{10}$

6. $4\frac{5}{6} - 2\frac{1}{6}$

7. $8 + 3\frac{4}{5}$

8. $5\frac{7}{8} - 3\frac{1}{3}$

9. $12\frac{8}{9} - 4$

10. $7\frac{3}{10} + 2\frac{3}{5}$

11. $4\frac{5}{8} + 2\frac{7}{12}$

12. $7 - 3\frac{3}{4}$

C Explain how you found the sum or difference in Exercises 7 and 9.

D Tell how you would round each addend in Exercise 11.

E Which exercises would be easiest to rewrite using decimals? Explain why.

Choose a Computation Method (4-7)

Find each answer. Tell what computation method you used.

13. $9\frac{1}{3} - 5\frac{7}{8}$

14. $2\frac{3}{4} + 15$

15. $11 - 5\frac{3}{5}$

16. $4\frac{1}{5} + 6\frac{4}{5}$

F Explain why you chose the method you used in Exercise 16.

Problem-Solving Skill: Exact Answer or Estimate? (4-8)

17. Janelle has $21. She estimates that 5 raffle tickets will cost $20. Can Janelle buy the tickets if each ticket costs $4.40? Explain.

G Tell how you decided whether to find an estimate or exact answer for Exercise 17.

MULTIPLE CHOICE

1. Find $9\frac{1}{3} - 2\frac{3}{4}$. (4-6)

A. $7\frac{4}{7}$ **B.** $7\frac{7}{12}$ **C.** $7\frac{1}{12}$ **D.** $6\frac{7}{12}$

2. Mrs. Anderson made $3\frac{1}{2}$ dozen apple muffins and $2\frac{1}{4}$ dozen bran muffins. How many muffins did she make altogether? (4-5)

A. $5\frac{3}{4}$ dozen   **B.** $5\frac{1}{4}$ dozen   **C.** $5\frac{1}{6}$ dozen   **D.** $1\frac{1}{4}$ dozen

> **Think It Through**
> For multiple-choice items, first **eliminate any unreasonable answers.**

FREE RESPONSE

Estimate each sum or difference. (4-4)

3. $\frac{3}{8} + \frac{7}{12}$ **4.** $\frac{11}{12} - \frac{1}{8}$ **5.** $6\frac{2}{5} + 3\frac{9}{10}$ **6.** $1\frac{1}{4} - \frac{7}{8}$

Find each sum or difference. Simplify if possible. (4-5, 4-6, 4-9)

7. $8\frac{5}{6} + 3\frac{5}{6}$ **8.** $3\frac{9}{16} - \frac{5}{16}$ **9.** $12\frac{7}{8} + 13$ **10.** $7\frac{2}{9} - 5$

11. $9 - 8\frac{3}{4}$ **12.** $2\frac{3}{8} + 6\frac{3}{5}$ **13.** $5\frac{5}{12} + 6\frac{7}{8}$ **14.** $4\frac{1}{3} - 2\frac{5}{12}$

Grandma Siegel is 65 years old. Her grandson Ian is 9 years old, and her granddaughter Caitlyn is 14 years old. Use the table at the right. (4-8, 4-9).

Botanic Garden Fees			
General Admission		**Garden Trains Exhibit**	
Adults	$6	Adults	$4.25
Under 12	$4	Under 12	$3.75
Seniors (62+)	$5	Seniors (62+)	$3.75

15. Grandma Siegel has $27. Does she have enough money to cover the general admission and trains exhibit for herself and her grandchildren? Tell whether an exact answer or estimate is needed.

16. Close Knit Outlet is having a sweater sale. The pre-tax sale price for any sweater is $17.95. About how much money should Ana bring to the outlet if she plans to buy 3 sweaters? (4-8, 4-9)

Writing in Math

17. When you are adding a mixed number in simplest form to a whole number, can you have a whole number solution? Why or why not? (4-5)

18. Give an example of when you need to rename a mixed number before subtracting. (4-6)

19. Which computation method would you use to find $5\frac{8}{15} + 2\frac{11}{12}$? Explain why. (4-7)

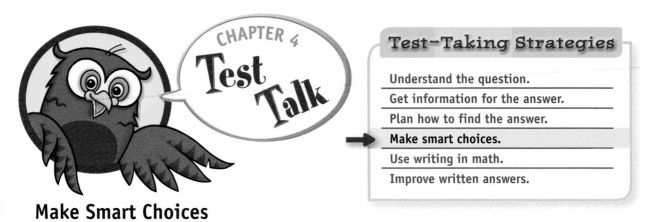

CHAPTER 4
Test Talk

Test-Taking Strategies
Understand the question.
Get information for the answer.
Plan how to find the answer.
Make smart choices.
Use writing in math.
Improve written answers.

Make Smart Choices

To answer a multiple-choice test question, you need to choose an answer from answer choices. The steps below will help you make a smart choice.

1. The following figures below are made with square tiles.

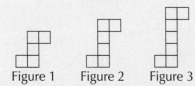

Figure 1   Figure 2   Figure 3

Which of the following shows Figure 4 based on this pattern?

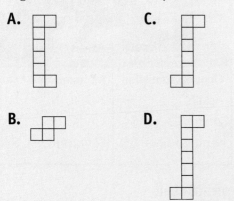

A.   C.

B.   D.

Understand the question.

• Look for important words. Finish the statement "I need to find ... ."

I need to find the next figure in the pattern.

Get information for the answer.

*The **picture** shows the first three figures of the pattern.*

Plan how to find the answer.

*I need to **look for a pattern** and use that pattern to choose the next figure. First I should look at the choices and eliminate those that do not make sense.*

Make Smart Choices.

• Eliminate wrong answers.

The number of tiles is increasing, so answer choice B is wrong.

Each figure shows a column of tiles with an extra tile at the top and bottom, one on the left side and one on the right. Answer choice A has both extra tiles on the right side, so answer choice A is wrong.

• Try working backward from an answer.

• Check answers for reasonableness; estimate.

The correct answer is either C or D. Both are reasonable because they both show the correct arrangement of tiles and both have more tiles than Figure 3.

*I'll use the pattern of the number of tiles to **make a smart choice.** The pattern is 5 tiles, 6 tiles, 7 tiles. So the next figure has to have 8 tiles.*

The correct answer is C.

2. The table below shows the number of marigolds planted in flats, or trays.

Number of flats	1	2	3	4	5
Number of marigolds	36	72	108	144	180

If f is the number of flats, which expression could be used to find the number of marigolds in f flats?

A. $180 \div f$

B. $36 + f$

C. $f - 36$

D. $36f$

Think It Through

*I need to find an expression that shows how many marigolds are in f flats. I should look for a pattern. The number of marigolds goes up 36 with each flat. Addition or multiplication might work. So I can **eliminate answer choices** A and C. Now I'll **work backward** and test answer choice B, 36 + f. If f = 1, then there are 36 + 1, or 37, marigolds. That's not right. So answer choice D must be correct. Just to be sure, I'll check if 36f works for f = 1, f = 2, f = 3, f = 4, and f = 5.*

Now it's your turn.

For each problem, give the answer and explain how you made your choice.

3. The table below shows the ages of Dominic and his mother at various times in their lives.

Age in years of Dominic's mother	35	40	45	50	55
Age in years of Dominic	6	11	16	21	26

If Dominic's mother is m years old, which expression could be used to find Dominic's age?

A. $m \div 5$

B. $m - 29$

C. $35m$

D. $m + 29$

4. Molly is making designs with rectangular tiles.

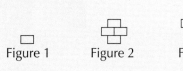

Figure 1   Figure 2   Figure 3

Which of the following shows Figure 4 based on this pattern?

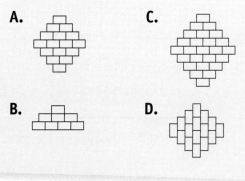

A.

C.

B.

D.

Self Check

We have hair color in common, because we both have brown hair.

Use **renaming** to add or subtract fractions. (Lessons 4-1, 4-2)

Find $\frac{5}{6} + \frac{5}{8}$.

1. Find the **lowest common denominator (LCD).** It is the **lowest common multiple (LCM)** of the two denominators.

6: 6, 12, 18, **24,** 30, 36, 42, 48
8: 8, 16, 24, 32, 40

2. Rename the fractions as equivalent fractions with the same denominator.

$$\frac{5}{6} = \frac{5 \times 4}{6 \times 4} = \frac{20}{24} \qquad \frac{5}{8} = \frac{5 \times 3}{8 \times 3} = \frac{15}{24}$$

3. Add. Then write improper fractions as mixed numbers in simplest form.

$$\frac{20}{24} + \frac{15}{24} = \frac{35}{24} = 1\frac{11}{24}$$

1. Find $\frac{6}{8} - \frac{1}{5}$ and $\frac{2}{3} + \frac{9}{10}$.

They are alike in that they have the same color hair.

Like denominators *are denominators that have the same value.* (p. 204)

They were unlike in that they are wearing different color shirts.

Unlike denominators *are denominators that have different values.* (p. 206)

Self Check

*The **lowest common multiple** is the smallest multiple two numbers both have.*

Look at the relationships between the numbers to discover the **pattern.** (Lesson 4-3)

Find the next three numbers in the pattern. Name the pattern.

$$12, 11\frac{1}{2}, 10\frac{1}{2}, 9, \underline{\quad}, \underline{\quad}, \underline{\quad}$$

$12 - \frac{1}{2} = 11\frac{1}{2}; \quad 11\frac{1}{2} - 1 = 10\frac{1}{2}; \quad 10\frac{1}{2} - 1\frac{1}{2} = 9;$

The pattern involves subtracting. Each number is subtracted by $\frac{1}{2}$ more.

$9 - 2 = 7; \qquad 7 - 2\frac{1}{2} = 4\frac{1}{2}; \qquad 4\frac{1}{2} - 3 = 1\frac{1}{2}.$ The next three numbers are $7, 4\frac{1}{2},$ and $1\frac{1}{2}.$

2. Find the next three numbers in the pattern: $\frac{3}{4}, \frac{6}{8}, \frac{9}{12}, \frac{12}{16}, \underline{\quad}, \underline{\quad}, \underline{\quad}.$

*The restaurant where my aunt works was renamed from "Large Taco" to "Taco Biggie." When fractions are **renamed** they have a new denominator but the same value.*

Self Check

Use **renaming** to add or subtract mixed numbers. (Lesson 4-4, 4-5, 4-6, 4-7)

Find $4\frac{8}{9} - 1\frac{5}{6}$.

1. Rewrite the fractions using the LCD.

9: 9, **18**, 27
6: 6, 12, **18**, 24

$$4\frac{8}{9} = 4\frac{8 \times 2}{9 \times 2} = 4\frac{16}{18} \qquad 1\frac{5}{6} = 1\frac{5 \times 3}{6 \times 3} = 1\frac{15}{18}$$

2. Subtract the fractions, then the whole numbers. Make sure the answer is in simplest form.

$$4\frac{16}{18} - 1\frac{15}{18} = \mathbf{3\frac{1}{18}}$$

3. Find $6\frac{5}{8} - 3\frac{1}{6}$ and $2\frac{2}{4} + 10\frac{2}{5}$.

Self Check

Decide whether you need an estimate or an exact answer when **solving problems.** (Lesson 4-8)

Decide whether an estimate or an exact answer is needed. Then solve.

Jillian walked $1\frac{1}{2}$ miles on Monday, $2\frac{1}{4}$ miles on Tuesday, and $1\frac{2}{5}$ miles on Wednesday. How far did she walk during the three days?

The question asks for the total, so an exact answer is needed. Find the total.

Find the total for Monday and Tuesday. $1\frac{1}{2} + 2\frac{1}{4} = 1\frac{2}{4} + 2\frac{1}{4} = 3\frac{3}{4}$.

Add Wednesday to the total. $3\frac{3}{4} + 1\frac{2}{5} = 3\frac{15}{20} + 1\frac{8}{20} = 4\frac{23}{20} = 5\frac{3}{20}$

Jillian walked $5\frac{3}{20}$ miles during the three days.

4. The student acting club sold 149 tickets to their spring play. They hope to donate at least $500 to charity from the money raised through ticket sales. If each ticket was sold for $3.75, will they be able to meet their goal?

1. $1\frac{11}{20}$ and $1\frac{17}{30}$; 2. $\frac{15}{18}$, $\frac{20}{24}$, $\frac{21}{28}$; 3. $3\frac{11}{24}$ and $12\frac{9}{10}$; 4. yes, the estimate for the total money raised is $4 \times 150 = \$600$

Chapter 4 Key Vocabulary and Concept Review 235

MULTIPLE CHOICE

Choose the correct letter for each answer.

1. Find $\frac{7}{8} + \frac{7}{8}$.

A. $\frac{7}{16}$ **C.** $1\frac{1}{2}$

B. $\frac{7}{8}$ **D.** $1\frac{3}{4}$

2. Find $\frac{11}{12} - \frac{2}{3}$.

A. $\frac{1}{4}$ **C.** $\frac{3}{4}$

B. $\frac{3}{5}$ **D.** 1

3. Choose the best estimate for $6\frac{1}{4} + 3\frac{3}{8}$.

A. 8   **C.** 11

B. 9   **D.** 12

4. Choose the best estimate for $5\frac{8}{9} - 3\frac{1}{8}$.

A. 5   **C.** 3

B. 4   **D.** 2

5. Find $7\frac{9}{10} + 2\frac{3}{10}$.

A. $5\frac{3}{5}$

B. $9\frac{1}{5}$

C. $9\frac{3}{5}$

D. $10\frac{1}{5}$

6. Find the sum of $3\frac{5}{6}$ and $2\frac{1}{4}$.

A. $1\frac{7}{12}$ **C.** $6\frac{1}{12}$

B. $5\frac{3}{5}$ **D.** $6\frac{1}{6}$

7. Find the difference between $3\frac{7}{10}$ and $\frac{2}{5}$.

A. $2\frac{3}{10}$ **C.** $3\frac{1}{2}$

B. $3\frac{3}{10}$ **D.** $4\frac{1}{10}$

8. Find $12\frac{3}{8} - 4\frac{7}{8}$.

A. $9\frac{1}{4}$ **C.** $7\frac{1}{2}$

B. $8\frac{1}{2}$ **D.** $7\frac{1}{4}$

9. Find the difference $8 - 7\frac{9}{10}$.

A. $17\frac{9}{10}$ **C.** $1\frac{1}{10}$

B. $17\frac{1}{10}$ **D.** $\frac{1}{10}$

10. Which number is NOT a common denominator for $\frac{3}{4}$, $\frac{5}{6}$, and $\frac{7}{8}$?

A. 72

B. 48

C. 24

D. 12

Think It Through
I should **watch for words like NOT.**

11. Name the next 3 numbers in the pattern 2, 4, 8, 16, 32, ▪, ▪, ▪.

A. 34, 36, 38

B. 48, 80, 128

C. 64, 128, 256

D. 42, 54, 68

For 12–14, refer to the table below.

School Play Ticket Information Adults:$6.50 Children: $3.50		
Day	Tickets Sold Adult	Tickets Sold Children
1	126	89
2	97	106
3	145	138
4	194	176

12. What was the total of the ticket sales for Day 3? Is an exact answer or estimate needed?

    A. $1,425.50; exact

    B. $1,000.50; exact

    C. $1,400; estimate

    D. $1,800; estimate

13. For all four days, were more children or adult tickets sold? About how many more? Is an exact answer or an estimate needed?

    A. adult; 37; exact

    B. adult; 70; estimate

    C. children; 80; estimate

    D. children; 37; exact

14. What would it cost for 1 grandparent, 1 parent, and 3 children to see the play? Is an exact answer or estimate needed?

    A. $23.50; exact

    B. $26.50; exact

    C. $23.00; estimate

    D. $27.00; estimate

FREE RESPONSE

Estimate each answer.

15. $2\frac{4}{5} + 1\frac{1}{3}$ **16.** $11\frac{1}{6} - 4\frac{7}{9}$

Find each answer. Simplify if possible.

17. $\frac{3}{4} + \frac{9}{16}$ **18.** $\frac{8}{9} - \frac{5}{9}$

19. $2\frac{7}{8} + 3\frac{1}{3}$ **20.** $5\frac{3}{4} - \frac{1}{6}$

21. Tell what computation method you would use to find $8 - 1\frac{2}{3}$.

Writing in Math

22. In the pattern below, how many triangles are needed to build the 5th shape? Explain the strategy you used.

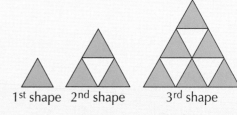

1st shape   2nd shape   3rd shape

23. Explain how to subtract $3\frac{5}{8}$ from $4\frac{1}{4}$.

24. Explain how you could use mental math to find $5\frac{3}{10} + 7\frac{3}{8} + 2\frac{1}{5} + 4\frac{5}{8}$.

Number and Operation

MULTIPLE CHOICE

1. In 1994, Leroy Burrell ran 100 meters in 9.85 seconds. Round his time to the nearest second.

   A. 9 seconds

   B. 9.8 seconds

   C. 9.9 seconds

   D. 10 seconds

2. Give the best estimate for the product 43×25.

   A. 800

   B. 1,000

   C. 1,500

   D. 2,000

FREE RESPONSE

3. Tamika made a fruit salad with $2\frac{1}{2}$ cups raspberries, $3\frac{3}{4}$ cups strawberries, and 4 cups sliced peaches. How many more cups of berries did she use than peaches?

4. One week, the prices for JGA stocks were 25.5, 24.75, 25.25, 29, and 30.5 points. What was the average for the 5 days?

5. Carnie answered $\frac{7}{8}$ of the test questions correctly. Write this fraction as a decimal.

Writing in Math

6. Explain how you would write 34.607 in expanded notation.

7. Explain how you would compare 3.57 and $3\frac{3}{5}$.

Geometry and Measurement

MULTIPLE CHOICE

8. An angle that measures 90° is

   A. a straight angle.

   B. a right angle.

   C. an obtuse angle.

   D. an acute angle.

9. Betsy's biology lab starts at 11:30 A.M. The lab lasts 1 hour 45 minutes. At what time does Betsy's lab end?

   A. 12:15 A.M.   **C.** 12:15 P.M.

   B. 1:15 A.M.   **D.** 1:15 P.M.

FREE RESPONSE

10. A pattern for a woven wall hanging calls for different colored ribbon. How many meters of ribbon are called for altogether?

Color	Length (cm)
Green	150
Yellow	120
Blue	150
Pink	120

11. Give all the names that apply to the figure.

Writing in Math

12. Explain the difference between the perimeter and area of a rectangle.

13. Name two things you would measure in feet. Explain your choices.

Data Analysis and Probability

MULTIPLE CHOICE

14. How many different coin and color possibilities are there if you toss a coin and spin the spinner?

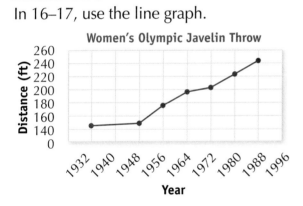

 A. 4   **C.** 8

 B. 6   **D.** 16

15. What type of graph would NOT be best for showing the ethnic makeup of a school's population?

 A. circle graph   **C.** line graph

 B. bar graph   **D.** pictograph

FREE RESPONSE

In 16–17, use the line graph.

Women's Olympic Javelin Throw

(Line graph: Distance (ft) on y-axis from 0, 140 to 260; Year on x-axis 1932, 1940, 1948, 1956, 1964, 1972, 1980, 1988, 1996.)

16. Which was the first year to have a distance greater than 200 feet?

17. What distance might you predict for 1996?

Writing in Math

18. There are 12 red counters and 6 blue counters in a bag. Explain how you would determine the probability of choosing a blue counter.

Algebra

MULTIPLE CHOICE

19. Which equation has the solution $x = 4.5$?

 A. $x - 2 = 6.5$

 B. $\frac{x}{3} = 13.5$

 C. $2x = 9$

 D. $x + 2 = 2.5$

20. Calculate the value of $2 \times 3.5 + 8 \div 0.5 + 1.5$.

 A. 11   **C.** 31.5

 B. 24.5   **D.** 47.5

21. Solve $\frac{n}{1.2} = 6$.

 A. $n = 0.2$ **C.** $n = 7.2$

 B. $n = 5$ **D.** $n = 72$

FREE RESPONSE

22. Find the next 3 numbers in this pattern. Then give the rule.
 1, 1, 2, 3, 5, 8, 13, ▢, ▢, ▢

23. Gary's best time for the 100-meter dash is 11.6 seconds. This time is 1.68 seconds more than the record time set by Carl Lewis in 1988. What was Lewis's time?

24. An orange has 62 calories. It has x fewer calories than a nectarine. Write an expression for the number of calories a nectarine has.

Writing in Math

25. Explain how you would find 8×52 mentally.

26. Explain how you would solve and check $\frac{n}{6} = 3.6$.

Set 4-1 (pages 204–205)

Find $\frac{11}{15} + \frac{8}{15}$.

$\frac{11}{15} + \frac{8}{15} = \frac{19}{15}$ The denominators are the same, so just add the numerators.

$= 1\frac{4}{15}$ Since 19 is greater than 15, write the answer as a mixed number.

Find $\frac{7}{8} - \frac{3}{8}$.

$\frac{7}{8} - \frac{3}{8} = \frac{4}{8}$ The denominators are the same, so just subtract the numerators.

$= \frac{1}{2}$ Simplify.

Remember when the numerator is greater than the denominator, your answer will be a mixed number.

1. $\frac{5}{7} + \frac{3}{7}$ **2.** $\frac{8}{9} - \frac{2}{9}$

3. $\frac{12}{13} - \frac{10}{13}$ **4.** $\frac{7}{8} + \frac{3}{8}$

5. $\frac{7}{10} - \frac{3}{10}$ **6.** $\frac{4}{15} + \frac{13}{15}$

Set 4-2 (pages 206–209)

Find $\frac{3}{4} + \frac{5}{6}$.

The LCD of 4 and 6 is 12.

$\frac{3}{4} = \frac{9}{12}$

$+ \frac{5}{6} = + \frac{10}{12}$

Add the fractions.

$\frac{9}{12}$

$+ \frac{10}{12}$

$\frac{19}{12}$

Simplify if possible.

$\frac{19}{12} = 1\frac{7}{12}$

Find $\frac{4}{5} - \frac{3}{10}$.

The LCD of 5 and 10 is 10.

$\frac{4}{5} = \frac{8}{10}$

$- \frac{3}{10} = - \frac{3}{10}$

Subtract the fractions.

$\frac{8}{10}$

$- \frac{3}{10}$

$\frac{5}{10}$

Simplify if possible.

$\frac{5}{10} = \frac{1}{2}$

Remember that the least common denominator (LCD) is the least common multiple (LCM) of the denominators.

1. $\frac{2}{5} + \frac{1}{4}$ **2.** $\frac{6}{7} - \frac{1}{2}$

3. $\frac{2}{3} + \frac{1}{4}$ **4.** $\frac{7}{9} - \frac{2}{3}$

5. $\frac{5}{8} - \frac{1}{6}$ **6.** $\frac{3}{10} + \frac{1}{8}$

7. $\frac{3}{8} + \frac{1}{3}$ **8.** $\frac{9}{10} - \frac{3}{5}$

9. $\frac{15}{16} - \frac{5}{8}$ **10.** $\frac{3}{8} + \frac{5}{12}$

Set 4-3 (pages 212–213)

Find the next 3 numbers.

$\frac{1}{3}$, 1, $1\frac{2}{3}$, $2\frac{1}{3}$, 3, ▨, ▨, ▨

The pattern is "add $\frac{2}{3}$."

$3 + \frac{2}{3} = 3\frac{2}{3}$; $3\frac{2}{3} + \frac{2}{3} = 4\frac{1}{3}$; $4\frac{1}{3} + \frac{2}{3} = 5$

The next three numbers are $3\frac{2}{3}$, $4\frac{1}{3}$, 5.

Remember you can subtract the numbers to discover a pattern.

1. 10, $9\frac{1}{4}$, $8\frac{1}{2}$, $7\frac{3}{4}$, ▨, ▨, ▨

2. 3, $3\frac{1}{10}$, $3\frac{1}{5}$, $3\frac{3}{10}$, $3\frac{2}{5}$, ▨, ▨, ▨

Estimate $1\frac{5}{6} + 2\frac{1}{4}$.

$1\frac{5}{6} + 2\frac{1}{4}$

$\downarrow \quad \downarrow$ Round to the nearest whole number.

$2 \ + \ 2 = 4$

$1\frac{5}{6} + 2\frac{1}{4} \approx 4$

Estimate $5\frac{5}{8} - 3\frac{1}{6}$.

$5\frac{5}{8} - 3\frac{1}{6}$

$\downarrow \quad \downarrow$ Round to the nearest whole number.

$6 \ - \ 3 = 3$

$5\frac{5}{8} - 3\frac{1}{6} \approx 3$

Remember you can think of the numbers on a number line to help you estimate.

1. $2\frac{1}{8} + 3\frac{4}{5}$ **2.** $2\frac{7}{8} - \frac{1}{3}$

3. $4\frac{2}{5} + 9\frac{3}{4}$ **4.** $12\frac{3}{8} - 9\frac{5}{7}$

5. $2\frac{1}{3} + 5\frac{4}{9}$ **6.** $\frac{8}{11} + \frac{4}{5}$

7. $11\frac{1}{4} - \frac{3}{10}$ **8.** $7\frac{1}{2} - 3\frac{7}{10}$

9. $2\frac{11}{12} + 8\frac{1}{16}$ **10.** $9\frac{1}{9} - 8\frac{7}{8}$

Find $8\frac{4}{5} + 6\frac{3}{4}$.

The LCD of 5 and 4 is 20.

$\frac{4}{5} = \frac{16}{20}$

$\frac{3}{4} = \frac{15}{20}$

Add.

$8\frac{16}{20}$

$+ \ 6\frac{15}{20}$

$\overline{\quad 14\frac{31}{20}}$

Simplify if possible.

$14\frac{31}{20} =$

$14 + \frac{20}{20} + \frac{11}{20}$

$= 15\frac{11}{20}$

Remember to write equivalent fractions with the least common denominator.

1. $13\frac{1}{6} + 9\frac{5}{12}$ **2.** $8\frac{7}{8} + 3\frac{1}{4}$

3. $6\frac{2}{9} + 3\frac{5}{6}$ **4.** $5\frac{4}{5} + 3\frac{1}{3}$

5. $4\frac{7}{10} + 8\frac{1}{4}$ **6.** $3\frac{5}{8} + 1\frac{3}{8}$

7. $15\frac{3}{4} + 7\frac{7}{10}$ **8.** $23\frac{9}{16} + 19\frac{3}{4}$

Find $13\frac{1}{6} - 7\frac{5}{6}$. Estimate: $13 - 8 = 5$

$13\frac{1}{6} = 12 + \frac{6}{6} + \frac{1}{6} = 12\frac{7}{6}$ ← Since $\frac{5}{6} > \frac{1}{6}$, rename $13\frac{1}{6}$ to show more sixths.

$- \ 7\frac{5}{6}$

$12\frac{7}{6}$

$- \ 7\frac{5}{6}$

$\overline{\quad 5\frac{2}{6}} = 5\frac{1}{3}$

Remember that you can rename a whole number as a mixed number.

1. $23 - 18\frac{1}{3}$ **2.** $4\frac{7}{8} - 2\frac{5}{8}$

3. $12\frac{1}{4} - 3\frac{1}{2}$ **4.** $18 - 9\frac{3}{5}$

5. $14\frac{1}{3} - 5\frac{2}{3}$ **6.** $12\frac{1}{4} - 7\frac{5}{6}$

7. $15\frac{3}{8} - 9\frac{5}{6}$ **8.** $14\frac{4}{9} - 6\frac{5}{6}$

Set 4-7 (pages 224–225)

Find $4\frac{3}{4} + 7\frac{1}{4}$.

Since the fractions are easy to add, use mental math.

$4\frac{3}{4} + 7\frac{1}{4} = 12$

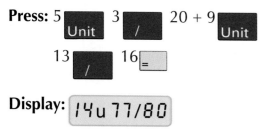

$\frac{3}{4} + \frac{1}{4} = 1; 4 + 7 + 1 = 12$

Find $2\frac{3}{7} + 4\frac{1}{4}$.

Since the fractions need to be renamed, use paper and pencil.

$$2\frac{3}{7} = 2\frac{12}{28}$$
$$+ 4\frac{1}{4} = + 4\frac{7}{28}$$
$$\overline{\phantom{+ 4\frac{1}{4} = }6\frac{19}{28}}$$

Find $5\frac{3}{20} + 9\frac{13}{16}$.

The fractions are not easy to add. So, use a calculator.

Press: 5 [Unit] 3 [/] 20 + 9 [Unit]

13 [/] 16 [=]

Display: $14u\,77/80$

Remember to decide which computation method would be the best for a given problem.

Find each answer. Tell what computation method you used.

1. $3\frac{1}{3} + 2\frac{1}{2} + 5\frac{2}{3}$

2. $9\frac{3}{8} - 4\frac{1}{25}$

3. $6\frac{1}{4} + 5\frac{2}{5}$

4. $18\frac{5}{12} - 16\frac{7}{8}$

5. $3\frac{1}{6} - 2\frac{3}{4}$

6. $8\frac{9}{10} + 3\frac{1}{2}$

7. $7\frac{7}{8} + 3\frac{1}{2} + 1\frac{1}{4} + \frac{1}{4} + 2\frac{1}{8}$

8. $5\frac{3}{10} + 8\frac{1}{6} + 3\frac{3}{4} + 2\frac{7}{8} + 1\frac{1}{2}$

Set 4-8 (pages 226–227)

The length of Maria's desk is $60\frac{3}{4}$ inches and the width is $34\frac{1}{4}$ inches. How much longer is the length than the width? Tell whether an exact answer or estimate is needed.

Finding the difference in measurements requires an exact answer.

$$60\frac{3}{4}$$
$$- 34\frac{1}{4}$$
$$\overline{\phantom{-34\frac{1}{4}}26\frac{2}{4} = 26\frac{1}{2}}$$

Her desk is $26\frac{1}{2}$ inches longer than it is wide.

Remember to look for key words that will help you determine whether to find an estimate or exact answer.

Lisa ran $1\frac{1}{2}$ mi on Monday, $2\frac{3}{4}$ mi on Wednesday, and $1\frac{7}{8}$ mi. on Friday.

1. What was Lisa's total distance for the three days?

2. How much farther did Lisa run on Wednesday than on Monday?

3. About how much farther did Lisa run on Wednesday than on Friday?

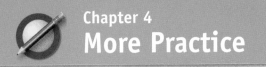

Take It to the NET
More Practice
www.scottforesman.com

Set 4-1 (pages 204–205)

Find each sum or difference. Simplify if possible.

1. $\frac{5}{6} - \frac{1}{6}$ **2.** $\frac{1}{8} + \frac{3}{8}$ **3.** $\frac{5}{16} - \frac{3}{16}$ **4.** $\frac{7}{9} - \frac{4}{9}$

5. $\frac{4}{9} + \frac{8}{9}$ **6.** $\frac{3}{4} + \frac{3}{4}$ **7.** $\frac{8}{15} - \frac{2}{15}$ **8.** $\frac{8}{11} - \frac{2}{11}$

9. $\frac{5}{6} + \frac{5}{6}$ **10.** $\frac{7}{10} + \frac{6}{10}$ **11.** $\frac{11}{8} - \frac{3}{8}$ **12.** $\frac{3}{7} + \frac{5}{7}$

13. $\frac{9}{20} - \frac{3}{20}$ **14.** $\frac{3}{16} + \frac{13}{16}$ **15.** $\frac{7}{12} + \frac{11}{12}$ **16.** $\frac{11}{18} - \frac{5}{18}$

17. Marcus had $\frac{3}{4}$ cup of milk in a bowl. He added $\frac{1}{2}$ cup of milk. How much did he have in all?

Set 4-2 (pages 206–209)

Find each sum or difference. Simplify if possible.

1. $\frac{7}{10} - \frac{5}{8}$ **2.** $\frac{7}{8} + \frac{1}{12}$ **3.** $\frac{15}{16} - \frac{3}{8}$ **4.** $\frac{9}{10} - \frac{1}{5}$

5. $\frac{1}{8} + \frac{5}{6}$ **6.** $\frac{2}{3} + \frac{4}{5}$ **7.** $\frac{5}{8} - \frac{7}{16}$ **8.** $\frac{3}{4} + \frac{7}{12}$

9. $\frac{7}{9} - \frac{2}{3}$ **10.** $\frac{1}{5} + \frac{1}{6}$ **11.** $\frac{3}{4} - \frac{1}{5}$ **12.** $\frac{8}{9} + \frac{1}{6}$

13. $\frac{7}{8} + \frac{1}{3}$ **14.** $\frac{3}{4} - \frac{1}{10}$ **15.** $\frac{3}{5} + \frac{1}{3}$ **16.** $\frac{11}{12} - \frac{1}{4}$

17. Tom and Leona measured the rainfall in their neighborhoods. Tom measured $\frac{5}{8}$ inch and Leona measured $\frac{3}{4}$ inch How much more rain fell in Leona's neighborhood?

Set 4-3 (pages 212–213)

Find the missing numbers, or draw the next 3 figures.

1. $3, 3\frac{4}{5}, 4\frac{3}{5}, 5\frac{2}{5},$, ,   **2.**   **3.**

x	y	z
12	24	36
21	42	63
30	60	90
?	?	117
?	96	?

4. $7\frac{9}{10}, 7\frac{1}{2}, 7\frac{1}{10}, 6\frac{7}{10},$, ,

5. Susana worked 1 hour on Monday, $2\frac{1}{2}$ hours on Tuesday, 4 hours on Wednesday. If this pattern continues, how long will she work on Friday?

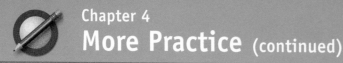

Set 4-4 (pages 216–217)

Estimate each sum or difference.

1. $2\frac{2}{3} + 1\frac{1}{5}$ **2.** $7\frac{3}{8} + 3\frac{7}{12}$ **3.** $2\frac{3}{4} - 1\frac{2}{9}$ **4.** $2\frac{5}{6} - 1\frac{1}{7}$

5. $9\frac{1}{3} + 5\frac{4}{5}$ **6.** $9\frac{7}{8} - 3\frac{3}{4}$ **7.** $12\frac{1}{15} + 7\frac{5}{16}$ **8.** $6\frac{3}{7} - 2\frac{3}{5}$

9. $4\frac{5}{8} + 2\frac{2}{3}$ **10.** $3\frac{9}{10} - 3\frac{1}{3}$ **11.** $9\frac{1}{3} + 3\frac{4}{5}$ **12.** $16\frac{1}{5} - 10\frac{3}{4}$

13. Lorissa worked $7\frac{3}{4}$ hours on Saturday and $5\frac{1}{3}$ hours on Sunday. Estimate her total weekend hours.

Set 4-5 (pages 218–219)

Find each sum. Simplify if possible.

1. $7\frac{5}{6} + 3\frac{1}{4}$ **2.** $9\frac{2}{3} + 2\frac{1}{2}$ **3.** $6\frac{3}{5} + 1\frac{3}{4}$ **4.** $8\frac{7}{9} + 3\frac{2}{3}$

5. $18\frac{3}{8} + 2\frac{1}{6}$ **6.** $12\frac{1}{2} + 6\frac{7}{8}$ **7.** $1\frac{2}{5} + 3\frac{1}{3}$ **8.** $10\frac{7}{10} + 3\frac{2}{5}$

9. $2\frac{1}{5} + 2\frac{3}{10}$ **10.** $5\frac{3}{5} + 4\frac{1}{4}$ **11.** $11\frac{7}{10} + 2\frac{3}{4}$ **12.** $9\frac{1}{2} + 6\frac{1}{4}$

13. Sonia has $1\frac{3}{4}$ cups of apples and $2\frac{1}{3}$ cups of grapes. How many cups of fruit does she have?

Set 4-6 (pages 220–223)

Find each difference. Simplify if possible.

1. $8 - 3\frac{2}{3}$ **2.** $7\frac{1}{6} - 2\frac{3}{4}$ **3.** $18\frac{1}{2} - 12\frac{7}{8}$ **4.** $5\frac{1}{4} - 2\frac{9}{10}$

5. $9\frac{2}{5} - 4\frac{5}{6}$ **6.** $3\frac{3}{4} - 1\frac{1}{4}$ **7.** $8\frac{1}{3} - 2\frac{7}{8}$ **8.** $6 - 5\frac{3}{4}$

9. $8\frac{1}{4} - 7\frac{5}{8}$ **10.** $4\frac{1}{3} - 3\frac{8}{9}$ **11.** $7\frac{3}{8} - 1\frac{7}{8}$ **12.** $3\frac{2}{5} - 1\frac{7}{10}$

13. Last week Joe ran $5\frac{7}{8}$ miles and Jocelyn ran $6\frac{1}{2}$ miles. How much farther did Jocelyn run?

14. In San Diego, California, the shortest day of the year has 10 hours of daylight. In Bangor, Maine, the shortest day of the year has $8\frac{14}{15}$ hours of daylight. How much more daylight does San Diego have on the shortest day than Bangor?

Take It to the NET
More Practice
www.scottforesman.com

Set 4-7 (pages 224–225)

Find each sum or difference. Tell what computation method you used.

1. $3\frac{1}{4} + 5\frac{5}{6}$

2. $2\frac{3}{10} + 9\frac{2}{5}$

3. $7\frac{13}{28} - 4\frac{11}{21}$

4. $7 + 2\frac{1}{2}$

5. $8\frac{4}{7} - 3\frac{4}{5}$

6. $5\frac{3}{8} - 2\frac{3}{16}$

7. $6 - 3\frac{2}{3}$

8. $3\frac{1}{4} + 8\frac{3}{4}$

9. $7\frac{1}{6} - 3\frac{2}{5}$

10. $11\frac{3}{4} - 8\frac{1}{8}$

11. $9\frac{14}{25} + 6\frac{11}{20}$

12. $9\frac{1}{2} - 4 + 2\frac{1}{2}$

Set 4-8 (pages 226–227)

For Exercises 1–3, use the table at the right. Tell whether an exact answer or an estimate is needed. Then solve.

1. How many more hours did Julian work on Monday than Tuesday?

2. About how many hours did Julian work in that week?

3. What was the total number of hours Julian worked on Monday and Tuesday?

Julian's Work Schedule	
Day	**Hours Worked**
Monday	$7\frac{3}{4}$
Tuesday	$4\frac{1}{4}$
Wednesday	$8\frac{1}{2}$
Thursday	$5\frac{1}{12}$
Friday	$6\frac{11}{12}$

Tell whether an exact answer or an estimate is needed. Then solve.

4. Calista wants to plant tomato seeds in her garden. Packets of seeds cost $0.89 each. How much money should Calista take to the store to buy six packets?

5. Satisfied customers often will acknowledge good service by leaving a tip of about $0.20 for each dollar spent. If a bill is $50.23, how much tip should a satisfied customer leave?

6. Dimitri lives near a river that floods. He should evacuate his home when the river reaches 28 feet. The river is now $21\frac{7}{10}$ feet and is predicted to rise another $6\frac{1}{2}$ feet this evening. Will Dimitri need to evacuate?

DIAGNOSING READINESS

A Vocabulary
(pages 40, 44, 160, 168)

Choose the best term from the box.

1. A quantity that can change or vary is called a __?__.

2. A __?__ combines a whole number and a fraction.

3. Multiplication and division are __?__.

4. The __?__ of a proper fraction is less than its __?__.

Vocabulary

- **mixed number** *(p. 168)*
- **improper fraction** *(p. 168)*
- **inverse operations** *(p. 44)*
- **denominator** *(p. 160)*
- **variable** *(p. 40)*
- **numerator** *(p. 160)*

B Multiplication and Division *(pages 24–27)*

Multiply or divide.

5. 3×8

6. $45 \div 9$

7. $(5 \times 6) \div 3$

8. $60 \div (4 \times 3)$

9. $72 \div (3 \times 3)$

10. $(88 \div 4) \times 5$

11. $(36 \div 9) \times 7$

12. $(12 \times 9) \div 4$

13. Mr. Bruckner bought 7 packs of pencils. There are 12 pencils in each pack. If he wants to divide the pencils evenly among 18 students, how many pencils will each student get? Will there be any pencils left over? If so, how many?

Do You Know...

How many bees would it take to produce $\frac{1}{2}$ teaspoon of honey?

You will find out in Lesson 5-11.

C Fractions and Mixed Numbers

(pages 160–163, 168–169, 216–217)

Write the shaded part as a fraction.

14.

15.

Round to the nearest whole number.

16. $3\frac{3}{4}$

17. $5\frac{5}{6}$

18. $\frac{3}{5}$

19. $9\frac{1}{5}$

20. $7\frac{3}{8}$

21. $\frac{2}{11}$

Write each mixed number as an improper fraction.

22. $3\frac{3}{8}$

23. $1\frac{4}{5}$

24. $2\frac{1}{3}$

D Solving Equations

(pages 48–51, 112–113)

Solve.

25. $7a = 28$

26. $g \div 9 = 6$

27. $55 = h + 13$

28. $36 = 3.6t$

29. $1.5y = 1.5$

30. $352 = 8m$

31. $71 = k - 583$

32. $n \div 43 = 2$

33. Jen takes pictures for the yearbook. Each roll of Jen's film allows her to take 36 photographs. Write and solve an equation to find the number of rolls of film Jen needs to take 1,260 photographs.

Think It Through

- I can **draw a picture** to show the main idea.

- I can **use what I know** about adding fractions to multiply with fractions.

Multiplying a Fraction and a Whole Number

✓ WARM UP

1. $\frac{1}{4} + \frac{1}{4} + \frac{1}{4}$ 2. $36 \div 4$

3. $\frac{2}{3} + \frac{2}{3}$ 4. $48 \div 8$

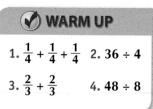

LEARN

What does it mean to multiply a fraction and a whole number?

Example A

One batch of an oatmeal muffin recipe uses $\frac{3}{4}$ cup of rolled oats. How many cups of rolled oats are needed to make 8 batches?

Find $8 \times \frac{3}{4}$.

The model shows 8 groups of $\frac{3}{4}$.

$8 \times \frac{3}{4} = \frac{3}{4} + \frac{3}{4} + \frac{3}{4} + \frac{3}{4} + \frac{3}{4} + \frac{3}{4} + \frac{3}{4} + \frac{3}{4} = \frac{24}{4} = 6.$

Six cups are needed for 8 batches.

Example B

Seline read 8 books. Three fourths of them were mysteries. How many mystery books did Seline read?

Find $\frac{3}{4}$ of 8, or $\frac{3}{4} \times 8$.

The model shows $\frac{3}{4}$ of 8 wholes.

$\frac{3}{4} \times 8 = 6.$

Seline read 6 mystery books.

✓ Talk About It

1. How are the products $8 \times \frac{3}{4}$ and $\frac{3}{4}$ of 8 the same? How are they represented differently?

2. Draw a number line to find $6 \times \frac{1}{6}$.

What are some ways to multiply a fraction and a whole number?

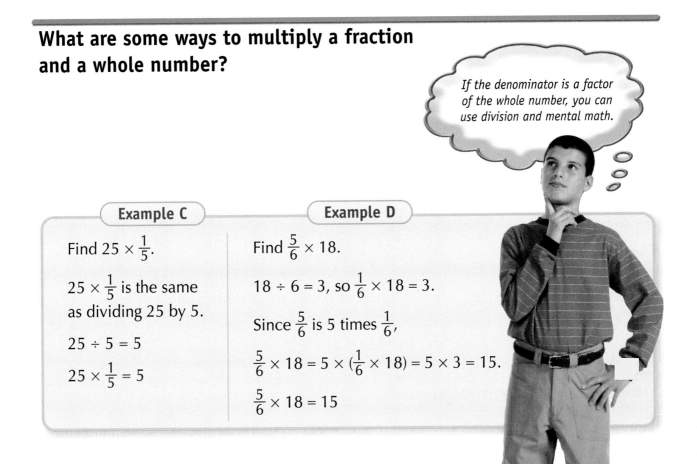

If the denominator is a factor of the whole number, you can use division and mental math.

Example C

Find $25 \times \frac{1}{5}$.

$25 \times \frac{1}{5}$ is the same as dividing 25 by 5.

$25 \div 5 = 5$

$25 \times \frac{1}{5} = 5$

Example D

Find $\frac{5}{6} \times 18$.

$18 \div 6 = 3$, so $\frac{1}{6} \times 18 = 3$.

Since $\frac{5}{6}$ is 5 times $\frac{1}{6}$,

$\frac{5}{6} \times 18 = 5 \times (\frac{1}{6} \times 18) = 5 \times 3 = 15$.

$\frac{5}{6} \times 18 = 15$

✔ Talk About It

3. Use mental math to find the number of cups of rolled oats needed for 20 batches in Example A.

4. Could you use division and mental math to find $\frac{3}{4}$ of 18? Explain.

5. **Number Sense** Explain how to find $\frac{7}{10}$ of 100.

CHECK ✔

For another example, see Set 5-1 on p. 292.

Find each product.

1. $12 \times \frac{1}{3}$ **2.** $\frac{5}{6} \times 24$ **3.** $\frac{2}{3}$ of 27   **4.** $\frac{7}{8}$ of 80

5. $45 \times \frac{3}{5}$ **6.** $\frac{1}{9} \times 36$ **7.** $\frac{4}{7}$ of 28   **8.** $\frac{11}{13} \times 39$

9. Reasoning Without multiplying, tell whether $18 \times \frac{8}{9}$ is greater than or less than 18. How do you know?

For more practice, see Set 5-1 on p. 295.

PRACTICE

Ⓐ Skills and Understanding

Find each product.

10. $\frac{2}{3} \times 12$ **11.** $15 \times \frac{4}{5}$ **12.** $\frac{3}{10} \times 90$ **13.** $45 \times \frac{8}{9}$

14. $\frac{2}{5}$ of 35 **15.** $\frac{5}{16}$ of 48 **16.** $\frac{7}{10}$ of 800 **17.** $\frac{1}{9}$ of 54

18. $\frac{5}{7} \times 28$ **19.** $72 \times \frac{5}{6}$ **20.** $\frac{9}{10}$ of 50 **21.** $\frac{24}{25}$ of 100

22. Reasoning Can you use division and mental math to find $15 \times \frac{3}{10}$? Explain.

23. Number Sense Find $30 \times \frac{3}{5}$. Change the numbers to decimals and multiply. Are the products the same? Explain.

Ⓑ Reasoning and Problem Solving

🎵 Math and Music

The graph at the right shows the fraction of students that make up each section of a 60-member orchestra. Find the number of students in each section.

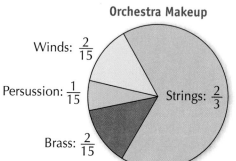

Orchestra Makeup

Winds: $\frac{2}{15}$

Persussion: $\frac{1}{15}$

Brass: $\frac{2}{15}$

Strings: $\frac{2}{3}$

24. Strings **25.** Brass

26. Percussion **27.** Winds

28. What fraction of the orchestra is shown by the brass and percussion sections combined?

29. The two dozen roses that Tamika ordered to distribute at the final curtain call are shown at the right. She gives half of them to the conductor. She gives half of the remaining roses to the pianist and the other half to the vocalist. How many roses does the vocalist get?

30. <u>Writing in Math</u> Is the explanation below correct? If not, tell why and write a correct response.

Find $42 \times \frac{6}{7}$.

$42 \times \frac{6}{7} = 42 \times \frac{1}{6} = 7$ and $7 \times 6 = 42$.

C Extensions

31. Algebra Simplify the expression $20 - \frac{1}{6}(55 + 35)$.

32. Reasoning Two thirds of a number is 18. Find the number.

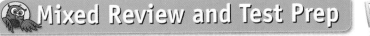

Take It to the NET
Test Prep
www.scottforesman.com

Tell whether an exact answer or estimate is needed. Then solve.

33. It costs $450 per day to maintain and run the arboretum. Admission to the arboretum is $2.50. Will the arboretum make a profit if at least 200 people pay admission each day? Explain.

Find each sum or difference. Tell what computation method you used.

34. $10\frac{1}{5} - 5\frac{3}{4}$

35. $\frac{4}{7} + \frac{8}{9}$

36. $6 - 3\frac{2}{5}$

37. Algebra Find $4 + 2 \times 3 - 4 \div 2$.

A. 3   **B.** 7   **C.** 8   **D.** 16

Enrichment

Writing Repeating Decimals as Fractions

A short way of writing the repeating decimal $0.323232\ldots$ is $0.\overline{32}$. You can write this repeating decimal as a fraction.

Write $1n = 0.323232\ldots$ Since two digits repeat, multiply both sides by 100 to get $100n = 32.323232\ldots$

$$100n = 32.323232\ldots$$
$$- \quad 1n = 0.323232\ldots$$
$$99n = 32$$

Subtract and solve for n.

$$n = \frac{32}{99}$$

To write $0.1\overline{643}$ as a fraction, write $1n = 0.1643643\ldots$

$$1,000n = 164.3643643\ldots$$
$$- \quad 1n = 0.1643643\ldots$$
$$999n = 164.2$$

Three digits repeat, so multiply both sides by 1,000 to get $1,000n = 164.3643643\ldots$

Subtract and solve for n. Simplify.

$$n = \frac{164.2}{999} = \frac{1,642}{9,990} = \frac{821}{4,995}$$

For 1–4, write each decimal as a fraction with whole numbers in the numerator and denominator.

1. $0.\overline{4}$ **2.** $0.\overline{25}$ **3.** $0.\overline{153}$ **4.** $0.2\overline{73}$

Key Idea
You can use common factors to help you multiply fractions.

Vocabulary
• greatest common factor (GCF) (p. 150)

Multiplying Fractions

LEARN

How do you find products of fractions?

For Newton School's award ceremony, $\frac{4}{5}$ of the auditorium seating is reserved. Faculty members occupy $\frac{1}{6}$ of that space. What part of the reserved space is occupied by faculty?

Example A

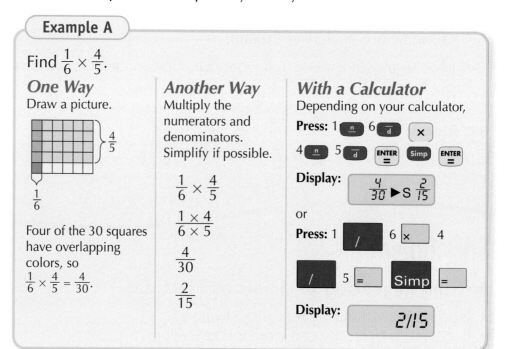

Find $\frac{1}{6} \times \frac{4}{5}$.

One Way
Draw a picture.

$\frac{4}{5}$

$\frac{1}{6}$

Four of the 30 squares have overlapping colors, so
$\frac{1}{6} \times \frac{4}{5} = \frac{4}{30}$.

Another Way
Multiply the numerators and denominators. Simplify if possible.

$\frac{1}{6} \times \frac{4}{5}$

$\frac{1 \times 4}{6 \times 5}$

$\frac{4}{30}$

$\frac{2}{15}$

With a Calculator
Depending on your calculator,

Press: 1 [n] 6 [d] [×]

4 [n] 5 [d] [ENTER =] [Simp] [ENTER =]

Display: $\frac{4}{30} \blacktriangleright S \frac{2}{15}$

or

Press: 1 [/] 6 [×] 4

[/] 5 [=] [Simp] [=]

Display: 2/15

Two fifteenths of the reserved space is for faculty.

How can you simplify before you multiply?

Example B

Find $\frac{2}{3} \times \frac{5}{8}$.

What You Write

Find $\frac{2}{3} \times \frac{5}{8}$.

Find the **GCF** of any numerator and any denominator.

The GCF of 2 and 8 is 2. Divide 2 and 8 by the GCF.

$\frac{\overset{1}{2}}{3} \times \frac{5}{\underset{4}{8}} = \frac{5}{12}$

Why It Works

$\frac{2}{3} \times \frac{5}{8} = \frac{10}{24}$ Multiply numerators. Multiply denominators.

$= \frac{10 \div 2}{24 \div 2}$ Simplify. Divide the numerator and the denominator by the GCF of 10 and 24.

$= \frac{5}{12}$ The GCF of 10 and 24 is 2.

TEST TALK

Think It Through
I can **use the greatest common factor** to simplify the fractions before multiplying.

Example C

Find $\frac{3}{4} \times \frac{8}{9}$.

What You Write

Find $\frac{3}{4} \times \frac{8}{9}$.   The GCF of 3 and 9 is 3.
                                         The GCF of 4 and 8 is 4.

$\frac{\overset{1}{\cancel{3}}}{\underset{1}{\cancel{4}}} \times \frac{\overset{2}{\cancel{8}}}{\underset{3}{\cancel{9}}} = \frac{2}{3}$ Divide the numerators and
                                                                                                                                  denominators by the GCFs.

Why It Works

$\frac{3}{4} \times \frac{8}{9} = \frac{24}{36}$ Multiply numerators.
                                                    Multiply denominators.

$= \frac{24 \div 12}{36 \div 12}$ Simplify. Divide the numerator
                                     and the denominator by the
                                     GCF of 24 and 36.

$= \frac{2}{3}$ The GCF of 24 and 36 is 12.

Sometimes you can't find a fraction of a whole number mentally.

Example D

Find $75 \times \frac{11}{30}$.

$75 \times \frac{11}{30} = \frac{75}{1} \times \frac{11}{30}$ Since 75 is a rational number,
                                                                 you can write it as $\frac{75}{1}$

$= \frac{\overset{5}{\cancel{75}}}{1} \times \frac{11}{\underset{2}{\cancel{30}}}$ Divide the numerator and
                                                                                     denominator by the GCF.

$= \frac{55}{2} = 27\frac{1}{2}$ Multiply. Write the product
                                    as a mixed number.

✔ Talk About It

1. Suppose in Example C, 4 and 8 were divided by 2 instead of the GCF. How would the answer be different?

Take It to the NET
More Examples
www.scottforesman.com

2. Would writing 75 as $\frac{300}{4}$ change the answer in Example D? Explain.

CHECK ✔

For another example, see Set 5-2 on p. 292.

Write an equation for each picture.

1. 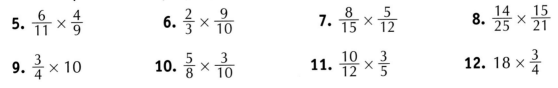   2.   3.   4.

Find each product. Simplify if possible.

5. $\frac{6}{11} \times \frac{4}{9}$ 6. $\frac{2}{3} \times \frac{9}{10}$ 7. $\frac{8}{15} \times \frac{5}{12}$ 8. $\frac{14}{25} \times \frac{15}{21}$

9. $\frac{3}{4} \times 10$ 10. $\frac{5}{8} \times \frac{3}{10}$ 11. $\frac{10}{12} \times \frac{3}{5}$ 12. $18 \times \frac{3}{4}$

13. **Number Sense** Find $\frac{1}{2} \times \frac{4}{5}$. Write the fractions as decimals and multiply. Are the products the same? Explain.

A Skills and Understanding

Write an equation for each picture.

14.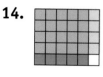

15.

16.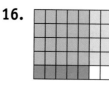

17.

Find each product. Simplify if possible.

18. $\frac{9}{14} \times \frac{28}{29}$

19. $\frac{4}{9} \times \frac{3}{10}$

20. $\frac{11}{18} \times \frac{27}{50}$

21. $\frac{10}{12} \times \frac{6}{8}$

22. $\frac{3}{11} \times \frac{22}{27}$

23. $\frac{5}{6} \times 32$

24. $\frac{7}{8} \times \frac{1}{7}$

25. $28 \times \frac{5}{12}$

26. Reasoning Which is greater, $\frac{4}{5} \times \frac{1}{2}$ or $\frac{4}{5} \times \frac{1}{4}$? Explain how you know.

B Reasoning and Problem Solving

Math and Everyday Life

Millie plants $\frac{2}{3}$ of her garden with vegetables and $\frac{1}{3}$ of it with flowers. Three fourths of the flower section is red geraniums; the rest of the flower section is daisies. What fraction of the entire garden is planted in

27. geraniums?

28. daisies?

29. How many acres will be planted in vegetables?

30. Writing in Math Has Candice simplified and multiplied the fractions correctly? Explain.

Area of Millie's garden: 2 acres

Find $\frac{4}{10} \times \frac{3}{9}$.

$\overset{2}{\underset{5}{\cancel{4}}} \times \overset{1}{\underset{3}{\cancel{3}}} = \frac{2}{15}.$

C Extensions

31. Use mental math to find $\frac{4}{5} \times \left(\frac{1}{4} \times 5 \right)$.

Algebra Use the Distributive Property to find each product mentally.

32. $\frac{1}{2} \times 2\frac{1}{2}$

33. $8 \times 4\frac{3}{4}$

34. $3\frac{2}{3} \times 9$

35. Algebra Simplify $\frac{7}{12} \left(\frac{5}{6} - \frac{1}{2} \right)$.

Mixed Review and Test Prep

Take It to the NET
www **Test Prep**
www.scottforesman.com

36. Find $\frac{1}{3} \times 5$. Simplify if possible.

37. Which is the GCF of 36 and 117?

   A. 1   **B.** 3   **C.** 4   **D.** 9

Practice Game

GCF Spin

Players: 2   **Materials:** Spinner (labeled 0–9)

1. Each player spins the spinner 4 times to build two numbers. Numbers may have 1, 2, or 3 digits in any combination.

2. Players find the GCF of the two numbers and record the GCF as a point value.

3. The player with the most points after 5 rounds is the winner.

Learning with Technology

Multiplication with the Fraction eTool

You can use the array feature to multiply fractions. To multiply $\frac{1}{3}$ and $\frac{4}{5}$, enter 3 for the horizontal axis and 5 for the vertical axis. Use the slider to shade the numerators, 1 column along the horizontal axis and 4 rows along the vertical axis.

1. How many rectangles are created when 3 and 5 are selected as denominators? What does this tell you about the product?

2. How many rectangles are included in the highlighting for both sliders? What does this tell you about the product?

Use the Fraction eTool to find each product.

3. $\frac{2}{3} \times \frac{3}{8}$ **4.** $\frac{1}{4} \times \frac{2}{3}$

 All text pages available online and on CD-ROM.

Key Idea
There are several ways to estimate products and quotients of fractions and mixed numbers.

Vocabulary
• compatible numbers (p. 18)
• rounding (p. 14)

Estimating with Fractions and Mixed Numbers

✓ **WARM UP**
1. $\frac{1}{3} \times 12$ 2. $\frac{1}{2} \times \frac{3}{4}$
3. $\frac{2}{3} \times 3$ 4. $\frac{3}{5} \times 50$

LEARN

What are some ways to estimate?

LaToya is making school banners for the tournament parade. It takes $\frac{7}{8}$ yard of felt to make each banner. Estimate the amount of felt needed for 25 banners.

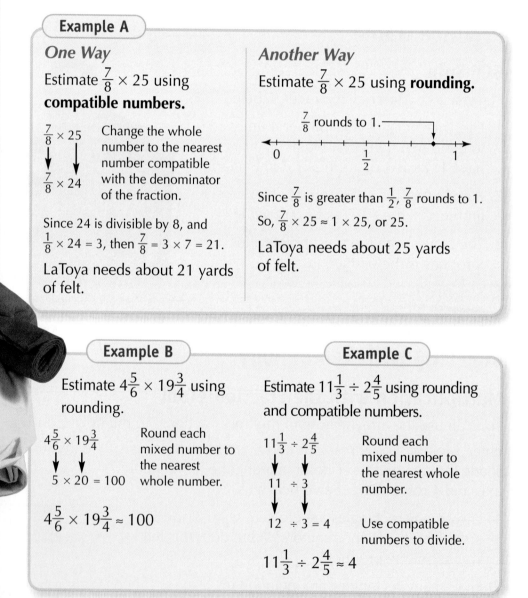

Example A

One Way

Estimate $\frac{7}{8} \times 25$ using **compatible numbers.**

$\frac{7}{8} \times 25$
$\downarrow \quad \downarrow$
$\frac{7}{8} \times 24$

Change the whole number to the nearest number compatible with the denominator of the fraction.

Since 24 is divisible by 8, and $\frac{1}{8} \times 24 = 3$, then $\frac{7}{8} = 3 \times 7 = 21$.

LaToya needs about 21 yards of felt.

Another Way

Estimate $\frac{7}{8} \times 25$ using **rounding.**

$\frac{7}{8}$ rounds to 1.

Since $\frac{7}{8}$ is greater than $\frac{1}{2}$, $\frac{7}{8}$ rounds to 1.
So, $\frac{7}{8} \times 25 \approx 1 \times 25$, or 25.

LaToya needs about 25 yards of felt.

Example B

Estimate $4\frac{5}{6} \times 19\frac{3}{4}$ using rounding.

$4\frac{5}{6} \times 19\frac{3}{4}$
$\downarrow \quad \downarrow$
$5 \times 20 = 100$

Round each mixed number to the nearest whole number.

$4\frac{5}{6} \times 19\frac{3}{4} \approx 100$

Example C

Estimate $11\frac{1}{3} \div 2\frac{4}{5}$ using rounding and compatible numbers.

$11\frac{1}{3} \div 2\frac{4}{5}$
$\downarrow \quad \downarrow$
$11 \div 3$
$\downarrow \quad \downarrow$
$12 \div 3 = 4$

Round each mixed number to the nearest whole number.

Use compatible numbers to divide.

$11\frac{1}{3} \div 2\frac{4}{5} \approx 4$

✓ Talk About It

1. In Example A, is 21 yards of felt enough? Without computing, explain how you know.

Take It to the NET
More Examples
www.scottforesman.com

For another example, see Set 5-3 on p. 292.

Estimate each product or quotient.

1. $\frac{3}{5} \times 16$ **2.** $20 \times \frac{4}{9}$ **3.** $12\frac{5}{8} \times 3\frac{1}{3}$ **4.** $29\frac{11}{12} \div 4\frac{4}{5}$

5. Number Sense Estimate $\frac{6}{7} \times 27$ using compatible numbers. Then estimate using rounding. Which estimate is closest to the actual product? Why?

PRACTICE

For more practice, see Set 5-3 on p. 295.

Ⓐ Skills and Understanding

Estimate each product or quotient.

6. $\frac{1}{3} \times 35$ **7.** $58 \times \frac{7}{8}$ **8.** $\frac{5}{7} \times 20$ **9.** $4\frac{2}{5} \times 5\frac{7}{8}$

10. $30\frac{1}{9} \div 19\frac{1}{2}$ **11.** $17\frac{7}{8} \times 2\frac{5}{6}$ **12.** $24 \div 5\frac{3}{8}$ **13.** $9\frac{5}{8} \div 2\frac{4}{7}$

14. Number Sense What benchmark fraction could you use to estimate the product in Exercise 8?

> **TEST TALK**
>
> **Think It Through**
> Sometimes I can use benchmark fractions to estimate a product or quotient.

Ⓑ Reasoning and Problem Solving

Ms. Candar's woodworking class is making wooden letters and signs for the parade floats. The amount of lumber needed to make each item appears in the table.

15. Estimate the amount of lumber needed to make the capital vowels *a*, *e*, *i*, *o*, and *u*.

16. Estimate the number of large signs that can be made from an 8-foot piece of lumber. Is your estimate an overestimate or underestimate?

Items	Length in feet
Lowercase wooden letter	$\frac{7}{12}$
Capital wooden letter	$\frac{3}{4}$
Small sign	$\frac{11}{12}$
Large sign	$1\frac{1}{3}$

17. <u>**Writing in Math**</u> Explain how you would estimate $\frac{5}{11} \times \frac{2}{9}$ using one or two benchmark fractions.

🦉 Mixed Review and Test Prep

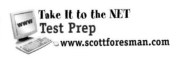
Take It to the NET
Test Prep
www.scottforesman.com

Find each product. Simplify if possible.

18. $18 \times \frac{7}{9}$ **19.** $\frac{2}{5} \times \frac{15}{22}$ **20.** $\frac{5}{8} \times \frac{4}{25}$

21. Which fraction is NOT equivalent to $\frac{8}{24}$?

A. $\frac{10}{30}$ **B.** $\frac{15}{45}$ **C.** $\frac{18}{54}$ **D.** $\frac{24}{75}$

Think It Through
I should **estimate** the product before working the problem.

Multiplying Mixed Numbers

✓ **WARM UP**
1. $\frac{3}{4} \times \frac{5}{8}$ 2. $\frac{9}{20} \times \frac{1}{2}$
3. $\frac{2}{3} \times \frac{5}{6}$ 4. $\frac{5}{6} \times \frac{9}{10}$

LEARN

How can you find the product of mixed numbers?

Example A

Find $5\frac{1}{2} \times 2\frac{2}{3}$. Estimate: $6 \times 3 = 18$

STEP 1

Write each mixed number as an improper fraction.

$5\frac{1}{2} \times 2\frac{2}{3} = \frac{11}{2} \times \frac{8}{3}$

STEP 2

Look for common factors and simplify.

$\frac{11}{\underset{1}{\cancel{2}}} \times \frac{\overset{4}{\cancel{8}}}{3} = \frac{11}{1} \times \frac{4}{3}$

STEP 3

Multiply. Write the product as a mixed number.

$\frac{11}{1} \times \frac{4}{3} = \frac{44}{3} = 14\frac{2}{3}$.

$14\frac{2}{3}$ is close to 18, so the answer is reasonable.

Example B

Franco has two dogs. His toy terrier is $9\frac{3}{16}$ inches tall. His Great Dane puppy is 3 times as tall as the terrier. How tall is his Great Dane?

Find $3 \times 9\frac{3}{16}$. Estimate: $3 \times 9 = 27$

One Way

$3 \times 9\frac{3}{16} = \frac{3}{1} \times \frac{147}{16}$

$= \frac{3 \times 147}{1 \times 16}$

$= \frac{441}{16}$

$= 27\frac{9}{16}$

Another Way

Use the Distributive Property.

$3 \times 9\frac{3}{16} =$

$3 \times (9 + \frac{3}{16}) =$

$(3 \times 9) + (3 \times \frac{3}{16}) =$

$27 \quad + \quad \frac{9}{16} \quad =$

$27\frac{9}{16}$

With a Calculator

Press: 3 ☐✕ 9 **Unit**

3 ☐ 16 /

Display: `441/16`

Press: **Ab/c** **=**

Display: `27u9/16`

The Great Dane is $27\frac{9}{16}$ inches tall.

✓ **Talk About It**

1. Which way in Example B would you use to find $8 \times 3\frac{3}{4}$? Why?

CHECK ✓

Find each product. Simplify if possible.

1. $2\frac{3}{4} \times 4\frac{2}{3}$

2. $5\frac{1}{2} \times 1\frac{1}{6}$

3. $\frac{5}{8} \times 7\frac{1}{3}$

4. $12 \times 1\frac{1}{2}$

5. Number Sense Is $2\frac{1}{2} \times 4\frac{3}{4}$ greater than or less than 15? Explain.

PRACTICE

For more practice, see Set 5-4 on p. 296.

A Skills and Understanding

Find each product. Simplify if possible.

6. $1\frac{1}{3} \times 2\frac{4}{5}$

7. $2\frac{3}{5} \times 4\frac{1}{6}$

8. $5\frac{1}{9} \times 13\frac{2}{3}$

9. $5 \times 2\frac{1}{2}$

10. $3\frac{1}{3} \times 1\frac{1}{5}$

11. $4\frac{1}{2} \times 1\frac{2}{3}$

12. $5\frac{1}{5} \times 1\frac{1}{2}$

13. $5\frac{1}{8} \times 16$

14. Number Sense Is $5\frac{2}{3} \times 2$ greater than or less than 11? Explain.

B Reasoning and Problem Solving

There are 3 types of poodle that differ mainly by height—standard, miniature, and toy. Mara's grandmother has one of each type.

15. Tartan, her standard poodle, is $20\frac{5}{8}$ inches tall. Tiki, her miniature, is $\frac{2}{3}$ Tartan's height. How tall is Tiki?

16. Mr. Samara's beagle is $1\frac{1}{2}$ times as tall as Gigi, her $8\frac{1}{4}$-inch tall toy poodle. How tall is Mr. Samara's beagle?

17. **Writing in Math** In *Duncan's Way*, the family loaded supplies on the baking boat. The amount of flour they loaded was $1\frac{1}{3}$ times the amount of sugar. If they loaded $10\frac{1}{2}$ pounds of sugar, how much flour did they load? Explain how you found your answer.

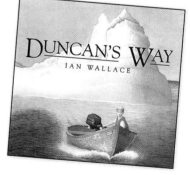

DUNCAN'S WAY
IAN WALLACE

🦉 Mixed Review and Test Prep

Take It to the NET
Test Prep
www.scottforesman.com

Estimate each answer.

18. $\frac{5}{6} \times 17$

19. $15\frac{1}{5} \times 2\frac{4}{9}$

20. $15\frac{1}{2} \div 2\frac{7}{8}$

21. $\frac{2}{9} \times 64$

22. $32\frac{3}{5} \div 2\frac{5}{9}$

23. $57 \times 1\frac{1}{4}$

24. Which is the least common multiple of 12 and 18?

    A. 4   **B.** 12   **C.** 24   **D.** 36

 All text pages available online and on CD-ROM.

Do You Know How?

Do You Understand?

Multiplying a Fraction and a Whole Number (5-1)

Find each product.

1. $\frac{1}{3} \times 6$ **2.** $\frac{1}{5} \times 10$

3. $\frac{4}{7} \times 21$ **4.** $36 \times \frac{3}{4}$

5. $56 \times \frac{5}{8}$ **6.** $30 \times \frac{3}{10}$

A Draw a picture to show Exercise 1.

B Tell how you found the product in Exercise 5.

Multiplying Fractions (5-2)

Find each product. Simplify if possible.

7. $\frac{2}{3} \times \frac{9}{16}$ **8.** $\frac{4}{5} \times \frac{3}{8}$

9. $\frac{1}{2} \times \frac{4}{7}$ **10.** $\frac{5}{8} \times \frac{7}{10}$

11. $\frac{3}{4} \times \frac{5}{12}$ **12.** $\frac{7}{11} \times \frac{22}{35}$

C Explain how you can simplify before multiplying in Exercise 11.

D Draw a picture for $\frac{3}{4} \times \frac{2}{3}$.

Estimating with Fractions and Mixed Numbers (5-3)

Estimate each product or quotient.

13. $\frac{4}{5} \times 16$ **14.** $3\frac{1}{5} \times 31$

15. $5\frac{5}{7} \times 5\frac{8}{9}$ **16.** $9\frac{2}{9} \times 3\frac{4}{9}$

17. $2\frac{3}{5} \times 4\frac{1}{6}$ **18.** $12\frac{4}{5} \div 3\frac{2}{3}$

19. $22\frac{1}{2} \div 10\frac{3}{8}$ **20.** $34\frac{3}{5} \div 7\frac{7}{12}$

E Describe two ways to estimate Exercise 17.

F What benchmark fraction could you use to estimate $\frac{7}{9} \times 48$?

Multiplying Mixed Numbers (5-4)

Find each product. Simplify if possible.

21. $2\frac{1}{3} \times 1\frac{2}{7}$ **22.** $1\frac{1}{2} \times 4$

23. $5\frac{5}{7} \times 7$ **24.** $9\frac{2}{9} \times 3\frac{4}{9}$

25. $2\frac{3}{5} \times 4\frac{1}{6}$ **26.** $1\frac{4}{5} \times 1\frac{2}{3}$

27. $4\frac{1}{2} \times 1\frac{2}{3}$ **28.** $1\frac{7}{8} \times 2\frac{2}{5}$

G Tell how you changed the mixed numbers to improper fractions in Exercise 28.

H Explain how you could use the Distributive Property in Exercise 23.

MULTIPLE CHOICE

1. Which is $\frac{4}{7} \times 28$? (5-1)

    A. $\frac{16}{28}$ **B.** $\frac{16}{7}$ **C.** 16   **D.** 49

2. Which is the product $\frac{2}{3} \times \frac{6}{7}$? (5-2)

    A. $\frac{4}{7}$ **B.** $\frac{14}{18}$ **C.** $\frac{9}{7}$ **D.** $\frac{7}{4}$

> **TEST TALK**
>
> **Think It Through**
> Before I multiply fractions, I should look for **common factors** in the numerators and denominators.

FREE RESPONSE

Find the product. (5-1)

3. $\frac{3}{5} \times 20$ **4.** $18 \times \frac{5}{6}$ **5.** $40 \times \frac{7}{8}$ **6.** $\frac{1}{2} \times 40$

Find each product. Simplify if possible. (5-2)

7. $\frac{2}{3} \times \frac{9}{14}$ **8.** $\frac{3}{5} \times \frac{10}{27}$ **9.** $\frac{1}{2} \times \frac{4}{5}$

10. $\frac{3}{8} \times \frac{4}{5}$ **11.** $\frac{1}{3} \times \frac{1}{2}$ **12.** $\frac{3}{4} \times \frac{8}{9}$

Estimate each product or quotient. (5-3)

13. $2\frac{3}{7} \times 13$ **14.** $3\frac{5}{6} \times 24$ **15.** $25 \div 4\frac{3}{8}$ **16.** $19\frac{7}{8} \div 3\frac{1}{3}$

Find each product. Simplify if possible. (5-4)

17. $1\frac{3}{5} \times 1\frac{3}{8}$ **18.** $5\frac{1}{5} \times 1\frac{1}{2}$ **19.** $6 \times 3\frac{1}{2}$

20. $9\frac{1}{3} \times 18$ **21.** $4\frac{2}{3} \times 2\frac{1}{2}$ **22.** $4\frac{1}{5} \times 2\frac{3}{11}$

23. A ride on the roller coaster takes $2\frac{3}{4}$ minutes. Mario rode 6 times. For how many minutes did he ride?

24. A coin is $\frac{3}{4}$ copper and $\frac{1}{4}$ nickel. It weighs $8\frac{1}{2}$ grams. How many grams of copper are in the coin?

Writing in Math

25. Is 120 a reasonable estimate for $120 \div 1\frac{2}{3}$? Explain. (5-3)

26. Explain how to use the distributive property to find $2\frac{1}{2} \times 8$. (5-4)

Understand Graphic Sources: Lists

Understanding graphic sources such as lists when you read in math can help you use the **problem-solving strategy,** *Make an Organized List,* in the next lesson.

In reading, understanding lists can help you understand what you read. In math, understanding lists can help you solve problems.

Vera made an organized list to show all the combinations of quarters, dimes, and nickels that make 55¢.

The headings at the top of the list tell me what items are included in the combinations

Quarters	Dimes	Nickels
2	0	1
1	3	0
1	2	2
1	1	4
1	0	6
0	5	1
0	4	3
0	3	5
0	2	7
0	1	9
0	0	11

Each row describes a different combination.

There are 11 different possible combinations.

The number of rows tells the number of different possible combinations.

1. How many different kinds of coins are used in the combinations of 55¢?

2. How many combinations have no quarters?

3. How could Vera have organized her list in a different way?

For 4–7, use the problem below and the list at the right.

Bill made an organized list to show the different outfits he could wear on vacation.

4. What items are in an outfit?

5. How many different types of shoes are there to choose from?

6. How many combinations include a blue shirt and sneakers?

7. **Writing in Math** How could Bill have organized his list in a different way?

Pants	Shirt	Shoes
shorts	red shirt	sneakers
shorts	red shirt	sandals
shorts	blue shirt	sneakers
shorts	blue shirt	sandals
shorts	white shirt	sneakers
shorts	white shirt	sandals
jeans	red shirt	sneakers
jeans	red shirt	sandals
jeans	blue shirt	sneakers
jeans	blue shirt	sandals
jeans	white shirt	sneakers
jeans	white shirt	sandals

For 8–10, use the problem below and the list at the right.

Ms. Von Helms began an organized list to show the different possible orders of 4 students who are going to perform in a talent show.

8. Does the list show all the different orders that are possible if Mark is first?

9. How many orders are possible if Mark performs first? if Jessica performs first?

10. **Writing in Math** How many more rows will Ms. Von Helms need to write to complete the list? Explain.

First	Second	Third	Fourth
Mark	Eric	Jessica	Tina
Mark	Eric	Tina	Jessica
Mark	Jessica	Eric	Tina
Mark	Jessica	Tina	Eric
Mark	Tina	Eric	Jessica
Mark	Tina	Jessica	Eric
Jessica	Mark	Eric	Tina
Jessica	Mark	Tina	Eric
Jessica	Eric	Mark	Tina
Jessica	Eric	Tina	Mark
Jessica	Tina	Mark	Eric
Jessica	Tina	Eric	Mark

For 11–12, use the problem below and the list at the right.

Cal wants to buy 3 caps in different colors. His choices are red, blue, black, and gray.

11. How many combinations do not include blue?

12. **Writing in Math** Why doesn't this list show a row that starts with black?

Cap 1	Cap 2	Cap 3
red	blue	black
red	blue	gray
red	black	gray
blue	black	gray

Problem-Solving Strategy

Key Idea
Learning how and when to make an organized list can help you solve problems.

Make an Organized List

 **LEARN**

How can you make an organized list to solve problems?

Locker Combinations A class was given the numbers 5, 7, and 9 to use for 3-digit locker combinations. Can they make enough different combinations for the 30 students in the class?

Read and Understand

What do you know?   Three numbers are available—5, 7, and 9. Each combination must have 3 digits. The digits can be repeated in a combination.

What are you trying to find?   How many different locker combinations using the digits 5, 7, and 9 can be made?

Plan and Solve

What strategy will you use?

Strategy: Make an Organized List

5	7	9
555	777	999
557	775	995
559	779	997
575	755	975
577	757	977
579	759	979
595	795	955
597	797	957
599	799	959

How to Make an Organized List

Step 1   Identify the items to be combined.

Step 2   Choose one of the items. Find combinations keeping that item fixed.

Step 3   Repeat Step 2 as often as needed.

Answer: There are 27 combinations possible. So, there are not enough for the 30 students.

Look Back and Check

Is your answer reasonable?   Yes, no combinations are repeated. There are 3 sets of 9 ways.

✔ Talk About It

1. Suppose digits cannot be repeated in the Locker Combinations problem. How many combinations are possible?

2. **Patterns** Explain how patterns were used to organize the Locker Combinations list.

For another example, see Set 5-5 on p. 293.

CHECK ✓

Solve by making an organized list. The lists have been started for you.

M   A   T   H
MAT
MAH
MTA
MTH
MHA
MHT

1. How many different arrangements of 3 letters can be made from the letters in the word MATH if no repetition of letters is allowed?

2. In how many ways can you make $0.60 using at least one quarter? You cannot use half dollars or pennies.

Q	D	N
2	1	0

PRACTICE

For more practice, see Set 5-5 on p. 296.

Solve by making an organized list.

3. Fumiko wants to lay out a patio in a design like the one shown at right. She has 50 bricks to use. How many bricks should she place in the middle row to use the greatest number of bricks? Draw a diagram or make a table, then look for a pattern.

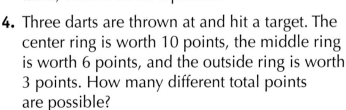

4. Three darts are thrown at and hit a target. The center ring is worth 10 points, the middle ring is worth 6 points, and the outside ring is worth 3 points. How many different total points are possible?

5. The chess club has 4 senior members. They are planning a special tournament in which every member plays every other member just once. How many games will be played?

6. **Writing in Math** Explain how you would find the number of different ways to arrange Marcus, Norio, Catana, and Alfons in a row.

STRATEGIES

- **Show What You Know**
  Draw a Picture
  Make an Organized List
  Make a Table
  Make a Graph
  Act It Out or Use Objects
- **Look for a Pattern**
- **Try, Check, and Revise**
- **Write an Equation**
- **Use Logical Reasoning**
- **Solve a Simpler Problem**
- **Work Backward**

Choose a tool

Mental Math

All text pages available online and on CD-ROM.

Vocabulary
- reciprocal
- multiplicative inverse

Think It Through
- I can **use models** to show division of fractions.
- I can **look for a pattern** to understand how division and multiplication are related.

Dividing Fractions

✔ **WARM UP**

1. $8 \times \frac{5}{4}$ 2. $12 \times \frac{7}{3}$

3. $\frac{5}{6} \times \frac{3}{2}$ 4. $\frac{3}{8} \times \frac{4}{3}$

LEARN

How can you model division of fractions?

Example A

Mr. Wagner makes wooden coasters for glasses. He cuts small round posts into $\frac{1}{2}$-inch thick slices. How many slices can he get from a 5-inch post?

Find $5 \div \frac{1}{2}$.

Think: "How many halves are in 5?"

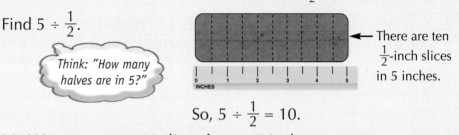

Divide 5 inches into $\frac{1}{2}$-inch sections.

← There are ten $\frac{1}{2}$-inch slices in 5 inches.

So, $5 \div \frac{1}{2} = 10$.

Mr. Wagner can get 10 slices from a 5-inch post.

Example B

Find $\frac{3}{4} \div 4$.

You can think of $\frac{3}{4} \div 4$ as "What is $\frac{3}{4}$ divided into 4 equal parts?"

So, $\frac{3}{4} \div 4 = \frac{3}{16}$.

Show $\frac{3}{4}$.

Divide $\frac{3}{4}$ into 4 equal parts.

Each of the four equal parts contains 3 sixteenths.

How can you divide fractions?

Activity

a. Study the patterns below. Compare the first and second columns.

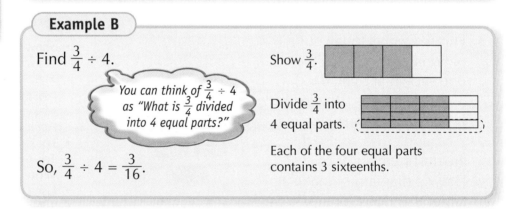

Pattern 1	
$6 \div \frac{3}{1} = 2$	$6 \times \frac{1}{3} = 2$
$3 \div \frac{4}{1} = \frac{3}{4}$	$3 \times \frac{1}{4} = \frac{3}{4}$
$4 \div \frac{1}{2} = 8$	$4 \times \frac{2}{1} = 8$

Pattern 2	
$\frac{3}{4} \div \frac{2}{1} = \frac{3}{8}$	$\frac{3}{4} \times \frac{1}{2} = \frac{3}{8}$
$\frac{1}{4} \div \frac{1}{12} = 3$	$\frac{1}{4} \times \frac{12}{1} = 3$
$\frac{3}{4} \div \frac{3}{8} = 2$	$\frac{3}{4} \times \frac{8}{3} = 2$

b. What do you notice about the divisors in the first column and the factors in the second column of each pattern?

c. How does the quotient compare to the dividend when the divisor is a fraction less than 1?

Dividing by a fraction is the same as multiplying by its **reciprocal**. The product of a number and its reciprocal is 1. For example, $\frac{3}{4} \times \frac{4}{3} = 1$, so $\frac{3}{4}$ and $\frac{4}{3}$ are reciprocals. Reciprocals are also called **multiplicative inverses**.

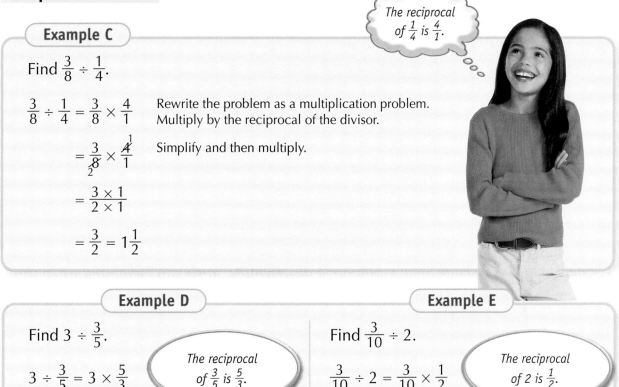

The reciprocal of $\frac{1}{4}$ is $\frac{4}{1}$.

Example C

Find $\frac{3}{8} \div \frac{1}{4}$.

$\frac{3}{8} \div \frac{1}{4} = \frac{3}{8} \times \frac{4}{1}$ Rewrite the problem as a multiplication problem. Multiply by the reciprocal of the divisor.

$= \frac{3}{\underset{2}{\cancel{8}}} \times \frac{\overset{1}{\cancel{4}}}{1}$ Simplify and then multiply.

$= \frac{3 \times 1}{2 \times 1}$

$= \frac{3}{2} = 1\frac{1}{2}$

Example D

Find $3 \div \frac{3}{5}$.

$3 \div \frac{3}{5} = 3 \times \frac{5}{3}$

$= \frac{\overset{1}{\cancel{3}}}{1} \times \frac{5}{\underset{1}{\cancel{3}}}$

$= \frac{1 \times 5}{1 \times 1} = 5$

The reciprocal of $\frac{3}{5}$ is $\frac{5}{3}$.

Example E

Find $\frac{3}{10} \div 2$.

$\frac{3}{10} \div 2 = \frac{3}{10} \times \frac{1}{2}$

$= \frac{3}{10} \times \frac{1}{2}$

$= \frac{3 \times 1}{10 \times 2} = \frac{3}{20}$

The reciprocal of 2 is $\frac{1}{2}$.

✔ Talk About It

1. How can you think of $3 \div \frac{1}{4}$? $\frac{1}{4} \div 3$?

2. How is dividing 5 by $\frac{1}{2}$ different from multiplying 5 by $\frac{1}{2}$?

3. Write and solve $36 \div 9$ as a multiplication problem.

CHECK ✓

For another example, see Set 5-6 on p. 293.

Write the reciprocal of each fraction or number.

1. $\frac{8}{9}$ **2.** $\frac{7}{10}$ **3.** 12   **4.** $\frac{4}{3}$

Find each quotient. Simplify if possible.

5. $8 \div \frac{2}{3}$ **6.** $\frac{2}{3} \div \frac{3}{4}$ **7.** $\frac{5}{8} \div \frac{7}{12}$ **8.** $\frac{5}{12} \div 3$

9. Number Sense When you divide a whole number by a fraction less than 1, is the quotient greater or less than the whole number?

A Skills and Understanding

Write the reciprocal of each fraction or number.

10. $\frac{3}{10}$ **11.** 6   **12.** $\frac{1}{15}$ **13.** 3

Find each quotient. Simplify if possible.

14. $9 \div \frac{3}{5}$ **15.** $\frac{5}{7} \div 20$ **16.** $\frac{2}{9} \div \frac{1}{3}$ **17.** $\frac{4}{5} \div 6$

18. $24 \div \frac{2}{3}$ **19.** $\frac{8}{9} \div 12$ **20.** $\frac{3}{10} \div \frac{5}{6}$ **21.** $\frac{11}{12} \div \frac{3}{4}$

22. $\frac{3}{8} \div 5$ **23.** $10 \div \frac{5}{9}$ **24.** $\frac{7}{8} \div \frac{1}{8}$ **25.** $\frac{9}{14} \div \frac{3}{7}$

26. $\frac{11}{13} \div \frac{13}{11}$ **27.** $6 \div \frac{6}{10}$ **28.** $\frac{1}{2} \div \frac{2}{3}$ **29.** $\frac{6}{7} \div \frac{1}{3}$

30. Reasoning Will $3 \div \frac{2}{5}$ have a whole number answer? Explain.

31. Number Sense Explain how to use decimals to find $6 \div \frac{3}{4}$.

B Reasoning and Problem Solving

Math and Everyday Life

Mr. Wagner also makes wooden games that use peg markers. He cuts the pegs from dowel rods.

32. How many $\frac{1}{2}$-inch pegs can he cut from an 18-inch dowel rod?

33. How many $\frac{3}{4}$-inch pegs can he cut from a 16-inch dowel rod?

34. How long a dowel rod would he need to make 24 pegs that are each $\frac{1}{2}$ inch?

35. Writing in Math Are the explanations correct? If not, tell why and write a correct response.

Find $4 \div \frac{2}{5}$.

I can rewrite this problem as $\frac{1}{4} \times \frac{5}{2}$ because dividing by a fraction is the same as multiplying by its reciprocal. $\frac{1}{4} \times \frac{5}{2} = \frac{5}{8}$.

Find $4 \div \frac{2}{5}$.

I can rewrite this problem as $\frac{4}{1} \times \frac{2}{5}$ because dividing by a fraction is the same as the reciprocal of the answer. $\frac{4}{1} \times \frac{2}{5} = \frac{8}{5}$, and the reciprocal of $\frac{8}{5}$ is $\frac{5}{8}$.

C Extensions

36. Number Sense Which number is its own reciprocal? Explain.

37. Number Sense Is there any number that does not have a reciprocal? Explain.

 **Mixed Review and Test Prep**

Take It to the NET
Test Prep
www.scottforesman.com

38. Without computing, is 3.05 ÷ 0.75 more than or less than 3.05? Explain how you know.

Find each product. Simplify if possible.

39. $4\frac{5}{6} \times \frac{3}{4}$

40. $7\frac{1}{2} \times 1\frac{1}{5}$

41. $16 \times 2\frac{1}{4}$

42. Which is the prime factorization of 576?

A. $8^2 \times 9$ **B.** $4^3 \times 3^2$ **C.** $2^4 \times 3^2 \times 4$ **D.** $2^6 \times 3^2$

43. Which is $\frac{2}{5}$ written as a decimal?

A. 2.5   **B.** 0.4   **C.** 0.25   **D.** 0.04

Discover Math in Your World

Discovery CHANNEL SCHOOL

Not-So-Sweet Honeybee

While "killer bees" look like domestic honeybees, they are much more quick-tempered and aggressive.

1. When threatened, a "killer bee" will pursue an intruder up to $\frac{1}{12}$ mile. A domestic bee will chase an intruder up to $\frac{1}{35}$ mile. How many times farther is the chase distance of a "killer bee?"

2. About 60,000 domestic bees produce 100 pounds of honey. An equal number of "killer bees" produces $\frac{3}{4}$ that amount. Calculate the bees-per-pound production of the "killer bee."

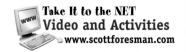 **Take It to the NET**
Video and Activities
www.scottforesman.com

All text pages available online and on CD-ROM.

Think It Through

I should **make an estimate** before using a calculator.

Dividing Mixed Numbers

LEARN

How can you find the quotient of mixed numbers?

Example A

Find $4\frac{1}{2} \div 3\frac{3}{4}$.   Estimate: $5 \div 4 = \frac{5}{4} = 1\frac{1}{4}$

STEP 1	Write each mixed number as an improper fraction.	$4\frac{1}{2} \div 3\frac{3}{4} = \frac{9}{2} \div \frac{15}{4}$
STEP 2	Find the reciprocal of the divisor. Rewrite as a multiplication problem.	$= \frac{9}{2} \times \frac{4}{15}$
STEP 3	Look for common factors, simplify, and then multiply.	$= \frac{\overset{3}{\cancel{9}}}{\underset{1}{2}} \times \frac{\overset{2}{\cancel{4}}}{\underset{5}{\cancel{15}}}$ $= \frac{6}{5} = 1\frac{1}{5}$

$1\frac{1}{5}$ is close to $1\frac{1}{4}$, so the answer is reasonable.

Example B

Find $26 \div 1\frac{5}{8}$.

Estimate: $26 \div 2 = 13$

$26 \div 1\frac{5}{8} = \frac{26}{1} \div \frac{13}{8}$

$= \frac{26}{1} \times \frac{8}{13}$

$= \frac{\overset{2}{\cancel{26}}}{1} \times \frac{8}{\underset{1}{\cancel{13}}}$

$= 16$

16 is close to 13, so the answer is reasonable.

Example C

Find $17\frac{8}{9} \div 3$ using a calculator.

Estimate: $18 \div 3 = 6$

Press: 17 $\boxed{\text{Unit}}$ 8 $\boxed{/}$ 9 $\boxed{\div}$ 3 $\boxed{=}$

Display: $\boxed{161/27}$

Press: $\boxed{\text{Ab/c}}$

Display: $\boxed{5u26/27}$

Since $5\frac{26}{27}$ is close to 6, the answer is reasonable.

✓ Talk About It

1. Explain how to estimate and then find $3\frac{2}{5} \div 8$ using paper and pencil.

2. **Reasoning** Does the commutative property work for division of mixed numbers? Explain using an example.

Find each quotient. Simplify if possible.

1. $2\frac{3}{8} \div 4\frac{2}{5}$ **2.** $4\frac{1}{2} \div 2\frac{7}{10}$ **3.** $2\frac{2}{3} \div 1\frac{1}{2}$ **4.** $3 \div 6\frac{1}{4}$

5. Number Sense When you divide a whole number by a mixed number, is the quotient greater or less than the dividend? Explain.

PRACTICE   *For more practice, see Set 5-7 on p. 297.*

A Skills and Understanding

Find each quotient. Simplify if possible.

6. $4\frac{1}{2} \div 1\frac{4}{9}$ **7.** $1\frac{1}{3} \div 1\frac{1}{6}$ **8.** $3\frac{4}{5} \div 1\frac{9}{10}$ **9.** $2\frac{5}{8} \div 3$

10. $3\frac{1}{9} \div 1\frac{7}{12}$ **11.** $8\frac{1}{4} \div 3\frac{2}{3}$ **12.** $11\frac{1}{4} \div 1\frac{5}{6}$ **13.** $14\frac{3}{8} \div 3\frac{1}{3}$

14. Algebra If $7 \div \frac{x}{3} = 7 \times \frac{x}{3}$, what is the value of x? Explain.

B Reasoning and Problem Solving

Robin makes wooden bird feeders and houses. The table at the right shows the amount of lumber needed for each item.

15. How many feeders can Robin make from an 8-ft board?

16. How many wren houses can be made from the amount of lumber needed for a martin house?

17. <u>Writing in Math</u> Explain why $5\frac{1}{2} \div \frac{1}{2}$ has a greater quotient than $5\frac{1}{2} \times \frac{1}{2}$.

Data File

Item	Lumber
Feeder	$2\frac{1}{2}$ ft
Wren house	$3\frac{1}{3}$ ft
Bluebird house	$4\frac{1}{2}$ ft
Martin house	32 ft

C Extensions

18. Representations Draw a model to show $3\frac{1}{2} \div 2$.

19. Algebra Simplify the expression $\frac{5}{6} \times \frac{2}{3} \div 2\frac{1}{4}$.

Mixed Review and Test Prep

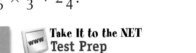

Take It to the NET
Test Prep
www.scottforesman.com

Find each quotient. Simplify if possible.

20. $\frac{7}{10} \div \frac{3}{8}$ **21.** $3 \div \frac{5}{6}$ **22.** $\frac{5}{6} \div \frac{2}{3}$

23. Which is 0.0000021 written in scientific notation?

   A. 21×10^{-6} **B.** 0.21×10^{-6} **C.** 2.1×10^{6} **D.** 2.1×10^{-6}

Do You Know How?

Do You Understand?

Problem-Solving Strategy: Make an Organized List (5-5)

Solve by making an organized list.

1. There are 5 pitchers and 3 catchers on the intramural baseball team. From how many pitcher-catcher pairs can the coach choose?

2. A spinner has 4 colors—red, yellow, blue, and green. If you spin two times, how many color pairs can you get?

Ⓐ Explain how you identified the pitchers and catchers in Exercise 1.

Ⓑ Discuss why you should carefully organize your list.

Dividing Fractions (5-6)

Write the reciprocal of each fraction or number.

3. $\frac{3}{7}$ **4.** 5   **5.** 1

Find each quotient.

6. $21 \div \frac{3}{7}$ **7.** $\frac{1}{6} \div 4$

8. $\frac{6}{7} \div 9$ **9.** $\frac{5}{9} \div \frac{5}{6}$

10. $\frac{2}{3} \div \frac{1}{3}$ **11.** $6 \div \frac{1}{2}$

12. $\frac{9}{2} \div \frac{1}{6}$ **13.** $\frac{18}{25} \div \frac{12}{15}$

Ⓒ Tell how you can think of $8 \div \frac{1}{4}$ and $\frac{2}{3} \div 4$.

Ⓓ Explain how to write and solve $56 \div 7$ as a multiplication problem.

Dividing Mixed Numbers (5-7)

Find each quotient. Simplify if possible.

14. $1\frac{1}{2} \div 1\frac{1}{4}$ **15.** $16 \div 2\frac{3}{4}$

16. $5\frac{2}{9} \div 1\frac{2}{3}$ **17.** $9\frac{3}{8} \div 3\frac{9}{10}$

18. $20\frac{4}{5} \div 4\frac{9}{10}$ **19.** $19 \div 1\frac{1}{5}$

20. $1\frac{4}{9} \div 2\frac{2}{3}$ **21.** $3\frac{21}{25} \div 1\frac{2}{5}$

Ⓔ Tell which method you would choose for $24\frac{1}{4} \div \frac{1}{4}$ and why.

Ⓕ How is dividing with mixed numbers different from dividing with fractions?

MULTIPLE CHOICE

1. Which is $\frac{1}{6} \div \frac{3}{8}$? (5-6)

A. $\frac{1}{16}$ **B.** $\frac{4}{9}$ **C.** $2\frac{1}{4}$ **D.** $2\frac{7}{8}$

2. Which is the quotient $4\frac{2}{3} \div 7$? (5-7)

A. $\frac{3}{98}$ **B.** $\frac{2}{3}$ **C.** $1\frac{1}{2}$ **D.** $32\frac{2}{3}$

> **Think It Through**
> Before I divide mixed numbers, I should **estimate** the quotient.

FREE RESPONSE

Solve by making an organized list. (5-5)

3. A spinner has 3 colors—red, yellow, and blue. If you spin two times, how many color pairs can you get?

Give the reciprocal of each fraction or number. (5-6)

4. $\frac{4}{7}$ **5.** 6   **6.** $\frac{8}{3}$ **7.** 12

Find each quotient. Simplify if possible. (5-6)

8. $\frac{5}{6} \div 20$ **9.** $18 \div \frac{6}{11}$ **10.** $\frac{1}{6} \div \frac{8}{3}$ **11.** $\frac{1}{5} \div \frac{14}{15}$

12. $\frac{2}{9} \div \frac{4}{81}$ **13.** $\frac{3}{4} \div \frac{5}{16}$ **14.** $\frac{7}{19} \div 14$ **15.** $48 \div \frac{16}{21}$

Find each quotient. Simplify if possible. (5-7)

16. $2\frac{1}{3} \div 1\frac{1}{14}$ **17.** $5\frac{2}{5} \div 1\frac{5}{9}$ **18.** $6\frac{2}{3} \div 4\frac{1}{5}$

19. $24 \div 1\frac{8}{9}$ **20.** $18 \div 2\frac{4}{15}$ **21.** $2\frac{3}{4} \div 1\frac{5}{11}$

22. $7\frac{3}{7} \div 3\frac{1}{5}$ **23.** $4\frac{4}{9} \div 7\frac{2}{3}$ **24.** $98 \div 4\frac{5}{12}$

25. Elka bought a 12-ft length of ribbon from which she wants to cut $\frac{3}{4}$-ft pieces. How many pieces can she cut? (5-7)

26. To make 11 puppets, Kevin used $5\frac{1}{2}$ yards of material. How much material did he use for each puppet?

Writing in Math

27. How is dividing 6 by $\frac{1}{3}$ different from multiplying 6 by $\frac{1}{3}$. (5-6)

28. Explain why when you divide a whole number other than zero by a proper fraction, the quotient is always greater than the whole number. (5-7)

Algebra

Key Idea
Relationships among fractional quantities can be written using algebra.

Think It Through
I need to use **order of operations** to simplify expressions.

Expressions with Fractions

LEARN

How can you write algebraic expressions with fractions?

Example A

At the bowling alley, Miguel works half the number of hours that Damaris works.

Write an algebraic expression for the number of hours Miguel works.

Let d equal the number of hours Damaris works.

Then $\frac{1}{2}d$ is the number of hours Miguel works.

Example B

Carlote's salary is $4 more than $\frac{1}{3}$ the salary of the bowling alley's manager.

Write an algebraic expression for Carlote's salary.

Let s equal the manager's salary.

Then $\frac{1}{3}s + 4$ is Carlote's salary.

How can you evaluate algebraic expressions with fractions?

Example C

Brett is half as old as Victor.

Find Brett's age if Victor is 14 years old.

Evaluate the expression $\frac{1}{2}v$ when $v = 14$.

$\frac{1}{2}v$ Substitute 14 for v.

$\frac{1}{2}(14) = 7$ Simplify.

Brett is 7 years old.

Example D

Evaluate $\frac{1}{5}m + 7$ when $m = 4\frac{1}{6}$.

$\frac{1}{5}\left(4\frac{1}{6}\right) + 7$ Substitute $4\frac{1}{6}$ for m.

$\frac{1}{5}\left(\frac{25}{6}\right) + 7$ Use order of operations and simplify.

$\frac{1}{\cancel{5}}\left(\frac{\cancel{25}^{5}}{6}\right) + 7$

$\frac{5}{6} + 7$

$7\frac{5}{6}$

✔ Talk About It

1. What is another way to write $\frac{1}{2}d$ and $\frac{1}{3}s$?

Write each word phrase as an algebraic expression.

1. two thirds Josh's age   **2.** 6 less than $\frac{1}{9}k$ **3.** 4 more than $\frac{1}{8}x$

Evaluate each expression for $n = \frac{3}{4}$ and $n = 2\frac{1}{2}$.

4. $8n$ **5.** $\frac{1}{2}n$ **6.** $2\frac{1}{2}n + 3\frac{1}{8}$

7. Number Sense How do the word phrases representing $\frac{1}{4}x + 5$ and $\frac{1}{4}(x + 5)$ differ?

PRACTICE

For more practice, see Set 5-8 on p. 297.

Ⓐ Skills and Understanding

Write each word phrase as an algebraic expression.

8. $\frac{5}{6}$ Yuri's height   **9.** 3 more than $\frac{1}{4}c$ **10.** 8 fewer than $\frac{1}{3}$ the amount

11. 5 less than r **12.** p decreased by 12   **13.** 8 more than 3 times a number

Evaluate each expression for $n = \frac{5}{6}$ and $n = 1\frac{1}{4}$.

14. $2\frac{1}{5}n$ **15.** $2 + \frac{3}{10}n$ **16.** $24n - 8$

17. Number Sense How do the word phrases representing $3 - \frac{2}{3}y$ and $\frac{2}{3}y - 3$ differ?

Ⓑ Reasoning and Problem Solving

18. A bowler's handicap is calculated using the expression $\frac{4}{5}(200 - a)$, where a is the bowler's average score. What is the handicap for a bowler whose average is 140? 180?

19. **Writing in Math** When given the phrase, "$\frac{1}{3}$ of two times a number," Callista wrote the expression $\frac{2}{3}x$. Is she correct? Explain.

🎧 Mixed Review and Test Prep

Take It to the NET
www **Test Prep**
www.scottforesman.com

20. How long will it take to walk $3\frac{1}{2}$ miles at a rate of $2\frac{1}{2}$ miles per hour?

21. How many $\frac{3}{4}$-pound servings are in 15 pounds?

22. $5\frac{1}{2} \div 3\frac{2}{3}$ equals

A. $\frac{6}{121}$ **B.** $\frac{2}{3}$ **C.** $1\frac{1}{2}$ **D.** $20\frac{1}{6}$

Algebra

Key Idea
You can solve equations with fractions using inverse operations, just as with whole numbers and decimals.

Think It Through
I know that **dividing by a fraction** is the same as **multiplying by its reciprocal.**

Solving Equations with Fractions

LEARN

How can you solve equations involving fractions and mixed numbers?

✓ **WARM UP**

Solve.

1. $8.2 + x = 10$

2. $x - 18 = 19$

3. $32 = 175 - x$

4. $1.8 = x - 8.6$

Example A

Solve $x + \frac{2}{3} = 8$.

$$x + \frac{2}{3} = 8$$

$$x + \frac{2}{3} - \frac{2}{3} = 8 - \frac{2}{3}$$

$$x = 7\frac{1}{3}$$

Check: $x + \frac{2}{3} = 8$

$$7\frac{1}{3} + \frac{2}{3} = 8$$

$$8 = 8$$

Example B

Solve $n - 4\frac{1}{2} = 6\frac{3}{8}$.

$$n - 4\frac{1}{2} = 6\frac{3}{8}$$

$$n - 4\frac{1}{2} + 4\frac{1}{2} = 6\frac{3}{8} + 4\frac{1}{2}$$

$$n = 6\frac{3}{8} + 4\frac{4}{8}$$

$$n = 10\frac{7}{8}$$

Check: $n - 4\frac{1}{2} = 6\frac{3}{8}$

$$10\frac{7}{8} - 4\frac{1}{2} = 6\frac{3}{8}$$

$$6\frac{3}{8} = 6\frac{3}{8}$$

Example C

Solve $\frac{4}{5}y = 32$.

$$\frac{4}{5}y = 32$$

$$\left(\frac{5}{4}\right)\frac{4}{5}y = 32\left(\frac{5}{4}\right)$$

$$y = \frac{\overset{8}{\cancel{32}}}{1} \times \frac{5}{\underset{1}{\cancel{4}}}$$

$$y = 40$$

Check: $\frac{4}{5}y = 32$

$$\frac{4}{5}(40) = 32$$

$$32 = 32$$

Example D

Solve $a \div \frac{2}{3} = 6\frac{1}{2}$.

$$a \div \frac{2}{3} = 6\frac{1}{2}$$

$$a \times \frac{3}{2} = 6\frac{1}{2} \qquad \boxed{6\frac{1}{2} = \frac{13}{2}}$$

$$a \times \frac{3}{2}\left(\frac{2}{3}\right) = \frac{13}{2}\left(\frac{2}{3}\right)$$

$$a = \frac{13}{3}$$

$$a = 4\frac{1}{3}$$

✓ **Talk About It**

1. How would you check the answer to the equation in Example D?

Take It to the NET
More Examples
www.scottforesman.com

For another example, see Set 5-9 on p. 294.

Solve each equation and check your answer.

1. $c + 4 = 7\frac{1}{2}$ **2.** $m - \frac{5}{6} = 4\frac{2}{3}$ **3.** $\frac{5}{6}b = 7\frac{1}{2}$ **4.** $w \div \frac{3}{4} = 4\frac{1}{2}$

5. Number Sense Is the solution of $\frac{5}{4}x = 20$ greater than or less than 20?

PRACTICE

For more practice, see Set 5-9 on p. 297.

Ⓐ Skills and Understanding

Solve each equation and check your answer.

6. $x + 2\frac{2}{3} = 5\frac{1}{6}$ **7.** $b - 5 = 6\frac{3}{8}$ **8.** $2p = \frac{5}{8}$ **9.** $x \div \frac{6}{7} = 1\frac{1}{6}$

10. $\frac{1}{3} + m = 4\frac{1}{4}$ **11.** $7\frac{6}{7} = p - 2\frac{1}{5}$ **12.** $\frac{1}{2} = \frac{5}{6}y$ **13.** $4\frac{3}{4} = w \div \frac{1}{5}$

14. Number Sense Is the solution of $y \div \frac{4}{3} = 15$ greater than or less than 15?

Ⓑ Reasoning and Problem Solving

15. After completing $36\frac{3}{4}$ miles of a bike race, Kimi still has $8\frac{3}{4}$ miles to go. Use the equation $b - 36\frac{3}{4} = 8\frac{3}{4}$ to find the total length of the race.

16. Tyrell divided a spool of ribbon into 12 pieces of the same length shown below. Use the equation $r \div 12 = 2\frac{1}{2}$ to find the number of feet of ribbon the spool held.

| 0 | 12 in. | 24 in. | 36 in. |

17. **Writing in Math** Marta said, "I'm thinking of a fraction. If I divide it by $\frac{1}{2}$, I get $\frac{7}{12}$." Describe how you would determine what fraction Marta was thinking of; then solve the problem.

🦉 Mixed Review and Test Prep

Take It to the NET
Test Prep
www.scottforesman.com

Choose a variable and write an expression for each phrase.

18. five more than $\frac{1}{3}$ Jill's score

19. three less than $\frac{7}{8}$ a number

20. Choose the expression with the greatest quotient.

A. $5\frac{1}{2} \div \frac{1}{4}$ **B.** $3\frac{1}{3} \div \frac{1}{4}$ **C.** $7 \div \frac{1}{4}$ **D.** $\frac{1}{10} \div \frac{1}{4}$

Problem-Solving Skill

Reading Helps!

Identifying steps in a process
can help you with...
writing to explain.

Key Idea
There are specific things you can do to write a good explanation in math.

Think It Through
When you write to explain, it is important that you **describe each step** in the solution clearly.

Writing to Explain

◀ **LEARN** ▬▬▬▬▬▬▬▬▬▬▬▬▬

How do you write a good explanation?

Wooden Pegs Camille plans to make a wooden rack for hanging keys and purses by drilling 6 peg holes, each $\frac{7}{8}$ inch in diameter, in a piece of wood $16\frac{5}{8}$ inches long.

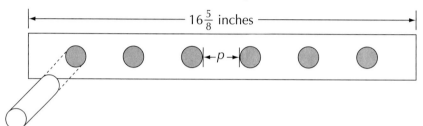

The space at each end of the rack is the same size as the space between any two pegs. What is the distance (p) between any two pegs? Show your work and explain in writing how you solved the problem.

To find the amount of space taken up by the peg holes, I multiplied the diameter of each hole by the number of peg holes $\left(\frac{7}{8} \times 6 = \frac{21}{4} = 5\frac{1}{4} \text{ in.}\right)$. I then subtracted this amount from $16\frac{5}{8}$ to find the amount of wood left between the holes (p) and at the ends $\left(16\frac{5}{8} - 5\frac{1}{4} = 11\frac{3}{8}\right)$. Using the picture, I counted the spaces between the holes and at the ends and got 7 spaces. Since all of these spaces are equal, I divided the $11\frac{3}{8}$ inches of wood space by 7; $\frac{91}{8} \div 7 = \frac{13}{8} = 1\frac{5}{8}$. So, the distance between any two pegs (p) is $1\frac{5}{8}$ inches.

Tips for Writing Good Explanations

- Include the work you did that led to that solution.
- Describe the steps and operations you used in the order you used them.
- Refer to any diagrams or data that provide important information or supporting details.

✔ Talk About It

1. What information from the diagram of the wooden rack was needed to solve the problem? How is the information used in the explanation?

CHECK ✔

For another example, see Set 5-10 on p. 294.

Explain your solution and show your work.

A number of sixth graders were asked which of 4 subjects they prefer. The number of students who prefer each subject appears in the table at the right.

Subject	Number of 6th graders
Math	330
Science	255
Reading	190
Social Studies	105

1. What fraction of students prefer science?

2. Which subject accounts for $\frac{3}{8}$ of the preferences?

PRACTICE

For more practice, see Set 5-10 on p. 297.

Explain your solution and show your work.

3. Mr. Masong began planting his garden. The section marked on the diagram shows 18 plants with 3 plants in each square. If he continues the pattern, find the number of plants that he will need to finish planting his garden.

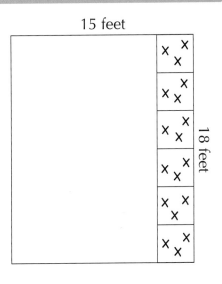

15 feet

18 feet

4. Patina participated in an academic game show consisting of two 25-question rounds. Correct answers in the first round were worth $75 each; in the second, they were worth $150 each. Patina correctly answered $\frac{4}{5}$ of the first-round questions and $\frac{2}{5}$ of the second-round questions. What fraction of the total possible money did Patina win?

5. The 12 members of the chorus are wearing matching robes and hats for the evening performances. The seamstress needs $4\frac{7}{8}$ yards of material for each robe and $1\frac{1}{8}$ yards for each hat. Calculate the total number of yards of material needed to make robes and hats for the entire chorus.

6. A truck driver started the year making $\frac{7}{20}$ dollar for each mile she drove. Halfway through the year, she received a raise and earned $\frac{19}{50}$ dollar per mile. She drove 48,000 miles in the first 6 months, and 45,000 miles in the last 6 months. Find her truck-driver earnings for the year.

All text pages available online and on CD-ROM.

Problem-Solving Applications

Honeybees Bees gather pollen and nectar for food. From the nectar they make honey. The food is stored in the honeycomb's cells. These cells are also where bees grow from eggs into adults.

Trivia Honey is made by a bee sucking nectar into its honey stomach, regurgitating it, adding enzymes, then allowing the water to evaporate.

1 It takes 24 days for some drone bees to develop from an egg to an adult. Worker bees need $\frac{7}{8}$ of that time to develop. How long does it take a worker bee to develop?

2 A bee spends $\frac{8}{20}$ of its development time as a larva or prepupa. If $\frac{1}{10}$ of the development time is in the prepupa stage, what fraction is spent as a larva?

3 An average worker bee produces $\frac{1}{12}$ teaspoon of honey in its lifetime. About how many worker bees would it take to produce $\frac{1}{2}$ teaspoon of honey?

Good News/Bad News *In theory, a bee could fly around the world with the energy from just one ounce of honey. Unfortunately, worker bees can only fly about 500 miles before they die because their bodies simply wear out.*

Using Key Facts

4 Almost $\frac{95}{100}$ of all bees are worker bees. How many worker bees are in a typical colony?

Key Facts
Honeybees

- A colony may have 55,000 bees.
- A queen can lay 200,000 eggs per year.
- Hives may have over 100,000 cells.
- The nectar from about 2,000,000 flowers is needed to make 1 pound of honey.

5 A typical hive needs to store at least 40 pounds of honey for winter food. How many flowers would a colony have to visit to make this much honey?

6 **Writing in Math** Hexagonal cells are efficient shapes for honeycombs. They leave little wasted space between cells or around each larva. Do you think that school lockers should be hexagonal in shape? How efficient would a honeycomb-configuration of lockers be? Include a drawing in your explanation.

7 **Decision Making** Emma and Jon counted 274 cells in one cross-section of honeycomb. Emma used front-end estimation and predicted that there would be approximately 20,000 cells in 100 of these cross-sections. Jon used rounding and estimated there would be about 30,000 cells. Which method of estimation would you use to predict the number of cells? Explain your choice.

Do You Know How?

Do You Understand?

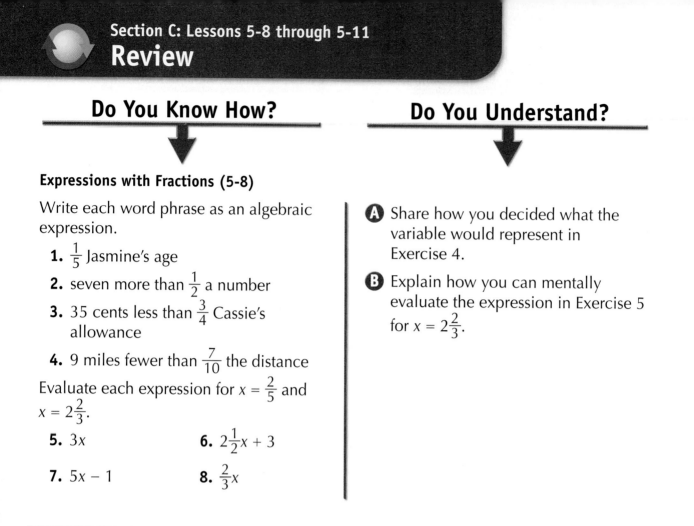

Expressions with Fractions (5-8)

Write each word phrase as an algebraic expression.

1. $\frac{1}{5}$ Jasmine's age

2. seven more than $\frac{1}{2}$ a number

3. 35 cents less than $\frac{3}{4}$ Cassie's allowance

4. 9 miles fewer than $\frac{7}{10}$ the distance

Evaluate each expression for $x = \frac{2}{5}$ and $x = 2\frac{2}{3}$.

5. $3x$

6. $2\frac{1}{2}x + 3$

7. $5x - 1$

8. $\frac{2}{3}x$

Ⓐ Share how you decided what the variable would represent in Exercise 4.

Ⓑ Explain how you can mentally evaluate the expression in Exercise 5 for $x = 2\frac{2}{3}$.

Solving Equations with Fractions (5-9)

Solve each equation and check your answer.

9. $\frac{2}{3} + b = 3$

10. $p - 2\frac{2}{3} = 5$

11. $5\frac{1}{2} = 1\frac{3}{4} + m$

12. $n - \frac{5}{6} = 1\frac{1}{3}$

13. $\frac{3}{5}g = 27$

14. $d \div \frac{1}{5} = \frac{7}{10}$

15. $4c = \frac{2}{7}$

16. $\frac{1}{2} = w \div \frac{3}{4}$

Ⓒ Share how you solved the equation in Exercise 11.

Ⓓ Explain how to check your answer in Exercise 14.

Problem-Solving Skill: Writing to Explain (5-10)

Explain your solution and show your work.

17. A tile setter is tiling a floor with tiles that measure $\frac{3}{4}$ ft on each side. If he uses 17 tiles along a wall, how long is the wall?

Ⓔ What information from the problem is needed to solve the problem?

MULTIPLE CHOICE

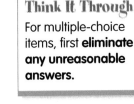

Think It Through
For multiple-choice items, first **eliminate any unreasonable answers.**

1. Which is the solution to $p - 2\frac{1}{9} = 2\frac{2}{3}$? (5-9)

  A. $\frac{1}{6}$ **B.** $\frac{5}{9}$ **C.** $4\frac{1}{4}$ **D.** $4\frac{7}{9}$

2. Which is the solution to $\frac{5}{7}m = 10$? (5-9)

  A. $7\frac{1}{7}$ **B.** $9\frac{2}{7}$ **C.** $10\frac{5}{7}$ **D.** 14

FREE RESPONSE

Write each word phrase as an algebraic expression. (5-8)

3. $\frac{4}{5}$ Luis' height

4. 5 inches more than $\frac{2}{3}$ the width

Evaluate each expression for $n = \frac{7}{8}$. (5-8)

  5. $16n$ **6.** $\frac{1}{7}n + 4$ **7.** $4n - 1$ **8.** $1\frac{1}{2} + n$

Solve each equation and check your answer. (5-9, 5-11)

  9. $p - \frac{4}{9} = 2$ **10.** $2\frac{1}{5} = r + 1\frac{1}{3}$ **11.** $d - 3\frac{4}{5} = 8$

  12. $6\frac{2}{3} + g = 10$ **13.** $\frac{4}{7} = b + \frac{1}{6}$ **14.** $y - 1\frac{5}{9} = 2\frac{2}{3}$

  15. $\frac{5}{8}p = 12$ **16.** $m \div \frac{2}{5} = 8$ **17.** $18 = \frac{3}{7}a$

  18. $1\frac{3}{4}t = 3\frac{2}{7}$ **19.** $p \div 4 = 5\frac{5}{7}$ **20.** $2\frac{2}{5} = j \div 1\frac{1}{5}$

Explain your solution and show your work. (5-10, 5-11)

21. Samuel wants to cover the top of a square table with a pattern made from assorted glass pieces. A bag of assorted glass contains about 300 pieces. Samuel has calculated that the shaded section of the tabletop, shown in the diagram at right, will require $\frac{3}{4}$ of one bag. Estimate the number of bags of glass Samuel will need to cover the entire tabletop.

Writing in Math

22. What ideas are used in solving equations regardless of whether they contain whole numbers, decimals, or fractions? (5-9)

23. Explain why the solution of $\frac{7}{8}x = 43$ is more than 43. (5-9)

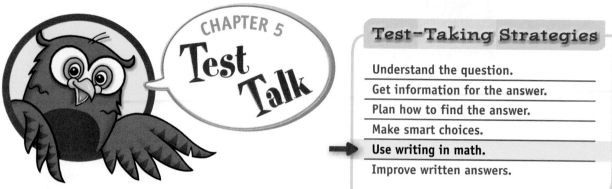

Test-Taking Strategies

Understand the question.

Get information for the answer.

Plan how to find the answer.

Make smart choices.

→ **Use writing in math.**

Improve written answers.

Use Writing in Math

Sometimes a test question asks for a written answer, such as an explanation, a description, or a comparison. See how one student followed the steps below to answer this test item by writing in math.

1. Ethan is planting petunias in a circular garden. He has determined that he needs about 125 petunias for Section 1 of the garden, shown in the drawing below.

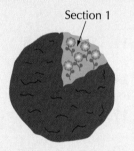

Section 1

ESTIMATE the number of petunias Ethan needs for the entire garden.

Estimated number of petunias: _____

Show your work or explain in words how you found your estimate.

Understand the question.

I need to estimate the number of petunias Ethan needs for the entire garden.

Get information for the answer.

I'll need to get information from the text and the picture.

Plan how to find the answer.

Each section of the garden will have about the same number of petunias. So, I can use multiplication.

Use writing in math.

• Make your answer brief but complete.

• Use words from the problem and use math terms accurately.

• Describe steps in order.

Estimated number of petunias: _____750_____

Show your work or explain in words how you found your estimate.

First, I estimated that Section 1 is about $\frac{1}{6}$ the entire garden. Then I multiplied 125 × 6. I got the estimate of 750.

• Is the question completely answered?

• Is the answer clear?

• Are the steps explained in order?

2. Lorenzo is building a shelving unit with 5 shelves, as shown below. Each shelf is $\frac{3}{4}$ inch thick, and there is a space of 14 inches between the shelves.

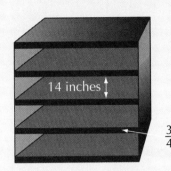

14 inches

$\frac{3}{4}$ inch

Find the total height in inches of the shelving unit.

$59\frac{3}{4}$ inches

Show or explain in words how you found your answer.

First I multiplied $5 \times \frac{3}{4}$. Next I multiplied 4×14. Then I added together the two products $3\frac{3}{4} + 56$. I got $59\frac{3}{4}$ inches for the total height.

Think It Through

I have found the total height of $59\frac{3}{4}$ inches. Now I need to explain how I found my answer.

I should describe the steps I used in order. I will begin by explaining how I found the total height of the 5 shelves. Next I'll tell how I found the total height of the 4 spaces. Then I'll explain how I added together the results to get the total height.

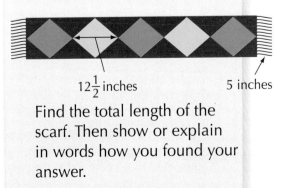

Now it's your turn.

For each problem, give a complete response.

3. Inez is hooking a rug. She used about 800 yards of yarn to complete section 1.

Section 1

ESTIMATE the number of yards of yarn Inez needs for the entire rug.

Estimated number of yards: _____

Show your work or explain in words how you found your estimate.

4. Lee knit a winter scarf that had 5 diamonds, as shown below. Each diamond is $12\frac{1}{2}$ inches long, and there is a 5-inch fringe at each end.

$12\frac{1}{2}$ inches   5 inches

Find the total length of the scarf. Then show or explain in words how you found your answer.

GCF stands for greatest common factor.

The **greatest common factor** of two numbers is the largest number that divides into both evenly. (pp. 150, 252)

Self Check

Multiply fractions and mixed numbers. (Lessons 5-1, 5-2, 5-3, 5-4)

There are different ways to multiply by fractions and mixed numbers. One way is to write each factor as a fraction. Then multiply the numerators and multiply the denominators.

$30 \times \frac{5}{6} = \frac{30}{1} \times \frac{5}{6}$ Simplify.

$= \frac{\overset{5}{\cancel{30}}}{1} \times \frac{5}{\cancel{6}_1}$ Divide 30 and 6 by the **GCF**, 6.

$= 25$

$\frac{1}{6} \times \frac{3}{4} = \frac{1}{\cancel{6}_2} \times \frac{\cancel{3}^1}{4}$

$= \frac{1}{8}$

$3\frac{1}{4} \times 2\frac{2}{3} = \frac{13}{\cancel{4}_1} \times \frac{\cancel{8}^2}{3}$ Estimate: $3 \times 3 = 9$

$= \frac{26}{3}$

$= 8\frac{2}{3}$ Since $8\frac{2}{3}$ is close to 9, the answer is reasonable.

1. Find $\frac{7}{8} \times 48$, $\frac{3}{5} \times \frac{15}{16}$, and $3\frac{1}{8} \times 4\frac{3}{5}$.

Self Check

After I've baked a cake, I invert the cake pan to remove the cake.

I can find the **multiplicative inverse**, or **reciprocal**, by turning a fraction upside down. (p. 266)

You can use multiplication to divide fractions. (Lessons 5-6, 5-7)

Multiply by the **reciprocal** of the divisor. The reciprocal is also called the **multiplicative inverse**.

$\frac{9}{10} \div \frac{3}{5} = \frac{9}{10} \times \frac{5}{3}$

$= \frac{\overset{3}{\cancel{9}}}{\cancel{10}_2} \times \frac{\cancel{5}^1}{\cancel{3}_1}$ Simplify and then multiply.

$= \frac{3}{2}$

$= 1\frac{1}{2}$

$17\frac{1}{2} \div 2\frac{1}{2} = \frac{35}{2} \div \frac{5}{2}$ Estimate: $18 \div 3 = 6$

$= \frac{35}{2} \times \frac{2}{5}$

$= \frac{\overset{7}{\cancel{35}}}{\cancel{2}_1} \times \frac{\cancel{2}^1}{\cancel{5}_1}$

$= 7$ Since 7 is close to 6, the answer is reasonable.

2. Find $\frac{3}{4} \div \frac{7}{8}$, $2\frac{2}{5} \div 6$, and $4\frac{1}{4} \div 1\frac{2}{3}$.

"*Equation*" sounds like it contains the word "*equal*."

Remember, an **equation** has an equal sign, but an **expression** doesn't. (p. 276)

Self Check

Algebraic expressions and equations may contain fractions. (Lessons 5-8, 5-9)

Iyo's age is 3 years older than $\frac{3}{4}$ Michael's age.	Evaluate $\frac{1}{6}n + 8$ when $n = 24$.	Solve $\frac{2}{5}y = 8$.
Write an algebraic expression for Iyo's age.	Substitute 24 for n. Then use order of operations.	$\frac{2}{5}y = 8$
Let m equal Michael's age.	$\frac{1}{6}(24) + 8$	$\left(\frac{5}{2}\right)\frac{2}{5}y = 8\left(\frac{5}{2}\right)$
Then $\frac{3}{4}m + 3$ is Iyo's age.	$4 + 8$	$y = \frac{\overset{4}{\cancel{8}}}{1} \times \frac{5}{\cancel{2}_1}$
	12	$y = 20$

3. Evaluate $\frac{7}{8}w - 5$ when $w = 40$, and solve $\frac{2}{3}p = 18$.

Self Check

Make an organized list and write to explain how to solve problems. (Lessons 5-5, 5-10)

Pamela's 4-digit locker combination uses all four of the digits 1, 3, 4, and 5. How many different locker combinations are possible? Explain your answer.

To make an organized list:

Step 1: Identify the items to be combined.

Step 2: Choose one of the items. Find combinations keeping that item fixed.

Step 3: Repeat Step 2 as often as needed.

1	3	4	5
1345	3145	4135	5134
1354	3154	4153	5143
1435	3415	4315	5314
1453	3451	4351	5341
1534	3514	4513	5413
1543	3541	4531	5431

I made an organized list. First I showed all the combinations starting with 1, then starting with 3, then 4, and then 5. There are 24 different locker combinations.

4. In how many ways can you make 30¢ without using pennies?

Answers: 1. 42; $\frac{9}{16}$; 14$\frac{3}{8}$ 2. $\frac{6}{7}$; $\frac{2}{5}$; $\frac{11}{20}$ 3. 30; $p = 27$ 4. 5 ways

MULTIPLE CHOICE

Choose the correct letter for each answer.

1. What is $\frac{7}{8} \times 72$?

   A. 9   C. 63

   B. 56   D. 70

2. Mandy has a garden in which $\frac{3}{5}$ of the plants are tomato plants. Of the tomato plants, $\frac{1}{3}$ are cherry tomato plants. What fraction of the plants in Mandy's garden are cherry tomato plants?

   A. $\frac{1}{3}$ C. $\frac{3}{5}$

   B. $\frac{1}{5}$ D. $\frac{1}{15}$

3. Estimate $\frac{2}{5} \times 36$ using compatible numbers.

   A. 7   C. 14

   B. 10   D. 72

4. Find $4\frac{1}{6} \times 2\frac{3}{5}$.

   A. $10\frac{5}{6}$ C. $8\frac{1}{10}$

   B. $10\frac{1}{8}$ D. $4\frac{23}{30}$

5. Carol is $1\frac{1}{3}$ times as tall as her younger brother. Her younger brother is 48 inches tall. How tall is Carol?

   A. 16 inches   C. 64 inches

   B. 56 inches   D. 66 inches

6. Find $3\frac{1}{3} \div 1\frac{1}{9}$.

   A. 3

   B. $3\frac{1}{27}$

   C. $3\frac{1}{9}$

   D. 9

Think It Through
I should **look for key words** in the problem.

7. Which is the reciprocal of $2\frac{1}{7}$?

   A. $2\frac{7}{1}$ C. $\frac{7}{10}$

   B. $1\frac{5}{7}$ D. $\frac{7}{15}$

8. Kiko has 6 boxes. This is only $\frac{2}{3}$ of the number she needs. How many boxes does she need?

   A. 4 boxes

   B. 8 boxes

   C. 9 boxes

   D. 10 boxes

9. Which expression represents three more than $\frac{2}{7}$ of a number, n?

   A. $\frac{2}{7}n \times 3$ C. $3n + \frac{2}{7}$

   B. $3 + \frac{2}{7}n$ D. $n \div \frac{2}{7} + 3$

10. Solve $x \div \frac{4}{5} = 3$.

    A. $x = \frac{4}{15}$ C. $x = 3\frac{3}{4}$

    B. $x = 2\frac{2}{5}$ D. $x = 3\frac{4}{5}$

For 11–12, use the ingredient list below.

Custard Pie Filling
Ingredients

4 eggs	$\frac{1}{4}$ teaspoon nutmeg
$\frac{2}{3}$ cup sugar	$2\frac{2}{3}$ cups milk
$\frac{1}{2}$ teaspoon salt	1 teaspoon vanilla

11. If you doubled the recipe, how much milk would you need?

A. $4\frac{1}{3}$ cups **C.** $5\frac{1}{3}$ cups

B. $4\frac{2}{3}$ cups **D.** $5\frac{2}{3}$ cups

12. Justin wants to make a custard pie that is $\frac{1}{4}$ the size of the pie that the recipe makes. How much sugar will he need for his pie?

A. $\frac{1}{3}$ cup **C.** $\frac{1}{6}$ cup

B. $\frac{1}{4}$ cup **D.** $\frac{1}{12}$ cup

FREE RESPONSE

Find each product. Simplify if possible.

13. $2\frac{3}{8} \times 6\frac{1}{4}$ **14.** $3\frac{1}{9} \times 4$

Write the reciprocal of each.

15. $\frac{6}{7}$ **16.** 12

Estimate.

17. $\frac{5}{7} \times 33$ **18.** $7\frac{4}{5} \div 2\frac{1}{4}$

For 19–20 find each quotient. Simplify if possible.

19. $7\frac{3}{4} \div 1\frac{2}{3}$ **20.** $\frac{3}{7} \div 6$

21. Write 6 fewer than $\frac{5}{6}$ a number h as an algebraic expression.

22. Evaluate $\frac{1}{8}n + 2\frac{1}{4}$ for $n = \frac{3}{4}$.

Solve each equation and check your answer.

23. $3\frac{3}{5}p = \frac{2}{5}$ **24.** $y + \frac{4}{5} = 3\frac{1}{10}$

Writing in Math

25. Explain how to find the reciprocal of a mixed number.

26. The digits 0, 1, 2, and 4 are in the 4-digit combination for a lock. Each number is used only once. How many different combinations are possible? Solve by making an organized list.

27. To make a border around her room, Erica painted balloons that were $2\frac{4}{5}$ inches wide. Leaving a space at each end, she painted 15 evenly spaced balloons along a 150-inch wall. What was the distance between any two balloons? Explain your solution and show your work.

Think It Through
- I need to make sure I **describe the steps and operations I used** in the order I used them.
- I can **draw a diagram or make a model** to help describe my work.

Number and Operation

MULTIPLE CHOICE

1. What is the product $\frac{2}{3} \times \frac{4}{5}$?

   A. $\frac{2}{5}$ **C.** $\frac{3}{4}$

   B. $\frac{8}{15}$ **D.** $\frac{5}{6}$

2. Estimate $1.47 + 2.8$ to the nearest whole number.

   A. 5   **C.** 3

   B. 4   **D.** 2

3. Which is the LCM of 28 and 36?

   A. 252   **C.** 4

   B. 126   **D.** 2

FREE RESPONSE

4. Aurora walks $3\frac{3}{4}$ miles each week. At this pace, how many weeks will it take her to walk 30 miles?

5. $4\frac{1}{7} \times 3\frac{2}{5}$

6. $5\frac{3}{5} \div \frac{7}{8}$

7. $3.4 + 2.08 + 6\frac{1}{5}$

8. $\frac{2}{3} \times 45$

9. $76 \div 3\frac{1}{4}$

10. $5\frac{1}{4} + 11\frac{3}{15}$

Think It Through
I should **describe steps in order.**

Writing in Math

11. Explain how you would add $2\frac{3}{5}$ and $\frac{1}{7}$.

12. Describe how to estimate $3{,}624 \div 38$ using compatible numbers.

Geometry and Measurement

MULTIPLE CHOICE

13. The side of a square measures 2.3 cm. What is its perimeter?

   A. 4.6 cm   **C.** 6.93 cm

   B. 5.29 cm   **D.** 9.2 cm

14. How many feet are in $3\frac{1}{3}$ yards?

   A. 7 feet   **C.** $13\frac{1}{3}$ feet

   B. 10 feet   **D.** 40 feet

15. Which polygon below has more than six sides?

   A. quadrilateral   **C.** octagon

   B. pentagon   **D.** hexagon

FREE RESPONSE

16. Find the area of a rectangle with length $5\frac{1}{6}$ ft and width $8\frac{3}{4}$ ft.

17. What is the name of a quadrilateral with no right angles and four sides of equal length?

18. Name a quadrilateral that is NOT a parallelogram.

19. Find the perimeter of a rectangle with length $14\frac{5}{16}$ in. and width 11 in.

20. Write an expression for the perimeter of a regular pentagon with side s.

Writing in Math

21. Maria cut 12 feet of ribbon into 16 pieces of equal length. Explain how to find the length of each piece.

Data Analysis and Probability

MULTIPLE CHOICE

22. Kristi has 4 nickels, 2 dimes, and 7 quarters. She pulls out one coin. What is the probability that the coin she pulls out is a quarter?

A. $\frac{7}{4}$ **C.** $\frac{7}{13}$

B. $\frac{7}{6}$ **D.** $\frac{1}{7}$

23. What is the median of this data set?

3, 5, 9, 7, 5, 8, 7, 11, 3, 4, 4

A. 5   **C.** 7

B. 6   **D.** 8

FREE RESPONSE

For 24–26, use the bar graph.

Favorite Colors

24. How many more people chose green than chose red?

25. How many people chose red, yellow, or blue?

26. How many votes are represented in the graph?

Writing in Math

27. What is meant by the probability of an event? Give an example.

Algebra

MULTIPLE CHOICE

28. Solve $y + 3\frac{1}{5} = 11$.

A. $y = 13\frac{1}{5}$ **C.** $y = 7\frac{1}{5}$

B. $y = 7\frac{4}{5}$ **D.** $y = 6\frac{4}{5}$

29. Which expression represents five more than two-thirds a number, m?

A. $\frac{2}{3}m - 5$ **C.** $5m + \frac{2}{3}$

B. $5 + \frac{2}{3}m$ **D.** $5 \div \frac{2}{3}m$

FREE RESPONSE

Write a rule for each table.

30.

x	2	3	6	10	16
y	$\frac{1}{2}$	$\frac{3}{4}$	$\frac{3}{2}$	$\frac{5}{2}$	4

31.

x	$\frac{1}{4}$	$\frac{1}{2}$	$\frac{3}{4}$	1
y	1	2	3	4

32.

x	60	50	40	30	20
y	49	39	29	19	9

33. Write an algebraic expression for 6 less than twice Matt's age. Then, find the value if Matt is 18 years old.

34. Write an algebraic expression for $12 more than $\frac{1}{5}$ Quincy's salary. Then, find the value if Quincy's salary is $25,000.

Writing in Math

35. Write an equation that includes a variable and a fraction on one side and can be solved by multiplying both sides by a fraction.

Set 5-1 (pages 248–251)

Find $\frac{2}{5} \times 15$.

$15 \div 5 = 3$, so $\frac{1}{5} \times 15 = 3$

Since $\frac{2}{5}$ is 2 times $\frac{1}{5}$,

$\frac{2}{5} \times 15 = 2 \times \left(\frac{1}{5} \text{ of } 15 \right) = 2 \times 3 = 6.$

$\frac{2}{5} \times 15 = 6$

Remember if the denominator is a factor of the whole number, you can use division and mental math.

1. $10 \times \frac{3}{5}$ **2.** $\frac{3}{4} \times 12$

3. $\frac{5}{7} \times 28$ **4.** $18 \times \frac{8}{9}$

5. $32 \times \frac{5}{8}$ **6.** $\frac{2}{3} \times 45$

7. $144 \times \frac{1}{6}$ **8.** $\frac{7}{12} \times 108$

Set 5-2 (pages 252–255)

Find $\frac{3}{4}$ of $\frac{2}{5}$. Simplify if possible.

Multiply the numerators and denominators.

$\frac{3}{4} \times \frac{2}{5} = \frac{3 \times 2}{4 \times 5} = \frac{6}{20}$

Simplify if possible.

$\frac{6}{20} = \frac{6 \div 2}{20 \div 2} = \frac{3}{10}$ Divide both the numerator and denominator by 2, the GCF of 6 and 20.

Remember you can also use the greatest common factor to simplify the fractions before multiplying.

1. $\frac{1}{4} \times \frac{5}{6}$ **2.** $\frac{6}{7} \times \frac{14}{15}$

3. $\frac{2}{9} \times \frac{3}{10}$ **4.** $\frac{2}{3} \times \frac{3}{7}$

5. $\frac{4}{9} \times \frac{5}{8}$ **6.** $\frac{9}{10} \times \frac{5}{6}$

7. $\frac{8}{11} \times \frac{1}{6}$ **8.** $\frac{12}{13} \times \frac{39}{44}$

Set 5-3 (pages 256–257)

Estimate $2\frac{5}{6} \times 31\frac{1}{3}$ using rounding.

$2\frac{5}{6} \times 31\frac{1}{3} \approx 3 \times 31 = 93$ Round each fraction to the nearest whole number.

$2\frac{5}{6} \times 31\frac{1}{3} \approx 93$

Estimate $18\frac{9}{10} \div 2\frac{3}{10}$.

$18\frac{9}{10} \div 2\frac{3}{10}$

$\downarrow \qquad \downarrow$

$19 \quad \div \quad 2$ Round each mixed number to the nearest whole number.

$\downarrow \qquad \downarrow$

$20 \quad \div \quad 2 = 10.$ Use compatible numbers to divide.

$18\frac{9}{10} \div 2\frac{3}{10} \approx 10$

Remember you can also use benchmark fractions to estimate a product or quotient.

1. $9\frac{1}{3} \times 2\frac{4}{5}$ **2.** $35 \times \frac{7}{8}$

3. $28 \div 3\frac{1}{4}$ **4.** $5\frac{1}{6} \times 4\frac{7}{9}$

5. $3\frac{3}{5} \div 2\frac{1}{8}$ **6.** $16\frac{11}{12} \div 7\frac{3}{10}$

7. $4\frac{1}{2} \times 11\frac{1}{3}$ **8.** $2\frac{5}{8} \div 7$

9. $100 \times 5\frac{3}{10}$ **10.** $16 \times 1\frac{5}{8}$

Find $1\frac{1}{8} \times 3\frac{3}{5}$.

$1\frac{1}{8} \times 3\frac{3}{5} = \frac{9}{8} \times \frac{18}{5}$ Write each mixed number as an improper fraction.

$= \frac{9}{{}_{4}8} \times \frac{\cancel{18}^{9}}{5}$ Look for common factors and simplify.

$= \frac{81}{20}$ Multiply.

$= 4\frac{1}{20}$ Write the product as a mixed number.

Remember to estimate the product before working the problem so that you can check if your answer is reasonable.

1. $2\frac{1}{3} \times 4\frac{3}{5}$ 2. $2\frac{6}{7} \times 1\frac{3}{4}$

3. $3\frac{1}{9} \times 5\frac{3}{7}$ 4. $4\frac{3}{8} \times 12$

5. $7\frac{1}{2} \times 6\frac{1}{5}$ 6. $10\frac{5}{12} \times 7\frac{1}{5}$

7. $3\frac{1}{6} \times 2\frac{2}{9}$ 8. $9\frac{1}{3} \times 8\frac{1}{2}$

When you make an organized list, follow these steps.

Step 1: Identify the items to be combined.
Step 2: Choose one of the items. Find combinations keeping that item fixed.
Step 3: Repeat Step 2 for each of the other items as often as needed.

Remember to keep each item fixed and find all the possible combinations for that item.

1. Jackie has a red shirt, a blue shirt, and a green shirt, and white pants, brown pants, and black pants. How many different outfits can Jackie make?

2. How many ways can you make $0.75 without using pennies or half dollars?

Find $\frac{6}{7} \div \frac{2}{3}$.

$\frac{6}{7} \div \frac{2}{3} = \frac{6}{7} \times \frac{3}{2}$ Rewrite the problem as a multiplication problem.

$= \frac{\cancel{6}^{3}}{7} \times \frac{3}{\cancel{2}_{1}}$ Look for common factors.

$= \frac{3 \times 3}{7 \times 1}$ Simplify and then multiply.

$= \frac{9}{7}$

$= 1\frac{2}{7}$ Write the product as a mixed number.

Remember that dividing by a fraction is the same as multiplying by its reciprocal. The product of a number and its reciprocal is 1.

1. $5 \div \frac{3}{5}$ 2. $\frac{4}{7} \div 6$

3. $\frac{5}{6} \div \frac{1}{12}$ 4. $\frac{9}{10} \div \frac{2}{3}$

5. $\frac{5}{8} \div 4$ 6. $\frac{1}{6} \div \frac{8}{9}$

7. $\frac{3}{8} \div \frac{1}{8}$ 8. $\frac{1}{4} \div \frac{13}{16}$

Set 5-7 (pages 270–271)

Find $3\frac{7}{8} \div 1\frac{1}{4}$.

$3\frac{7}{8} \div 1\frac{1}{4} = \frac{31}{8} \div \frac{5}{4}$ Write each mixed number as an improper fraction.

$= \frac{31}{8} \times \frac{4}{5}$ Find the reciprocal of the divisor. Rewrite as a multiplication problem.

$= \frac{31}{{}_2 8} \times \frac{\cancel{4}^1}{5}$ Look for common factors, simplify, and then multiply.

$= \frac{31}{10} = 3\frac{1}{10}$ Write the answer as a mixed number.

Remember when changing a mixed number to an improper fraction, the denominator does not change.

1. $3\frac{4}{5} \div 8\frac{1}{5}$ **2.** $2\frac{7}{8} \div 1\frac{1}{12}$

3. $2\frac{1}{4} \div 2\frac{1}{8}$ **4.** $1\frac{1}{3} \div 2\frac{3}{5}$

5. $12\frac{5}{6} \div 3$ **6.** $9\frac{1}{6} \div 3\frac{1}{4}$

Set 5-8 (pages 274–275)

Write an algebraic expression for

2 more than $\frac{1}{3}$ the width.

Let w equal the width.

$2 + \frac{1}{3}w$ "More than" tells you to add.

Remember to look for key words to know which operation(s) to use.

1. 3 more than $\frac{1}{2}$ Ann's age

2. 5 less than $\frac{1}{4}$ the number of students

Set 5-9 (pages 276–277)

Solve $b - 2\frac{3}{5} = 4$.

$b - 2\frac{3}{5} = 4$ Use addition to undo subtraction.

$b - 2\frac{3}{5} + 2\frac{3}{5} = 4 + 2\frac{3}{5}$

$b = 6\frac{3}{5}$

Remember that to keep an equation balanced, you need to do the same operation to both sides.

1. $m - 2\frac{3}{4} = 5$ **2.** $2\frac{2}{3} = 1\frac{1}{6} + p$

3. $15 = \frac{5}{7}n$ **4.** $a \div 16 = 1\frac{3}{32}$

5. $w \div \frac{5}{6} = \frac{11}{12}$ **6.** $g + 4\frac{4}{7} = 8\frac{1}{9}$

Set 5-10 (pages 278–279)

When you are writing to explain your solution,
- include the work you did that lead to that solution.
- describe the steps and operations you used in the order you used them.
- refer to any diagrams or data that provide important information or supporting details.

Remember identifying important information and supporting details can help you to explain your solution.

Explain your solution and show your work.

1. Jamie decorates picture frames with lace. How many yards of lace does she need to decorate 14 frames if Jamie uses $2\frac{1}{4}$ yards for each frame?

Take It to the NET
More Practice
www.scottforesman.com

Set 5-1 (pages 248–251)

Find each product.

1. $\frac{5}{8} \times 24$

2. $\frac{1}{4} \times 16$

3. $27 \times \frac{2}{9}$

4. $\frac{3}{4} \times 20$

5. $\frac{5}{13} \times 39$

6. $\frac{3}{5} \times 25$

7. $40 \times \frac{7}{8}$

8. $\frac{3}{7} \times 42$

9. $132 \times \frac{7}{12}$

10. $\frac{5}{16} \times 80$

11. $\frac{11}{25} \times 175$

12. $95 \times \frac{4}{19}$

13. Tomas bought 6 pounds of fruit. Maria bought $\frac{2}{3}$ the amount of fruit that Tomas bought. How many pounds of fruit did Maria buy?

Set 5-2 (pages 252–255)

Write a multiplication problem for each picture.

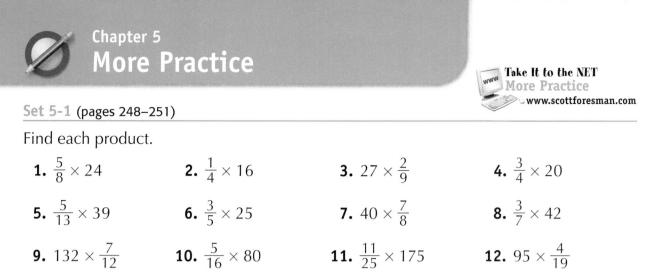

1.

2.

3.

Find each product. Simplify if possible.

4. $\frac{3}{4} \times \frac{8}{9}$

5. $\frac{8}{15} \times \frac{1}{4}$

6. $\frac{4}{5} \times \frac{3}{7}$

7. $\frac{1}{9} \times \frac{2}{5}$

8. $\frac{5}{12} \times \frac{4}{7}$

9. $\frac{7}{8} \times \frac{1}{7}$

10. $\frac{11}{12} \times \frac{3}{10}$

11. $\frac{2}{5} \times 16$

12. $\frac{7}{10} \times \frac{5}{14}$

13. $\frac{5}{12} \times \frac{3}{20}$

14. $\frac{9}{10} \times \frac{45}{100}$

15. $\frac{5}{8} \times \frac{20}{30}$

16. Juanita needed $\frac{3}{4}$ cup of onions for her recipe. She only had $\frac{5}{6}$ of the amount she needed. How much did Juanita have?

Set 5-3 (pages 256–257)

Estimate each product or quotient.

1. $\frac{5}{6} \times 13$

2. $\frac{2}{5} \times 21$

3. $12\frac{1}{6} \div 3\frac{7}{8}$

4. $57 \times 2\frac{5}{6}$

5. $4\frac{4}{5} \div 2\frac{1}{4}$

6. $4\frac{3}{4} \times 17$

7. $5\frac{6}{7} \times 3\frac{1}{9}$

8. $12\frac{1}{5} \div 5\frac{9}{10}$

9. $15 \times 10\frac{1}{4}$

10. $11\frac{2}{3} \div 2\frac{7}{8}$

11. $4\frac{4}{5} \times 9\frac{5}{6}$

12. $7 \div 2\frac{5}{8}$

13. Yvette has $3\frac{3}{4}$ rolls of ribbon. If there is $3\frac{1}{3}$ yards of ribbon on each roll, about how many yards of ribbon does Yvette have?

Set 5-4 (pages 258–259)

Find each product. Simplify if possible.

1. $3\frac{1}{3} \times 5\frac{1}{5}$ **2.** $1\frac{4}{5} \times 3\frac{1}{2}$ **3.** $1\frac{3}{5} \times 1\frac{3}{8}$ **4.** $4\frac{3}{4} \times 2\frac{1}{7}$

5. $8\frac{9}{10} \times 3\frac{7}{8}$ **6.** $5\frac{4}{9} \times 2\frac{2}{9}$ **7.** $4\frac{5}{9} \times 1\frac{1}{8}$ **8.** $6\frac{2}{3} \times 18$

9. $4\frac{1}{2} \times 2\frac{2}{5}$ **10.** $6\frac{2}{5} \times 3\frac{1}{2}$ **11.** $8 \times 3\frac{1}{4}$ **12.** $7\frac{1}{6} \times 1\frac{1}{5}$

13. $5\frac{3}{4} \times 8\frac{2}{3}$ **14.** $7\frac{1}{2} \times 12\frac{2}{7}$ **15.** $15\frac{1}{8} \times 2\frac{2}{3}$ **16.** $24\frac{3}{5} \times 4\frac{1}{8}$

17. Alberto can run one lap around the track in $2\frac{3}{5}$ minutes. How long would it take him to run $5\frac{1}{2}$ laps around the track, if he runs the same pace the entire time?

Set 5-5 (pages 264–265)

Solve by making an organized list.

1. How many different 3-digit numbers can be made from the digits 1, 2, 3, 4, and 5 if the digits are not repeated?

2. In how many ways can you make $0.80 in coins without using half dollars or pennies?

3. Josephine has four stuffed animals. How many different ways can she arrange them on a shelf?

Set 5-6 (pages 266–269)

Write the reciprocal of each fraction or number.

1. $\frac{2}{5}$ **2.** 7 **3.** $\frac{8}{3}$ **4.** $\frac{1}{12}$

Find each quotient. Simplify if possible.

5. $3 \div \frac{3}{10}$ **6.** $\frac{8}{15} \div 4$ **7.** $\frac{7}{8} \div \frac{5}{8}$ **8.** $\frac{4}{5} \div 12$

9. $9 \div \frac{3}{5}$ **10.** $\frac{4}{5} \div \frac{7}{10}$ **11.** $\frac{3}{7} \div \frac{5}{6}$ **12.** $\frac{8}{9} \div \frac{2}{3}$

13. $\frac{1}{2} \div \frac{1}{2}$ **14.** $\frac{5}{8} \div 5$ **15.** $\frac{9}{10} \div \frac{5}{18}$ **16.** $\frac{5}{12} \div \frac{5}{18}$

17. $\frac{6}{7} \div \frac{9}{21}$ **18.** $\frac{1}{6} \div 6$ **19.** $24 \div \frac{3}{8}$ **20.** $\frac{9}{14} \div \frac{3}{28}$

21. A developer plans to divide 18 acres of land into $\frac{3}{4}$-acre building sites. How many building sites will there be?

Take It to the NET
www More Practice
www.scottforesman.com

Set 5-7 (pages 270–271)

Find each quotient. Simplify if possible.

1. $3\frac{4}{5} \div 1\frac{9}{10}$
2. $\frac{2}{3} \div 10\frac{1}{3}$
3. $4\frac{1}{2} \div 1\frac{4}{9}$

4. $5\frac{1}{5} \div 6\frac{1}{6}$
5. $9\frac{7}{10} \div 3\frac{1}{3}$
6. $8\frac{7}{8} \div 2\frac{3}{4}$

7. Mona has a $6\frac{3}{4}$-yard length of ribbon that she wants to cut into $1\frac{1}{8}$-yard pieces. How many pieces will she have?

Set 5-8 (pages 274–275)

Write each word phrase as an algebraic expression.

1. $\frac{5}{8}$ of the blue markers
2. 5 less than $\frac{2}{5}$ Ed's height

3. $1\frac{2}{5}$ miles more than $\frac{1}{2}$ Jack's distance
4. $25 plus $6 per hour for x hours

Evaluate each expression for $n = \frac{3}{4}$ and $n = 1\frac{1}{6}$.

5. $3\frac{1}{5}n$
6. $4 + \frac{7}{8}n$
7. $5n - 2$

8. $n \div 4$
9. $2\frac{5}{8}n + 3$
10. $1\frac{1}{3}n - n$

Set 5-9 (pages 276–277)

Solve each equation and check your answer.

1. $\frac{7}{8}p = 14$
2. $m - 2\frac{5}{8} = 1\frac{3}{7}$
3. $3 + w = 9\frac{2}{7}$

4. $k \div 1\frac{1}{4} = 12$
5. $\frac{2}{7}a = 4\frac{5}{6}$
6. $\frac{5}{6} = z - 4\frac{2}{3}$

7. $3\frac{1}{2} + 4\frac{1}{3} = d$
8. $x \div \frac{3}{4} = 3\frac{1}{9}$
9. $n - 2\frac{1}{5} = \frac{14}{5}$

10. Jerome wants to walk $5\frac{1}{3}$ miles. In the morning, he walked $1\frac{7}{8}$ miles. How much farther does he have to walk to reach his goal?

Set 5-10 (pages 278–279)

Explain your solution and show your work.

1. Hayley planted 3 rows of flowers. She planted 16 flowers in each row. In Row A, $\frac{3}{8}$ of the flowers blossomed. In Row B, $\frac{3}{4}$ of the flowers blossomed, and in Row C, $\frac{7}{8}$ of the flowers blossomed. How many plants blossomed?

Chapter 5 More Practice   297

A Vocabulary

(pages 150, 152, 160, 164)

Choose the best term from the box.

1. A __?__ is a number that names part of a whole or part of a group.

2. Fractions that name the same amount are called __?__.

3. The __?__ is the greatest number that divides two or more numbers with no remainder.

4. The solution of a multiplication problem is called the __?__.

Vocabulary

- **equivalent fractions** *(p. 164)*
- **fraction** *(p. 160)*
- **product** *(Gr. 5)*
- **least common multiple** *(p. 152)*
- **greatest common factor** *(p. 150)*
- **quotient** *(Gr. 5)*

B Fraction Concepts

(pages 164–167)

Write a simplified fraction for each shaded portion.

5.
6.
7.
8.

Write two equivalent fractions.

9. $\frac{2}{5}$ 10. $\frac{6}{10}$ 11. $\frac{3}{4}$

12. $\frac{12}{15}$ 13. $\frac{1}{6}$ 14. $\frac{1}{2}$

15. At the bake sale, Marta sold $1\frac{1}{4}$ times as many muffins as Tina did. If Tina sold 4 dozen muffins, how many did Marta sell?

Do You Know...

What is the length of the largest American flag?
You will find out in Lesson 6-11.

C Multiplication & Division *(pages 30, 32, 94)*

Multiply.

16. 23×9

17. 18×12

18. 16×23

19. 67×28

Divide.

20. $108 \div 9$

21. $126 \div 14$

22. $210 \div 25$

23. $782 \div 34$

24. Becky wants to buy 4 T-shirts. Each shirt costs $12.98, including tax. What will be the total cost?

25. Tonya bought 3 bracelets for a total of $54, excluding tax. How much did each bracelet cost?

D Solving Equations *(pages 44–47)*

Solve for the variable.

26. $24 + c = 53$

27. $y - 15 = 129$

28. $5b = 45$

29. $\frac{v}{4} = 8$

30. $3g = 123$

31. $x + 14 = 37$

32. $\frac{t}{8} = 9$

33. $27 = m - 9$

34. The area of a rectangle is 18 ft². If the width is 3 ft, what is the length? (Area = length × width)

35. The height of a triangle is $\frac{3}{8}$ the length of the base. Find the height of the triangle if the base measures 16 inches.

Understanding Ratios

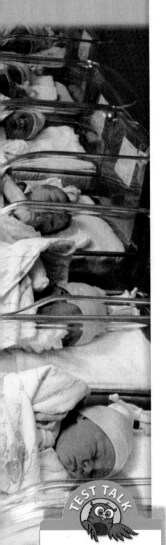

LEARN

What is a mathematical way to compare quantities?

Ms. Aeriko surveyed her students to find out the number of students who celebrate a birthday each month.

A **ratio** is a comparison of two quantities that can be written as *a* to *b*, *a:b*, or $\frac{a}{b}$.

The quantities in the ratio are called **terms.** The first term in the ratio above is *a*, and the second term is *b*.

✔ **WARM UP**

Write a fraction for each shaded portion.

1.

2.

Data File

Birthdays	
Month	Number of Students
January	4
February	5
April	7
May	1
June	5
August	2
September	1
October	3

Example A

Write a ratio comparing the students with August birthdays to the students with April birthdays.

There are 2 students who have August birthdays and 7 students who have April birthdays.

The ratio is 2 to 7, 2:7, or $\frac{2}{7}$.

Example B

Write a ratio comparing the students with October birthdays to the total number of students.

There are 3 students who have October birthdays. The total number of students is 4 + 5 + 7 + 1 + 5 + 2 + 1 + 3 = 28.

The ratio is 3 to 28, 3:28, or $\frac{3}{28}$.

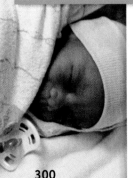

Think It Through
I can use a **fraction** to describe a part of a set or a part of a whole.

✔ **Talk About It**

1. What is the ratio comparing the total number of students to students with January birthdays?

2. How do you decide which number to give as the first term of a ratio?

3. **Number Sense** A fraction compares a part to a whole. Which ratios in the examples compare a part to a whole? Do all ratios compare a part to a whole?

CHECK ✓

A person's blood type is denoted with the letters A, B, and O and the symbols + and −. The blood type A+ is read *A positive*. The blood type B− is read *B negative*. Write a ratio for each comparison in three different ways.

Data File

Blood Donors

Type	Donors
A+	60
B+	25
AB+	9
O+	120
A−	27
B−	0
AB−	6
O−	12
Total	259

1. O+ donors to A+ donors
2. AB− donors to total donors
3. What does the ratio $\frac{120}{12}$ represent in the table? Explain.
4. **Number Sense** How are the ratios $\frac{9}{25}$ and $\frac{25}{9}$ different? Explain.

PRACTICE

For more practice, see Set 6-1 on p. 349.

A Skills and Understanding

A recipe for Vegetable Tossed Salad calls for the ingredients pictured. Write a ratio for each comparison in three different ways.

5. tomatoes to peppers
6. tomatoes to all ingredients
7. Suppose you added 3 stalks of celery to the mix. What would be the ratio of stalks of celery to tomatoes? Stalks of celery to the total number of vegetables?
8. **Number Sense** Explain why the denominator of a fraction can never be zero but any term of a ratio can be zero.

Vegetable Tossed Salad
Ingredients:
6 tomatoes   1 onion
2 peppers   2 cucumbers

B Reasoning and Problem Solving

Janice is making a quilt with different colored squares—12 green, 9 rose, and 4 white. Write each ratio in three different ways.

9. green to rose
10. white to green
11. rose to all colors
12. green to other colors
13. **Writing in Math** Give an example of a ratio that compares a part to a part and explain how it is different from a fraction.

Mixed Review and Test Prep

Take It to the NET
Test Prep
www.scottforesman.com

Solve.

14. $\frac{3}{2} \times n = 12$
15. $\frac{x}{2} = 12$
16. $b \div 8 = 6$

17. What is the sum $2\frac{3}{5} + 7\frac{1}{8}$ written in simplest form?

A. $9\frac{1}{20}$ B. $9\frac{1}{10}$ C. $9\frac{4}{13}$ D. $9\frac{29}{40}$

TEST TALK

Think It Through

- I know that **multiplying and dividing by 1** does not change the amount.

- I can use **divisibility rules** to help me choose numbers that are easy to divide by.

Equal Ratios

LEARN

How can you find equal ratios?

In the survey, the ratio of left-handed tourists to the total number of tourists is $\frac{24}{60}$.

Sometimes you need to find ratios that are equal to a known ratio. You can create equal ratios by multiplying and dividing both terms of the ratio by the same nonzero amount.

Left-Handed People Taking Over!

Monterey, CA
A survey of 60 tourists found that 24 were left-handed. These results are high compared to those of other surveys.

✔ **WARM UP**

Tell whether the number is divisible by 2, 3, 4, 5, 6, 9, or 10.

1. 483   2. 648

3. 108   4. 3,540

Example A

Find three ratios that are equal to $\frac{24}{60}$.

One Way
Use multiplication.

Multiply both terms by the same nonzero number.

$$\frac{24 \times 2}{60 \times 2} = \frac{48}{120}$$

$$\frac{24 \times 3}{60 \times 3} = \frac{72}{180}$$

$$\frac{24 \times 4}{60 \times 4} = \frac{96}{240}$$

Another Way
Use division.

Divide both terms by the same nonzero number.

$$\frac{24 \div 12}{60 \div 12} = \frac{2}{5}$$

$$\frac{24 \div 6}{60 \div 6} = \frac{4}{10}$$

$$\frac{24 \div 4}{60 \div 4} = \frac{6}{15}$$

So, $\frac{2}{5}, \frac{4}{10}, \frac{6}{15}, \frac{24}{60}, \frac{48}{120}, \frac{72}{180}$, and $\frac{96}{240}$ are all equal ratios.

Example B

Decide whether the ratios $\frac{3}{27}$ and $\frac{5}{40}$ are equal.

Divide by the GCF of 3 and 27.

$$\frac{3}{27} = \frac{3 \div 3}{27 \div 3} = \frac{1}{9}$$

Divide by the GCF of 5 and 40.

$$\frac{5}{40} = \frac{5 \div 5}{40 \div 5} = \frac{1}{8}$$

Since $\frac{1}{9} \neq \frac{1}{8}$, $\frac{3}{27}$ is not equal to $\frac{5}{40}$.

Example C

For any class field trip, a school requires every 10 students to have one chaperone. Do all the ratios in the table equal 10:1?

Number of Students	30	50	80	100
Number of Chaperones	3	5	8	10

$10:1 = 10 \div 1 = 10$

$30:3 = 30 \div 3 = 10$

$50:5 = 50 \div 5 = 10$

$80:8 = 80 \div 8 = 10$

$100:10 = 100 \div 10 = 10$

Because the quotients are the same, the ratios are equal.

Example D

Write the ratio 96:60 in simplest form.

$\frac{96}{60} = \frac{96 \div 3}{60 \div 3} = \frac{32}{20}$ This is not in simplest form because both 32 and 20 have 4 as a factor.

$\frac{32}{20} = \frac{32 \div 4}{20 \div 4} = \frac{8}{5}$

8:5 is in simplest form because the only number that divides both 8 and 5 is 1.

TEST TALK

Think It Through

I can **use the GCF** of 96 and 60.

$\frac{96}{60} = \frac{96 \div 12}{60 \div 12} = \frac{8}{5}$

✔ Talk About It

1. Which ratio in Example C is in simplest form? Explain how you know.

2. Are the ratios 5:2 and 35:14 equal? Tell how you decided.

3. Can you find an equal ratio by adding the same nonzero amount to each term in the ratio? Why or why not?

Take It to the NET
More Examples
www.scottforesman.com

CHECK ✔

For another example, see Set 6-2 on p. 346.

Give three ratios that are equal to each ratio.

1. $\frac{4}{9}$ **2.** 8 to 5   **3.** 6:10   **4.** $\frac{8}{3}$ **5.** $\frac{12}{60}$

Tell whether the ratios in each pair are equal.

6. $\frac{20}{12}$ and $\frac{15}{9}$ **7.** 3 to 5 and 12 to 15   **8.** $\frac{24}{3}$ and $\frac{16}{3}$

9. Write the ratio 52 to 4 in simplest form.

10. Number Sense Are the ratios 5 to 1 and 6 to 1 equal? Explain.

A Skills and Understanding

Give three ratios that are equal to each ratio.

11. $\frac{5}{6}$ **12.** 8 to 3   **13.** 7:8   **14.** $\frac{8}{6}$ **15.** 7 to 10   **16.** $\frac{20}{10}$

17. 12:36   **18.** $\frac{42}{28}$ **19.** 0.5 to 2   **20.** 1:0.25   **21.** $\frac{1.2}{3.6}$ **22.** 4.5 to 9

Tell whether the ratios in each pair are equal.

23. $\frac{18}{36}$ and $\frac{3}{6}$ **24.** 5 to 7 and 7 to 9   **25.** 6:4 and 30:20   **26.** $\frac{9}{32}$ and $\frac{3}{8}$

27. $\frac{30}{75}$ and $\frac{4}{10}$ **28.** 14 to 7 and 12 to 5   **29.** 45:54 and 60:72   **30.** $\frac{15}{24}$ and $\frac{7}{12}$

Write each ratio in simplest form.

31. $\frac{75}{15}$ **32.** 42 to 21   **33.** 15:87   **34.** $\frac{4.5}{90}$

35. Number Sense Are the ratios $\frac{12}{3}$ and 24:3 equal? How can you tell by just looking at them?

B Reasoning and Problem Solving

Math and Science

The Data File shows bone counts for an adult human.

36. Express the number of bones in the skull to the total number of bones as a ratio.

37. Find the ratio of the number of bones in the arms to the number of bones in the ears. Give two ratios that are equal to this ratio.

38. The ratio of the number of bones in the hip to the number of bones in the sternum is 2:3. Is there another ratio in the table that is 2:3?

39. Writing in Math Is the explanation below correct? Explain.

> Are the ratios 5:18 and 30:128 equal?
>
> I made a table of ratios equal to 5:18. When I got to 30:108, I stopped, because 30:108 is not equal to 30:128. The ratios are not equal.
>
> | | ×2 | ×3 | ×4 | ×5 | ×6 |
> |----|----|----|----|----|-----|
> | 5 | 10 | 15 | 20 | 25 | 30 |
> | 18 | 36 | 54 | 72 | 90 | 108 |

Data File

Bones of the Adult Human Body	
Location	**Number**
Skull	22
Ears (pair)	6
Vertebrae	26
Sternum	3
Throat	1
Ribs	24
Pectoral girdle	4
Arms (pair)	60
Hip bones	2
Legs (pair)	58
Total	206

C Extensions

40. Algebra Copy the grid at the right. Then graph the ratios from the table and connect the points. The first ratio has been graphed for you. Describe any patterns you notice.

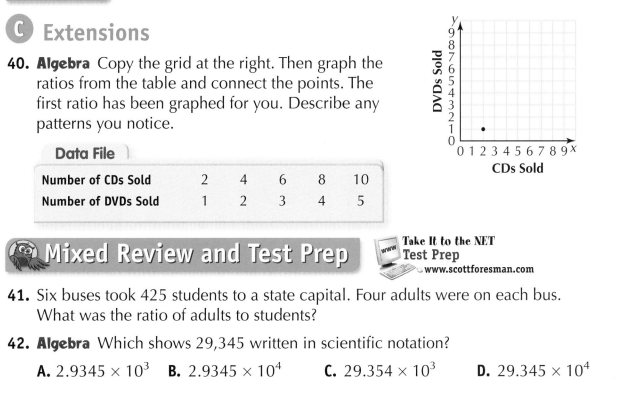

Data File

Number of CDs Sold	2	4	6	8	10
Number of DVDs Sold	1	2	3	4	5

Mixed Review and Test Prep

Take It to the NET
Test Prep
www.scottforesman.com

41. Six buses took 425 students to a state capital. Four adults were on each bus. What was the ratio of adults to students?

42. Algebra Which shows 29,345 written in scientific notation?

A. 2.9345×10^3 **B.** 2.9345×10^4 **C.** 29.354×10^3 **D.** 29.345×10^4

Enrichment

The Golden Ratio

The ancient Greeks believed that rectangles with a length to width ratio of approximately $\frac{1.618}{1}$ were most pleasing to the eye. They called this ratio the *Golden Ratio* and used it to design the Parthenon.

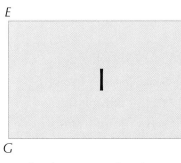

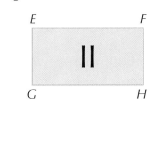

1. Which rectangle above appeals most to you?

2. Measure the sides of rectangles I and II to the nearest millimeter and then express the ratio $\frac{EF}{EG}$ for each rectangle as a decimal. Which rectangle has a length to width ratio closest to the *Golden Ratio*? Was this the rectangle you chose as most appealing?

TEST TALK

Think It Through

I can **use logical reasoning** to compare rates.

$1.50lb

Rates and Unit Rates

LEARN

Activity

Can you compare ratios?

WARM UP

Tell whether the ratios in each pair are equal.

1. $\frac{23}{24}$; 99:100

2. $\frac{5}{15}$, $\frac{7}{21}$

3. 9:5; $\frac{81}{45}$

TANGY Orange Juice
24 oz
$1.25

TANGY Orange Juice
20 oz
$1.25

Crunchy Nuggets
20 oz
$1.75

Crunchy Nuggets
20 oz
$1.95

Really Rich Rolls
6 rolls
$1.80

Really Rich Rolls
10 rolls
$2.50

a. One ratio for the orange juice is $\frac{\$1.25}{20 \text{ oz}}$. The first term is expressed in dollars. What unit of measure is used to express the second term? Write a ratio for the larger bottle of orange juice that includes units of measure.

b. Compare the two orange juice ratios. Are they equal? Is there a way to decide which ratio is greater?

c. Write and compare the two cereal ratios. Then, write and compare the two ratios for the rolls.

d. For which pair of items was it easiest to compare? For which pair was it hardest to compare? Explain.

Are there special kinds of ratios?

A **rate** is a ratio that compares two quantities with different units of measure. A common rate you already know is miles per hour. Some other examples of rates are shown at the right.

If the comparison is to 1 unit, the rate is called a **unit rate**. All of the common rates at the right are unit rates. Notice that 22 miles per gallon, $1.50 per pound, and 72 heartbeats per minute could also be given as 22 miles per 1 gallon, $1.50 per 1 pound, and 72 heartbeats per 1 minute.

Data File

Some Common Rates

• 22 miles per gallon
• 3 cups of water to 1 can of lemonade mix
• $1.50 per pound
• 72 heartbeats per minute

Example A

Give the unit rate for 12 gallons of water in 3 minutes.

One Way
Find an equal ratio.

$$\frac{12 \text{ gallons}}{3 \text{ minutes}} = \frac{x \text{ gallons}}{1 \text{ minute}}$$

$$\frac{12 \div 3}{3 \div 3} = \frac{4}{1}$$

Unit rate: $\frac{4 \text{ gallons}}{1 \text{ minute}}$

Another Way
Find the quotient of the terms.

$$\text{Rate} = \frac{12 \text{ gallons}}{3 \text{ minutes}}$$

$$12 \div 3 = 4$$

Unit rate: $\frac{4 \text{ gallons}}{1 \text{ minute}}$

The unit rate is 4 gallons per minute.

✔ Talk About It

1. What are the unit rates for the rolls on the previous page? Which package of rolls is the better buy?

How can unit rates help you make comparisons?

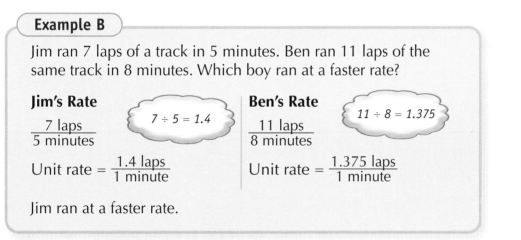

Example B

Jim ran 7 laps of a track in 5 minutes. Ben ran 11 laps of the same track in 8 minutes. Which boy ran at a faster rate?

Jim's Rate

$\frac{7 \text{ laps}}{5 \text{ minutes}}$ $7 \div 5 = 1.4$

Unit rate $= \frac{1.4 \text{ laps}}{1 \text{ minute}}$

Ben's Rate

$\frac{11 \text{ laps}}{8 \text{ minutes}}$ $11 \div 8 = 1.375$

Unit rate $= \frac{1.375 \text{ laps}}{1 \text{ minute}}$

Jim ran at a faster rate.

✔ Talk About It

2. How could you find Jim's rate in laps per hour?

Take It to the NET
More Examples
www.scottforesman.com

For another example, see Set 6-3 on p. 346.

CHECK ✔

Write each as a unit rate.

1. 300 miles in 5 hours

2. 250 calories in 10 crackers

Which is the better buy?

3. 6 T-shirts for $31.50, or 5 T-shirts for $27.50

4. 3 boxes for $6.89, or 5 boxes for $10.93

5. Number Sense Ken runs 4 laps in 6 minutes. What is his rate for 1 hour?

A Skills and Understanding

Write each as a unit rate.

6. 120 students to 6 teachers

7. 9 lb for $13.50

8. 260 miles to 13 gallons of gas

9. 8 ounces every 4 hours

10. 300 miles in 5 hours

11. 18 marbles for 6 boys

12. $12 for 3 books

13. $375 for working 30 hours

Which is the better buy?

14. one gallon of milk for $1.99, or $\frac{1}{2}$ gallon of milk for $0.98

15. $3.96 for 36 oz of cheese, or $6.30 for 42 oz of cheese

16. 16 oz of sour cream for $1.50, or 32 oz of sour cream for $2.75

Which is the lower rate?

17. 2,133 km in 6 hours, or 1,498 km in 7 hours

18. 144 students on 3 buses, or 208 students on 4 buses

19. Number Sense Cristy runs 3 miles in 30 minutes. What is her rate per hour?

B Reasoning and Problem Solving

Math and Science

Give three different rates that describe the speed of the following land animals.

20. lion   **21.** zebra   **22.** grizzly bear

23. A cheetah runs 64 mph. How far can a cheetah run in 15 minutes?

24. The speed of a squirrel is 12 mph. If a squirrel could maintain this speed for 5 minutes, how far would it run?

25. Connections Describe how you could change a rate of feet per second to a rate of feet per hour.

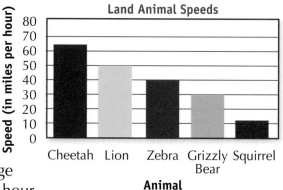

Land Animal Speeds

(Bar graph: Speed in miles per hour vs. Animal)
- Cheetah: ~65
- Lion: ~50
- Zebra: ~40
- Grizzly Bear: ~30
- Squirrel: ~12

26. Writing in Math Is the explanation below correct? If not, tell why not, and write the correct response.

> Explain why $64,480 per year and $1,240 per week are equal rates.
>
> They are equal rates because they are both unit rates.
> One rate is $64,480 for 1 year, and the other is $1,240 for 1 week.

C Extensions

Speed is a type of rate. It is calculated by evaluating the ratio $\frac{\text{distance}}{\text{time}}$. For example, 60 mph = $\frac{300 \text{ miles}}{5 \text{ hours}}$.

27. What ratio can you use to calculate the time it takes to cover 500 miles at a rate of 40 mph?

28. If the speed limit on a highway is 65 miles per hour, what is the shortest time a person can drive 410 miles on this highway without exceeding the speed limit? Express your answer in hours and minutes.

 **Mixed Review and Test Prep**

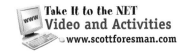 **Take It to the NET**
Test Prep
www.scottforesman.com

Give three ratios that are equal to each ratio.

29. $\frac{8}{24}$ **30.** $\frac{5}{12}$ **31.** $\frac{10}{16}$ **32.** $\frac{30}{10}$

33. Which is the expanded form for 5.072?

A. $(5 \times 0) + (7 \times 0.1) + (2 \times 0.01)$

B. $(5 \times 1) + (7 \times 0.1) + (2 \times 0.01)$

C. $(5 \times 1) + (7 \times 0.01) + (2 \times 0.001)$

D. $(5 \times 10) + (7 \times 0.01) + (2 \times 0.001)$

Discovery CHANNEL SCHOOL

Discover Math in Your World

The Not-So-Mammoth Mastodon

Often confused as being synonymous, the mastodon and the mammoth were two different animals. Standing at a maximum height of 10 feet and weighing up to 13,228 pounds, the mastodon was shorter and heavier than today's Asian elephants.

1. Express the weight of a mastodon in pounds per foot and pounds per inch.

2. Suppose the tusk of a male mastodon was about 9 feet long and weighed about 135 pounds. What was the weight of a tusk in pounds per foot? Pounds per inch?

Take It to the NET
Video and Activities
www.scottforesman.com

All text pages available online and on CD-ROM.

Visualize

Visualizing when you read in math can help you use the **problem-solving strategy,** *Use Objects,* in the next lesson.

In reading, visualizing can help you "see" what is happening in a story. In math, visualizing can help you "see" what is happening in a problem and use objects to solve the problem.

At Lakeside resort, the ratio of motorboats to rowboats is 3 to 4. If there are 35 boats, how many are rowboats?

When I visualize the problem, I see a long line of 35 boats.

Count out 3 red cubes for every 4 blue ones.

Use objects, such as little cubes. Use red cubes for motorboats and blue cubes for rowboats.

1. How many cubes are needed to represent all the boats?

2. What fraction of all the boats are rowboats?

For 3–5, use the problem below.

At the puppet show, the ratio of adults' tickets sold to children's tickets was 3 to 5. In all, 56 tickets were sold. How many tickets sold were children's tickets?

3. Visualize the problem. Describe what you see.

4. Now act it out and use objects by representing the problem with small pieces of colored paper.

5. **Writing in Math** Could fewer than 28 children's tickets have been sold? Explain.

For 6–8, use the problem below.

Ned planted a border of 48 petunias in a single line around the perimeter of his square garden. He started in one corner with a white petunia and evenly spaced them all the way around, alternating between white and red petunias. What is the color of the flowers in the other 3 corners?

6. Visualize the problem. Describe what you see.

7. Now act it out and use small colored objects to represent the problem.

8. **Writing in Math** How many flowers are on each side? Explain how you found your answer.

For 9–12, use the problem and picture below.

Helen put up a wallpaper border of ballerinas on a wall of her dance studio. Each repeat of the pattern shows the same 4 ballerinas. If the length of the wall is 308 inches, how many of the ballerinas are pink?

9. Visualize the problem. Describe what you see

10. **Writing in Math** How many repeats of the pattern were needed? Explain.

11. Now use small colored objects to act out the problem.

12. How many objects did you need to represent the problem?

Wallpaper Border #217   Height: 7" Repeat: 22"

Problem-Solving Strategy

Reading Helps!

Visualizing

can help you with...

the problem-solving strategy, *Use Objects*.

Key Idea
Learning how and when to use objects can help you solve problems.

Use Objects

LEARN

How can you use objects to solve a problem?

Brass Section There are 20 members in the brass section of an orchestra. Three out of every five musicians in the brass section are new to the orchestra. How many members of the brass section are new to the orchestra?

Read and Understand

What do you know? There are 20 members in the brass section. Three out of every five are new.

What are you trying to find? How many members out of the 20 in the brass section are new to the orchestra?

Plan and Solve

What strategy will you use? **Strategy: Use Objects**

How to Use Objects

Step 1 Choose objects.
Step 2 Show the known information.
Step 3 Use the objects to solve the problem.

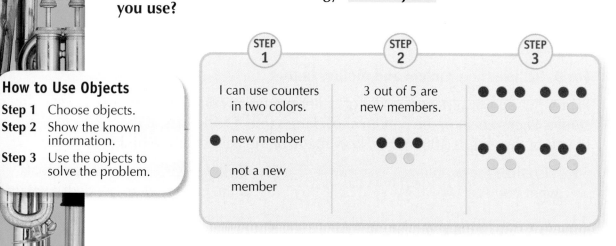

Answer: There are 12 new members in the brass section.

Look Back and Check

Is your work correct? Yes. The model shows 20 members and that 3 out of every 5 are new.

✔ Talk About It

1. What do the red and yellow counters show in Step 2?

For another example, see Set 6-4 on p. 347.

CHECK ✓

Use objects to solve each problem. Give the answer in a complete sentence.

1. There are 24 players on a baseball team. Two out of every three players were on the team last year. How many players were on the team last year?

2. Erik has 30 tomato plants. One out of every 5 plants has yellow tomatoes. How many plants have yellow tomatoes?

PRACTICE

For more practice, see Set 6-4 on p. 350.

Solve each problem. Give the answer in a complete sentence.

3. Cathy has a large aquarium containing 50 fish. Three out of every 5 fish are guppies. How many fish are guppies? The green color tiles represent guppies. The blue tiles represent other fish. Use the color tiles pictured below to solve the problem.

4. Of the 120 members in the Trevian marching band, 2 out of every 5 members are girls. How many girls are in the band?

5. A rock band needed 250 hours of studio work to record 45 minutes of music. What is the ratio of minutes of music to minutes of studio work?

6. Lisa is older than Susan. Glenn is younger than Susan. Rodney's age is between Glenn's and Susan's. What is the order of the four children from youngest to oldest?

7. How many boys are in a class of 32 students if the ratio of boys to girls is 3:5?

8. **Reasoning** Pets, Incorporated has 36 kittens and puppies. Two out of every 3 of these young animals are kittens. How many of the animals are puppies?

9. **Writing in Math** A math test had 24 items. For every 5 correct answers, Carrie had 1 incorrect answer. Explain how to find how many items Carrie had correct.

STRATEGIES

- **Show What You Know**
  Draw a Picture
  Make an Organized List
  Make a Table
  Make a Graph
  Act It Out or Use Objects
- **Look for a Pattern**
- **Try, Check, and Revise**
- **Write an Equation**
- **Use Logical Reasoning**
- **Solve a Simpler Problem**
- **Work Backward**

Choose a tool

Mental Math

TEST TALK

Think It Through

Stuck? I won't give up. I can:

- Reread the problem.
- Tell what I know.
- Identify key facts and details.
- Tell the problem in my own words.
- Show the main idea.
- Try a different strategy.
- Retrace my steps.

Do You Know How?

Do You Understand?

Understanding Ratios (6-1)

Write a ratio for each comparison in three ways.

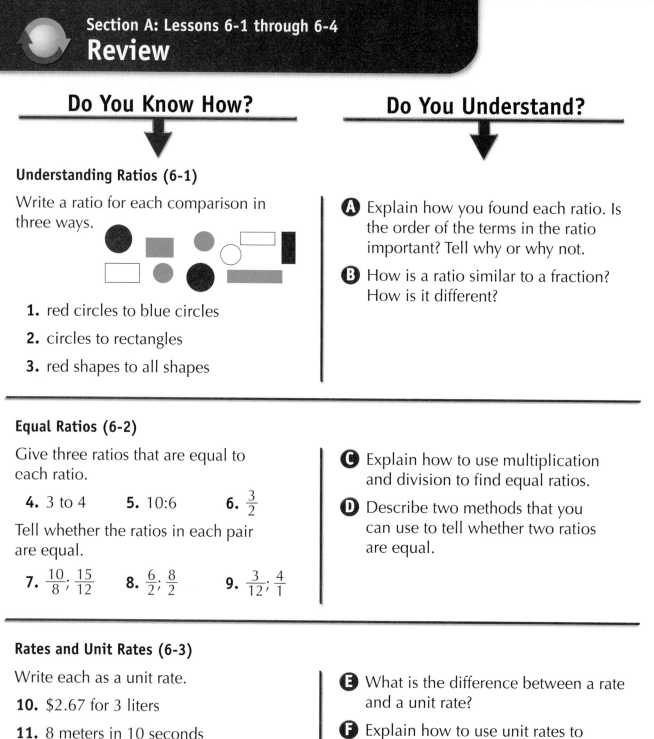

1. red circles to blue circles

2. circles to rectangles

3. red shapes to all shapes

A Explain how you found each ratio. Is the order of the terms in the ratio important? Tell why or why not.

B How is a ratio similar to a fraction? How is it different?

Equal Ratios (6-2)

Give three ratios that are equal to each ratio.

4. 3 to 4   5. 10:6   6. $\frac{3}{2}$

Tell whether the ratios in each pair are equal.

7. $\frac{10}{8}$; $\frac{15}{12}$ 8. $\frac{6}{2}$; $\frac{8}{2}$ 9. $\frac{3}{12}$; $\frac{4}{1}$

C Explain how to use multiplication and division to find equal ratios.

D Describe two methods that you can use to tell whether two ratios are equal.

Rates and Unit Rates (6-3)

Write each as a unit rate.

10. $2.67 for 3 liters

11. 8 meters in 10 seconds

12. 164 miles on 8 gallons of gas

E What is the difference between a rate and a unit rate?

F Explain how to use unit rates to decide which is a better buy: 5 lb for $5.60 or 7 lb for $8.05.

Use Objects (6-4)

Use objects to solve the problem. Give the answer in a complete sentence.

13. At a dinner, the guests could choose between beef or chicken. Of the 35 guests, 3 out of 5 chose chicken. How many guests chose chicken?

G What other strategies could you use to find the number of guests who chose chicken?

MULTIPLE CHOICE

1. Which ratio is equal to 3 to 5? (6-2)

   A. $\frac{5}{3}$

   B. $\frac{12}{20}$

   C. 3:10

   D. 12:15

2. Which is the best buy? (6-3)

   A. $9.95 for 5 lb

   B. $13.23 for 7 lb

   C. $6.15 for 3 lb

   D. $8.60 for 4 lb

FREE RESPONSE

T-shirts Galore recorded the number of each color T-shirt they sold. Write a ratio for each comparison in three ways. (6-1)

3. red T-shirts to white T-shirts

4. black T-shirts to purple T-shirts

5. blue T-shirts to all other T-shirts

6. white T-shirts to all T-shirts

Data File

T-shirt Sales	
Color	Amount
red	15
blue	9
black	12
white	28
purple	8

Give three ratios that are equal to each ratio. (6-2)

7. $\frac{6}{5}$

8. 12 to 8

9. 36:48

10. 3 to 1

11. $\frac{2}{7}$

Write each ratio in simplest form. (6-2)

12. 54 to 16

13. $\frac{64}{88}$

14. 33 to 270

15. 96:8

Write each as a unit rate. (6-3)

16. 171 miles in 3 hours

17. $290 for 25 hours of work

18. 2 cups of flour for 4 dozen cookies

19. $2.88 for 32 oz

20. Mrs. McGregor has 12 rose bushes around her house. Two out of every 3 rose bushes have red flowers. How many rose bushes have red flowers? (6-4)

Writing in Math

21. Yvette did 30 sit ups and 18 push ups. She wrote the ratio 3:5 to compare the number of sit ups to the number of push ups. Is this correct? Explain your answer. (6-1, 6-2)

22. Explain how to decide if 5 cans for $3.25 or 12 cans for $8.16 is the better buy.

Key Idea
A proportion is a statement that two ratios are equal.

Vocabulary
• proportion
• cross products

Understanding Proportions

✔ **WARM UP**

Write = or ≠.

1. $\frac{3}{4}$ $\frac{9}{12}$ 2. $\frac{8}{16}$ $\frac{4}{8}$

3. $\frac{20}{12}$ $\frac{5}{3}$ 4. $\frac{3}{1}$ $\frac{1}{3}$

5. $\frac{24}{6}$ $\frac{4}{1}$ 6. $\frac{12}{15}$ $\frac{3}{5}$

LEARN

What is a proportion?

A **proportion** states that two ratios are equal. You can use the first two Value Vehicle ratios to write a proportion: $\frac{1 \text{ day}}{\$20} = \frac{2 \text{ days}}{\$40}$.

In a proportion, the units must be the same across the top and bottom, or down the left and right sides. In this case, days are across the top and dollars across the bottom.

For Value Vehicle, the ratios of days to the cost of renting a car are all equal. We say that these quantities **vary proportionally.** The What-A-Deal Wheels ratios are NOT all equal, so these quantities do NOT vary proportionally.

In the proportion $\frac{1}{20} = \frac{2}{40}$, 1×40 and 20×2 are cross products. The **cross products** of the terms in a proportion are equal.

Value Vehicle

Days	Cost
1	$20
2	$40
3	$60
4	$80

What-A-Deal Wheels

Days	Cost
1	$20
2	$35
3	$48
4	$59

Example

Decide if the ratios $\frac{3 \text{ ft}}{8 \text{ sec}}$ and $\frac{9 \text{ ft}}{24 \text{ sec}}$ form a proportion.

What You Do	**Why It Works**
Look at the units.	Multiply both sides of the proportion by 24×8 and simplify.
$\frac{3 \text{ ft}}{8 \text{ sec}} \overset{?}{=} \frac{9 \text{ ft}}{24 \text{ sec}}$ — The units are the same across the top and bottom.	$\frac{24 \times 8 \times 3}{8} = \frac{9 \times 24 \times 8}{24}$
Look at the cross products.	$24 \times 3 = 9 \times 8$ ← cross products
$3 \times 24 \overset{?}{=} 8 \times 9$ ← The cross products are equal.	$72 = 72$
$72 = 72$	

Since the units are the same and the cross products are equal, the ratios form a proportion.

✔ **Talk About It**

1. Do the ratios $\frac{4 \text{ ft}}{6 \text{ ft}}$ and $\frac{12 \text{ sec}}{18 \text{ sec}}$ form a proportion? Why or why not?

Decide if the ratios form a proportion.

1. $\frac{2 \text{ tbs}}{1 \text{ oz}}$; $\frac{4 \text{ oz}}{8 \text{ tbs}}$

2. $\frac{100 \text{ mi}}{4 \text{ h}}$; $\frac{125 \text{ mi}}{5 \text{ h}}$

3. $\frac{5 \text{ ft}}{8 \text{ s}}$; $\frac{10 \text{ s}}{6 \text{ ft}}$

4. Number Sense Which proportion is written correctly? Explain.

    a. 12 inches:1 foot = 4 feet:48 inches   **b.** 12 inches:1 foot = 48 inches:4 feet

PRACTICE

For more practice, see Set 6-5 on p. 350.

Ⓐ Skills and Understanding

Decide if the ratios form a proportion.

5. $\frac{14 \text{ in.}}{10 \text{ min}}$; $\frac{70 \text{ in.}}{50 \text{ s}}$

6. $\frac{6 \text{ mi}}{10 \text{ mi}}$; $\frac{15 \text{ yd}}{25 \text{ yd}}$

7. $\frac{8 \text{ oranges}}{\$5}$; $\frac{11 \text{ oranges}}{\$7}$

8. \$75:5 h; \$35:2 h

9. 1ft:8 s; 4 ft:33 s

10. 3:25; 6:50

11. Number Sense Explain why $\frac{\$1.25}{5 \text{ oz}}$ and $\frac{20 \text{ oz}}{\$5}$ do not form a proportion.

Ⓑ Reasoning and Problem Solving

12. Which two boys' successes to attempts ratios are equal?

13. Reasoning How can you tell by looking at the graph whether Nate or Anthony was more successful?

14. Algebra Find three x- and y-values for $\frac{5 \text{ tickets}}{\$40} = \frac{x \text{ tickets}}{\$y}$.

15. Writing in Math Some standard sizes for photographs are 3.5-by-5 inches, 4-by-6 inches, 5-by-7 inches, and 8-by-10 inches. Do the ratios of the dimensions vary proportionally? Explain how you know when quantities vary proportionally.

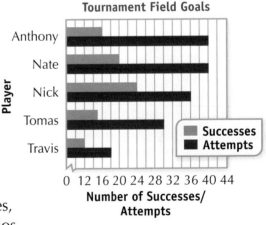

Tournament Field Goals

Number of Successes/ Attempts

■ Successes
■ Attempts

🦉 Mixed Review and Test Prep

Take It to the NET
Test Prep
www.scottforesman.com

16. Kevin successfully completed 5 out of 6 serves at the volleyball game. If he served 30 times, how many serves did he complete successfully?

17. Which is the GCF of 12 and 18?

    A. 3   **B.** 6   **C.** 36   **D.** 216

18. Which is the LCM of 54 and 72?

    A. 9   **B.** 18   **C.** 216   **D.** 972

Key Idea
There are different methods for solving proportions.

Think It Through
I can **make a table** and **look for a pattern** to solve proportions.

Solving Proportions

LEARN

WARM UP
Find each pair of cross products.
1. $\frac{2}{3} = \frac{8}{12}$ 2. $\frac{18}{6} = \frac{15}{5}$
3. $\frac{24}{36} = \frac{4}{6}$ 4. $\frac{5}{10} = \frac{7}{14}$

Activity

How can you use ratio tables to solve proportions?

Solve these problems by copying and completing the ratio tables. In each problem, the quantities vary proportionally.

a. For every 3 CD-of-the-month club subscriptions sold to men, 8 subscriptions are sold to women. At this rate, how many subscriptions would be sold to women if 18 are sold to men? Look at the pattern.

The yellow counters below show the number of CD subscriptions sold to men. The red counters show the number sold to women.

Subscriptions Sold to Men	3	6	9	12	15	18
Subscriptions Sold to Women	8	16	?	?	?	?

b. Of the last 100 vehicles sold at a particular dealership, 60 were sport utility vehicles (SUVs). At this rate, how many SUVs would be sold out of the next 40 vehicles sold?

Total Vehicles Sold	100	10	20	30	40
Total SUVs Sold	60	6	?	?	?

c. In Problem a, how did you know what numbers to write in the row titled Subscriptions Sold to Women?

d. In Problem b, $\frac{100}{60}$ was first simplified to $\frac{10}{6}$. Then what was done to complete the table?

What are other methods for solving proportions?

Sometimes it is not easy to make a table to solve a proportion.

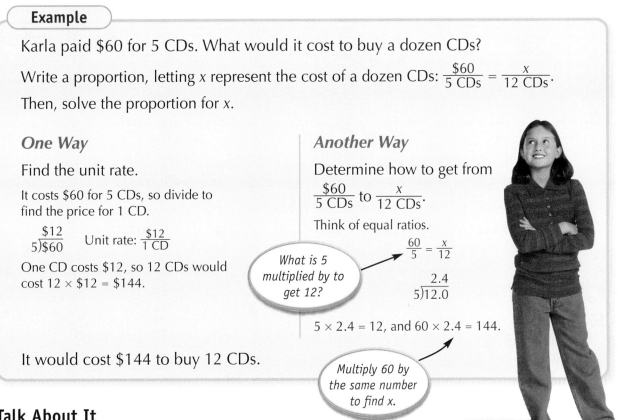

Example

Karla paid $60 for 5 CDs. What would it cost to buy a dozen CDs?

Write a proportion, letting x represent the cost of a dozen CDs: $\frac{\$60}{5 \text{ CDs}} = \frac{x}{12 \text{ CDs}}$.

Then, solve the proportion for x.

One Way

Find the unit rate.

It costs $60 for 5 CDs, so divide to find the price for 1 CD.

$$5\overline{)\$60}^{\$12} \qquad \text{Unit rate: } \frac{\$12}{1 \text{ CD}}$$

One CD costs $12, so 12 CDs would cost $12 \times \$12 = \$144$.

Another Way

Determine how to get from $\frac{\$60}{5 \text{ CDs}}$ to $\frac{x}{12 \text{ CDs}}$.

Think of equal ratios.

$$\frac{60}{5} = \frac{x}{12}$$

$$5\overline{)12.0}^{2.4}$$

What is 5 multiplied by to get 12?

$5 \times 2.4 = 12$, and $60 \times 2.4 = 144$.

It would cost $144 to buy 12 CDs.

Multiply 60 by the same number to find x.

✔ Talk About It

1. In the first method in the Example, what two numbers were used to find the unit price?

2. In the second method in the Example, would you use the same operation if you wrote the proportion $\frac{5 \text{ CDs}}{\$60} = \frac{12 \text{ CDs}}{x}$?

3. **Estimation** How could you have estimated a value for x in the proportion above?

CHECK ✓

For another example, see Set 6-6 on p. 347.

Solve each proportion using any method.

1. $\frac{\$25}{4 \text{ hours}} = \frac{x}{12 \text{ hours}}$

2. $\frac{16 \text{ ft}}{5 \text{ s}} = \frac{48 \text{ ft}}{x}$

3. $\frac{5 \text{ gal}}{20 \text{ qt}} = \frac{x}{6 \text{ qt}}$

4. Lauren's car averages 24 miles for each gallon of gasoline. How many gallons are needed for a trip of 216 miles?

5. If rent for 2 weeks is $750, how much rent is paid for 5 weeks?

6. **Estimation** Melinda earned $380 working 40 hours. Use *estimation* to decide if she earned between $8 and $9 an hour or between $9 and $10 an hour. Tell how you decided.

A Skills and Understanding

Solve each proportion using any method.

7. $\dfrac{9\text{ m}}{b\text{ s}} = \dfrac{6\text{ m}}{8\text{ s}}$

8. $\dfrac{\$31.50}{5\text{ hours}} = \dfrac{f}{7\text{ hours}}$

9. $\dfrac{220\text{ mi}}{4\text{ h}} = \dfrac{82.5\text{ mi}}{y\text{ h}}$

10. $\dfrac{300\text{ mi}}{p\text{ h}} = \dfrac{180\text{ mi}}{6\text{ h}}$

11. $\dfrac{\$93.75}{y\text{ h}} = \dfrac{\$62.50}{10\text{ h}}$

12. $\dfrac{2.4\text{ ft}}{4.5\text{ s}} = \dfrac{p\text{ ft}}{1.8\text{ s}}$

13. The local museum requires 3 chaperones for every 15 students. How many chaperones would be necessary for 125 students?

14. A model of a park has a length of 5 inches. The park has an actual length of 18 feet and a width of 27 feet. How wide is the model?

15. **Number Sense** Sol drove 440 miles in 8 hours. Calculate his speed by finding the unit rate of miles per hour (mph). Explain how you found your answer.

B Reasoning and Problem Solving

16. At Happy Day Kiddie Kamp, the ratio of counselors to campers is 2 to 15. How many counselors should be hired if 120 children sign up for the camp?

17. Chucky's Deli sells 60 salads for every 96 sandwiches. At this rate, how many salads will be sold for every 32 sandwiches?

Math and Science

The famous scientist and artist Leonardo da Vinci felt that the parts of a perfect body should be related by certain ratios. His famous 1492 drawing, *Vitruvian Man,* is shown here. The armspan is equal to the man's height. Some of the other ratios are listed below the drawing.

18. If the hand in a drawing measures 21 inches, how long should the foot be?

19. If the length of the big toe of a sculpture is 6 centimeters, how long should the hand be?

20. Suppose the distance from the elbow to the end of the hand on a statue measures 18 inches. How long should the distance from the shoulder to the elbow be?

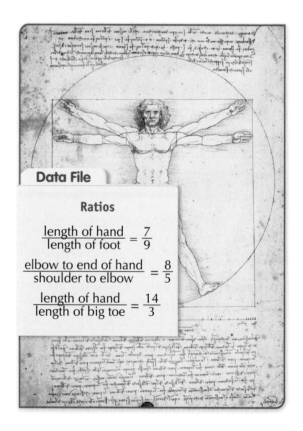

Data File

Ratios

$\dfrac{\text{length of hand}}{\text{length of foot}} = \dfrac{7}{9}$

$\dfrac{\text{elbow to end of hand}}{\text{shoulder to elbow}} = \dfrac{8}{5}$

$\dfrac{\text{length of hand}}{\text{length of big toe}} = \dfrac{14}{3}$

21. <u>Writing in Math</u> Is the explanation below correct? If not, tell why and write the correct response.

Uma has 12 boys in her class of 20 students. Felix has 15 boys in his class of 24 students. Which class has the greater ratio of boys to students?

I need to look at the ratios $\frac{12 \text{ boys}}{20 \text{ students}}$ and $\frac{15 \text{ boys}}{24 \text{ students}}$.

When I simplify the ratio of boys to students in Uma's class, I get $\frac{12 \div 4}{20 \div 4} = \frac{3 \text{ boys}}{5 \text{ students}}$. The simplified ratio for Felix's class is $\frac{5 \text{ boys}}{8 \text{ students}}$.

Since $\frac{3}{5} > \frac{5}{8}$, the ratio is greater in Uma's class.

Think It Through

I should ask myself if there is **another way to solve the problem** as a way to check my answer.

C Extensions

22. Algebra Give four values for $\frac{x}{y}$ to make $\frac{50}{24} = \frac{x}{y}$ a proportion.

Mixed Review and Test Prep

Take It to the NET
Test Prep
www.scottforesman.com

Decide if the ratios form a proportion.

23. $\frac{10 \text{ ft}}{4 \text{ sec}}; \frac{5 \text{ sec}}{2 \text{ ft}}$

24. $\frac{3}{4}; \frac{12}{16}$

25. $\frac{\$40}{8 \text{ hr}}; \frac{\$55}{11 \text{ hr}}$

26. Which is $\frac{2}{3} \div \frac{3}{5}$?

A. $\frac{2}{5}$

B. $\frac{10}{9}$

C. $\frac{9}{10}$

D. $\frac{5}{2}$

Enrichment

Dimensional Analysis

One way of changing units from one unit of measure to another is to use a formula. Another way is to analyze the units and use them to divide and simplify rates. This method is called **dimensional analysis.**

You can use dimensional analysis to calculate the number of times a person's heart beats in one hour, assuming it beats an average of 68 times per minute.

$$\frac{68 \text{ beats}}{\text{minute}} \cdot \frac{60 \text{ minutes}}{1 \text{ hour}} = \frac{(68)(60) \text{beats}}{1 \text{ hour}} = \frac{4,080 \text{ beats}}{\text{hour}}$$

Using dimensional analysis and the given heart rate, calculate:

1. the number of heartbeats per day.

2. the number of heartbeats per year.

Key Idea
Another method for solving proportions is to use cross products.

Vocabulary
• cross products (p. 316)

Think It Through

I can **draw a picture** to show the proportion.

Solving Proportions Using Cross Products

LEARN

How can you use cross products to solve proportions?

Example A

Granola Bars How many ounces of granola are needed to make 9 dozen bars?

The picture below shows the proportion.

```
|    12 oz    |  |       ? oz      |
|   4 dozen   |  |     9 dozen     |
```

So, $\frac{12}{4} = \frac{x}{9}$, where x is the number of ounces of granola needed.

Solve $\frac{12}{4} = \frac{x}{9}$.

$12 \cdot 9 = 4x$ Write the cross products.

$108 = 4x$ Multiply.

$\frac{108}{4} = \frac{4x}{4}$ Solve for the variable.

$27 = x$

For 9 dozen granola bars, 27 ounces of granola are needed.

> **GRANOLA BARS**
> Sift together $1\frac{1}{4}$ cups flour 1 tsp baking soda, $\frac{1}{2}$ tsp salt. Add 1 cup brown sugar 1 tsp vanilla, and 2 eggs. Beat until smooth. Stir in 12 oz of granola and cup chopped nuts. Spread into greased 9" x 13" pan and bake at 350 for about 25 minutes until brown.
>
> Makes 4 dozen bars.

Example B

Use a calculator to solve $\frac{58.5}{k} = \frac{25}{6.2}$.

Press: 58.5 ⊠ 6.2 ⊟ ⊞ 25.

Display: ⌈ 14.508 ⌉

Why It Works

$\frac{58.5}{k} = \frac{25}{6.2}$

$(58.5)(6.2) = 25k$

$\frac{(58.5)(6.2)}{25} = k$ *Round to the nearest tenth.*

$14.5 \approx k$

✔ **Talk About It**

1. **Estimation** In Example B, 58 is about 2 times 25. How can you use that fact to estimate the value of k?

Solve each proportion using cross products. Round to the nearest hundredth as needed.

1. $\frac{6}{8} = \frac{p}{12}$　　　**2.** $\frac{g}{6} = \frac{1}{4}$　　　**3.** $\frac{4}{m} = \frac{20}{36}$　　　**4.** $\frac{2.4}{4.5} = \frac{d}{1.8}$

5. Number Sense How can you tell without solving $\frac{45}{20} = \frac{h}{50}$ that h is greater than 100?

PRACTICE

For more practice, see Set 6-7 on p. 350.

Ⓐ Skills and Understanding

Solve each proportion using cross products. Round to the nearest hundredth as needed.

6. $\frac{b}{3} = \frac{8}{4}$　　　**7.** $\frac{3}{5} = \frac{14}{c}$　　　**8.** $\frac{8.4}{h} = \frac{11.2}{6.8}$　　　**9.** $\frac{3}{10} = \frac{k}{60}$

10. $\frac{p}{12.6} = \frac{5}{15}$　　**11.** $\frac{45}{77.4} = \frac{10}{m}$　　**12.** $\frac{w}{24} = \frac{0.875}{6}$　　**13.** $\frac{35}{8} = \frac{27}{j}$

14. Number Sense Franci can read 40 pages in 30 minutes. How can you mentally calculate the number of pages she can read in 45 minutes?

Ⓑ Reasoning and Problem Solving

The table at the right gives the ratio of pedal turns to rear-wheel turns for each gear of a 5-speed bicycle.

15. On Miguel's bike, the rear wheel turns 770 times per mile. How many times would he have to pedal to travel 1 mile in first gear? fifth gear?

16. If Miguel pedals 385 times to go 1 mile, what gear is the bicycle in?

17. <u>Writing in Math</u> For a bike trip, there are to be 4 chaperones for every 20 students. How many chaperones are needed for 120 students? Explain how you found your answer.

Data File

5-speed Bicycle

Gear	Pedal Turns: Rear-wheel Turns
First	9:14
Second	4:7
Third	1:2
Fourth	3:7
Fifth	5:14

🦉 Mixed Review and Test Prep

Take It to the NET
www **Test Prep**
www.scottforesman.com

Solve each proportion.

18. $\frac{\$3}{4\text{ oz}} = \frac{m}{6\text{ oz}}$　　　**19.** $\frac{\$14}{4\text{ hr}} = \frac{\$35}{v\text{ hr}}$　　　**20.** $\frac{165\text{ mi}}{3\text{ hr}} = \frac{r\text{ mi}}{2\text{ hr}}$

21. Which is 6.54×18.9?

　　A. 25.44　　　**B.** 117.72　　　**C.** 123.606　　　**D.** 123.66

Problem-Solving Skill

Key Idea
There are specific things you can do to write a good explanation in math.

Think It Through
I should make sure my explanations are clear and well organized so that others can understand them.

Writing to Explain

LEARN

How do you write a good explanation?

When you write to explain, it is important that you describe each step in the solution clearly.

Orange Drink Kimberley has the two recipes for orange drink shown below.

Orange-Drink Recipe 1	**Orange-Drink Recipe 2**
• 2 cans orange juice concentrate • 3 cans of cold water	• 4 cans orange juice concentrate • 8 cans of cold water

Which recipe do you think has more of an orange taste? Write and explain how you decided.

Writing a Math Explanation

- State your answer.

- Break your explanation into steps so it is easier to follow.

- Use pictures or diagrams, if they help in the explanation.

- If computation is part of the solution, show the computation.

I think that Recipe 1 has more of an orange taste. Here is why.

This shows Recipe 2. 4 circles show cans of juice and 8 circles show cans of water.

I drew the line to show equal groups. Each group has 2 cans of juice and 4 cans of water.

Recipe 2 uses 2 cans of juice for 4 cans of water. Recipe 1 uses 2 cans of juice for 3 cans of water. Recipe 1 has more juice per can of water, so Recipe 1 has more orange flavor.

✔ Talk About It

1. How does the picture help in the explanation?

2. Is there another way to explain the solution to the problem? Explain.

1. For every 6 girls on a bus, there are 5 boys. If there are 18 girls on the bus, how many boys are on the bus? Write to explain how to find the answer.

2. Perry goes for a walk every morning. Today he walked more miles than he did yesterday and in less time. On which day did he walk faster? Write to explain how to find the answer.

3. Lynette earns $5 by delivering newspapers. She saves $3 and she spends the rest. If she saved $27 one month, how much money did she spend? Explain how to find the answer.

4. Filipi and Junko are on a swim team. Their training swim is 200 meters and usually takes them 3 minutes. Explain how long, at this rate, it would take them to complete an 800-meter swim.

5. Deliah's car travels 180 miles on 4 gallons of gas. Explain how far the car will travel on 7 gallons of gas.

Reasonableness For Problems 6–8, rewrite each problem so that it makes sense.

6. Jake walks 35 miles to school in one hour.

7. Ben receives an allowance of $4 each week. At this rate, he will receive about $100 in allowance per month.

8. Janice knows that 1 kilometer is a little more than $\frac{1}{2}$ mile. If she runs 10 kilometers in 1 hour, then she runs at a rate of 4 miles per hour.

Model railroad hobbyists can collect toy trains and equipment that are precise replicas of the actual trains. There are four popular scales which appear in the table at the right.

9. How many inches long is the actual locomotive if an O scale model is 18 inches long?

10. How long, in inches, would an S scale model of a 768-inch locomotive be?

11. Write a proportion to convert 13.5 inches to feet.

Scale Name	Scale (inches) Model: Actual
H	$\frac{1}{24}$
HO	$\frac{1}{87}$
O	$\frac{1}{48}$
S	$\frac{1}{64}$

Do You Know How?

Do You Understand?

Understanding Proportions (6-5)

Decide if the ratios form a proportion.

1. $\frac{25 \text{ mi}}{5 \text{ h}}$; $\frac{15 \text{ mi}}{3 \text{ h}}$

2. $\frac{3 \text{ in.}}{8 \text{ ft}}$; $\frac{6 \text{ ft}}{16 \text{ in.}}$

3. $\frac{10 \text{ cm}}{5 \text{ m}}$; $\frac{1 \text{ cm}}{2 \text{ m}}$

4. $\frac{9 \text{ lb}}{\$13.50}$; $\frac{4 \text{ lb}}{\$6.00}$

A Explain how you decided whether the ratios form a proportion.

B How can you tell without calculating whether $\frac{4 \text{ in.}}{21 \text{ ft}}$; $\frac{1 \text{ ft}}{7 \text{ in.}}$ is a proportion?

Solving Proportions (6-6)
Solving Proportions Using Cross Products (6-7)

Solve each proportion using any method.

5. $\frac{6 \text{ cans}}{\$4.50} = \frac{x \text{ cans}}{\$1.50}$

6. $\frac{2 \text{ in.}}{5 \text{ ft}} = \frac{7 \text{ in.}}{y \text{ ft}}$

7. $\frac{9.6 \text{ mi}}{2 \text{ h}} = \frac{24 \text{ mi}}{y \text{ h}}$

8. $\frac{2 \text{ L}}{\$3.98} = \frac{5 \text{ L}}{x}$

Solve each proportion using cross products.

9. $\frac{3 \text{ in.}}{120 \text{ mi}} = \frac{5 \text{ in.}}{t \text{ mi}}$

10. $\frac{15}{b} = \frac{21}{7}$

11. $\frac{5 \text{ h}}{\$53.25} = \frac{8 \text{ h}}{m}$

12. $\frac{t}{90} = \frac{16}{100}$

C Explain what method you used to solve the proportion in Exercise 5.

D Describe how to use cross products to find the missing value in a proportion.

Writing to Explain (6-8)

13. Fly By Night Airlines keeps the ratio of discount-fare seats to full-fare seats at 2 to 15. How many discount-fare tickets should be sold for a 240 full-fare seat flight?

14. Four shovels of sand are used for every 5 shovels of concrete. How many shovels of sand are needed for 25 shovels of concrete?

15. The ratio of weight on Earth to weight on the moon is 6:1. If you weigh 138 pounds on Earth, how much would you weigh on the moon?

E Describe how you could use proportions to solve each problem.

F What should you include to write a good explanation to a math problem?

MULTIPLE CHOICE

1. Which of the following is NOT a proportion? (6-5)

A. $\dfrac{3 \text{ in.}}{12 \text{ ft}} = \dfrac{1 \text{ in.}}{4 \text{ ft}}$
  B. $\dfrac{\$9}{3 \text{ lb}} = \dfrac{\$6}{2 \text{ lb}}$
  C. $\dfrac{360 \text{ mi}}{7.2 \text{ h}} = \dfrac{50 \text{ h}}{1 \text{ mi}}$
  D. $\dfrac{4 \text{ laps}}{12 \text{ min}} = \dfrac{6 \text{ laps}}{18 \text{ min}}$

2. Jack runs 3 miles in 27 minutes. At this rate, how long will it take him to run 10 miles? (6-6, 6-7, 6-8)

A. 1.1 hours   **B.** 90 minutes   **C.** 81 minutes   **D.** 57 minutes

FREE RESPONSE

Decide if the ratios form a proportion. (6-5)

3. $\dfrac{64 \text{ mi}}{2 \text{ h}}, \dfrac{160 \text{ mi}}{5 \text{ h}}$
  4. $\dfrac{3 \text{ cm}}{15 \text{ km}}, \dfrac{5 \text{ cm}}{25 \text{ km}}$
  5. $\dfrac{6 \text{ gal}}{\$3.48}, \dfrac{\$0.58}{1 \text{ gal}}$

6. $\dfrac{2 \text{ tsp}}{1 \text{ oz}}, \dfrac{4 \text{ oz}}{8 \text{ tsp}}$
  7. $\dfrac{6 \text{ acres}}{10 \text{ acres}}, \dfrac{15 \text{ ft}}{25 \text{ ft}}$
  8. $\dfrac{6 \text{ ft}}{10 \text{ s}}, \dfrac{9 \text{ ft}}{15 \text{ s}}$

9. $\dfrac{14}{17}, \dfrac{70}{55}$
  10. $\dfrac{1 \text{ mi}}{7 \text{ min}}, \dfrac{7 \text{ mi}}{49 \text{ min}}$
  11. $\dfrac{3}{8}, \dfrac{6}{9.5}$

12. $\dfrac{2 \text{ tsp}}{12 \text{ oz}}, \dfrac{1.5 \text{ tsp}}{9 \text{ oz}}$
  13. $\dfrac{4}{6}, \dfrac{0.9}{1.3}$
  14. $\dfrac{12.7 \text{ cm}}{20 \text{ m}}, \dfrac{8.9 \text{ cm}}{14.06 \text{ m}}$

Think It Through
I can use what I know about **equal ratios** to solve a proportion.

Solve each proportion using any method. (6-6, 6-7)

15. $\dfrac{\$97.50}{13 \text{ h}} = \dfrac{\$y}{6 \text{ h}}$
  16. $\dfrac{7 \text{ in.}}{35 \text{ ft}} = \dfrac{9 \text{ in.}}{n \text{ ft}}$
  17. $\dfrac{2 \text{ cups}}{5 \text{ gal}} = \dfrac{x \text{ cups}}{8 \text{ gal}}$

18. $\dfrac{65 \text{ mi}}{4 \text{ h}} = \dfrac{130 \text{ mi}}{b \text{ h}}$
  19. $\dfrac{1 \text{ in.}}{2.54 \text{ cm}} = \dfrac{t \text{ in.}}{254 \text{ cm}}$
  20. $\dfrac{3 \text{ tbsp}}{2 \text{ gal}} = \dfrac{x \text{ tbsp}}{15 \text{ gal}}$

21. $\dfrac{8.4}{y} = \dfrac{11.2}{6.8}$
  22. $\dfrac{2.4}{4.5} = \dfrac{w}{1.8}$
  23. $\dfrac{24 \text{ lb}}{12 \text{ ft}} = \dfrac{x \text{ lb}}{28 \text{ ft}}$

24. $\dfrac{4 \text{ lbs}}{\$89} = \dfrac{9 \text{ lbs}}{m}$
  25. $\dfrac{\$13,500}{9 \text{ mos}} = \dfrac{x}{10 \text{ mos}}$
  26. $\dfrac{160.95}{37} = \dfrac{26.10}{n}$

Writing in Math

27. Justin earns $7 for each lawn he mows. If he earned $28 yesterday, how many lawns did he mow? Explain how you found the answer. (6-8)

28. Maggie puts $5 out of every $20 she earns into her savings account. She says that to put $25 in her savings account, she needs to earn $220. Is this reasonable? Explain your answer. (6-8)

29. Andrew drove 120 miles on 5 gallons of gas. He says his car uses 1 gallon to go 24 miles. Does this make sense? Explain your answer. (6-8)

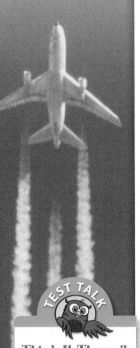

Algebra

Key Idea
You can use formulas to solve problems involving unit rates.

Vocabulary
• formula

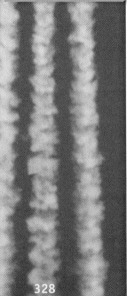

Think It Through
I **substitute** the known values into a formula in order to find the missing value.

Using Formulas

LEARN

What is a formula?

An airplane travels at a steady rate, *r,* and flies a specific distance, *d,* in *t* hours. How are rate, distance, and time related?

distance = rate × time
$$d = r \times t$$

A **formula** is a rule that uses symbols to relate two or more quantities. The formula above relates distance, rate, and time.

How do you use a formula to solve a problem?

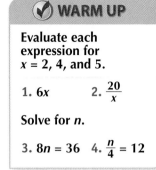

Example A	Example B
A plane travels at a rate of 400 miles per hour. How far will the plane travel in 5 hours?	The width of a box is 8 inches. How many centimeters wide is the box?
Use the formula that relates distance, rate, and time.	Use the formula that relates centimeters, *c,* to number of inches, *i.*
$d = r \times t$	$c = 2.54i$
$d = \frac{400 \text{ miles}}{\text{hour}} \times 5 \text{ hours}$	$c = 2.54\frac{\text{cm}}{\text{inch}} \cdot 8 \text{ inches}$
$d = 2{,}000$ miles	$c = 20.32$ cm
The plane will travel 2,000 miles.	The box is 20.32 centimeters wide.

✔ **Talk About It**

1. Use the rate $\frac{400 \text{ miles}}{1 \text{ hour}}$ in Example A to write a proportion that could be used to find the distance traveled in 5 hours.

2. How long will it take a car traveling at a rate of 68 miles per hour to go 510 miles?

3. Write a proportion that you can use to find the number of centimeters in 1 foot.

Take It to the NET
More Examples
www.scottforesman.com

1. At Euro Furniture Design, all dimensions for custom orders must be given in centimeters. Use the formula $c = 2.54i$ to find the dimensions of a 9 ft by 5 ft dining room table in centimeters.

2. **Estimation** A car traveled 140 miles at a rate of 50 miles per hour. Estimate the number of hours the car traveled.

PRACTICE

For more practice, see Set 6-9 on p. 351.

Ⓐ Skills and Understanding

At Veggies 'N' More, vegetables and fruits are sold by the pound. Use the formula *total cost = unit price × weight* to find the cost of each.

3. 4 lb of carrots   4. 8 lb of tomatoes

5. **Estimation** Jasmine purchased a bag of grapes for $6.30. Estimate how many pounds of grapes she purchased.

$1.89/lb $2.19/lb $1.89/lb

Ⓑ Reasoning and Problem Solving

Acceleration is the rate at which velocity changes with respect to time. To calculate acceleration, you divide the change in velocity by the amount of time. You can use the formula $a = \frac{v}{t}$ where a represents the acceleration (in meters per second squared), v is the change in velocity, and t is the time it takes to make the change.

6. The velocity of water flowing over Lara Falls is 12 meters per second. Before going over the falls, the velocity of the water is 6 meters per second. It takes 3 seconds to make the change in velocity. What is the acceleration of the water?

7. **Writing in Math** Can a car that gets 21 miles per gallon of gasoline travel 325 miles on 18 gallons of gasoline? Explain.

Mixed Review and Test Prep

Take It to the NET
Test Prep
www.scottforesman.com

Rewrite the problem so that it makes sense.

8. The president of a company earns $125,000 per year. At this salary, she will earn $1,000,000 in 6 years.

9. Which is the solution for the proportion $\frac{6}{8} = \frac{15}{d}$?

   A. $d = 8$ **C.** $d = 17$

   B. $d = 10$ **D.** $d = 20$

Key Idea
Proportions are
used to make scale
drawings.

Vocabulary
• scale drawing
• scale

Materials
• ruler
• centimeter grid
  paper or

 tools

Think It Through
To make a scale
drawing, I need to
**draw a picture on
grid paper.**

Scale Drawings and Maps

LEARN

What is a scale drawing?

For a 1933 movie, a 24-inch poster of a gorilla
was enlarged to make a building banner that
was 50 feet high.

In a **scale drawing,** the dimensions of an
object are reduced by the same ratio or
scale. The dimensions of the scale drawing
and the original figure are proportional. A
house plan is a scale drawing. So is a map.

Activity

How do you make a scale drawing?

Step 1 Find the dimensions of your classroom.

Step 2 Decide what scale to use so that your drawing
will fit on your piece of paper.

Step 3 Use a ruler to draw your classroom on grid paper.
Convert the dimensions using the scale.

a. What scale did you use
for your drawing? Explain
your choice.

How is your scale drawing
like your classroom? How
is it different?

c. How many centimeters
wide is your drawing?
How does this compare
to the actual width of
your classroom?

d. Set up a proportion
that shows the
relationship between
the scale drawing and
the actual classroom.

Example:
Actual Length = 34 feet
Actual Width = 22 feet

Scale: 1 cm = 1 ft

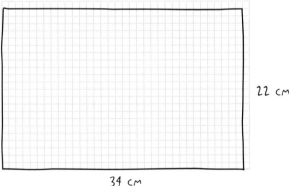

22 cm

34 cm

COOPER-
SCHOEDSACK
PRODUCTION

How can you use scale drawings?

Example A

The scale in the drawing at the right is 1 cm:2 m. What is the actual length of the living room?

Let y be the actual length of the living room in meters. Use the scale to set up a proportion.

$\dfrac{1 \text{ cm}}{2 \text{ m}} = \dfrac{4 \text{ cm}}{y \text{ m}}$ ← scale length
← actual length

$1(y) = 2(4)$ Solve the proportion.

$y = 8$

The actual length of the living room is 8 meters.

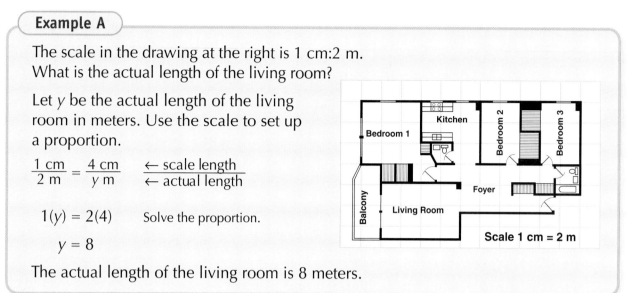

Scale 1 cm = 2 m

✔ Talk About It

1. Could the proportion in the example have been written as $\dfrac{2 \text{ m}}{1 \text{ cm}} = \dfrac{y}{4 \text{ cm}}$? Explain.

2. Find the length of the kitchen.

How can you use the scale on a map?

Example B

What is the actual distance from Jacksonville to Fort Pierce?

Let d be the actual distance between the two cities.

$\dfrac{1 \text{ in.}}{112 \text{ mi}} = \dfrac{2 \text{ in.}}{d \text{ mi}}$ ← map distance
←actual distance

$1 \cdot d = 2 \times 112$ Solve the proportion.

$d = 224$

The actual distance from Jacksonville to Fort Pierce is about 224 miles.

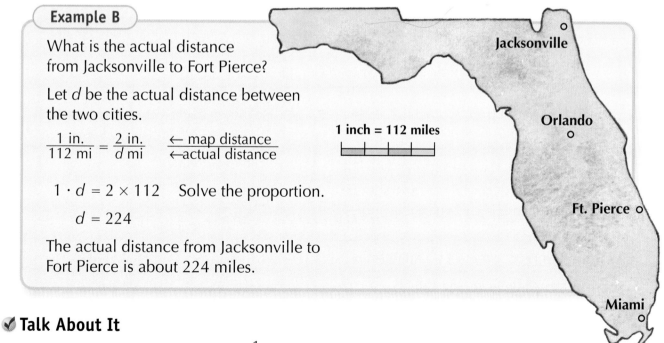

1 inch = 112 miles

✔ Talk About It

3. About how many miles does $2\frac{1}{4}$ inches represent on the map in Example B?

1. On a map with scale 2 cm:25 km, what would be the dimensions of a 145 km by 80 km rectangle?

2. **Reasoning** If a scale on a map is 1 in. = 250 miles, what would be the map distance if the actual distance between two cities is 1,000 miles?

Ⓐ Skills and Understanding

Use the scale drawing to answer exercises 3–4.

3. Marisa left home and walked to the beach. What was the actual distance she walked?

4. It took Marisa 30 minutes to walk to the beach from home. If she walks at the same pace, how long will it take her to walk from her home to the theater?

5. If Marisa were to walk from her house to the theater, from the theater to the beach, and from the beach to her house, what would be the total actual distance she walked?

6. **Reasoning** If the actual distance between Chicago and Cincinnati is about 300 miles, what would the distance be on a map with a scale of 0.5 in. = 50 miles?

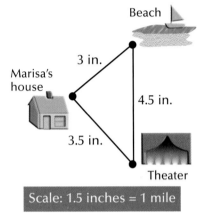

Scale: 1.5 inches = 1 mile

Ⓑ Reasoning and Problem Solving

Math and Social Studies

Although California is the third largest state by area, it is the most populated, with more than 33 million people! In fact, it contains four of the nation's 20 largest cities: Los Angeles, San Diego, San Jose, and San Francisco. A map of California is shown at the right. Find the distance

7. from San Francisco to Los Angeles.

8. from Los Angeles to San Diego.

9. from San Francisco to San Diego.

10. **Reasoning** If the map is enlarged, would the scale remain the same? Explain.

1 inch = 192 miles

11. **Writing in Math** The scale on a map of Chicago's lakefront is 2.5 cm = 4 km. Rich wants to know how far it is from the Field Museum to the Museum of Science and Industry. Explain how Rich could calculate the actual distance between the two museums.

C Extensions

12. **Reasoning** The Gateway Arch in St. Louis is 192 meters tall. Make a scale drawing of the arch that fits on one sheet of paper. Tell what scale you used to make your drawing.

Mixed Review and Test Prep

Take It to the NET
Test Prep
www.scottforesman.com

Use the formula $d = r \cdot t$ to solve each problem.

13. George drives at a rate of 30 miles per hour. How long will it take him to drive 150 miles?

14. Irene runs at a rate of 6 miles per hour. If she ran for 7 hours last week, how many total miles did she run?

15. Which ratio is equal to 4:10?

   A. $\frac{5}{2}$ **B.** 10:4   **C.** $\frac{6}{15}$ **D.** 1 to 4

Learning with Technology

The Geometry Drawing eTool

You can use the Geometry Drawing eTool to make scale drawings. Draw a small rectangle. Then, use the scale transformation tool to draw a new rectangle with sides that are three times as long as the sides of your small rectangle.

1. Measure the sides of each rectangle. Write ratios comparing the lengths of the shortest to longest sides of the 2 rectangles. Do the ratios form a proportion?

2. Find the perimeters of each rectangle. How does the ratio of perimeters compare to the ratio of the length of the shortest sides?

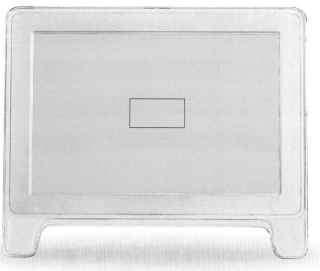

Problem-Solving Applications

The Stars and Stripes After the Revolutionary War, there were many versions of the American flag until President Taft, in 1912, set the first standards regarding the flag's proportions and arrangement of stars. The last change to the flag occurred on July 4, 1960, when a star was added to represent Hawaii, America's 50th state.

Trivia The rules of flag etiquette state that the flag should not be flown with the blue field down, except as a signal of distress in instances of extreme danger.

1 In 1777, the U.S. flag changed from the Grand Union flag, shown at the right, to the Stars and Stripes. One of the first styles of this flag, with 13 stars in a circle, is shown below. This early style of the flag was flown during the nation's bicentennial in 1976. Use mental math to find the number of years between 1777 and 1976.

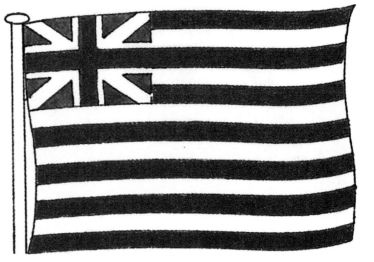

2 The current American flag is shown on the next page. What fraction of the stars are in the top row? Write your answer in simplest form.

3 In 2002, the largest Stars and Stripes measured 255 feet wide, and had a width to length ratio of about 1 to 1.98. Find the length of this flag.

Good News/Bad News You can still view the flag that inspired Francis Scott Key to write the poem that is used in the National Anthem. The bad news is that the flag is not in very good shape. Its original dimensions were 30 x 42 feet. It has been so battered and torn over time that, after restoration, it now measures only 30 x 34 feet.

Using Key Facts

4 Suppose you need to make a U.S. flag for a school project. The flag's length must be $9\frac{1}{2}$ feet. How wide should the flag be?

5 The flag that was placed on the moon measured 5 feet long and 3 feet wide. Compare this length to width ratio to the official length to width ratio. Do the ratios form a proportion?

Key Facts
Official Flag Ratios

Dimension	Ratio of Dimension to Flag's Width
•Length	19:10
•Blue field width	7:13
•Blue field length	76:100
•Stripe width	1:13

6 **Decision Making** Design your own flag. Record the colors and ratios of the design so that someone else could create a duplicate of your flag.

7 **Writing in Math** Using the pictures or information from this lesson, write your own word problem that involves ratios. Solve your problem and write the answer in a complete sentence.

Do You Know How?

Do You Understand?

Using Formulas (6-9, 6-11)

1. A car traveled at a rate of 45 miles per hour for 3 hours. Use the formula $d = r \times t$ to find the distance the car traveled.

2. Myra's truck can travel 16 miles on 1 gallon of gasoline. How many gallons will Myra need to travel 296 miles? Use the formula $m = \dfrac{d}{g}$ where m represents miles per gallon, d is the distance traveled, and g is the number of gallons of gasoline used.

A When can you use a formula?

B Use the rate $\dfrac{45 \text{ miles}}{3 \text{ hours}}$ to write a proportion that could be used to find the distance traveled in 1 hour.

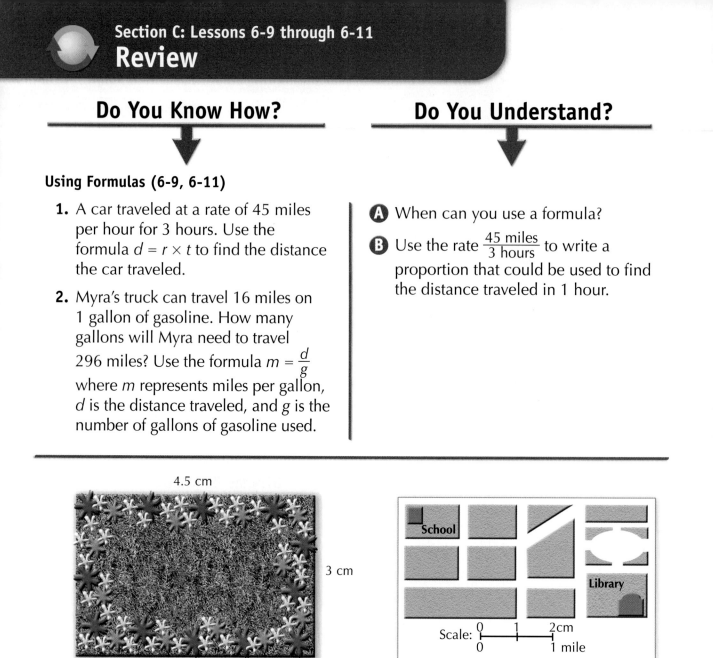

4.5 cm

3 cm

Garden

Map

School

Library

Scale: 0   1   2cm / 0   1 mile

Scale Drawings and Maps (6-10)

3. Express the length to width ratio of the garden pictured above in simplest form.

4. The scale in the drawing of the garden above is 3 cm = 7 ft. Find the actual dimensions of the garden.

5. Use the map at the above right and a metric ruler to find the shortest distance between the school and the library.

C Describe how to use proportions to find the actual length of an object from a scale drawing.

D Explain what the scale on a map tells you.

MULTIPLE CHOICE

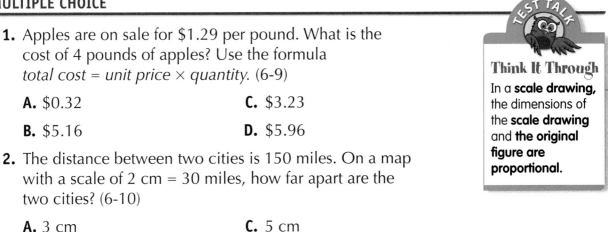

Think It Through

In a **scale drawing,** the dimensions of the **scale drawing** and **the original figure are proportional.**

1. Apples are on sale for $1.29 per pound. What is the cost of 4 pounds of apples? Use the formula *total cost = unit price × quantity.* (6-9)

   A. $0.32   **C.** $3.23

   B. $5.16   **D.** $5.96

2. The distance between two cities is 150 miles. On a map with a scale of 2 cm = 30 miles, how far apart are the two cities? (6-10)

   A. 3 cm   **C.** 5 cm

   B. 7.5 cm   **D.** 10 cm

FREE RESPONSE

3. Mr. Bruckner drove from his house to the beach without stopping. He drove at a rate of 55 miles per hour and it took him 5.5 hours. Use the formula *distance = rate × time* to find how far it is from Mr. Bruckner's house to the beach. (6-9)

4. In 11 seconds, a race car goes from 44 meters per second to 77 meters per second. Find the acceleration of the race car. Use the formula $a = \frac{f - s}{t}$ where *a* represents the acceleration (in meters per second squared), *f* is the final speed, *s* is the starting speed, and *t* is the time it took to make the change. (6-9, 6-11)

5. On a blueprint of a house, the kitchen measures 5 in. long and 3 in. wide. The scale of the blueprint is 1 in. = 3 ft. What are the actual dimensions of the kitchen? (6-10)

6. Jessica looks on a map and finds that the amusement park is 3.5 cm from the hotel where she is staying. The scale of the map is 2 cm = 3 mi. How many miles away is the amusement park from the hotel? (6-10)

Writing in Math

7. What makes a drawing a scale drawing? (6-10, 6-11)

8. When you use a proportion to solve scale drawing problems, can the proportion be set up in more than one way? Explain. (6-10, 6-11)

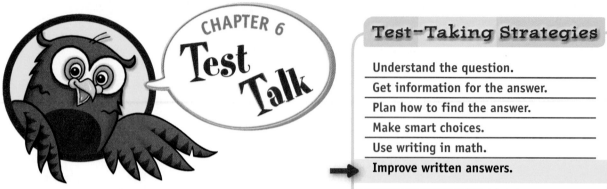

CHAPTER 6

Test Talk

Test-Taking Strategies

| Understand the question. |
| Get information for the answer. |
| Plan how to find the answer. |
| Make smart choices. |
| Use writing in math. |
| → Improve written answers. |

Improve Written Answers

You can follow the tips below to learn how to improve written answers on a test. It is important to write a clear answer and include only information needed to answer the question.

1 The French Club is selling candles for a fundraiser. As a bonus, the club receives gift certificates for free pizzas. The table shows how many gift certificates the club might earn.

Number of boxes of candles sold	40	80	120	160
Number of pizza gift certificates	3	6	9	12

Use an equation, ratio, or rule to explain how the number of boxes of candles is related to the number of gift certificates. Then find the number of gift certificates the club would receive for selling 240 boxes of candles.

Improve Written Answers

- Check if your answer is complete.

  *In order to **get as many points as possible,** I must explain how the number of boxes of candles is related to the number of gift certificates <u>and</u> I must find the number of gift certificates the club would receive for selling 240 boxes of candles.*

- Check if your answer makes sense.

  I should check that my equation, ratio, or rule works for every pair of numbers in the table. Then I should check that it works for the number of gift certificates I said the club would earn for selling 240 boxes of candles.

- Check if your explanation is clear and easy to follow.

  *I should reread my explanation to be sure it is **accurate and clear.** I shouldn't include any unnecessary information.*

The rubric below is a scoring guide for Test Questions 1 and 2.

Scoring Rubric

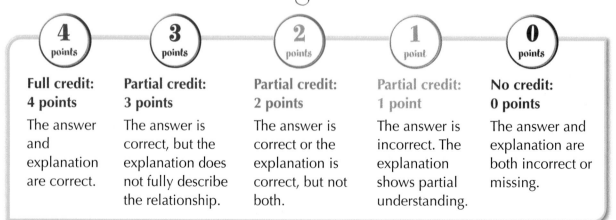

4 points	**3** points	**2** points	**1** point	**0** points
Full credit: 4 points	**Partial credit: 3 points**	**Partial credit: 2 points**	**Partial credit: 1 point**	**No credit: 0 points**
The answer and explanation are correct.	The answer is correct, but the explanation does not fully describe the relationship.	The answer is correct or the explanation is correct, but not both.	The answer is incorrect. The explanation shows partial understanding.	The answer and explanation are both incorrect or missing.

Lourdes used the scoring rubric on page 338 to score a student's answer to Test Question 1. The student's paper is shown below.

> As the number of boxes of candles increases, the number of pizza gift certificates also increases. The club would receive 18 pizza gift certificates for selling 240 boxes of candles.

Think It Through

The explanation seems incomplete. This would be a better way to describe the relationship: The ratio of the number of boxes of candles to the number of pizza gift certificates is $\frac{40}{3}$. The answer of 18 gift certificates is correct. Since the answer is correct, but the explanation does not fully describe the relationship, the score is 3 points.

Now it's your turn.

Score the student's paper. If it does not get 4 points, rewrite it so that it does.

2 Janie is planning to attend a summer music camp. The table shows how many music teachers will be at the camp.

Number of students	25	50	75	100
Number of music teachers	2	4	6	8

Use an equation, ratio, or rule to explain how the number of students is related to the number of music teachers. Then find the number of music teachers that would be at the camp if there are 225 students.

> The ratio of students to music teachers is 25 to 2. For 225 students there would be 10 music teachers.

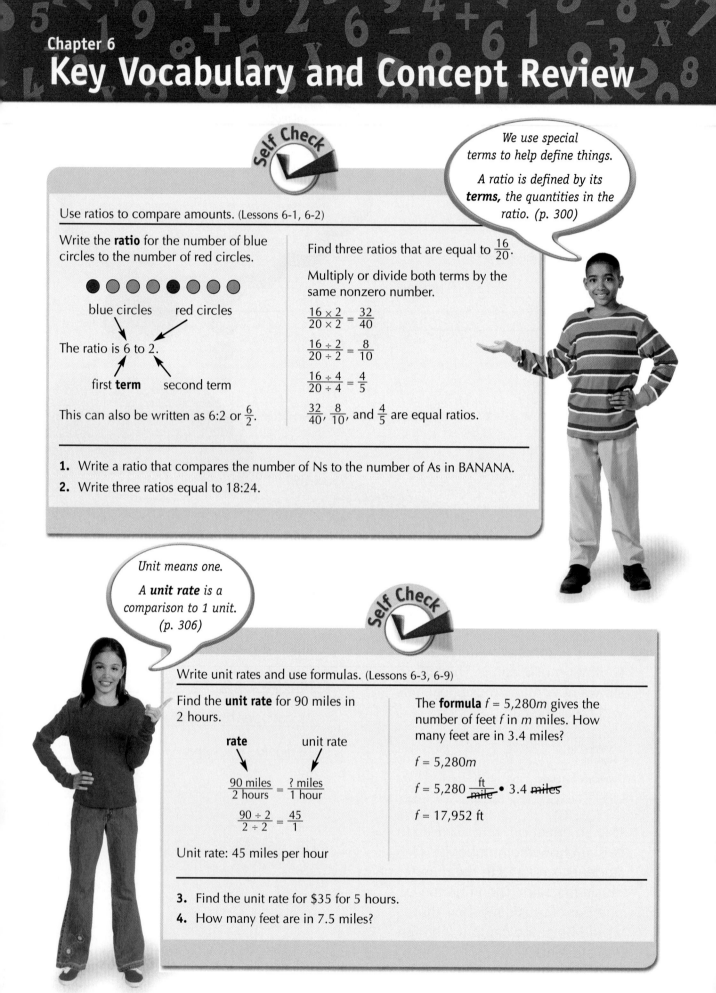

Self Check

We use special terms to help define things.

A ratio is defined by its **terms,** the quantities in the ratio. (p. 300)

Use ratios to compare amounts. (Lessons 6-1, 6-2)

Write the **ratio** for the number of blue circles to the number of red circles.

● ● ● ● ● ● ● ●

blue circles   red circles

The ratio is 6 to 2.

first **term**   second term

This can also be written as 6:2 or $\frac{6}{2}$.

Find three ratios that are equal to $\frac{16}{20}$.

Multiply or divide both terms by the same nonzero number.

$$\frac{16 \times 2}{20 \times 2} = \frac{32}{40}$$

$$\frac{16 \div 2}{20 \div 2} = \frac{8}{10}$$

$$\frac{16 \div 4}{20 \div 4} = \frac{4}{5}$$

$\frac{32}{40}$, $\frac{8}{10}$, and $\frac{4}{5}$ are equal ratios.

1. Write a ratio that compares the number of Ns to the number of As in BANANA.
2. Write three ratios equal to 18:24.

Unit means one.

A **unit rate** is a comparison to 1 unit. (p. 306)

Self Check

Write unit rates and use formulas. (Lessons 6-3, 6-9)

Find the **unit rate** for 90 miles in 2 hours.

rate   unit rate

$$\frac{90 \text{ miles}}{2 \text{ hours}} = \frac{? \text{ miles}}{1 \text{ hour}}$$

$$\frac{90 \div 2}{2 \div 2} = \frac{45}{1}$$

Unit rate: 45 miles per hour

The **formula** $f = 5{,}280m$ gives the number of feet f in m miles. How many feet are in 3.4 miles?

$f = 5{,}280m$

$f = 5{,}280 \frac{\text{ft}}{\text{mile}} \cdot 3.4 \text{ miles}$

$f = 17{,}952 \text{ ft}$

3. Find the unit rate for $35 for 5 hours.
4. How many feet are in 7.5 miles?

I draw an X over it.

When I find the **cross products** in a proportion, I multiply like this. (p. 316)

$1 \times 12 = 4 \times 3$

Use proportions. (Lessons 6-5, 6-6, 6-7, 6-10)

Do the ratios $\frac{6 \text{ gallons}}{\$9}$ and $\frac{10 \text{ gallons}}{\$15}$ form a **proportion?**

Check the **cross products.**

$$6 \times 15 \overset{?}{=} 9 \times 10$$

$$90 = 90$$

The units are the same and the cross products are equal, so the ratios form a proportion.

The **scale** on a **scale drawing** is 2 cm: 15 km. What is the actual distance represented by 5 cm on the drawing?

$$\frac{2 \text{ cm}}{15 \text{ km}} = \frac{5 \text{ cm}}{x \text{ km}} \quad \leftarrow \text{scale length} \\ \leftarrow \text{actual length}$$

$2x = 5(15)$ Write the cross products.

$2x = 75$ Multiply.

$\frac{2x}{2} = \frac{75}{2}$ Solve for x.

$x = 37.5$; The actual distance is 37.5 km.

5. Solve $\frac{12}{m} = \frac{24}{18}$.

Use objects or write to explain to solve problems. (Lessons 6-4, 6-8)

You can model some problems with objects.

Of the 12 kittens at the pet shop, 2 out of 3 have stripes. How many kittens have stripes.

● = striped   ○ = not striped

●●○ ●●○ ●●○ ●●○

Eight kittens have stripes.

A drawing can help explain your thinking.

Would you rather be given 2 quarters every 6 days or 4 quarters every 10 days? Why?

I'd rather have 4 quarters every 10 days. Here's why.

My picture shows that 4 quarters in 10 days can be split into 2 equal groups of 2 quarters in 5 days. That's better than 2 quarters in 6 days.

A grading scale compares a numerical test score to a letter grade.

The **scale** in a **scale drawing** is a ratio that compares the dimensions in the drawing to the dimensions of the real object. (p. 330)

6. There are 30 passengers. Four out of 5 are adults. How many are adults?

Answers: 1. 2:3 **2.** Sample answer: 3:4, 9:12; 36:48 **3.** $7 per hour **4.** 39,600 ft **5.** $m = 9$ **6.** 24

Chapter 6 Key Vocabulary and Concept Review

MULTIPLE CHOICE

Choose the correct letter for each answer.

1. Which ratio compares the number of circles to the number of diamonds?

   A. 4 to 2   **C.** 4 to 3

   B. 2 to 4   **D.** 2 to 3

2. Which ratio is equal to 8:2?

   A. $\frac{1}{4}$ **C.** $\frac{20}{5}$

   B. 3 to 12   **D.** 16:2

3. Which pair below are equal ratios?

   A. $\frac{4}{6}$; 6:4   **C.** 4 to 3; 7 to 6

   B. $\frac{6}{9}$; $\frac{1}{3}$ **D.** 12 to 10; $\frac{18}{15}$

4. Find the unit rate for 120 miles in 4 hours.

   A. $\frac{30 \text{ mi}}{1 \text{ h}}$ **C.** $\frac{60 \text{ mi}}{2 \text{ h}}$

   B. $\frac{1 \text{ mi}}{3 \text{ h}}$ **D.** $\frac{40 \text{ mi}}{1 \text{ h}}$

5. There are 35 students in Richard's class. Two out of every 7 students are wearing jeans. How many students in the class are wearing jeans?

   A. 2   **C.** 10

   B. 5   **D.** 14

6. Which proportion is written correctly?

   A. $\frac{2 \text{ in.}}{5 \text{ ft}} = \frac{3 \text{ in.}}{72 \text{ in.}}$ **C.** $\frac{1 \text{ gal}}{4 \text{ qt}} = \frac{2 \text{ pints}}{1 \text{ quart}}$

   B. $\frac{2 \text{ ft}}{5 \text{ ft}} = \frac{24 \text{ in.}}{60 \text{ in.}}$ **D.** $\frac{3 \text{ ft}}{1 \text{ yd}} = \frac{3 \text{ yd}}{9 \text{ ft}}$

7. Solve the proportion $\frac{42 \text{ mi}}{3 \text{ h}} = \frac{y \text{ mi}}{5 \text{ h}}$

   A. $y = 2.8$ mi   **C.** $y = 70$ mi

   B. $y = 15$ mi   **D.** $y = 84$ mi

8. Which is the best buy?

   A. 20 oz for $4.60   **C.** 9 oz for $2.25

   B. 16 oz for $4.00   **D.** 24 oz for $5.76

9. A car travels at a rate of 65 miles an hour. At this rate, how far will the car travel in 5 hours?

   A. 13 miles   **C.** 325 miles

   B. 70 miles   **D.** 845 miles

10. Ceila is 56 inches tall. Using the formula $c = 2.54i$, where c represents the number of centimeters, and i is the number of inches, find Ceila's height in centimeters.

    A. 145.56 cm

    B. 142.24 cm

    C. 39.37 cm

    D. 22.05 cm

TEST TALK

Think It Through
- I should **look for key words** in the problem.
- I can **eliminate** unreasonable answers.

11. What is the actual distance between Mathville and Fractiontown?

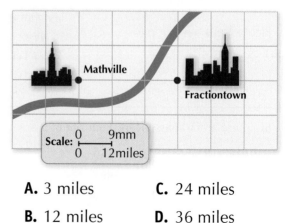

    Scale: 0 — 9mm
            0 — 12miles

    A. 3 miles   **C.** 24 miles

    B. 12 miles   **D.** 36 miles

Write a ratio for each comparison.

Color	red	blue	silver	white
Number of balloons	12	8	15	16

12. blue to red

13. silver to all colors

14. red to all other colors

Give three ratios that are equal to each ratio.

15. 15:6 **16.** $\frac{12}{16}$

Write each ratio in simplest form.

17. 150:234 **18.** 3.5 to 0.5

Write each as a unit rate.

19. $6.12 for 9 gal

20. 312 mi on 13 gal

Decide if the ratios form a proportion.

21. $\frac{5 \text{ ft}}{8 \text{ mi}}$, $\frac{15 \text{ ft}}{18 \text{ mi}}$

22. $\frac{9 \text{ tbsp}}{3 \text{ gal}}$, $\frac{12 \text{ tbsp}}{4 \text{ gal}}$

Solve each proportion.

23. $\frac{156 \text{ mi}}{6 \text{ gal}} = \frac{y \text{ mi}}{11 \text{ gal}}$

24. $\frac{16}{22} = \frac{40}{w}$

25. Patty drives at a rate of 42 miles per hour for 7 hours. How far does she drive? Use the formula $d = rt$.

26. There are 60.96 centimeters in 2 feet. How many centimeters are in 1 yard?

27. The scale on a map is 2.5 cm to 30 mi. If two cities are 8 cm apart on the map, what is the actual distance between the two cities?

Writing in Math

28. Beginning with the ratio $\frac{4 \text{ in.}}{5 \text{ days}}$ make a table of quantities that vary proportionally. Tell how you know that the values in the table vary proportionally.

29. Travis is training for a duathlon. He bikes and runs each day. The ratio of miles biked to miles run is 4 to 1. If he runs 5 miles, how many miles does he bike? Solve and explain your reasoning.

30. Explain how to use objects to solve the problem below. Give the answer in a complete sentence.

Loretta has 36 stuffed animals. Four out of every 9 stuffed animals are bears. How many bears are in Loretta's stuffed animal collection?

Think It Through

- Using objects involves **showing the known information with objects**.
- I need to make sure **the objects I use can help me solve the problem**.

Number and Operation

MULTIPLE CHOICE

1. Find $6 + 4^2 \div 2$.

   A. 5   **C.** 14

   B. 11   **D.** 26

2. Which ratio is equal to 12:3?

   A. 1 to 4   **C.** 8 to 2

   B. 3:1   **D.** $\frac{8}{3}$

FREE RESPONSE

3. Which is the better buy?

14 oz
¢2.52

32 oz
¢6.72

4. Find 5.2×9.36.

5. What is the GCF of 8, 12, and 24?

6. Find the LCM of 10, 30, and 45.

7. Jeffrey is $6\frac{1}{5}$ feet tall. Christina is $5\frac{1}{4}$ feet tall. How much taller is Jeffrey?

8. Jon's grandfather needs $8\frac{1}{4}$ cups of raisins to make 2 fruitcakes. A 15-ounce box of raisins contains $2\frac{3}{4}$ cups. How many boxes should Jon's grandfather buy?

Writing in Math

9. Explain why $\frac{4\text{ lb}}{\$7.56}$ and $\frac{\$5.67}{3\text{ lb}}$ do not form a proportion.

10. Compare fractions and ratios. How are they the same? How are they different?

Geometry and Measurement

MULTIPLE CHOICE

11. Which ratio is equal to $\frac{1\text{ yard}}{91.44\text{ centimeters}}$?

   A. $\frac{5\text{ yd}}{457.2\text{ cm}}$ **C.** $\frac{3\text{ ft}}{1\text{ yd}}$

   B. $\frac{457.2\text{ cm}}{5\text{ yd}}$ **D.** $\frac{3\text{ ft}}{91.44\text{ cm}}$

12. How many inches are in 4 feet?

   A. 24 in.   **C.** 40 in.

   B. 36 in.   **D.** 48 in.

FREE RESPONSE

13. Find the circumference of a circle with a diameter of 7 cm. Use $\frac{22}{7}$ for π.

14. What is the name of a triangle with three angles that measure less than 90°?

15. Find the area of a triangle with base 12 in. and height 8 in. Use the formula $A = \frac{1}{2}bh$.

16. Use the proportion to find the number of centimeters in 1 foot.

$$\frac{2.54\text{ cm}}{1\text{ in.}} = \frac{x\text{ cm}}{12\text{ in.}}$$

Writing in Math

17. An insect in a picture is $\frac{1}{2}$ inch long and a label says "enlarged 12 times." Explain how you would find the insect's actual length.

18. Describe how to find the time elapsed between 11:46 A.M. and 2:13 P.M.

Data Analysis and Probability

MULTIPLE CHOICE

19. What is the probability of spinning red?

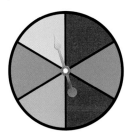

A. $\frac{2}{4}$ **B.** $\frac{1}{6}$ **C.** $\frac{6}{2}$ **D.** $\frac{1}{3}$

20. What is the median of the set of data below?

4, 10, 7, 4, 8, 1, 9, 6

A. 4 **B.** 6 **C.** 6.5 **D.** 8

FREE RESPONSE

21. Use the bar graph to write a comparison between the number of students who play baseball and the number of students who play tennis.

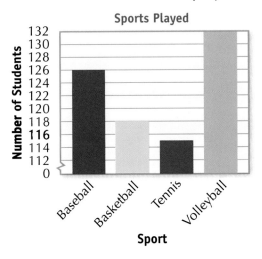

Writing in Math

22. Explain how to find the probability of rolling a sum of 5 on two numbered cubes.

Algebra

MULTIPLE CHOICE

23. Solve the proportion. $\frac{3 \text{ in.}}{12 \text{ s}} = \frac{y \text{ in.}}{20 \text{ s}}$

A. y = 1.8 in. **C.** y = 5 in.

B. y = 4 in. **D.** y = 6 in.

24. Find $\frac{x}{2}$ + 8 for x = 10.

A. 5 **C.** 13

B. 8 **D.** 17

FREE RESPONSE

25. Use the formula *distance = rate × time* to find how long it would take to travel 189 miles at a rate of 54 miles per hour.

26. Evaluate the expression $\frac{3}{5}x - 4$ for x = 10, 15, and 20.

27. Write the word phrase as an algebraic expression.

24 less than a number

28. Solve for the variable.

$$\frac{3}{7}a = 9$$

29. Use the Distributive Property to find 4 × 109 mentally.

Writing in Math

30. A map has a scale of 3 cm = 15 mi. Carl measured the distance between two cities to be 4 cm. He set up and solved the following proportion. Is his answer correct? Explain.

$$\frac{4}{15} = \frac{3}{y}$$
$$4y = 15 \times 3$$
$$y = 11.25 \text{ miles}$$

The two cities are 11.25 miles apart.

Set 6-1 (pages 300–301)

Write a ratio for the comparison in three ways.

⭐ ☐ ☆ ★ ● ■

Stars to circles

There are 3 stars and 1 circle.

3:1   3 to 1 $\frac{3}{1}$

Remember that a ratio is a comparison of like or unlike quantities. The order of the terms is important.

Write a ratio for each comparison in three ways.

1. red shapes to blue shapes

2. squares to stars

3. white shapes to all shapes

4. blue stars to other stars

Set 6-2 (pages 302–305)

Find three ratios equal to $\frac{14}{24}$.

One Way Multiply.

$\frac{14 \times 2}{24 \times 2} = \frac{28}{48}$

$\frac{14 \times 3}{24 \times 3} = \frac{42}{72}$

Another Way Divide.

$\frac{14 \div 2}{24 \div 2} = \frac{7}{12}$

Write the ratio 48:15 in simplest form.

$\frac{48}{15} = \frac{48 \div 3}{15 \div 3} = \frac{16}{5}$ Divide by the GCF of 48 and 15.

Remember to find equal ratios, you must do the same operation to both terms.

Give three ratios that are equal to each ratio.

1. $\frac{4}{10}$ **2.** $\frac{3}{5}$ **3.** $\frac{22}{30}$

4. $\frac{8}{12}$ **5.** $\frac{20}{12}$ **6.** $\frac{1}{9}$

7. $\frac{25}{40}$ **8.** $\frac{36}{6}$ **9.** $\frac{78}{30}$

Write each ratio in simplest form.

10. $\frac{224}{480}$ **11.** 42:68   **12.** 500 to 125

Set 6-3 (pages 306–309)

Write 25 miles in 5 hours as a unit rate.

One Way Use equivalent fractions.

$\frac{25}{5} = \frac{?}{1}$

$\frac{25 \div 5}{5 \div 5} = \frac{5}{1}$

Another Way Find the quotient of the terms.

$25 \div 5 = 5$

Unit rate $= \frac{5 \text{ miles}}{1 \text{ hour}}$

Remember that a unit rate is a comparison where the second term is 1 unit.

Write each as a unit rate.

1. $6.00 for 12 oranges

2. 336 miles on 12 gallons

3. 16 people to 4 pizzas

4. $288 for 36 hours of work

5. 30 minutes for 15 laps

6. $7.17 for 3 pounds of meat

Set 6-4 (pages 312–313)

There are 12 books on the shelf. One out of every 4 books is a mystery book. How many books on the shelf are mystery books?

Use objects.   ◯ = "mystery book"

⬤ = "not a mystery book"

There are 3 mystery books on the shelf.

Remember to choose an object that you can use to represent known information. Write your answer in a complete sentence.

1. There are 24 girls on the team. Two out of every three girls are age 12. How many 12-year-old girls are on the team?

Set 6-5 (pages 316–317)

Decide if the ratios form a proportion.

$\dfrac{2 \text{ mi}}{24 \text{ min}}, \dfrac{5 \text{ mi}}{60 \text{ min}}$ Find the cross products.
$2 \times 60 = 120$
$24 \times 5 = 120$

The cross products are equal, so the ratios form a proportion.

Remember that in a proportion, the cross products are equal.

Decide if the ratios form a proportion.

1. $\dfrac{\$28}{7 \text{ h}}, \dfrac{\$45}{9 \text{ h}}$ **2.** $\dfrac{16 \text{ oz}}{2 \text{ tbsp}}, \dfrac{24 \text{ oz}}{3 \text{ tbsp}}$

3. $\dfrac{8}{10}, \dfrac{12}{15}$ **4.** $\dfrac{50}{24}, \dfrac{10}{6}$

Set 6-6 (pages 318–321)

Solve the proportion.

$\dfrac{\$132}{20 \text{ h}} = \dfrac{\$y}{40 \text{ h}}$

$\dfrac{\$132 \times 2}{20 \text{ h} \times 2} = \dfrac{\$264}{40 \text{ h}}$ Think of equal ratios.

Remember that ratios that form a proportion are equal ratios.

1. $\dfrac{312 \text{ mi}}{6 \text{ h}} = \dfrac{936 \text{ mi}}{x \text{ h}}$ **2.** $\dfrac{\$7.96}{2 \text{ lb}} = \dfrac{\$n}{5 \text{ lb}}$

3. $\dfrac{4 \text{ in.}}{12 \text{ ft}} = \dfrac{3 \text{ in.}}{x \text{ ft}}$ **4.** $\dfrac{5 \text{ gal}}{2 \text{ days}} = \dfrac{y \text{ gal}}{8 \text{ days}}$

Set 6-7 (pages 322–323)

Solve $\dfrac{12}{3} = \dfrac{x}{5}$ using cross products.

$\dfrac{12}{3} = \dfrac{x}{5}$

$3x = 12 \times 5$ Write the cross products.

$3x = 60$ Multiply.

$x = 20$ Solve for x.

Remember that the cross products of the terms in a proportion are equal.

Solve each proportion using cross products.

1. $\dfrac{6}{8} = \dfrac{x}{12}$ **2.** $\dfrac{12}{16} = \dfrac{9}{y}$

3. $\dfrac{32}{6} = \dfrac{x}{9}$ **4.** $\dfrac{21}{4} = \dfrac{x}{5}$

Set 6-8 (pages 324–325)

Which is the better buy: 12 oz for $3.84 or 18 oz for $6.30? Tell how you decided.

> 12 oz for $3.84 is a better buy.
> I found the unit price for each and then compared.
>
> 12 oz for $3.84 unit price: $0.32 per oz
> 18 oz for $6.30 unit price: $0.35 per oz

Remember that you can draw pictures to explain your thinking.

1. Which is the better buy, 3 rolls for $3.57 or 8 rolls for $8.48? Tell how you decided.

2. Three out of every 7 students have blue eyes. If there are 28 students, how many students have blue eyes? Explain how you found the answer.

Set 6-9 (pages 328–329)

Patricia bikes at a rate of 15 miles per hour. At this rate, how far will she bike in 2.5 hours?

Use the formula *distance = rate × time.*

$d = \dfrac{15 \text{ mi}}{1 \text{ h}} \times 2.5 \text{ h}$

$d = 37.5 \text{ mi}$

Patricia can bike 37.5 miles in 2.5 hours.

Remember to insert the data into the formula and solve for the missing variable.

Use a formula to solve each problem.

1. A train traveled for 5 hours at a rate of 52 miles per hour. How far did the train travel?

2. Marcus earns $6.25 per hour. Use the formula *total earnings = pay rate × time* to find how much Marcus earns in 39 hours.

Set 6-10 (pages 330–333)

If a scale on a map is 2 cm = 125 mi, how long would the distance on the map be if the actual distance is 750 miles?

$\dfrac{2 \text{ cm}}{125 \text{ mi}} = \dfrac{y \text{ cm}}{750 \text{ mi}}$ Set up a proportion.

$750(2) = 125y$ Solve the proportion using cross products.

$\dfrac{1,500}{125} = \dfrac{125y}{125}$

$12 = y$

The distance on the map would be 12 cm.

Remember to check that the labels are the same for each ratio in the proportion.

1. The scale of a drawing is 1 in. = 7.5 ft. A building is 4 in. in the drawing. What is the actual height of the building?

2. Two cities are located 1.5 in. apart on a map. The scale of the map is 1 in. = 25 mi. How far apart are the two cities?

3. A model train is built using the scale 1:60. The actual length of the dining car is 2,100 cm. Find the length of the dining car of the model train.

Take It to the NET
More Practice
www.scottforesman.com

Set 6-1 (pages 300–301)

The data at the right shows the number of students who play each type of sport. Write a ratio for each comparison in three ways.

1. basketball to soccer

2. swimming to tennis

3. baseball to all other sports

4. soccer to all sports

5. baseball to basketball

6. all sports to tennis

7. Of the students who play tennis, 12 are girls. Write a ratio comparing the number of girls that play tennis to the number of boys who play tennis.

Data File

Sport Participation

Sport	Number of Students
Baseball	42
Basketball	26
Tennis	18
Soccer	53
Swimming	20

Set 6-2 (pages 302–305)

Give three ratios that are equal to each ratio.

1. 3 to 5

2. 12:6

3. 2 to 9

4. 7:11

5. $\frac{25}{14}$

6. $\frac{18}{30}$

7. 4 to 20

8. $\frac{21}{6}$

Tell whether the ratios in each pair are equal.

9. 4 to 6 and 12 to 8

10. 8:3 and 24:9

11. $\frac{7}{12}$ and $\frac{12}{7}$

12. $\frac{15}{5}$ and $\frac{3}{1}$

13. 9 to 11 and 27 to 33

14. 16:6 and 8:3

Write each ratio in simplest form.

15. 165 to 135

16. 126:495

17. $\frac{84}{248}$

18. The table shows the number of boys and girls in each class. Which classes have equal ratios of boys to girls?

Teacher	Number of Boys	Number of Girls
Mrs. Alvarez	25	20
Mr. Collins	20	16
Ms. Cable	18	16

Set 6-3 (pages 306–309)

Write each as a unit rate.

1. 144 miles in 3 hours

2. 420 students to 20 teachers

3. 5 cups for 8 servings

4. $248.20 for 34 hours

Which is the better buy?

5. 2 liters of lemonade for $2.38, or 5 liters of lemonade for $5.80

6. 6 cans of juice for $3.90, or 24 cans of juice for $16.32

7. 12 oz box of cereal for $4.29, or 16 oz box of cereal for $5.89

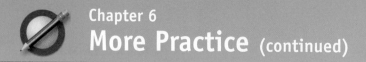
Set 6-4 (pages 312–313)

Use objects to solve each problem. Give the answer in a complete sentence.

1. Jasper's little league team won 3 out of every 4 games they played. If they played 12 games this season, how many did they win?

2. This year, 84 people attended the community fair. If 2 out of every 7 who attended were adults, how many children attended the fair?

Set 6-5 (pages 316–317)

Decide if the ratios form a proportion.

1. $\dfrac{6 \text{ tbsp}}{10 \text{ cups}}$, $\dfrac{9 \text{ tbsp}}{15 \text{ cups}}$

2. $\dfrac{24 \text{ laps}}{30 \text{ min}}$, $\dfrac{4 \text{ laps}}{6 \text{ min}}$

3. $\dfrac{8 \text{ in.}}{24 \text{ ft}}$, $\dfrac{3 \text{ in.}}{9 \text{ ft}}$

4. $\dfrac{5 \text{ apples}}{\$4}$, $\dfrac{7 \text{ apples}}{\$9}$

5. $\dfrac{32}{6}$, $\dfrac{35}{9}$

6. $\dfrac{10}{45}$, $\dfrac{9}{2}$

7. Find a value for each variable to form the proportion $\dfrac{5 \text{ cups}}{6 \text{ tbsp}} = \dfrac{x}{y}$.

Set 6-6 (pages 318–321)

Solve each proportion using any method.

1. $\dfrac{96 \text{ mi}}{3 \text{ h}} = \dfrac{x \text{ mi}}{5 \text{ h}}$

2. $\dfrac{20 \text{ oz}}{5 \text{ servings}} = \dfrac{x \text{ oz}}{3 \text{ servings}}$

3. $\dfrac{2 \text{ in.}}{5 \text{ min}} = \dfrac{8 \text{ in.}}{y \text{ min}}$

4. $\dfrac{4 \text{ buses}}{60 \text{ students}} = \dfrac{x \text{ buses}}{90 \text{ students}}$

5. $\dfrac{\$75}{10 \text{ h}} = \dfrac{\$y}{21 \text{ h}}$

6. $\dfrac{3 \text{ qt}}{8 \text{ in.}} = \dfrac{5 \text{ qt}}{x \text{ in.}}$

7. Kim uses 4 yards of ribbon to make 3 large bows. How many yards of ribbon will she need to make 24 large bows?

8. Marc's car used 6 gallons of gasoline to travel 96 miles. How many gallons of gasoline will his car use to travel 152 miles?

Set 6-7 (pages 322–323)

Solve each proportion using cross products.

1. $\dfrac{r}{35} = \dfrac{13}{5}$

2. $\dfrac{40}{8} = \dfrac{x}{3}$

3. $\dfrac{15}{y} = \dfrac{20}{11}$

4. $\dfrac{7}{28} = \dfrac{10}{n}$

5. $\dfrac{t}{18} = \dfrac{11}{12}$

6. $\dfrac{12}{7} = \dfrac{p}{28}$

7. At track practice, Nick ran 500 yards in 2.5 minutes. At this rate, how long will it take Nick to run 1 mile? [Hint: 1 mile = 1,760 yards]

8. As a house painter, Tai works 6 hours and earns $71.70. If Tai works 8 hours, how much does he earn?

Take It to the NET
More Practice
www.scottforesman.com

Set 6-8 (pages 324–325)

For each problem, explain how you found your answer.

1. The ratio of an executive's expenses to income is 5 to 8. What are the executive's expenses for a month when the income is $9,800?

2. In a package of colored balloons, 3 out of every 8 balloons are red. If there are 18 red balloons in the package, how many total balloons are there?

3. Adams School orders 3 cartons of skim milk for every 7 students. If there are 581 students in the school, how many cartons of skim milk are ordered?

4. The ratio of teachers to students at a middle school is 1 to 36. If there are 720 students in the school, how many teachers are there?

Set 6-9 (pages 328–329)

At Crafts Plus More, ribbon and fabric are sold by the yard. Use the formula *cost = unit price × quantity* to find the cost of each.

1. 4 yd red ribbon

2. 6.1 yd blue fabric

3. 2.3 yd patterned fabric

4. 3.5 yd lace

5. The new car Travis bought gets 33 miles to a gallon of gas. At this rate, how far can Travis travel on 12 gallons of gas?

6. Use the formula $d = r \times t$ to find the time it takes a train to travel 434 miles at a rate of 62 mph.

Red ribbon:	$0.75/yard
Lace:	$0.98/yard
Blue fabric:	$1.78/yard
Patterned fabric:	$2.12/yard

Set 6-10 (pages 330–333)

1. The scale in a drawing is 1 cm to 3 ft. In the drawing, the height of a flagpole is 3.5 cm. What is the actual height of the flagpole?

2. On a map, the scale is 2 inches to 15 miles. If two cities are 75 miles apart, how far apart are they on the map?

3. Jan's garden is 5 feet wide and 8 feet long. She wants to make a scale drawing of the garden. If she uses the scale 3 inches = 4 feet, what will be the dimensions of the garden in the scale drawing?

4. The distance from *A* to *B* on the map is 4.2 cm. The distance from *B* to *C* is 1.4 cm. *B* is on a straight road from *A* to *C*. The scale on the map is 1 cm: 125 km. What is the actual distance from *A* to *C*?

5. A map uses the scale 1 cm = 319 km. If South America is 27.7 cm long on the map, about what is the actual length of South America?

 DIAGNOSING READINESS

A Vocabulary
(pages 18, 76, 160, 300)

Choose the best term from the box.

1. __?__ are numbers that use place value to show values less than 1.

2. The word form of the number 0.04 is four __?__.

3. __?__ are numbers that are easy to compute mentally.

4. A __?__ compares two quantities.

Vocabulary

- **fractions** *(p. 160)*
- **decimals** *(p. 76)*
- **hundredths** *(p. 76)*
- **compatible numbers** *(p. 18)*
- **ratio** *(p. 300)*
- **tenths** *(p. 76)*

B Decimals and Fractions
(pages 172–175)

Write each shaded part as a fraction in simplest form and a decimal.

5. 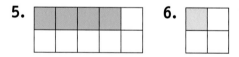 **6.**

Write each fraction as a decimal.

7. $\frac{3}{5}$ **8.** $\frac{1}{10}$ **9.** $\frac{41}{100}$

Write as a fraction in simplest form.

10. 0.35   **11.** 0.2   **12.** 0.05

13. Chris spent 1.6 hours doing homework. Lori spent $1\frac{4}{5}$ hours doing homework. Who spent more time doing homework?

Do You Know...

What city has the world's busiest airport?

You will find out in Lesson 7-11.

STEPHEN BIESTY'S INCREDIBLE
EXPLOSIONS
EXPLODED VIEWS OF ASTONISHING THINGS

C Addition and Subtraction

(pages 86–89)

Add.

14. $12 + $1.34
15. 0.45 + 0.7
16. 8.05 + 0.39
17. $1.89 + $1.03

Subtract.

18. 5.3 − 2.2
19. $17 − $4.52
20. 7.09 − 3.4
21. $23.50 − $5.26

22. Patty bought a shirt for $12.96, a book for $5.95, and a drink for $1.19. How much did she spend?

23. Jasper had $13.83. He bought a sandwich and a drink for $6.28. How much money does he have left?

D Multiplication

(pages 90–93, 248–251)

Multiply.

24. $\frac{1}{2} \times 26$
25. $\frac{2}{3} \times 18$

26. $\frac{3}{8} \times 48$
27. $\frac{3}{7} \times 21$

28. $5 \times 2.62
29. 0.3×5.17

30. 1.8×6.09
31. 2.1×0.05

32. Cindy had $57.48. She deposited $\frac{1}{4}$ of her money in a savings account. How much did she put into the account?

33. Mixed nuts sell for $7.49 per pound. How much would 0.4 pound of mixed nuts cost?

Key Idea
A percent is
another way to
compare parts to
a whole.

Vocabulary
• percent

Materials
• ruler

Understanding Percent

LEARN

What is a percent?

About 7 out of every 10 square miles of Earth's total surface area is water. What percent of Earth's surface is water?

A **percent** is a ratio in which the first term is compared to 100. The percent is the number of hundredths that represents the part to the whole.

Example A

What You **See**	What You **Write**	What You **Say**
	$\frac{7}{10} = \frac{70}{100} = 70\%$	"seventy percent"

Example B

It is easy to use percents when working with tenths, fifths, and fourths.

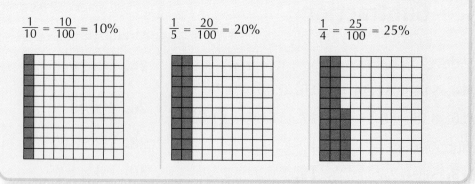

$\frac{1}{10} = \frac{10}{100} = 10\%$ $\frac{1}{5} = \frac{20}{100} = 20\%$ $\frac{1}{4} = \frac{25}{100} = 25\%$

✔ **Talk About It**

1. How can you write 4:5 as a percent?

2. Why is it easy to use percents when working with tenths, fifths and fourths?

3. What percent of Earth's surface is land?

How does percent relate to the whole?

Even though $\frac{1}{2} = \frac{50}{100} = 50\%$, percent is relative to the size of the whole. For the pizzas below, 50% of pizza A is smaller than 50% of pizza B because the whole pizzas are not the same size.

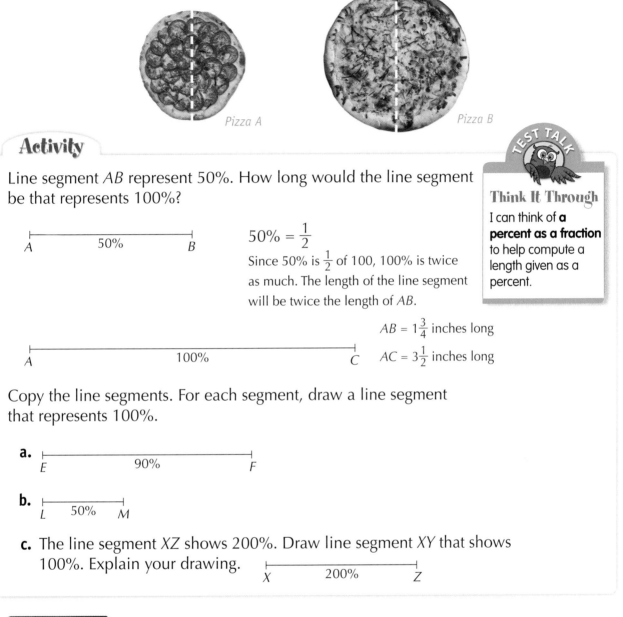

Pizza A   Pizza B

Activity

Line segment AB represent 50%. How long would the line segment be that represents 100%?

A |———— 50% ————| B

$50\% = \frac{1}{2}$

Since 50% is $\frac{1}{2}$ of 100, 100% is twice as much. The length of the line segment will be twice the length of AB.

Think It Through

I can think of **a percent as a fraction** to help compute a length given as a percent.

$AB = 1\frac{3}{4}$ inches long

A |———————— 100% ————————| C $AC = 3\frac{1}{2}$ inches long

Copy the line segments. For each segment, draw a line segment that represents 100%.

a. E |———— 90% ————| F

b. L |— 50% —| M

c. The line segment XZ shows 200%. Draw line segment XY that shows 100%. Explain your drawing.   X |——— 200% ———| Z

CHECK ✓

For another example, see Set 7-1 on p. 400.

Write the percent of each figure that is shaded.

1.

2.

3.

4. Number Sense The picture shows 25% of a bracelet. How long is the bracelet? Draw your answer.

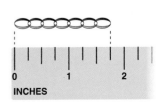

Ⓐ Skills and Understanding

Write the percent of each figure that is shaded.

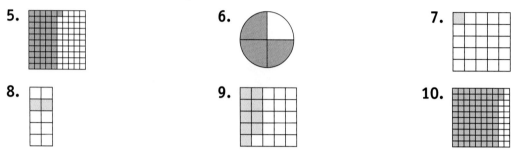

5. **6.** **7.**

8. **9.** **10.**

11. Number Sense The line segment below represents 300% of the length of a leaf Nick found. Draw line segment *ML* that represents the actual length of the leaf.

M   N

Ⓑ Reasoning and Problem Solving

Each line segment shows 100%. Copy each segment. Show where 25%, 50%, and 75% of each segment is.

12.

Q   R

13.

V   W

🎯 Math and Social Studies

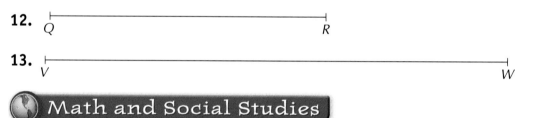

The bar graph shows the most important inventions of the twentieth century as chosen by teenagers.

Teen-Ranked Most Important Inventions of the 20th Century

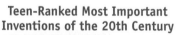
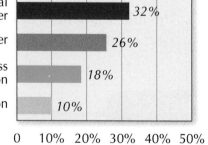

14. Which item was chosen by the most teenagers? the fewest?

15. Which two items together make up more than 50%?

16. Is the sum of the percents in the graph greater than or less than 100%?

17. Which invention was chosen by about $\frac{1}{5}$ of the teenagers surveyed?

18. **Writing in Math** Give a reason why the percents in the graph do not equal 100%.

19.  Is 25% always the same amount? Explain if the student's answer below is correct. If it is not, write the correct response.

> 25% means $\frac{25}{100}$ or 25 parts out of 100. As a drawing, this is 25 squares out of 100 squares. The size of the squares doesn't matter, only the number of squares. So, 25% is always the same amount.

C Extensions

20. Estimation To meet their goal, the math club needed to sell 60 boxes of holiday cards. The members sold 120 boxes. Did they sell 100% or 200% of their actual goal? Explain.

Mixed Review and Test Prep

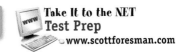

Take It to the NET
Test Prep
www.scottforesman.com

21. The scale on a map is 2 cm:25 miles. If two cities are 5 cm apart on the map, what is the actual distance between the two cities?

Find each answer.

22. $\frac{2}{3} + \frac{3}{4}$ **23.** $\frac{5}{6} \times \frac{4}{5}$ **24.** $\frac{7}{8} - \frac{1}{5}$ **25.** $\frac{2}{3} \div \frac{5}{6}$

26. Algebra Which is the solution to the equation $\frac{d}{4.2} = 3.6$?

     A. $d = 0.1512$ **B.** $d = 1.512$ **C.** $d = 15.12$ **D.** $d = 151.2$

Learning with Technology

Fractions eTool and Percents

You can use the Fractions eTool to explore percent. Select 5 and 10 as the denominators in the Array workspace. Drag the corner of the array to show 20% of 50.

1. How can you use the array representing 20% of 50 to find 10% of 50?

2. Select 6 and 10 as the denominators. Drag the corner of the array to show 50% of 60. Use the array representing 50% of 60 to find 25% of 60. Then find 5% and 40% of 60.

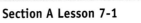

Key Idea
Fractions, decimals, and percents all name parts of a whole.

Materials
• 10 × 10 grids
• colored pencils or markers
• centimeter grid paper

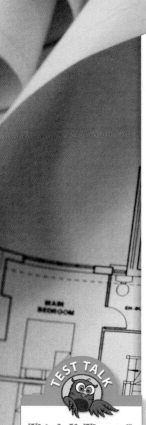

Think It Through
I can think about fractions with **denominators of 100** when changing between fractions, decimals, and percents.

ST FLOOR

Fractions, Decimals, and Percents

LEARN

How are fractions, decimals, and percents related to each other?

Fractions, decimals, and percents are three ways to show portions of a whole.

$\frac{40}{100}$ or 40 out of 100 of the squares are shaded.

$\frac{40}{100} = 0.40 = 40\%$

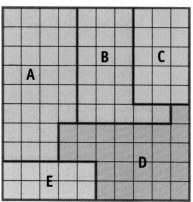

Activity

The floor plan shows a large room divided into five smaller sections A through E.

a. Compare the number of squares in each section to the total number of squares. Write each comparison as a fraction, decimal, and percent.

b. What denominator did you use for each fraction?

c. Which sections can you combine to make exactly 50% of the total area?

d. Draw another floor plan on a 10 × 10 grid with 6 sections. Give the area of each section as a fraction, decimal, and percent of the total area.

Take It to the NET
More Examples
www.scottforesman.com

How do you change between fractions, decimals, and percents?

Example A

Write 60% as a fraction and decimal.

$60\% = \frac{60}{100} = 0.60$

Example B

Write 0.38 as a fraction and percent.

$0.38 = \frac{38}{100} = 38\%$

Percent means per 100.

Example C

Write $\frac{3}{8}$ as a percent.

One Way

Use a proportion.

$\frac{3}{8} = \frac{n}{100}$

$8 \cdot n = 3 \cdot 100$

$8n = 300$

$n = 37.5$

So, $\frac{3}{8} = 37.5\%$.

Another Way

Divide.

$$\begin{array}{r} 0.375 \\ 8\overline{)3.000} \\ -24 \\ \hline 60 \\ -56 \\ \hline 40 \\ -40 \\ \hline 0 \end{array}$$

$0.375 = \frac{37.5}{100} = 37.5\%$

So, $\frac{3}{8} = 37.5\%$.

Example D

Write 0.5% as a fraction and decimal.

$0.5\% = \frac{0.5}{100} = 0.005$

Example E

Write 0.525% as a fraction and percent.

$0.525 = \frac{52.5}{100} = 52.5\%$

✔ Talk About It

1. Using Examples C–E, describe the movement of the decimal point when changing from a decimal to a percent and a percent to a decimal.

2. **Mental Math** Explain how you can use mental math to write $\frac{13}{50}$ as a percent and a decimal.

3. **Number Sense** Find the decimal and percent equivalent for $\frac{3}{11}$.

CHECK ✔

For another example, see Set 7-2 on p. 400.

Describe the shaded portion of each as a fraction, decimal, and percent.

1.

2.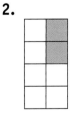

Write each in two other ways.

3. 78%   4. 0.85   5. $\frac{3}{5}$ 6. 7.5%   7. 0.333   8. $\frac{5}{16}$

9. **Mental Math** Is 65% greater than or less than $\frac{1}{2}$? Explain your answer.

A Skills and Understanding

Describe the shaded portion of each as a fraction, decimal, and percent.

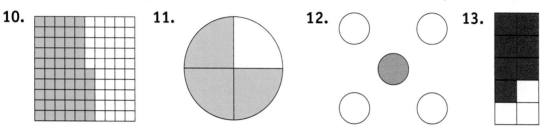

10. **11.** **12.** **13.**

Write each in two other ways.

14. 32% **15.** 0.05 **16.** 0.548 **17.** 22.5% **18.** 0.8

19. 13% **20.** $\frac{7}{8}$ **21.** $\frac{3}{10}$ **22.** 0.12 **23.** $\frac{11}{25}$

24. 98% **25.** 0.44 **26.** $\frac{2}{5}$ **27.** $\frac{19}{20}$ **28.** 36%

29. 1.5% **30.** $\frac{7}{10}$ **31.** 0.752 **32.** 0.6% **33.** $\frac{9}{250}$

34. Estimation Estimate $\frac{11}{23}$ and $\frac{8}{12}$ as percents.

B Reasoning and Problem Solving

35. Kyle and Martin shared a pizza. Kyle ate $\frac{1}{3}$ of the pizza and Martin ate 30% of the pizza. Who ate more?

36. Order the distances from least to greatest.
0.85 mile, $\frac{4}{5}$ mile, 82% of a mile

Math and Social Studies

The table shows six medal-winning countries in the 2002 Winter Olympics, which were held in Salt Lake City, Utah.

For 37–40, you may use a calculator. Round your answer to the nearest whole percent.

37. About what percent of the 2002 medals were won by the USA?

38. The USA won 10 gold medals. About what percent of the medals won by the USA were gold?

39. Which country won about $\frac{1}{4}$ of the 2002 medals?

40. Number Sense Altogether, 234 medals were awarded. About what percent of those were won by the top six countries?

Data File

2002 Winter Olympics	
Country	**Number of medals won**
Germany	35
USA	34
Norway	24
Canada	17
Russia	16
Austria	16

41. <u>Writing in Math</u> Is the explanation below correct? If not, tell why and write a correct response.

> What fraction of the original price would you pay during a 25%-off sale?
>
> The original price is equal to 100%. If 25% is taken off, that leaves 100% − 25% = 75%. 75% written as a fraction is $\frac{3}{4}$. So, you would pay $\frac{3}{4}$ the original price.

C Extensions

To write 125% as a fraction and as a decimal, first use the definition of percent:

$125\% = \frac{125}{100}$. Then simplify: $\frac{125}{100} = \frac{5}{4} = 1\frac{1}{4}$ and $\frac{125}{100} = 1.25$

Write each percent as a fraction and a decimal.

42. 120%   **43.** 150%   **44.** 225%   **45.** 203%

Mixed Review and Test Prep

Take It to the NET
Test Prep
www.scottforesman.com

46. Ramone received 85 points out of a possible 100 points on his last math test. What was his score as a percent?

47. Which set of numbers is in order from least to greatest?

A. $1\frac{1}{6}$, $1\frac{1}{3}$, $1\frac{7}{8}$ **B.** $\frac{2}{3}$, $\frac{5}{6}$, $\frac{7}{9}$ **C.** $\frac{8}{9}$, $\frac{8}{11}$, $\frac{8}{13}$ **D.** $\frac{1}{5}$, $\frac{1}{6}$, $\frac{1}{7}$

Practice Game

Match Them

Players: 2 or 3   **Materials:** 40 Fraction and Percent Cards

1. Shuffle the cards and place them face down in 5 rows of 8 cards.

2. The first player turns over 2 cards. If the numbers on the cards equal each other, the player keeps both cards and takes another turn. If the cards are not equal, the cards are returned to their original face-down position in the array.

3. The game ends when all cards have been correctly matched. The winner is the player with the most cards at the end of the game.

All text pages available online and on CD-ROM.

Problem-Solving Skill

Key Idea
There are specific things you can do to write a good explanation in math.

Think It Through
I should make sure my explanations are clear and well organized so that others can understand them.

Writing to Explain

LEARN

How can you write a good explanation?

When you **write to explain,** it is important that you describe each step in the solution clearly.

Allowance Alejandro said that he spent 110% of his allowance on sports equipment. Is this possible? Write to explain why or why not.

Tips for Writing Good Explanations

Break explanations into parts to make them easy to follow.

Use specific numbers for examples to explain why something works or does not work.

Give alternate explanations if appropriate.

Alejandro could not spend 110% of his allowance <u>unless</u> he had some extra money. Here is why.

Suppose Alejandro's allowance is $10 a week. This is the total, or 100%. If he spent 100%, he would have nothing left.

Now suppose Alejandro has $1 left from a previous week. Then he would have $11. If he spent $11, he would have spent more than $10, or more than 100%. $11 is 110% of $10, so if Alejandro had extra money, he could have spent more than 110% of his weekly allowance.

Alternate way: One dollar is 10% of $10. So, if he spent $11, he spent 100%, plus an additional 10%, or 110% of his allowance.

✔ **Talk About It**

1. What are the parts in the explanation above?

Mr. Edward conducted a survey. The results are given in the circle graph at the right.

1. Does the circle graph make sense? Explain your answer.

2. Darien says he spends 25% of the day in school. Does Darien's statement make sense? Explain your answer. Give an alternate explanation.

Favorite Primary Colors

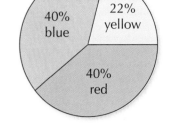

PRACTICE

For more practice, see Set 7-3 on p. 404.

3. How can you tell by looking at a decimal that the equivalent percent is less than 10%? Give an example as part of your explanation.

For Problems 4–6, decide if the circle graph makes sense. Explain your answer.

4. **Favorite Sport**   5. **Math Club Budget**   6. **Transportation to Work**

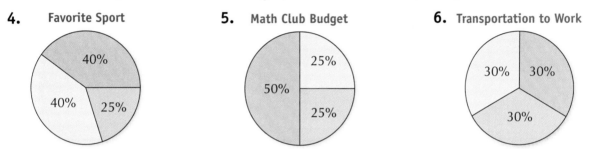

7. Raul got 7 out of 10 answers correct on a math test and 18 out of 25 answers correct on a science test. On which test did Raul get a greater percent correct? Explain.

8. If 50% of the students in your school are involved in sports, are there exactly 50 students involved in sports? Explain.

9. Can 25% of something be greater than 50% of something else? Explain and give an example in your explanation.

10. In Ms. Kim's class, 65% of the students are wearing T-shirts and 48% of the students are wearing jeans. Is this possible? Explain.

11. There are 100 members in the Computer Club. Thirty-five percent of the members are seventh graders, 10% are sixth graders, and the rest are eighth graders. Is it true to say that most of the members are seventh graders? Explain.

Reasonableness Tell whether each statement makes sense, and explain why or why not. If it does not make sense, rewrite it so that it does.

12. The student attendance for a school assembly was 115%.

13. One fourth of the coins in Jon's pocket were worth $\frac{1}{20}$ of a dollar.

Do You Know How?

Do You Understand?

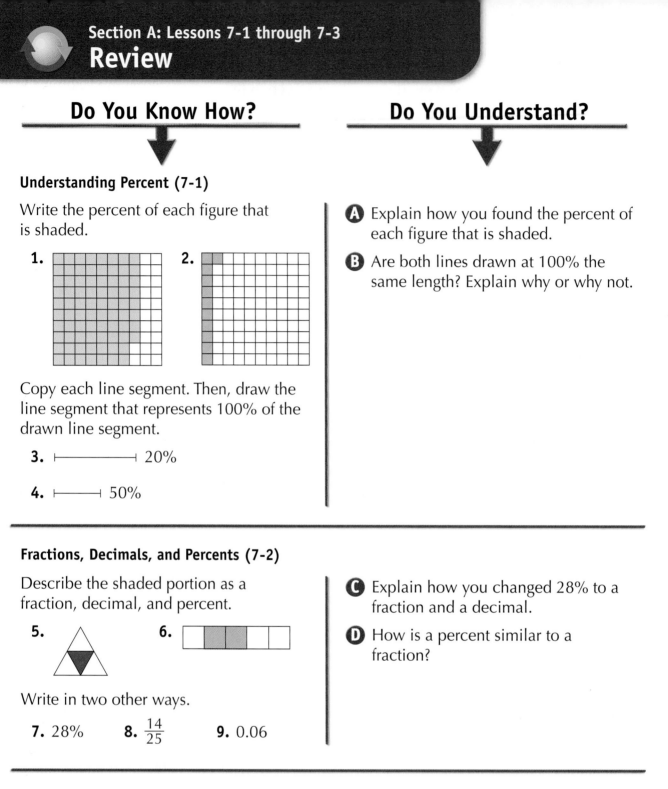

Understanding Percent (7-1)

Write the percent of each figure that is shaded.

1.   **2.**

A Explain how you found the percent of each figure that is shaded.

B Are both lines drawn at 100% the same length? Explain why or why not.

Copy each line segment. Then, draw the line segment that represents 100% of the drawn line segment.

3. ⊢———⊣ 20%

4. ⊢——⊣ 50%

Fractions, Decimals, and Percents (7-2)

Describe the shaded portion as a fraction, decimal, and percent.

5.   **6.**

C Explain how you changed 28% to a fraction and a decimal.

D How is a percent similar to a fraction?

Write in two other ways.

7. 28%   **8.** $\frac{14}{25}$ **9.** 0.06

Problem-Solving Skill: Writing to Explain (7-3)

10. Ramon walked 25% of the race and ran the rest of the race. If he walked 2 miles, how far did he run?

11. June said that she sold 200% of her toys at the garage sale. Is this possible? Explain.

E Explain how you determined how far Ramon ran.

F Compare 100% and 200%. Describe a situation in which you would use a percent greater than 100%.

MULTIPLE CHOICE

1. Which is $\frac{237}{500}$ written as a percent? (7-2)

   A. 2.37%   **B.** 4.74%   **C.** 23.7%   **D.** 47.4%

2. On a test, Tatiana got 21 out of 30 questions correct. What percent of the questions did she answer correctly? (7-2)

   A. 21%   **B.** 42%   **C.** 63%   **D.** 70%

FREE RESPONSE

Write the percent of each figure that is shaded. (7-1)

3.

4.

Draw a line segment that represents 100% of each line segment below. (7-1)

5. ⊢————⊣ 75%   **6.** ⊢—————⊣ 20%

Write in two other ways. (7-2)

7. 18%   **8.** 0.86   **9.** $\frac{7}{8}$ **10.** 66%   **11.** 0.045

12. $\frac{211}{500}$ **13.** $\frac{3}{8}$ **14.** $\frac{12}{15}$ **15.** 25%   **16.** $\frac{4}{25}$

17. Write and explain whether the statement makes sense.

At the junior high, 62% of the students study a foreign language and 48% do not. (7-3)

Writing in Math

18. Explain how to show a percent on a 10 × 10 grid. (7-1)

19. How do you change a percent to a fraction? to a decimal? (7-2)

20. Vick constructed a circle graph with the following parts: 20% red, 30% green, 40% yellow, and 25% purple. Does this make sense? Why or why not? (7-3)

21. Can 35% of something be greater than 60% of something else? Explain. (7-3)

Think It Through
I should **make my answers brief but complete.**

Think It Through

I can use what I know about **multiplying a fraction and a whole number** to mentally find a percent of a number.

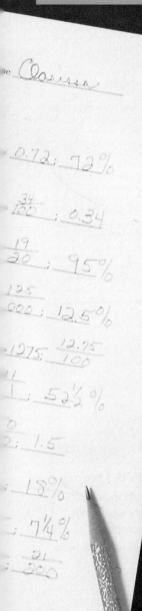

Mental Math: Finding a Percent of a Number

LEARN

How can you use fractions to mentally find a percent of a number?

To maintain her B average, Clarissa must score at least 80% on the next math quiz. The next quiz will have 40 questions. What is the minimum number of questions Clarissa needs to answer correctly?

Find 80% of 40.

The table below shows some common percents and their fraction equivalents.

Percent	10%	20%	25%	$33\frac{1}{3}$%	40%	50%	60%	$66\frac{2}{3}$%	75%	80%
Fraction	$\frac{1}{10}$	$\frac{1}{5}$	$\frac{1}{4}$	$\frac{1}{3}$	$\frac{2}{5}$	$\frac{1}{2}$	$\frac{3}{5}$	$\frac{2}{3}$	$\frac{3}{4}$	$\frac{4}{5}$

You can use the fraction equivalents to find a percent of a whole number mentally, especially when the denominator easily divides into the whole number.

Example

One Way

Think: 80% is $\frac{4}{5}$.

$\frac{4}{\overset{}{5}} \times \overset{8}{\cancel{40}} = 32$

So, 80% of 40 is 32.

Another Way

Think: 80% is 8 × 10%.

10% of 40 is 4,
8 × 4 = 32

So, 80% of 40 is 32.

Clarissa needs to answer at least 32 questions correctly.

✔ **Talk About It**

1. How could you use 20% to find 80% of 40 in the Example?

2. Is 25% of 151 easy to do mentally? Explain.

3. **Number Sense** Which is easiest to compute mentally? Explain your answer.

   20% of 47   20% of 62   20% of 85

Find the percent of each number mentally.

1. 50% of 80   **2.** 20% of 15   **3.** 80% of 25   **4.** $33\frac{1}{3}$% of 36

5. Number Sense If 10% of 120 is 12, what is 20% of 120? Explain how you decided.

PRACTICE

For more practice, see Set 7-4 on p. 404.

Ⓐ Skills and Understanding

Find the percent of each number mentally.

6. $66\frac{2}{3}$% of 12   **7.** 25% of 44   **8.** 10% of 1,570   **9.** 40% of 35

10. 60% of 60   **11.** $33\frac{1}{3}$% of 27   **12.** 75% of 72   **13.** 80% of 60

14. 20% of 125   **15.** 60% of 65   **16.** 40% of 55   **17.** 75% of 48

18. Number Sense If 10% of 80 is 8, what is 5% of 80? Explain how you decided.

Ⓑ Reasoning and Problem Solving

19. Copy and complete the table.

50% of 200	25% of 200	10% of 200	5% of 200	1% of 200
100				

20. Use your completed table to find: 6% of 200, 9% of 200, and 22% of 200.

21. Jocelyn received a 98% on her last math test. If there were 50 questions on the test, how many did she answer correctly?

22. At Central Middle School, 75% of the students said they prefer rock music. If there are 720 students at Central, how many prefer rock music?

23. **Writing in Math** An item originally priced $250 was marked down 50%. A sign said to take another 50% off. Does this mean the item costs $0? Explain.

🦉 Mixed Review and Test Prep

Take It to the NET
Test Prep
www.scottforesman.com

24. A recent survey of 100 teenage boys showed that 25% played golf, 35% played tennis, and 40% played baseball. How many boys played each sport?

25. Which fraction is equivalent to 28%?

A. $\frac{14}{100}$ **B.** $\frac{7}{25}$ **C.** $\frac{10}{28}$ **D.** $\frac{7}{10}$

26. Find 394.75×0.10.

A. 39,475   **B.** 3,947.5   **C.** 39.475   **D.** 3.9475

Estimating with Percents

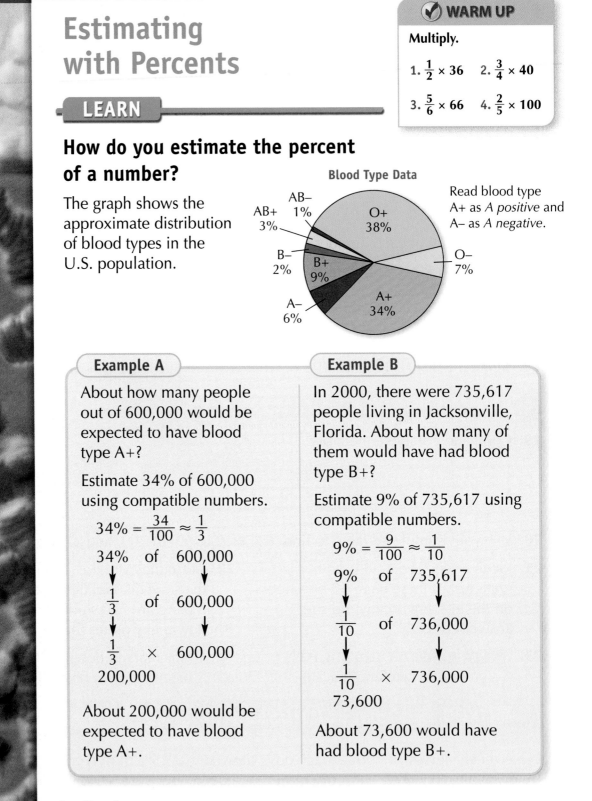

How do you estimate the percent of a number?

The graph shows the approximate distribution of blood types in the U.S. population.

Blood Type Data

Read blood type A+ as *A positive* and A– as *A negative*.

AB– 1%
AB+ 3%
O+ 38%
B– 2%
B+ 9%
O– 7%
A– 6%
A+ 34%

✓ WARM UP
Multiply.
1. $\frac{1}{2} \times 36$ 2. $\frac{3}{4} \times 40$
3. $\frac{5}{6} \times 66$ 4. $\frac{2}{5} \times 100$

Example A

About how many people out of 600,000 would be expected to have blood type A+?

Estimate 34% of 600,000 using compatible numbers.

$$34\% = \frac{34}{100} \approx \frac{1}{3}$$

34%   of   600,000
↓   ↓
$\frac{1}{3}$ of   600,000
↓   ↓
$\frac{1}{3}$ ×   600,000
200,000

About 200,000 would be expected to have blood type A+.

Example B

In 2000, there were 735,617 people living in Jacksonville, Florida. About how many of them would have had blood type B+?

Estimate 9% of 735,617 using compatible numbers.

$$9\% = \frac{9}{100} \approx \frac{1}{10}$$

9%   of   735,617
↓   ↓
$\frac{1}{10}$ of   736,000
↓   ↓
$\frac{1}{10}$ ×   736,000
73,600

About 73,600 would have had blood type B+.

✓ Talk About It

1. Could 735,600 have been used in Example B instead of 736,000? Explain.

2. **Number Sense** How could you estimate 6% of 600,000? of 736,000?

1. In 2000, Seattle, WA had 563,374 residents. Using the graph on page 368, about how many of those residents would be expected to have had blood type O+?

Estimate.

2. 43% of 28   **3.** 78% of 123   **4.** 12% of 1,875   **5.** 58% of 93

6. Number Sense Explain how to estimate 54% of 214. How can you use your estimate to find 154% of 214?

PRACTICE

For more practice, see Set 7-5 on p. 404.

Ⓐ Skills and Understanding

Estimate.

7. 71% of 61   **8.** 38% of 94   **9.** 48% of 219   **10.** 17% of 118

11. 34% of 55   **12.** 7% of 287   **13.** 26% of 338   **14.** 98% of 548

15. 4% of 405   **16.** 67% of 657   **17.** 41% of 523   **18.** 82% of 83

19. Number Sense 49 percent of what number is about 18?

Ⓑ Reasoning and Problem Solving

20. A student scored 83% on a test with 120 items. About how many questions did the student answer correctly?

21. Red blood cells have no way to repair themselves, and they have a very limited life span, usually about 33% of 1 year. About how many days does a red blood cell live?

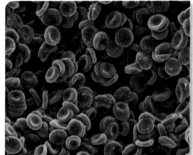

22. Algebra Use estimation to find x if 30% of x is about $70.

23. ~~Writing in Math~~ A store had 78 T-shirts in stock. Of those shirts, about 60% were sold during a sidewalk sale. The store manager says there are about 48 shirts left. Does this seem right? Explain your answer.

🦉 Mixed Review and Test Prep

Take It to the NET
Test Prep
www.scottforesman.com

Find each mentally.

24. 10% of 520   **25.** $66\frac{2}{3}$% of 60   **26.** 50% of 84   **27.** 20% of 45

Solve each proportion.

28. $\frac{5}{6} = \frac{m}{24}$ **29.** $\frac{7}{b} = \frac{28}{20}$ **30.** $\frac{1}{2} = \frac{p}{8}$ **31.** $\frac{3}{4} = \frac{15}{b}$

32. Which is the solution of $\frac{2}{3}x = 18$?

   A. $x = 6$ **B.** $x = 9$ **C.** $x = 12$ **D.** $x = 27$

Think It Through

- I should **estimate first** to see if my exact answer is reasonable.

- I should only **use a calculator when numbers are large** or to check my answer.

Finding a Percent of a Number

LEARN

What number sentence can you use to find a percent of a number?

The circle graph shows how water is typically used at home. If a household used 346 gallons of water, how much was used for laundry and cleaning?

Find 21% of 346. Estimate: $\frac{1}{5} \times 350 = 70$

Water Used At Home

Bathroom: 74%

Kitchen: 5%

Laundry/ Cleaning: 21%

Example A

One Way
Write the percent as a decimal.

21% of 346

$0.21 \times 346 = 72.66$

Since 72.66 is close to 70, the answer is reasonable.

Another Way
Write a proportion.

$\frac{\text{part}}{\text{whole}} = \frac{\text{percent value}}{100}$

$\frac{x}{346} = \frac{21}{100}$

$100x = 7{,}266$

$\frac{100}{100}x = \frac{7{,}266}{100}$

$x = 72.66$

With a Calculator
Depending on your calculator,

Press: 0.21 × [ ] 346 =

Display: **72.66**

or

Press: 21 [▸%] [×]

346 [ENTER =]

Display: **72.66**

The household used 72.66 gallons of water for laundry and cleaning.

Sometimes, you need to find a number when a percent of it is known.

Example B

Janelle tipped her waitress $8.25, which was 15% of the total bill. What was her total bill?

So, 15% of the total bill is $8.25. Write a proportion to find 15% of   is $8.25.

$\text{part} \longrightarrow \frac{\text{tip amount}}{\text{total bill}} = \frac{\text{percent value}}{100}$
$\text{whole} \longrightarrow$

$\frac{8.25}{x} = \frac{15}{100}$

$825 = 15x$ Find cross products.

$\frac{825}{15} = \frac{15x}{15}$ Divide.

$55 = x$ Solve for x.

Janelle's total bill was $55.

✔ Talk About It

1. How could you solve Example B using a calculator?

CHECK ✓

For another example, see Set 7-6 on p. 404.

Find the percent of each number.

1. 43% of 120   **2.** 30% of 63   **3.** 55% of 750   **4.** 8% of 900

Find the total amount.

5. 20% of ___ is 2.   **6.** 35% of ___ is 42.   **7.** 90% of ___ is 63.   **8.** 7% of ___ is 6.16.

9. Estimation Is 24% of $89 greater than or less than $16? Explain.

PRACTICE

For more practice, see Set 7-6 on p. 404.

Ⓐ Skills and Understanding

Find the percent of each number.

10. 52% of 300   **11.** 25% of 16   **12.** 38% of 1,500   **13.** 24% of 45

14. 19% of 184   **15.** 12.5% of 87   **16.** 3.2% of $15.80   **17.** 73% of 55

Find the total amount.

18. 30% of ___ is 75   **19.** 45% of ___ is 90   **20.** 62% of ___ is 62   **21.** 73% of ___ is 146

22. 25% of ___ is 20   **23.** 100% of ___ is 5   **24.** 3% of ___ is 0.63   **25.** 7.5% of ___ is 13.2

26. Estimation Is the exact answer for 32% of $83 greater than or less than $40? Explain.

Ⓑ Reasoning and Problem Solving

27. Use a proportion to find what percent of 150 is 90.

28. Water is the most abundant compound in the human body. It makes up about 60% of the average adult's body weight. If 114 pounds of an adult male's total weight is water, what is his total weight?

29. <u>Writing in Math</u> 7.5% of 1,875 is about 10% of 1,900, or 190. Is this estimate greater than or less than the exact answer? Explain.

🦉 Mixed Review and Test Prep

Take It to the NET
Test Prep
www.scottforesman.com

Estimate.

30. 22% of 65   **31.** 52% of 78   **32.** 32% of 32

33. Which is the unit rate for 90 miles in 3 hours?

　A. $\frac{270 \text{ miles}}{1 \text{ hour}}$ **B.** $\frac{30 \text{ miles}}{2 \text{ hours}}$ **C.** $\frac{30 \text{ miles}}{1 \text{ hour}}$ **D.** $\frac{180 \text{ miles}}{6 \text{ hours}}$

 All text pages available online and on CD-ROM.

Activate Prior Knowledge

Activating prior knowledge when you read in math can help you use the **problem-solving strategy,** *Solve a Simpler Problem,* in the next lesson.

In reading, activating prior knowledge can help you connect new ideas to what you know. In math, activating prior knowledge can help you connect a new problem to one you know how to solve.

Mr. Clearwater needs to pick 2 students from French Club to attend a language fair. How many different ways can he choose the 2 students if there are 8 students in the club?

I'll start with simpler problems that I know how to solve.

List each club member.

List the other students that can be paired with the member.

3 students		
Student 1	Student 2	Student 3
Student 2	Student 3	
Student 3		
2 +	1 =	3 ways

I'll find the number of choices if there are 3 students or 4 students in the club.

4 students			
Student 1	Student 2	Student 3	Student 4
Student 2	Student 3	Student 4	
Student 3	Student 4		
Student 4			
3 +	2 +	1 =	6 ways

1. What is the pattern for finding the number of ways to choose the 2 students when there are 3 students in the club? 4 students?

2. How can these simpler problems help you solve the original problem?

For 3–5, use the picture at the right.

Julio is buying jeans today. How much money will he save with a 30% discount?

3. You know that you can use mental math to find 10% of a number. Write a simpler problem about buying the jeans using 10%.

4. What is the amount saved with a 10% discount?

5. **Writing in Math** How can you use the answer to the simpler problem to solve the original problem?

For 6–7, use the chart at the right and the problem below.

Samantha is making sandwiches at her restaurant. Each sandwich has one meat and one cheese. How many different sandwiches are possible if Samantha can choose from 5 different meats and 4 different cheeses?

6. Write simpler problems like this one using a fewer number of meats and cheeses.

7. **Writing in Math** How can you use these simpler problems to solve the original problem?

MEATS	CHEESES
Ham	Swiss
Beef	American
Turkey	Provolone
Chicken	Cheddar
Pastrami	

For 8–9, use the bankbook shown at the right.

If the trend continues, what will the bank balance be after the 12th deposit?

8. Write simpler problems that you can solve using the information you already know.

9. **Writing in Math** How can you use these simpler problems to solve the original problem?

First Statewide Bank

Date	Transactions	Withdrawals	Deposits	Balance
3/3			$40.00	
3/10				$80.00
3/17				$120.00
3/24				$160.00

Problem-Solving Strategy

Key Idea
Learning how and when to solve a simpler problem can help you solve problems.

Solve a Simpler Problem

LEARN

How can you solve a complex problem by first solving a simpler problem?

First Car Emma wants to buy a car that is priced at $8,000. She put a deposit on the car that is 15% of the price. How much was the deposit?

Read and Understand

What do you know?   The price of the car is $8,000.

Emma paid a deposit of 15% of the price.

What are you trying to find?   Find the amount of the deposit.

Plan and Solve

What strategy will you use?   Strategy: **Solve a Simpler Problem**

How to Solve a Simpler Problem

Step 1 Break apart or change the problem into one or more problems that are simpler to solve.

Step 2 Solve the simpler problem(s).

Step 3 Use the answer(s) to the simpler problem to help you solve the original problem.

It is easy to find 10%.

Break apart 15% into 10% and 5%.

10% of $8,000 = $800

5% is half of 10%.

5% of $8,000 = $\frac{1}{2} \times$ $800 = $400

So, 15% of $8,000 is $800 + $400, or $1,200.

Answer: Emma paid a $1,200 deposit.

Look Back and Check

Is your work correct?   Yes. The ratio 1,200 to 8,000 equals 15 to 100, or $\frac{15}{100}$, which is 15%.

✔ Talk About It

1. What number was broken apart to make your calculations easier?

2. What simpler problems were solved in the First Car problem?

3. Find 11% of 1,200 by solving two simpler problems.

Think It Through

When to Solve a Simpler Problem

Think about solving a simpler problem when:

- a problem can be broken into smaller problems.
- smaller numbers can be used to get a solution.

When might you solve a simpler problem?

Table-Tennis Tournament Twelve people played each other one time in a table-tennis tournament. How many games were played?

Solve the problem with fewer than 12 people and look for a pattern.

First, solve the problem for 4 people. Label people A, B, C, and D. List the people played by each person.	Then, solve the problem for 5 people. Label people A, B, C, D, and E. List the people played by each person.
A B C D	A B C D E
B C D	B C D E
C D	C D E
D	D E
	E
4 people: 3 + 2 + 1 = 6 games	5 people: 4 + 3 + 2 + 1 = 10 games

The pattern involves finding the sum of the counting numbers from 1 through 1 less than the number of people in the tournament.

12 people: 11 + 10 + 9 + 8 + 7 + 6 + 5 + 4 + 3 + 2 + 1 = 66 games

✔ Talk About It

4. What simpler problems were solved in the Table-Tennis Tournament problem?

5. What pattern was found?

CHECK ✔

For another example, see Set 7-7 on p. 401.

Solve the simpler problems. Then use your solutions to help you solve the original problem.

1. **Wood Cuts** Clint cut a 12-foot board into 22 equal-length pieces. Each cut took 30 seconds. How long did it take him to make all the cuts?

   Simpler Problems: How many cuts are needed to cut the board into 3 pieces? into 4 pieces?

Ⓐ Using the Strategy

Solve the simpler problems. Then use your solutions to help solve the original problem.

2. What is the sum of the first 10 odd numbers?

> Simpler Problems: What is the sum of the first two odd numbers? the first three odd numbers?

3. How many different combinations can Harry make with the clothes at the right?

> Simpler Problems: How many different combinations can Harry make with 2 shirts and 2 pairs of pants? 2 shirts and 3 pairs of pants?

8 shirts

6 pants

4. How many different combinations can Shannon make with 4 skirts, 5 blouses, and 6 sweaters?

🌞 Math and Everyday Life

At the Tiny Trees nursery, tree seedlings are raised in square plots that are side by side. Each square side is a 1-foot section of fence.

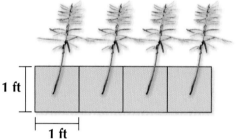

1 ft

1 ft

5. The length of fencing needed for one square tree plot is 4 feet. The length of fencing needed for a row of 2 square tree plots is 7 feet. The length needed for a row of 3 square plots is 10 feet. If this pattern continues, what is the total length of fencing needed for a row of 25 tree plots?

6. If a 1-foot section of fencing costs $3, how much would it cost to fence a row of 30 tree plots?

7. Calculator When 3 points are marked on a line segment, as shown at the right, 3 line segments can be identified. How many segments can be counted if you mark 12 points on a line segment?

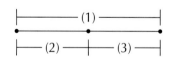

8. What is the total number of triangles in the figure below?

9. What is the total number of squares in the figure below?

B **Mixed Strategy Practice**

Solve each problem. Write each answer in a complete sentence.

10. To help raise money for new library books, Manuel decided to give 1¢ the first day and each day thereafter, give double the previous day's amount. How much money will Manuel give in 10 days?

11. Mrs. Forseth gave old library books to interested students. Andy took $\frac{1}{2}$ the books and then Barb took $\frac{1}{2}$ of the remaining books. Cathy took $\frac{1}{3}$ of the books that were left after Andy and Barb. Desmond and Ellie shared the remaining 8 books. How many books did Mrs. Forseth give to the students?

12. There are 9 Supreme Court Justices. The Justices shake hands with each other before the first session of the term. How many handshakes are there?

13. **Writing in Math** Ivory Coast Travel Agency placed this poster in its office window. Solve the problem, then explain how you did it.

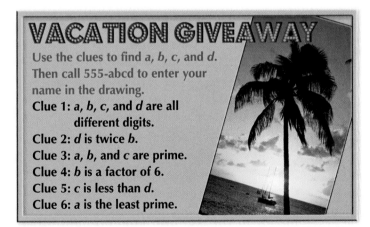

VACATION GIVEAWAY

Use the clues to find *a*, *b*, *c*, and *d*.
Then call 555-abcd to enter your name in the drawing.
Clue 1: *a*, *b*, *c*, and *d* are all different digits.
Clue 2: *d* is twice *b*.
Clue 3: *a*, *b*, and *c* are prime.
Clue 4: *b* is a factor of 6.
Clue 5: *c* is less than *d*.
Clue 6: *a* is the least prime.

STRATEGIES

- **Show What You Know**
  Draw a Picture
  Make an Organized List
  Make a Table
  Make a Graph
  Act It Out or Use Objects
- **Look for a Pattern**
- **Try, Check, and Revise**
- **Write an Equation**
- **Use Logical Reasoning**
- **Solve a Simpler Problem**
- **Work Backward**

Choose a tool — Mental Math

Think It Through

Stuck? I won't give up. I can:
- Reread the problem.
- Tell what I know.
- Identify key facts and details.
- Tell the problem in my own words.
- Show the main idea.
- Try a different strategy.
- Retrace my steps.

Mixed Review and Test Prep

Take It to the NET
Test Prep
www.scottforesman.com

Find each percent.

14. 65% of 210   **15.** 2% of 18   **16.** 80% of ▮ is 48

17. Which is equivalent to 8%?

    A. $\frac{4}{5}$ **B.** 0.8   **C.** $\frac{2}{25}$ **D.** $\frac{1}{8}$

 All text pages available online and on CD-ROM.

Do You Know How?

Do You Understand?

Mental Math: Finding a Percent of a Number (7-4)

Find the percent of each number mentally.

1. 20% of 65
2. $33\frac{1}{3}$% of 27
3. 80% of 50
4. 25% of 84
5. 40% of 30
6. 75% of 48
7. $66\frac{2}{3}$% of 99
8. 10% of 2,440

A For Exercise 2, explain how you used mental math to find the answer.

B Explain how to find 15% of 2,440 using your answer from Exercise 8.

Estimating with Percents (7-5)

Estimate.

9. 28% of 52
10. 98% of 76
11. 22% of 43
12. 12% of 342
13. 53% of 77
14. 78% of 92

C Explain how you estimated 22% of 43.

D Describe compatible numbers and give an example of how they can be used to estimate a percent.

Finding a Percent of a Number (7-6)

Find the percent of each number.

15. 4% of 12
16. 47% of 810
17. 34% of 49
18. 104% of 22
19. 12% of 16
20. 71% of 35
21. $8\frac{1}{2}$% of 76
22. 7.75% of 300

E Explain how you can use a proportion to find the percent of a number.

F When finding 90% of a number, is the answer greater than or less than the original number? Explain how you know.

Problem-Solving Strategy:
Solve a Simpler Problem (7-7)

23. Mr. Sims earns $48,000 a year and gives 12% of this money to charity. How much does he give to charity?

24. There are 7 teams in the baseball league. If each team plays the other teams 2 times each, how many games will be played?

G Describe how you used a simpler problem to solve each.

H Explain how solving a simpler problem helps you solve a more complex problem.

MULTIPLE CHOICE

1. Which is 10% of 1,580? (7-4)

   A. 0.158   **B.** 1.58   **C.** 15.8   **D.** 158.0

2. Miguel collected aluminum cans for recycling. He collected 150 cans. If 58% of those cans were soda cans, how many soda cans did he collect? (7-6)

   A. 58 soda cans   **B.** 87 soda cans   **C.** 108 soda cans   **D.** 116 soda cans

FREE RESPONSE

Find the percent of each number mentally. (7-4)

3. 10% of 5,240   **4.** 60% of 150   **5.** 75% of 64   **6.** 25% of 16

7. 100% of 6   **8.** 20% of 65   **9.** 50% of 88   **10.** $33\frac{1}{3}$% of 33

Estimate. (7-5)

11. 12% of 37   **12.** 27% of 90   **13.** 78% of 22   **14.** 99% of 253

15. 40% of 44   **16.** 76% of 24   **17.** 48% of 98   **18.** 58% of 74

Find the percent of each number. (7-6)

19. 26% of 48   **20.** 59% of 12   **21.** 13.6% of 50   **22.** 30% of 25

23. 2.9% of 120   **24.** 98% of 245   **25.** 0.3% of 12   **26.** 5% of 36

27. Matina and her family went out to dinner. The bill was $127.94. If Matina wants to leave a 15% tip, how much money should she leave? (7-7)

28. To accommodate a wheelchair, a builder replaces the original $3\frac{1}{4}$-foot counter tops with ones that are $2\frac{1}{2}$ feet high. What percent of the original height is the height of the replacement counter tops? Round your answer to the nearest whole percent.

Writing in Math

29. Zachary has 60 baseball cards. He put 45% of them in an album. He says he has 15 cards left over. Does this seem right? Explain your answer. (7-5)

30. Greg painted a design every 4.5 inches of a 36-inch-long poster board. He did not paint a design on either end. If it took him 5 minutes to paint each design, how long did it take him to paint all the designs? Explain your answer. (7-7)

Think It Through
I should **check to make sure my answer makes sense.**

Algebra

Key Idea
Discounts and sales tax are given as percents.

Vocabulary
• discount

Think It Through
I can **find the amount taken away** if I know **the percent of the whole that remains.**

Sales Tax and Discount

LEARN

How do you find the sale price of an item?

When stores have sales, prices of items are lowered. The **discount** is the amount to be taken off the original price. The discount can be given as a percent. Joyce wants to buy a pair of jeans at the Bargain Outlet. What is the sale price of the jeans after the discount?

WARM UP
Find each value.

1. 5% of 50
2. 25% of 84
3. 20% of 15
4. 10% of 18

Example A

One Way

Find the discount amount and subtract it from the original price.

Discount: 20% of $36.95

Estimate: $\frac{1}{5} \times \$35 = \$7$

$20\% \times 36.95 = 0.20 \times 36.95$
$= \$7.39$

Sale Price = regular price − discount
Estimate: $37 − $7 = $30

Sale Price = $36.95 − $7.39
$= \$29.56$

Since $29.56 is close to $30, the answer is reasonable.

Another Way

The discount is 20%. So, the sale price is 100% − 20%, or 80% of the regular price.

Find 80% of $36.95.

Estimate: $\frac{4}{5} \times \$35 = \$28$

80% of $36.95

0.80×36.95

$29.56

$29.56 is close to $28, so the answer is reasonable.

The total cost of the jeans after the discount is $29.56.

✔ Talk About It

1. In Example A, what does 80% represent?

2. **Number Sense** Suppose Joyce bought a pair of jeans and a sweatshirt. Explain how you would find the amount of money she saved.

How do you calculate sales tax?

A part of the receipt from Joyce's purchase in Example A is shown at the right. If the sales tax is 6% of the subtotal, what was her total bill?

Bargain Outlet

1 pair jeans..$36.95
Discount........($7.39)
Sale Price......$29.56
Subtotal $29.56

Tax 6% ....
TOTAL ......

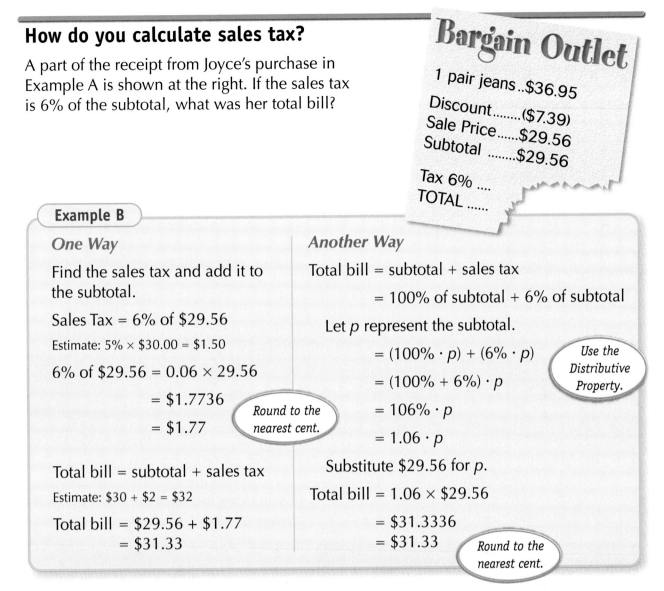

Example B

One Way

Find the sales tax and add it to the subtotal.

Sales Tax = 6% of $29.56

Estimate: 5% × $30.00 = $1.50

6% of $29.56 = 0.06 × 29.56

= $1.7736

= $1.77   *Round to the nearest cent.*

Total bill = subtotal + sales tax

Estimate: $30 + $2 = $32

Total bill = $29.56 + $1.77
= $31.33

Another Way

Total bill = subtotal + sales tax

= 100% of subtotal + 6% of subtotal

Let *p* represent the subtotal.

= (100% · *p*) + (6% · *p*)   *Use the Distributive Property.*

= (100% + 6%) · *p*

= 106% · *p*

= 1.06 · *p*

Substitute $29.56 for *p*.

Total bill = 1.06 × $29.56

= $31.3336

= $31.33   *Round to the nearest cent.*

The total for Joyce's bill was $31.33.

✔ Talk About It

3. Why is 106% written as 1.06?

4. Explain how to estimate 5% of $29.56. How would you estimate 106% × $29.56?

CHECK ✓

For another example, see Set 7-8 on p. 402.

Find the sale price or total cost.

1. Regular Price: $145
Discount: 15%
Sale Price: __?__

2. Subtotal: $64.89
Sales Tax: 6%
Total Cost: __?__

3. Estimation Estimate the total cost of a boat with a selling price of $2,350 and a sales tax of 8.5%. Explain how you found the estimate.

For more practice, see Set 7-8 on p. 405.

A Skills and Understanding

Find the sale price or total cost.

4. Regular Price: $250
Discount: 10%
Sale Price: __?__

5. Regular Price: $25.50
Discount: 25%
Sale Price: __?__

6. Regular Price: $79.95
Discount: 40%
Sale Price: __?__

7. Subtotal: $120.63
Sales Tax: 4%
Total Cost: __?__

8. Subtotal: $89.99
Sales Tax: 8.5%
Total Cost: __?__

9. Subtotal: $348.40
Sales Tax: 6.25%
Total Cost: __?__

10. Regular Price: $15
Discount: $33\frac{1}{3}$%
Sale Price: __?__

11. Subtotal: $525
Sales Tax: 7%
Total Cost: __?__

12. Regular Price: $279.49
Discount: 20%
Sale Price: __?__

13. Number Sense Janine wants to buy a sweatshirt for $24.99. The sales tax is 5.5%. Janine has $27.00. Explain how Janine can use estimation to decide if she has enough money.

B Reasoning and Problem Solving

14. The original price of a shirt was $23.48. Maria bought the shirt for $17.61. If there was no sales tax on the shirt, how much was the discount?

15. The total bill for lunch was $12.72. If $0.72 of the price is sales tax, what was the sales tax rate to the nearest whole percent?

Math and Social Studies

Sales tax is controlled by the state government. Therefore, the sales tax rate depends on which state you are in. Sales tax rates range from 0% in states like Oregon and Delaware to 7.25% in California. Use the table of sales tax rates to answer the following questions.

16. What would be the sales tax on a $12 item in Georgia? in West Virginia?

17. The sales tax rate in South Carolina is 0.5% more than the rate in North Carolina. In South Carolina, what would be the total cost with tax of an item that costs $23.98?

18. Which would have the greater sales tax amount, a $50 item in Texas or a $65 dollar item in Virginia?

19. Write the sales tax rate for Arkansas as a decimal.

20. In Minnesota, what would be the total cost with tax of an item that costs $300?

Data File

Sales Tax Rates

State	Sales Tax
Arkansas	5.125%
Florida	6%
Georgia	4%
Idaho	5%
Illinois	6.25%
Louisiana	4%
Minnesota	6.5%
North Carolina	4.5%
Ohio	5%
Tennessee	6%
Texas	6.25%
Virginia	4.5%
West Virginia	6%

21. **Writing in Math** Explain if the student's answer below is correct. If it is not, write the correct response.

> How can you use the sales tax on the receipt to estimate the amount of a 15% tip?
>
> *The sales tax is $1.89. Round this to $2.00. 15% of $2.00 is $0.30. So you should leave $0.30 as the tip.*

The Rio Restaurant

Beef dinner special	..$18.95
House salad	.......$ 3.50
Iced tea	.........$ 1.25
Slice of cake	......$ 1.50
Subtotal	..........$25.20
Tax (7.5%)	........$ 1.89
TOTAL	.........$27.09

Thank you!

C Extensions

For 22–23, use the information at the right.

22. Lea bought 3 T-shirts that were discounted 25% and a pair of jeans at regular price. The sales tax was 6.25%. How much did Lea have to pay in all?

23. Julio bought two pairs of jeans. If one pair was discounted 15% and the other 20% and the sales tax was 4.5%, how much did he spend in all?

Jeans	$35.00
T-shirts	$12.99
Sweatshirts	$20.50
Shorts	$17.50

Mixed Review and Test Prep

Take It to the NET
Test Prep
www.scottforesman.com

24. A telephone rang 30 times. Each ring lasted three seconds. Two seconds elapsed between rings. How long did the ringing last?

25. **Algebra** Solve $w - 2\frac{5}{8} = 3\frac{5}{6}$.

A. $w = 1\frac{5}{24}$ **B.** $w = 5\frac{11}{24}$ **C.** $w = 5\frac{10}{14}$ **D.** $w = 6\frac{11}{24}$

DISCOVERY
CHANNEL
SCHOOL

Discover Math in Your World

Take It to the NET
Video and Activities
www.scottforesman.com

A Whale of a Baby

The average adult female humpback whale is about 45 feet long and weighs between 85,000 to 90,000 pounds. A newborn humpback calf is about 14 feet long and can weigh about 5,000 pounds.

1. About what percent of its adult length is a calf at birth?

2. Each day, newborn humpback whales grow about $\frac{1}{2}$ inch and gain about 100 pounds. What percent of its birth weight does a calf gain each day?

Algebra

Key Idea
The amount of increase or decrease in costs can be given as a percent.

Percent of Increase and Decrease

WARM UP
Write each decimal as a percent.

1. 0.19   2. 0.125

3. 1.10   4. 0.0325

LEARN

How can you use percents to show change?

Prices at a local electronics shop have changed over the last decade. By what percent did the prices increase or decrease?

Data File

	Electronics prices	
Item	1994	2004
Stereo system	$98.95	$135.95
Cellular phone	$245.00	$159.00

		Example A	**Example B**
		Stereo System	Cellular Phone
STEP 1	Subtract to find the amount of increase or decrease.	Amount of Increase: $135.95 - $98.95 = $37	Amount of Decrease: $245.00 - $159.00 = $86
STEP 2	Write and solve a proportion to find the percent of increase or decrease.	$\dfrac{\text{percent change}}{100} = \dfrac{\text{increase amount}}{\text{original amount}}$ $\dfrac{x}{100} = \dfrac{37}{98.95}$ $x = \dfrac{37}{98.95} \times 100$ $x \approx 0.374 \times 100$ $x \approx 37.4$ The price of the stereo system increased by about 37.4%.	$\dfrac{\text{percent change}}{100} = \dfrac{\text{decrease amount}}{\text{original amount}}$ $\dfrac{x}{100} = \dfrac{86}{245}$ $245x = 8{,}600$ $x \approx 35.1$ The price of a cellular phone decreased by about 35.1%.

✓ **Talk About It**

1. In Examples A and B, what was the amount of increase or decrease divided by?

2. Why was $\dfrac{37}{98.95}$ multiplied by 100 in Example A?

3. **Number Sense** Explain how you could estimate the price increase in the stereo system by using 10% of $98.95.

For another example, see Set 7-9 on p. 402.

CHECK ✓

Find the percent of increase or decrease. If necessary, round answers to the nearest tenth of a percent.

1. A $20 item is increased to $25.

2. A $72 item is on sale for $54.

3. A price decreased from $120 to $114.

4. The number increased from 54 to 58.

5. Reasoning Will the item with the greatest change in price also be the item with the greatest percent change? Explain.

PRACTICE

For more practice, see Set 7-9 on p. 405.

A Skills and Understanding

Find the percent of increase or decrease. If necessary, round answers to the nearest tenth of a percent.

6. Ticket price increased from $27 to $54.

7. 200 people attended the fair last year; 286 attended the fair this year.

8. The average age on the football team increased from 12 to 13.

9. Reasoning If an original amount is $25 and it increases to $50, without calculating, is the percent increase 25%, 50%, 100%, or 200%? Explain.

B Reasoning and Problem Solving

10. Maris receives an employee discount. She bought a $75 jacket for $60. What percent discount do employees receive?

11. *Depreciation* is a decrease in value of an item over time. If a new car costs $23,500 and depreciates to $19,975 a year later, what is the percent of depreciation?

12. The original price of a ticket was $48. The price increased by 25%. What is the new price?

13. **Writing in Math** The sides of a square are each increased 100%. Does this increase the area 100%? Explain.

Mixed Review and Test Prep

Take It to the NET
Test Prep
www.scottforesman.com

14. What is the total cost of an item with a price of $75 and a sales tax rate of 4%?

15. Which is 234,000,000 written in scientific notation?

A. 23.4×10^7 **B.** 2.34×10^8 **C.** 2.34×10^6 **D.** 0.234×10^6

16. Find 210% of 90.

A. 189   **B.** 180.9   **C.** 18.9   **D.** 1.89

 All text pages available online and on CD-ROM.

Algebra

Key Idea
You can find simple interest by multiplying by a percent.

Vocabulary
• principal
• interest
• simple interest

Simple Interest

LEARN

How do you calculate simple interest?

When you first deposit money in a savings account, your deposit is called **principal.** The bank takes the money and invests it. In return, the bank pays you **interest** based on the **interest rate. Simple interest** is interest paid only on the principal. The formula for finding simple interest is $I = p \cdot r \cdot t$.

Suppose you invest $500 for 3 years at a simple interest rate of 5% per year. How much money will you have at the end of the 3 years?

Example

		What You **Think**	What You **Write**
STEP 1	Find the simple interest.	I need to find the interest amount on $500 invested at 5% for 3 years. I represents the interest, p represents the principal, r represents the interest rate per year, t represents the time in years.	$I = p \cdot r \cdot t$ $I = \$500 \cdot 5\% \cdot 3$ $I = 500 \times 0.05 \cdot 3$ $I = \$75$
STEP 2	Find the total.	To find the total at the end of 3 years, I need to add the principal and amount of interest earned. Total = principal + interest $T = p + I$	$T = p + I$ $T = \$500 + \$75$ $T = \$575$

You will have $575 after 3 years.

✓ Talk About It

1. In the Example, was the interest earned each year the same amount?

2. **Number Sense** If you know the simple interest earned in 1 year, how do you find the interest earned in 6 months? Explain.

Find the amount of interest and the total amount.

1. $1,000 for 4 years at a simple interest rate of 10% per year

2. $250 for 2 years at a simple interest rate of 7.5% per year

3. **Estimation** Mr. Masters used his credit card to purchase a living room set that costs $2,547.45. Estimate the total price of the furniture if the simple interest is 8% per year and he takes 3 years to pay it.

PRACTICE

For more practice, see Set 7-10 on p. 405.

Ⓐ Skills and Understanding

Find the amount of interest and the total amount.

4. $5,000 for 2 years at a simple interest rate of 9% per year

5. $300 for 8 years at a simple interest rate of 12% per year

6. $870 for 9 months at a simple interest rate of 6% per year

7. **Mental Math** You have $100 to invest. Which is the better investment: 5 years at 5% simple interest per year, or 10 years at 3% simple interest per year?

Think It Through
I can **use a calculator** whenever the computation involves many factors or factors with many digits.

Ⓑ Reasoning and Problem Solving

8. Sal borrowed $12,000 at a simple interest rate of 6.75%. If he borrowed the money for 5 years, how much interest did he have to pay?

9. Mr. Lee invested some money at a simple interest rate of 5.5%. He earned $1,760 in simple interest after 4 years. How much money did he invest?

10. Jack earned $63 in simple interest in one year. If the original amount he invested was $1,400, what was the simple interest rate?

11. **Writing in Math** Les wants to borrow $1,000. He saw the two bank advertisements at the right. From which bank should he borrow? Explain your answer.

Main Street Bank — 7.8% per year on a 3-year loan

Elm Street BANK — 9.5% per year on a 2-year loan

🦉 Mixed Review and Test Prep

Take It to the NET
Test Prep
www.scottforesman.com

Find the percent of increase or decrease.

12. 500 increased to 575

13. $75 decreased to $15

14. Solve $\frac{k}{32} = 5$.

   A. $k = 160$ **B.** $k = 16$ **C.** $k = 0.16$ **D.** $k = 16\%$

Problem-Solving Applications

Airports Preparing a flight for departure involves much more than checking tickets and baggage. Major airports employ thousands of people to take care of everything that needs to be done.

Trivia Los Angeles International Airport has nearly 8,000 parking spaces in 8 parking garages. If all the cars left at once, they'd form a line over 24 miles long!

1 Over 61.6 million passengers used the main airport of Los Angeles in 2001. This was about 75% of all the airline passengers in the region. About how many airline passengers traveled in the region?

2 Some baggage systems carry bags through a terminal at speeds of 20 miles per hour. Multiply this by 1.6 to find the speed in kilometers per hour.

Good News/Bad News *Since so little building space is available in Japan, one city built their airport on an artificial island. Unfortunately, the island tends to sink and the terminal has to be kept level by adjusting 900 jacks.*

3 **Writing in Math** Write a word problem that uses percents and involves airports. Write the answer in a complete sentence.

Key Facts
Busiest Airports in 2000

Location	Passengers
• Atlanta	80,162,407
• Chicago	72,144,244
• Dallas/Fort Worth	60,687,122
• London	64,606,826
• Los Angeles	66,424,767

Using Key Facts

4 Where is the world's busiest airport? Write the word name for the number of passengers that this airport serves.

5 A jet holds 48,445 gallons of fuel. A fuel truck holds 6,341 gallons of fuel. Estimate the number of trucks that are needed to fill the jet's tanks.

6 **Decision Making** An airport's gift shop is lowering its prices by 10%. Show two ways of finding the sale price of an $80 item. Which method do you find easier to use? Explain.

Do You Know How?

Do You Understand?

Sales Tax and Discount (7-8)

Find the sale price or total cost.

1. Price: $175
Discount: 25%

2. Subtotal: $78.89
Sales Tax: 4.5%

3. Price: $22.50
Discount: 20%

4. Subtotal: $103.54
Sales Tax: 6.0%

A Describe the steps you took to find the sale price for Exercise 3.

B Explain how you find the total cost of an item including sales tax.

Percent of Increase and Decrease (7-9)

Find the percent of increase or decrease. If necessary, round answers to the nearest tenth of a percent.

5. A $52 item is on sale for $40.

6. Membership increases from 36 people to 72 people.

7. One hundred ten T-shirts were sold last week and only 80 T-shirts were sold this week.

8. Marta's gymnastics practice changed from 4 days a week to 6 days a week.

9. The bakery had 25 loaves of bread, now they have 5 loaves of bread.

10. In a year, Hunter's CD collection increased from 10 CDs to 90 CDs.

C Describe how you find the percent increase.

D Explain how you can tell if the percent of increase will be more than 100%.

Simple Interest (7-10)

Find the amount of interest and the total amount.

11. $1,000 for 2 years at a simple interest rate of 8.25% per year.

12. $850 for 5 years at a simple interest rate of 5.5% per year.

13. $15,000 for 8 years at a simple interest rate of 6.75% per year.

E Explain how you found the amount of interest for Exercises 11 and 12.

F Tell what operation or operations are needed to find the total amount.

MULTIPLE CHOICE

1. An item originally priced at $240 is discounted 25%. What is the sale price? (7-8)

    A. $60   **B.** $180   **C.** $215   **D.** $300

2. Lita increased the number of push-ups she does each day from 20 to 25. By what percent did she increase her number of push-ups? (7-9)

    A. 4%   **B.** 5%   **C.** 20%   **D.** 25%

FREE RESPONSE

Find the sale price or total cost. (7-8, 7-11)

3. Regular Price: $25
Discount: 15%

4. Subtotal: $229.50
Sales Tax: 4%

5. Subtotal: $37.95
Sales Tax: 6.25%

Find the percent of increase or decrease. If necessary, round answers to the nearest tenth of a percent. (7-9, 7-11)

6. The number of balloons decreased from 25 to 18.

7. Sales increased from $55 a day to $110 a day.

8. Last year the average age was 12 years old, this year it is 11 years old.

9. The average life expectancy increased from 47 years to 77 years.

Find the amount of interest and the total amount. (7-10)

10. $7,000 for 2 years at a simple interest rate of 8.5%

11. $850 for 10 years at a simple interest rate of 3.75%

12. Juan paid $880 interest on an $8,000 loan he took out for 2 years. What was the simple interest rate per year? (7-10)

13. Jasmine practices the piano for 50 minutes. If she wants to increase her practice time by 10%, how many minutes should she practice? Explain how you found the answer. (7-9)

Writing in Math

14. Each side of a rectangle is increased 20%. Explain how this affects the perimeter. (7-9)

15. Tamara wants to invest $3,000. Which is the better investment: 4% for 8 years or 2.25% for 12 years? Explain. (7-10)

CHAPTER 7

Test Talk

Test-Taking Strategies

Understand the question.

Get information for the answer.

→ Plan how to find the answer.

Make smart choices.

Use writing in math.

Improve written answers.

Plan How to Find the Answer

After you understand a test question and get needed information, you need to plan how to find the answer. Think about problem-solving skills and strategies and computation methods you know.

① Sharon purchased some gym shorts at 30% off the ticketed price. What was the sale price of the shorts?

Gym Shorts
$15.00

A. $4.50

B. $7.00

C. $10.50

D. $14.70

Understand the question.

I need to find the sale price of the gym shorts.

Get information for the answer.

*The percent of discount is given in the **text**. The **picture** gives the ticketed price.*

Plan how to find the answer.

• Think about problem-solving skills and strategies.

*This is a **multiple-step problem.** First I need to find 30% of $15.00. I can write 30% as a decimal and multiply. That gives me the amount of the discount. Then I need to subtract the amount of the discount from the ticketed price.*

• Choose computation methods.

I can use mental math to estimate the answer to each step. But I will use paper and pencil to do the actual computations.

2 The director of an airport prepared this circle graph describing last month's passengers.

Airport Passengers

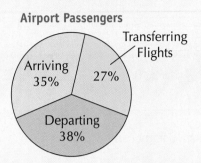

Arriving 35%

Transferring Flights 27%

Departing 38%

On Monday, the airport served 12,416 passengers. Based on the graph, which gives the best estimate of the number of arriving passengers?

A. 400   **C.** 4,000

B. 3,000   **D.** 6,000

Think It Through

*I need to **estimate** the number of passengers who arrived at the airport on Monday. The **graph** gives the percent of passengers who arrived last month, and the **text** gives the total number of passengers for Monday. I'll **estimate by rounding.** I'll use $\frac{1}{3}$ for 35% since 35% is close to $33\frac{1}{3}$%, and I'll use 12,000 for the number of passengers. Then I'll use mental math to multiply $\frac{1}{3} \times 12,000$.*

Now it's your turn.

For each problem, describe a plan for finding the answer.

3 Davie bought a DVD. He had to pay 6% sales tax. What was the total amount Davie had to pay for the DVD with sales tax?

DVD'S $32.00

A. $1.92

B. $30.08

C. $33.92

D. $51.20

4 This chart shows last year's distribution of gym uniform sizes.

Gym Uniform Sizes	
Extra-Small	9%
Small	22%
Medium	38%
Large	18%
Extra-Large	13%

This year there are 485 gym students. Based on the data in the chart, which is the best estimate for the number of large gym uniforms that will be needed?

A. 10   **C.** 100

B. 50   **D.** 200

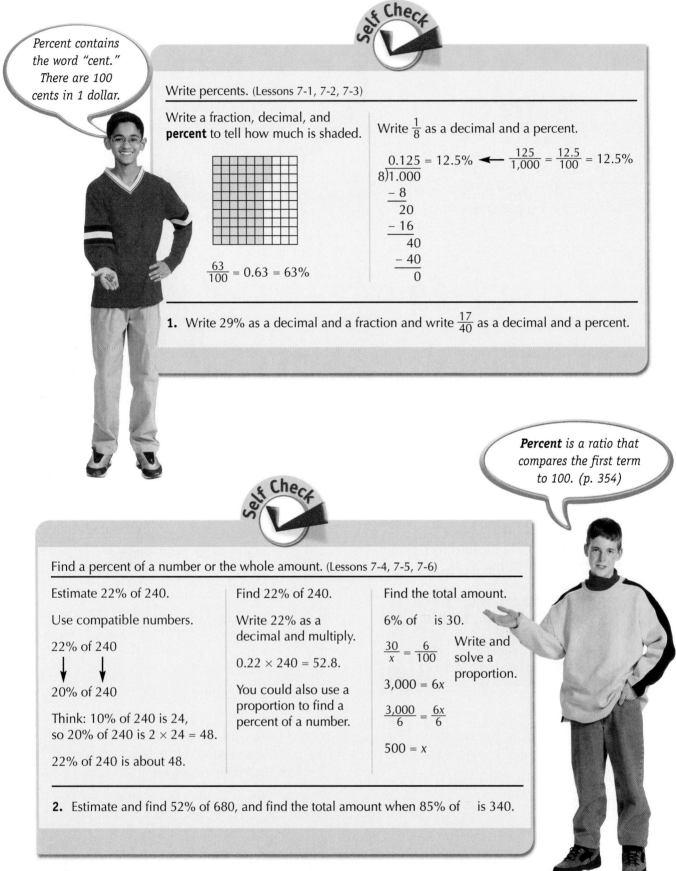

Self Check

Percent contains the word "cent." There are 100 cents in 1 dollar.

Write percents. (Lessons 7-1, 7-2, 7-3)

Write a fraction, decimal, and **percent** to tell how much is shaded.

$$\frac{63}{100} = 0.63 = 63\%$$

Write $\frac{1}{8}$ as a decimal and a percent.

$$\begin{array}{r} 0.125 \\ 8\overline{)1.000} \\ -8 \\ \hline 20 \\ -16 \\ \hline 40 \\ -40 \\ \hline 0 \end{array} = 12.5\% \longleftarrow \frac{125}{1{,}000} = \frac{12.5}{100} = 12.5\%$$

1. Write 29% as a decimal and a fraction and write $\frac{17}{40}$ as a decimal and a percent.

Percent is a ratio that compares the first term to 100. (p. 354)

Self Check

Find a percent of a number or the whole amount. (Lessons 7-4, 7-5, 7-6)

Estimate 22% of 240.

Use compatible numbers.

22% of 240
↓   ↓
20% of 240

Think: 10% of 240 is 24, so 20% of 240 is 2 × 24 = 48.

22% of 240 is about 48.

Find 22% of 240.

Write 22% as a decimal and multiply.

0.22 × 240 = 52.8.

You could also use a proportion to find a percent of a number.

Find the total amount.

6% of   is 30.

$$\frac{30}{x} = \frac{6}{100}$$

Write and solve a proportion.

3,000 = 6x

$$\frac{3{,}000}{6} = \frac{6x}{6}$$

500 = x

2. Estimate and find 52% of 680, and find the total amount when 85% of   is 340.

"Dis-" means not, as in "dishonorable."

Discount is the amount of money you do not pay. It's subtracted from the price. (p. 380)

Self Check

Find discounts and interest. (Lessons 7-8, 7-10)

What is the sale price of a $25 back pack after a 15% **discount**?

Find the discount.

$25 × 0.15 = $3.75

Subtract from the regular price.

$25 − $3.75 = $21.25

$600 is invested for 2 years at a **simple interest rate** of 5% per year.

Find the interest.

$\ell = p \cdot r \cdot t$

$\ell = \$600 \cdot 5\% \cdot 2$

$\ell = 600 \cdot 0.05 \cdot 2$

$\ell = \$60$

Find the total.

$T = p + \ell$

$T = \$600 + \$60$

$T = \$660$

ℓ = **interest**
p = **principal**
r = annual interest rate
t = time in years
T = total

3. Find the total value of an account after 4 years if $8,000 is invested at a simple interest rate of 6% per year.

Self Check

Solve a simpler problem and write to explain. (Lessons 7-3, 7-7)

Solve a problem by breaking it into simpler problems.

Find 60% of $14,000.
Break apart 60% into 50% and 10%.
50% of $14,000 = $7,000
10% of $14,000 = $1,400
So, 60% of $14,000 is $8,400.

Break explanations into parts so they are easy to follow.

Explain how you solved the problem at the left.

60% is the same as 50% + 10%. So I found 50% of $14,000, which is $7,000. Then I found 10% of $14,000, which is $1,400. Finally, I added the results, $7,000 + $1,400 = $8,400.

4. Find 11% of 4,200. Explain how you solved the problem.

Answers: 1. 0.29; $\frac{29}{100}$; 0.425; 42.5% 2. Sample estimate: 340; 353.6; 400 3. $9,920 4. 462; explanations will vary.

Chapter 7 Key Vocabulary and Concept Review 395

MULTIPLE CHOICE

Choose the correct letter for each answer.

1. Which is 20% of 50?

    A. 1   **C.** 20

    B. 10   **D.** 100

2. A $35 toaster is on sale for $28. Which is the percent of decrease?

    A. 4%   **C.** 20%

    B. 7%   **D.** 25%

3. Which is 32% of 56?

    A. 0.1792   **C.** 17.92

    B. 1.792   **D.** 179.2

4. Estimate 38% of 44.

    A. 9   **C.** 22

    B. 17   **D.** 38

5. Which percent is equivalent to $\frac{5}{8}$?

    A. 4%   **C.** 62.5%

    B. 6.25%   **D.** 40%

6. Cassie bought a sweater that was discounted 25%. If the original price was $60, how much did Cassie pay for the sweater?

    A. $15   **C.** $45

    B. $25   **D.** $75

7. Miko invested $500 for 6 years at a simple interest rate of 4% per year. How much interest did she earn?

    A. $20   **C.** $200

    B. $120   **D.** $620

8. Mr. and Mrs. Sanchez's dinner bill is $80. If they want to leave a 15% tip, how much should they leave?

    A. $8   **C.** $16

    B. $12   **D.** $24

Marianna bought a bicycle. The original price was $120. The bike was discounted $33\frac{1}{3}$%. She also paid a sales tax of 6%.

9. How much was the bike discounted?

    A. $20   **C.** $40

    B. $36   **D.** $80

10. How much did Marianna pay for the bike including sales tax?

    A. $42.40   **C.** $127.20

    B. $84.80   **D.** $128.00

11. Mr. Matolka took a survey of the colors of jackets his students wear. He collected the data below. What percent of his students wear a blue jacket?

    A. 8%   **C.** 32%

    B. 25%   **D.** 40%

Data File

Jacket Colors

Color	Number of Students
red	6
black	5
blue	8
white	2
other	4
Total	25

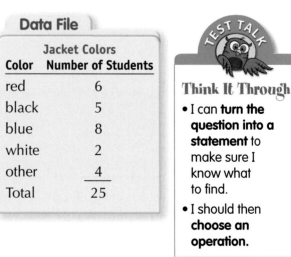

Think It Through

• I can **turn the question into a statement** to make sure I know what to find.

• I should then **choose an operation.**

FREE RESPONSE

Write each in two other ways.

12. 20%

13. $\frac{19}{20}$

14. 2.6%

15. 0.09

Find the percent of each number.

16. 80% of 80

17. 20% of 55

18. 96% of 135

19. 1% of 64

Find the percent of increase or decrease. If necessary, round to the nearest tenth of a percent.

20. The price increases from $12 to $20.

21. Membership decreases from 75 to 55 members.

22. 10 shirts were sold yesterday, 40 were sold today.

23. Theo's Jewelers bought a necklace for $75. The necklace was sold for $125.

Write the percent of each figure that is shaded.

24. 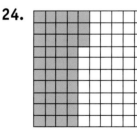 **25.**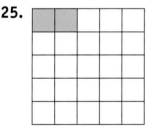

26. Nicholas deposited $350 into a savings account with a simple interest rate of 2.5% per year. How much money did he have after 3 years?

27. What is the total cost of a $32 item with a sales tax of 4.25%?

Writing in Math

28. Josie said she was going to save 110% of her allowance. Does this make sense? Explain why or why not.

29. Explain how to use the problem-solving strategy Solve a Simpler Problem to find 15% of $27,000.

Think It Through
- I should **make my answers brief but complete.**
- I should **describe steps in order.**

30. Edgar bought the items listed below at the store. If he received a discount of 25% off each item and then paid a sales tax of 5%, what was his total bill? Explain how you found the total amount.

Outlet Store

T-shirt	$12.00
jeans	$36.00
socks	$3.50
shampoo	$7.50
Subtotal	$59.00
Discount: 25%	
Sales Tax: 5%	
Total:	

Number and Operation

MULTIPLE CHOICE

1. What is $\frac{2}{3} + \frac{4}{5}$?

   A. $\frac{6}{8}$ **C.** $\frac{8}{15}$

   B. $\frac{6}{15}$ **D.** $1\frac{7}{15}$

2. Estimate 18% of 63.

   A. 8   **C.** 13

   B. 9   **D.** 18

FREE RESPONSE

3. Julie earns $750 each week. If she saves 10% of her salary each week, how much will she have saved after 4 weeks?

4. Sam exercises for 0.75 hour each weekday and 2.5 hours each day on the weekend. How many hours does he exercise in one week?

5. What is 32% of 450?

6. What percent of 25 is 13?

7. 35% of what number is 52.5?

Writing in Math

8. Explain how to add 3.096 and 4.27. Then find the sum.

9. Write and solve a problem that involves decimals and has an answer of 78.9.

10. In Mrs. Mill's class, 36% of the students are boys and 74% of the students are girls. Does this make sense? Explain.

Geometry and Measurement

MULTIPLE CHOICE

11. An equilateral triangle is $5\frac{1}{3}$ ft on each side. What is its perimeter?

   A. 15 ft   **C.** 18 ft

   B. 16 ft   **D.** $21\frac{1}{3}$ ft

12. How many inches are in 2 feet?

   A. 12 in.   **C.** 36 in.

   B. 24 in.   **D.** 48 in.

FREE RESPONSE

13. Missy biked 36 miles last week. This week, she increased her distance by 20%. How far did she bike this week?

14. Ramone drove 300 miles in 6 hours. Use the formula $d = r \times t$ to find the speed at which Ramone drove.

15. Use the formula $i = 2.54c$ to find the number of centimeters in a yard.

Writing in Math

16. Explain why the perimeter of a square with side length $2\frac{1}{4}$ ft is 9 ft. Use the picture below for help.

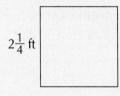

$2\frac{1}{4}$ ft

17. An 8-foot beam of wood must be cut into 16 equal pieces. Explain how to determine how far apart each cut should be made.

Data Analysis and Probability

MULTIPLE CHOICE

Cards with the letters for the word
MISSISSIPPI are put into a bag.
A card is selected at random.

18. What is the probability of NOT
selecting the letter I?

A. $\frac{1}{11}$ **B.** $\frac{4}{11}$ **C.** $\frac{7}{11}$ **D.** 1

19. What is the probability of selecting
the letter M, S, I, or P?

A. $\frac{1}{11}$ **B.** $\frac{4}{11}$ **C.** $\frac{7}{11}$ **D.** 1

FREE RESPONSE

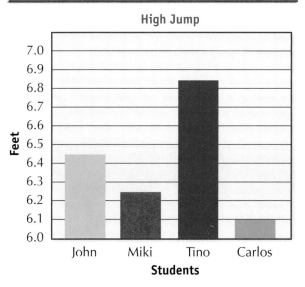

High Jump

20. According to the graph above, how
much higher did Tino jump than
Carlos?

Writing in Math

21. In a survey of favorite color, 35%
chose red, 65% chose blue, and
15% chose green. Explain whether
this statement makes sense.

Algebra

MULTIPLE CHOICE

22. Solve $x + 7.4 = 12$

A. $x = 4.4$ **C.** $x = 5.6$

B. $x = 4.6$ **D.** $x = 19.4$

23. Which expression represents 5 less
than twice w?

A. $5 - 2w$ **C.** $2w - 5$

B. $2 - 5w$ **D.** $5w - 2$

FREE RESPONSE

24. Find the next number in the pattern.

$$\frac{1}{2}, \frac{2}{3}, \frac{3}{4}, \frac{4}{5}, \underline{\quad}$$

25. Find the next 3 numbers in the
pattern.

6, 7, 14, 15, 30, 31, ___ , ___ , ___

26. What is the interest on an investment
of $3,000 for 5 years at a simple
interest rate of 4.2% per year?

27. Write a word expression for $7 + x$.

28. A fitness club requires dues of $35
each month. Write an expression for
the cost of dues for n months.

Writing in Math

29. A student calculated the cost of an
item priced at $45 with a sales tax
of 6%. Is his answer correct?
Explain.

Total cost = price + sales tax
sales tax: $45 x 6% = $45 x 0.6 = $27
Total cost = $45 + $27
The total cost would be $72.

Set 7-1 (pages 354–357)

Find the percent of the figure that is shaded.

Remember that a percent is a comparison to 100.

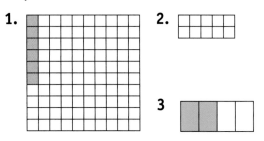

1.

2.

3

The figure has 48 out of 100 squares shaded. So, 48% of the figure is shaded.

Set 7-2 (pages 358–361)

Write 22% as a fraction and a decimal.

To find the fraction:
Place the percent over 100.

$$22\% = \frac{22}{100}$$

To find the decimal:
The second decimal place is hundredths.
Move the decimal point two places to the left.

$$22\% = 0.22$$

Remember to change a fraction to a percent, you can also set up a proportion.

Write in two other ways.

1. $\frac{4}{5}$ **2.** 3%   **3.** $\frac{5}{8}$

4. 0.15   **5.** $\frac{1}{10}$ **6.** 88%

7. $\frac{7}{10}$ **8.** 0.032   **9.** 16%

Set 7-3 (pages 362–363)

Of the 28 classmates Saiyo surveyed, $\frac{3}{4}$ like going to the mall as a leisure activity, and $\frac{3}{7}$ like going to the movies. Is this possible? Explain.

When you write an explanation, break your explanation into parts. Use specific numbers for examples to explain why something works or does not work. Give alternate explanations.

No. $\frac{3}{4}$ of 28 is 21, and $\frac{3}{7}$ of 28 is 12; 21 + 12 = 33. It is possible that several of the classmates indicated a preference for both activities.

Remember to give alternate explanations when you explain.

1. Decide if the circle graph makes sense. Explain your answer.

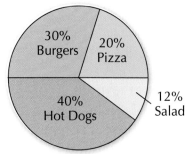

Students' Lunch Choices

30% Burgers

20% Pizza

40% Hot Dogs

12% Salad

2. Selina stated that she spends $\frac{1}{4}$ of her morning getting dressed. Does Selina's statement make sense? Explain.

Find 60% of 60 using mental math.

You can use fraction equivalents.

$60\% = \frac{3}{5}$

$\frac{3}{5} \times 60 = 36$

So, 60% of 60 is 36.

This is easy to multiply mentally, because 5 is a factor of 60.

Remember when the denominator of a fraction is a factor of the number, it is easy to multiply the fraction and number.

1. 20% of 25   **2.** 75% of 16

3. $33\frac{1}{3}\%$ of 45   **4.** 80% of 50

5. 25% of 84   **6.** $66\frac{2}{3}\%$ of 33

Estimate 53% of 531.

Use compatible numbers to make it easy to multiply mentally.

53% of 531 is about 50% of 530.

$50\% = \frac{1}{2}$ $\frac{1}{2} \times 530 = 265$

So, 53% of 531 is about 265.

Remember you can use compatible numbers and fraction equivalents to estimate percents.

1. 68% of 47   **2.** 43% of 73

3. 46% of 146   **4.** 16% of 87

5. 26% of 49   **6.** 78% of 66

Find 17% of 45.

Change the percent to a decimal and multiply.

$17\% \times 45 = 0.17 \times 45$

$= 7.65$

Remember to find the percent of a number, you can also set up a proportion.

1. 47% of 20   **2.** 36% of 40

3. 63% of 48   **4.** 78% of 18.6

5. 20% of ▢ is 15

6. 18% of ▢ is 180

Leo put a 12% deposit on a computer that cost $3,500. How much was Leo's deposit?

Solve a Simpler Problem

Step 1 Break apart or change the problem into one or more problems that are simpler to solve.

Step 2 Solve the simpler problem(s).

Step 3 Use the answer(s) to the simpler problem to help you solve the original problem.

$12\% = 10\% + 1\% + 1\%$

10% of $3,500 = $350   1% of $3,500 = $35

So, 12% of $3,500 = $350 + $35 + $35 = $420

Leo's deposit was $420.

Remember to break apart the problem into one or more problems that are simpler to solve.

1. Marsha put a 16% down payment on a car that cost $9,000. How much was her down payment?

2. For a 100-km bicycle race, markers were placed at the starting line, the finish line, and at every 10 km in between. How many markers were used for this race?

Set 7-8 (pages 380–383)

Find the cost of a $36 item after a
discount of 30%.

One Way

Discount = 30% of $36
= 0.30 × $36
= $10.80

Sale Price = regular price – discount
= $36 – $10.80
= $25.20

Another Way

Since the discount is 30%,
the sale price is 100% – 30% = 70%

70% of 36
0.70 × 36
$25.20

Find the total cost for a subtotal of $199
and a sales tax of 7%.

Total cost = subtotal + 7% of subtotal
= 107% · subtotal
= 1.07% × 199
= $212.93

Remember a discount reduces the price
of an item and sales tax increases the
price.

1. Price: $25
Discount: 15%
Sale Price: _?_

2. Subtotal: $148.50
Sales Tax: 6%
Total Cost: _?_

3. Price: $575
Discount: 20%
Sale Price: _?_

4. Subtotal: $83.60
Sales Tax: 5%
Total Cost: _?_

5. Price: $97
Discount: 40%
Sale Price: _?_

6. Subtotal: $13.76
Sales Tax: 4.25%
Total Cost: _?_

7. Price: $202.60
Discount: 10%
Sale Price: _?_

8. Subtotal: $19.95
Sales Tax: 7%
Total Cost: _?_

Set 7-9 (pages 384–385)

Find the percent of increase when 20 is
increased to 28.

28 – 20 = 8   Find the amount
of increase.

$\frac{8}{20}$ × 100 = 40%   Divide the amount of
increase by the original
amount and multiply by 100
to find the percent.

Remember to divide the amount of
change by the original amount.

1. A $28 item is increased to $35.

2. 60 people attended last week and
48 people attended this week.

3. The average age increased from 8 to 9.

Set 7-10 (pages 386–387)

Find the amount of interest and the total
amount for $5,000 invested for 2 years at
an interest rate of 9.4%.

$I = p × r × t$
$I = 5,000 × 0.094 × 2$
$I = 940

Total = $5,000 + $940 = $5,940

Remember to add the interest to the
principal to find the total amount.

1. $6,000 for 3 years at a simple interest
rate of 6.25% per year.

2. $700 for 5 years at a simple interest
rate of 8% per year.

3. $9,000 for 6 years at a simple interest
rate of 10.9% per year.

Chapter 7
More Practice

Take It to the NET
More Practice
www.scottforesman.com

Set 7-1 (pages 354–357)

Write the percent of each figure that is shaded.

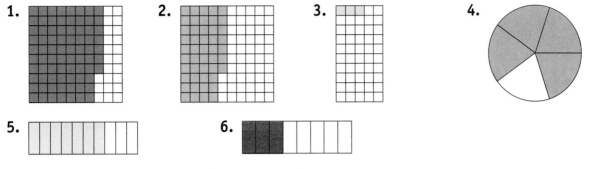

Copy the line segment. Draw the segment that represents 100%.

7. ⊢——⊣ 20%   **8.** ⊢—⊣ 40%   **9.** ⊢————⊣ 50%

10. Maggie answered 80% of the test questions correctly on a math test with 50 questions. Miguel answered 80% of the test questions correctly on an English test with 100 questions. Did they both answer the same number of questions correctly? Explain your answer.

Set 7-2 (pages 358–361)

Describe the shaded portion of each as a fraction, decimal, and percent.

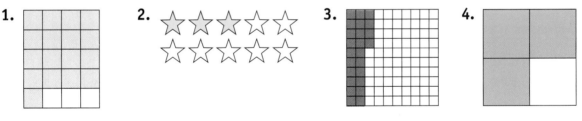

Write each in two other ways.

5. 0.36   **6.** 2%   **7.** $\frac{9}{10}$ **8.** 0.8%

9. $\frac{27}{50}$ **10.** 0.05   **11.** 3%   **12.** $\frac{1}{5}$

13. $\frac{3}{8}$ **14.** 0.045   **15.** 0.18   **16.** 13%

17. Leon sold 50 out of 75 T-shirts. What percent did he sell? Round your answer to the nearest whole percent.

18. The label on an orange drink reads "20% real fruit juice." What fractional part is real fruit juice?

19. The House of Representatives has 435 members, of whom 52 are from California. About what percent of the members are from California?

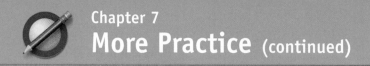

Set 7-3 (pages 362–363)

1. A survey shows that 36% of the students prefer volleyball and 73% prefer soccer. Explain whether or not this is possible.

Decide if each circle graph makes sense. Explain your answer.

2.

3.

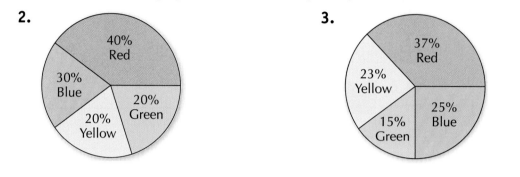

Set 7-4 (pages 366–367)

Find each using mental math.

1. 40% of 40   2. 25% of 84   3. 50% of 120   4. 20% of 90

5. $66\frac{2}{3}$% of 120   6. 10% of 590   7. 80% of 35   8. 75% of 92

9. 60% of 55   10. 25% of 4   11. 60% of 70   12. $33\frac{1}{3}$% of 33

13. Sanji worked 35 hours last week. If he worked 60% of his hours on Friday and Saturday, how many hours did he work Friday and Saturday?

Set 7-5 (pages 368–369)

Estimate.

1. 27% of 42   2. 51% of 198   3. 98% of 12   4. 83% of 122

5. 18% of 53   6. 74% of 238   7. 3% of 63   8. 11% of 493

9. The bill for dinner was $58.36. Jonathan wants to leave an 18% tip. About how much tip money should he leave?

Set 7-6 (pages 370–371)

Find the percent of each number.

1. 15% of $27   2. 32% of 48   3. 3.5% of $540   4. 27% of 50

5. 7.5% of 240   6. 82% of 32   7. 9% of 315   8. 0.5% of 120

9. $33\frac{1}{3}$% of 48   10. 25% of 24   11. 1.5% of 120   12. 34% of 250

Find the total amount.

13. 5% of ▊ is 15   14. 12.5% of ▊ is 6.5   15. 98% of ▊ is 49

16. Sarah answered 90% of the questions on a test correctly. If there were 30 questions on the test, how many did she answer correctly?

Take It to the NET
More Practice
www.scottforesman.com

Set 7-7 (pages 374–377)

1. The Werner's dinner bill is $75 and they want to leave a 15% tip. Explain how you can solve a simpler problem to calculate the tip amount. Then find the tip amount.

2. The lockers on one side of a hallway are numbered consecutively from 1 to 50. What is the sum of these locker numbers

3. There are 64 teams in the state soccer tournament. A team is eliminated if it loses a game. How many games must be played to determine the state soccer champion?

Set 7-8 (pages 380–383)

Find the sale price or total cost.

1. Regular Price: $165
   Discount: 15%
   Sale Price: __?__

2. Regular Price: $1,500
   Discount: 40%
   Sale Price: __?__

3. Subtotal: $24.89
   Sales Tax: 6.5%
   Total Cost: __?__

4. Subtotal: $12,000
   Sales Tax: 8.25%
   Total Cost: __?__

5. Regular Price: $39.99
   Discount: 25%
   Sale Price: __?__

6. Subtotal: $98.99
   Sales Tax: 7%
   Total Cost: __?__

7. A $40 sweater was on sale for 10% off. Mary received an additional 20% off the sale price because she was an employee. How much did Mary pay for the sweater?

Set 7-9 (pages 384–385)

Find the percent of increase or decrease. If necessary, round answers to the nearest tenth of a percent.

1. Andy's work hours increased from 20 to 30.

2. The average age decreased from 12 to 10.

3. The wholesale cost for a jacket is $50. The store charges $80 for the jacket. What percent is the price increase?

Set 7-10 (pages 386–387)

Find the amount of interest and the total.

1. $4,000 for 3 years at a simple interest rate of 5.4% per year

2. $5,750 for 20 years at a simple interest rate of 7% per year

3. $990 for 4 years at a simple interest rate of 2.8% per year

4. Paulo borrowed $5,000 for 5 years. If he paid $1,625 in simple interest, what was the interest rate?

CHAPTER 8

Algebra: Integers and Rational Numbers

DIAGNOSING READINESS

A Vocabulary
(pages 44, 45, 160)

Choose the best term from the box.

1. If you divide 8 by 2, the answer is a __?__.

2. A __?__ describes equal parts of a whole or part of a group.

3. Addition and subtraction are __?__.

4. An __?__ states that two quantities have the same value.

> **Vocabulary**
> - **equation** *(p. 44)* • **inverse operations** *(p. 45)*
> - **fraction** *(p. 160)* • **whole number** *(Gr. 5)*

B Adding and Subtracting Whole Numbers
(pages 24–29)

5. $12 + 9 - 13$ **6.** $15 - (6 + 9)$

7. $25 + 16 - 23$ **8.** $52 + 68 + 23$

9. $28 + 28 - 28$ **10.** $42 - (29 + 4)$

11. $72 - 48 + 56$ **12.** $88 - 59 + 47$

13. $55 + 77 - 33$ **14.** $775 - 228 + 248$

15. At Newton High School, there are 398 freshmen, 406 sophomores, 384 juniors, and 392 seniors. If 573 students are involved in a school sport, how many students are not involved in a school sport?

Do You Know...

What is the most amount of rain to fall in one day? in one year?
You will find out in Lesson 8-14.

C Multiplying and Dividing Whole Numbers
(pages 24–29)

16. 8×7

17. $91 \div 7$

18. $84 \div 4$

19. 12×8

20. $24 \times 3 \div 18$

21. $36 \div (36 \times 9)$

22. $85 \div 5 \times 3$

23. $(5 \times 8) \div 2$

24. $25(10 + 3)$

25. 6×32

26. Darien needs a minimum of $100 to open a savings account. He currently has $72. How many hours would he have to baby-sit at a rate of $6 per hour to have enough money to open the account?

D Solving Equations with Whole Numbers
(pages 44–47, 48–51)

Solve each equation.

27. $a - 12 = 24$

28. $5 + b = 33$

29. $d + 14 = 21$

30. $c - 15 = 15$

31. $6x = 84$

32. $\frac{n}{4} = 16$

33. $\frac{m}{7} = 5$

34. $8y = 104$

35. The attendance at a concert was 35,892 on Friday. This was 3,285 less than the attendance on Saturday. Use the equation $35{,}892 = a - 3{,}285$ to find Saturday's attendance.

Algebra

Key Idea
Just as there are numbers greater than zero, there are numbers less than zero.

Vocabulary
• opposites
• integers
• absolute value

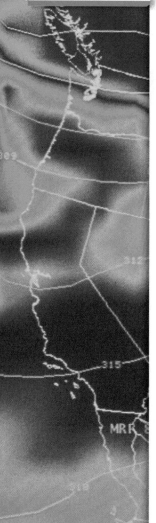

Think It Through
I can **use a number line** to show integers.

Understanding Integers

LEARN

What are integers?

Meteorologists use integers to describe temperatures. A number line is like a thermometer.

WARM UP
Tell if the number is a decimal, fraction, whole number, or mixed number.

1. $5\frac{1}{2}$ 2. $\frac{3}{4}$ 3. 0.63

Numbers that are the same distance from 0 are called **opposites.** −5 and 5 are opposites.

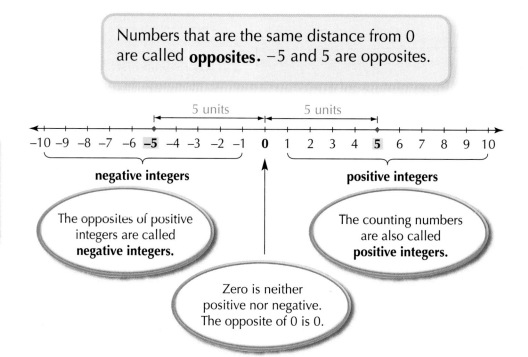

Integers are the counting numbers, their opposites, and zero.

It is important to read positive and negative integers correctly.

Number	How you read it
−5	negative 5
−(−6)	the opposite of negative 6

The **absolute value** of an integer is its distance from zero. Since distance is positive, the absolute value of either a positive or a negative integer is positive. The absolute value of 5 is written $|5|$. On the number line above, both 5 and −5 are 5 units from 0. So, $|5| = 5$ and $|-5| = 5$.

✔ Talk About It

1. What is another name for the opposite of −6?

2. Does $|-11| = |11|$? Explain.

Take It to the NET
More Examples
www.scottforesman.com

408

```
  D   H   A           F     C   I     B   G         E           K
←─┼─●─┼─●─┼─●─┼─┼─┼─┼─●─┼─┼─●─┼─●─┼─┼─●─┼─●─┼─┼─┼─┼─●─┼─┼─┼─┼─●─→
     -10         -5             0           5           10
```

In 1–5, use the number line above. Write the integer for each point.
Then give its opposite and its absolute value.

1. *A*　　　**2.** *B*　　　**3.** *C*　　　**4.** *D*　　　**5.** *E*

6. Number Sense Write an integer to represent a $13 debt. Describe a
situation representing the opposite of this integer.

Ⓐ Skills and Understanding

In 7–11, use the number line above. Write the integer for
each point. Then give its opposite and absolute value.

7. *F*　　　**8.** *G*　　　**9.** *H*　　　**10.** *I*　　　**11.** *K*

12. Draw a number line and graph the points −10, 4, −3, 6, −1, and 8.

13. Number Sense The Dead Sea is 1,312 feet below sea level.
Write this elevation as an integer.

Ⓑ Reasoning and Problem Solving

The table gives highest and lowest
elevations for some cities in the
United States. Use integers to describe
the two elevations for each city.

14. Boston　　　**15.** Denver

16. Los Angeles　**17.** New Orleans

18. **Writing in Math** Describe an
everyday situation that suggests
an integer and its opposite.

Data File

Elevations (in feet, relative to sea level)		
	Highest	**Lowest**
Boston	330 above	0 sea level
Denver	5,494 above	5,140 above
Los Angeles	5,081 above	0 sea level
New Orleans	15 above	6 below

🦉 Mixed Review and Test Prep

Take It to the NET
Test Prep
www.scottforesman.com

19. Ms. Flores borrowed $300 from her bank for 6 months. The bank
charges an interest rate of 1.5% per month. Find the interest
charged and total amount Ms. Flores owed the bank.

20. Thirty-seven is what percent of 296?

21. Find $\frac{1}{5}$ of 750.

A. 25　　　**B.** 75　　　**C.** 150　　　**D.** 175

Algebra

Key Idea
You can use a number line to compare and order integers.

Think It Through
Whenever I want to **order three or more integers,** I can **compare them two at a time.**

Comparing and Ordering Integers

LEARN

How can you compare and order integers?

When comparing two integers on a number line, the integer that is farther to the right is greater.

Example A

One day in January, the temperature at dawn was −2°F. At noon the temperature was 7°F. At which time was the temperature greater?

Compare −2 and 7.
Draw a number line and locate the numbers.

$$\xleftarrow{\;-10\quad -8\quad -6\quad -4\quad -2\quad 0\quad 2\quad 4\quad 6\;7\;8\quad 10\;}\rightarrow$$

What You **Think**	What You **Write**
Since 7 is to the right of −2 on a number line, 7 is greater than −2. The temperature was greater at noon.	7 > −2, or −2 < 7

Example B

Order −2, 5, and −8 from least to greatest.
Draw a number line and locate the numbers.

$$\xleftarrow{\;-10\quad -8\quad -6\quad -4\quad -2\quad 0\quad 2\quad 4\;5\;6\quad 8\quad 10\;}\rightarrow$$

What You **Think**	What You **Write**
When comparing two integers, the integer that is farther to the left is less. So −8 is less than −2 and −2 is less than 5.	−8, −2, 5

✓ Talk About It

1. **Number Sense** How do you know that any positive integer is greater than any negative integer?

2. Explain how −12 is less than −3, but $|-12|$ is greater than $|-3|$.

Use <, >, or = to compare.

1. −18 ☐ 3   **2.** −5 ☐ −10   **3.** 4 ☐ |−4| **4.** 0 ☐ −3

Order from least to greatest.

5. 10, −8, −9   **6.** 7, −13, 0   **7.** −1, 1, −5, −2   **8.** −2, |−5|, −1, |4|

9. Number Sense Compare 8 and −12 using the symbols > and <.

PRACTICE

For more practice, see Set 8-2 on p. 466.

Ⓐ Skills and Understanding

Use >, <, or = to compare.

10. −13 ☐ 0   **11.** −2 ☐ −18   **12.** 13 ☐ |−13| **13.** 5 ☐ −1   **14.** −6 ☐ −3

15. 2 ☐ 8   **16.** −18 ☐ −20   **17.** |−7| ☐ −7   **18.** 12 ☐ 24   **19.** 6 ☐ −1

Order from least to greatest.

20. −5, −4, 3, −1   **21.** −1, −8, 3, −7   **22.** |−2|, −6, −3, 5

23. 32, 19, −16, |−28|, 20, 5, 0   **24.** 28, −52, 4, −15, −3, −21, −16, |7|

25. Reasoning What is the least positive integer? The greatest negative integer? Explain.

Ⓑ Reasoning and Problem Solving

In 26–27, use the table at the right.

26. Order the high temperatures of all the cities from greatest to least.

27. Order the low temperatures of all the cities from least to greatest.

28. **Writing in Math** Explain why |x| = |−x| for integer values of x.

Data File

High and Low Record Temperatures (°F)		
	High	**Low**
Juneau, AK	90	−22
Jacksonville, FL	105	7
Chicago, IL	104	−27
Bismarck, ND	109	−44
Houston, TX	107	11
Seattle, WA	99	2

🦉 Mixed Review and Test Prep

Take It to the NET
Test Prep
www.scottforesman.com

29. David is buying a $560 refrigerator that is on sale for 25% off. Tax is 6%. How much will the refrigerator cost with the discount and tax?

    A. $420   **B.** $445.20   **C.** $526.40   **D.** $593.60

Give an integer to describe each situation.

30. The temperature drops 5°C.   **31.** You add $50 to your savings account.

Algebra

Key Idea
Just as there are positive and negative integers, there are also positive and negative decimals and fractions.

Vocabulary
• rational number

Declined

0.4%

−0⁰³

TEST TALK

Think It Through
Sometimes it helps to **write fractions as decimals** or **decimals as fractions**.

+0⁵⁷

Understanding Rational Numbers

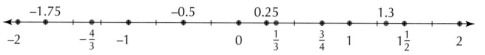

<table>
</table>

WARM UP

Use <, >, or = to compare.

1. $\frac{1}{2}$ ◯ 4

2. 0.7 ◯ $\frac{3}{5}$

3. $1\frac{3}{4}$ ◯ 1.75

LEARN

What is a rational number?

A **rational number** is any number that can be written as a quotient $\frac{a}{b}$, where a and b are integers and $b \neq 0$. For example, $3\frac{1}{8}$, −0.28, and 5 are all rational numbers because they can be written as $\frac{25}{8}$, $-\frac{28}{100}$, and $\frac{5}{1}$, respectively. The number line below shows some rational numbers.

```
        −1.75              −0.5      0.25           1.3
 ←──┬──•─┬──•─┬──┬──┬──•──•─┬──┬──┬──•─•─┬──•──→
   −2   −4⁄3 −1          0  1⁄3  3⁄4  1  1½      2
```

✓ Talk About It

1. Why are $-2\frac{1}{6}$, 3, and 1.25 rational numbers?

2. Name three rational numbers that are between −5 and −4.

How can rational numbers be compared and ordered?

Example A

Compare $-4\frac{1}{3}$ and $-1\frac{1}{4}$.

What You **Think**	What You **Write**
On a number line $-4\frac{1}{3}$ is to the left of $-1\frac{1}{4}$.	$-4\frac{1}{3} < -1\frac{1}{4}$ or $-1\frac{1}{4} > -4\frac{1}{3}$

Example B

Order −0.5, 2.3, and $-1\frac{1}{4}$ from least to greatest.

What You **Think**	What You **Write**
Think of $-1\frac{1}{4}$ as −1.25. −1.25 is less than −0.5 and −0.5 is less than 2.3.	$-1\frac{1}{4}$, −0.5, 2.3

✓ Talk About It

3. Order −2.25, $-2\frac{1}{8}$, $-2\frac{3}{4}$, and −2.1 from least to greatest. Did you write all the numbers as fractions or as decimals?

Graph each rational number on the same number line.

1. $-1\frac{3}{8}$ **2.** 0.75 **3.** $-\frac{7}{8}$ **4.** $-\frac{1}{8}$

Use > or < to compare.   Order from least to greatest.

5. -3.7 ◻ $-4\frac{1}{2}$ **6.** $-2\frac{1}{2}$ ◻ $-2\frac{3}{4}$ **7.** $-2.4, \frac{5}{8}, -\frac{5}{8}$ **8.** $0.5, -5\frac{1}{3}, -12, 0$

9. Number Sense Name three rational numbers that are between -3 and -4.

PRACTICE

For more practice, see Set 8-3 on p. 466.

Ⓐ Skills and Understanding

Graph each rational number on the same number line.

10. -1.5 **11.** 1.25 **12.** $-\frac{5}{8}$ **13.** $-\frac{1}{4}$ **14.** $\frac{7}{8}$

Use > or < to compare.   Order from least to greatest.

15. -3.1 ◻ $-2\frac{1}{2}$ **16.** $-\frac{5}{8}$ ◻ -0.55 **17.** $-\frac{3}{4}, -\frac{7}{8}, -1\frac{1}{2}, -\frac{1}{4}$ **18.** $0.25, -2, -0.5$

19. Reasoning Why are integers rational numbers?

Ⓑ Reasoning and Problem Solving

20. A **Venn diagram** can be used to show how sets of numbers are related. Copy the table below. Indicate the sets to which the numbers belong.

	Natural	Whole	Integers	Rational
10	Yes	Yes	Yes	Yes
−6				
0				
2.7				
−3.5				

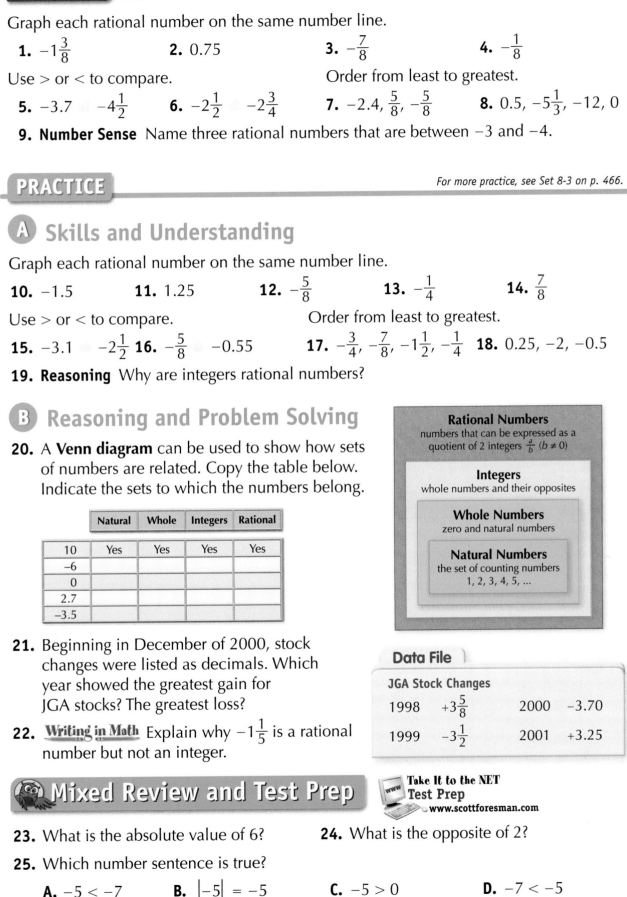

Rational Numbers
numbers that can be expressed as a quotient of 2 integers $\frac{a}{b}$ $(b \neq 0)$

Integers
whole numbers and their opposites

Whole Numbers
zero and natural numbers

Natural Numbers
the set of counting numbers
1, 2, 3, 4, 5, ...

21. Beginning in December of 2000, stock changes were listed as decimals. Which year showed the greatest gain for JGA stocks? The greatest loss?

22. **Writing in Math** Explain why $-1\frac{1}{5}$ is a rational number but not an integer.

Data File

JGA Stock Changes

1998	$+3\frac{5}{8}$	2000	−3.70
1999	$-3\frac{1}{2}$	2001	+3.25

Mixed Review and Test Prep

Take It to the NET
Test Prep
www.scottforesman.com

23. What is the absolute value of 6?   **24.** What is the opposite of 2?

25. Which number sentence is true?

A. $-5 < -7$ **B.** $|-5| = -5$ **C.** $-5 > 0$ **D.** $-7 < -5$

Problem-Solving Skill

Reading Helps!

Identifying the main idea
can help you with...
choosing an operation.

Key Idea
Some problems can be solved by using an operation.

Choose an Operation

LEARN

How can you decide what the main idea is for a problem?

Draw a picture of the action in a problem. The picture shows the main idea and helps you choose an operation.

Stopping Distances The table at the right shows the number of feet needed to completely stop a car traveling at different speeds on dry, level asphalt.

Data File

Speed (mph)	Total Stopping Distance (ft)
10	15
20	40
30	75
40	120
50	175
60	240
70	315

Example A	Example B
The stopping distance at 30 mph is about how many times as great as at 10 mph?	How many more feet does it take to stop at 70 mph than at 50 mph?

Read and Understand

Show the main idea.	30 mph: 75 ft 10 mph: 15 ft	70 mph: 315 ft 50 mph: 175 ft

How many times as great is 75 than 15?

15 [ ] How many 15s are in 75?

75 [   ]

How many more feet?

315 ft

175 ft ?

Plan and Solve

Choose an operation. Divide to find how many times as great one number is than another.

$$75 \div 15 = ?$$
distance at 30 mph | distance at 10 mph | times as great

Subtract to find how many more feet.

$$315 - 175 = ?$$
distance at 70 mph | distance at 50 mph | additional distance

✔ Talk About It

1. Write the answers for Examples A and B in complete sentences.

2. **Number Sense** Suppose a classmate said she could use addition to solve Example B. Would she be correct? Explain.

CHECK ✓

For another example, see Set 8-4 on p. 463.

Use the picture to choose an operation. Solve the problem.

1. During off-hours, Dante's drive to work takes 24 minutes. His drive during rush hour takes 1 hour 12 minutes. How many times as great is Dante's drive during rush hour than during off-hours?

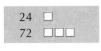

PRACTICE

For more practice, see Set 8-4 on p. 467.

Draw a picture to show the main idea. Use the picture to choose an operation. Solve the problem.

2. If the main span of the Golden Gate bridge is 4,200 ft, how many feet are traveled by a car that crosses $\frac{2}{3}$ the distance of the span?

3. According to the information at the right, how many pounds does a package weigh that costs $27.20 to send?

4. How much does a $3\frac{1}{2}$-pound package cost to send overnight?

5. An outside thermometer reads 7°F at 9:30 A.M. If the temperature rises at a rate of 5°F per hour, what will the thermometer read at 1:30 P.M.?

6. Ann wants to mail 12 party invitations. Each invitation weighs 0.6 ounce. How much do the invitations weigh in all?

7. Mrs. Lehi hires a dog-walking service for the 4 weeks she will be on vacation. If the service walks her dog $\frac{1}{2}$ hour each day, how many hours will the service walk her dog?

8. Mr. Ruiz hires the dog walking service to walk his dog $\frac{1}{2}$-hour each day while he is on a 15-day vacation. How much will he have to pay the service?

9. <u>Writing in Math</u> Write a word problem that can be solved using multiplication or division. Draw a picture to show the main idea and give the solution in a complete sentence.

All text pages available online and on CD-ROM.

Do You Know How?

Do You Understand?

Understanding Integers (8-1)

For 1–5, write the integer for each point. Then give its opposite and absolute value.

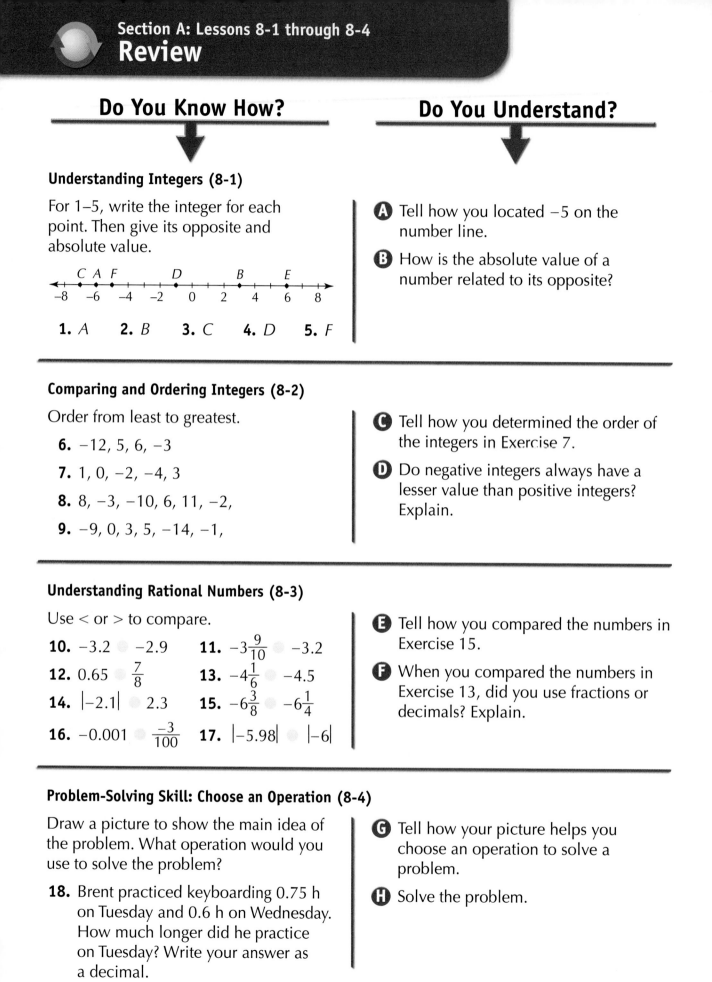

1. A   2. B   3. C   4. D   5. F

A Tell how you located −5 on the number line.

B How is the absolute value of a number related to its opposite?

Comparing and Ordering Integers (8-2)

Order from least to greatest.

6. −12, 5, 6, −3

7. 1, 0, −2, −4, 3

8. 8, −3, −10, 6, 11, −2,

9. −9, 0, 3, 5, −14, −1,

C Tell how you determined the order of the integers in Exercise 7.

D Do negative integers always have a lesser value than positive integers? Explain.

Understanding Rational Numbers (8-3)

Use < or > to compare.

10. -3.2 ⚪ -2.9 11. $-3\frac{9}{10}$ ⚪ -3.2

12. 0.65 ⚪ $\frac{7}{8}$ 13. $-4\frac{1}{6}$ ⚪ -4.5

14. $|-2.1|$ ⚪ 2.3 15. $-6\frac{3}{8}$ ⚪ $-6\frac{1}{4}$

16. -0.001 ⚪ $\frac{-3}{100}$ 17. $|-5.98|$ ⚪ $|-6|$

E Tell how you compared the numbers in Exercise 15.

F When you compared the numbers in Exercise 13, did you use fractions or decimals? Explain.

Problem-Solving Skill: Choose an Operation (8-4)

Draw a picture to show the main idea of the problem. What operation would you use to solve the problem?

18. Brent practiced keyboarding 0.75 h on Tuesday and 0.6 h on Wednesday. How much longer did he practice on Tuesday? Write your answer as a decimal.

G Tell how your picture helps you choose an operation to solve a problem.

H Solve the problem.

MULTIPLE CHOICE

1. Which set is ordered from least to greatest? (8-2)

    A. −6, −9, 2, 5   **C.** −9, −6, 2, 5

    B. −9, −6, 5, 2   **D.** −6, −9, 5, 2

2. Which number sentence is true? (8-3)

    A. $-9.8 < -9\frac{3}{4}$ **C.** $-9.25 = -9\frac{3}{8}$

    B. $-9\frac{1}{2} > -9.48$ **D.** $-9.01 < -9.03$

FREE RESPONSE

Write the number that represents each point on the number line below. Then, give the absolute value and opposite of each number. (8-1)

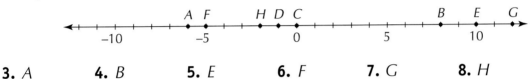

3. A **4.** B **5.** E **6.** F **7.** G **8.** H

In 9–11, write an integer to represent the situation. (8-1)

9. The scuba diver was 85 ft below sea level.

10. At noon, it was 6°F below zero.

11. Ana made an investment profit of $192.

Locate each number on the same number line. (8-3)

12. $1\frac{1}{8}$ **13.** −0.75

14. $-1\frac{7}{8}$ **15.** 1.5

> **TEST TALK**
>
> **Think It Through**
> I **remember** that values on a number line increase as I move to the right.

Write in order from least to greatest. (8-2, 8-3)

16. −5, 0, −3, −2, 4

17. $-1.9, 0.6, -3\frac{3}{10}, 0.5, 0.1, -\frac{1}{5}$

For 18–19, draw a picture to show the main idea. Then solve the problem. (8-4)

18. A certain type of label is sold in packages of 300. If you need 1,935 labels, how many packages will you have to buy? Will there be any labels left over? If so, how many?

19. There are 136 fifth and sixth graders at an assembly. The number of fifth graders is 8 less than half the number of students at the assembly. How many sixth graders are at the assembly?

Writing in Math

20. You want to buy $2\frac{1}{2}$ pounds of green beans that are on sale for $0.68 per lb. What can you do to help you decide which operation to use? Which operation would you choose?

Algebra

Key Idea
You can use a number line to add integers.

Vocabulary
• absolute value (p. 408)

TEST TALK

Think It Through
When adding integers on the number line, I need to **start at zero.**

Adding Integers

LEARN

How can you add integers using a number line?

Think of walking along a number line. Walk forward for positive integers and walk backward for negative integers.

Example A

On the first down after getting the football, a football team gained 5 yards. On the next down, it lost 7 yards. Has the team gained or lost yardage after two downs?

Find 5 + (−7).

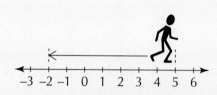

Start at zero, facing the positive integers. Walk forward 5 steps for 5.

The team has lost 2 yards.

Then walk backward 7 steps for −7. You stop at −2.

So, 5 + (−7) = −2.

Example B

Find −4 + (−2).

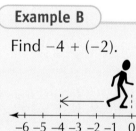

Start at zero, facing the positive integers. Walk backward 4 steps for −4.

Then walk backward 2 steps for −2. You stop at −6.

So, −4 + (−2) = −6.

Example C

Find −6 + 11.

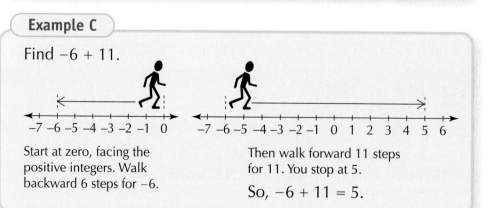

Start at zero, facing the positive integers. Walk backward 6 steps for −6.

Then walk forward 11 steps for 11. You stop at 5.

So, −6 + 11 = 5.

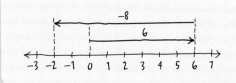

Example D

Draw a number line to find 6 + (−8).

Start at zero. Move forward 6 units.
Then move backward 8 units.

So, 6 + (−8) = −2.

✔ **Talk About It**

1. Refer to Example B. Is the sum of two negative integers positive or negative? Explain.

2. Refer to Examples A and C. Is the sum of a positive integer and a negative integer positive or negative? Explain.

3. **Number Sense** Explain how you would use a number line to find 8 + (−7) + (−2).

Is there another way to add integers?

Another way to add integers is to use the rules given below.

Rules for Adding Integers

Adding Two Integers with the Same Sign

- Find the sum of the absolute values of the two numbers.

- Give the sum the same sign as the addends.

Adding Two Integers with Different Signs

- Find the difference of the absolute values of the two numbers.

- Give the difference the sign of the addend with the greater absolute value.

Example E

Find −4 + (−18).

The sum of the absolute values is $|-4| + |-18| = 22$.

Give the sum the same sign as the addends.

So, −4 + (−18) = −22.

Example F

Find 17 + (−29).

The difference of the absolute values is $|-29| - |17| = 12$.

Give the difference the same sign as the addend with the greater absolute value.

So, 17 + (−29) = −12.

✔ **Talk About It**

4. **Number Sense** Explain how you would use the rules for adding integers to find (−3) + (−1) + 2.

1. Draw a number line to find $-4 + (-5)$.

For 2–4, draw a number line or use the rules for adding integers to find each sum.

2. $-8 + 6$ **3.** $-5 + (-14)$ **4.** $-18 + 30$

5. Reasoning What is the sum of any integer and its opposite?

PRACTICE

For more practice, see Set 8-5 on p. 467.

Ⓐ Skills and Understanding

6. Draw a number line to find $5 + (-9)$.

7. Draw a number line to find $-8 + (-5) + 6$.

Draw a number line or use the rules for adding integers to find each sum.

8. $12 + (-9)$ **9.** $-4 + (-7)$ **10.** $8 + (-16)$ **11.** $-20 + (-4)$ **12.** $-31 + 0$

13. $13 + 23$ **14.** $-18 + 18$ **15.** $-50 + (-5)$ **16.** $-3 + 2 + 8$ **17.** $-7 + 3 + (-2)$

18. Number Sense When is the sum of one positive integer and one negative integer positive?

Ⓑ Reasoning and Problem Solving

Algebra Use the rule to complete each table.

19. Rule: Add -3

Input	Output
5	
7	
0	

20. Rule: Add 17

Input	Output
9	
-14	
34	

21. Rule: Add -8

Input	Output
-13	
57	
21	

For 22–25, evaluate each expression for $t = -12$.

22. $45 + t$ **23.** $-12 + t + 24$ **24.** $t + -21$ **25.** $t + |-8| + 5$

In the game of golf, *par* is the number of times an expert can be expected to hit the ball in order to complete the course. Strokes under par are indicated with negative integers.

For 26–28, use the table at the right.

26. What does Steven's score of 0 for Round 2 represent?

27. What was the best score of any one round? Who had that score?

28. Who had the better score for the four rounds? What was his score?

GOLF STROKES

Round	1	2	3	4
Steven	+2	0	+1	-1
Mel	-3	-1	+1	-2

PRACTICE

29.  Explain how to find the sum −5 + 12 + 5 using mental math.

C Extensions

Calculator Use a calculator to find −29 + (−38).

Press: (-)29 + (-)38 ENTER =

Display: −67

For 30–32, use a calculator to find each sum.

30. 64 + −117   **31.** −256 + 148   **32.** −381 + −479

33. Show the sums −7 + (5 + (−3)) and (−7 + 5) + (−3) on two different number lines. What is the name of the property shown?

Think It Through
When using mental math, I can **add opposites** to get zero.

Mixed Review and Test Prep

Take It to the NET
Test Prep
www.scottforesman.com

34. A car travels about 0.9 mi per minute, at a speed of 55 mph. Estimate the distance this car will travel in 25 minutes.

35. Which number has the least value?

A. −7.0   **B.** −7.7   **C.** −7.17   **D.** −7

Discovery CHANNEL SCHOOL

Discover Math in Your World

Take It to the NET
Video and Activities
www.scottforesman.com

Pressure Probes

By placing probes in the path of an oncoming tornado, research engineers can measure the barometric pressure drop of the tornado's core. Probe measurements are shown in the graph at the right.

1. At 120 seconds, the air pressure was 918 millibars (mb). At 240 seconds, the pressure was 913 mb. Use an integer to express this decrease in pressure.

2. Write an equation to find the drop in pressure from average sea-level of 1,013.25 mb to the lowest pressure recorded on the graph.

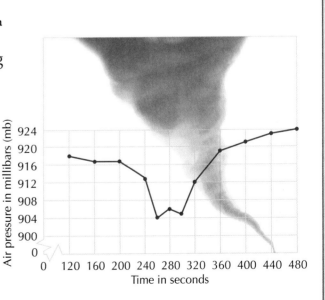

All text pages available online and on CD-ROM.

Algebra

Key Idea
Subtracting an integer is the same as adding its opposite.

Think It Through

When subtracting integers on the number line, I need to **start at zero**.

Subtracting Integers

LEARN

WARM UP

1. −8 + (−8)

2. 13 + (−5)

3. 4 + (−11)

4. 15 + (−15)

How do you read expressions that have negative signs and subtraction?

It is important to understand the difference between a minus sign and a negative sign. They look the same, but one is an operation between two numbers indicating subtraction and the other tells you that a number is negative.

Number or Expression	How to Read It
−7	negative 7
−(−6)	the opposite of negative 6
3 − 4	3 minus 4
3 − (−4)	3 minus negative 4
−6 − 7	negative 6 minus 7
−6 − (−7)	negative 6 minus negative 7

✔ **Talk About It**

1. What is another way to read −7?

How can you subtract integers on a number line?

Example A

Find 3 − 5.

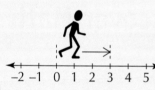

Start at zero, facing the positive integers. Walk forward 3 steps for 3.

The subtraction sign, (−), means *turn around.*

Then walk forward 5 steps for 5. You stop at −2.

So, 3 − 5 is −2.

Example B

Find −5 − 2.

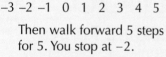

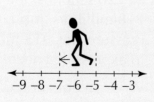

Start at zero, facing the positive integers. Walk backward 5 steps for −5.

The subtraction sign, (−), means *turn around.*

Then walk forward 2 steps for 2. You stop at −7.

So, −5 − 2 = −7.

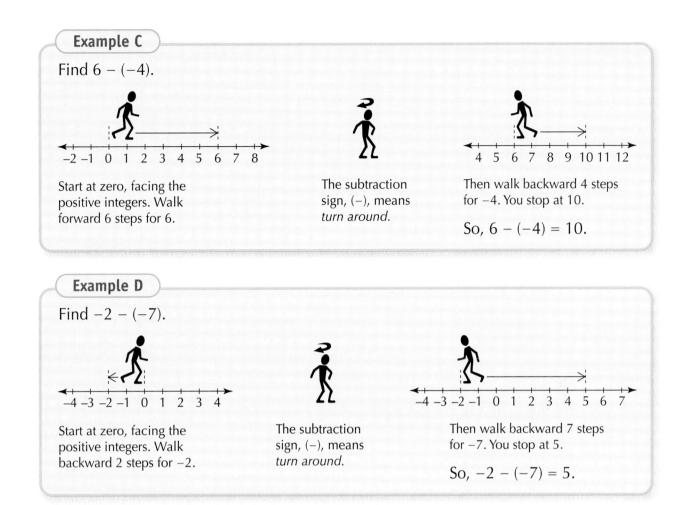

Example C

Find $6 - (-4)$.

Start at zero, facing the positive integers. Walk forward 6 steps for 6.

The subtraction sign, $(-)$, means *turn around.*

Then walk backward 4 steps for -4. You stop at 10.

So, $6 - (-4) = 10$.

Example D

Find $-2 - (-7)$.

Start at zero, facing the positive integers. Walk backward 2 steps for -2.

The subtraction sign, $(-)$, means *turn around.*

Then walk backward 7 steps for -7. You stop at 5.

So, $-2 - (-7) = 5$.

✔ **Talk About It**

2. When you subtract a positive integer, is the difference greater than or less than the integer you subtract from?

What is a rule for subtracting integers?

A class made the table at the right to show some sums and differences they found on number lines.

In each row, the answer is the same!

I see a rule for subtracting. I can add the opposite of the second number to the first number.

	Subtraction	Addition
A.	$3 - (-2) = 5$	$3 + 2 = 5$
B.	$-4 - 1 = -5$	$-4 + (-1) = -5$
C.	$1 - 5 = -4$	$1 + -5 = -4$
D.	$-6 - (-8) = 2$	$-6 + 8 = 2$

Rule for Subtracting Integers

Subtracting an integer is the same as adding its opposite.

✔ **Talk About It**

3. How can you change $8 - (-3)$ to addition?

Draw a number line or use the rules for subtracting integers to find each difference.

1. $-6 - 3$ **2.** $10 - (-6)$ **3.** $-8 - (-8)$ **4.** $7 - 12$

Evaluate each expression for $n = -3$.

5. $n - (-19)$ **6.** $n - 4$ **7.** $-1 - n$ **8.** $15 - n$

9. Number Sense Without computing, how do you know if $-9 - (-5)$ is negative?

PRACTICE

For more practice, see Set 8-6 on p. 467.

Ⓐ Skills and Understanding

Draw a number line or use the rules for subtracting integers to find each difference.

10. $-17 - 17$ **11.** $7 - 8$ **12.** $-6 - (-6)$ **13.** $36 - (-14)$ **14.** $5 - |14|$

15. $0 - (-9)$ **16.** $-34 - 0$ **17.** $-20 - (-45)$ **18.** $8 - 17$ **19.** $6 - |-13|$

In 20–23, evaluate each expression for $a = -4$.

20. $37 - a$ **21.** $7 - |a| - (-11)$ **22.** $a - 16$ **23.** $a - (-33) - 30$

24. Number Sense Without computing, how do you know if $2 - (-2)$ is positive?

Ⓑ Reasoning and Problem Solving

Math and Social Studies

For 25–27, find the difference in elevation.

25. Dead Sea and Mount Everest

26. Mount Rainier and Death Valley

27. Dead Sea and Death Valley

28. Find the difference between the highest and lowest recorded temperatures given below.

El Azizia, Libya, September 13, 1922: 136°F
Vostok, Antarctica, July 21, 1983: −129°F

29. Writing in Math Is Sally's explanation correct? If not, tell why and write a correct explanation.

> Can the Commutative Property be used for subtracting integers? Give an example.
>
> Yes. The expression $-2 - 3$ has the same difference as $3 - (-2)$. The value of each expression is 5.

Elevation Records

Location	Elevation (feet)
Dead Sea, Israel	-1,302
Mount Everest, Nepal/Tibet	29,035
Death Valley, CA	-282
Mount Rainier, WA	14,410

TEST TALK

Think It Through
I know that **subtracting an integer is the same as adding its opposite.**

C Extensions

Evaluate using the rules for operations with rational numbers.

30. $-3\frac{1}{8} + \frac{1}{8}$ **31.** $-7\frac{2}{3} - \frac{2}{3}$ **32.** $-7 + 1\frac{1}{2}$ **33.** $2.05 - 5.56$

Mixed Review and Test Prep

Take It to the NET
Test Prep
www.scottforesman.com

For 34–36, order from least to greatest.

34. 8, 3, −15, −2   **35.** $-10\frac{1}{3}, 5\frac{2}{3}, 8, -2\frac{2}{3}$ **36.** $-4\frac{1}{10}, -3.8, -3.75, -4.01$

37. Greg's scores for 4 rounds of golf were 3 below par, 2 below par, 4 above par, and even par. What was Greg's total score for the 4 rounds?

     A. −1   **B.** 0   **C.** 1   **D.** 2

Learning with Technology

Using a Calculator to Add and Subtract Rational Numbers

You can use a calculator to compute rational numbers.

Depending on your calculator, to find $-5.6 + (-8.7)$

Press: (-)5.6 [+] (-)8.7 [ENTER =]   **Press:** 5.6 [+○−] [+] 8.7 [+○−] [=]

Display: -14.3 **Display:** -14.3

Notice that [(-)] and [+○−] are not operation keys. If you try to use these keys to perform addition or subtraction, an error message will be displayed.

Depending on your calculator, to find $-\frac{3}{8} - \left(-\frac{2}{5}\right)$,

Press: (-)3 [n] 8 [d] [−] (-)2 [n] 5 [d] [ENTER =]   **Press:** 3 [+○−] [/] 8 [−] 2 [+○−] [/] 5 [=]

Display: $\frac{1}{40}$ **Display:** $\frac{1}{40}$

Use your calculator to find each sum or difference.

   1. $-29 - (-94)$ **2.** $\frac{5}{8} + \left(-\frac{7}{192}\right)$ **3.** $-4.6 - (-9.7)$ **4.** $0.35 + \left(-3\frac{4}{5}\right)$

   5. How would you compute Exercise 4 without using fraction keys?

Algebra

Key Idea
When you multiply integers, the product can be positive, negative, or zero.

Multiplying Integers

LEARN

How do you multiply integers?

Example A

Find 4×3.

$4 \times 3 = 3 + 3 + 3 + 3 = 12$.   So, $4 \times 3 = 12$.

The product of two positive integers is positive.

Example B

Find $4 \times (-3)$.

$4 \times (-3) = (-3) + (-3) + (-3) + (-3) = -12$. So, $4 \times (-3) = -12$.

The product of a positive integer and a negative integer is negative.

Example C

Find $(-3)(4)$.

Because of the Commutative Property of Multiplication, $(-3)(4) = (4)(-3) = -12$.

The product of a negative integer and a positive integer is negative.

In algebra, $(-3)(4)$ means -3×4.

Example D

Find $-3 \times (-4)$.

The table shows that the products increase by 3. Continuing the pattern gives 3, 6, 9, 12.

So, $-3 \times (-4) = 12$.

The product of two negative integers is positive.

$-3 \times 4 = -12$
$-3 \times 3 = -9$
$-3 \times 2 = -6$
$-3 \times 1 = -3$
$-3 \times 0 = 0$
$-3 \times (-1) = \square$
$-3 \times (-2) = \square$
$-3 \times (-3) = \square$
$-3 \times (-4) = \square$

Think It Through
I can **use the Commutative Property of Multiplication** when multiplying integers.

Rules for Multiplying Integers

• The product of two integers with the same sign is positive.
• The product of two integers with different signs is negative.

✓ Talk About It

1. Number Sense Explain how to find the product $(-2)(5)(-6)$.

1. $5 \times (-6)$ **2.** $(-7)(-9)$ **3.** 8×12 **4.** $(-17)^2$

For 5–8, evaluate each expression when $b = -4$.

5. $-1b$ **6.** $17b$ **7.** $-38b$ **8.** $b \times |-12| \times (-5)$

9. Number Sense Use order of operations to find $9 - (-6) + (-5) \times 3$.

PRACTICE

For more practice, see Set 8-7 on p. 467.

A Skills and Understanding

10. $(-8)(-7)$ **11.** $20 \times (-10)$ **12.** -2×0 **13.** $17 \times (-6)$ **14.** $-3 \times (-12)$

15. 19×2 **16.** $(-1)(-55)$ **17.** -45×4 **18.** $(-5)^3$ **19.** $(-8)(-8)(-1)$

Number Sense In 20–22 use order of operations to evaluate each expression.

20. $-6 + (3)(-2) + (-5)$ **21.** $4 + (-8)(-3) - 12$ **22.** $-15 + 11 + (-1)(-9)$

For 23–26, evaluate each expression when $c = 6$.

23. $-2c$ **24.** $|-5| \times c$ **25.** $-30c - (-9)$ **26.** $-24 + 2c - 7$

27. Number Sense Is the product of 3 negative integers positive or negative?

B Reasoning and Problem Solving

The underlying rock ledge of Canada's Horseshoe Falls erodes about 2 feet each year.

28. Write the erosion rate as a negative integer.

29. How much will the rock ledge erode in a 7-year period?

30. **Writing in Math** Is Maria's work correct? If not, tell why.

$$-6 \times (-9) + 3 = -54 + 3 = -51$$

Mixed Review and Test Prep

Take It to the NET
Test Prep
www.scottforesman.com

Evaluate $7 - y$ for the given values of y.

31. $y = 4$ **32.** $y = -7$ **33.** $y = 10$ **34.** $y = 0$ **35.** $y = -26$

36. Does $-x$ represent a negative number? Explain.

37. Which sentences are true?

   I. $-7 + 9 = 2$ II. $-7 + 9 = -2$ III. $-7 + (-9) = 16$ IV. $-7 + (-9) = -16$

   A. I and IV   **B.** I and II   **C.** II and IV   **D.** II and III

Algebra

Key Idea
You can use what you know about multiplying integers to help you divide integers.

Think It Through
I remember that **multiplication and division are inverse operations;** that is, they "undo" each other.

Dividing Integers

LEARN

How can you divide integers?

A decrease of temperature with an increase in altitude is known as the lapse rate. Suppose the lapse rate is $-5°F$ per 1,000 feet. The change in temperature from 2,000 to 5,000 feet is $3 \times (-5)$, or $-15°F$.

Example

In the table at the right, the change in temperature from 3,500 to 7,500 feet is $-16°F$. What is the lapse rate in degrees per 1,000 feet?

Temperature	Altitude (ft)
47° F	3,500
39° F	5,500
31° F	7,500

To calculate the lapse rate, you need to find $-16 \div 4$.

You know:	Related division fact:	Sign of quotient:
$4 \times 4 = 16$	$16 \div 4 = 4$	$+$
$-4 \times 4 = -16$	$-16 \div (-4) = 4$	$+$
$4 \times (-4) = -16$	$-16 \div 4 = -4$	$-$
$-4 \times (-4) = 16$	$16 \div (-4) = -4$	$-$

The lapse rate is $-4°F$ per 1,000 feet.

The rules for dividing integers can be found in the Example above.

Rules for Dividing Integers

- The quotient of two integers with the same sign is positive.
- The quotient of two integers with different signs is negative.

✓ Talk About It

1. Explain why $-16 \div 4$ was used to find the lapse rate per 1,000 ft in the Example.

2. Name two division facts for $8 \times (-9) = -72$.

3. Why is the quotient $81 \div (-3)$ negative?

For another example, see Set 8-8 on p. 464.

1. $\frac{-45}{9}$ **2.** $\frac{-66}{-11}$ **3.** $-32 \div (-8)$ **4.** $24 \div (-12)$

For 5–8, evaluate each expression when $m = -18$

5. $\frac{m}{-9}$ **6.** $54 \div m$ **7.** $m \div 6$ **8.** $\frac{-108}{m}$

9. Reasoning Without computing, tell if the quotient $-280 \div (-35)$ is less than or greater than zero. Explain how you know.

PRACTICE

For more practice, see Set 8-8 on p. 468.

Ⓐ Skills and Understanding

10. $\frac{60}{-5}$ **11.** $\frac{-50}{-25}$ **12.** $\frac{-28}{7}$ **13.** $\frac{64}{8}$ **14.** $\frac{0}{-8}$

15. $-51 \div (-17)$ **16.** $-30 \div 30$ **17.** $38 \div (-2)$ **18.** $-144 \div -12$ **19.** $100 \div (-1)$

Number Sense Use order of operations to evaluate each expression.

20. $-36 \div 4 \times (-6) + 50$ **21.** $3^2 + (-5)^2 - (-1)^3$ **22.** $53 - 12 + (-10)(-3)$

For 23–26, evaluate each expression when $c = -9$.

23. $-630 \div c$ **24.** $\frac{c}{-3} - (-3)$ **25.** $\frac{72}{c} - 8$ **26.** $c^2 \div 81$

27. Reasoning Without computing, tell if the quotient $123 \div (-3)$ is greater than or less than zero. Explain how you know.

Ⓑ Reasoning and Problem Solving

for 28–29, use the table at the right.

28. Find the difference in elevation from Telescope Peak to the floor of Death Valley.

29. There are 3 feet in a yard. Express the Death Valley elevation in yards.

Data File

Site (Death Valley National Park)	Elevation (feet)
Telescope Peak	11,049
Park Headquarters	−190
Floor of Death Valley	−282

30. Writing in Math Explain why $-\frac{8}{2} = \frac{-8}{2} = \frac{8}{-2}$.

🦉 Mixed Review and Test Prep

www Take It to the NET
Test Prep
www.scottforesman.com

For 31–32, write a numerical expression, and then evaluate it.

31. 3 minus the opposite of 5

32. Mr. Akins deposits $420, and then writes a check for $339.

33. Evaluate $n \times (-16)$ when $n = -4$.

    A. −64 **C.** −12

    B. −20 **D.** 64

34. Evaluate $5x$ when $x = -13$.

    A. −65 **C.** 18

    B. −8 **D.** 65

Algebra

Key Idea
You can solve equations with integers the same way you solve equations with whole numbers, decimals, and fractions.

Think It Through
I can **use substitution** to check my answer for an equation.

Solving Equations with Integers

LEARN

How can you solve equations with integers?

When solving equations with integers, remember to use inverse operations and the properties of equality.

Example A

From 1:00 A.M. to 1:30 A.M. on a January night, the temperature dropped 18°F. After it dropped, the outside temperature was −12°F. What was the temperature at 1:00 A.M.?

Let t = the temperature at 1:00 A.M.

Temperature at 1:00 A.M.	Drop in temperature	Temperature at 1:30 A.M.
t	− 18	= −12

Remember that addition and subtraction are inverse operations.

$t - 18 = -12$

$t - 18 + 18 = -12 + 18$ ← To undo subtracting 18, add 18 to both sides.

$t = 6$

The temperature at 1:00 A.M. was 6°F.

Check: $t - 18 = -12$

$6 - 18 = -12$ ← Substitute 6 for t.

$-12 = -12$

Example B

Solve $-5n = 30$.

$-5n = 30$

$\frac{-5n}{-5} = \frac{30}{-5}$

$n = -6$

Example C

Solve $y + 8 = -15$.

$y + 8 = -15$

$y + 8 - 8 = -15 - 8$

$y = -23$

Example D

Solve $\frac{a}{-3} = -9$.

$\frac{a}{-3} = -9$

$\frac{a}{-3} \times (-3) = -9 \times (-3)$

$a = 27$

✔ Talk About It

1. Tell which inverse operation was used to solve each equation in Examples A through D.

2. Explain how to check the answers in Examples B through D.

For another example, see Set 8-9 on p. 464.

CHECK ✓

Solve and check each equation.

1. $\frac{n}{-5} = -9$ **2.** $-3d = 57$ **3.** $t - 8 = -42$ **4.** $m + 88 = -4$

5. After Richeal spent $48 for a jacket, she was $23 in debt. Use the equation $n - 48 = -23$ to find how much money Richeal had before she bought the jacket.

6. Reasoning Without solving the equation $m - (-3) = 8$, tell if m is less than, greater than, or equal to 8. Tell how you decided.

PRACTICE

For more practice, see Set 8-9 on p. 468.

A Skills and Understanding

Solve and check each equation.

7. $n - 13 = -7$ **8.** $y + 53 = 11$ **9.** $a - (-18) = 28$ **10.** $s - 84 = -147$

11. $-5d = 85$ **12.** $\frac{m}{-7} = -14$ **13.** $30h = -210$ **14.** $\frac{w}{6} = -2$

15. $c - 57 = 6$ **16.** $x + (-21) = -59$ **17.** $-180 = 12g$ **18.** $-27t = -81$

19. Reasoning Without solving, tell whether each variable is greater than, less than, or equal to -8. Tell how you decided.

a. $k + 18 = 2$ **b.** $n + (-2) + 2 = 0$ **c.** $t + 1 = -15$

B Reasoning and Problem Solving

20. Bob looked at his watch 10 seconds before the launch of a rocket. The next time he looked, it was 20 seconds past the launch. Solve $-10 + s = 20$ to find the number of seconds that had passed.

21. Elena was 47 feet below the surface of the water. She swam up to 18 feet below the surface. Solve $-47 + w = -18$ to find the number of feet she rose.

22. Writing in Math Use -102, 17, and the variable b to write a multiplication equation. Then solve it.

🦉 Mixed Review and Test Prep

Take It to the NET
www **Test Prep**
www.scottforesman.com

23. $\frac{-250}{-25}$ **24.** -6×41 **25.** $720 \div (-9)$

26. $-85 \div 5$ **27.** $-2 \times (-3) \times (-8)$

28. Evaluate $18a$ when $a = -\frac{1}{6}$.

  A. -108 **B.** -3 **C.** 3 **D.** 108

All text pages available online and on CD-ROM.

Identify Steps in a Process

Identifying the steps in a process can help you use the **problem-solving strategy, *Work Backward,*** in the next lesson.

In reading, identifying the steps in a process can help you organize what you read. In math, it can help you work backward to solve problems in which you know the result of a series of steps.

By noon, the Cookie Shoppe had sold only 50 of the cookies in their display case that were available at the beginning of the day. Then the bakers baked 200 cookies. Of these 200 cookies, they threw away 20 because they were burnt. If the Cookie Shoppe had 450 cookies left at the end of the day, how many cookies did they begin with?

Draw a diagram to show each step and the end result.

First I'll identify the steps in the problem.

Starting number	→	Number sold	→	Number baked	→	Number thrown away	→	Ending number
n	−	50	+	200	−	20	=	450

Then work backward from the result doing the reverse of each step.

1. How many steps from the starting number were taken to get the result 450?

2. As you work backward, how can you reverse the step where the cookies were baked?

432

For 3–5, use the picture at the right and the problem below.

Theresa played Ben's number game. She wound up with 41. Ben says he can find her beginning number.

3. Draw a diagram to show the steps involved in the problem.

4. Now work backward. How can Ben reverse the step where Theresa multiplied by 4?

5. **Writing in Math** Explain the steps Ben should use to find the beginning number.

Think of a number.
Add 6.
Then multiply by 4.
Now divide by 2.
Then subtract 7.

What number did you get?

For 6–8, use the game board pictured at the right and the problem below.

Candace moved forward 3 squares, then backward 2 squares, then forward 5 squares. She landed on a blue square. What was the color of the square where Candace began?

6. Draw a diagram to show the steps involved in the problem.

7. Now work backward. How can you reverse the step where Candace moved forward 5 squares?

8. **Writing in Math** Explain the steps you would use to find out the color of the square where Candace began.

For 9–10, use the picture at the right and the problem below.

Jim went shopping with Paul. Jim bought a computer cable and a rewriteable CD. Then Jim bought lunch for both of them. Each boy's lunch cost $6. Jim had $8 left. How much money did he start with?

9. Draw a diagram to show the steps involved in the problem.

10. **Writing in Math** Now work backward. Explain the steps you would use to solve the problem.

Problem-Solving Strategy

Key Idea
Learning how and when to work backward can help you solve problems.

Work Backward

LEARN

How can you work backward to solve a problem?

Elevator Test After completing repairs on an elevator, a maintenance engineer tested his work by sending the elevator up 12 floors, down 18 floors, and back up 20 floors. If the elevator ended up on the 30th floor, on which floor did the engineer begin his test?

Read and Understand

What do you know?

The elevator went up 12 floors, then down 18 floors, then back up 20 floors. It ended up on the 30th floor.

What are you trying to find?

Find the floor from which the engineer began his test.

Plan and Solve

What strategy will you use?

Strategy: **Work Backward**

How to Work Backward

Step 1   Identify what you are trying to find.

Step 2   Draw a diagram to show each change, starting from the unknown.

Step 3   Start at the end. Work backward using the inverse of each change.

The starting floor is what you are trying to find.

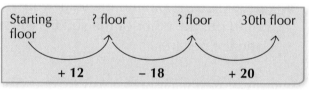

Work backward from the 30th floor.

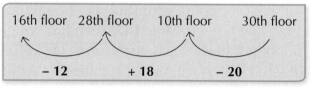

The engineer began his test on the 16th floor.

Look Back and Check

What can you do to check your answer?

Start on the 16th floor and work forward.
$16 + 12 = 28$; $28 - 18 = 10$; $10 + 20 = 30$

✔ Talk About It

1. What unknown information needs to be identified in the Elevator Test problem?

2. What inverse operation was used to "undo" adding 20? Subtracting 18? Adding 12?

When do you work backward to solve a problem?

Temperature at Midnight One January night, the temperature fell 13°F between midnight and 6 A.M. By 9 A.M., the temperature had doubled from what it had been at 6 A.M. By noon, it had risen another 8 degrees to 32°F. What was the temperature at midnight?

The temperature at midnight is what you are trying to find.

Midnight temp. $\xrightarrow[-13]{}$? °F $\xrightarrow[\times 2]{}$? °F $\xrightarrow[+8]{}$ 32°F Noon temp.

Work backward from the temperature at noon.

25°F $\xleftarrow[+13]{}$ 12°F $\xleftarrow[\div 2]{}$ 24°F $\xleftarrow[-8]{}$ 32°F

When to Work Backward

Think about working backward when:
There is an end result after a series of steps.
- 30th floor
- 32°F

You are asked to find the quantity in the first step.
- On which floor did the engineer begin his test?
- What was the temperature at midnight?

✔ Talk About It

3. What inverse operation was used to undo adding 8? Multiplying by 2? Subtracting 13?

4. Give the answer to the Temperature at Midnight problem in a complete sentence. Explain how you can check your answer.

CHECK ✔

For another example, see Set 8-10 on p. 464.

1. For the Fund-Raising problem, use the picture that is given to help you work backward. Solve and check your work.

Fund Raising Al, Sheldon, Carlos, and Natalie each sold three-year calendar books to raise money for their new school gymnasium. Sheldon raised twice as much money as Al. Carlos raised $100 more than Sheldon, and Natalie raised half as much as Carlos. Natalie raised $110. How much money did each of the others raise?

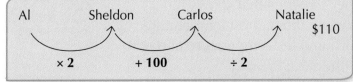

A Using the Strategy

Work Backward to Solve a Problem. For the Lakes problem, use the picture that is given to help you work backward. Solve and check your work.

2. **Lakes** Lake Erie is about half as wide as Lake Michigan. Lake Erie is five miles wider than Lake Ontario. Lake Superior is approximately three times as wide as Lake Ontario. If Lake Superior is 159 miles wide, about how wide is Lake Michigan?

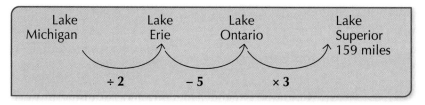

For 3–4, solve using the steps in How to Work Backward.

3. Joe chose a number, subtracted 8 from it, multiplied the difference by 7, added 10 to that, and finally divided by 5. The result was 9. What was Joe's number?

4. A movie begins at 1:00 P.M. Karin has a 15-minute walk to the bus from her home and a 5-minute walk from the bus to the theater. The bus ride takes 38 minutes. What is the latest bus she can take to make it in time for the movie?

BUS DEPARTURES

A.M.	P.M.
10:10	12:05
10:30	12:15
11:00	12:25
11:35	12:40

For 5–6, use the Temperature Change problem.

Temperature Change The greatest change in temperature during a 24-hour period occurred in Browning, Montana. On January 23, 1916, the highest temperature had been 44°F. As the morning of January 24, 1916 dawned, the temperature had dropped 100°F from the highest temperature of the previous day.

5. What was the temperature at dawn on January 24, 1916?

6. Write a number sentence that shows the difference between the highest temperature on January 23rd and the temperature at dawn on January 24th.

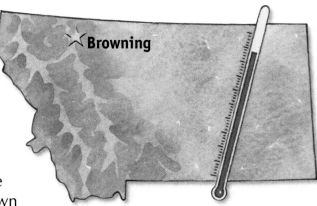

B Mixed Strategy Practice

Solve each problem. Write the answer in a complete sentence.

7. By the end of her first week of classes, Kiyoko finished reading a certain number of pages from the 713-page novel *War and Peace*. During her second week she read the same number of pages that she read the first week. She had 119 pages left to read. What page of the book did she begin reading at the start of her second week? Explain how you got your answer.

8. Calvin loaned his sister an amount of money from the $42.00 he had in his wallet. He then bought a DVD for $23.50, and was left with $12.75. What was the amount of money his sister borrowed?

9. You spend $\frac{1}{3}$ of the money you have at a bake sale. Your friend then pays back the $2.50 that he borrowed from you. Later, you spend $4.00 on a movie ticket and $1.25 for a snack. You are left with $5.25 at the end of the day. How much money did you have before the bake sale?

10. <u>Writing in Math</u> Write a word problem that can be solved by working backward.

STRATEGIES

- **Show What You Know**
  Draw a Picture
  Make an Organized List
  Make a Table
  Make a Graph
  Act It Out or Use Objects
- **Look for a Pattern**
- **Try, Check, and Revise**
- **Write an Equation**
- **Use Logical Reasoning**
- **Solve a Simpler Problem**
- **Work Backward**

Choose a tool
Mental Math

TEST TALK

Think It Through
Stuck? I won't give up. I can:
- Reread the problem.
- Tell what I know.
- Identify key facts and details.
- Tell the problem in my own words.
- Show the main idea.
- Try a different strategy.
- Retrace my steps.

Mixed Review and Test Prep

Take It to the NET
Test Prep
www.scottforesman.com

Find each answer.

11. $-\frac{84}{3}$

12. $-360 \div 4$

13. $1440 \div -12$

14. -7×0

15. $-3 \times (-17)$

16. $2 \times (-3) \times (-4) \times (-5)$

Order from least to greatest.

17. $\frac{-169}{3}$, -62, $-58\frac{5}{8}$, $\frac{-300}{5}$, -62.1

18. -4, -1, $|-2|$, 0, $|7|$, $-\frac{1}{3}$

19. Solve. $13a = -52$

    A. $a = 4$ **B.** $a = 3$ **C.** $a = -4$ **D.** $a = -2$

20. Solve. $\frac{x}{-3} = -6$

    A. $x = 218$ **B.** $x = 18$ **C.** $x = 2$ **D.** $x = -2$

Do You Know How?

Do You Understand?

Adding Integers (8-5), Subtracting Integers (8-6)

1. $-3 + 14$

2. $5 + (-7)$

3. $-1 + (-24)$

4. $-9 - (-32)$

5. $3 - 13$

6. $4 - (-6)$

7. Evaluate $31 - t$ for $t = -5$.

A How can using a number line help you add or subtract integers?

B Can the difference of two integers ever be greater than either of the two numbers? Explain.

Multiplying Integers (8-7), Dividing Integers (8-8)

8. -8×7

9. 19×4

10. $-12 \times (-11)$

11. $63 \div (-7)$

12. $-42 \div (-2)$

13. $-90 \div 15$

14. Evaluate $-108 \div m$ for $m = -9$.

C How can you use repeated addition to solve Exercise 8?

D What related multiplication fact can help you find the quotient in Exercise 11?

Solving Equations with Integers (8-9)

15. $\frac{a}{-7} = 7$

16. $-6d = -66$

17. $t - 19 = -4$

18. $b + 8 = -4$

19. $\frac{x}{12} = -6$

20. $c + (-7) = 7$

21. $r - (-2) = 20$

22. $8y = -96$

23. $a - 2 = -8$

24. $b \div (-4) = 15$

E Tell how you solved the equations in Exercises 15 and 16 by using inverse operations.

F Explain how you can check the solution to an equation.

Problem-Solving Strategy: Work Backward (8-10)

25. Produce Prices At a local grocery store, a pound of peaches costs twice as much as a pound of broccoli. Two pounds of apples cost $0.50 more than a pound of peaches. A head of lettuce costs half as much as two pounds of apples. If a head of lettuce costs $0.98, what is the cost of each other item?

G Tell the steps you used to work backward to solve Problem 25.

H What can you do to check your work when you use the work backward strategy?

MULTIPLE CHOICE

1. Evaluate $x - (-2)$ for $x = 3$. (8-6)

    A. -5 **C.** 1

    B. -1 **D.** 5

2. Evaluate $\frac{n}{-36}$ for $n = -108$. (8-8)

    A. -144 **C.** 3

    B. -3 **D.** 144

FREE RESPONSE

Solve. (8-5 – 8-8)

3. $-16 + 40$ **4.** $-22 + (-33)$ **5.** $-8 - 7$ **6.** $-9 - (-5)$ **7.** $4 - 21$

8. $\frac{-18}{-2}$ **9.** $13 \times (-1)$ **10.** $-44 \div 4$ **11.** $-18(3)$ **12.** $\frac{57}{-3}$

13. Suppose the decrease in temperature from 2,800 ft to 5,800 ft is $-15°$F. What is the lapse rate in degrees per 1,000 ft? (8-8)

14. With their spelunking club, Rishi and Jyotsna plan to explore a cave passage that has an elevation of -56 ft. They plan to descend at a rate of -8 ft/min. How long will it take to reach the cave passage? (8-8)

Solve each equation. (8-9)

15. $b + (-1) = -9$ **16.** $a - (-10) = 4$ **17.** $y + 12 = -7$

18. $h + (-3) = 3$ **19.** $\frac{n}{7} = -22$ **20.** $t \div 4 = -8$

21. $15m = -75$ **22.** $\frac{h}{-6} = 42$ **23.** $-3t = 126$

Work backward to solve Problem 24. (8-10)

24. Tina, Darla, Gene, and Bob worked at a school car wash on Saturday. Darla washed half as many cars as Tina did. Gene washed 4 more than Darla. Bob washed 5 fewer than Gene. If Bob washed 8 cars, how many cars did each of the other students wash? What was the total number of cars washed?

Think It Through
I need to **reverse the steps** from the number that is given.

Writing in Math

25. Name the words in Problem 24 that give you clues about which inverse operations you need to use when you work backward. (8-10)

26. Explain how a number line can help you find $7 + (-8)$. (8-5)

27. Explain why when you square a negative integer the result is positive. (8-7)

Algebra

Key Idea
The location of a point on the coordinate plane can be described by an ordered pair of numbers.

Vocabulary
- coordinate plane
- quadrant
- ordered pair
- origin
- x-coordinate
- y-coordinate
- x-axis
- y-axis

Materials
- grid paper or
- **tools**

Graphing Ordered Pairs

LEARN

What is a coordinate plane?

The term *pixel* is a contraction of *picture elements* and is used to describe the dots on a computer display. Computer programmers use ordered pairs to position pixels on a display.

A **coordinate plane** is a grid containing two number lines that intersect in a right angle at zero. The number lines, which are called the **x- and y-axes,** divide the plane into four **quadrants.**

An **ordered pair** (x, y) of numbers gives the coordinates and location of a point.

The **x-coordinate** shows the position left or right of the y-axis.

The **y-coordinate** shows the position above or below of the x-axis.

If a point lies on an axis, it does not lie in a quadrant. Point S lies on the y-axis.

*To locate any point, I need to know its horizontal and vertical distance and direction from (0, 0) or the **origin.***

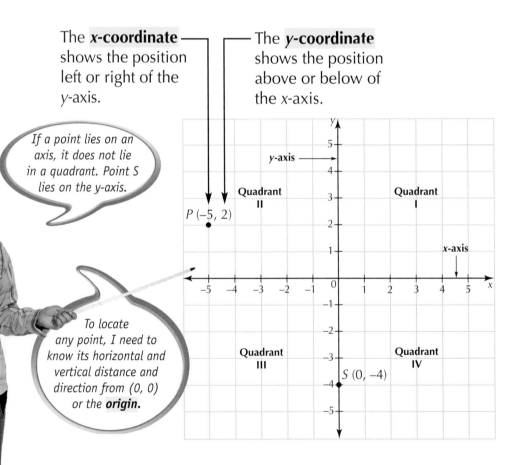

✔ Talk About It

1. Where would the point *Q* lie if both its x- and y-coordinate are negative?

2. Where would the point *R* lie if its y-coordinate is 0?

How can you graph a point on a coordinate plane?

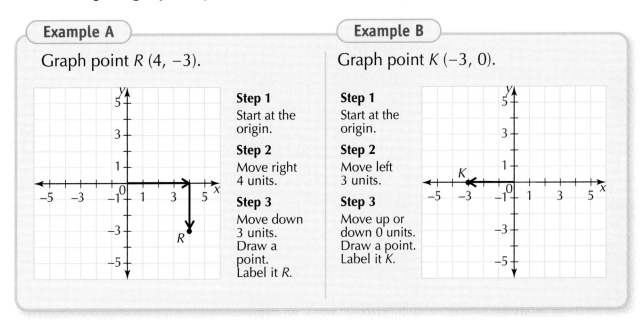

Example A

Graph point R (4, −3).

Step 1
Start at the origin.

Step 2
Move right 4 units.

Step 3
Move down 3 units. Draw a point. Label it R.

Example B

Graph point K (−3, 0).

Step 1
Start at the origin.

Step 2
Move left 3 units.

Step 3
Move up or down 0 units. Draw a point. Label it K.

How can you use a coordinate plane to locate points on a map?

Example C

A map of Pythagoras Park is shown at the right. The park fountain is located at the origin.

Give the coordinates of the tennis courts and tell what is located at (7, 12).

The tennis courts are located 8 units to the left of the origin and 6 units below. So its coordinates are (−8, −6).

Count 7 units to the right and 12 units up. The club house is located at that point.

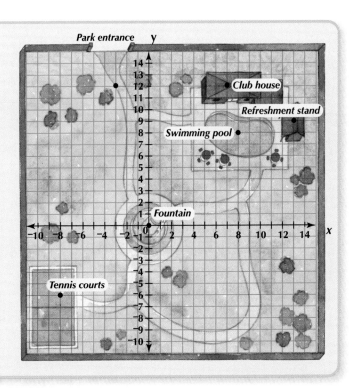

✔ Talk About It

3. In which quadrant do the majority of points lie in Example C?

4. **Reasoning** Where on the coordinate plane would you graph any point whose x-coordinate is zero? Whose y-coordinate is zero?

Give the ordered pair for each point.

1. *A*   **2.** *B*   **3.** *C*

Name the point for each ordered pair and the quadrant or axis on which it lies.

4. (0, −5)   **5.** (−5, −2)   **6.** (1, 1)

Draw a coordinate plane. Graph and label the points given.

7. *Y* (0, −3)   **8.** *W* (−3, 3)   **9.** *V* (−4, −1)

10. Reasoning What is true about every point on the *x*-axis?

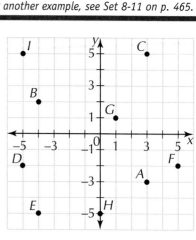

PRACTICE

For more practice, see Set 8-11 on p. 469.

Ⓐ Skills and Understanding

Give the ordered pair for each point.

11. *W*   **12.** *L*   **13.** *R*

14. *S*   **15.** *J*   **16.** *U*

Name the point for each ordered pair and the quadrant or axis on which it lies.

17. (−5, 2)   **18.** (1, −1)   **19.** (4, −5)

20. (−4, −5)   **21.** (4, 2)   **22.** (0, −5)

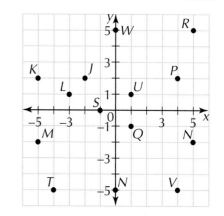

Draw a coordinate plane. Graph and label the points.

23. *A* (−1, −2)   **24.** *B* (5, 0)   **25.** *C* (1, −3)   **26.** *D* (3, 4)   **27.** *E* (−2, 4)

28. Reasoning What is true about the coordinates of points in Quadrants I and III?

Ⓑ Reasoning and Problem Solving

Math and Social Studies

Use the grid map of Washington, D.C., to complete the table below.

	Location	Coordinates
29.	Ellipse	
30.		(−5, −3)
31.		(2, −7)
32.		(2, 3)
33.	Washington Monument	

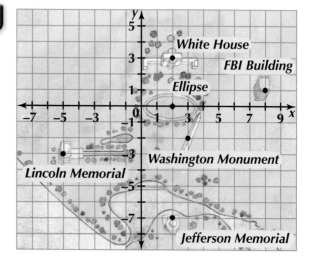

34. Reasoning Which is located closer to the Ellipse, the Jefferson Memorial or the White House? Explain how you know.

35. <u>**Writing in Math**</u> In *G is for Googol*, the *y*-axis is called the vertical axis, and the *x*-axis is called the horizontal axis. Explain why these alternate names are appropriate.

C Extensions

36. Locate and label points *A* (−2, 2), *B* (2, 2), *C* (2, −2), and *D* (−2, −2) on a coordinate plane. Connect the points in order to form square *ABCD*. If point *B* is moved 3 units up and *D* is moved 3 units down, what will be the new coordinates of *B* and *D*? After *B* and *D* are moved, what shape does *ABCD* form?

Mixed Review and Test Prep

Take It to the NET
Test Prep
www.scottforesman.com

37. Marni withdrew money from her bank account. She used $\frac{1}{2}$ the money to buy clothes. She spent $20 for books and was left with $10. How much money did Marni withdraw?

Solve each equation.

38. $-35t = -105$ **39.** $\frac{a}{-6} = 18$ **40.** $m + 9 = -33$ **41.** $h - (-99) = 145$

42. For which values of *a* and *b* does $|a + b| = |a| + |b|$?

  A. $a = -1; b = 1$ **B.** $a = -3; b = 4$ **C.** $a = -4; b = -3$ **D.** $a = 4; b = -3$

Practice Game

Players: 2–4 **Materials:** Number cards, −20 to 20 (2 sets)

Interesting Integers

1. Shuffle the cards and place them face down.

2. Each player takes 2 cards and computes the sum.

3. The player with the greatest sum takes all the cards played. If two or more players have the same greatest sum, cards are divided equally among them.

4. The winner is the player with the most cards when all cards have been played.

Algebra

Key Idea
Patterns and tables can be used to represent situations.

Vocabulary
• relation
• function

TEST TALK

Think It Through
I can **use what I know about** equations, patterns, and tables to evaluate a function.

Patterns and Tables

LEARN

What is a function?

WARM UP
Evaluate for $x = -4$.
1. $-7x$ 2. $\frac{20}{x}$
3. $x - (-3)$ 4. $12 - x$

Any set of ordered pairs (x, y) is called a **relation.** A **function** is a relation in which there is only one y-value for each x-value.

Example A

Determine if the relation is a function.

x	y
−2	0
−1	1
0	2
1	3

(−2, 0)   You can write
(−1, 1)   the data in the
(0, 2)   table as a set of
(1, 3)   ordered pairs.

The relation is a function because exactly one y-value is assigned to each x-value.

Example B

Determine if the relation is a function.

x	y
−2	−4
−1	−2
0	0
−2	4

(−2, −4)
(−1, −2)
(0, 0)
(−2, 4)

The relation is not a function because two y-values, −4 and 4, are assigned to the same x-value, −2.

✔ Talk About It

1. The relation at the right is a function. Why?

m	−1	0	1	2
n	7	7	7	7

How can you use a function to solve a problem?

Example C

When the space shuttle is in the first stage of its return to Earth, it descends about 3.5 miles per minute. Use an equation and table to find how far the shuttle descends in 8 minutes.

Let t represent the number of minutes.
Let d represent the number of miles the shuttle descends.

The equation is $d = -3.5t$.

t	1	2	3	4	5	6	7	8
d	−3.5	−7.0	−10.5	−14	−17.5	−21	−24.5	−28

When $t = 8$,
$d = -3.5(8)$
$= -28$

In 8 minutes, the shuttle descends 28 miles.

Use the function $y = 3x - 5$ to complete the table.

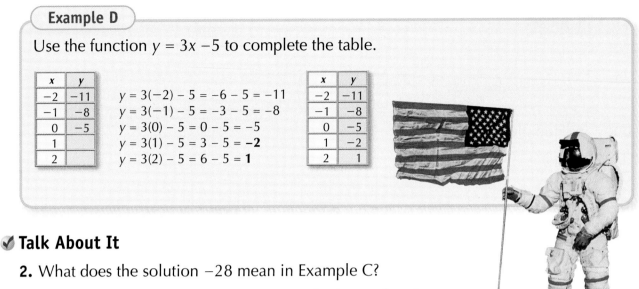

x	y
-2	-11
-1	-8
0	-5
1	
2	

$y = 3(-2) - 5 = -6 - 5 = -11$
$y = 3(-1) - 5 = -3 - 5 = -8$
$y = 3(0) - 5 = 0 - 5 = -5$
$y = 3(1) - 5 = 3 - 5 = \mathbf{-2}$
$y = 3(2) - 5 = 6 - 5 = \mathbf{1}$

x	y
-2	-11
-1	-8
0	-5
1	-2
2	1

✔ Talk About It

2. What does the solution -28 mean in Example C?

3. Reasoning In Example C, how can you find a *t*-value if you know a *d*-value?

4. In Example D, what is the value of *y* when $x = 10$? $x = -10$?

How can you write a rule for a function?

You can write a rule and an equation that tells how to find one value of the function when the other value is known.

a	b
-2	-6
-1	-3
0	0
1	3
2	6

What You Think

What can I do to
-2 to get -6,
-1 to get -3,
 0 to get 0,
 1 to get 3...?

I can multiply *a* by 3 to get *b*.

What You Write

Rule: Each *b*-value equals 3 times its corresponding *a*-value.

Equation: $b = 3a$, or $3a = b$

✔ Talk About It

5. In Example E, what happens to the *b*-values as the *a*-values increase by 1?

6. At a supermarket salad bar, the price of a salad depends on its weight. Suppose a salad costs $0.29 per ounce. Complete the table below. Write a rule and equation to describe this function.

w	1	2	3	4	5
p	$0.29	$0.58	$0.87		

Take It to the NET
www **More Examples**
www.scottforesman.com

Tell whether each relation is a function.

1.

x	2	1	0	−1
y	6	5	4	3

2.

a	1	6	9	1
b	−3	−2	−1	3

3.

u	−3	0	0	3
v	0	2	−2	0

Copy and complete each table.

4. $t = 4 - v$

v	t
0	
3	
6	
9	

5. $y = 2x + 3$

x	y
−4	
−2	
0	
2	

6. $b = \dfrac{a}{-3}$

a	b
−6	
−3	
0	
3	

7. Write a rule and an equation to describe the function.

x	4	6	8	10
y	−3	−1	1	3

8. Patterns Apples sell for $0.15 each. Make a table to find the cost of 4, 8, 12, and 16 apples. Use $t = 0.15a$.

Ⓐ Skills and Understanding

Tell whether each relation is a function.

9.

r	9	3	4	9
s	6	8	9.5	2

10.

x	−2	3	5	8
y	5	1.2	6	9

11.

m	−7	−5	−7	−5
n	3	1	−3	−1

Copy and complete each table.

12. $n = \dfrac{m}{-2}$

m	n
6	
10	
14	
18	

13. $y = x - (-8)$

x	y
−10	
−5	
0	
5	

14. $b = 12a - 4$

a	b
−2	
0	
2	
4	

15. $y = 15 - x$

x	y
12	
13	
14	
15	

For 16–18, write a rule and an equation to describe the function.

16.

x	9	11	13	15
y	3	5	7	9

17.

x	−6	−3	0	3
y	2	1	0	−1

18.

x	$\frac{-2}{5}$	$\frac{-1}{5}$	0	$\frac{1}{5}$
y	−2	−1	0	1

19. Patterns The water level in the backyard pond decreased by 2.5 inches each day. Make a table to find the change in the water level over a 6-day period. Use $t = -2.5d$.

PRACTICE

B Reasoning and Problem Solving

20. Lawn Profits Rishi borrowed $245 from his grandmother to buy a lawn mower. He plans to charge $18 to mow an average-size lawn. Let p represent his profit in dollars and m represent the number of lawns he mows. Use the equation $p = 18m - 245$ to complete the table below.

Think It Through
I can **look for patterns in the table to tell if the values of a function are true.**

m	0	5	10	15	20	25	30	35
p	−245	−155	−65	25	115			

For 21–22 refer to the table in the Lawn Profits problem.

21. Reasoning What does the ordered pair (10, −65) represent? The ordered pair (20, 115)?

22. Estimate how many lawns Rishi must mow before he makes a profit.

23. __Writing in Math__ Wanda made the table at the right for the given function. Is her table correct? If not, make changes in the table so that the values are correct.

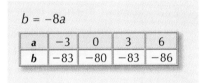

$b = -8a$

a	−3	0	3	6
b	−83	−80	−83	−86

C Extensions

24. A plumber charges $67.50 per hour. Write an equation to represent the relationship between the number of hours worked, h, and the total charge for labor, c. Make a table that shows the charges for 4 different numbers of hours worked.

Mixed Review and Test Prep

Take It to the NET
Test Prep
www.scottforesman.com

25. Armando has a football game at 1:30 P.M. It takes 25 minutes to travel by bus from the school to the stadium, $\frac{1}{3}$ hour for a quick lunch, $1\frac{1}{2}$ hour to practice at the school, and $\frac{1}{4}$ hour to get ready at home. At what time should Armando begin getting ready?

26. Evaluate $\frac{1}{5}n - \frac{1}{2}$ when $n = \frac{2}{3}$.

27. Name the ordered pair for Point A on the coordinate plane at the right.

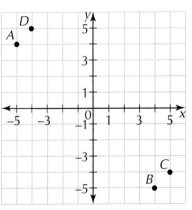

   A. (−4, 5)   **C.** (4, −5)

   B. (5, −4)   **D.** (−5, 4)

All text pages available online and on CD-ROM.

Algebra

Key Idea
You can use what you know about graphing ordered pairs to graph an equation.

Vocabulary
• T-table
• linear equation

Think It Through
An equation, table, and graph can all represent the same function.

Graphing Equations

LEARN

How can you graph an equation?

Example A

The Math Club is selling seed packets to raise money. They buy 40 packets at $0.05 each. They are selling the packets for $1 each. How many packets must be sold to make a profit of $5?

The Math Club spent 40(0.05), or $2.

Let x represent the number of packets sold. Then $1 \cdot x$ is the amount the club will earn for selling x packets. Let y be the amount of profit.

Graph the equation $y = x - 2$.
First make a **T-table** like the one at the right. List at least three values for x.

$y = x - 2$	
x	y
-1	-3
0	-2
1	-1

Graph each ordered pair from the T-table onto a coordinate plane. Draw a line to connect the points. This line contains all the points that make the equation $y = x - 2$ true. Since the graph of this equation is a straight line, the equation $y = x - 2$ is called a **linear equation.**

Points on the line represent the number of packets sold and the club's profit. The point (7,5) means the students must sell 7 packets to make a profit of $5.

Example B

Graph $y = -2x$.

$y = -2x$	
x	y
-2	4
-1	2
0	0
1	-2

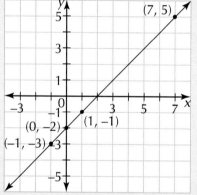

1. In Example B, is either of the points for the ordered pairs $(\frac{1}{2}, -1)$ or $(1\frac{1}{2}, -3)$ on the graph of the equation? Explain your answer.

2. **Number Sense** In Examples A and B, why do you think x-values such as -2, -1, 0, and 1 were used in the T-tables?

CHECK ✓

For another example, see Set 8-13 on p. 465.

For 1–4, make a T-table. Then graph each equation.

1. $y = x + 3$
2. $y = 3 - x$
3. $y = 3x$
4. $y = -1x$

5. Is $(-5, -15)$ a solution to $y = -3x$? Explain how you know.

6. **Reasoning** How can you tell if the point $(3, -1)$ is on the graph for the equation $y = x + (-4)$?

PRACTICE

For more practice, see Set 8-13 on p. 469.

Ⓐ Skills and Understanding

For 7–14, make a T-table. Then graph each equation.

7. $y = x + 4$
8. $y = x + (-1)$
9. $y = x$
10. $y = -1 - x$
11. $y = -2 - x$
12. $y = -3x$
13. $y = -x - 3$
14. $y = -4 + x$

15. Is $(-7, -1)$ a solution to $y = x + 8$? Explain how you know.

16. **Reasoning** How can you rewrite the equation $-x + y = -7$ so that making a T-table is easier?

Ⓑ Reasoning and Problem Solving

For each pair of equations, graph both lines on the same coordinate plane. Then tell what you notice about them.

17. $y = 2x$
    $y = -2x$
18. $y = x - 4$
    $y = x + 4$
19. $y = -1$
    $y = 1$

20. **Writing in Math** Explain why the graph of the equation $y = 2 - x$ does not pass through the third quadrant.

🦉 Mixed Review and Test Prep

Take It to the NET
Test Prep
www.scottforesman.com

21. Write a rule and equation to describe the function.

x	6	0	−6	−12
y	−12	0	12	24

22. Which describes a point that is located in the third quadrant?

   A. x and y are both negative.
   B. x and y are both positive.
   C. x is negative and y is positive.
   D. x is positive and y is negative.

Problem-Solving Applications

Extreme Weather The winds, precipitation, and temperatures associated with extreme weather can be very destructive, particularly for the unprepared. Meteorologists continually search for more reliable methods of predicting threatening weather. Even with accurate predictions, however, it is doubtful that the power of nature will be overcome.

Trivia Hailstones once fell in Kansas that were the size of bowling balls!

North Dakota

Réunion

Cherrapunji, India

❶ The island of Réunion had a record one-day rainfall that was 57 inches greater than North Dakota's average annual rainfall. This record one-day rainfall was also 968 inches less than the record one-year rainfall in India. North Dakota's annual rainfall is 17 inches. Find the two record rainfalls.

Using Key Facts

❷ To be upgraded from a tropical storm to a hurricane, a storm must produce sustained wind speeds of almost 75 mph. What fraction of a hurricane's extreme gust speed is this?

❸ One of the worst storms of tornadoes was in 1974 when 148 tornadoes struck 13 states. What percent of the 50 states were struck?

❹ Newfoundland is one of the world's foggiest places, with an average of about 120 foggy days each year. Draw a circle graph that shows the number of days with and without fog.

Key Facts Extreme Winds	
Type of Wind	**Approximate Speed**
• Chinooks	100 mph
• Hurricane gusts	200 mph
• Tornado winds	300 mph
• Jet stream	300 mph

Good News/Bad News *Hurricanes transfer heat from the tropics to cooler areas of the globe, but they cause huge amounts of damage in the process.*

5 Sound travels through air at about $\frac{1}{5}$ mile per second. If you see a flash of lightning and then hear thunder 7 seconds later, about how far away from you was the lightning strike?

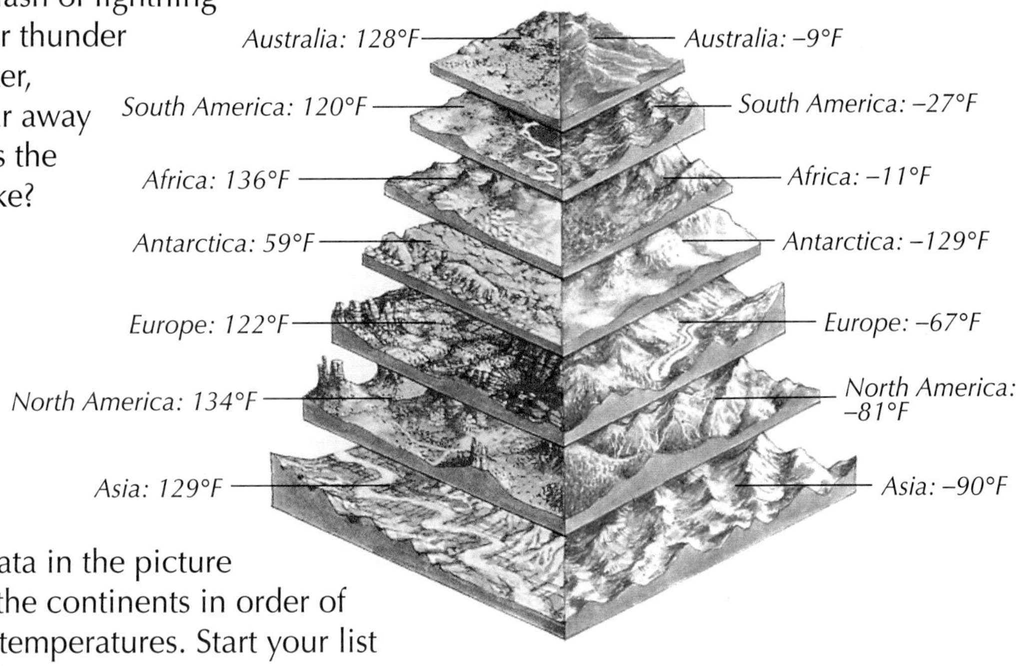

Maximum Temperature

Australia: 128°F
South America: 120°F
Africa: 136°F
Antarctica: 59°F
Europe: 122°F
North America: 134°F
Asia: 129°F

Minimum Temperature

Australia: −9°F
South America: −27°F
Africa: −11°F
Antarctica: −129°F
Europe: −67°F
North America: −81°F
Asia: −90°F

6 Use the data in the picture above to list the continents in order of extreme low temperatures. Start your list with the coldest continent.

7 Decision Making The picture above shows that the range of temperatures in North America is 215°F. On what other continent would you like to live? How much different is the temperature range of your preferred continent from that of North America?

8 Writing in Math Write your own word problem involving the information in this lesson. Write your answer in a complete sentence.

Do You Know How?

Do You Understand?

Graphing Ordered Pairs (8-11)

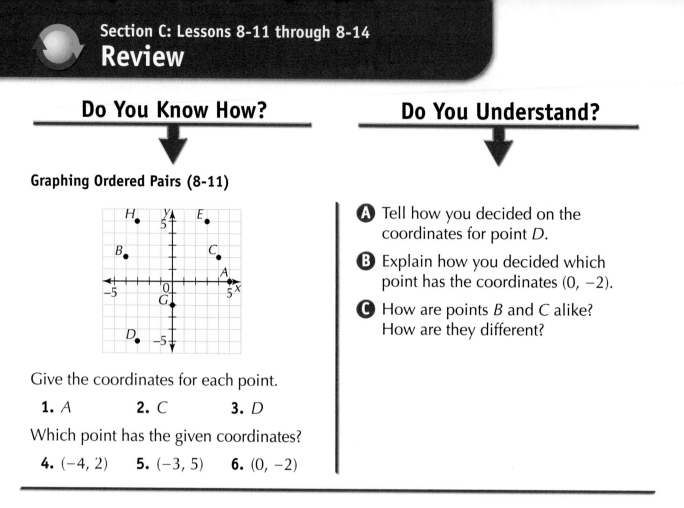

Give the coordinates for each point.

1. *A* **2.** *C* **3.** *D*

Which point has the given coordinates?

4. (−4, 2) **5.** (−3, 5) **6.** (0, −2)

A Tell how you decided on the coordinates for point *D*.

B Explain how you decided which point has the coordinates (0, −2).

C How are points *B* and *C* alike? How are they different?

Patterns and Tables (8-12)

7. Complete the table for the equation *y* = 4*x*.

x	−2	−1		1	2	
y			0			12

8. Write a rule and an equation for the table below.

x	−2	−1	0	1	2	3
y	3	4	5	6	7	8

D Share how you completed the table for Exercise 7.

E Tell whether *y* = 4*x* is a function and why.

Graphing Equations (8-13)

Make a T-table for each equation. Graph each equation.

9. *y* = −4*x* **10.** *y* = 1 − *x*

11. *y* = −*x* − 4 **12.** *y* = 2*x*

F Explain how you determined the values to use for Exercise 9.

G What is true about the lines you graphed for Exercises 9 and 12?

H What *x*-values would you use in a T-table for $y = \frac{3}{4}x$?

Diagnostic Checkpoint

MULTIPLE CHOICE

1. Which equation represents the relationship in the table at the right? (8-12)

x	y
−2	−5
0	−3
2	−1
4	1

A. $y = x - 3$ **C.** $y = 3 - x$

B. $y = 3x$ **D.** $y = 3 + x$

> **Think It Through**
> A **function** is a **relation** that can be **represented by a graph**.

2. Which T-table is correct for the equation $y = x - 8$? (8-13)

A.

x	y
−2	−10
−1	−11
0	−12
1	−13

B.

x	y
−2	6
−1	7
0	8
1	9

C.

x	y
−2	−10
−1	−9
0	−8
1	−7

D.

x	y
−2	10
−1	11
0	12
1	13

FREE RESPONSE

For 3–14, use the coordinate plane at the right. (8-11)

Give the ordered pair for each point.

3. M **4.** P **5.** T **6.** Q

Name the point for each ordered pair.

7. $(-3, 0)$ **8.** $(-4, -5)$

9. $(0, 1)$ **10.** $(2, -3)$

11. $(2, 0)$ **12.** $(4, -4)$

13. $(0, -2)$ **14.** $(4, 0)$

15. Cathy earns $5.75 per hour baby-sitting. How many hours will she have to work in order to buy a backpack that costs $39? Let h be the number of hours Cathy baby-sits and let m be the total amount earned after each hour. Write an equation and make a table to solve the problem. (8-12, 8-14)

Make a T-table and graph each equation. (8-13)

16. $y = x - 3$ **17.** $y = 4 - x$ **18.** $y = x + 1$ **19.** $y = 2$

Writing in Math

20. Refer to your table in Problem 15. Explain what the first ordered pair means. (8-12)

21. Describe the relationship between the lines you graphed in Exercises 16 and 18. (8-13)

Test-Taking Strategies

Understand the question.

Get information for the answer.

Plan how to find the answer.

Make smart choices.

Use writing in math.

Improve written answers.

Plan How to Find the Answer

After you understand a test question and get needed information, you need to plan how to find the answer. Think about problem-solving skills and strategies and computation methods you know.

1. The table shows a pair of values for x and y when $y = x - 3$.

$y = x - 3$

x	y
-1	-4
0	
1	
2	

Part A

Complete the table for the other values of x.

Part B

Graph the equation $y = x - 3$ on the coordinate plane.

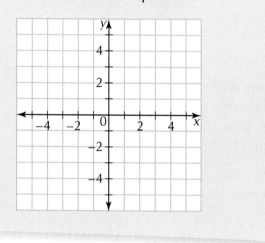

Understand the question.

I need to find values of y for certain values of x when y = x – 3. Then I need to graph the equation.

Get information for the answer.

*The numbers I need to work with are given in the **table**.*

Plan how to find the answer.

- Think about problem-solving skills and strategies.

  *Part A: I can find the other values of y to **complete the table** by substituting the given values of x into the equation.*

  *Part B: I can **make the graph** by plotting each ordered pair from the table. Then I should connect the points with a line.*

- Choose computation methods.

  I can use mental math to complete the values in the table.

2. Which equation describes the relation shown in the table?

x	y
2	−6
3	−9
4	−12
5	−15

A. $y = x - 3$

B. $y = 3x$

C. $y = \dfrac{x}{-3}$

D. $y = -3x$

Think It Through

I need to choose the equation that describes the relation given in the table. What can I do to 2 to get −6? to 3 to get −9? to 4 to get −12? to 5 to get −15? These are simple numbers, so I can use mental math. Once I figure out the rule in words, I need to translate it into an equation.

Now it's your turn.

For each problem, describe a plan for finding the answer.

3. The table shows a pair of values for x and y when $y = -2x$.

Part A

Copy and complete the table for the other values of y.

$y = -2x$

x	y
−2	4
−1	
0	
1	

Part B

Graph the equation $y = -2x$ on a grid.

4. Which equation describes the relation shown in the table?

x	y
3	−1
1	−3
0	−4
2	−2

A. $y = x + 4$

B. $y = 4x$

C. $y = \dfrac{x}{4}$

D. $y = x - 4$

Key Vocabulary and Concept Review

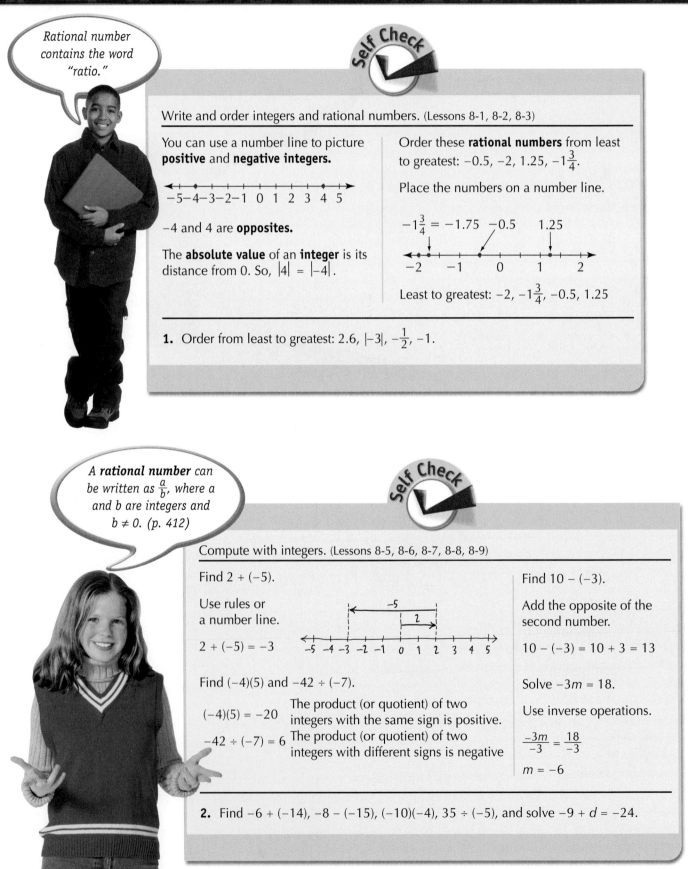

Rational number contains the word "ratio."

Self Check

Write and order integers and rational numbers. (Lessons 8-1, 8-2, 8-3)

You can use a number line to picture **positive** and **negative integers**.

$$-5\;-4\;-3\;-2\;-1\;\;0\;\;1\;\;2\;\;3\;\;4\;\;5$$

-4 and 4 are **opposites**.

The **absolute value** of an **integer** is its distance from 0. So, $|4| = |-4|$.

Order these **rational numbers** from least to greatest: $-0.5, -2, 1.25, -1\frac{3}{4}$.

Place the numbers on a number line.

$$-1\frac{3}{4} = -1.75 \quad -0.5 \qquad 1.25$$

$$-2 \qquad -1 \qquad 0 \qquad 1 \qquad 2$$

Least to greatest: $-2, -1\frac{3}{4}, -0.5, 1.25$

1. Order from least to greatest: $2.6, |-3|, -\frac{1}{2}, -1$.

A **rational number** can be written as $\frac{a}{b}$, where a and b are integers and $b \neq 0$. (p. 412)

Self Check

Compute with integers. (Lessons 8-5, 8-6, 8-7, 8-8, 8-9)

Find $2 + (-5)$.

Use rules or a number line.

$$2 + (-5) = -3$$

$$-5\;-4\;-3\;-2\;-1\;\;0\;\;1\;\;2\;\;3\;\;4\;\;5$$

Find $(-4)(5)$ and $-42 \div (-7)$.

$(-4)(5) = -20$ The product (or quotient) of two integers with the same sign is positive.

$-42 \div (-7) = 6$ The product (or quotient) of two integers with different signs is negative

Find $10 - (-3)$.

Add the opposite of the second number.

$$10 - (-3) = 10 + 3 = 13$$

Solve $-3m = 18$.

Use inverse operations.

$$\frac{-3m}{-3} = \frac{18}{-3}$$

$$m = -6$$

2. Find $-6 + (-14)$, $-8 - (-15)$, $(-10)(-4)$, $35 \div (-5)$, and solve $-9 + d = -24$.

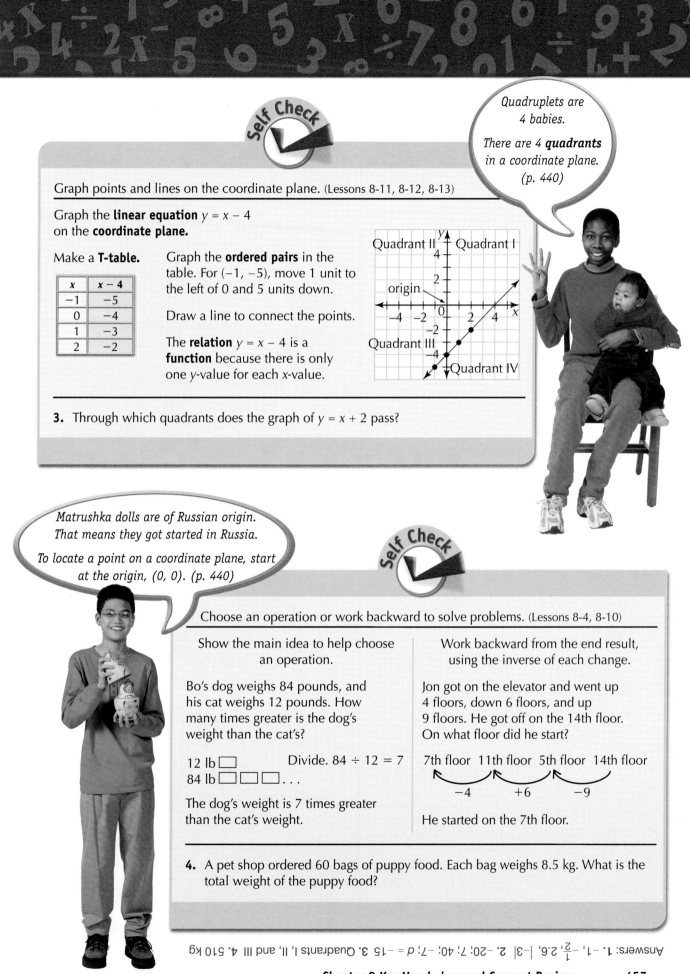

(p. 440)

Quadruplets are 4 babies.

There are 4 **quadrants** in a coordinate plane. (p. 440)

Self Check

Graph points and lines on the coordinate plane. (Lessons 8-11, 8-12, 8-13)

Graph the **linear equation** $y = x - 4$ on the **coordinate plane.**

Make a **T-table.**

x	x − 4
−1	−5
0	−4
1	−3
2	−2

Graph the **ordered pairs** in the table. For (−1, −5), move 1 unit to the left of 0 and 5 units down.

Draw a line to connect the points.

The **relation** $y = x - 4$ is a **function** because there is only one *y*-value for each *x*-value.

Quadrant II   Quadrant I
origin
Quadrant III   Quadrant IV

3. Through which quadrants does the graph of $y = x + 2$ pass?

Matrushka dolls are of Russian origin. That means they got started in Russia.

To locate a point on a coordinate plane, start at the origin, (0, 0). (p. 440)

Self Check

Choose an operation or work backward to solve problems. (Lessons 8-4, 8-10)

Show the main idea to help choose an operation.

Bo's dog weighs 84 pounds, and his cat weighs 12 pounds. How many times greater is the dog's weight than the cat's?

12 lb ☐
84 lb ☐☐☐...

Divide. $84 \div 12 = 7$

The dog's weight is 7 times greater than the cat's weight.

Work backward from the end result, using the inverse of each change.

Jon got on the elevator and went up 4 floors, down 6 floors, and up 9 floors. He got off on the 14th floor. On what floor did he start?

7th floor   11th floor   5th floor   14th floor
−4   +6   −9

He started on the 7th floor.

4. A pet shop ordered 60 bags of puppy food. Each bag weighs 8.5 kg. What is the total weight of the puppy food?

Answers: 1. −1, −$\frac{1}{2}$, 2.6, |−3| 2. −20; 7; 40; −7; *d* = −15 3. Quadrants I, II, and III 4. 510 kg

Chapter 8 Key Vocabulary and Concept Review 457

Chapter Test

MULTIPLE CHOICE

Choose the correct letter for each answer.

1. Which point is the opposite of −3?

```
   B        A         C         D
 <-+--+--+--+--+--+--+--+--+--+--+--+->
  -6 -5 -4 -3 -2 -1  0  1  2  3  4  5  6
```

 A. A   **C.** C

 B. B   **D.** D

2. Which integer is the greatest?

 A. −4   **C.** −7

 B. 0   **D.** −3

3. Which of the following sets of numbers is in order from least to greatest?

 A. $-1.6, -\frac{5}{6}, 1.2, 2$

 B. $\frac{1}{4}, 0, -0.5, -1.2$

 C. $-3.1, -1, -1\frac{2}{5}, 0.4$

 D. $\frac{1}{10}, -1.5, 1.75, -2.1$

4. Find −12 + 7.

 A. −19   **C.** 5

 B. −5   **D.** 19

5. Find 8 × (−6).

 A. −56   **C.** 48

 B. −48   **D.** 56

6. Which answer is a negative integer?

 A. 18 + (−12)

 B. −5 × −3

 C. 3 − (−8)

 D. 32 ÷ (−4)

7. Find −4 − (−12).

 A. −16   **C.** 8

 B. −8   **D.** 16

8. Solve y + 6 = −2.

 A. y = −8   **C.** y = 4

 B. y = −4   **D.** y = 8

9. The temperature at 1:00 P.M. was 88°F. This was 12°F warmer than at 8:00 A.M. Earlier on the same day, the temperature fell 7°F from midnight to 4:00 A.M. Then it rose 6°F from 4:00 A.M. to 8:00 A.M. What was the temperature at midnight?

Think It Through
I can **try working backward from an answer.**

 A. 25°F   **C.** 75°F

 B. 65°F   **D.** 77°F

10. Which point is NOT located on the line with the equation y = x − 3?

 A. R (−1, −4)   **C.** T (2, −1)

 B. S (1, 4)   **D.** U (3, 0)

11. Which point is located at (−2, 3)?

 A. A   **B.** B   **C.** C   **D.** D

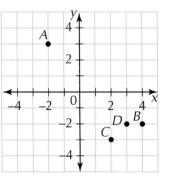

For 12–14, use the number line below. Write the integer for each point. Then give its opposite and absolute value.

$$A \quad\quad\quad C \quad E \quad\quad D \quad\quad B$$

```
◄─┼──┼──┼──┼──┼──┼──┼──┼──┼──┼──►
 -5 -4 -3 -2 -1  0  1  2  3  4  5
```

12. E **13.** B **14.** A

Use <, >, or = to compare.

15. $-7 \quad -4$ **16.** $|-3| \quad -3$

17. $3.5 \quad -4.3$ **18.** $-5.85 \quad -5\frac{3}{5}$

Order from least to greatest.

19. $6, -10, 3, |4|, -1$

20. $-1\frac{3}{4}, -1.8, 1.65$

Add or subtract.

21. $-5 - (-4)$

22. $3 + (-18)$

23. $-11 + (-7)$

24. $-21 + 13$

Multiply or divide.

25. -9×-4

26. $-56 \div 8$

27. 12×-9

28. $-42 \div -6$

Solve each equation.

29. $\frac{n}{-4} = 20$ **30.** $p - (-14) = 7$

31. $m + 6 = -1$ **32.** $-3c = 51$

Graph and label the points on the same coordinate plane.

33. $A(-1, 5)$ **34.** $B(0, -2)$

Make a T-table. Then graph each equation.

35. $y = 2 - x$ **36.** $y = \frac{1}{2}x$

37. Write a rule and an equation for the function below.

x	1	−1	−3
y	−1	−3	−5

Writing in Math

38. Write a word problem. Draw a picture to show the main idea and give the solution in a complete sentence.

39. Explain how you can tell if the answer to an addition problem will be positive or negative.

40. Jocelyn works at a store. For every T-shirt she sells, she earns $3. How many T-shirts will she have to sell to earn at least $50? Explain how you found your answer.

Think It Through
I can **look for key words** in the problem to help me **choose an operation**.

Number and Operation

MULTIPLE CHOICE

1. What is the sum of (−4) and (−9)?

   A. 36   **C.** −5

   B. 13   **D.** −13

2. Which expression has a value of 26?

   A. $2^4 + 10$ **C.** $-19 - (-7)$

   B. $5 \times (4 + 6)$ **D.** $18 - 5 \times 2$

FREE RESPONSE

3. Order −4, 7 −1.5, 0, 2, and $-\frac{4}{5}$ from least to greatest.

4. What is the least common multiple of 3, 5, and 12?

5. Becky biked 3.2 miles from her house to Maria's house. The two girls then biked $5\frac{1}{4}$ miles to the mall and another 2.6 miles to Janet's house. How many miles did Becky bike?

Writing in Math

6. Explain how to add $\frac{3}{8}$ and $\frac{3}{10}$. Then add.

7. Shoes 'N' More is having a sale. A pair of sneakers with a regular price of $44.00 is marked 45% off. Chris says the sneakers cost $19.80. Is this correct? Explain.

8. Explain how you can tell if the answer to a division problem will be positive or negative.

Geometry and Measurement

MULTIPLE CHOICE

9. A scale drawing of a building shows the building with a height of 5.5 in. The scale of the drawing is 2 in. = 30 ft. What is the actual height of the building?

   A. 30 ft   **C.** 82.5 ft

   B. 60 ft   **D.** 165 ft

10. Which of the following statements is true?

    A. A regular hexagon has 6 equal sides.

    B. The perimeter and area of a square are always equal.

    C. All triangles have one right angle.

    D. Some quadrilaterals have more than 4 sides.

FREE RESPONSE

11. What is the circumference of a circle with a diameter of 14 cm? (Use $\frac{22}{7}$ for π.)

Writing in Math

12. The temperature increased 3°F, then decreased 8°F, and then increased another 6°F. The final temperature was 42°F. Explain how to find the initial temperature.

13. Explain the difference between an acute angle and an obtuse angle.

Data Analysis and Probability

MULTIPLE CHOICE

14. The circle graph shows the percent of students in each category. If 125 students participated in the track meet, how many were in a running event?

Track and Field

Running 52%

Throwing 20%

Jumping 28%

A. 52 students   **C.** 65 students

B. 60 students   **D.** 104 students

15. What is the probability of rolling an odd number on a fair number cube?

A. $\frac{1}{6}$ **C.** $\frac{1}{2}$

B. $\frac{1}{3}$ **D.** 1

FREE RESPONSE

16. Marta is 4 years older than Jared. Jared is twice as old as Kim. Marta is 12 years old. How old is Kim?

17. If two coins are tossed, what is the probability that they will both land heads up?

Writing in Math

18. Describe how the line graph that shows an increase in temperature from 8:00 A.M. to 6:00 P.M. would look.

Algebra

MULTIPLE CHOICE

19. Solve $a + (-7) = 1$.

A. $a = 7$ **C.** $a = 6$

B. $a = -8$ **D.** $a = 8$

20. Yolanda deposited $47 into her checking account. Which expression shows the amount now in her account, if c equals the amount in Yolanda's account before the deposit?

A. $c - \$47$ **C.** $c + \$47$

B. $\$47c$ **D.** $\frac{\$47}{c}$

FREE RESPONSE

21. Copy and complete the table of values for the equation $y = -3 - x$.

x	y
0	
1	
2	
3	

22. Solve the proportion $\frac{4}{5} = \frac{7}{n}$.

23. Solve for p: $-\frac{1}{3}p = -27$.

Use a proportion to solve.

24. 20 is 4% of what number?

25. 75% of what number is 24?

Writing in Math

26. Write a rule and an equation that tell how to find the value of y when the value of x is known.

x	-4	-2	3	6
y	-6	-4	1	4

Set 8-1 (pages 408–409)

Write the integer and its absolute value for each point on the number line.

A: 2; $|2| = 2$

B: −3; $|-3| = 3$

C: 0; $|0| = 0$

Remember the absolute value of an integer is the number of units the integer is from zero on a number line.

Write the integer and its absolute value for each point on the number line.

1. A **2.** B **3.** C

4. D **5.** E **6.** F

Set 8-2 (pages 410–411)

Compare −15 and −7. Which is greater?

Since −7 is farther to the right on the number line than −15, −7 is greater.

$-7 > -15$

Write −5, −9, 4, −10, and 9 in order from least to greatest.

Locate the values on the number line.

The numbers from least to greatest are −10, −9, −5, 4, 9.

Remember zero is neither positive nor negative.

Use >, <, or = to compare.

1. −5 ⚪ −2 **2.** 0 ⚪ −1

3. $|-15|$ ⚪ 15 **4.** −21 ⚪ −22

Write the numbers in order from least to greatest.

5. 15, 13, −8, 0, −4, 1

6. −2, −5, −3, 11, 3, −1

7. −15, −45, 0, −8, −27

Set 8-3 (pages 412–413)

Graph $-\frac{2}{5}$, $-\frac{3}{5}$, and 0.8 on the number line.

Compare −0.45 and −0.40. Which is greater?

The number −0.45 is farther to the left on the number line, so −0.40 is greater.

Remember all positive decimals and fractions have opposites that are located to the left of zero on the number line.

Graph each rational number on the same number line.

1. −0.5 **2.** $1\frac{7}{8}$ **3.** 1.25 **4.** $-\frac{5}{8}$

Use >, <, or = to compare.

5. $-\frac{1}{8}$ ⚪ $-\frac{1}{4}$ **6.** 0.79 ⚪ $\frac{4}{5}$

7. 0 ⚪ −0.1 **8.** −8.01 ⚪ −8.1

TWX stock is selling for $34 per share. Michael has $225 to invest. Will this amount be enough to purchase 7 shares?

Show the main idea.

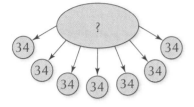

Multiply to find if 7 shares will cost more or less than $225.

Since 7 × 34 = $238, Michael does not have enough money.

Remember that drawing pictures of the main idea can help you choose an operation to solve the problem.

Draw a picture to show the main idea. Solve the problem.

1. The yearbook staff wants to use 12 pages for individual pictures of 192 sixth graders. How many pictures will go on each page?

2. The head of a tropical fish is $\frac{1}{3}$ as long as its midsection. Its tail is as long as its head and midsection combined. The total length of the fish is 48 cm. How long is each part?

Use a number line to add 6 + (−4).

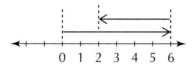

Start at 0, move 6 steps to the right for 6. Then move 4 steps to the left for −4.

So, 6 + (−4) = 2.

Remember the rules when you add integers.

1. 12 + (−5)   2. −1 + (−9)

3. 10 + (−15)   4. −7 + (−8)

5. −11 + 11   6. 1 + (−4)

Find 5 − (−3).

5 −   (−3)
5 + (−(−3)) | 5 minus −3 is the same as
5 +   3 | 5 plus the opposite of −3.
  8 | The opposite of −3 is 3.

Remember that to subtract an integer, you add its opposite.

1. −15 − 3   2. −6 − (−9)

3. 7 − (−15)   4. −1 − 8

5. 3 − 4   6. −36 − 41

Find the product −13 × (−12).

Both integers are negative, so the product is positive.

−13 × −12 = 156

Find the product −4 × 16.

Since one integer is negative and the other is positive, the product is negative.

−4 × 16 = −64

Remember the product of two integers with the same sign is positive.

1. −24 × (−4)   2. 6 × (−30)

3. (−37)(−3)   4. −16 × 7

5. (−33)(−5)   6. (17)(8)

Set 8-8 (pages 428–429)

Find the quotient $-42 \div 14$.

One of the signs is negative and the other is positive, so the quotient is negative.

$-42 \div 14 = -3$

Find the quotient $-38 \div (-19)$.

The signs are both negative, so the quotient is positive.

$38 \div (-19) = 2$

Remember the rules when dividing integers.

The quotient of two numbers with the same sign is positive.

The quotient of two numbers with different signs is negative.

1. $-85 \div 5$ **2.** $30 \div (-15)$

3. $\dfrac{105}{3}$ **4.** $-48 \div (-4)$

5. $-63 \div (-9)$ **6.** $\dfrac{-33}{11}$

Set 8-9 (pages 430–431)

Solve the equation $m - (-18) = 3$.

You can rewrite $m - (-18)$ as $m + 18$.

$m - (-18) = 3$
$m + 18 = 3$
$m + 18 + (-18) = 3 + (-18)$
$m = 3 + (-18)$
$m = -15$

Remember to use the rules for adding, subtracting, multiplying, and dividing integers when solving equations with integers.

1. $n + 16 = -20$ **2.** $\dfrac{x}{-5} = -34$

3. $y \div (-8) = 9$ **4.** $t - (-10) = -12$

Set 8-10 (pages 434–437)

Work backward to solve the problem.

The distance from a suburb of Chicago to Springfield, Illinois, is about 180 miles. A train travels at a rate of 60 miles per hour and makes a 20-minute stop after each hour. If the train arrives in Springfield at 3:00 P.M., what time did it leave the suburb?

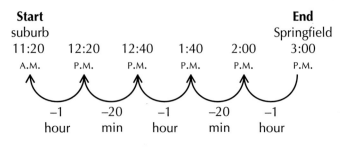

| **Start** suburb | | | | | **End** Springfield |
| 11:20 A.M. | 12:20 P.M. | 12:40 P.M. | 1:40 P.M. | 2:00 P.M. | 3:00 P.M. |

−1 hour   −20 min   −1 hour   −20 min   −1 hour

The train left at 11:20 A.M.

Remember to use inverse operations when you work backward.

Make and use a diagram to work backward to solve each problem.

1. Marta multiplied a number by 6, divided the product by 9, and then subtracted 14. Then she doubled the difference. The result was 20. What was her number?

2. Derek rented a car for a week. His bill came to $50. How many miles did he drive?

RENT-A-CAR
$35 a week
100 miles free!
$0.15 for each mile after the first 100 miles.

Locate *H* (−4, 5).

Start at the origin. Move 4 units to the left, for −4. Move 5 units up for 5. Label the point with its coordinates.

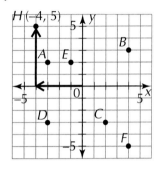

Remember that the first coordinate tells you how far to move right or left from the origin. The second coordinate tells you how far up or down to move from the origin.

In 1−6, use the graph at the left. Give the ordered pair for each point.

1. *A* **2.** *B* **3.** *C*

4. *D* **5.** *E* **6.** *F*

7. Graph and label the points *G* (2, 1), *J* (−2, 4), *K* (−4, −1), and *M* (0, −3) on the same coordinate plane.

A relation is a function if there is only one *y*-value for each *x*-value.

x	−1	0	1	2
y	0	3	6	9

x	−4	−1	0	−1
y	−6	−3	1	5

This is a function because for each *x*-value there is only one *y*-value.

This is not a function because there are two *y*-values for −1.

Complete the table for the equation $y = x - 4$.

x	y	
−2	−6	If *x* = −2, then *y* = −2 − 4 = −6.
−1	−5	If *x* = −1, then *y* = −1 − 4 = −5.
0	−4	If *x* = 0, then *y* = 0 − 4 = −4.
2	−2	If *x* = 2, then *y* = 2 − 4 = −2.

Remember to substitute the value for one variable into the equation to determine the value of the other variable.

Tell whether each relation is a function.

1.

x	2	12	18	2
y	−6	−4	−2	6

2.

x	−4	0	4	8
y	−5	−1	3	7

Copy and complete the table for each equation.

3. $n = 6 - m$

m	−1	0	1	
n				

4. $y = \frac{x}{4}$

x	−12	−8	0	
y				

Make a T-table for the equation $y = x - 5$. Then graph the equation.

x	y
0	−5
1	−4
4	−1

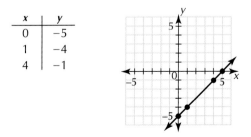

Remember, ordered pairs that make an equation true can be used to graph an equation.

Complete the T-table for each equation. Then graph each equation.

1. $y = 4 - x$

x	y
−2	
0	
2	

2. $y = -5x$

x	y
−1	
0	
1	

Chapter 8 Reteaching   465

Set 8-1 (pages 408–409)

Write the integer for each point on the number line.

1. A   **2.** B   **3.** C   **4.** D   **5.** E   **6.** F

Write the opposite and absolute value for each point on the number line.

7. A   **8.** B   **9.** C   **10.** D   **11.** E   **12.** F

13. Today's low temperature was 9°F below zero. Write this temperature as an integer.

Set 8-2 (pages 410–411)

Use >, <, or = to compare.

1. -8 -13 **2.** -2 -5 **3.** 0 6

4. $|-13|$ 13 **5.** -4 4 **6.** -2 -33

Order from least to greatest.

7. $-8, 3, -3, 8$ **8.** $-1, -5, 0, 4$ **9.** $-12, 7, -3, 20$

10. $-2, -4, -22, 0$ **11.** $14, -9, -10, 6$ **12.** $11, -4, 0, 3$

13. The outdoor temperature at the bank read $-5°F$. The outdoor temperature on Jeff's thermometer at home read $-4°F$. Which temperature is colder? Explain.

Set 8-3 (pages 412–413)

Graph each rational number on the same number line.

1. 0.75 **2.** $-1\frac{3}{4}$ **3.** $-\frac{4}{16}$ **4.** 0.375 **5.** $1\frac{21}{24}$ **6.** -1.25

Use >, <, or = to compare.

7. -3.2 $-3\frac{2}{3}$ **8.** $-4\frac{4}{5}$ -4.8 **9.** $1\frac{3}{8}$ $1\frac{5}{6}$

10. $-2\frac{9}{20}$ -2.45 **11.** -1.25 $-1\frac{1}{4}$ **12.** $\frac{2}{3}$ $-0.\overline{3}$

13. Order $0.84, -1.3, -\frac{4}{5}, \frac{1}{2}$, and -1.5 from least to greatest.

14. Order $-3\frac{1}{3}, 5\frac{1}{2}, 0, \frac{-7}{4}$, and $5\frac{5}{6}$ from greatest to least.

15. Martin is working on a research report. He has completed $\frac{2}{3}$ of the report. Is he more or less than $\frac{4}{5}$ of the way finished? Explain.

Take It to the NET
www More Practice
www.scottforesman.com

Set 8-4 (pages 414–415)

Draw a picture to show the main idea. Use the picture to choose an operation. Solve the problem.

Mark's Lawn and Garden Service

	Old Rates
Mowing	$10.00
Blowing/Sweeping	$5.00
Leaf Raking	$10.00
Tree Planting	ea. $20.00

1. Mark started his own lawn and garden service last summer. He wants to increase the amount he charges for each service shown on the chart by $2.00. With the new rates, how much would it cost a customer to have his yard mowed, 2 trees planted, and the driveway swept?

2. Micah bought and donated 5 basketballs as a contribution to his intramural team. Each basketball cost $9.20. Micah's father paid half of the final cost. How much did all the basketballs cost? How much did Micah pay?

Set 8-5 (pages 418–421)

1. $-4 + 3$	**2.** $-5 + (-4)$	**3.** $9 + (-9)$
4. $7 + 7$	**5.** $-6 + 12$	**6.** $-11 + (-16)$
7. $-4 + 10$	**8.** $-11 + 7$	**9.** $18 + (-28)$
10. $-8 + 10$	**11.** $24 + (-12)$	**12.** $-4 + 15$

13. One share of stock was $17 on Monday. During the week the stock price fell $3, then increased $5. What was the price of one share by the end of the week?

Set 8-6 (pages 422–425)

1. $-6 - 3$	**2.** $-7 - (-7)$	**3.** $3 - (-5)$
4. $-1 - (-10)$	**5.** $8 - 8$	**6.** $-2 - 3$
7. $12 - 6$	**8.** $4 - 8$	**9.** $-6 - 0$
10. $9 - (-3)$	**11.** $-2 - (-8)$	**12.** $-4 - 5$

13. Brendan read that the average temperature on the surface of Earth is 15°C. The average temperature on the surface of Mars is -50°C. Find the difference between the two temperatures.

Set 8-7 (pages 426–427)

1. $-9 \times (-6)$	**2.** $7 \times (-12)$	**3.** $-4 \times (-15)$
4. 4×25	**5.** $8 \times (-8)$	**6.** -43×0
7. $21 \times (-6)$	**8.** $-9 \times (-3)$	**9.** -2×32
10. $-1 \times (-11)$	**11.** $-2 \times (-8)$	**12.** -10×22

13. Use order of operations to compute $-8 + (-5) \times (-3) - 6$.

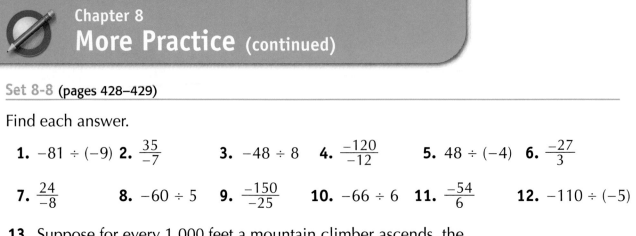

Set 8-8 (pages 428–429)

Find each answer.

1. $-81 \div (-9)$ **2.** $\frac{35}{-7}$ **3.** $-48 \div 8$ **4.** $\frac{-120}{-12}$ **5.** $48 \div (-4)$ **6.** $\frac{-27}{3}$

7. $\frac{24}{-8}$ **8.** $-60 \div 5$ **9.** $\frac{-150}{-25}$ **10.** $-66 \div 6$ **11.** $\frac{-54}{6}$ **12.** $-110 \div (-5)$

13. Suppose for every 1,000 feet a mountain climber ascends, the temperature drops 4°F. How much will the temperature drop if a climber ascends 5,000 feet?

Set 8-9 (pages 430–431)

Solve each equation.

1. $\frac{b}{4} = -6$ **2.** $-4n = 36$ **3.** $s - (-12) = 24$ **4.** $m + 4 = -13$

5. $-3c = 36$ **6.** $x + 7 = 5$ **7.** $n \div 5 = -16$ **8.** $\frac{a}{15} = -3$

9. A plane flying at an elevation of 3,000 feet is preparing to land at the airport. The descent takes 6 minutes. Use the equation $6n = -3,000$ to find the number of feet per minute the plane will descend.

Set 8-10 (pages 434–437)

Work backward to solve each problem.

1. Jackie jogged a total of 15 miles over a five-day period. Each day she jogged 0.25 mile more than she did each previous day. On the last day she jogged 3.5 miles. How many miles did Jackie jog each day?

2. Rick bought a package of lined paper, a set of 2 pens, 1 protractor, and some folders for school. Use the data in the table to find how many folders Rick bought, if he paid the clerk $10.00 and received $1.71 in change.

Supplies	Price with Tax
Lined paper	$0.75 per pack
Pens	$3.89 set of 2
Protractor	$1.29
Folder	$0.59

3. Cort wants to finish mowing three lawns by 3:00 P.M. It takes him $1\frac{1}{2}$ hours to mow the first lawn, and twice as long to mow the second lawn. The third lawn, which is across the street, takes him $1\frac{1}{4}$ hours to mow. Cort plans to take a $\frac{1}{2}$-hour break between the second and third lawns. What time should he plan to start mowing?

Write the ordered pair for each point.

1. A   **2.** B   **3.** C

4. D   **5.** E   **6.** F

7. G   **8.** H   **9.** I

10. K   **11.** L   **12.** M

13. Graph and label the points N (2, 3), P (0, 2), Q (−5, 0), R (−2, −3), and S (4, −4) on the same coordinate plane.

Tell whether each relation is a function.

1.

x	−3	−1	3	3
y	0	1	0	3

2.

x	−2	−1	0	1
y	−5	−4	−3	−2

3.

x	−2	0	2	4
y	5	5	5	5

Copy and complete the table for each equation.

4. $y = x + 10$

x	y
−10	
−2	
0	
2	

5. $y = 7x$

x	y
−1	
0	
1	
5	

6. $y = x - 7$

x	y
−3	
0	
3	
7	

7. Janelle deposits $35 in her savings account. Complete the table below to find the total amount, T, she has saved when m months have passed. Use the equation $T = 35m$.

m	1	3	6	9	12
T					

Make a T-table with at least three ordered pairs for each equation. Then graph each equation.

1. $y = -\dfrac{x}{2}$ **2.** $y = x - (-4)$ **3.** $y = 0$ **4.** $y = 8 - x$ **5.** $y = \dfrac{x}{3}$

6. Explain why (6, −1) is not a point on the graph of the equation $y = 4 - x$.

DIAGNOSING READINESS

A Vocabulary
(Grade 5)

Choose the best term from the box.

1. A ___?___ is a polygon with three sides.

2. A pair of items that are the same size and shape are described as ___?___.

3. A(n) ___?___ is formed by two rays that have the same endpoint.

4. Two figures that are the same shape with sides that are proportional are called ___?___ figures.

Vocabulary

- **triangle** *(Grade 5)*   • **similar** *(Grade 5)*
- **quadrilateral** *(Grade 5)*   • **angle** *(Grade 5)*
- **congruent** *(Grade 5)*

B Adding and Subtracting Whole Numbers
(pages 32–35)

Add or subtract mentally.

5. $64 + 30 + 86$ **6.** $180 - (28 + 85)$

7. $90 + 75 + 90$ **8.** $360 - (125 + 210)$

9. $66 + 31 - 97$ **10.** $270 - (103 + 49)$

11. $360 - 2(55)$ **12.** $101 + 24 + 55$

13. To train for a triathalon, Dan swam for 6 miles, biked for 38 miles, and ran for 14 miles. How many total miles did Dan cover?

14. A triangle has sides measuring 70 feet, 240 feet, and 250 feet. Find the sum of the sides.

Do You Know...

How many rooms were planned to be in Neuschwanstein Castle?

You will find out in Lesson 9-15.

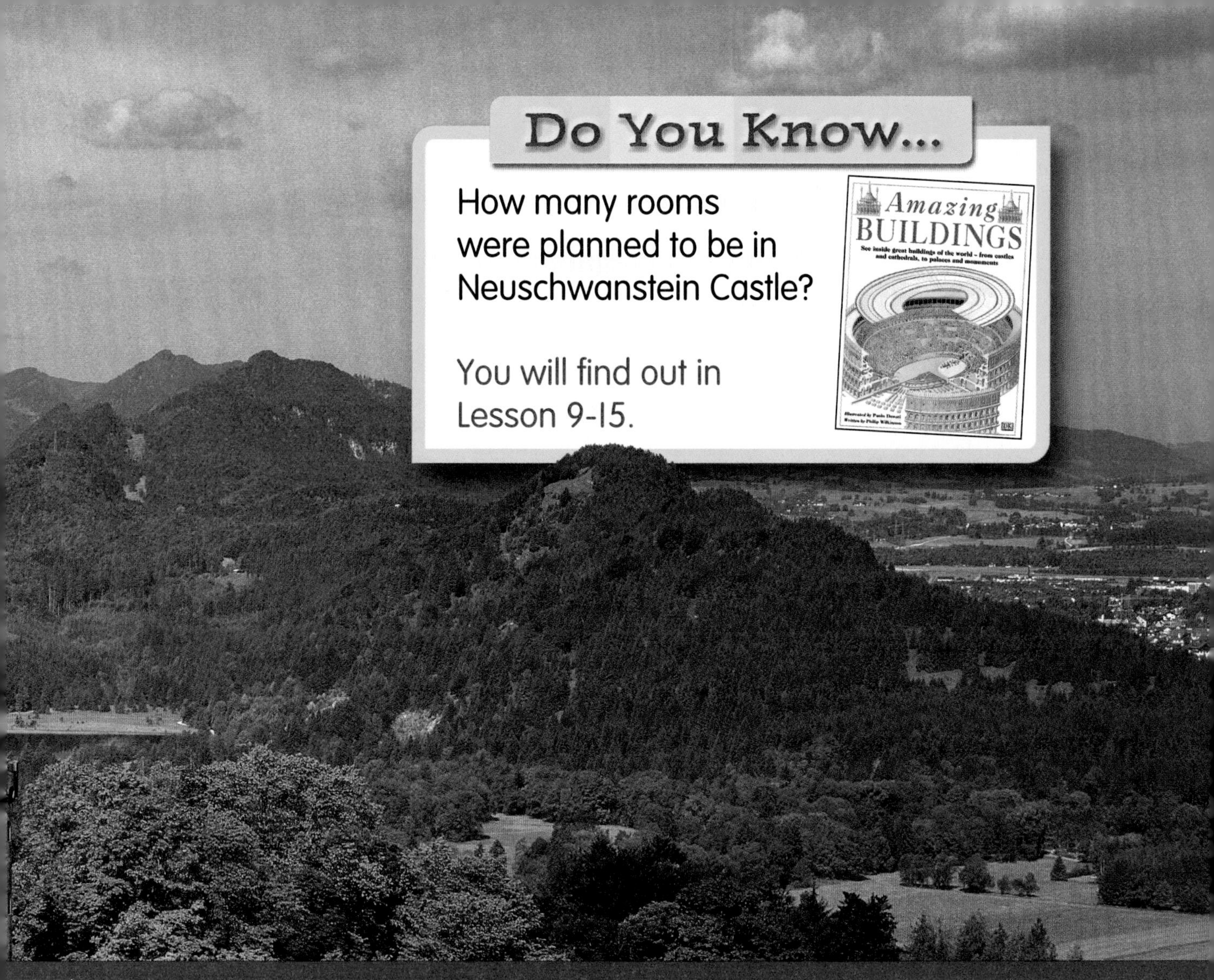

C Graphing and Measurement

(page 440, Grade 5)

Graph each ordered pair on a coordinate grid.

15. $R(2, 0)$ **16.** $S(5, -2)$

17. $M(-3, 1)$ **18.** $V(-2, -1)$

19. $P(0, 3)$ **20.** $W(1, 4)$

21. In which quadrant does a point with a negative x-coordinate and a positive y-coordinate lie?

22. Draw two parallel line segments $\overline{AB}$ and $\overline{CD}$. Make $\overline{AB}$ 3 inches long and $\overline{CD}$ $4\frac{1}{2}$ inches long.

D Solving Equations

(pages 48–51, 318–321)

Solve for x.

23. $x + 52 = 90$

24. $16 + x + 71 = 180$

25. $x + 102 = 180$

26. $x + 18 = 90$

27. $14 + 29 + x = 180$

28. $x + 72 + 90 = 180$

29. $123 + 76 + 123 + x = 360$

30. $122 + 88 = x + 94$

31. Explain how to solve the proportion $\frac{x}{16} = \frac{4}{20}$.

Vocabulary
• point
• line
• ray
• line segment
• midpoint
• congruent line segments
• plane
• intersecting lines
• parallel lines
• perpendicular lines
• skew lines

Materials
• ruler or straight edge

Think It Through
I need to **use mathematics vocabulary precisely** to understand and describe geometric relationships.

Geometric Ideas

LEARN

Which terms are commonly used in geometry?

	What You **Draw**	What You **Say**	What You **Write**
Point An exact location in space	•*P*	"point *P*"	*P* or point *P*
Line A straight path of points that goes on forever in two directions.	*X* •——→ *Y*	"line *XY*"	$\overleftrightarrow{XY}$ (or $\overleftrightarrow{YX}$)
Ray Part of a line with one endpoint, extending forever in only one direction	*E* •——→ *F*	"ray *EF*"	$\overrightarrow{EF}$
Line segment Part of a line with two endpoints	*R* •——• *Q*	"line segment *RQ*" (or "segment *RQ*")	$\overline{RQ}$ (or $\overline{QR}$) *RQ* without the bar over it refers to the length of $\overline{RQ}$.
Midpoint The point halfway between the endpoints of a line segment	•——•——• *E*	"midpoint *E*"	*E* or midpoint *E*
Congruent line segments Line segments with the same length	*M* •——• *N* *T* •——• *W*	"line segment *MN* is congruent to line segment *TW*"	$\overline{MN} \cong \overline{TW}$
Plane A flat surface that extends forever in all directions	•*B* •*C* •*A*	"plane *ABC*"	⧄ *ABC*

✔ Talk About It

1. Why are there two possible names shown for both the line and the line segment on page 472, but only one for the ray?

2. Which statement is written correctly, $AB = 8$ ft or $\overline{AB} = 8$ ft?

3. Name two congruent segments in the diagram at the right. What can you conclude about point H?

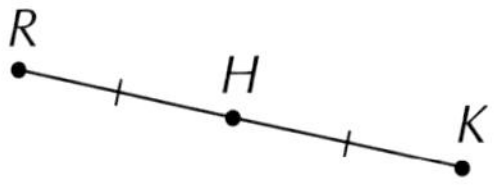

How do you classify pairs of lines?

Lines can be classified by their relationship to other lines. These special relationships also apply to line segments and rays.

	What You **Draw**	What You **Say**	What You **Write**
Intersecting lines pass through the same point.	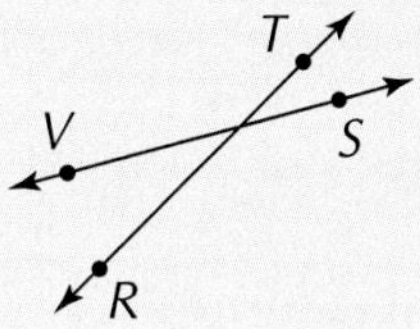	"Line VS intersects line RT."	$\overleftrightarrow{VS}$ intersects $\overleftrightarrow{RT}$.
Parallel lines are in the same plane but do not intersect.	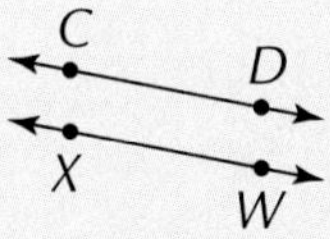	"Line CD is parallel to line XW."	$\overleftrightarrow{CD} \parallel \overleftrightarrow{XW}$
Perpendicular lines are intersecting lines that form right angles (square corners).	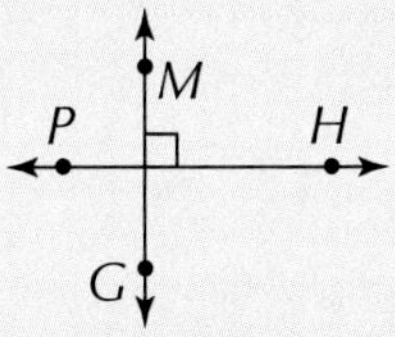	"Line MG is perpendicular to line PH."	$\overleftrightarrow{MG} \perp \overleftrightarrow{PH}$
Skew lines lie in different planes. They do not intersect and are not parallel.	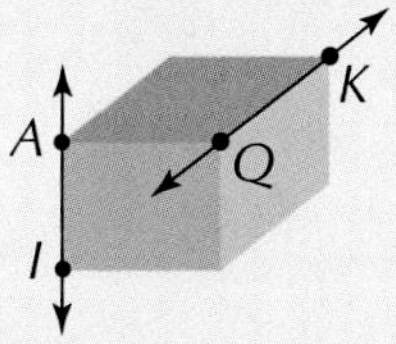	"Line AJ and line QK are skew."	$\overleftrightarrow{AJ}$ and $\overleftrightarrow{QK}$ are skew.

✔ Talk About It

4. In your classroom, what would be an example of parallel line segments? perpendicular line segments? skew line segments?

5. **Reasoning** The intersection of two different lines is a point. What is the intersection of two different planes?

Name the following.

1.
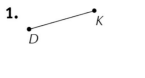

2.

3. *B*

4. *N* *Y*

Use the cube at the right. Are the line segments listed below parallel, perpendicular, or skew?

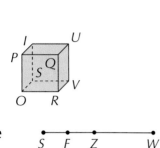

5. $\overline{QR}$ and $\overline{UV}$ **6.** $\overline{PQ}$ and $\overline{UV}$ **7.** $\overline{PO}$ and $\overline{PQ}$

8. Reasoning Point *Z* is the midpoint of $\overline{SW}$, and point *F* is the midpoint of $\overline{SZ}$. If *SW* = 20 cm, find *SF*.

S   F   Z   W

PRACTICE   *For more practice, see Set 9-1 on p. 536.*

Ⓐ Skills and Understanding

Use the diagram at the right. Name the following.

9. three rays   **10.** three line segments

11. two perpendicular lines   **12.** two parallel line segments

13. two lines that intersect $\overleftrightarrow{CM}$

Draw a diagram to illustrate each situation.

14. $\overline{PQ} \cong \overline{ST}$ **15.** $\overrightarrow{GY} \perp \overrightarrow{GU}$ **16.** $\overleftrightarrow{VK} \parallel \overleftrightarrow{EN}$

17. $\overleftrightarrow{XY}$ intersects $\overleftrightarrow{UW}$ at point *K*   **18.** Point *C* is the midpoint of $\overline{DN}$.

19. Reasoning How many different lines can be drawn through just one point? How many different lines can be drawn through two points?

Ⓑ Reasoning and Problem Solving

🦋 Math and Science

Optical illusions trick the brain into misjudging the properties of a figure.

20. In Figure 1, which red line segment is longest?

21. In Figure 2, are the green line segments parallel?

22. **Writing in Math** Diane said, "Two lines that don't intersect are parallel." Is she right? Explain.

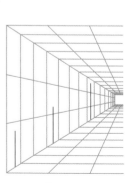

Figure 1

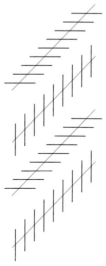

Figure 2

Extensions

Planes can be classified by their relationship to other planes.

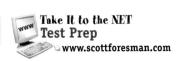

Intersecting planes   **Perpendicular planes**   **Parallel planes**

Refer to the building drawn at the right. Give an example of parts of the building that suggest each pair of planes.

23. Parallel planes   **24.** Perpendicular planes

25. Intersecting, but not perpendicular, planes

Mixed Review and Test Prep

 Take It to the NET Test Prep www.scottforesman.com

26. Algebra Graph the equation $y = x - 3$.

27. Which of the following numbers represents a value greater than 1?

    A. $3 \div 10$ **B.** 85%   **C.** $4 \div 3$ **D.** 0.10

Enrichment

Networks

Materials: Tracing paper

1. Place a sheet of tracing paper over Figure 1. Can you trace over each segment without lifting your pencil and without retracing any segment? Can you trace Figure 2?

Figures 1 and 2 are examples of **networks.** A network is a set of points connected by paths. The following steps can be used to determine if a network can be traced as described in Exercise 1.

Figure 1   **Figure 2**

• Count the number of paths at each point, as shown at the right.

• How many points have an odd number of paths? If there are more than 2, the network cannot be traced.

←2 paths
←4 paths
←3 paths

2. Which figures below can be traced without retracing or lifting your pencil?

Figure 3   **Figure 4**   **Figure 5**   **Figure 6**

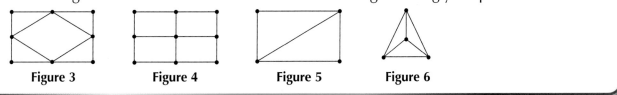

Vocabulary
- angle
- sides
- vertex
- degrees
- acute angle
- right angle
- obtuse angle
- straight angle

Materials
- ruler or straightedge
- protractor
- tracing paper

Measuring and Drawing Angles

LEARN

Activity

How can you measure angles?

An **angle** is formed by two rays that have the same endpoint. Angle *DEF* (written ∠*DEF*) is shown at the right. Its **sides** are $\overrightarrow{ED}$ and $\overrightarrow{EF}$. Point *E* is called the **vertex** (plural: vertices). The **interior** and **exterior** of ∠*DEF* are also shown.

We usually measure angles in **degrees** (°).

1° angle

a. Trace each angle and extend its sides. Follow the directions below to measure the angle with a **protractor**.

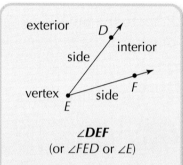

exterior
side
vertex
interior
side

∠**DEF**
(or ∠*FED* or ∠*E*)

When three letters are used, the middle letter names the vertex.

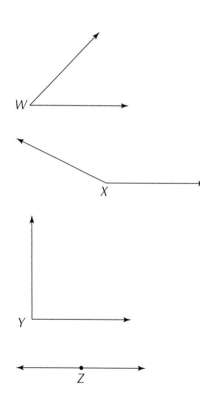

W

X

Y

Z

To Measure an Angle

Place the protractor's center on the angle's vertex.

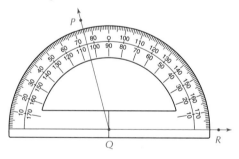

Place the 0° mark on one side of the angle. Read the measure where the other side of the angle crosses the protractor.
The measure of ∠*PQR* is 105°.

You can write this as m∠*PQR* = 105°.

b. There are two scales of numbers on a protractor. How do you know which one to use?

c. Use the following classifications to classify the four angles you measured.

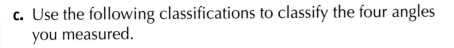

Acute angle
between 0° and 90°

Right angle
exactly 90°

Obtuse angle
between 90° and 180°

Straight angle
exactly 180°

How do you draw an angle with a given measure?

a. Follow the directions at the right to draw an angle with each measure.

52°   90°

165°   180°

b. Classify the four angles you drew.

To Draw an Angle of 68°

Draw a ray. Place the protractor's center on the endpoint. Line up the ray with the 0° mark. Using the degree scale, place a point at 68°. Draw the other ray.

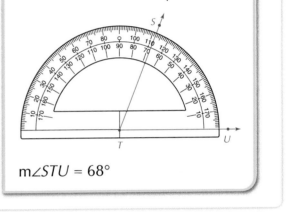

m∠STU = 68°

CHECK ✓

For another example, see Set 9-2 on p. 532.

Classify each angle as acute, right, obtuse, or straight. Then measure the angle. (Hint: Trace each angle and draw longer sides if necessary.)

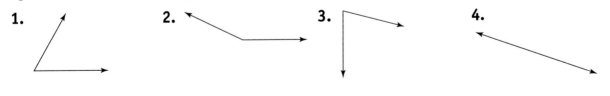

1.   **2.**   **3.**   **4.**

Draw an angle with each measure.

5. 112°   **6.** 85°   **7.** 137°   **8.** 20°

9. Reasoning Point *P* is in the same plane as ∠FGH, but it is not in the interior or the exterior of the angle. Where is point *P* located?

A Skills and Understanding

Classify each angle as acute, right, obtuse, or straight. Then measure the angle. (Hint: Trace each angle and draw longer sides if necessary.)

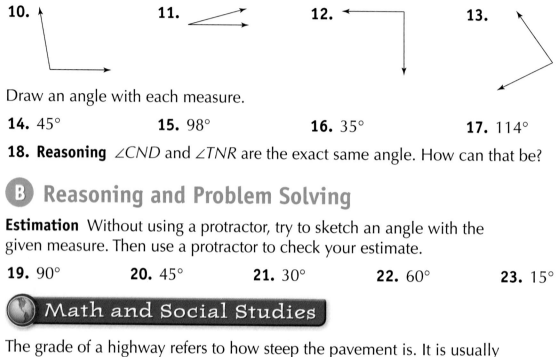

10.   **11.**   **12.**   **13.**

Draw an angle with each measure.

14. 45°   **15.** 98°   **16.** 35°   **17.** 114°

18. Reasoning ∠*CND* and ∠*TNR* are the exact same angle. How can that be?

B Reasoning and Problem Solving

Estimation Without using a protractor, try to sketch an angle with the given measure. Then use a protractor to check your estimate.

19. 90°   **20.** 45°   **21.** 30°   **22.** 60°   **23.** 15°

Math and Social Studies

The grade of a highway refers to how steep the pavement is. It is usually given as a percent. Highway grades of 5% or greater require extreme caution by truck drivers. A grade steeper than 10% is rarely found on highways.

A grade of 6% is modeled in the scale drawing below.

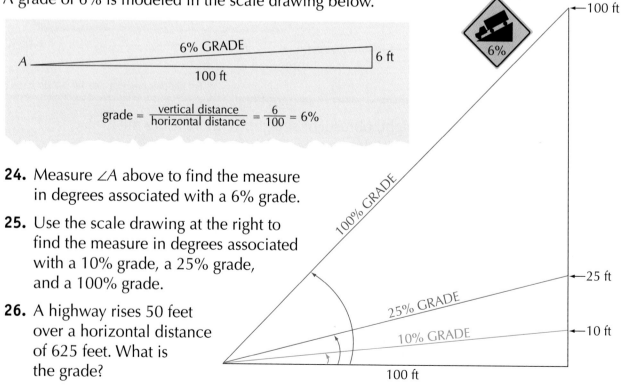

6% GRADE

A _____ 6 ft

100 ft

$$\text{grade} = \frac{\text{vertical distance}}{\text{horizontal distance}} = \frac{6}{100} = 6\%$$

24. Measure ∠*A* above to find the measure in degrees associated with a 6% grade.

25. Use the scale drawing at the right to find the measure in degrees associated with a 10% grade, a 25% grade, and a 100% grade.

26. A highway rises 50 feet over a horizontal distance of 625 feet. What is the grade?

100% GRADE

25% GRADE

10% GRADE

100 ft

—100 ft

—25 ft

—10 ft

6%

27. Writing in Math Tracy says that the measure of ∠XYZ is 130°. Teruo says it's 50°. Which student is right? What mistake did the other student make?

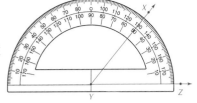

TEST TALK

Think It Through
I can **make an organized list** and then **look for a pattern.**

C Extensions

28. How many *different* angles are formed by three rays with a common endpoint? 4 rays? 5 rays? 6 rays?

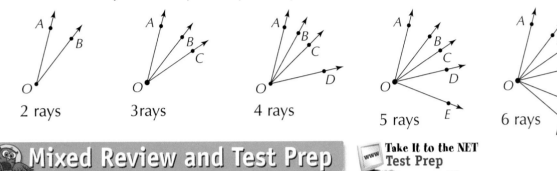

2 rays   3 rays   4 rays   5 rays   6 rays

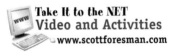

Mixed Review and Test Prep

Take It to the NET
Test Prep
www.scottforesman.com

29. Are $\overline{GH}$ and $\overline{MN}$ congruent? How do you know?

G   H   M   N

30. Algebra Which expression means "9 less than a number"?

A. $9n$ **B.** $n - 9$ **C.** $9 - n$ **D.** $\dfrac{n}{9}$

Discovery
CHANNEL
SCHOOL™

Discover Math in Your World

Take It to the NET
Video and Activities
www.scottforesman.com

The Siege Machine

The trebuchet was the successor of the catapult, capable of throwing heavier objects farther and with more accuracy. Constructed near an enemy's castle during a siege, the trebuchet was used to hurl decaying matter into the castle complex with the intent to spread disease.

1. The throwing range of the trebuchet is a function of the loading angle, which is the angle formed by the projectile arm and the ground. Classify a loading angle of 45°.

2. A projectile arm can be mounted on a supporting frame of parallel and perpendicular timbers. Classify the angle formed by perpendicular line segments.

Key Idea
Some pairs of angles have special relationships based on their position or their measures.

Vocabulary
• congruent angles
• vertical angles
• adjacent angles
• complementary angles
• supplementary angles

Angle Pairs

LEARN

What are some special pairs of angles?

Understanding the relationships between certain pairs of angles can help you determine angle measures.

✓ **WARM UP**

Trace the diagram.

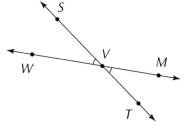

1. Use a protractor to measure ∠*PKT* and ∠*XKV*.

2. Use a protractor to measure ∠*PKX* and ∠*TKV*.

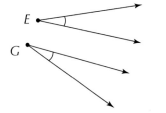

Congruent angles have the same measure. You can write ∠*E* ≅ ∠*G*. The little symbols inside the angles, called arcs, are drawn to show congruent angles.

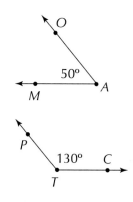

Vertical angles are a pair of angles formed by intersecting lines. They have no side in common. Vertical angles are congruent. ∠*WVS* and ∠*TVM* are vertical angles. So are ∠*WVT* and ∠*SVM*.

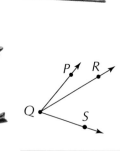

Adjacent angles are a pair of angles with a common vertex and a common side, but no common interior points. ∠*PQR* and ∠*RQS* are adjacent angles.

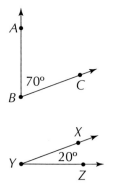

Complementary angles are two angles whose measures add up to 90°. ∠*ABC* and ∠*XYZ* are complementary angles.

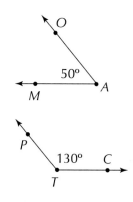

Supplementary angles are two angles whose measures add up to 180°. ∠*OAM* and ∠*PTC* are supplementary angles.

✔ Talk About It

1. When two lines intersect, how many pairs of vertical angles are formed?

2. **Reasoning** Which pair of adjacent angles at the right are complementary? Which are supplementary? How do you know?

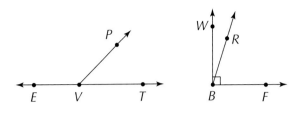

How can you find measures in special pairs of angles?

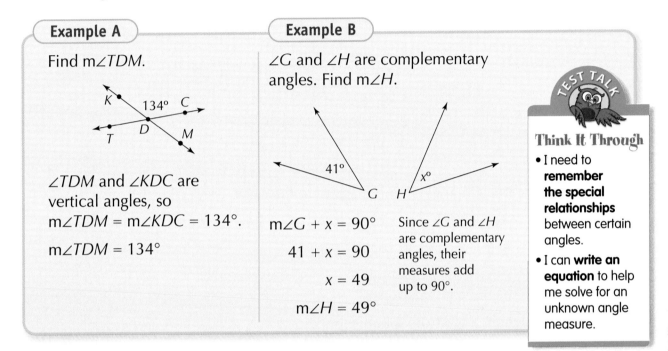

Example A

Find m∠TDM.

∠TDM and ∠KDC are vertical angles, so
m∠TDM = m∠KDC = 134°.

m∠TDM = 134°

Example B

∠G and ∠H are complementary angles. Find m∠H.

m∠G + x = 90°   Since ∠G and ∠H are complementary angles, their measures add up to 90°.

41 + x = 90

x = 49

m∠H = 49°

Think It Through
- I need to **remember the special relationships** between certain angles.
- I can **write an equation** to help me solve for an unknown angle measure.

✔ Talk About It

3. ∠U and ∠V are supplementary and m∠U = 138°. Find m∠V.

CHECK ✓

For another example, see Set 9-3 on p. 532.

Find x.

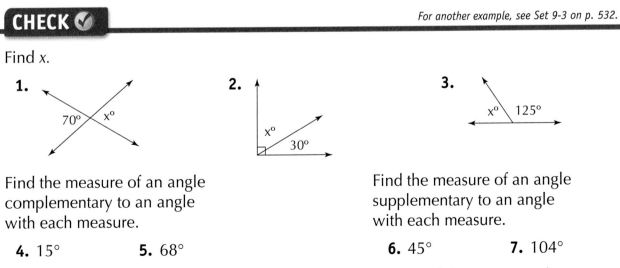

1.   70°   x°

2.   x°   30°

3.   x°   125°

Find the measure of an angle complementary to an angle with each measure.

4. 15°   5. 68°

Find the measure of an angle supplementary to an angle with each measure.

6. 45°   7. 104°

8. **Reasoning** Two congruent angles are complementary. Find the measure of each angle.

Ⓐ Skills and Understanding

Find *x*.

9.

128°

x°

10.

x° / 66°

11.

22°

x°

Find the measure of an angle complementary to an angle with each measure.

12. 13°   **13.** 71°   **14.** 6°   **15.** 88°

Find the measure of an angle supplementary to an angle with each measure.

16. 95°   **17.** 111°   **18.** 37°   **19.** 175°

20. Reasoning Are all right angles congruent? Explain?

Ⓑ Reasoning and Problem Solving

Find the measure of each angle in the diagram at the right.

21. ∠PON   **22.** ∠ROQ   **23.** ∠TON   **24.** ∠TOR

25. Are ∠ROQ and ∠TOS vertical angles? Explain.

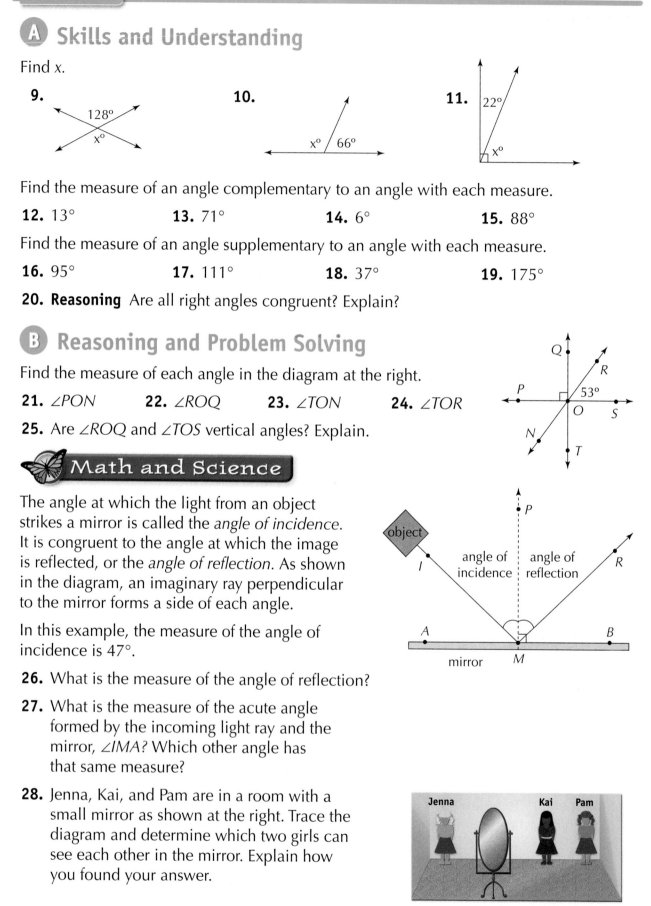

Math and Science

The angle at which the light from an object strikes a mirror is called the *angle of incidence*. It is congruent to the angle at which the image is reflected, or the *angle of reflection*. As shown in the diagram, an imaginary ray perpendicular to the mirror forms a side of each angle.

In this example, the measure of the angle of incidence is 47°.

26. What is the measure of the angle of reflection?

27. What is the measure of the acute angle formed by the incoming light ray and the mirror, ∠IMA? Which other angle has that same measure?

28. Jenna, Kai, and Pam are in a room with a small mirror as shown at the right. Trace the diagram and determine which two girls can see each other in the mirror. Explain how you found your answer.

29. <u>Writing in Math</u> Can two acute angles be supplementary? Can two obtuse angles be supplementary? Explain.

C Extensions

Draw $\overleftrightarrow{AB}$, $\overleftrightarrow{CD}$, and $\overleftrightarrow{EF}$ all intersecting in point *P*.

30. Identify four different pairs of adjacent angles.

31. Identify three different pairs of supplementary angles.

32. Identify all the pairs of vertical angles.

33. Are there any complementary angles in your diagram? If so, identify them.

Mixed Review and Test Prep

Take It to the NET
Test Prep
www.scottforesman.com

34. Write four and nineteen thousandths in standard form.

35. Estimation What is the best estimate of the measure of ∠*FGH*?

A. 30°   **B.** 60°   **C.** 90°   **D.** 120°

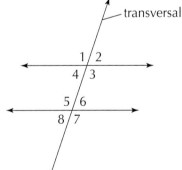

Enrichment

> Sometimes, numbers are used as a convenient way to name angles. A number without a degree symbol written in the angle's interior is a label, not a measure.

Angles and Parallel Lines

Special names are given to pairs of angles formed by two lines that are intersected by a third line, called a **transversal.**

On a sheet of notebook paper, draw two parallel lines 2 to 3 inches apart. Then draw a transversal that is not perpendicular to the parallel lines. Label the angles as shown in the diagram.

1. Use a protractor to carefully measure both pairs of alternate interior angles. What do you notice?

2. Use a protractor to carefully measure both pairs of alternate exterior angles. What do you notice?

3. Use a protractor to carefully measure all four pairs of corresponding angles. What do you notice?

4. Repeat Exercises 1–3 with a new pair of parallel lines and transversal. Do you get the same results?

5. Would you get the same results if the lines are not parallel? Draw a new diagram and measure the angles to check.

alternate interior angles
∠4 and ∠6; ∠3 and ∠5

alternate exterior angles
∠1 and ∠7; ∠2 and ∠8

corresponding angles
∠1 and ∠5; ∠4 and ∠8;
∠2 and ∠6; ∠3 and ∠7

Key Idea
You can use a compass and straightedge to construct geometric figures.

Vocabulary
• construction
• arc
• perpendicular bisector
• angle bisector

Materials
• GeoTool™ or compass
• ruler or straightedge
• tracing paper

Think It Through
• I can **draw a picture** with a variety of geometric tools.
• I need to remember that **using numeric measures is not done in a construction.**

Constructions

LEARN

Activity

What are some constructions involving segments?

A **construction** is a geometric drawing made with just two tools: an unmarked ruler, called a **straightedge,** and a **compass.** A compass can be used to draw a circle or a part of a circle, called an **arc.**

compass

center | knob
slider

WARM UP

Draw an example of each figure.

1. $\overline{JK}$ 2. $\overrightarrow{AB}$

3. $\overleftrightarrow{NM}$ 4. $\angle DHQ$

a. Trace $\overline{AB}$. Then follow the steps to construct a segment congruent to $\overline{AB}$.

A ———————— B

STEP 1

Draw a line and label point P.

P

STEP 2

Adjust the compass to a setting equal to AB by placing the center of the compass on point A and moving the slider to point B. Tighten the knob.

A   B

STEP 3

Place the center at P and draw an arc that intersects the line. Label point Q, the point of intersection. $\overline{PQ} \cong \overline{AB}$

P   Q

The **perpendicular bisector** of a line segment is a line that is perpendicular to the segment and contains the segment's midpoint.

b. Trace $\overline{CD}$. Then follow the steps to construct the perpendicular bisector of $\overline{CD}$.

C ——— D

STEP 1

Adjust the compass to any setting greater than $\frac{1}{2}CD$. Place the center on C and draw an arc. With the same setting, place the center on D and draw another arc.

C   D

STEP 2

Label the points of intersection R and S. Draw $\overleftrightarrow{RS}$. $\overleftrightarrow{RS}$ is the perpendicular bisector of $\overline{CD}$.

R
C   D
S

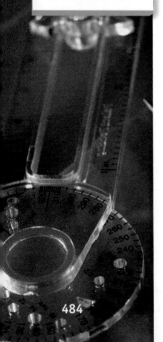

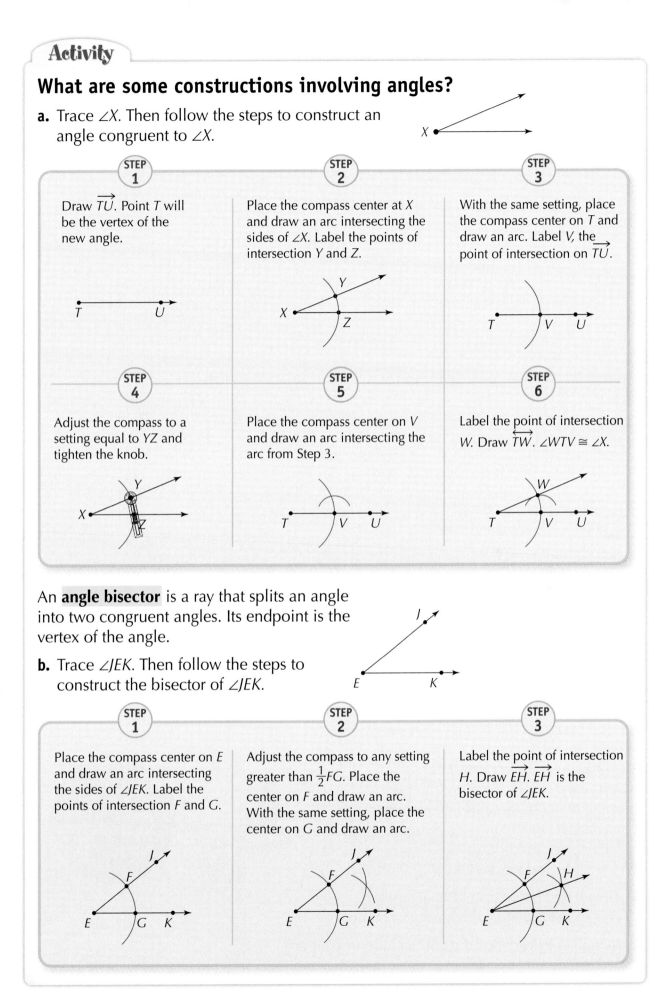

Activity

What are some constructions involving angles?

a. Trace ∠X. Then follow the steps to construct an angle congruent to ∠X.

STEP 1

Draw $\overrightarrow{TU}$. Point *T* will be the vertex of the new angle.

STEP 2

Place the compass center at *X* and draw an arc intersecting the sides of ∠X. Label the points of intersection *Y* and *Z*.

STEP 3

With the same setting, place the compass center on *T* and draw an arc. Label *V*, the point of intersection on $\overrightarrow{TU}$.

STEP 4

Adjust the compass to a setting equal to *YZ* and tighten the knob.

STEP 5

Place the compass center on *V* and draw an arc intersecting the arc from Step 3.

STEP 6

Label the point of intersection *W*. Draw $\overleftrightarrow{TW}$. ∠WTV ≅ ∠X.

An **angle bisector** is a ray that splits an angle into two congruent angles. Its endpoint is the vertex of the angle.

b. Trace ∠JEK. Then follow the steps to construct the bisector of ∠JEK.

STEP 1

Place the compass center on *E* and draw an arc intersecting the sides of ∠JEK. Label the points of intersection *F* and *G*.

STEP 2

Adjust the compass to any setting greater than $\frac{1}{2}FG$. Place the center on *F* and draw an arc. With the same setting, place the center on *G* and draw an arc.

STEP 3

Label the point of intersection *H*. Draw $\overrightarrow{EH}$. $\overrightarrow{EH}$ is the bisector of ∠JEK.

Trace $\overline{MP}$ and ∠V at the right.

1. Construct a segment congruent to $\overline{MP}$.

   M ●————————● P

2. Construct an angle congruent to ∠V.

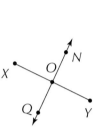

Make another tracing of $\overline{MP}$ and ∠V.

3. Construct the perpendicular bisector of $\overline{MP}$.

4. Construct the bisector of ∠V.

5. **Reasoning** $\overleftrightarrow{NQ}$ is the perpendicular bisector of $\overline{XY}$. What is the measure of ∠NOY? Which segments are congruent?

PRACTICE

For more practice, see Set 9-4 on p. 537.

A Skills and Understanding

Trace $\overline{HG}$ and ∠C at the right.

H ●————————● G

6. Construct a segment congruent to $\overline{HG}$.

7. Construct an angle congruent to ∠C.

Make another tracing of $\overline{HG}$ and ∠C.

8. Construct the perpendicular bisector of $\overline{HG}$.

9. Construct the bisector of ∠C.

10. **Reasoning** $\overrightarrow{QB}$ bisects ∠PQR. If m∠PQR = 82°, find m∠PQB.

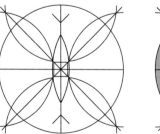

B Reasoning and Problem Solving

Math and Art

Beautiful designs can be created using a straightedge and a compass. The design shown here includes construction of a perpendicular bisector and four angle bisectors. Many of these design elements are used by people of many cultures to decorate such objects as pottery, eggs, jewelry, and window glass.

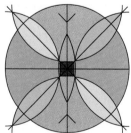

11. Create and color your own geometric design using a straightedge and a compass.

12. Which constructions did you include in your art?

486

13. **Writing in Math** Walt attempted to construct the

perpe

what he did wrong.

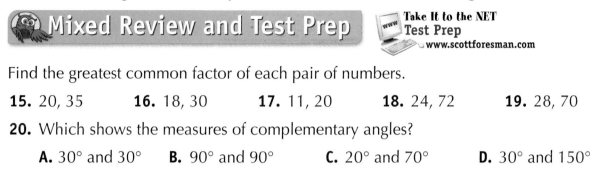

C Extensions

14. Draw an angle. Then use a protractor and ruler to draw the angle bisector.

Mixed Review and Test Prep

Take It to the NET
Test Prep
www.scottforesman.com

Find the greatest common factor of each pair of numbers.

15. 20, 35   **16.** 18, 30   **17.** 11, 20   **18.** 24, 72   **19.** 28, 70

20. Which shows the measures of complementary angles?

   A. 30° and 30°   **B.** 90° and 90°   **C.** 20° and 70°   **D.** 30° and 150°

Enrichment
Constructing Perpendicular Lines

Case 1 Draw a line. Mark and label a point P on the line. Follow the steps below to construct a line through P perpendicular to the line.

   Step 1 Place the center of the compass at P. Use the same setting to draw two arcs that intersect the line at points C and D.

   Step 2 Increase the compass setting and draw two intersecting arcs, one with the center at C and another with the center at D. Label the point of intersection E.

   Step 3 Draw $\overleftrightarrow{PE}$. $\overleftrightarrow{PE} \perp \overleftrightarrow{CD}$.

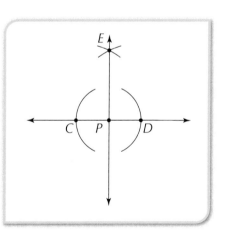

Case 2 Draw a line. Mark and label a point Q not on the line. Follow the steps below to construct a line through Q perpendicular to the line.

   Step 1 Place the center at Q. Use the same setting to draw two arcs that intersect the line at points V and W.

   Step 2 Using the same compass setting, draw two intersecting arcs, one with the center at V and another with the center at W. Label the point of intersection Z.

   Step 3 Draw $\overleftrightarrow{QZ}$. $\overleftrightarrow{QZ} \perp \overleftrightarrow{VW}$.

Construct $\overleftrightarrow{PQ} \perp \overleftrightarrow{MN}$ if

   1. P is on $\overleftrightarrow{MN}$.   **2.** P is not on $\overleftrightarrow{MN}$.

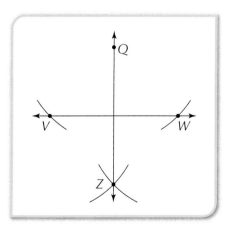

Understand Graphic Sources: Pictures

Understanding graphic sources such as pictures when you read in math can help you use the **problem-solving strategy, *Draw a Picture,*** in the next lesson.

In reading, understanding pictures can help you understand what you read. In math, understanding pictures can help you solve problems.

Look for information in the picture.

Sometimes labels or symbols are used to give some specific information.

12 ft   13 ft

5 ft

This picture includes some dimensions. For example, I can tell that the ladder is 13 feet long.

1. Can you tell any angle measures from the picture? Explain.

2. How high above the ground is the top of the ladder?

For 3–6, use the picture at the right.

3. What does the picture show?

4. What are the length and width of the kitchen? How did you use the picture to find your answer?

5. How many closets are located on this level of the house?

6. **Writing in Math** Explain how you would use the picture to find the length and width of this level of the house.

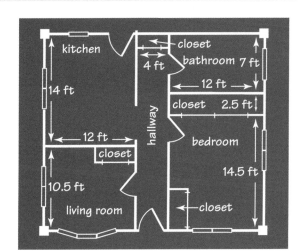

For 7–9, use the picture at the right.

7. How many suns are in both the square and the circle?

8. How many stars are in the triangle, but not in the square?

9. **Writing in Math** Could you add the number of stars in the square, the number of stars in the triangle, and the number of stars in the circle to find the total number of stars? Explain.

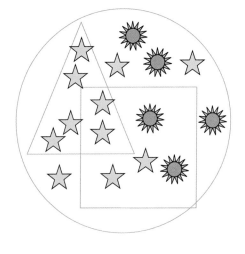

For 10–12, use the map of Texas.

10. What does the star symbol on the map represent? How do you know?

11. If you want to drive from Austin to Dallas, in which general direction should you travel?

12. **Writing in Math** Do you need to use the scale to determine if Dallas or San Antonio is farther from Houston? Explain.

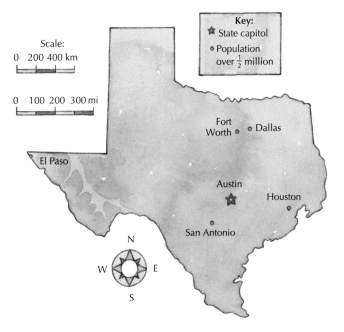

Problem-Solving Strategy

Understanding graphic sources
such as pictures

can help you with...

the problem-solving strategy,
Draw a Picture.

Key Idea
Learning how
and when to
draw a picture
can help you
solve problems.

Draw a Picture

LEARN

How do you draw a picture to solve a problem?

Box Pile Victoria was stacking boxes in a display window. The boxes were stacked in the shape of a triangle. How many boxes are needed altogether if there are 7 boxes on the bottom row?

bottom row: 3 boxes
total: 6 boxes

Read and Understand

What do you know? Boxes are being stacked.
3 on the bottom gives 6 altogether.

What are you trying to find? The total number of boxes needed if there are 7 boxes in the bottom row

Plan and Solve

What strategy will you use? Strategy: **Draw a Picture**

How to Draw a Picture

Step 1 Draw a picture to represent the situation.

Step 2 Finish the picture to show the action in the story.

Step 3 Interpret the picture to find the answer.

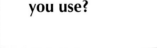

6 boxes

10 boxes

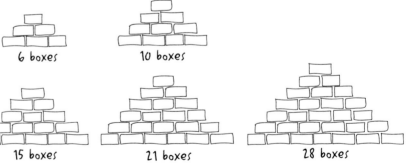

15 boxes

21 boxes

28 boxes

Answer: There are 28 boxes needed if there are 7 on the bottom row.

Look Back and Check

Is your answer reasonable? Yes, the pattern continues in the triangle shapes. The bottom row has one more box than the bottom row of the previous stack. I counted carefully.

✔ Talk About It

1. What pattern can be seen in the triangle shapes on page 490?

2. **Reasoning** Without drawing the picture, can you tell how many boxes are needed if there are 8 boxes on the bottom row? Explain.

CHECK ✓

For another example, see Set 9-5 on p. 533.

Draw a picture to solve the problem. Write the answer in a complete sentence.

1. **Duets** Mr. Taglia has six flute students. At a music festival, every student is to play one duet with every other student. Copy and finish the picture to determine how many duets will be performed.

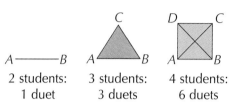

A———B   2 students: 1 duet

A△B   3 students: 3 duets

A▢B   4 students: 6 duets

PRACTICE

For more practice, see Set 9-5 on p. 537.

Draw a picture to solve the problem. Write the answer in a complete sentence.

2. A pilot is 3,800 ft below the clouds. A plane at a lower altitude is 5,500 ft above the ground. The clouds are at 12,000 ft altitude. Find the difference in altitude between the planes.

3. Suzanne needs to rent a bike. Wheels-to-Go charges $10 for the first hour and $4 for each additional hour. Bud's Bikes charges $18 for the first hour and $2 for each additional hour. Which plan would be less expensive if Suzanne rents the bike for 6 hours?

4. The sixth and seventh grades have the same number of volleyball teams. Each sixth-grade team is to play each seventh-grade team once. How many games will be played if there are 5 teams in each grade?

5. Mrs. Doering pays 40¢ each time she drives on the toll way. In how many ways can she make exactly 40¢ using only nickels, dimes, and quarters?

6. A tree branch divides into 2 branches. Each smaller branch divides into 3 branches. Each of these divides into 5 branches. How many branches of all sizes are there?

STRATEGIES

- **Show What You Know**
  Draw a Picture
  Make an Organized List
  Make a Table
  Make a Graph
  Act It Out or Use Objects
- **Look for a Pattern**
- **Try, Check, and Revise**
- **Write an Equation**
- **Use Logical Reasoning**
- **Solve a Simpler Problem**
- **Work Backward**

Choose a tool

Mental Math

Think It Through

Stuck? I won't give up. I can:
- Reread the problem.
- Tell what I know.
- Identify key facts and details.
- Tell the problem in my own words.
- Show the main idea.
- Try a different strategy.
- Retrace my steps.

Do You Know How?

Do You Understand?

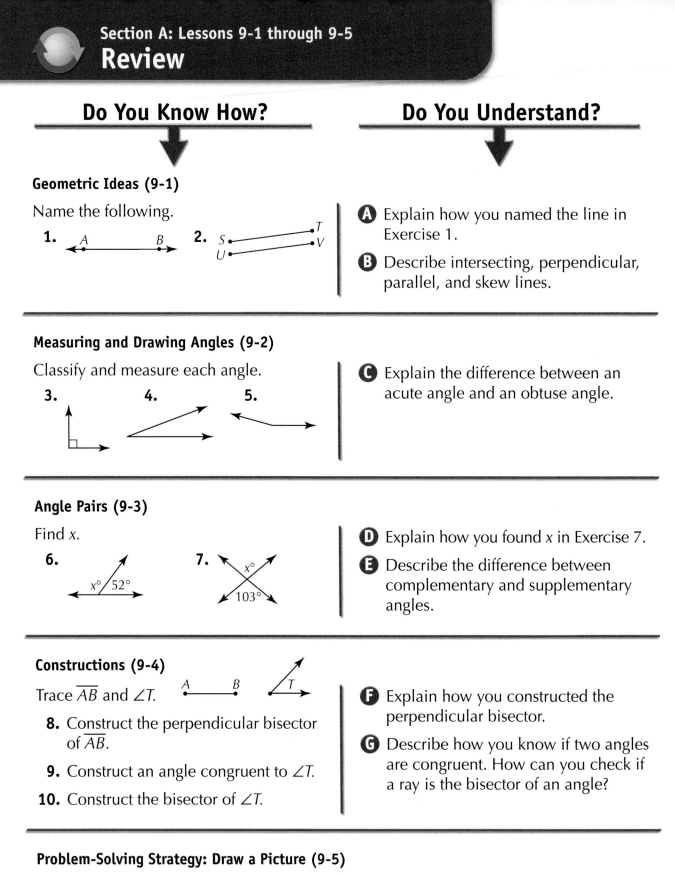

Geometric Ideas (9-1)

Name the following.

1. A ———— B

2. S ———— T
    U ———— V

A Explain how you named the line in Exercise 1.

B Describe intersecting, perpendicular, parallel, and skew lines.

Measuring and Drawing Angles (9-2)

Classify and measure each angle.

3.

4.

5.

C Explain the difference between an acute angle and an obtuse angle.

Angle Pairs (9-3)

Find x.

6. $x°$ $52°$

7. $x°$ $103°$

D Explain how you found x in Exercise 7.

E Describe the difference between complementary and supplementary angles.

Constructions (9-4)

Trace $\overline{AB}$ and $\angle T$.   A ——— B   T

8. Construct the perpendicular bisector of $\overline{AB}$.

9. Construct an angle congruent to $\angle T$.

10. Construct the bisector of $\angle T$.

F Explain how you constructed the perpendicular bisector.

G Describe how you know if two angles are congruent. How can you check if a ray is the bisector of an angle?

Problem-Solving Strategy: Draw a Picture (9-5)

Draw a picture to solve the problem.

11. Tony is building a fence around his garden. He places a picket every foot. If the garden is 3 ft wide and 5 ft long, how many pickets will Tony need?

H Explain the picture you drew. How did it help you solve the problem?

MULTIPLE CHOICE

1. Two lines that lie in different planes and do not pass through the same point are called __?__. (9-1)

    A. intersecting   **B.** parallel   **C.** perpendicular   **D.** skew

2. What is the measure of an angle supplementary to an angle with a measure of 78°? (9-3)

    A. 12°   **B.** 22°   **C.** 102°   **D.** 112°

FREE RESPONSE

Use the diagram at the right. Name the following. (9-1)

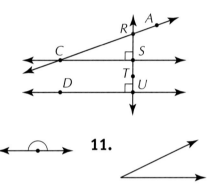

3. two rays   **4.** three lines   **5.** two parallel lines

6. two perpendicular line segments

Classify each angle as acute, right, obtuse, or straight. Then trace and measure the angle. (9-2)

7.   **8.**   **9.**   **10.**   **11.**

Draw or construct the following. (9-2, 9-3, 9-4)

12. an angle measuring 62°   **13.** vertical angles measuring 137° each

14. segment $\overline{EF}$ with a perpendicular bisector

15. the bisector of an angle measuring 130°.

Find x. (9-3)

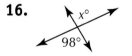   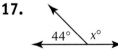   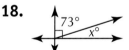

16.   **17.**   **18.**

Writing in Math

TEST TALK

Think It Through
I can **draw pictures to help explain my thinking.**

19. Katrina has a shelf that is 25 inches long. She places a figurine at each end and then spaces the other figurines 3 inches apart. How many figurines did Katrina put on the shelf if each figurine is 1 inch wide? Draw a picture to solve the problem and write the answer in a complete sentence. (9-5)

20. Can two vertical angles also be complementary angles? Why or why not? (9-3)

Vocabulary
• polygon
• triangle
• quadrilateral
• pentagon
• hexagon
• heptagon
• octagon
• nonagon
• decagon
• dodecagon
• diagonal
• regular polygon

Materials
• compass
• ruler or straightedge

Think It Through
I can **draw a picture** to show an example of each type of polygon.

Polygons

LEARN

Activity

How do you identify polygons?

A **polygon** is a closed plane figure made up of line segments. A polygon is identified according to how many sides it has. Some polygons have special names.

triangle	3 sides
quadrilateral	4 sides
pentagon	5 sides
hexagon	6 sides
heptagon	7 sides
octagon	8 sides
nonagon	9 sides
decagon	10 sides
dodecagon	12 sides

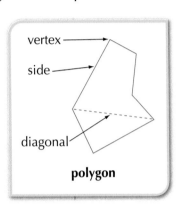

polygon

A **diagonal** is a line segment that connects two vertices of a polygon and is not a side.

A **regular polygon** has sides of equal length and angles of equal measure.

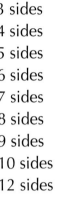

regular polygon

a. Draw and label an example of a heptagon, a nonagon, and a decagon.

b. Draw a pentagon. Then draw all of its diagonals.

c. Follow the steps below to construct a regular hexagon.

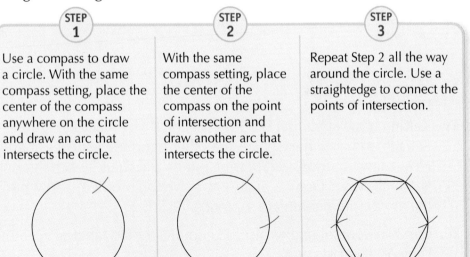

STEP 1	STEP 2	STEP 3
Use a compass to draw a circle. With the same compass setting, place the center of the compass anywhere on the circle and draw an arc that intersects the circle.	With the same compass setting, place the center of the compass on the point of intersection and draw another arc that intersects the circle.	Repeat Step 2 all the way around the circle. Use a straightedge to connect the points of intersection.

Name each polygon. Then tell if it appears to be a regular polygon.

1.   **2.**   **3.**   **4.**   **5.**

6. Reasoning How many angles are there in an *n*-sided polygon?

PRACTICE   For more practice, see Set 9-6 on p. 537.

Ⓐ Skills and Understanding

Name each polygon. Then tell if it appears to be a regular polygon.

7.   **8.**   **9.**   **10.**   **11.**

12. Reasoning Draw a closed figure that is not a polygon.

Ⓑ Reasoning and Problem Solving

13. Draw a figure that is not a polygon but is made up of 5 line segments.

14. If you draw one diagonal in a quadrilateral, what polygon is formed twice? What happens if you draw a diagonal in a pentagon? a hexagon?

Constructions For Exercises 15 and 16, do the construction on page 494. Then extend it to construct each figure.

15. regular triangle   **16.** regular dodecagon

From *one* vertex of the given regular figure, how many diagonals can you draw?

17. quadrilateral **18.** pentagon   **19.** hexagon   **20.** decagon   **21.** *n*-gon

22. Writing in Math Is the figure at the right a regular hexagon? Explain.

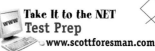

Think It Through
I can **look for a pattern** to help me count diagonals.

Mixed Review and Test Prep   Take It to the NET
Test Prep
www.scottforesman.com

23. Draw an obtuse angle. Construct the angle bisector.

24. Draw a picture to solve the problem. Six people are competing in a chess tournament. If every person plays every other person once, how many chess games will be played?

A. 6   **B.** 12   **C.** 15   **D.** 24

Key Idea
Understanding some special relationships will help you to draw and classify triangles, and find missing angles.

Vocabulary
• acute triangle
• right triangle
• obtuse triangle
• equilateral triangle
• isosceles triangle
• scalene triangle

Materials
• ruler
• protractor
• scissors

Think It Through
I can use additional sample triangles to **try, check, and revise** my prediction.

Triangles

LEARN

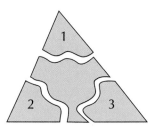

✓ **WARM UP**
Use a protractor to draw an angle with the given measure.

1. 75°   2. 24°

3. 90°   4. 150°

Activity

What is the sum of the measures of the angles of a triangle?

a. Use a ruler to draw a large triangle.

b. Cut out two identical copies of the triangle. Label the angles in each triangle 1, 2, and 3.

c. Tear off each angle of one triangle. Position the angles as three adjacent angles.

d. What appears to be true about the sum of the measures of the three angles?

e. Check your prediction by using a protractor to measure each of the angles in the matching triangle. Record the measures. What is the sum of the measures?

f. Repeat Steps a–e with two more triangles.

g. In each triangle, what is the sum of the measures of the angles?

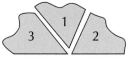

How can you find angle measures in a triangle?

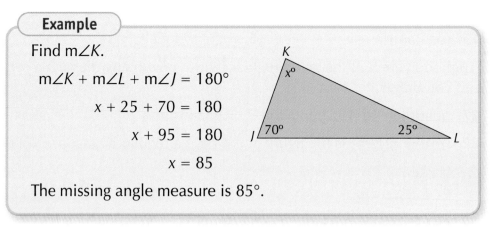

Example

Find m∠K.

m∠K + m∠L + m∠J = 180°

x + 25 + 70 = 180

x + 95 = 180

x = 85

The missing angle measure is 85°.

✓ **Talk About It**

1. In the Example, explain how to solve the equation x + 95 = 180.

2. Can a triangle have two right angles? two obtuse angles? Explain.

Activity

How can you draw and classify triangles?

Triangles can be classified by their angles or their sides.

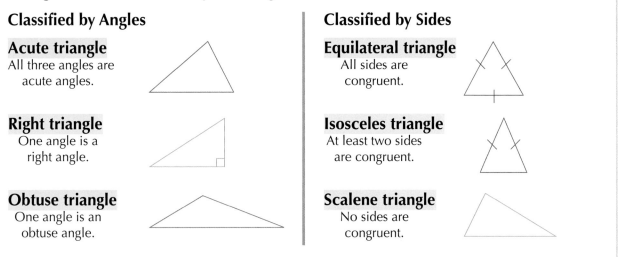

Classified by Angles

Acute triangle
All three angles are acute angles.

Right triangle
One angle is a right angle.

Obtuse triangle
One angle is an obtuse angle.

Classified by Sides

Equilateral triangle
All sides are congruent.

Isosceles triangle
At least two sides are congruent.

Scalene triangle
No sides are congruent.

Follow Steps a–c to draw a triangle with a 5-cm side between 40° and 50° angles.

a. Draw a 5-cm segment.

b. Draw a 40° angle at one end of the segment and a 50° angle at the other end. Extend the sides until they meet.

c. Classify the triangle by its angles and by its sides. You can use your protractor and ruler to check measurements.

d. Draw and label an accurate example of each type of triangle defined above.

Take It to the NET
www More Examples
www.scottforesman.com

CHECK ✓

For another example, see Set 9-7 on p. 533.

Find the missing angle measure. Then classify the triangle by its angles and by its sides.

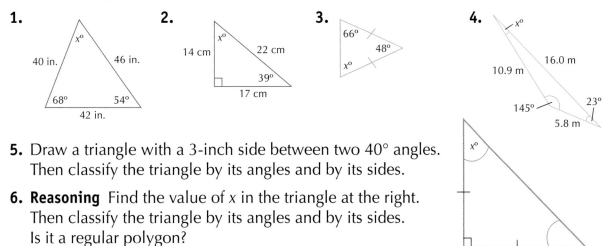

1.
40 in. 46 in. $x°$ 68° 54° 42 in.

2.
14 cm 22 cm $x°$ 39° 17 cm

3.
66° 48° $x°$

4.
$x°$ 16.0 m 10.9 m 145° 23° 5.8 m

5. Draw a triangle with a 3-inch side between two 40° angles. Then classify the triangle by its angles and by its sides.

6. Reasoning Find the value of x in the triangle at the right. Then classify the triangle by its angles and by its sides. Is it a regular polygon?

A Skills and Understanding

Find the missing angle measure. Then classify the triangle by its angles and by its sides.

7.

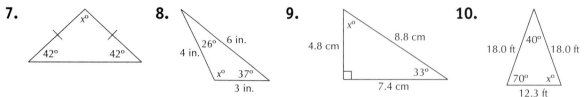

8.

9.

10.

11. Draw a triangle with a 7-cm side between a 110° and a 30° angle. Then classify the triangle by its angles and by its sides.

12. Reasoning Find the value of *y* in the triangle at the right. Then classify the triangle by its angles and by its sides. Is it a regular polygon?

B Reasoning and Problem Solving

13. What type of angle is the largest angle in an acute triangle? in a right triangle? in an obtuse triangle?

14. Draw a triangle with a 120° angle between sides of 2 in. and 3 in. (Hint: Start with the 120° angle.)

15. Construction Draw a segment. Label it $\overline{RS}$. Then complete the following construction.

   a. Adjust the compass to a setting equal to *RS*. Place the center of the compass at one endpoint of the segment and draw an arc. Repeat from the other endpoint.

   b. Connect the endpoints to the point where the arcs intersect.

   c. What type of triangle did you construct? Explain.

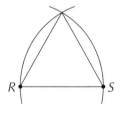

Math and Social Studies

A geodesic dome is a structure that looks like a sphere and is made up of a complex network of triangles. It was invented by Buckminster Fuller in the 1940s.

You can create a 40-cm diameter model of a geodesic dome by taping together twenty full-size copies of the pattern shown here.

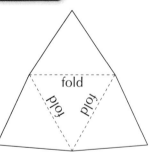

Dashed segments, 12.36cm
Solid segments, 10.93cm

16. Classify the center triangle by its sides.

17. Classify the other three triangles by their sides.

18. Writing in Math Is an equilateral triangle also isosceles? Explain.

C Extensions

19. Use a ruler to draw three different large isosceles triangles. Measure the angles with a protractor. Record the measures. What special relationship do you notice?

Mixed Review and Test Prep

Take It to the NET
Test Prep
www.scottforesman.com

20. Draw an example of a decagon.

21. The flag of Denmark is shown at the right. What type of angles are formed by the intersection of the white bars?

A. acute   **C.** obtuse

B. right   **D.** straight

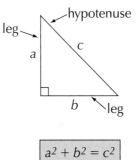

Learning with Technology

Using a Calculator with the Pythagorean Theorem

The names of the sides of a right triangle are shown at the right.

The famous Pythagorean Theorem states that in any right triangle, $a^2 + b^2 = c^2$, where a and b are the lengths of the legs and c is the length of the hypotenuse.

You can use the Pythagorean Theorem to find the length of the hypotenuse of a right triangle if you know the lengths of the legs.

$$a^2 + b^2 = c^2$$

Suppose the legs are 3 in. and 4 in. long.	Suppose the legs are 4 cm and 7 cm long.
$a^2 + b^2 = c^2$	$a^2 + b^2 = c^2$
$3^2 + 4^2 = c^2$	$4^2 + 7^2 = c^2$
$9 + 16 = c^2$	$16 + 49 = c^2$
$25 = c^2$	$65 = c^2$
$5 = c$ Use mental math to find c.	$8.06 \approx c$

Enter 65 $\sqrt{}$ on a calculator to find the value of c. Round to the nearest hundredth.

$\approx$ means "approximately equal to."

The hypotenuse is 5 in. long.   The hypotenuse is about 8.06 cm long.

Find the length of each hypotenuse. Round decimals to the nearest hundredth.

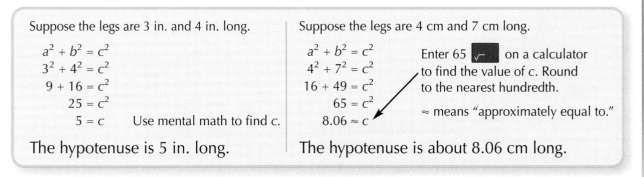

1. 8 ft, 6 ft

2. 8 m, 4 m

3. 5 cm, 12 cm

4. 1 mi, 1 mi

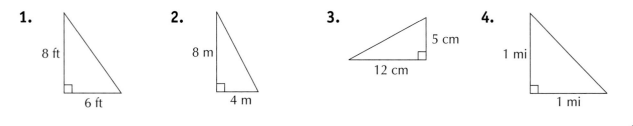

Vocabulary
• quadrilateral
  (p. 494)
• trapezoid
• parallelogram
• rhombus
• rectangle
• square

Materials
• compass
• ruler
• protractor

Quadrilaterals

LEARN

What are the properties of some quadrilaterals?

Quadrilaterals can be classified according to the special properties of their sides and angles.

✓ **WARM UP**

The measures of two
angles of a triangle are
given. Give the measure
of the third angle.

1. 74°, 26°

2. 22°, 136°

3. 90°, 60°

A **trapezoid** is a quadrilateral with only one pair of parallel sides.	A **parallelogram** is a quadrilateral with both pairs of opposite sides parallel. Opposite sides as well as opposite angles are congruent.

Matching tick marks and arcs indicate congruent sides and congruent angles.

A **rhombus** is a parallelogram with all sides congruent.	A **rectangle** is a parallelogram with four right angles.	A **square** is a rectangle with all sides congruent. A square is also a rhombus.

Every quadrilateral can be divided into two triangles. Since the sum of the angle measures in each triangle is 180°, the sum of the measures of the angles in any quadrilateral is 2 × 180°, or 360°.

Example

The measures of three angles of a quadrilateral are 145°, 90°, and 56°. Find the measure of the fourth angle.

$$145 + 90 + 56 + x = 360$$
$$291 + x = 360$$
$$x = 69$$

The measure of the fourth angle is 69°.

✓ **Talk About It**

1. The measures of two angles of a parallelogram are 115° and 65°. Find the measures of the third and fourth angles.

Classify each polygon in as many ways as possible.

1. **2.** **3.** **4.**

The measures of three angles of a quadrilateral are given. Find the measure of the fourth angle.

5. 80°, 120°, 66°   **6.** 30°, 150°, 30°   **7.** 90°, 90°, 90°

8. Find *PR* and m∠*R* in the rectangle at the right.

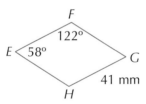

9. Reasoning The measure of one angle of a rhombus is 45°. Find the measures of the other three angles.

PRACTICE

For more practice, see Set 9-8 on p. 538.

A **Skills and Understanding**

Classify each polygon in as many ways as possible.

10.    **11.**   **12.**   **13.**

The measures of three angles of a quadrilateral are given. Find the measure of the fourth angle.

14. 51°, 140°, 120°   **15.** 80°, 110°, 80°   **16.** 70°, 70°, 70°

17. Find *EH* and m∠*H* in the rhombus at the right.

18. Reasoning The measure of one angle of a parallelogram is 110°. Find the measures of the other three angles.

B **Reasoning and Problem Solving**

19. Use a ruler and protractor to draw a 3-inch by 5-inch rectangle.

20. Construction Construct a square. Explain your method.

21. <u>Writing in Math</u> Draw a parallelogram with 4-inch and 6-inch sides and a 75° angle. Explain how you did it.

Mixed Review and Test Prep

Take It to the NET
Test Prep
www.scottforesman.com

22. Can a triangle have angles with measures of 65°, 80°, and 55°? Explain.

23. Which number is NOT between 18.047 and 18.407?

A. 18.049   **B.** 18.249   **C.** 18.4   **D.** 18.42

Vocabulary
• circle
• center
• radius
• diameter
• chord
• central angle
• arc (p. 484)
• sector
• semicircle

Materials
• compass
• ruler
• protractor

TEST TALK

Think It Through
I can **use logical reasoning** to determine the sum of the angle measures before I measure them.

Circles

LEARN

Which terms are commonly used when you talk about circles?

A **circle** is a closed plane figure made up of all the points the same distance from the **center.** A circle is named by its center. Circle O is shown below.

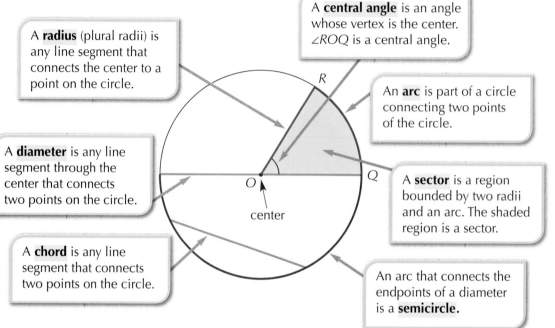

A **radius** (plural radii) is any line segment that connects the center to a point on the circle.

A **diameter** is any line segment through the center that connects two points on the circle.

A **chord** is any line segment that connects two points on the circle.

A **central angle** is an angle whose vertex is the center. ∠ROQ is a central angle.

An **arc** is part of a circle connecting two points of the circle.

A **sector** is a region bounded by two radii and an arc. The shaded region is a sector.

An arc that connects the endpoints of a diameter is a **semicircle.**

✔ Talk About It

1. How are a radius and a diameter in the same circle related?

2. **Reasoning** Describe the longest chord of a circle.

Activity

How many degrees are there in a circle?

You can investigate central angles to find how many degrees are in a circle.

a. Use your compass to construct a large circle. Then draw two intersecting diameters.

b. You should have 4 adjacent central angles in your drawing. What is the sum of their measures? Check your answer by measuring the angles with a protractor.

c. Repeat steps a and b with a different circle.

Identify the figure shown in red.

1. 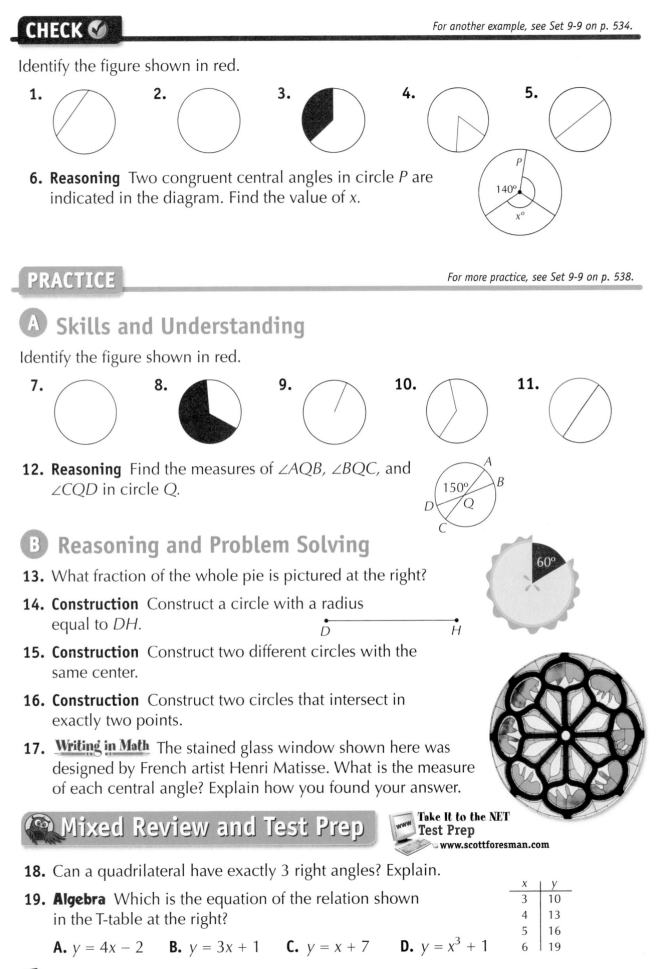   **2.**   **3.**   **4.**   **5.**

6. Reasoning Two congruent central angles in circle *P* are indicated in the diagram. Find the value of *x*.

P
140°
x°

PRACTICE

For more practice, see Set 9-9 on p. 538.

A Skills and Understanding

Identify the figure shown in red.

7.   **8.**   **9.**   **10.**   **11.**

12. Reasoning Find the measures of ∠*AQB*, ∠*BQC*, and ∠*CQD* in circle *Q*.

A
150°
B
D   Q
C

B Reasoning and Problem Solving

13. What fraction of the whole pie is pictured at the right?

60°

14. Construction Construct a circle with a radius equal to *DH*.

D •————————• H

15. Construction Construct two different circles with the same center.

16. Construction Construct two circles that intersect in exactly two points.

17. Writing in Math The stained glass window shown here was designed by French artist Henri Matisse. What is the measure of each central angle? Explain how you found your answer.

Mixed Review and Test Prep

Take It to the NET
www Test Prep
www.scottforesman.com

18. Can a quadrilateral have exactly 3 right angles? Explain.

19. Algebra Which is the equation of the relation shown in the T-table at the right?

x	y
3	10
4	13
5	16
6	19

A. $y = 4x - 2$ **B.** $y = 3x + 1$ **C.** $y = x + 7$ **D.** $y = x^3 + 1$

Do You Know How?

Do You Understand?

Polygons (9-6)

Name each polygon. Then tell if it appears to be a regular polygon.

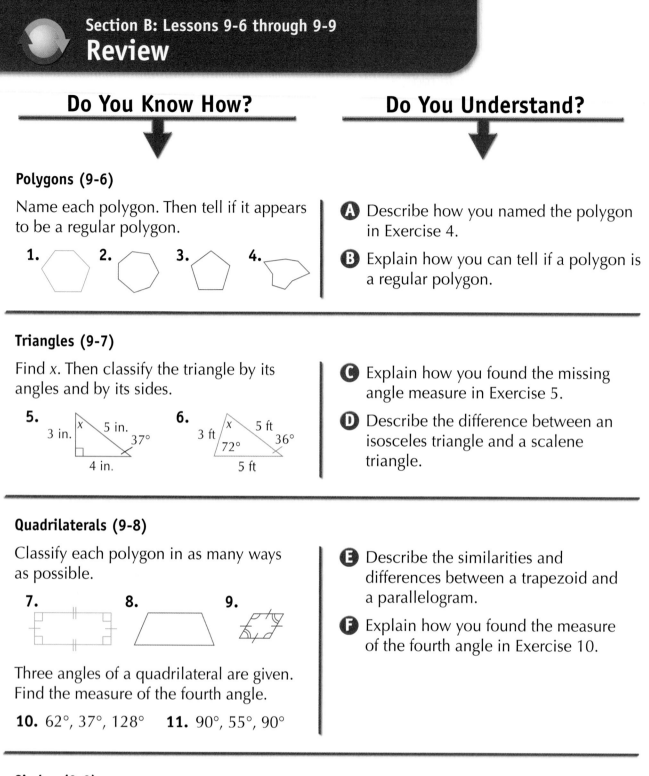

1.   2.   3.   4.

A Describe how you named the polygon in Exercise 4.

B Explain how you can tell if a polygon is a regular polygon.

Triangles (9-7)

Find x. Then classify the triangle by its angles and by its sides.

5.
3 in.   x   5 in.
37°
4 in.

6.
3 ft   x   5 ft
72°   36°
5 ft

C Explain how you found the missing angle measure in Exercise 5.

D Describe the difference between an isosceles triangle and a scalene triangle.

Quadrilaterals (9-8)

Classify each polygon in as many ways as possible.

7.   8.   9.

Three angles of a quadrilateral are given. Find the measure of the fourth angle.

10. 62°, 37°, 128°   11. 90°, 55°, 90°

E Describe the similarities and differences between a trapezoid and a parallelogram.

F Explain how you found the measure of the fourth angle in Exercise 10.

Circles (9-9)

Identify the figure shown in red.

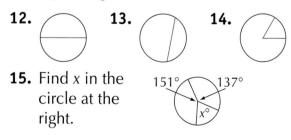

12.   13.   14.

15. Find x in the circle at the right.

151°   137°
x°

G How are an arc and a sector related?

H Describe how you found the missing angle measure in Exercise 15.

MULTIPLE CHOICE

1. Which polygon has twelve sides? (9-6)

   A. quadrilateral   **C.** decagon

   B. dodecagon   **D.** hexagon

2. Any line segment that connects two points on a circle is called a(n) __?__. (9-9)

   A. radius   **C.** sector

   B. chord   **D.** arc

Think It Through
I know that the **name of a polygon indicates the number of sides the polygon has.**

FREE RESPONSE

Name each polygon in as many ways as possible. Then tell if it appears to be a regular polygon (9-6, 9-8)

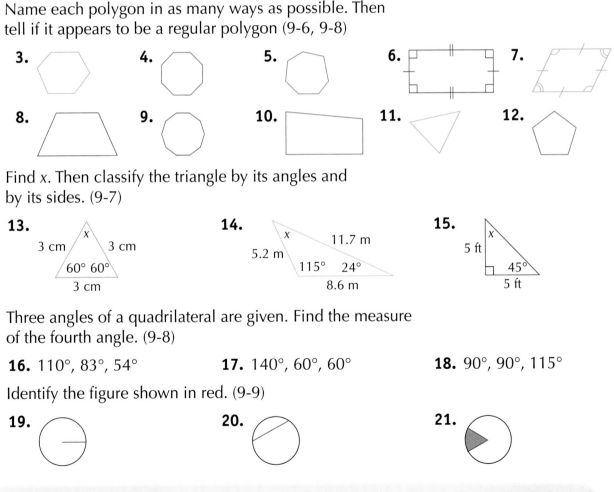

3.

4.

5.

6.

7.

8.

9.

10.

11.

12.

Find *x*. Then classify the triangle by its angles and by its sides. (9-7)

13. 3 cm   *x*   3 cm   60° 60°   3 cm

14. *x*   11.7 m   5.2 m   115°   24°   8.6 m

15. 5 ft   *x*   45°   5 ft

Three angles of a quadrilateral are given. Find the measure of the fourth angle. (9-8)

16. 110°, 83°, 54°

17. 140°, 60°, 60°

18. 90°, 90°, 115°

Identify the figure shown in red. (9-9)

19.

20.

21.

Writing in Math

22. A circle is divided into 5 equal sectors. What is the measure of each central angle? Explain your answer. (9-9)

Key Idea
Many geometric figures, as well as figures in the real world, have the same shape. Some also have the same size.

Vocabulary
• congruent figures
• similar figures

Materials
• $\frac{1}{2}$-inch grid paper
• $\frac{1}{4}$-inch grid paper
• 1-inch grid paper

Think It Through
Sometimes I can make substitutions, when I need to **use objects.**

Congruent and Similar Figures

LEARN

Activity

How do you compare the sizes and shapes of figures?

A $\frac{1}{2}$-inch grid has been placed over a picture of a dog.

a. Copy the picture, square by square, onto each grid.

$\frac{1}{2}$-inch grid   1-inch grid $\frac{1}{4}$-inch grid

b. Explain how each of your drawings compares in size and shape to the original picture.

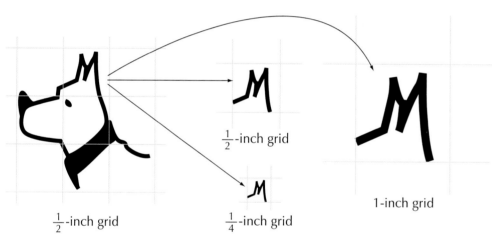

$\frac{1}{2}$-inch grid

$\frac{1}{2}$-inch grid

$\frac{1}{4}$-inch grid

1-inch grid

✓ **WARM UP**

Find the missing angle measure.

1.

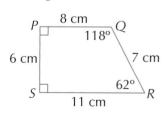

2. The measure of one angle of a parallelogram is 110°. Find the measures of the other three angles.

Congruent figures have the same size and shape. **Similar figures** have the same shape. They may or may not have the same size.

These trapezoids are congruent.

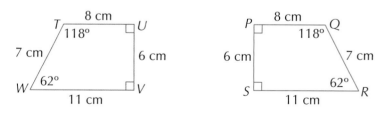

In congruent polygons:

• Corresponding angles are congruent.

Corresponding angles:
$\angle T \cong \angle Q$, $\angle U \cong \angle P$, $\angle V \cong \angle S$, $\angle W \cong \angle R$

• Corresponding sides are congruent.

Corresponding sides:
$\overline{TU} \cong \overline{PQ}$, $\overline{UV} \cong \overline{PS}$, $\overline{WV} \cong \overline{SR}$, $\overline{TW} \cong \overline{QR}$

These triangles are similar.

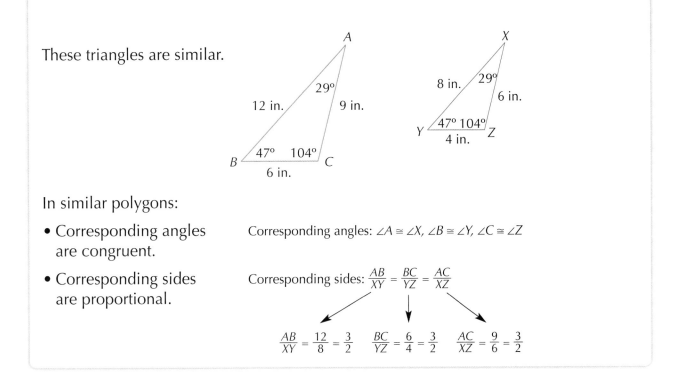

In similar polygons:

- Corresponding angles are congruent.

    Corresponding angles: $\angle A \cong \angle X$, $\angle B \cong \angle Y$, $\angle C \cong \angle Z$

- Corresponding sides are proportional.

    Corresponding sides: $\dfrac{AB}{XY} = \dfrac{BC}{YZ} = \dfrac{AC}{XZ}$

$$\frac{AB}{XY} = \frac{12}{8} = \frac{3}{2} \qquad \frac{BC}{YZ} = \frac{6}{4} = \frac{3}{2} \qquad \frac{AC}{XZ} = \frac{9}{6} = \frac{3}{2}$$

How can you find missing measures?

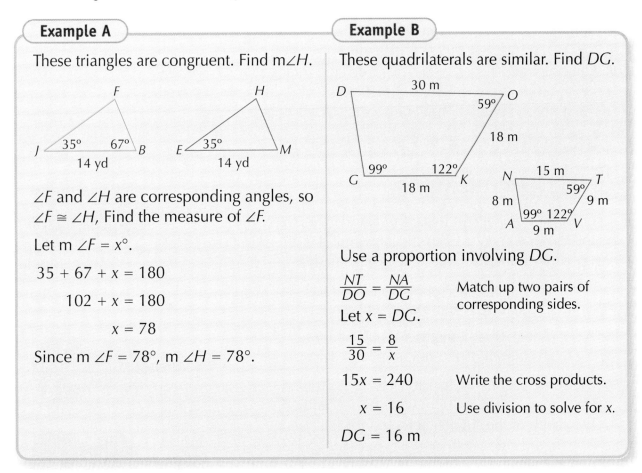

Example A

These triangles are congruent. Find m∠H.

$\angle F$ and $\angle H$ are corresponding angles, so $\angle F \cong \angle H$, Find the measure of $\angle F$.

Let m $\angle F = x°$.

$35 + 67 + x = 180$

$102 + x = 180$

$x = 78$

Since m $\angle F = 78°$, m $\angle H = 78°$.

Example B

These quadrilaterals are similar. Find DG.

Use a proportion involving DG.

$\dfrac{NT}{DO} = \dfrac{NA}{DG}$ Match up two pairs of corresponding sides.

Let $x = DG$.

$\dfrac{15}{30} = \dfrac{8}{x}$

$15x = 240$ Write the cross products.

$x = 16$ Use division to solve for x.

$DG = 16$ m

✔ **Talk About It**

1. In Example B, give a different proportion that could be used to find *DG*.

1. These triangles are congruent. Find m∠V and ON.

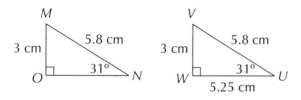

2. These parallelograms are similar. Find m∠R, m∠H, and SR.

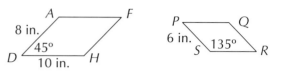

3. Reasoning Are all squares similar? congruent? Explain.

Ⓐ Skills and Understanding

4. These pentagons are congruent. Find RN, HG, m∠R, and m∠N.

5. These triangles are similar. Find m∠T, JC, and CK.

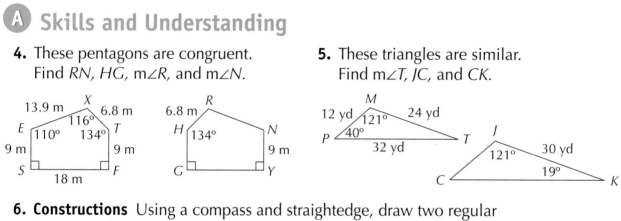

6. Constructions Using a compass and straightedge, draw two regular hexagons that are similar, one with corresponding sides twice the length of the other. (Hint: Follow the steps on page 494.)

Ⓑ Reasoning and Problem Solving

♪ Math and Music

Lance and his younger siblings, Lydia and Walt, play the violin. Lance uses a full-size violin. His siblings' violins are the same shape, but smaller.

7. What is the length of the body of Lydia's violin to the nearest tenth of a centimeter?

8. What is the overall length of Walt's violin to the nearest tenth of a centimeter?

9. The screens of two television sets are similar. The larger screen is 20 in. wide by 15 in. high. The width of the smaller screen is 16 in. How high is it?

10. By law, all United States flags must be similar to a rectangle 1 unit wide by 1.9 units long. What is the width of a flag that is 57 in. long?

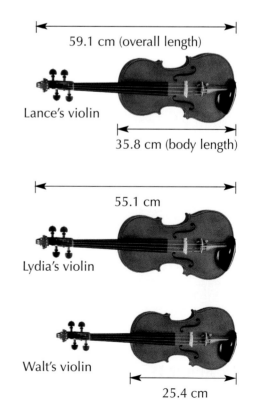

59.1 cm (overall length)

Lance's violin

35.8 cm (body length)

55.1 cm

Lydia's violin

Walt's violin

25.4 cm

11. <u>Writing in Math</u> How are similar and congruent polygons alike? How are they different?

C Extensions

12. Similar triangles and shadows can be used to find the height of very tall objects. Regina, who is 5 feet tall, casts a 2-foot shadow. At the same time, a flagpole casts a 12-foot shadow. The triangles suggested in this situation are similar. Find the height of the flagpole.

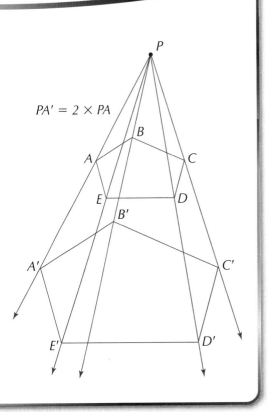

Mixed Review and Test Prep

Take It to the NET
Test Prep
www.scottforesman.com

13. Jonas is designing a quilt with a border as shown at the right. Explain how he can find the measure of ∠DBC if he knows that the measure of ∠ABC is 68°.

14. Draw a circle. Then draw and label a radius, a diameter, a chord, a central angle, an arc, and a sector. You may want to use colored pencils.

15. What is the value of $3 + 4 \times 5^2$?

A. 300 **B.** 103 **C.** 70 **D.** 43

Enrichment

Enlargements and Reductions

Materials: ruler

Draw a pentagon and label the vertices A, B, C, D, and E. Then follow the steps to draw a similar pentagon with sides twice as long as the original.

1. Draw a point P.
2. Draw rays from P through each vertex.
3. Measure PA. Then locate the point on $\overrightarrow{PA}$ that is twice this distance from P. Label it A' ("A prime").
4. Similarly, locate B', C', D', and E'.
5. Connect A', B', C', D', and E'.

Begin with a new pentagon. Follow the steps above, except change steps 3 and 4 so that each new point you find is half the distance from P. Is the new pentagon similar to the original one? How do the sides compare?

Transformations

LEARN

Activity

What are some basic transformations?

A **slide,** or **translation,**
moves a figure in a
straight direction.

A **flip,** or **reflection,** of
a figure gives its mirror
image over a line.

A **glide reflection** is
a slide followed by
a flip.

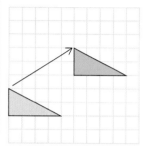

A **turn,** or **rotation,** moves
a figure about a point.

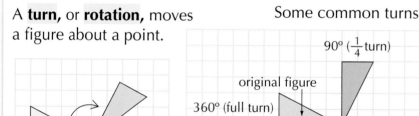

Some common turns

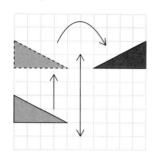

*These turns are
clockwise (like the movement
of a clock's hands). Counterclockwise
turns are in the opposite
direction.*

Use a separate grid for each exercise. Draw the triangle with
the given vertices. Apply the transformation, state the
coordinates of the new triangle, and tell if it is congruent to
the original. You may use tracing paper to help.

a. (2, 2), (7, 2), (7, 4) Slide to the right 6 units and up 2 units.

b. (1, 3), (5, 3), (1, 9) Slide to the left 3 units and down 4 units.

c. (1, 6), (1, 3), (6, 6) Flip over the y-axis.

d. (−2, −4), (−7, −4), (−7, −1) Flip over the x-axis.

e. (0, 0), (5, 0), (5, 2) Turn 90° clockwise about (0, 0).

f. (0, 0), (0, −6), (−3, −6) Turn 180° counterclockwise about (0, 0).

g. (−2, 2), (−2, 7), (−5, 7) Slide down 6 units. Then flip over the y-axis.

Tell whether the figures in each pair are related by a slide, a flip, a glide reflection, or a turn. If a turn, describe it.

1. **2.** **3.** **4.**

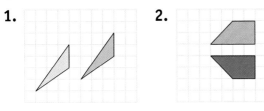
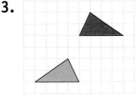
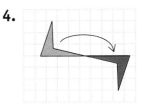

5. Reasoning What happens if you turn a figure 180° and then turn the resulting figure 180° about the same point?

PRACTICE

For more practice, see Set 9-11 on p. 539.

Ⓐ Skills and Understanding

Tell whether the figures in each pair are related by a slide, a flip, a glide reflection, or a turn. If a turn, describe it.

6. **7.** **8.** **9.**

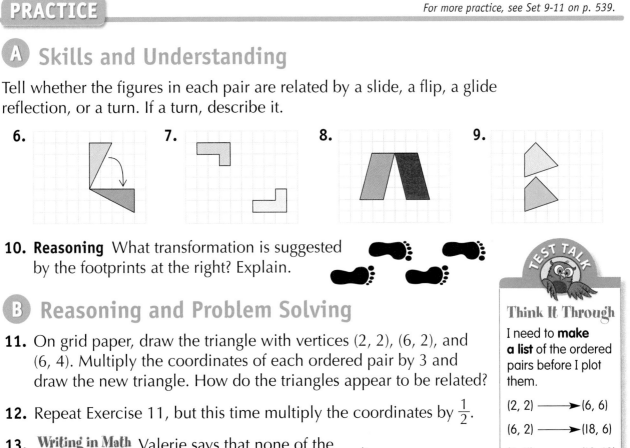

10. Reasoning What transformation is suggested by the footprints at the right? Explain.

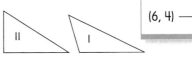

Ⓑ Reasoning and Problem Solving

11. On grid paper, draw the triangle with vertices (2, 2), (6, 2), and (6, 4). Multiply the coordinates of each ordered pair by 3 and draw the new triangle. How do the triangles appear to be related?

12. Repeat Exercise 11, but this time multiply the coordinates by $\frac{1}{2}$.

13. **Writing in Math** Valerie says that none of the transformations in this lesson can move triangle I onto triangle II. Is she right? Explain.

> **TEST TALK**
>
> **Think It Through**
> I need to **make a list** of the ordered pairs before I plot them.
>
> (2, 2) ——→ (6, 6)
>
> (6, 2) ——→ (18, 6)
>
> (6, 4) ——→ (18, 12)

Mixed Review and Test Prep

Take It to the NET
Test Prep
www.scottforesman.com

14. If two polygons are similar, how are their corresponding sides related?

15. Which of the following represents 9 squared?

   A. 9^3 **B.** 2×9 **C.** 9^2 **D.** 2^9

Problem-Solving Skill

Key Idea
There are specific things you can do to write a good comparison in math.

Materials
• coordinate grid paper or

 **tools**

Think It Through

• I can use brainstorming to help me decide how objects are alike or different.

• I'll use geometric terms accurately in my description.

Writing to Compare

LEARN

How do you write a good comparison?

When you **write to compare**, you need to analyze the information given to compare and contrast it.

Flips, Slides, and **Turns** Draw the quadrilateral with vertices at (0, 0), (4, 0), (8, 4), and (0, 4). Label it Figure 1. Turn Figure 1 90° counterclockwise about the origin. Label the result Figure 2. Slide Figure 2 to the left 6 units. Label the result Figure 3. Write statements that compare Figures 1 and 3.

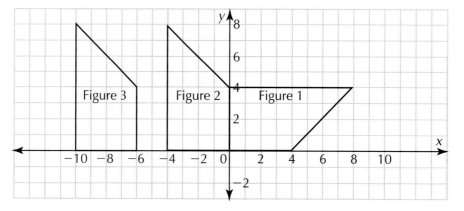

Writing a Math Comparison

• Compare properties of the figures such as length, angle measure, classification, and position.

• Use geometric terms to write the statements that tell how the figures are alike and how they are different.

Figures 1 and 3 each have two right angles. Figures 1 and 3 are both trapezoids.

Figure 1 is located in Quadrant I, but Figure 3 is located in Quadrant II. The parallel sides in Figure 1 are horizontal, but in Figure 3 they are vertical.

✔ Talk About It

1. What are some other comparison statements you could make?

2. Are Figures 1 and 3 congruent? Explain.

For another example, see Set 9-12 on p. 535.

1. Robin is describing these two shapes to a friend.

   a. Write two statements about how the shapes are alike.

   b. Write two statements about how the shapes are different.

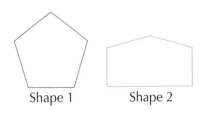

Shape 1   Shape 2

For more practice, see Set 9-12 on p. 539.

2. On grid paper, draw the triangle with vertices at (0, 0), (6, 0), and (6, −4). Label it Figure 1. Turn Figure 1 180° about the origin. Label the result Figure 2. Flip Figure 2 over the *y*-axis. Label the result Figure 3.

   a. Write two statements about how Figures 1 and 3 are alike.

   b. Write two statements about how Figures 1 and 3 are different.

3. Compare the traffic signs at the right.

   a. Write a statement about how their shapes are alike.

   b. Write a statement about how their shapes are different.

4. Denise and Ian wrote two number patterns.

   > Denise's pattern: 67, 62, 57, 52, . . .
   >
   > Ian's pattern: 80, 75, 70, 65, 60, . . .

   a. Write a statement about how the patterns are alike.

   b. Write a statement about how the patterns are different.

5. Compare the quilt patterns at the right.

   a. Use geometry terms to write two statements about how the patterns are alike.

   b. Use geometry terms to write two statements about how the patterns are different.

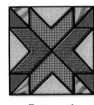 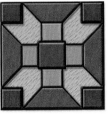

Pattern 1   Pattern 2

6. Compare the wallpaper samples at the right.

   a. Use geometry terms to tell how the samples are alike.

   b. Use geometry terms to tell how the samples are different.

 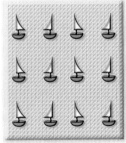

Sample 1   Sample 2

Symmetry

LEARN

What are symmetric figures?

Symmetry in architecture is found in all cultures and time periods. Many figures exhibit symmetry. A figure has **reflection symmetry** if it can be reflected onto itself. The line of reflection is a **line of symmetry.** Some figures have more than one line of symmetry.

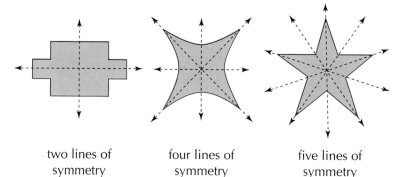

Line of symmetry

two lines of symmetry   four lines of symmetry   five lines of symmetry

When a figure rotates onto itself in less than a full turn, the figure has **rotational symmetry.** The flower at the right has rotational symmetry. A turn of 72° ($\frac{1}{5}$-turn) rotates the figure onto itself.

$180°(\frac{1}{2}$-turn) rotational symmetry

$120°(\frac{1}{3}$-turn) rotational symmetry

$90°(\frac{1}{4}$-turn) rotational symmetry

$72°(\frac{1}{5}$-turn) rotational symmetry

Think It Through
I can **use objects,** such as tracing paper, to help me check for symmetry.

✔ Talk About It

1. Which figures on this page have both reflection and rotational symmetry?

2. Why is a 72° turn equivalent to a $\frac{1}{5}$-turn?

3. **Reasoning** If a figure has $\frac{1}{4}$-turn rotational symmetry, how many congruent parts does it have?

Take It to the NET
More Examples
www.scottforesman.com

Tell if each figure has reflection symmetry, rotational symmetry, or both. If it has reflection symmetry, how many lines of symmetry are there? If it has rotational symmetry, what is the smallest turn that will rotate the figure onto itself?

1.  2. 3. 4. 5.

6. **Reasoning** Describe the symmetry of a regular hexagon.

PRACTICE

For more practice, see Set 9-13 on p. 539.

Ⓐ Skills and Understanding

Tell if each figure has reflection symmetry, rotational symmetry, or both. If it has reflection symmetry, how many lines of symmetry are there? If it has rotational symmetry, what is the smallest turn that will rotate the figure onto itself?

7. 8. 9. 10. 11.

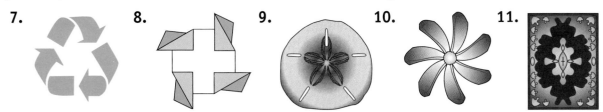

12. **Reasoning** Describe the symmetry of a circle.

Ⓑ Reasoning and Problem Solving

13. Which uppercase vowels have reflection symmetry? rotational symmetry? both?

14. Which words and numbers at the right have reflection symmetry? rotational symmetry? both? Print examples of your own.

15. **Writing in Math** Draw a figure that has four lines of symmetry, as well as rotational symmetry. You may use grid or dot paper if you like. Describe the symmetry.

MOM   M
808   SWIMS   A
      HIKE   T
             1961   H
             MOW

🦉 Mixed Review and Test Prep

Take It to the NET
www Test Prep
www.scottforesman.com

16. How are a rhombus and a trapezoid alike? How are they different?

17. What transformation relates the hammers at the right.

   A. reflection   **B.** rotation   **C.** glide reflection   **D.** translation

Key Idea
You can use what you know about transformations to create interesting tessellations.

Vocabulary
• tessellation

Materials
• construction paper
• scissors
• ruler
• tape
• markers or colored pencils

Tessellations

LEARN

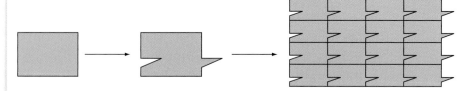

Activity

How can you create a tessellation based on a rectangle?

A **tessellation** is a pattern of congruent figures that fills the plane without gaps or overlaps. A rectangle is one of the polygons that can tessellate the plane. You can alter the sides of a rectangle to produce a new shape that tessellates the plane.

You can extend this idea to change a rectangle into an interesting shape that tessellates the plane.

a. Cut out a rectangular piece of paper about 6 cm by 12 cm. Label the sides as shown.

b. Draw and cut any shape out of side 1. Do <u>not</u> cut off a corner. If you cut off a numeral, simply remember which side is which.

c. Without turning the shape over, slide it straight across, and tape it onto side 3.

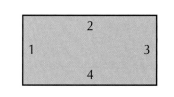

d. Similarly, cut into side 2, slide it straight across, and tape it onto side 4.

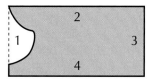

e. Repeat the process one or two more times, cutting into any <u>unaltered</u> part of the rectangle, except a corner. Remember to slide each piece straight across to the opposite side, and then tape it in place.

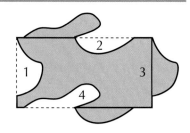

f. Does your shape look like any particular object? If so, you might want to add a few artistic details. To draw the tessellation, make repeated tracings around the shape. Color your drawing.

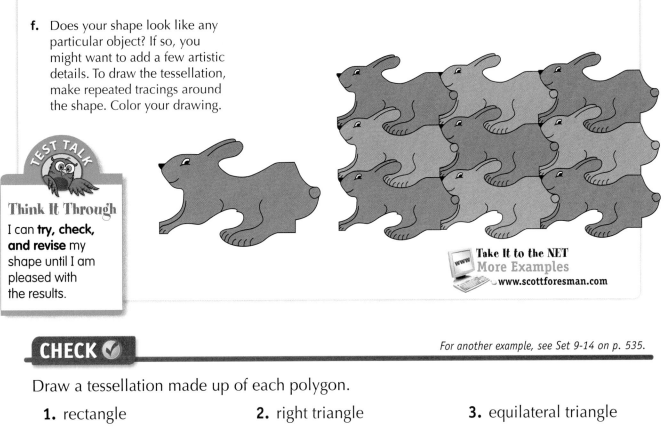

Think It Through
I can **try, check, and revise** my shape until I am pleased with the results.

Take It to the NET
More Examples
www.scottforesman.com

CHECK ✓

For another example, see Set 9-14 on p. 535.

Draw a tessellation made up of each polygon.

1. rectangle **2.** right triangle **3.** equilateral triangle

Does each shape tessellate? If so, trace the figure and draw the tessellation. (Hint: Sometimes you need to rotate or flip the shape.)

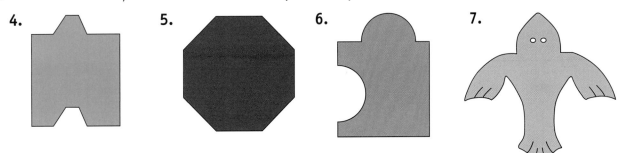

4. **5.** **6.** **7.**

8. Reasoning In the tessellation at the right, what transformation could you use to move shape *A* onto shape *B*? shape *A* onto shape *C*?

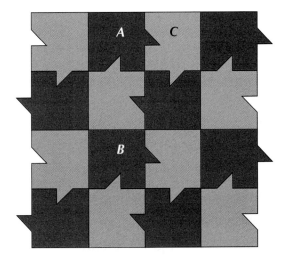

A Skills and Understanding

Draw a tessellation made up of each polygon.

9. square **10.** parallelogram **11.** isosceles triangle

Does each shape tessellate? If so, trace the figure and draw the tessellation.
(Hint: Sometimes you need to rotate or flip the shape.)

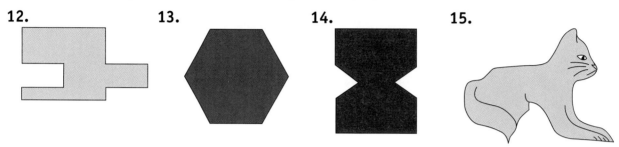

12. **13.** **14.** **15.**

16. Reasoning In the bunny tessellation on page 517, what transformation could you use to move a gray bunny onto a cream-colored bunny?

B Reasoning and Problem Solving

Math and Art

The Dutch artist M. C. Escher (1898 to 1972) is renowned for his interesting tessellations. Inspired by Escher's tessellating shapes of fish and lizards, Jon and Miguel created the art below.

17. What transformation would move fish *A* to fish *B*?

18. What transformation would move lizard *C* to lizard *D*? lizard *C* to lizard *E*?

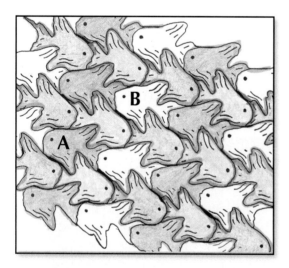

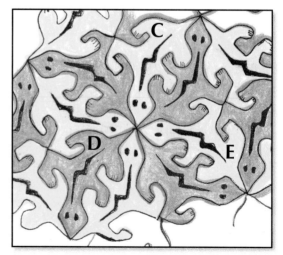

19. <u>**Writing in Math**</u> Joanne says that a circle does not tessellate the plane. Is she right? Explain.

C Extensions

20. Follow these steps to change a square into a shape that tessellates the plane.

a. Cut out a square piece of paper about 8 cm on a side. Label the sides and vertices as shown.

b. Draw and cut any shape out of side 1. Do not cut off a corner.

c. Rotate the piece about point *A* and tape it to side 2. Be sure to tape the piece the same distance from point *A* as it was before you cut it.

d. Similarly, cut into side 3, rotate the piece about point *B*, and tape the piece to side 4.

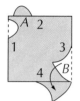

e. Repeat the process a few more times, cutting into any <u>unaltered</u> part of the square except a corner. Remember this plan:

- Rotate pieces from side 1 onto side 2, and from side 2 onto side 1. (Be sure to tape the piece the same distance from *A*.)

- Rotate pieces from side 3 onto side 4, and from side 4 onto side 3. (Be sure to tape the piece the same distance from *B*.)

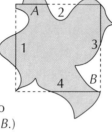

f. Add artistic details and draw the tessellation.

Mixed Review and Test Prep

Take It to the NET
Test Prep
www.scottforesman.com

21. Draw a figure that has exactly 2 lines of symmetry.

22. What is the measure of an angle that is a supplement of a 45° angle?

    A. 45°   **B.** 90°   **C.** 135°   **D.** 180°

Learning with Technology

The Geometry Drawing eTool and Tessellations

Draw an equilateral triangle, parallelogram, trapezoid, and pentagon. Find the interior angle measurements of each polygon. Try to tessellate each of the polygons separately.

1. Which of the polygons listed above will tessellate?

2. Is there a relationship between a polygon's interior angle measurements and its ability to tessellate? Explain.

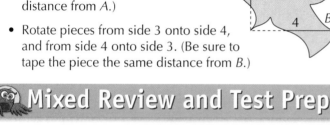

All text pages available online and on CD-ROM.

DK Problem-Solving Applications

Amazing BUILDINGS
See inside great buildings of the world – from castles and cathedrals, to palaces and monuments

Neuschwanstein Castle King Ludwig II, nicknamed the Mad King of Bavaria, was obsessed with the design and construction of magnificent buildings. Perhaps his most famous project was Neuschwanstein Castle. After directing the construction for 17 years, the King mysteriously died and plans to finish most of the castle were dropped.

Trivia King Ludwig II loved operas. Huge murals relating to operas were painted on the interior walls of the castle. The castle itself was not planned by an architect, but by an opera-scenery designer.

1 When King Ludwig II died, the exterior of the castle was $\frac{3}{4}$ complete. What fraction of the exterior was incomplete? What percent was incomplete?

2 The king lived in the castle for only 172 days. Write and solve an equation to find how many days less than a year this was. (Use 1 year = 365 days).

3 When the king lived in the castle, only 15 rooms were completed. The castle was planned to have about 5.47 times as many rooms. How many rooms were planned?

Using Key Facts

4 What percent of the workers at the castle were considered craftsmen? laborers? Round your answers to the nearest tenth.

Key Facts
Neuschwanstein Castle

- Construction started in 1869 and ended in 1892.
- Construction involved about 200 craftsmen and 100 laborers.
- The castle grounds cover about $\frac{1}{2}$ acre.
- The throne room has over a million floor tiles.
- The throne room's chandelier weighs about 1,000 pounds.
- The king's bedroom took over 4 years to finish.

5 To get to the castle, visitors have to walk for about 25 minutes up a winding road. What fraction of an hour does the walk take? Simplify your answer.

6 <u>Writing in Math</u> Use 3 geometric terms to describe parts of Neuschwanstein Castle. Use complete sentences.

7 **Decision Making** Draw a plan for your own dream castle. Use as many different shapes as you can and label each shape.

Good News/Bad News King Ludwig II was a great supporter of the arts. He was a friend and financer of the opera composer Richard Wagner. Unfortunately, some government officials feared that Wagner was a political threat to them. This caused the king many troubles.

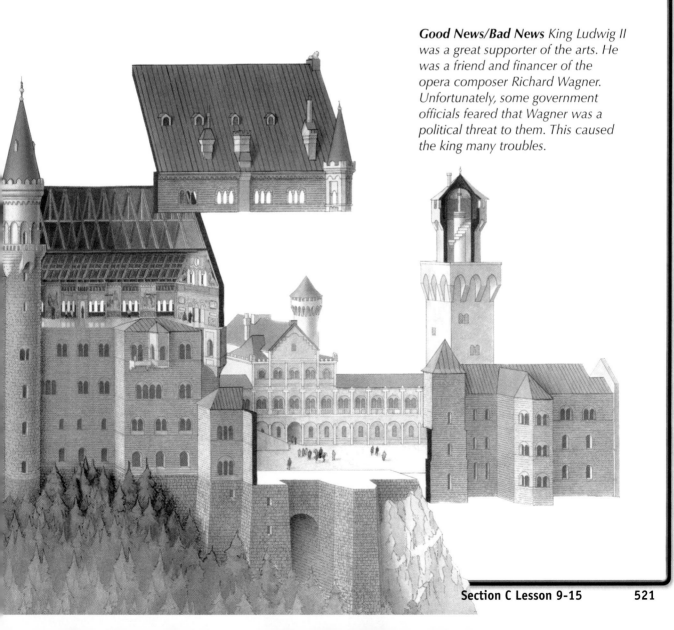

Do You Know How?

Do You Understand?

Congruent and Similar Figures (9-10)

1. These quadrilaterals are similar. Find the measure of ∠E, EF, and FG.

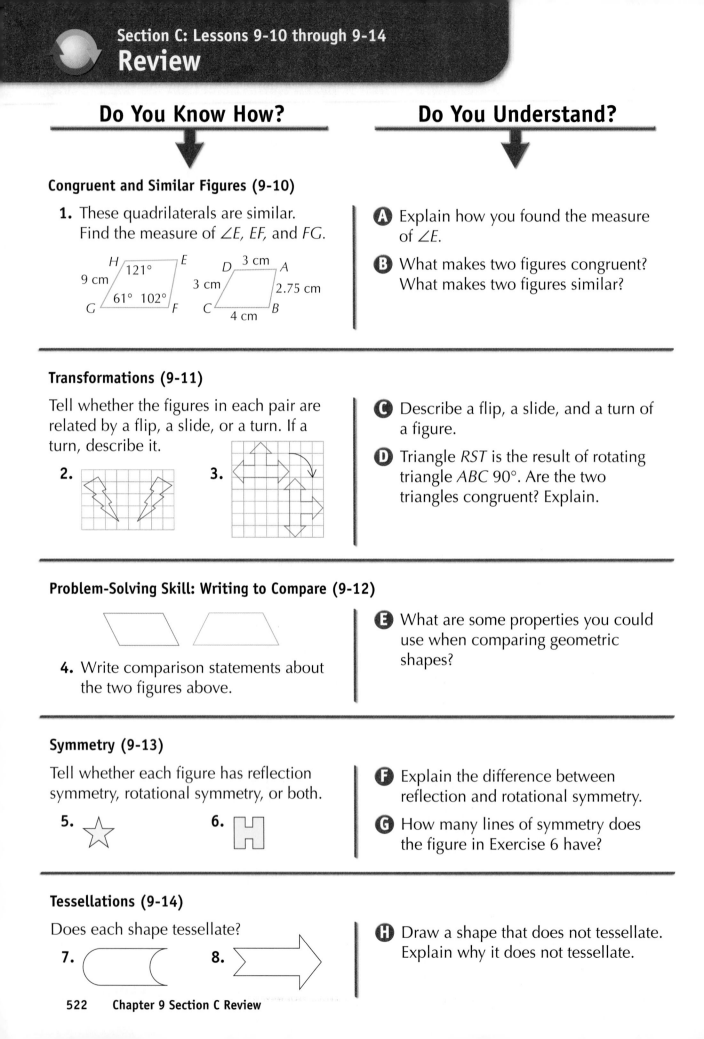

Ⓐ Explain how you found the measure of ∠E.

Ⓑ What makes two figures congruent? What makes two figures similar?

Transformations (9-11)

Tell whether the figures in each pair are related by a flip, a slide, or a turn. If a turn, describe it.

2.

3.

Ⓒ Describe a flip, a slide, and a turn of a figure.

Ⓓ Triangle *RST* is the result of rotating triangle *ABC* 90°. Are the two triangles congruent? Explain.

Problem-Solving Skill: Writing to Compare (9-12)

4. Write comparison statements about the two figures above.

Ⓔ What are some properties you could use when comparing geometric shapes?

Symmetry (9-13)

Tell whether each figure has reflection symmetry, rotational symmetry, or both.

5.

6.

Ⓕ Explain the difference between reflection and rotational symmetry.

Ⓖ How many lines of symmetry does the figure in Exercise 6 have?

Tessellations (9-14)

Does each shape tessellate?

7.

8.

Ⓗ Draw a shape that does not tessellate. Explain why it does not tessellate.

MULTIPLE CHOICE

1. Which type of transformation is a slide? (9-11)

    A. translation   **B.** reflection   **C.** tessellation   **D.** rotation

2. Which shape does NOT tessellate? (9-14)

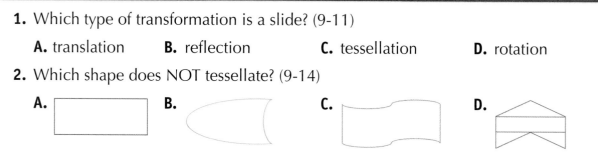

    A.   **B.**   **C.**   **D.**

FREE RESPONSE

3. These triangles are similar. Find $m\angle M$ and PQ. (9-14, 9-15)

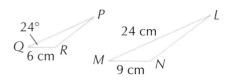

Tell whether the figures in each pair are related by a flip, a slide, a glide reflection, or a turn. If a turn, describe it. (9-11)

4.   **5.**   **6.**

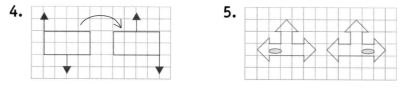

Tell if each figure has reflection symmetry, rotational symmetry, or both. If it has reflection symmetry, how many lines of symmetry are there? If it has rotational symmetry, what is the smallest turn that will rotate the figure onto itself? (9-13)

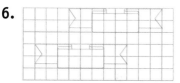

Think It Through
I should **use math terms accurately.**

7.   **8.**   **9.**

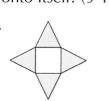

Writing in Math

10. Write two statements about how Figures A and B are alike. Write two statements about how Figures A and B are different. (9-12)

Figure A   Figure B

11. Do all figures with rotational symmetry also have reflection symmetry? Explain your answer. (9-13)

Test-Taking Strategies

Understand the question.

Get information for the answer.

Plan how to find the answer.

Make smart choices.

Use writing in math.

Improve written answers.

Plan How to Find the Answer

After you understand a test question and get needed information, you need to plan how to find the answer. Think about problem-solving skills and strategies and computation methods you know.

❶ Look at Triangle 1 drawn on the coordinate grid below.

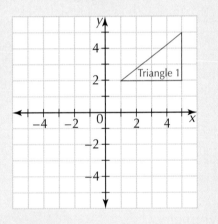

Part A
Reflect Triangle 1 over the x-axis. Label the result Triangle 2.

Part B
Write the ordered pairs for the vertices of Triangle 2.

_____

Understand the question.

I need to reflect Triangle 1 over the x-axis. Then I need to write the ordered pairs for the vertices of the Triangle 2.

Get information for the answer.

The figure I need to work with is on the **coordinate grid.**

Plan how to find the answer.

• Think about problem-solving skills and strategies.

Part A: I can reflect Triangle 1 by counting units on the grid. Triangle 1 and Triangle 2 should be the same distance from the x-axis. I can **use objects** *such as tracing paper to check my drawing.*

Part B: I should start at the origin and move to each vertex, counting across and then up or down. The horizontal distance is the first coordinate of the ordered pair. Moving right is positive; left is negative. The vertical distance is the second coordinate. Up is positive; down is negative.

• Choose computation methods.

I only need to count units on the grid.

2 The flag of Thailand is shown below.

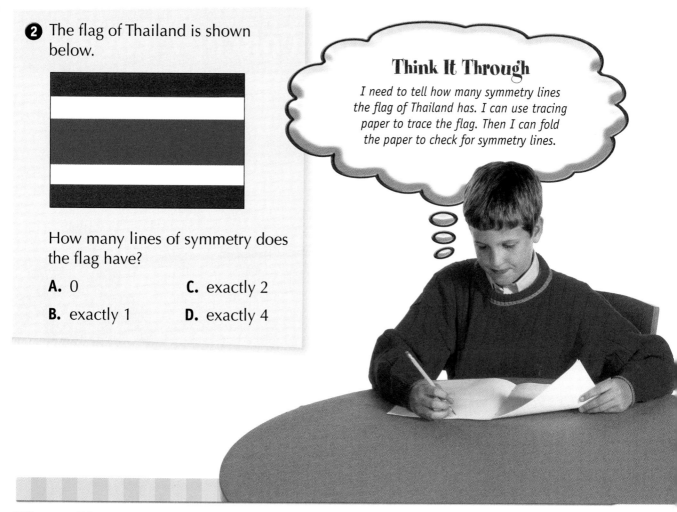

How many lines of symmetry does the flag have?

A. 0

B. exactly 1

C. exactly 2

D. exactly 4

Think It Through

I need to tell how many symmetry lines the flag of Thailand has. I can use tracing paper to trace the flag. Then I can fold the paper to check for symmetry lines.

Now it's your turn.

For each problem, describe a plan for finding the answer.

3 Draw Triangle 1 on a coordinate grid with vertices at (0, 0), (4, 0), and (4, −3).

Part A
Slide Triangle 1 to the left 3 units. Label the result Triangle 2.

Part B
Write the ordered pairs for the vertices of Triangle 2.

4 The flag of Aruba is shown below. It features a red 4-pointed star.

Which of the following is the smallest rotation that will rotate the red star onto itself?

A. 45°

B. 90°

C. 180°

D. 360°

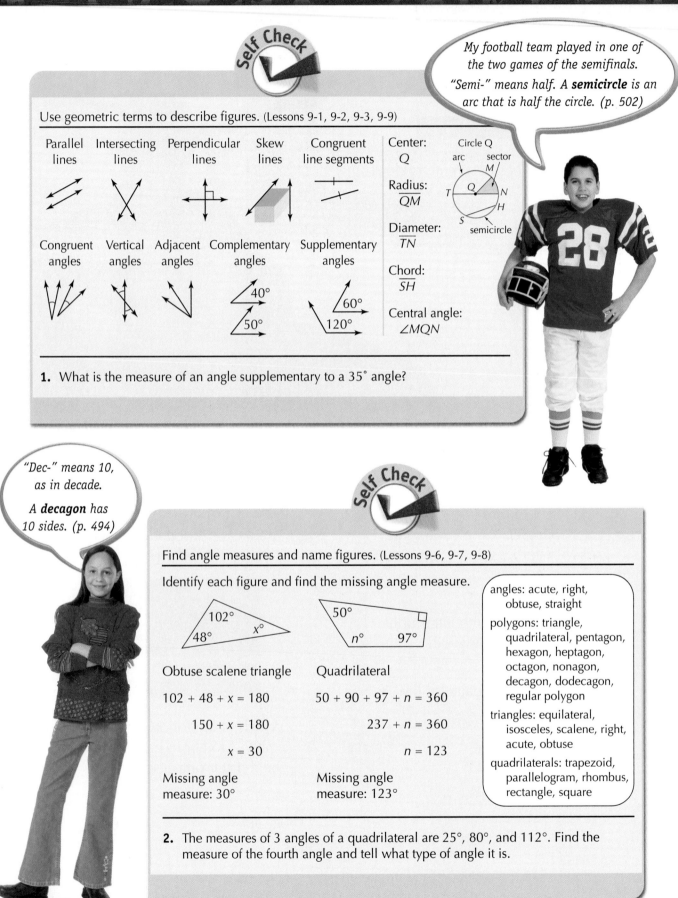

Self Check

My football team played in one of the two games of the semifinals. *"Semi-"* means half. A **semicircle** is an arc that is half the circle. (p. 502)

Use geometric terms to describe figures. (Lessons 9-1, 9-2, 9-3, 9-9)

Parallel lines   Intersecting lines   Perpendicular lines   Skew lines   Congruent line segments

Congruent angles   Vertical angles   Adjacent angles   Complementary angles   Supplementary angles

40°
50°

60°
120°

Center: Q

Radius: $\overline{QM}$

Diameter: $\overline{TN}$

Chord: $\overline{SH}$

Central angle: $\angle MQN$

Circle Q
arc   sector
semicircle

1. What is the measure of an angle supplementary to a 35° angle?

"Dec-" means 10, as in decade.

A **decagon** has 10 sides. (p. 494)

Self Check

Find angle measures and name figures. (Lessons 9-6, 9-7, 9-8)

Identify each figure and find the missing angle measure.

102°
48°
x°

50°
n°
97°

Obtuse scalene triangle

$102 + 48 + x = 180$

$150 + x = 180$

$x = 30$

Missing angle measure: 30°

Quadrilateral

$50 + 90 + 97 + n = 360$

$237 + n = 360$

$n = 123$

Missing angle measure: 123°

angles: acute, right, obtuse, straight

polygons: triangle, quadrilateral, pentagon, hexagon, heptagon, octagon, nonagon, decagon, dodecagon, regular polygon

triangles: equilateral, isosceles, scalene, right, acute, obtuse

quadrilaterals: trapezoid, parallelogram, rhombus, rectangle, square

2. The measures of 3 angles of a quadrilateral are 25°, 80°, and 112°. Find the measure of the fourth angle and tell what type of angle it is.

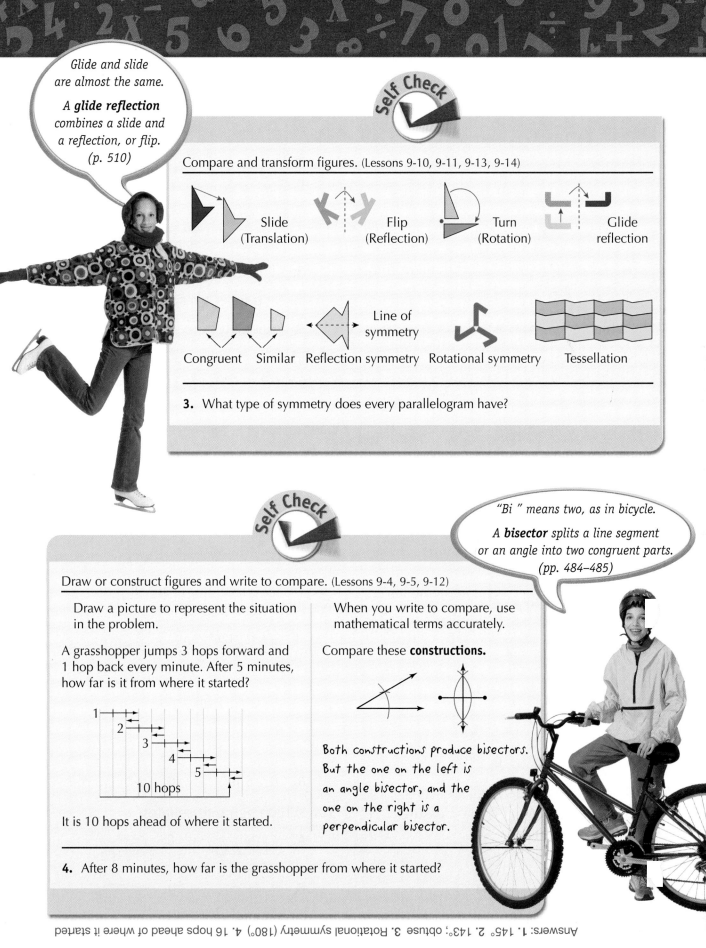

Glide and slide are almost the same.

A glide reflection combines a slide and a reflection, or flip. (p. 510)

Self Check

Compare and transform figures. (Lessons 9-10, 9-11, 9-13, 9-14)

Slide (Translation) Flip (Reflection) Turn (Rotation) Glide reflection

Congruent Similar Reflection symmetry Line of symmetry Rotational symmetry Tessellation

3. What type of symmetry does every parallelogram have?

Self Check

"Bi" means two, as in bicycle.

A **bisector** splits a line segment or an angle into two congruent parts. (pp. 484–485)

Draw or construct figures and write to compare. (Lessons 9-4, 9-5, 9-12)

Draw a picture to represent the situation in the problem.

A grasshopper jumps 3 hops forward and 1 hop back every minute. After 5 minutes, how far is it from where it started?

1
2
3
4
5
10 hops

It is 10 hops ahead of where it started.

When you write to compare, use mathematical terms accurately.

Compare these **constructions.**

Both constructions produce bisectors. But the one on the left is an angle bisector, and the one on the right is a perpendicular bisector.

4. After 8 minutes, how far is the grasshopper from where it started?

Answers: 1. 145° 2. 143°; obtuse 3. Rotational symmetry (180°) 4. 16 hops ahead of where it started

Chapter 9 Key Vocabulary and Concept Review 527

MULTIPLE CHOICE

Choose the correct letter for each answer.

1. Which is true of the picture?

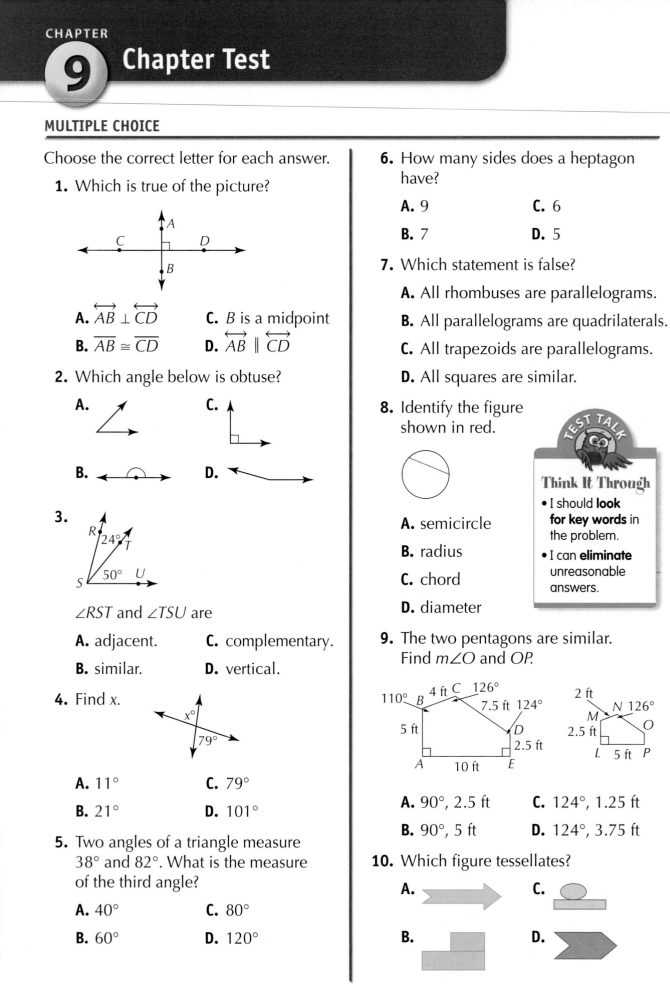

A. $\overleftrightarrow{AB} \perp \overleftrightarrow{CD}$ **C.** *B* is a midpoint

B. $\overline{AB} \cong \overline{CD}$ **D.** $\overleftrightarrow{AB} \parallel \overleftrightarrow{CD}$

2. Which angle below is obtuse?

A.   **C.**

B.   **D.**

3.

   ∠*RST* and ∠*TSU* are

   A. adjacent.   **C.** complementary.

   B. similar.   **D.** vertical.

4. Find *x*.

   A. 11°   **C.** 79°

   B. 21°   **D.** 101°

5. Two angles of a triangle measure 38° and 82°. What is the measure of the third angle?

   A. 40°   **C.** 80°

   B. 60°   **D.** 120°

6. How many sides does a heptagon have?

   A. 9   **C.** 6

   B. 7   **D.** 5

7. Which statement is false?

   A. All rhombuses are parallelograms.

   B. All parallelograms are quadrilaterals.

   C. All trapezoids are parallelograms.

   D. All squares are similar.

8. Identify the figure shown in red.

   A. semicircle

   B. radius

   C. chord

   D. diameter

   TEST TALK

   Think It Through
   - I should **look for key words** in the problem.
   - I can **eliminate** unreasonable answers.

9. The two pentagons are similar. Find *m∠O* and *OP*.

   A. 90°, 2.5 ft   **C.** 124°, 1.25 ft

   B. 90°, 5 ft   **D.** 124°, 3.75 ft

10. Which figure tessellates?

    A.   **C.**

    B.   **D.**

11. A triangle on the coordinate grid has vertices at $(-3,4)$, $(-1,1)$, and $(-3,0)$. If the triangle is translated 3 units down and then flipped over the *y*-axis, what would be the coordinates of the new triangle's vertices?

A. $(3,3); (1,4); (3,7)$

B. $(3,1); (1,-2); (3,-3)$

C. $(-3,1); (-3,-3); (-1,-2)$

D. $(3,0); (1,1); (3,4)$

FREE RESPONSE

Draw a diagram to illustrate each.

12. Point *Y* is the midpoint of $\overline{GH}$.

13. $\overrightarrow{MN}$ intersects parallel lines $\overleftrightarrow{AC}$ and $\overleftrightarrow{UV}$.

Classify each angle.

14. $125°$ **15.** $32°$ **16.** $98°$

17. Find the measure of an angle supplementary to an angle with a measure of $68°$.

Trace $\overline{PQ}$ and $\angle C$.

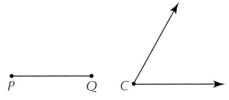

18. Construct a segment congruent to $\overline{PQ}$.

19. Construct the bisector of $\angle C$.

For 20–23, classify each polygon in as many ways as possible. Then tell if it is a regular polygon.

20. **21.**
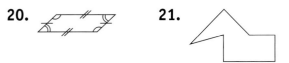

22. **23.**

Tell whether the figures in each pair are related by a slide, a flip, or a turn. If a turn, describe it.

24. **25.**

Tell if each figure has reflection symmetry, rotational symmetry, or both.

26. **27.**

Writing in Math

28. If two triangles are similar and one is an acute isosceles triangle, is the other one also an acute isosceles triangle? Explain.

29. Compare the figures below. Write two statements about how the figures are alike and two statements about how the figures are different.

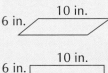
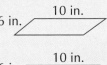

Think It Through
- I can **draw a picture** to help explain my thinking.
- I should **make my answer brief but complete.**

30. Draw a picture to solve the problem. A tour bus travels 15 mi north, $6\frac{2}{3}$ mi west, $8\frac{2}{3}$ mi south, and 23 mi east. How far has the tour bus traveled when it crosses its own path?

Number and Operation

MULTIPLE CHOICE

1. Which is 34,000,000 written in scientific notation?

   A. 3.4×10^6 **C.** 34×10^6

   B. 3.4×10^7 **D.** 0.34×10^8

2. Which is equivalent to 5%?

   A. 0.5   **C.** 0.20

   B. $\frac{1}{5}$ **D.** $\frac{1}{20}$

3. Find $35 \times \frac{3}{5}$.

   A. $4\frac{1}{5}$ **C.** 15

   B. 7   **D.** 21

FREE RESPONSE

4. Find $7\frac{3}{4} - 2\frac{4}{5}$.

5. Find the GCF of 12 and 32.

6. The temperature in the evening was 5°C. The temperature dropped 12°C overnight and then rose 3°C by 7:00 A.M. What was the temperature at 7:00 A.M.?

Writing in Math

7. Explain how to find the least common denominator of two fractions.

8. A shirt is on sale for 25% off the original price. If the original price is $32.50, what is the sale price? Explain how you found your answer.

Geometry and Measurement

MULTIPLE CHOICE

9. Which two lines are perpendicular?

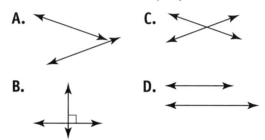

10. If Point T is the midpoint of $\overline{AB}$ and $\overline{UV}$, which of the following is true?

    A. $\overline{AB} \perp \overline{UV}$ **C.** $\overline{AT} \cong \overline{BT}$

    B. $\overline{AT} \cong \overline{UT}$ **D.** $\overline{AB} \cong \overline{UV}$

11.

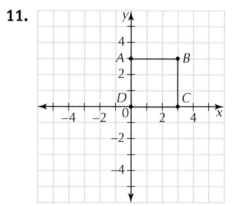

    $ABCD$ is reflected over the x-axis, then rotated 90° clockwise about the origin. What are the new coordinates of Point A?

    A. $(0,0)$ **C.** $(-3,-3)$

    B. $(0,-3)$ **D.** $(-3,0)$

FREE RESPONSE

12. The angles of a quadrilateral measure 102°, 67°, 98° and $x°$. Find x.

Writing in Math

13. Describe the similarities and differences between an equilateral triangle and a scalene triangle.

Data Analysis and Probability

MULTIPLE CHOICE

14. What is the probability of pulling a red sock without looking from a drawer containing 4 white socks, 2 black socks, and 2 red socks?

A. $\frac{1}{8}$　　　　　**C.** $\frac{2}{6}$

B. $\frac{1}{4}$　　　　　**D.** $\frac{1}{2}$

FREE RESPONSE

Use the bar graph to answer 15–16.

Rainfall Totals

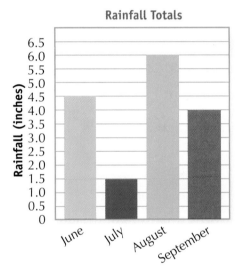

15. How much more rain fell in September than in July?

Writing in Math

16. What was the average rainfall per month over the 4 months? Explain how you found your answer.

17. Which type of graph is best to display the data below? Explain your choice.

Favorite Color

Color	# of votes
Red	45
Blue	55
Green	36
Yellow	24

Algebra

MULTIPLE CHOICE

18. Solve for the variable.

$$\frac{4}{5}x = 2\frac{2}{5}$$

A. $x = 1\frac{1}{2}$　　　　**C.** $x = 5$

B. $x = 3$　　　　　**D.** $x = 12$

19. Solve $y + (-5) = 16$.

A. $y = 21$　　　　**C.** $y = 11$

B. $y = -21$　　　　**D.** $y = -11$

FREE RESPONSE

20. To make 18 muffins, Josie needs $2\frac{1}{4}$ cups of flour. How much flour does she need to make 24 muffins?

21. Find $b \div (-6)$ when $b = -108$.

Solve for the variable.

22. $\frac{-5}{6}y = \frac{3}{5}$　　　　**23.** $\frac{m}{2.3} = -5.2$

24. $\frac{1}{4}d = 1.7$　　　　**25.** $-4.95a = 89.1$

26. $x - 12 = -25$　　　**27.** $r + 115 = 13$

Writing in Math

28. Explain how to graph the line given by the equation $y = 4x - 2$.

29. Rectangles A and B are similar. The length of rectangle A is 3.5 cm. The length of rectangle B is 10.5 cm. If the width of rectangle A is 1.4 cm, what is the width of rectangle B? Explain your answer.

Think It Through

I can draw a picture to help explain my thinking.

Set 9-1 (pages 472–475)

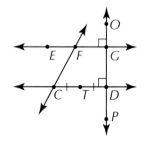

Use the diagram above to name

three rays. $\quad\overrightarrow{FE}\;\overrightarrow{CF}\;\overrightarrow{FG}$

three line segments. $\quad\overline{EG}\;\overline{CD}\;\overline{CF}$

two parallel rays. $\quad\overrightarrow{FG}\parallel\overrightarrow{CD}$

Remember that if two lines form a right angle, they are perpendicular lines.

Use the diagram at the left to name

1. a midpoint.

2. two perpendicular rays.

3. two parallel lines.

Set 9-2 (pages 476–479)

Classify the angle as acute, right, obtuse, or straight. Then measure the angle.

Since the angle measures 115°, it is obtuse.

Remember that you can use a protractor to measure and draw angles.

1. 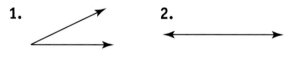 **2.**

Set 9-3 (pages 480–483)

Find *x*.

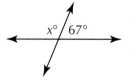 The angle measuring *x* is supplementary to the angle measuring 67°.

$x + 67 = 180; x = 113°$

Remember that the measures of complementary angles add up to 90° and the measures of supplementary angles add up to 180°.

1. 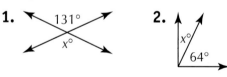 **2.**

Set 9-4 (pages 484–487)

Construct the bisector of ∠*A*.

Step 1: Draw an arc intersecting ∠*A* at points *P* and *Q*.

Step 2: Draw intersecting arcs with the same compass setting.

Step 3: Draw a ray from point *A* to the arcs.

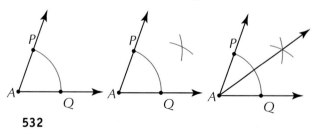

Remember that two congruent angles have the same measure.

1. Construct a segment congruent to segment $\overline{XY}$.

2. Construct an angle congruent to ∠*A*.

Set 9-5 (pages 490–491)

When you draw a picture, follow these steps.

Step 1: Draw a picture to represent the situation.

Step 2: Finish the picture to show the action in the story.

Step 3: Interpret the picture to find the answer.

Remember to check that your answer is reasonable.

1. Loni is making a quilt. Each square of the quilt is made up of 4 triangles. If the quilt is made by making 5 rows of 6 squares each, how many triangles will be on the quilt?

Set 9-6 (pages 494–495)

Name the polygon. Then tell if it appears to be a regular polygon.

The polygon has 6 sides, so it is a hexagon. The sides are of equal length and the angles are of equal measure, so it is a regular hexagon.

Remember that a regular polygon has congruent sides and congruent angles.

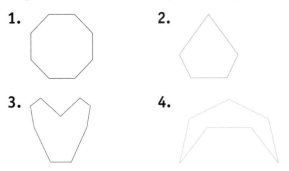

Set 9-7 (pages 496–499)

Find the missing angle measure.

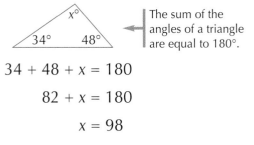

The sum of the angles of a triangle are equal to 180°.

$$34 + 48 + x = 180$$
$$82 + x = 180$$
$$x = 98$$

The missing angle measure is 98°.

Remember that the sum of the angle measures of a triangle is 180°.

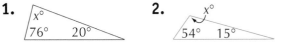

Set 9-8 (pages 500–501)

Classify the polygon in as many ways as possible.

The polygon has four sides. It is a quadrilateral.

Both pairs of opposite sides are parallel. It is a parallelogram.

Remember that the sum of the measures of a quadrilateral is 360°.

1.   2.

3. The angles of a quadrilateral measure 106°, 118°, 54°, and x°. Find x.

Set 9-9 (pages 502–503)

Identify the figure shown in red.

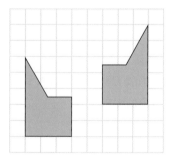

The shaded region is bound by two radii and an arc. The shaded region is a sector.

Remember that the diameter of a circle passes through the center of the circle. Identify the figure shown in red.

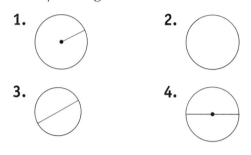

1.
2.
3.
4.

Set 9-10 (pages 506–509)

These trapezoids are congruent.
Find m∠*J* and *KL*.

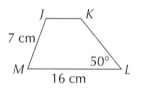 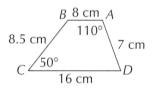

Corresponding angles are congruent.

∠*A* ≅ ∠*J*   So, m∠*J* = 110°

Corresponding sides are congruent.

$\overline{BC} \cong \overline{KL}$ So, *KL* = 8.5 cm

Remember that similar figures have the same shape and may or may not have the same size.

The triangles at the right are similar.

1. Find *ZY*.

2. Find m∠*Y*.

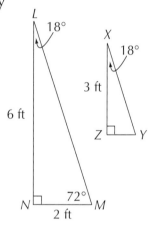

Set 9-11 (pages 510–511)

Tell whether the figures in each pair are related by a slide, a flip, a glide reflection, or a turn. If a turn, describe it.

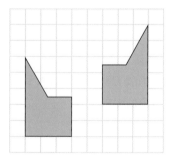

The figures above show a slide followed by a reflection.

The figures are related by a glide reflection.

Remember that turns move a figure about a point.

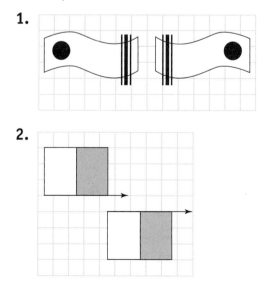

1.

2.

Write a statement about how the shapes are alike and a statement about how the shapes are different.

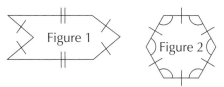

Both figures are hexagons.

Figure 1 does not have sides of equal length and angles of equal measure. Figure 2 is a regular hexagon.

Remember that you can compare length, angle measure, and position of figures.

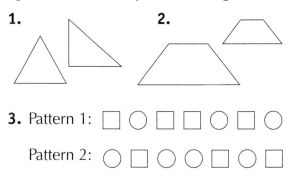

3. Pattern 1: □ ○ □ □ ○ □ ○

   Pattern 2: ○ □ ○ ○ □ ○ □

Tell what type of symmetry the figure has.

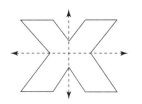

The figure has both reflection symmetry and rotational symmetry.

It has 2 lines of symmetry.

A 180° turn will rotate the figure onto itself.

Remember that a figure has reflection symmetry if it can be reflected onto itself.

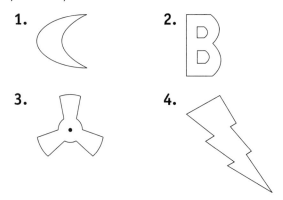

Does this figure tessellate? If so, trace the figure and draw the tessellation.

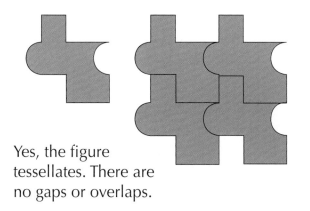

Yes, the figure tessellates. There are no gaps or overlaps.

Remember that for a figure to tessellate, there can be no gaps or overlaps.

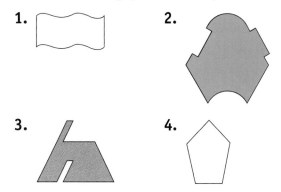

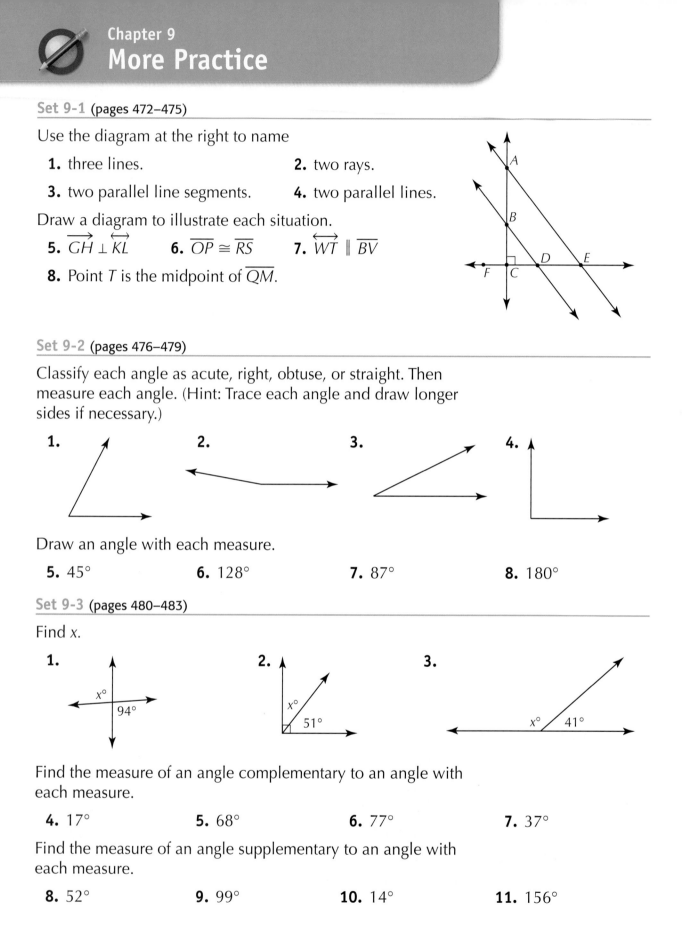

Set 9-1 (pages 472–475)

Use the diagram at the right to name

1. three lines.

2. two rays.

3. two parallel line segments.

4. two parallel lines.

Draw a diagram to illustrate each situation.

5. $\overrightarrow{GH} \perp \overleftrightarrow{KL}$ **6.** $\overline{OP} \cong \overline{RS}$ **7.** $\overleftrightarrow{WT} \parallel \overline{BV}$

8. Point T is the midpoint of $\overline{QM}$.

Set 9-2 (pages 476–479)

Classify each angle as acute, right, obtuse, or straight. Then measure each angle. (Hint: Trace each angle and draw longer sides if necessary.)

1.

2.

3.

4.

Draw an angle with each measure.

5. 45°   **6.** 128°   **7.** 87°   **8.** 180°

Set 9-3 (pages 480–483)

Find x.

1.

$x°$

$94°$

2.

$x°$

$51°$

3.

$x°$ $41°$

Find the measure of an angle complementary to an angle with each measure.

4. 17°   **5.** 68°   **6.** 77°   **7.** 37°

Find the measure of an angle supplementary to an angle with each measure.

8. 52°   **9.** 99°   **10.** 14°   **11.** 156°

Take It to the NET
www More Practice
www.scottforesman.com

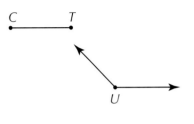

Set 9-4 (pages 484–487)

Trace $\overline{CT}$ and ∠U at the right.

1. Construct a segment congruent to $\overline{CT}$.

2. Construct an angle congruent to ∠U.

3. Construct the perpendicular bisector of $\overline{CT}$.

4. Construct the bisector of ∠U.

Set 9-5 (pages 490–491)

Draw a picture to solve each problem.
Write each answer in a complete sentence.

1. Lisette is pushing 6 square tables together to form a long
rectangular table. If each square table is 3 ft on each side and
the tables are pushed together end to end (so that the long
rectangular table will be 3 ft wide), how long will the table be?

2. At summer camp, a group of campers separated into pairs
to play a game. If there were 6 campers in the group, how
many different pairs could be made?

Set 9-6 (pages 494–495)

Name each polygon. Then tell if it appears to be a regular polygon.

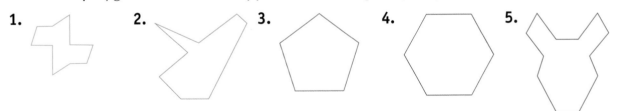

1.   **2.**   **3.**   **4.**   **5.**

6. Draw a figure that is NOT a polygon but is made up of 6 segments.

Set 9-7 (pages 496–499)

Find the missing angle measure. Then classify the triangle by
its angles and sides.

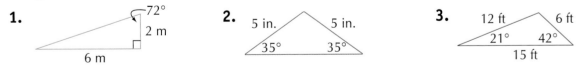

1.   72°   2 m   6 m   **2.** 5 in.   5 in.   35°   35°   **3.** 12 ft   6 ft   21°   42°   15 ft

4. Draw a triangle with a 3-inch side included between a
105° angle and a 25° angle. Then classify the triangle by its
angles and sides.

5. Draw a triangle with a 90° angle between sides of 3 inches
and 4 inches. Then classify the triangle by its angles and sides.

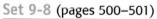
Set 9-8 (pages 500–501)

Classify each polygon in as many ways as possible.

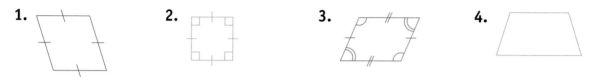

1.　　　　　　　**2.**　　　　　　　**3.**　　　　　　　**4.**

The measures of three angles of a quadrilateral are given. Find the measure of the fourth angle.

5. 36°, 95°, 140°　　　　**6.** 88°, 88°, 92°　　　　**7.** 118°, 55°, 42°

8. Use a ruler and protractor to draw a parallelogram with sides of length 4 cm and 6 cm and an angle measuring 100°.

Set 9-9 (pages 502–503)

Identify the figure shown in red.

1.　　　**2.**　　　**3.**　　　**4.**　　　**5.**

6. How are the radius and the diameter in the same circle related?

7. Find the measure of ∠RST in circle S at the right.

Set 9-10 (pages 506–509)

1. The rectangles at the right are similar. Find PQ and m∠Q.

2. The trapezoids at the right are congruent. Find UV and m∠X.

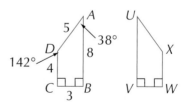

3. Box A and Box B are similar. Box A is 2 ft wide, 3 ft long, and 1 ft deep. Box B is 4.6 ft wide. How deep is Box B?

4. A TV monitor measures 17.5 in. by 24.5 in. A movie screen measures 20 ft by 28 ft. Are the two rectangular screens similar? Explain.

5. Are all squares similar? Explain.

Take It to the NET
More Practice
www.scottforesman.com

Set 9-11 (pages 510–511)

Tell whether the figures in each pair are related by a slide, a flip, a glide reflection, or a turn. If a turn, describe it.

1.   2.   3.   4.

5. Draw a triangle on grid paper with vertices at (3,2), (0,0), and (1,4). Slide the triangle 3 units to the right and then flip it over the *y*-axis. What are the coordinates of the vertices of the new triangle?

Set 9-12 (pages 512–513)

1. Compare the figures at the right.

 a. Write two statements about how the figures are alike.

 b. Write two statements about how the figures are different.

2. Look at the two number patterns at the right.

 a. Write a statement about how the patterns are alike.   3, 15, 23, 35, 43, 55, . . .

 b. Write a statement about how the patterns are different.   7, 12, 27, 32, 47, 52, . . .

Set 9-13 (pages 514–515)

Tell if each figure has reflection symmetry, rotational symmetry, or both. If it has reflection symmetry, how many lines of symmetry are there? If it has rotational symmetry, what is the smallest turn that will rotate the figure onto itself?

1.   2.   3.   4.

5. Which capital letters have reflection symmetry? rotational symmetry?

Set 9-14 (pages 516–519)

Draw a tessellation made up of each polygon.

 1. hexagon   **2.** quadrilateral

Does each shape tessellate? If so, trace the figure and draw the tessellation.

3.   4.   5.   6.

DIAGNOSING READINESS

A Vocabulary

(pages 494, 500, 502, Gr. 5)

Choose the best term from the box.

1. __?__ is the distance around a closed figure.

2. The length of the __?__ of a circle is twice the length of its __?__.

3. A __?__ has sides of equal length and angles of equal measure.

4. __?__ is the number of square units needed to cover a closed figure.

5. The number of cubic units needed to fill a solid figure is a measure of __?__.

Vocabulary

- **diameter** *(p. 502)*
- **radius** *(p. 502)*
- **perimeter** *(Gr. 5)*
- **rectangle** *(p. 500)*
- **regular polygon** *(p. 494)*
- **volume** *(Gr. 5)*
- **area** *(Gr. 5)*

B Units of Measurement

(Gr. 5)

Choose the best unit of measurement for each object's length, capacity, weight, or mass.

Choose inch, foot, yard, or mile.

6. a caterpillar   7. a football field

Choose centimeter, meter, or kilometer.

8. a plane ride   9. a textbook

Choose ounce, pound, or ton.

10. a truck   11. a butterfly

Choose gram or kilogram.

12. a person   13. a pencil

Choose cup, quart, or gallon.

14. a bathtub   15. a can of soup

Choose milliliter or liter.

16. an eyedropper   17. a fish tank

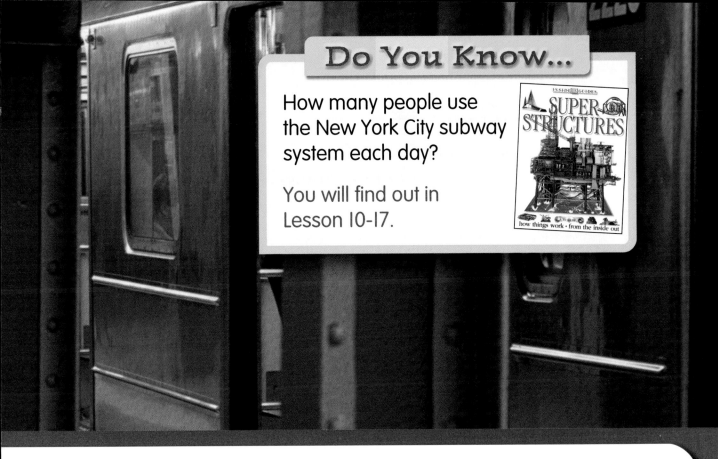

Do You Know...

How many people use the New York City subway system each day?

You will find out in Lesson 10-17.

C Plane Figures
(pages 494, 496, Gr. 5)

Classify each figure. Be as specific as possible.

18.

19.

20.

21.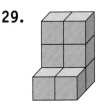

How many square units does each figure cover?

22.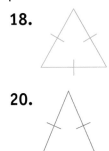

23.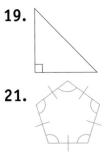

Tell how many sides each polygon has.

24. octagon

25. heptagon

26. quadrilateral

27. dodecagon

D Solid Figures
(Gr. 5)

Draw front, side, and top views of each solid made from unit cubes.

28.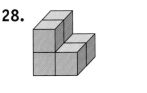

29.

30.

31.

32. Sort the solid figures below into two groups. Group A should be solids with all flat surfaces. Group B should be solids with curved surfaces.

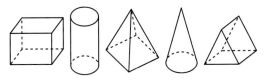

Key Idea
You can use multiplication and division to change from one unit of customary measurement to another.

Vocabulary
• capacity

Customary Measurement

LEARN

How can you change from one unit of length to another?

Customary units of length include inches, feet, yards, and miles. The relationship between these units is shown at the right.

Data File

foot (ft)	1 ft = 12 in.
yard (yd)	1 yd = 3 ft
	1 yd = 36 in.
mile (mi)	1 mi = 5,280 ft
	1 mi = 1,760 yd

Example A

Each letter on a hospital roof helipad is 2.5 feet wide. What is the width of each letter in inches?

To change from larger units to smaller units, multiply.

Think: 1 foot = 12 inches
$2.5 \times 12 = 30$
2.5 ft = 30 in.

Each letter is 30 inches wide.

Example B

The emergency wing of the hospital is 97 feet in length. What is the length of the wing in yards?

To change from smaller units to larger units, divide.

Think: 3 feet = 1 yard
$97 \div 3 = 32.\overline{3}$
97 ft = $32.\overline{3}$ yd

The length of the wing is $32.\overline{3}$ yards.

$$\begin{array}{r} 32.33... \\ 3\overline{)97.00} \\ -96 \\ \hline 1\,0 \\ -9 \\ \hline 10 \end{array}$$

✓ **Talk About It**

1. In Example B, how many feet are in $\frac{1}{3}$ yard? how many inches?

What units can you use to measure weight?

Weight is a measure of how heavy something is. Customary units of weight include ounces, pounds, and tons.

Data File

| pound (lb) | 1 lb = 16 ounces (oz) |
| ton (T) | 1 T = 2,000 lb |

Think It Through
I can also **use a proportion** to change units of measurement.

$\frac{1 \text{ lb}}{16 \text{ oz}} = \frac{p}{40 \text{ oz}}$

Example C

What is the weight of a 40-ounce book in pounds?

An ounce is a smaller unit than a pound, so divide.

$40 \div 16 = 2.5$

The weight of the book is 2.5 lb.

$$\begin{array}{r} 2.5 \\ 16\overline{)40.0} \\ -32 \\ \hline 8\,0 \\ -8\,0 \\ \hline 0 \end{array}$$

How can you measure the amount a container can hold?

Capacity is the amount a container can hold. Customary units of capacity include fluid ounces, cups, pints, quarts, and gallons.

Data File

cup (c)	1 c = 8 fluid ounces (oz)
pint (pt)	1 pt = 2 c
quart (qt)	1 qt = 2 pt
gallon (gal)	1 gal = 4 qt

Example D

The daycare center has 16 quarts of milk delivered each day. How many children will the milk serve if each child drinks 1 cup?

Find the number of cups in 16 quarts.

Change quarts to pints. — Use 1 qt = 2 pt. Since a quart is larger than a pint, multiply.

$16 \times 2 = 32$

Change pints to cups. — Use 1 pt = 2 c. Since a pint is larger, multiply.

$32 \times 2 = 64$

There are 64 cups in 16 quarts.
The milk will serve 64 children.

Example E

How many pints are in 4 gallons 2 quarts?

Find the number of pints in 4 gallons.

Change gallons to quarts. — Use 1 gal = 4 qt. Since a gallon is larger than a quart, multiply.

$4 \times 4 = 16$

$16 + 2 = 18$ qt

Change quarts to pints. — Use 1 qt = 2 pt. Since a quart is larger, multiply.

$18 \times 2 = 36$

There are 36 pints in 4 gal 2 qt.

TEST TALK

Think It Through
I can find the answer by **solving two simpler problems.**

✔ Talk About It

2. In Example D, how can you find the number of gallons of milk delivered each day?

CHECK ✓

For another example, see Set 10-1 on p. 610.

Copy and complete.

1. 96 in. = ▢ ft   **2.** 2.5 lb = ▢ oz   **3.** 2 gal = ▢ pt   **4.** 5 ft = ▢ in.   **5.** 80 oz = ▢ lb

6. How many inches are in 3 yd?   **7.** How many pints are in 8 gal?

8. During a marathon, volunteers passed out 21 quarts of water at one station. How many one-cup servings did this provide?

9. Number Sense A patio is 130 inches long on one side. Can you express this length as a whole number of feet? Explain.

A Skills and Understanding

Copy and complete.

10. 0.5 ft = ☐ in.   **11.** 48 oz = ☐ lb   **12.** 18 yd = ☐ ft   **13.** 4.5 qt = ☐ c

14. 0.5 mi = ☐ ft   **15.** 18 in. = ☐ ft   **16.** 3 mi = ☐ yd   **17.** 5 mi = ☐ ft

18. 12 c = ☐ gal   **19.** 0.5 T = ☐ lb   **20.** 6 ft = ☐ in.   **21.** 44 oz = ☐ lb

22. 4 pt = ☐ qt   **23.** 72 ft = ☐ yd   **24.** 8.5 lb = ☐ oz

25. How many feet are in 7 yd 2 ft?

26. Number Sense There are 48 one-cup servings in
a punch bowl. How many quarts should Brittany
add to have a total of 80 servings?

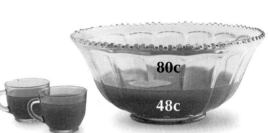

B Reasoning and Problem Solving

27. At one store, a gallon of milk costs $3.92 and
a quart of milk costs $0.94. Which is the better buy?

28. Tub A has a capacity of 40 gal. Tub B has a capacity of 161 qt.
Which tub can hold more?

Math and Everyday Life

The Social Committee estimates that 360 people
will attend the school picnic.

29. One serving of hamburger will be 4 oz.
If each person gets one hamburger,
how many pounds of ground beef should
the committee buy?

30. Which fruit drink at the right is the
better buy?

31. How many gallons of fruit drink are needed
for the picnic if each person gets one cup?

32. Assuming the committee purchases the
less-expensive brand, what is the total cost
for the fruit drink?

33. If each person at the school picnic gets one cup
of fruit drink, what is the cost of the less-expensive
fruit drink per person, rounded to the nearest cent?

34. **Writing in Math** One serving of chili is 1 cup.
Hannah figures that 3 gallons will serve 64 people.
Is she right? Explain.

544

C Extensions

You can add and subtract combinations of customary units.

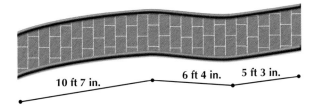

7 lb 8 oz
+ 11 lb 9 oz
18 lb 17 oz
19 lb 1 oz

Think: 16 oz = 1 lb, so add 1 lb to 18 lb to get 19 lb, with 1 oz left.

4 gal 5 qt
5 gal 1 qt
− 2 gal 3 qt
2 gal 2 qt

Think: 5 gal = 4 gal + 4 qt, so 5 gal 1 qt = 4 gal + 4 qt + 1 qt = 4 gal 5 qt

35. How long is this walkway in yards, feet, and inches?

10 ft 7 in.   6 ft 4 in.   5 ft 3 in.

36. Find the total weight of the packages below.

14 oz

7 lb 12 oz

4 lb 9 oz

37. Algebra The picture at the right measures 1 ft 6 in. across and 2 ft down. It is centered in a mat that will fit inside a frame that is 30 in. by 36 in. Find the *x* and *y* dimensions of the mat.

30 in.

1 ft. 6 in.

36 in.

2 ft.

x

y

Add or subtract.

38.   20 gal
     − 4 gal 1 qt

39.   8 lb 9 oz
     + 30 lb 9 oz

Mixed Review and Test Prep

Take It to the NET
Test Prep
www.scottforesman.com

40. $4.55 \times 1,000$

41. $7,765.4 \div 100$

42. 0.55×10

43. $6.9 \div 100$

44. $1,200 \times 1,000$

45. $0.007 \div 1,000$

46. A school worker uses $2\frac{3}{4}$ cartons of paper towels out of $4\frac{1}{4}$ cartons. How many cartons remain?

47. A typist can type $8\frac{1}{2}$ pages in one hour. How many pages can she type in 3 hours?

48. The sides of a triangle are all 4 units long. What type of triangle is it?

   A. obtuse   **B.** equilateral   **C.** scalene   **D.** right

Key Idea
In the metric system, you use decimals and powers of 10 to measure length, mass, and capacity.

Vocabulary
• metric system
• meter
• liter
• mass
• gram
• kilo-
• centi-
• milli-

Think It Through
I can **use approximate comparisons** to help choose units.

Metric Measurement

LEARN

WARM UP
1. 43.6 × 100
2. 2,344.8 ÷ 100
3. 173.65 × 1,000
4. 739.1 ÷ 1,000

What are metric units of measure?

In the **metric system,** the **meter** (m) is the basic unit of length. The basic unit for measuring capacity is the **liter** (L). **Mass** is the amount of matter in an object. When astronauts go into space, their weight decreases, but their mass remains the same. The basic unit for measuring mass is the **gram** (g).

The metric system also uses prefixes to describe amounts that are larger or smaller than the basic unit. The most common prefixes are **kilo-,** meaning 1,000; **centi-,** meaning $\frac{1}{100}$; and **milli-,** meaning $\frac{1}{1,000}$.

	Name	Abbreviation	Number of Base Units	Approximate Comparison
Length	**Kilo**meter	km	1,000	Length of 9 football fields
	Meter	m	1	Half the height of a door
	Centimeter	cm	$\frac{1}{100}$	Width of your smallest finger
	Millimeter	mm	$\frac{1}{1,000}$	Thickness of a dime
Capacity	Liter	L	1	A large bottle of water
	Milliliter	mL	$\frac{1}{1,000}$	The amount an eyedropper holds
Mass	**Kilo**gram	kg	1,000	Mass of a quart of milk
	Gram	g	1	Mass of a large paper clip

Example A

Janella has a European cookbook. The amounts for the ingredients are given in metric units. Which unit will the cookbook use for a spoonful of milk?

Think: The unit should be a unit of capacity. The capacity of a spoon is closer to that of an eyedropper than a bottle of water.

To measure spoonfuls, the cookbook will use milliliters.

✓ Talk About It

1. In Example A, which metric unit will the cookbook use for $2\frac{1}{2}$ pounds of potatoes?

2. How are millimeters and milliliters similar? How are they different?

How do you change from one metric unit of measure to another?

To change a measurement from one unit to another, multiply or divide by a power of 10.

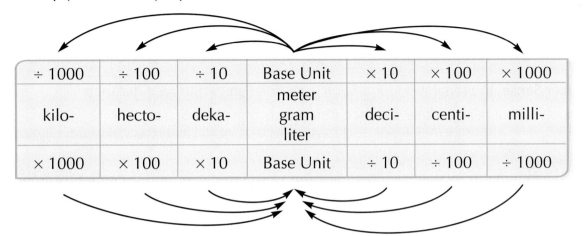

÷ 1000	÷ 100	÷ 10	Base Unit	× 10	× 100	× 1000
kilo-	hecto-	deka-	meter gram liter	deci-	centi-	milli-
× 1000	× 100	× 10	Base Unit	÷ 10	÷ 100	÷ 1000

Example B

Ropes that form the lanes in a pool are 2.5 cm wide. What is the width of the rope in millimeters?

To change from larger units to smaller units, multiply.

Think: 1 cm = 10 mm
$$2.5 \times 10 = 25$$
$$2.5 \text{ cm} = 25 \text{ mm}$$

The width of the rope is 25 mm.

Example C

For a triathlon, Mr. Abdar will swim 1,500 meters. How far is this in kilometers?

To change from smaller units to larger units, divide.

Think: 1,000 m = 1 km
$$1,500 \div 1,000 = 1.5$$
$$1,500 \text{ m} = 1.5 \text{ km}$$

Mr. Abdar will swim 1.5 km.

Example D

The mass of a seed is 8.45 grams. Find the mass of the seed in milligrams.

Since a gram is a larger unit than a milligram, multiply.

$$8.45 \times 10^3 = 8.450. = 8,450$$
$$8.45 \times 1,000 = 8,450$$

The mass of the seed is 8,450 mg.

TEST TALK

Think It Through
I can also **use a proportion** to change units of measurement.

$$\frac{1 \text{ g}}{1,000 \text{ mg}} = \frac{8.45 \text{ g}}{x \text{ mg}}$$

✔ Talk About It

3. What decimal part of a gram is 1 milligram?

4. By what power of ten would you divide to change millimeters to meters?

5. Number Sense Which is greater, 0.25 kL or 2,500 L?

Name the most appropriate metric unit for each measurement.

1. capacity of a tea cup   **2.** mass of a coin   **3.** height of a desk

Copy and complete.

4. 600 mL = ▨ L   **5.** 1.2 km = ▨ m   **6.** 3.2 kg = ▨ g   **7.** 3 cm = ▨ mm

8. 1.3 L = ▨ kL   **9.** 7.2 km = ▨ m   **10.** 950 mL = ▨ L   **11.** 5.4 cm = ▨ mm

12. Number Sense In preparation for a 5 km race, Jon runs $\frac{4}{5}$ the race distance each day. What is Jon's daily distance in meters?

PRACTICE

For more practice, see Set 10-2 on p. 614.

A Skills and Understanding

Name the most appropriate metric unit for each measurement.

13. length of an ant   **14.** mass of a bowling ball   **15.** capacity of a car's gas tank

Copy and complete.

16. 98 g = ▨ kg   **17.** 310 mL = ▨ L   **18.** 9 cm = ▨ mm   **19.** 2.3 kg = ▨ g

20. 970 mL = ▨ L   **21.** 3.25 km = ▨ m   **22.** 2,221 m = ▨ km   **23.** 35.4 cm = ▨ mm

24. 4.3 mm = ▨ cm   **25.** 7.8 kg = ▨ g   **26.** 60 cm = ▨ mm   **27.** 3.20 L = ▨ mL

28. Number Sense How many grams must be added to the right pan of the balance to equal the 2 kg in the left pan?

B Reasoning and Problem Solving

29. An average orange has a mass of 270 g. What is the mass of 8 oranges in kilograms?

30. Linda has 4.6 L of lemonade to serve 20 guests. How many milliliters should she pour into each glass?

31. Nutritionists recommend drinking eight glasses of water each day. Assuming a glass holds 240 mL, does the recommended daily water intake exceed 1 L?

32. A vitamin supplement provides 500 mg of calcium, which is about 42% of the recommended daily allowance. About what is the recommended daily allowance for calcium in grams?

Each glass holds 240 mL.

Math and Science

Density is the ratio of the mass of an object to its volume, and is calculated by using the formula $density = \frac{mass}{volume}$.

One way to identify an unknown substance is to calculate its density and compare it to the densities of known substances. For example, suppose a 5 mL sample of a liquid has a mass of 5 g. Since $\frac{5\ g}{5\ mL} = 1.0\ \frac{g}{mL}$, the liquid is water.

For 33–36, use the density chart at the right to identify the following liquid samples.

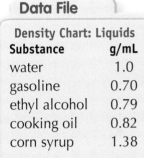

Data File

Density Chart: Liquids

Substance	g/mL
water	1.0
gasoline	0.70
ethyl alcohol	0.79
cooking oil	0.82
corn syrup	1.38

33. mass: 690 g   volume: 0.5 L

34. mass: 790 mg   volume: 1 L

35. mass: 0.738 kg   volume: 0.0009 kL

36. **Writing in Math** Yolanda needs to change 2,560 mL to liters. Her work is shown below.

$$1\ mL = \frac{1}{1,000}\ L.\ So,\ 2,560\ mL = 2,560 \times \frac{1}{1,000} = 2.56\ L.$$

Is her reasoning correct? Explain.

C Extensions

37. Maggie wants to strengthen each edge of this box with tape. How many meters of tape will she need?

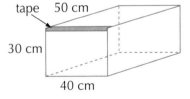

tape 50 cm

30 cm

40 cm

Mixed Review and Test Prep

Take It to the NET
Test Prep
www.scottforesman.com

Copy and complete.

38. 50 oz = ▮ lb

39. $3\frac{1}{2}$ qt = ▮ pt

40. $1\frac{1}{3}$ yd = ▮ in.

41. 36 c = ▮ qt

42. 60 in. = ▮ ft

43. $\frac{3}{4}$ mi = ▮ yd

44. **Algebra** Solve $x + (-3) = 10$.

45. **Algebra** Solve $-5a = 10$.

46. Find $2\frac{3}{8} + 4\frac{5}{16}$.

  A. $6\frac{8}{24}$ **C.** $6\frac{11}{16}$

  B. $6\frac{1}{3}$ **D.** $6\frac{13}{16}$

47. Which is the product $1\frac{2}{5} \times 2\frac{3}{5}$?

  A. $2\frac{6}{25}$ **C.** $3\frac{16}{25}$

  B. $3\frac{1}{5}$ **D.** $18\frac{1}{5}$

Key Idea
The smaller the unit of measure you use, the more precise the measurement will be.

Materials
• customary ruler
• metric ruler

Think It Through
I can **estimate** the measure by **rounding**.

Units of Measure and Precision

LEARN

Activity

Which measurement is the most precise?

All measurements are approximations. The paper clip at the right measures about 2 inches. A more precise measurement is about $1\frac{13}{16}$ inches. An even more precise measurement is about 46 mm. The smaller the units on the scale of a measuring instrument, the more **precise** the measurement is.

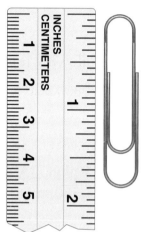

a. Measure and record the length, width, and thickness of your math book to the nearest quarter inch, eighth inch, sixteenth inch, centimeter, and millimeter.

b. Compare your measurements with other classmates. For which units of measure are the results the same? Explain why.

Example

To the nearest whole, half, quarter, eighth, and sixteenth inch, how long is this pencil? To the nearest centimeter and millimeter, how long is it?

The length of the pencil to the nearest

whole inch: 3   half inch: $3\frac{1}{2}$ quarter inch: $3\frac{1}{4}$ eighth inch: $3\frac{2}{8}$

sixteenth inch: $3\frac{5}{16}$ centimeter: 8   millimeter: 83

✓ **Talk About It**

1. Which measurement in the Example is the most precise? Explain.

Measure each segment to the nearest eighth inch and nearest centimeter.

1. ├────────────┤   **2.** ├─────────────────┤   **3.** ├──────────────────────────┤

Measure each segment to the nearest sixteenth inch and nearest millimeter.

4. ├──────────────────────────┤   **5.** ├──────────────────────────────────┤

6. Connections Which measurement is more precise, pounds or grams? Explain.

PRACTICE   *For more practice, see Set 10-3 on p. 614.*

Ⓐ Skills and Understanding

Measure each segment to the nearest eighth inch and nearest centimeter.

7. ├──────────┤   **8.** ├────────────────────┤   **9.** ├────┤

Measure each segment to the nearest sixteenth inch and nearest millimeter.

10. ├──────────────────────┤   **11.** ├──────────────────────────────┤

12. Connections Which measurement is less precise, cups or milliliters? Explain.

Ⓑ Reasoning and Problem Solving

13. Using the Global Positioning System (GPS), a geologist finds the distance between two mountain peaks. Which measurement is most precise, 1,068 m, 1,067.52 m, or 1,067.5 m?

14. The height of a mountain peak is 8,848 m. Express this height in kilometers.

15. <u>**Writing in Math**</u> In *Castle Diary,* Tobias writes that chain mail body armor was made by linking tiny wire loops. One coat of armor might contain 30,000 rings. If $1\frac{7}{8}$ inches of wire were needed to make each ring, how much wire was needed to make one coat? Express your answer in yards, feet, and inches.

🦉 Mixed Review and Test Prep

Take It to the NET
www Test Prep
www.scottforesman.com

Copy and complete.

16. 4.5 m = ▩ cm   **17.** 68 mL = ▩ L   **18.** 50.2 g = ▩ kg

19. 0.04 kL = ▩ mL   **20.** 0.8 g = ▩ mg   **21.** 290 mm = ▩ m

22. In $\triangle ABC$, $m\angle C = 90°$, $AC = 5$, and $BC = 5$. Which best describes $\triangle ABC$?

    A. isosceles   **B.** equilateral   **C.** right   **D.** isosceles, right

Key Idea
Since many countries of the world use the metric system, you need to know how customary and metric units of measurement are related.

Materials
• customary ruler
• yardstick
• metric ruler
• meter stick

Relating Customary and Metric Measurements

LEARN

WARM UP
1. 64 oz = ☐ lb
2. 400 L = ☐ kL
3. $3\frac{2}{3}$ yd = ☐ ft
4. 1,600 mL = ☐ L

Activity

How do customary and metric units compare?

a. Compare a yardstick to a meter stick. Use the relationships you find between units of length to complete each statement.

1 m is about ☐ ft.   1 in. is about ☐ cm.

b. Use the weight/mass relationships to complete each statement.

Weight/Mass	
1 kg ≈ 2 lb	28 g ≈ 1 oz

1 lb is about ☐ kg.   1 lb is about ☐ g.

c. Use the capacity relationships to complete each statement.

Capacity	
1 L ≈ 1 qt	30 mL ≈ 1 oz

1 gal is about ☐ L.   1 pt is about ☐ mL.

How can you convert between measurement systems?

You can convert between customary and metric measures using the table below. Only the equivalent for inches and centimeters is exact. All the other equivalents are approximate.

Customary and Metric Unit Equivalents		
Length	Weight/Mass	Capacity
1 in. = 2.54 cm	1 oz ≈ 28.35 g	1 L ≈ 1.06 qt
1 m ≈ 39.37 in.	1 kg ≈ 2.2 lb	1 gal ≈ 3.79 L
1 mi ≈ 1.61 km	1 metric ton (t) ≈ 1.102 T	

Example A

An imported pair of jeans has a waist measure of 76.2 cm. Convert this measure to inches.

A centimeter is a smaller unit than an inch, so divide.

$76.2 \div 2.54 = 30$

$$\begin{array}{r} 30 \\ 254\overline{)7620} \\ -\underline{7620} \\ 0 \end{array}$$

76.2 cm = 30 in.

Example B

A race is 13 miles. Convert this distance to kilometers.

A mile is a larger unit than a kilometer, so multiply.

$13 \times 1.61 = 20.93$ km

$$\begin{array}{r} 1.61 \\ \times\ \ 13 \\ \hline 20.93 \end{array}$$

13 mi ≈ 20.93 km

TEST TALK

Think It Through
I can **use a proportion** to convert inches to centimeters.

$$\frac{1\ in.}{2.54\ cm} = \frac{x\ in.}{76.2\ cm}$$

✔ Talk About It

1. Explain how you could use compatible numbers to estimate the conversion from centimeters to inches in Example A.

For another example, see Set 10-4 on p. 610.

CHECK ✔

Copy and complete. Round to the nearest tenth.

1. 50 in. =   cm

2. 25.8 L ≈   gal

3. 55 lb ≈   kg

4. **Estimation** Use 1 mi ≈ $\frac{3}{2}$ km to estimate the number of miles in 120 km.

PRACTICE

For more practice, see Set 10-4 on p. 614.

Ⓐ Skills and Understanding

Copy and complete. Round to the nearest tenth.

5. 300 yd ≈   m

6. 60.4 kg ≈   lb

7. 130.2 m ≈   yd

8. 8 fluid oz ≈   mL

9. 5 oz ≈   g

10. 6 pt ≈   L

11. **Estimation** Use 1 in. ≈ $\frac{5}{2}$ cm to estimate the number of cm in 1 ft.

Ⓑ Reasoning and Problem Solving

12. The speed limit on most highways in Denmark is 110 km/h. Convert this speed limit to miles per hour, rounded to the nearest tenth mile.

13. A European car can travel 8.3 km on 1 liter of gas. Express this unit rate in miles per gallon, rounded to the nearest tenth mile.

14. **Writing in Math** There are 1,760 yards in a mile and 1,000 meters in a kilometer. Explain how the distance of a mile compares to that of a kilometer.

🦉 Mixed Review and Test Prep

Take It to the NET
Test Prep
www.scottforesman.com

For each pair of measurements, determine the more precise measurement.

15. 0.5 mi; 2,638 ft

16. 2 m; 198.95 cm

17. 36 in.; $35\frac{11}{16}$ in.

18. Which point is in the fourth quadrant?

   A. (4, 7)   **B.** (−4, 7)   **C.** (−4, −7)   **D.** (4, −7)

19. In which quadrant is (−3, 2)?

   A. I   **B.** II   **C.** III   **D.** IV

All text pages available online and on CD-ROM.

Vocabulary
• elapsed time

Elapsed Time

LEARN

How can you find how much time passes between two events?

Japan has a high-speed train network that connects Tokyo with most of the country's other major cities. To use the train schedule, you need to know how to find the difference between two times, or **elapsed time**.

WARM UP

1. 0.4 h =   min

2. 92 min =   h   min

3. $2\frac{4}{5}$ h =   min

4. 4 h 10 min =   h

Tokaido Shinkansen Schedule

Depart Tokyo	Arrive (Time)
6:33 A.M.	Okayama (10:41 A.M.)
7:38 A.M.	Hiroshima (12:16 P.M.)
4:37 P.M.	Hakata (10:41 P.M.)
10:46 P.M.	Mishima (11:40 P.M.)

Example A

How long does the commute from Tokyo to Hakata take?

One Way
Count on from the starting time to the ending time.

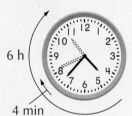

6 h

4 min

Count the whole hours:
4:37 to 10:37 is 6 hours.

Count the minutes from 10:37 to 10:41:
00:37 to 00:41 is 4 minutes.

Add the hours and minutes.
6 hours 4 minutes

Another Way
Subtract the ending time from the starting time.

$$\begin{array}{r} 10 \text{ h } 41 \text{ min} \\ - 4 \text{ h } 37 \text{ min} \\ \hline 6 \text{ h } 4 \text{ min} \end{array}$$

The commute from Tokyo to Hakata takes 6 hours 4 minutes.

Example B

Norio boarded the train in Tokyo and rode for 54 minutes. In which city did he arrive?

You can add to find the ending time.

$$\begin{array}{r} 10 \text{ h } 46 \text{ min} \\ + \phantom{10 \text{ h } 0}54 \text{ min} \\ \hline 10 \text{ h } 100 \text{ min} = 11 \text{ h } 40 \text{ min} \end{array}$$

Rename 100 min as 1 hr 40 min.

Norio arrived in Mishima.

Example C

Another train to Hiroshima will be added to the schedule. It will arrive at 7:18 P.M. If the commute from Tokyo to Hiroshima takes 4 hours 38 minutes, at what time should the train leave Tokyo?

You can subtract to find the starting time.

$$\begin{array}{r} 6\ \text{h}\ 78\ \text{min} \\ \cancel{7\ \text{h}\ 18\ \text{min}} \\ -\ 4\ \text{h}\ 38\ \text{min} \\ \hline 2\ \text{h}\ 40\ \text{min} \end{array}$$

18 min < 38 min
Rename to subtract.
7 h 18 min = 6 h 78 min

The train should leave at 2:40 P.M.

✔ Talk About It

1. The distance from Tokyo to Hakata is about 652 km. How can you estimate the train's speed in km per hour? miles per hour?

2. Can you use mixed numbers to find the elapsed times in Examples B and C? Explain.

3. Explain how you could count back to find the starting time in Example C.

How can you find the difference in elapsed times?

In 1977, the first woman wheelchair racer completed the Boston Marathon race with a finish time of 3:48:51. Twenty-three years later, the winning finish time for the women's wheelchair division was 2:00:52. How much longer did it take to complete the 26.2-mile course in 1977?

Example D

Find the difference in finish times.

$$\begin{array}{r} 3\ \text{h}\ 47\ \text{min}\ 111\ \text{s} \\ \cancel{3\ \text{h}\ 48\ \text{min}\quad 51\ \text{s}} \\ -\ 2\ \text{h}\ 00\ \text{min}\quad 52\ \text{s} \\ \hline 1\ \text{h}\ 47\ \text{min}\quad 59\ \text{s} \end{array}$$

Since 51 seconds < 52 seconds, rename to subtract.

1 min = 60 s, so
3h 48 min 51 s = 3 h 47 min 111s

It took 1 hour 47 minutes 59 seconds longer to complete the race in 1977.

✔ Talk About It

4. In Example D, are finish times elapsed times? Explain.

5. The winning finish time for the men's wheelchair division in 1977 was 2:40:10. Explain how you could count on to find the difference in the men's and women's finishing times that year.

For another example, see Set 10-5 on p. 611.

Find each elapsed time.

1. 6:19 A.M. to 8:03 A.M.   **2.** 11:51 A.M. to 2:10 P.M.   **3.** 4:27 P.M. to 1:08 A.M.

Find each starting time or ending time using the given elapsed time.

4. Start Time: 4:13 P.M.
Elapsed Time: 5 h 49 min

5. End Time: 11:05 A.M.
Elapsed Time: 0 h 58 min

6. Start Time: 12:58 A.M.
Elapsed Time: 22 h 10 min

Add or subtract.

7.   9 min 15 s
     + 15 min 49 s

8.   4 h   3 min 29 s
     − 2 h 15 min

9.   15 h   6 min 28 s
     − 7 h 29 min 56 s

10. Number Sense When adding or subtracting units of time, when do you rename?

For more practice, see Set 10-5 on p. 615.

A **Skills and Understanding**

Find each elapsed time.

11. 3:48 A.M. to 1:00 P.M.   **12.** 2:11 P.M. to 8:49 P.M.   **13.** 7:54 P.M. to 12:16 A.M.

Find each starting time or ending time using the given elapsed time.

14. End Time: 7:30 P.M.
Elapsed Time: 11 h 4 min

15. Start Time: 5:27 A.M.
Elapsed Time: 6 h 3 min

16. End Time: 10:43 P.M.
Elapsed Time: 9 h 15 min

Add or subtract.

17.   34 min 49 s
     + 3h 28 min 19 s

18.   3 h 13 min   8 s
     − 1 h 15 min 19 s

19.   14 h 59 min
     − 14 h 41 min 33 s

20. Number Sense Rename 1 day as 23 h ▧ min ▧ s.

B **Reasoning and Problem Solving**

☀ **Math and Everyday Life**

Poultry should be cooked long enough to be safe for eating. Recommended cooking times for several poultry types are given in the table at the right.

21. A 5-lb duck is put into the oven at 2:20 P.M. At about what time should the duck be finished cooking?

22. About how long will it take to cook a 0.68-kg pheasant?

Data File

Cooking Times	
Poultry	**Cook:**
Capon	20 to 30 min/lb
Duck	18 to 20 min/lb
Pheasant	30 min/lb
Turkey	15 to 20 min/lb

23. <u>Writing in Math</u> Is the method for subtracting the times correct? If not, explain why and show the correct subtraction.

Find the difference.

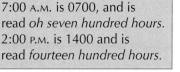

```
  18 h 60 min 60 s
  19 h
- 7 h 41 min 37 s
  11 h 19 min 23 s
```

C Extensions

Astronauts and military people use a 24-hour clock. Instead of starting at 1:00 again after 12:00 noon, the clock continues from 1300 up to 2400. When this 24-hour system is used, there is no need for A.M. or P.M.

> 7:00 A.M. is 0700, and is read *oh seven hundred hours*. 2:00 P.M. is 1400 and is read *fourteen hundred hours*.

Using a 24-hour system can sometimes make it easier to find elapsed time. For the example at the right, 2:39 P.M. was renamed as 14 h 39 min.

```
   14 h 39 min
   2 h 39 min P.M.
-  6 h 14 min A.M.
   8 h 25 min
```

Use a 24-hour system to find each elapsed time.

24. 11:08 A.M. to 7:43 P.M.   **25.** 7:32 A.M. to 1:58 P.M.

Mixed Review and Test Prep

Take It to the NET
Test Prep
www.scottforesman.com

Copy and complete. Round to the nearest tenth.

26. 24 kg ≈ ___ lb   **27.** 50 mi ≈ ___ km   **28.** 120 L ≈ ___ qt

29. Which number is prime?

    A. 8,832   **B.** 1   **C.** 143   **D.** 157

Discovery CHANNEL SCHOOL

Discover Math in Your World

Take It to the NET
Video and Activities
www.scottforesman.com

Bird Brain

Bird navigation studies have revealed that homing pigeons have trace amounts of magnetite in their brain tissue. Magnetite is an iron compound that is sensitive to magnetic fields and is believed to make the pigeons aware of north-south magnetic orientation.

1. Some homing pigeons have returned to their home lofts after being released from unfamiliar locations as far as 1,800 km away. Express this distance in miles.

2. In one study, a homing pigeon was set free at 7:06 A.M. and returned to its loft at 10:21:30 A.M. Find the elapsed flight time.

Draw Conclusions

Drawing conclusions when you read in math can help you use the **problem-solving strategy,** *Use Logical Reasoning,* in the next lesson.

In reading, drawing conclusions can help you make sense of things as you think through a story. In math, drawing conclusions can help you use logical reasoning as you think through a problem.

Juan and Amie work in the same office. They ride trains to work each morning and arrive at the same time. Juan's ride is 55 minutes. Amie's ride is 25 minutes longer. If Amie catches her train at 6:55 A.M., when does Juan arrive at work?

Continue using the facts and logical reasoning until the problem is solved.

First I'll identify the facts given in the problem.

Facts	Conclusions
Juan's ride is 55 minutes. Amie's ride is 25 minutes longer.	→ Amie's ride is 80 minutes.
Amie catches her train at 6:55 A.M.	→ Amie arrives at work at 8:15 A.M.
Juan and Amie get to work at the same time.	→ Juan arrives at 8:15 A.M.

Look at the facts and draw conclusions.

1. How can you draw the conclusion that Amie's ride is 80 minutes?

2. How can you draw the conclusion that Amie arrives at work at 8:15 A.M.?

For 3–5, use the problem below.

Glenn made a pot of stew and dinner rolls. The stew was ready
10 minutes after the rolls were done. The stew took $2\frac{1}{2}$ hours to cook.
The rolls took 45 fewer minutes. If Glenn started the rolls at 4:45 P.M.,
when was the stew ready?

   3. How long did the rolls take to make? Which fact(s)
   allowed you to draw that conclusion?

   4. When were the rolls done? Which fact(s) allowed you to
   draw that conclusion?

   5. **Writing in Math** Explain how to use your answer from
   Exercise 4 to find the time that the stew was ready.

For 6–8, use the problem and clocks below.

The clocks below show the local times in four states that lie in
different time zones. Tamara lives in New Mexico. She talked
online to Maggie in Minnesota for 3 hours beginning at
2:30 P.M. in New Mexico. What time was it in Minnesota when
the girls were done?

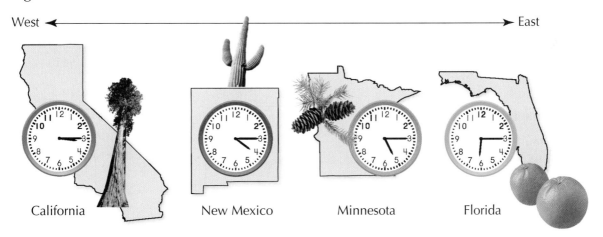

West ← → East

California   New Mexico   Minnesota   Florida

   6. What time was it in Minnesota when Tamara first got online with
   Maggie? Which fact(s) allowed you to conclude that?

   7. **Writing in Math** Explain how to use your answer from Exercise 6
   to find the time in Minnesota when the girls were done.

   8. Tamara called a friend in California and a friend in Florida 2 hours
   before she got on-line with Maggie. What were the local times in
   California and Florida when Tamara made the calls?

Problem-Solving Strategy

Reading Helps!

Drawing conclusions

can help you with...

the problem-solving strategy,
Use Logical Reasoning.

Key Idea
Learning how and when to use logical reasoning can help you solve problems.

ZÜRICH

NEW YORK

Use Logical Reasoning

LEARN

How do you use the logical reasoning strategy?

Local Time A rock band leaves Dallas, Texas for Honolulu, Hawaii at 8:55 P.M. Their flight will take 9 hours 48 minutes. What will the time be in Honolulu when they arrive?

Read and Understand

What do you know? It is 8:55 P.M. in Dallas when the flight to Honolulu departs.
The flight takes 9 hours 48 minutes.

What are you trying to find? Find the time it will be in Honolulu when the flight arrives.

Plan and Solve

What strategy will you use?

Strategy: Use Logical Reasoning

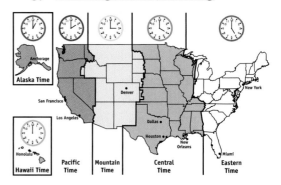

How to Use Logical Reasoning

Step 1 Find a U.S. Time Zones map.

Step 2 Use the map to find out the time in Honolulu when it is 8:55 P.M. in Dallas.

Step 3 Use the time difference and flying time to determine the time it will be in Honolulu when the flight arrives.

The map shows that the time in Honolulu is 4 hours earlier than the time in Dallas.

If it is 8:55 P.M. in Dallas, then it is 4:55 P.M. in Honolulu. If the plane leaves Dallas at 4:55 P.M. Honolulu time, then it arrives in Honolulu at 2:43 A.M. local time.

Look Back and Check

Is your answer reasonable?

Yes, the flight takes 9 h 48 min ≈ 10 h.
4:55 P.M. ≈ 5:00 P.M.
5:00 P.M. + 10 h ≈ 3:00 A.M.

PARIS

LONDON

✔ Talk About It

1. Suppose the plane leaves Dallas at 12 noon local time. What time would it land in Honolulu?

2. **Reasoning** If you travel from west to east, should you set your watch ahead or back? Explain.

CHECK ✓

For another example, see Set 10-6 on p. 611.

Use the time zone map on page 560 to solve the problem.

1. **Wakeup Call** The rock band's publicist lives in Miami. She plans to call the lead singer one hour before the 8 P.M. performance in Honolulu. What time will it be in Miami when the publicist makes her call?

PRACTICE

For more practice, see Set 10-6 on p. 615.

For 2–3, use the analog clocks below. The clocks show the times in London, Tokyo, and Sydney when it is noon on Tuesday in New York.

| New York noon Tuesday | London P.M. Tuesday | Tokyo A.M. Wednesday | Sydney A.M. Wednesday |

2. When it is 3 P.M. on Tuesday in New York, what day and time is it in Tokyo?

3. Tarnella left New York at 10:15 A.M. on Friday and arrived in Los Angeles 6 hours later. She changed planes and arrived in Sydney 14 hours 50 minutes after reaching Los Angeles. What was the day and time in Sydney when Tarnella arrived?

4. Mr. Centruso's class is electing officers. The candidates for class president are Justin, Clarissa, and Liam. The candidates for class secretary are Bernice, Simone, Marcus, and Tina. List all the possible president-secretary teams that could be elected.

5. **Writing in Math** Enrique measured a pencil to the nearest half inch and said it was $4\frac{1}{2}$ inches long. What is the shortest possible actual length of the pencil in inches? Write and explain your solution.

STRATEGIES

- **Show What You Know**
  Draw a Picture
  Make an Organized List
  Make a Table
  Make a Graph
  Act It Out or Use Objects
- **Look for a Pattern**
- **Try, Check, and Revise**
- **Write an Equation**
- **Use Logical Reasoning**
- **Solve a Simpler Problem**
- **Work Backward**

Choose a tool

Mental Math

Sydney Opera House

All text pages available online and on CD-ROM.

Do You Know How?

Do You Understand?

**Customary Measurement (10-1),
Metric Measurement (10-2)**

Copy and complete.

1. 156 in. = ▓ ft   **2.** 3.5 L = ▓ mL

3. 4.5 mm = ▓ cm   **4.** 0.5 T = ▓ lb

Ⓐ Explain how you decided to multiply or divide to solve Exercises 1 and 2.

Ⓑ For 1–4, classify the units as measures of length, capacity, weight, or mass.

Units of Measure and Precision (10-3)

Measure each segment to the nearest sixteenth inch and nearest millimeter.

5. ├──────────────────┤

6. ├──────────┤

Ⓒ Explain why smaller units of measure are more precise.

Ⓓ For Exercise 6, tell how you chose the nearest millimeter for your measure.

Relating Customary and Metric Measurements (10-4)

Copy and complete. Round to the nearest tenth.

7. 12.7 cm = ▓ in.   **8.** 25 L ≈ ▓ gal

9. 10 oz ≈ ▓ g   **10.** 4 mi ≈ ▓ km

Ⓔ For Exercises 7 and 8, which answer is exact and which is an estimate? Explain.

Ⓕ For 9–10, tell what operations you used to find your answers.

Elapsed Time (10-5)

Find each elapsed time.

11. 9:15 P.M. to 1:12 A.M.

12. 10:42 A.M. to 6:30 P.M.

Ⓖ Tell how you found each elapsed time.

Ⓗ Explain how to count on to find the elapsed time in Exercise 12.

Problem-Solving Strategy: Use Logical Reasoning (10-6)

Use logical reasoning to solve.

13. An actress working in New York, NY, must telephone her agent in Hollywood, CA. The agent is expecting the call at exactly 8:15 A.M. local time. What time will it be in New York when the actress places her call?

Ⓘ Explain the steps you followed to solve the problem.

Ⓙ Without a time zone map, can you estimate a time difference? Explain.

MULTIPLE CHOICE

1. Tony made 5 gallons of lemonade for a picnic. Which of the following is the best estimate for the number of liters of lemonade that he made? (10-4)

A. about 1.32 L   **B.** about 5 L

C. about 5.3 L   **D.** about 18.95 L

2. What is the length of this segment to the nearest sixteenth inch? (10-3)

|⊢—————————————————————⊣|

A. $3\frac{7}{16}$ inch   **B.** $3\frac{1}{2}$ inch   **C.** $3\frac{9}{16}$ inch   **D.** $3\frac{11}{16}$ inch

FREE RESPONSE

Copy and complete. (10-1, 10-2)

3. 192 ft =   in.   **4.** 7 c =   pt   **5.** 20 oz =   lb   **6.** 6 gal =   qt

7. 5.8 cm =   mm   **8.** 0.2 kg =   g   **9.** 3.9 L =   mL   **10.** 450 m =   km

Find each elapsed time. (10-5)

11. 6:18 P.M. to 9:05 P.M.   **12.** 11:29 A.M. to 1:15 P.M.   **13.** 4:30 P.M. to 12:45 A.M.

Find each starting time or ending time using the given elapsed time. (10-5)

14. End Time: 5:30 P.M.
Elapsed Time: 3 h 48 min

15. Start Time: 8:17 A.M.
Elapsed Time: 8 h 50 min

16. End Time: 2:09 P.M.
Elapsed Time: 5 h 12 min

Use the data at the right and logical reasoning to solve. (10-6)

17. Karen, Bill, Ted, and Aleesha each have one of the coins listed at the right. Bill has the thickest coin. Karen's coin is thicker than Ted's coin. Aleesha's coin is less than 0.14 cm thick. Which coin does each person have?

Data File

U.S. Coin Dimensions

Coin	Thickness
Penny	1.55 mm
Nickel	0.195 cm
Dime	0.00135 m
Quarter	1.75 mm

Writing in Math

18. Explain the steps you would follow to find the length, in inches, of a rope that is 4 yards long. Give the answer in a complete sentence. (10-1)

19. Describe two different ways you can use to find the difference in time between 11:45 A.M. and 1:15 P.M. (10-5)

Algebra

Key Idea
There are different ways to find the distance around a polygon.

Vocabulary
• perimeter
• regular polygon (p. 494)

Materials
• dot paper
• metric ruler

Think It Through
I can **use the Distributive Property** to write the formula for the perimeter of a rectangle in 2 ways:

$P = 2\ell + 2w$

or

$P = 2(\ell + w)$.

Perimeter

LEARN

How can you find the distance around a polygon?

You can find the **perimeter** (P), or distance around a polygon, by adding the lengths of its sides.

Activity

a. Use dot paper to draw regular and irregular polygons with 3 and 4 sides. Measure sides of your polygons in mm.

b. Copy and complete the tables at the right.

c. In a **regular polygon**, what is the relationship between the number of sides, the length of each side, and the perimeter? State a rule for this relationship. Does this rule work for irregular polygons? Explain.

d. Test your rule on regular polygons having 5, 6, and 8 sides.

Regular Polygons		
Number of Sides	Side Lengths (mm)	Perimeter
3		
4		

Irregular Polygons		
Number of Sides	Side Lengths (mm)	Perimeter
3		
4		

What are some ways to find perimeter?

Example A

Find the perimeter of the regulation college basketball court at the right.

Estimate: $50 + 100 + 50 + 100 = 300$

One Way
Add the lengths of all four sides.
$P = 94 + 50 + 94 + 50 = 288$

Another Way
Since there are two equal lengths and two equal widths, use the formula
$P = 2\ell + 2w$.
$P = 2(94) + 2(50)$
$\quad = 188 + 100$
$\quad = 288$

P = perimeter
ℓ = length
w = width

The perimeter of the basketball court is 288 ft.

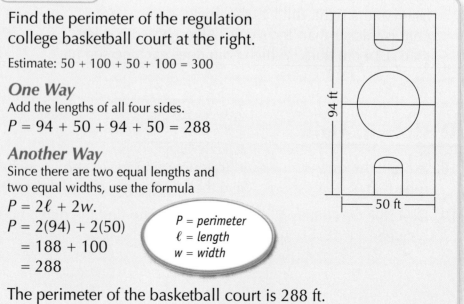

94 ft

50 ft

Find the perimeter of the square.

Since a square has four sides that are all the same length, use the formula $P = 4s$, where s represents the length of one side.

$P = 4s$
$ = 4(18.3)$
$ = 73.2$

The perimeter of the square is 73.2 cm.

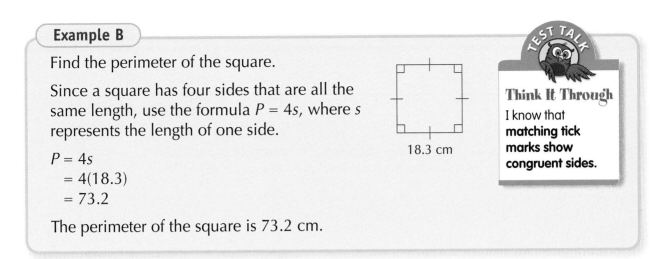

18.3 cm

Think It Through
I know that **matching tick marks show congruent sides.**

Sometimes, you are not given the lengths of all the sides of a polygon.

Example C

Find the perimeter of the figure below.

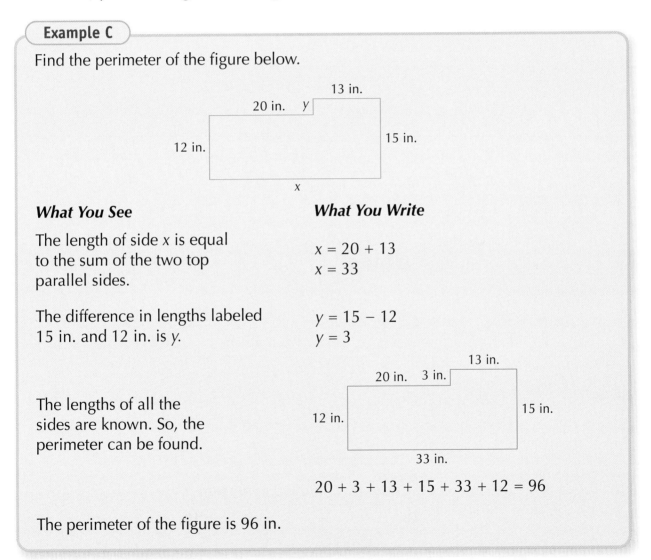

13 in.
20 in.   y
12 in.
15 in.
x

What You See

The length of side x is equal to the sum of the two top parallel sides.

The difference in lengths labeled 15 in. and 12 in. is y.

The lengths of all the sides are known. So, the perimeter can be found.

What You Write

$x = 20 + 13$
$x = 33$

$y = 15 - 12$
$y = 3$

13 in.
20 in.   3 in.
12 in.
15 in.
33 in.

$20 + 3 + 13 + 15 + 33 + 12 = 96$

The perimeter of the figure is 96 in.

✔ Talk About It

1. Explain how you could estimate the perimeter in Example B.

2. A rectangle has a length of 12.8 m, and a width of 4.3 m. Estimate the perimeter of this rectangle. Then explain how to use a formula to find its perimeter.

CHECK ✓

Find the perimeter of each figure.

1. square
sides 13.5 cm long

2. rectangle
length 8 in., width 4 in.

3. regular hexagon
sides 18.45 m long

Estimate the perimeter of each figure. Then find the perimeter.

4.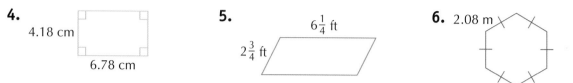
4.18 cm
6.78 cm

5. $6\frac{1}{4}$ ft
$2\frac{3}{4}$ ft

6. 2.08 m

Find the length of each unknown side. Then find the perimeter.

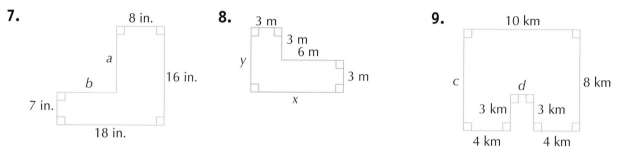

7. 8 in.
a
b
16 in.
7 in.
18 in.

8. 3 m
3 m
6 m
y
3 m
x

9. 10 km
c
d
8 km
3 km
3 km
4 km
4 km

10. Reasoning The perimeter of a rectangle is 24 ft. Its length is 8 ft. Find its width.

PRACTICE

For more practice, see Set 10-7 on p. 615.

A **Skills and Understanding**

Find the perimeter of each figure.

11. regular decagon
sides 1.2 mm long

12. rectangle
length 11 ft, width 12 ft

13. equilateral triangle
sides 150 cm long

Estimate the perimeter of each figure. Then find the perimeter.

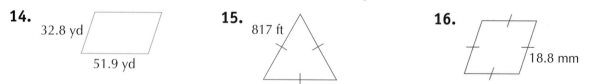

14. 32.8 yd
51.9 yd

15. 817 ft

16. 18.8 mm

Find the length of each unknown side. Then find the perimeter.

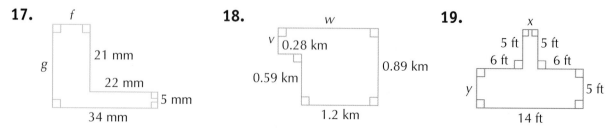

17. f
g
21 mm
22 mm
5 mm
34 mm

18. w
v 0.28 km
0.89 km
0.59 km
1.2 km

19. x
5 ft 5 ft
6 ft 6 ft
y
5 ft
14 ft

20. Reasoning The perimeter of a regular octagon is 18 ft. Find the length of each side.

B Reasoning and Problem Solving

Find the total length of each blue border.

21. squares and rectangles

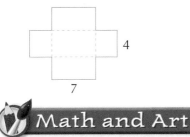

22. equilateral triangles

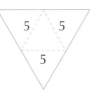

23. regular pentagons

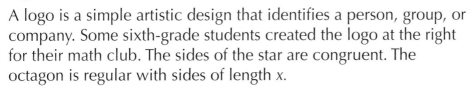

Math and Art

A logo is a simple artistic design that identifies a person, group, or company. Some sixth-grade students created the logo at the right for their math club. The sides of the star are congruent. The octagon is regular with sides of length x.

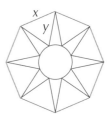

24. Write an expression for the length of ribbon needed to go around the star and octagon.

25. How many feet of ribbon are needed if $x = 5$ in. and $y = 4$ in.?

26. **Writing in Math** Explain why the expression $8(x + 2y)$ can also be used to find the length of needed ribbon.

C Extensions

27. Algebra Nan has square tables each measuring 34 inches on a side. She wants to arrange 10 tables end-to-end to form one long table and decorate the long table with a table skirt. Copy and complete the table at the right. Describe the relationship between the number of tables and the number of sides. Use this relationship to find the perimeter of the long table Nan plans to arrange.

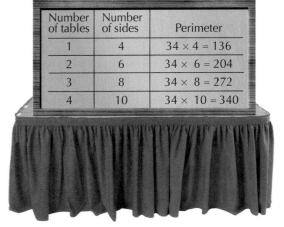

Number of tables	Number of sides	Perimeter
1	4	$34 \times 4 = 136$
2	6	$34 \times 6 = 204$
3	8	$34 \times 8 = 272$
4	10	$34 \times 10 = 340$

Mixed Review and Test Prep

Take It to the NET
Test Prep
www.scottforesman.com

28. Houston is two time zones to the east of Seattle. A flight left Houston at 1:15 P.M. local time and landed in Seattle 4 hours 20 minutes later. What time was it in Seattle when the plane landed?

29. Which represents 3 times the sum 5 and x?

   A. $3x + 5$ **B.** $3(x + 5)$ **C.** $3(5) + x$ **D.** $3 + 5 + x$

Algebra

Key Idea
You can use the dimensions of a square or rectangle to find its area.

Vocabulary
• area

Materials
• 12-inch rulers
• meter sticks
• yardsticks
• masking tape
• scissors
• large sheets of paper

Area of Squares and Rectangles

LEARN

Activity

How is area measured?

The **area** of a figure is the amount of surface it covers. Area is measured by the number of unit squares of the same size that can make up the figure. The unit square used to measure the area of the rectangle below is a square centimeter (cm^2). Since 8 square centimeters make up the rectangle, its area is 8 cm^2.

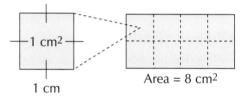

1 cm²

1 cm

Area = 8 cm²

a. Use a 12-inch ruler to make a 1 square-foot unit. In a similar fashion, make units of 1 square yard and 1 square meter.

b. Working with a partner, count and record the number of square-foot units that will cover a large area in your classroom. Repeat this procedure using square-yard and square-meter units.

c. Compare your results. How close to actual do you think your measurements are? Explain.

How can you use a formula to find area?

Instead of counting unit squares, you can use a formula to find area.

Example A

Find the area of a square that is 3.5 m on each side (s).

Use the formula $A = s^2$.

$A = (3.5)^2$
$A = 12.25$ Think: The unit is 1m².

The area is 12.25 m².

Example B

Find the area of a rectangle with a length (ℓ) of 9 ft and a width (w) of 6 ft.

Use the formula $A = \ell \times w$.

$A = 9 \times 6$
$A = 54$ Think: The unit is 1 square foot.

The area is 54 square feet.

✔ Talk About It

1. A square has an area of 36 m². How can you find the length of its sides?

For another example, see Set 10-8 on p. 611.

CHECK ✓

Find the area of each figure.

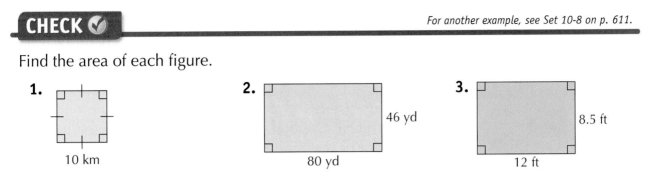

1. 10 km

2. 46 yd / 80 yd

3. 8.5 ft / 12 ft

4. **Algebra** If the area of a rectangle is 480 ft² and its length is 24 ft, what is its width?

PRACTICE

For more practice, see Set 10-8 on p. 615.

A Skills and Understanding

Find the area of each figure.

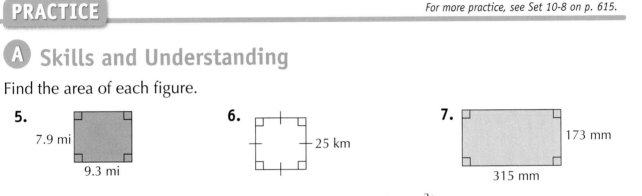

5. 7.9 mi / 9.3 mi

6. 25 km

7. 173 mm / 315 mm

8. **Number Sense** How many square centimeters are in 1m²?

B Reasoning and Problem Solving

The diagram at the right shows how a school field was sectioned off for the end-of-year picnic.

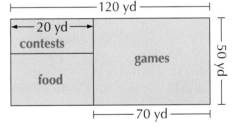

9. What is the area of the section set aside for games?

10. What is the area of the food section in square feet?

11. **Writing in Math** Can the distance of a race be measured in square miles? Explain.

🕷 Mixed Review and Test Prep

Take It to the NET
Test Prep
www.scottforesman.com

Find the perimeter of each figure.

12. regular pentagon with side 7.6 cm

13. isosceles triangle with sides 9 m, 20 m, 20 m

14. Juanita's haircut costs $28. If she tips her stylist 20%, what is her total cost?

    A. $56   **B.** $50.40   **C.** $33.60   **D.** $22.40

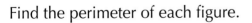 All text pages available online and on CD-ROM.

Algebra

Key Idea
You can change the area of a figure without changing its perimeter.

Materials
- $\frac{1}{4}$-inch grid paper

Think It Through
I can use **divisibility rules to help me find pairs of factors** for the dimensions of my rectangles.

Relating Area and Perimeter

LEARN

Activity

For the school carnival, twenty-four feet of rope will be used to mark off an area for ticket sales. What are the dimensions of the rectangular region that will provide the greatest area?

a. Draw a rectangle with a length of 7 units and a width of 5 units. Continue to draw and label as many rectangles as you can that have perimeters of 24 units. Lengths and widths should be whole units.

b. Find the area of each rectangle. Record your data in a table like the one shown below.

Rectangle	Length	Width	Perimeter	Area
1	7	5	24 units	35 square units
2			24 units	

c. What do you notice about the dimensions of the rectangle with the greatest area?

Activity

The carnival's concession area will be 48 square yards. What are the dimensions of the rectangular area that will take the least amount of rope to mark off?

a. Draw as many rectangles as you can with an area of 48 square units, using whole units for length and width.

b. Find each perimeter. Record your data in a chart like the one shown below.

Rectangle	Length	Width	Area	Perimeter
1	48	1	48 square units	
2			48 square units	

c. Which rectangle has the shortest perimeter?

d. Find the difference in length and width for each rectangle. What do you notice about the perimeter of the rectangle for which this difference is greatest? is least?

Using whole units and the perimeter given, find the dimensions of the rectangle with the greatest area.

1. $P = 20$ **2.** $P = 32$ **3.** $P = 60$ **4.** $P = 100$

Using whole units and the area given, find the dimensions of the rectangle with the shortest perimeter.

5. $A = 30$ **6.** $A = 36$ **7.** $A = 64$ **8.** $A = 120$

9. Number Sense A rectangle is 9 m long and 6 m wide. What happens to the area if the length is doubled? if both the length and width are doubled?

PRACTICE

For more practice, see Set 10-9 on p. 616.

A Skills and Understanding

Using whole units and the perimeter given, find the dimensions of the rectangle with the greatest area.

10. $P = 18$ **11.** $P = 38$ **12.** $P = 40$ **13.** $P = 202$

Using whole units and the area given, find the dimensions of the rectangle with the shortest perimeter.

14. $A = 49$ **15.** $A = 72$ **16.** $A = 188$ **17.** $A = 150$

18. Number Sense The side of a square measures 36 in. What is its area in square inches? in square feet? in square yards?

B Reasoning and Problem Solving

19. A backyard is to be fenced off with 96 m of fencing. The back of the house is to be used as one side of the rectangular enclosure. What whole number dimensions yield the largest area that can be enclosed by the fencing?

20. <u>Writing in Math</u> Renny says the closer to a square the dimensions of a rectangle are, the greater the area. Is he correct? Explain.

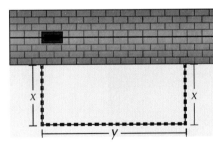

🦉 Mixed Review and Test Prep

Take It to the NET
www Test Prep
www.scottforesman.com

Find the area of each figure.

21. rectangle
$\ell = 7.2$m; $w = 3$m

22. square
$s = 9.7$ ft

23. rectangle
$\ell = 6\frac{2}{3}$ yd; $w = 2$yd

24. Choose the most reasonable estimate for 74% of 21.

   A. 10   **B.** 15   **C.** 19   **D.** 20

Algebra

Key Idea
You can use the formula for the area of a rectangle, to find the formulas for the area of a parallelogram and the area of a triangle.

Vocabulary
• base
• height

Area of Parallelograms and Triangles

LEARN

How can you use the formula for the area of a rectangle to find the area of a parallelogram?

You can use what you know about the area of a rectangle to find the area of a parallelogram. Look at the parallelogram below. If the triangle is cut out and moved to the opposite side, a rectangle is formed. The parallelogram and the rectangle have the same area.

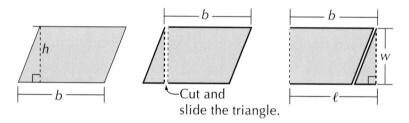

Cut and slide the triangle.

The **base** of the parallelogram (b) equals the length of the rectangle (ℓ). The **height** of the parallelogram (h), which is perpendicular to the base, equals the width of the rectangle (w).

$$A = \ell \cdot w$$
$$A = b \cdot h$$

> **Area of a Parallelogram**
> $$A = bh$$

Example A

Brigita is tiling her shower with parallelogram-shaped stone tiles. What is the area of the tile below?

Use the formula $A = bh$.

$A = 4 \times 2$
$A = 8$ Think: The unit is 1 in².

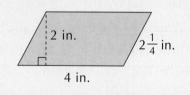

2 in.

$2\frac{1}{4}$ in.

4 in.

The area of the tile is 8 in².

✓ Talk About It

1. A rectangle and a parallelogram have the same base and height. How are their areas related?

2. In Example A, why isn't 4 multiplied by $2\frac{1}{4}$?

How can you use the formula for the area of a parallelogram to find the area of a triangle?

Now that you know how to find the area of a parallelogram, you can find the area of a triangle. Since two congruent triangles can form a parallelogram, the area of the triangle must be one half the area of the parallelogram that has the same base and height.

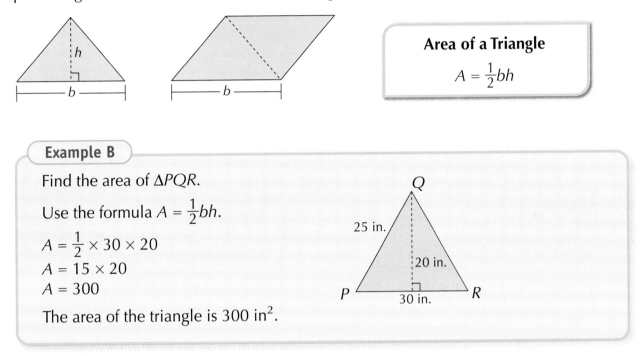

Area of a Triangle

$A = \frac{1}{2}bh$

Example B

Find the area of $\triangle PQR$.

Use the formula $A = \frac{1}{2}bh$.

$A = \frac{1}{2} \times 30 \times 20$

$A = 15 \times 20$

$A = 300$

The area of the triangle is 300 in.^{2}.

✓ Talk About It

3. In Example B, why isn't 30 multiplied by 25?

4. Explain how to find the height of a triangle if its area is 20 m^2 and its base measures 4 m.

Take It to the NET
More Examples
www.scottforesman.com

CHECK ✓

For another example, see Set 10-10 on p. 612.

Find the area of each parallelogram or triangle.

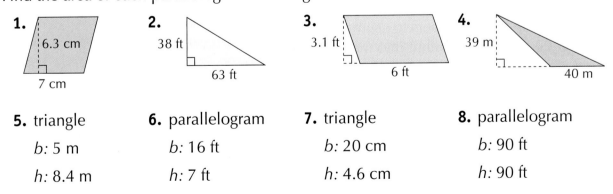

1. 6.3 cm / 7 cm

2. 38 ft / 63 ft

3. 3.1 ft / 6 ft

4. 39 m / 40 m

5. triangle
   b: 5 m
   h: 8.4 m

6. parallelogram
   b: 16 ft
   h: 7 ft

7. triangle
   b: 20 cm
   h: 4.6 cm

8. parallelogram
   b: 90 ft
   h: 90 ft

9. **Estimation** Estimate the area of a triangle with base of 10.86 m and height of 10.86 m.

A Skills and Understanding

Find the area of each parallelogram or triangle.

10. 320 ft, 150 ft

11. 4.1 m, 3.4 m

12. 27.5 cm, 32.5 cm

13. 58 in., 26 in.

14. parallelogram
b: 1.3 m
h: 0.4 cm

15. triangle
b: 2 in.
h: $4\frac{1}{3}$ in.

16. triangle
b: 1.5 cm
h: 1.5 cm

17. parallelogram
b: $1\frac{1}{4}$ ft
h: $3\frac{1}{2}$ ft

18. triangle
b: 12 cm
h: 8 cm

19. parallelogram
b: 18 in.
h: $1\frac{1}{2}$ in.

20. parallelogram
b: 12.4 yd
h: 12.4 yd

21. triangle
b: $13\frac{1}{2}$ ft
h: $5\frac{1}{2}$ ft

22. Number Sense A triangle has a base of 150 cm and a height of 850 cm. Find the area of the triangle in square meters.

B Reasoning and Problem Solving

Math and Social Studies

The intersection of city streets often creates areas of land shaped like parallelograms and triangles. City planners and surveyors need to calculate these areas. Use the diagram at the right to find the area of

385 ft, 290 ft, 760 ft, 760 ft, 225 ft

23. the triangular region.   **24.** the parallelogram region.

25. What is the area of the triangular region in square yards?

26. Use compatible numbers to estimate the number of 15,000 ft² lots that will fit into the parallelogram region.

27. **Writing in Math** Is the explanation below correct? If not, tell why and write a correct response.

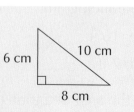

Find the area of the right triangle.

In a right triangle, any side can be used as a height. So, the area of this right triangle is $\frac{1}{2}(6 \times 10) = 30$ cm².

6 cm, 10 cm, 8 cm

C Extensions

You can find the area of an irregular figure by dividing it into familiar shapes, and then adding the area of each part. The figure below has been divided in two different ways.

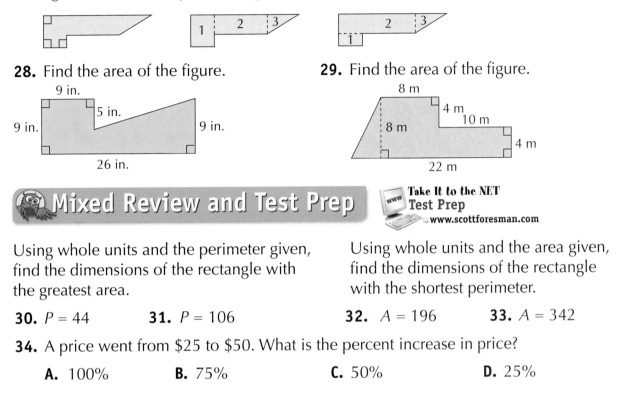

28. Find the area of the figure.

9 in.

5 in.

9 in.

9 in.

26 in.

29. Find the area of the figure.

8 m

4 m

10 m

8 m

4 m

22 m

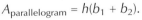
Mixed Review and Test Prep

Take It to the NET www Test Prep www.scottforesman.com

Using whole units and the perimeter given, find the dimensions of the rectangle with the greatest area.

30. $P = 44$ **31.** $P = 106$

Using whole units and the area given, find the dimensions of the rectangle with the shortest perimeter.

32. $A = 196$ **33.** $A = 342$

34. A price went from $25 to $50. What is the percent increase in price?

   A. 100%   **B.** 75%   **C.** 50%   **D.** 25%

Enrichment

Area of a Trapezoid

A trapezoid is a quadrilateral with one pair of parallel sides. The parallel sides are called bases and labeled b_1 and b_2.

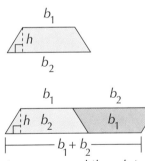

To find the formula for the area of a trapezoid, use two congruent trapezoids to form a parallelogram. The area of this parallelogram is given at the right.

$A_{parallelogram} = h(b_1 + b_2)$.

Since the area of one of the trapezoids is half the area of the parallelogram, the formula for the area of a trapezoid is $A = \frac{1}{2}h(b_1 + b_2)$.

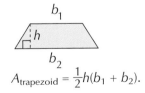

$A_{trapezoid} = \frac{1}{2}h(b_1 + b_2)$.

For 1–2, find the area of each trapezoid.

1. $b_1 = 9$ cm, $b_2 = 17$ cm; $h = 6$ cm   **2.** $b_1 = 8$ m, $b_2 = 15$ m; $h = 5$ m

Algebra

Key Idea
Like polygons, circles have dimensions that can be used to find the distance around the outside.

Vocabulary
• circumference
• diameter (p. 502)
• pi
• radius (p. 502)

Materials
• 5 circular objects, or paper circles
• string or paper ruler
• metric ruler, or paper ruler
• calculator

Circumference

LEARN

Activity

How are the measurements of a circle related?

a. Find 5 circular objects, such as a can, a lid, a clock, a plate, a wheel, and so on.

b. Wrap a string around the outside of each object. Then use a metric ruler to measure the length of the string to the nearest millimeter. This length is the **circumference** (C) of the circle.

c. Measure the **diameter** (d) of each object to the nearest millimeter.

d. Copy and complete the table. Use a calculator to find $\frac{C}{d}$.

e. Describe any patterns you see in the $\frac{C}{d}$ values.

Object	Circumference (C)	Diameter (d)	$\frac{C}{d}$

How can you find circumference?

The ratio of the circumference to the diameter of every circle is the same. The Greek letter π (read **pi**) is used to represent this ratio. Since the digits in π never end or repeat, approximate values are commonly used, like 3.14 and $\frac{22}{7}$.

Circumference of a Circle
$$C = \pi d$$

Test Talk

Think It Through
I can **use greatest common factors** to simplify fractions before multiplying.

Example A

The diameter of a steering wheel is $17\frac{1}{2}$ in. Find its circumference.
Estimate: $C = \pi d \approx 3 \times 18 = 54$

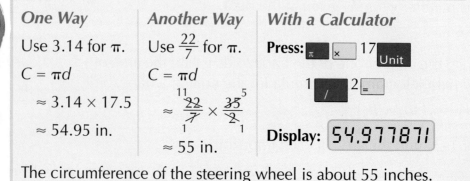

One Way	*Another Way*	*With a Calculator*
Use 3.14 for π.	Use $\frac{22}{7}$ for π.	**Press:**
$C = \pi d$	$C = \pi d$	
$\approx 3.14 \times 17.5$	$\approx \overset{11}{\underset{1}{\cancel{\frac{22}{7}}}} \times \overset{5}{\underset{1}{\cancel{\frac{35}{2}}}}$	
≈ 54.95 in.	≈ 55 in.	**Display:** 54.977871

The circumference of the steering wheel is about 55 inches.

Since the diameter of a circle is twice the **radius**, $C = \pi d$ is the same as $C = \pi(2r)$, or $C = 2\pi r$.

Example B

Find the circumference of a circle with radius $r = 3.5$ cm.
Estimate: $C = 2\pi r \approx 2 \cdot 3 \cdot 4 = 24$

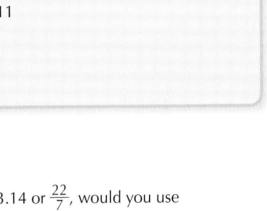
3.5 cm

One Way

Use 3.14 for π.

$C = 2\pi r$

$\approx 2 \times 3.14 \times 3.5$

≈ 21.98

Another Way

Use $\frac{22}{7}$ for π.

$C = 2\pi r$

$\approx 2 \times \overset{11}{\cancel{\frac{22}{7}}} \times \overset{1}{\cancel{\frac{7}{2}}}_1$

$\approx 2 \times 11$

≈ 22

The circumference is approximately 22 cm.

✔ **Talk About It**

1. Why is each answer in Example A different?

2. A circle has a radius of 4 m. Which value of π, 3.14 or $\frac{22}{7}$, would you use to find the circumference? Explain.

How can you find the diameter when you know the circumference?

If you know the circumference of a circle, you can use π to find the diameter or radius.

Example C

If the circumference of a Ferris wheel is 134 meters, what is its diameter?
Find d when $C = 134$ m. Use 3.14 for π.

$$C = \pi d$$
$$134 = 3.14d$$
$$\frac{134}{3.14} = \frac{3.14}{3.14}d$$
$$42.68 = d \qquad \text{Round the answer to the nearest hundredth.}$$

The diameter of the Ferris wheel is about 42.68 m.

✔ **Talk About It**

3. The circumference of a bicycle wheel is $84\frac{3}{4}$ in. How would you find the radius of the wheel?

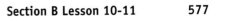

Take It to the NET
www More Examples
www.scottforesman.com

Find each circumference. Use 3.14 or $\frac{22}{7}$ for π.

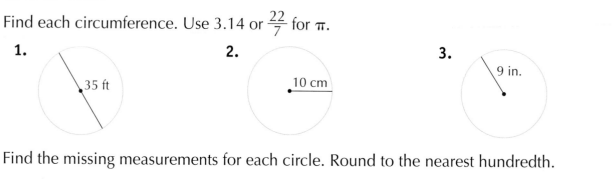

1.
35 ft

2.
10 cm

3.
9 in.

Find the missing measurements for each circle. Round to the nearest hundredth.

4. $d = 10.3$ m, $C \approx$ ▨

5. $r = 17$ ft, $C \approx$ ▨

6. $C \approx 10.6$ cm, $d =$ ▨

7. Estimation Earth's circumference is about 25,000 mi. Estimate the diameter of Earth.

PRACTICE

For more practice, see Set 10-11 on p. 616.

A Skills and Understanding

Find each circumference. Use 3.14 or $\frac{22}{7}$ for π.

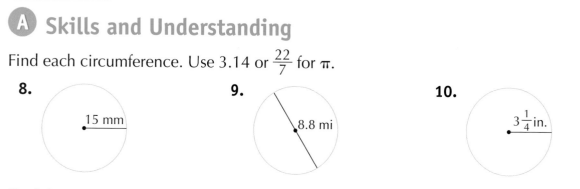

8.
15 mm

9.
8.8 mi

10.
$3\frac{1}{4}$ in.

Find the missing measurements for each circle. Round to the nearest hundredth.

11. $C \approx 58.404$ cm, $d =$ ▨

12. $r = 9.8$ km, $C \approx$ ▨

13. $C \approx 47.1$ yd, $r =$ ▨

14. Estimation The minute hand of a wristwatch is 1.2 cm long. Does the point of the hand move more or less than 2 inches in one hour?

B Reasoning and Problem Solving

🌐 **Math and Social Studies**

Since it was first introduced in 1869, the unicycle and its wheel have undergone some interesting transformations. Some unusual wheel diameters and heights are given in the table at the right.

15. If the unicycle with the largest wheel is ridden 1 km, how many complete rotations will the wheel make?

16. If the unicycle with the smallest wheel is ridden 1 m, how many complete rotations will the wheel make?

17. What is the approximate height of the tallest unicycle in feet?

Data File

Unicycles

	Diameter
Smallest Wheel	20 mm
Largest Wheel	185 cm

	Height
Shortest	20 cm
Tallest	31 m

18. <u>Writing in Math</u> Explain how to find the radius of a circle with $C \approx 198$ m.

C Extensions

Find the perimeter of each figure.

19.

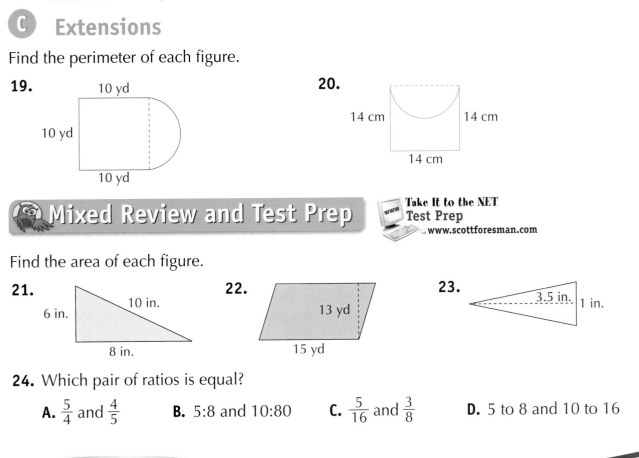

10 yd

10 yd

10 yd

20.

14 cm   14 cm

14 cm

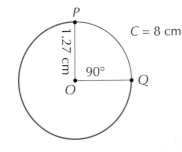

Mixed Review and Test Prep

Take It to the NET
Test Prep
www.scottforesman.com

Find the area of each figure.

21.

10 in.

6 in.

8 in.

22.

13 yd

15 yd

23.

3.5 in.   1 in.

24. Which pair of ratios is equal?

A. $\frac{5}{4}$ and $\frac{4}{5}$ **B.** 5:8 and 10:80   **C.** $\frac{5}{16}$ and $\frac{3}{8}$ **D.** 5 to 8 and 10 to 16

Enrichment

Arc Length

An arc length, written m$\overarc{PQ}$, is a portion of the circumference of a circle with center O. If you know the measure of $\angle POQ$, written m$\angle POQ$, you can use the proportion given below to find the arc length.

$$\frac{m\overarc{PQ}}{C} = \frac{m\angle POQ}{360°}$$

The circle at the right has a circumference of 8 cm and m$\angle POQ$ is 90°. Find m$\overarc{PQ}$.

Use the proportion above. Let $x = $ m$\overarc{PQ}$.

$$\frac{x}{8} = \frac{90}{360}$$
$$360x = 720$$
$$x = 2$$

So, m$\overarc{PQ}$ = 2 cm

P

1.27 cm

90°

O Q

$C = 8$ cm

For 1–4, use the angle measure and circumference to find the arc length.

1. m$\angle XOZ = 30°$; $C = 50.24$ m

3. m$\angle AOB = 118°$; $C = 63.68$ m

2. m$\angle TOV = 60°$; $C = 22.92$ m

4. m$\angle COD = 180°$; $C = 62.8$ m

Algebra

Key Idea
You can use the dimensions of a circle and π to find its area.

Area of a Circle

LEARN

✓ **WARM UP**

Using π = 3.14, find the circumference of a circle with the given measurement.

1. *d* = 8 cm

2. *r* = 1.9 ft

How do you find the area of a circle?

You can use what you know about the parts of a circle and the area of a parallelogram to help you find the area of a circle.

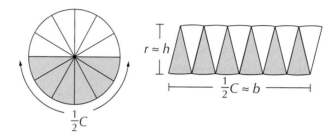

The sections of the circle above have been rearranged to approximate a parallelogram. The formula for the area of the parallelogram can be used to find the formula for the area of the circle.

$A = b \times h$ Area of a parallelogram

$\quad = \frac{1}{2}C \times h$ The base, *b*, is $\frac{1}{2}$ the circumference.

$\quad = \frac{1}{2}(2\pi r) \times r$ The height, *h*, is the radius, *r*.

$\quad = \pi r \times r$ $r \times r = r^2$

$A = \pi r^2$

Area of a Circle

$A = \pi r^2$

Example

The radius of a target's bull's-eye is 7 cm. Find the area of the bull's-eye.

One Way	Another Way	With a Calculator
Use 3.14 for π.	Use $\frac{22}{7}$ for π.	**Press:** π ×
$A = \pi r^2$	$A = \pi r^2$	7 x^2 =
$\approx 3.14 \times 7^2$	$\approx \frac{22}{7} \times 7^2$	
$\approx 3.14 \times 49$	$\approx \frac{22}{7} \times \frac{\overset{7}{49}}{1}$	**Display:** 153.93804
≈ 153.86	$\approx \frac{22}{\underset{1}{7}} \times \frac{\overset{7}{49}}{1}$	
	≈ 154	

The area of the bull's-eye is about 154 cm².

✔ Talk About It

1. Which answer in the Example is the most precise? Explain.

Take It to the NET
More Examples
www.scottforesman.com

For another example, see Set 10-12 on p. 612.

CHECK ✔

Find the area of each circle to the nearest whole number. Use 3.14 or $\frac{22}{7}$.

1.
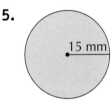
28 ft

2.

10 m

3.
21 in.

4. Reasoning If the circumference of a circle is 10π, what is the area of the circle?

PRACTICE

For more practice, see Set 10-12 on p. 616.

Ⓐ Skills and Understanding

Find the area of each circle to the nearest whole number. Use 3.14 or $\frac{22}{7}$.

5.
15 mm

6.
4.6 mi

7.
$4\frac{1}{2}$

8. d = 18 in.　　**9.** r = 14 km　　**10.** d = 2 yd　　**11.** r = 0.5 mi

12. Reasoning Which has the larger area, a square with side 10 m or a circle with a diameter of 10 m? Explain.

Ⓑ Reasoning and Problem Solving

13. Find the area covered by the water sprinkler at the right to the nearest 10 ft².

14. A small radio station broadcasts in all directions to a distance of 40 mi. How many square miles are in the station's broadcast area?

15. Writing in Math Explain how to find the area of a semicircle with a radius of 9 mm.

25 ft

🦉 Mixed Review and Test Prep

Take It to the NET
Test Prep
www.scottforesman.com

Find the missing measurements for each circle. Round to the nearest hundredth.

16. d = 6.1 cm, C ≈ ▮　　**17.** r = 8.3 mi, C ≈ ▮　　**18.** C ≈ 12 mm, d = ▮

19. A book costs $19.00 plus 5% tax. Which is the total cost?

　　A. $0.95　　**B.** $9.50　　**C.** $19.95　　**D.** $28.50

Problem-Solving Skill

Key Idea
Some problems have extra information, and some do not have enough information to solve them.

TEST TALK

Think It Through

I need to **use details** about each payment option to help me solve the problem.

Extra or Missing Information

LEARN

Do word problems contain only the information needed to solve them?

Better Deal Wynona has saved $875 to buy a 485 Chiplock computer. Which way of paying will cost her less?

Chiplock 485

$75.00 down, $47.50 per month for 1 year
-OR-
Cash Deal $575.50

Read and Understand

Step 1: What do you know?

Tell what you know in your own words.   Wynona wants to buy a computer.

Identify key facts and details.   Wynona has saved $875. She has two options for paying for the computer.

Step 2: What are you trying to find?

Tell what the question is asking.   Which option will cost less and how much less?

Show the main idea.

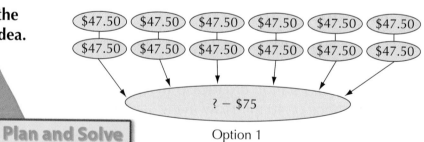

Option 1

Plan and Solve

There is more than enough information to solve the problem.

Option 1: The total cost is $75 + ($47.50 × 12) = $645.
Option 2: The total cost is $575.50.

Option 2 will cost less. Wynona will save $69.50 with Option 2.

Look Back and Check

Is the answer reasonable?   Since 12 × $47.50 ≈ 12($50) + $75 = $675, it is reasonable to think that the cash deal of $575.50 is the better deal.

✔ Talk About It

1. What is the extra information in the Better Deal problem?

2. After paying the $75 down payment, about how much would the monthly payments have to be to get the computer for the cash price of $575.50?

CHECK ✔

For another example, see Set 10-13 on p. 613.

Decide if the problem has extra or missing information. Solve if you have enough information.

1. Earth's moon, on average, is 238,900 miles from Earth. Its diameter measures about 2,160 miles. The diameter of Earth is about 7,926 miles. About what percent of Earth's diameter is the diameter of its moon?

PRACTICE

For more practice, see Set 10-13 on p. 617.

Decide if each problem has extra or missing information. Solve if you have enough information.

For 2–4, use the diagram at the right.

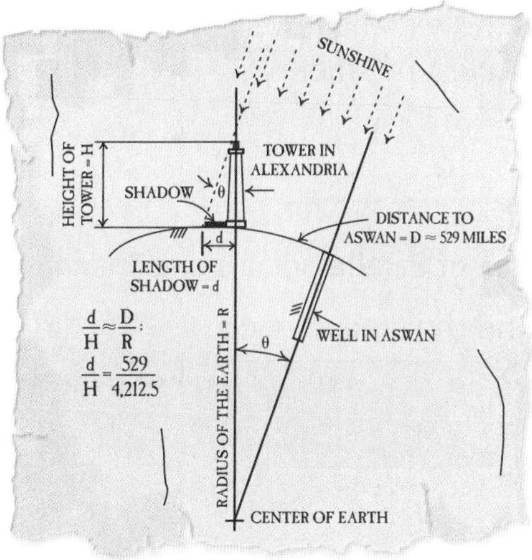

2. In about 240 B.C., a Greek scholar named Eratosthenes calculated the circumference of the Earth using shadows and the distance between two cities. The distance between Aswan and Alexandria is approximately 529 miles. Eratosthenes calculated the Earth's radius *(R)* to be 4,212.5 mi. Use his radius to find Earth's circumference.

3. Use the ratio $\frac{d}{H} = \frac{529}{4{,}212.5}$ to find the height of the tower of Alexandria *(H)*.

4. The actual diameter of Earth is about 7,926 miles. What is the approximate difference between Eratosthenes' diameter of Earth and the actual diameter?

5. Terrance plans to make a rope ladder for a treehouse. Each rung will be made from rope that is 2 inches thick. The rungs will be 10 inches apart. How much rope will be needed to make the ladder?

6. **Writing in Math** For 1–5, if there is missing information, make up the information that is needed and solve the problem.

Diagram labels:
SUNSHINE
HEIGHT OF TOWER = H
SHADOW θ
TOWER IN ALEXANDRIA
DISTANCE TO ASWAN = D ≈ 529 MILES
LENGTH OF SHADOW = d
RADIUS OF THE EARTH = R
WELL IN ASWAN
CENTER OF EARTH

$$\frac{d}{H} \approx \frac{D}{R};$$
$$\frac{d}{H} = \frac{529}{4{,}212.5}$$

STRATEGIES

- **Show What You Know**
  Draw a Picture
  Make an Organized List
  Make a Table
  Make a Graph
  Act It Out or Use Objects
- **Look for a Pattern**
- **Try, Check, and Revise**
- **Write an Equation**
- **Use Logical Reasoning**
- **Solve a Simpler Problem**
- **Work Backward**

Choose a tool

Mental Math

All text pages available online and on CD-ROM.

Do You Know How?

Do You Understand?

**Perimeter (10-7),
Area of Squares and Rectangles (10-8)**

Find the perimeter and area of each.

1. rectangle

$\ell = 4$ cm; $w = 3.5$ cm

2. square

$s = 1\frac{1}{2}$ yd

A Describe a way you could find each perimeter that is different than the method you used.

Relating Area and Perimeter (10-9)

Using whole units, find the dimensions of the rectangle with the greatest area or shortest perimeter.

3. $P = 10$

4. $A = 3,000$

B Tell how you found the dimensions of each rectangle in Exercises 3 and 4.

Area of Parallelograms and Triangles (10-10)

Find the area of each.

5.
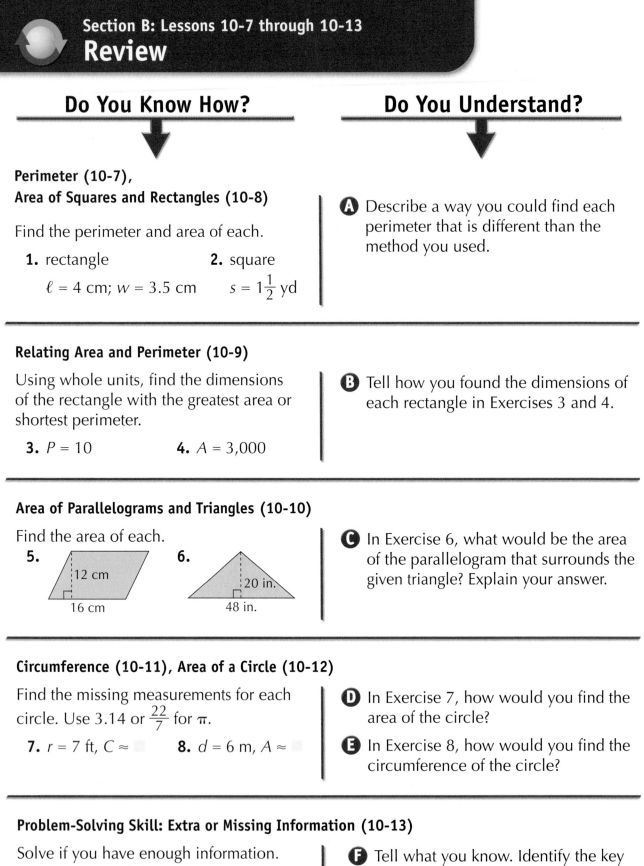
12 cm

16 cm

6.

20 in.

48 in.

C In Exercise 6, what would be the area of the parallelogram that surrounds the given triangle? Explain your answer.

Circumference (10-11), Area of a Circle (10-12)

Find the missing measurements for each circle. Use 3.14 or $\frac{22}{7}$ for π.

7. $r = 7$ ft, $C \approx$ ▉

8. $d = 6$ m, $A \approx$ ▉

D In Exercise 7, how would you find the area of the circle?

E In Exercise 8, how would you find the circumference of the circle?

Problem-Solving Skill: Extra or Missing Information (10-13)

Solve if you have enough information.

9. Tanesha used 58 congruent triangular pieces of cloth to make a quilt. Each piece is an equilateral triangle with a perimeter of 12 inches. The height of each triangle is 3 inches. What is the area of each triangle?

F Tell what you know. Identify the key facts and details. What are you trying to find?

G Did the problem have extra or missing information? Explain.

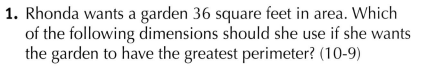
Think It Through
Always **read each part of the question** and review answer choices carefully.

MULTIPLE CHOICE

1. Rhonda wants a garden 36 square feet in area. Which of the following dimensions should she use if she wants the garden to have the greatest perimeter? (10-9)

   A. $\ell = 18$ ft, $w = 2$ ft   **B.** $\ell = 9$ ft, $w = 4$ ft

   C. $\ell = 3$ ft, $w = 12$ ft   **D.** $\ell = 6$ ft, $w = 6$ ft

2. A regular hexagon has a perimeter of 48 cm. Find s. (10-7)

   A. 4 cm   **B.** 6 cm   **C.** 8 cm   **D.** 12 cm

FREE RESPONSE

Find the perimeter and area of each rectangle or square. (10-7, 10-8)

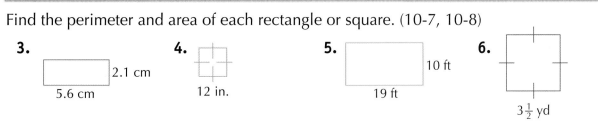

3. 2.1 cm, 5.6 cm   4. 12 in.   5. 10 ft, 19 ft   6. $3\frac{1}{2}$ yd

Find the perimeter and area of each parallelogram or triangle. (10-7, 10-10)

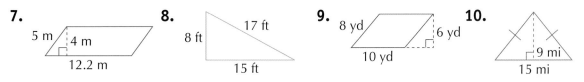

7. 5 m, 4 m, 12.2 m   8. 8 ft, 17 ft, 15 ft   9. 8 yd, 6 yd, 10 yd   10. 9 mi, 15 mi

Find the circumference and area of each circle. Use 3.14 or $\frac{22}{7}$ for π. (10-11, 10-12)

11. $2\frac{1}{2}$ m   12. 3.1 ft   13. 1 yd   14. 20 cm

For Exercises 15–16, decide if the problem has extra or missing information. Solve if you have enough information. (10-13)

15. How many feet of fencing do you need to enclose the triangular garden in the table at right?

16. Vivian used 20 feet of fencing to enclose her garden. What is the shape of Vivian's garden?

Flower Garden Shapes	
Shape	Area (ft²)
Rectangle	18
Triangle	10
Square	25

Writing in Math

17. Explain the difference between the perimeter and area of a polygon. (10-7, 10-8, 10-9, 10-10)

18. If you know the diameter of a circle, how can you find its area? (10-12)

Key Idea
Solids can be described by their faces, sides, edges, and vertices.

Vocabulary
- polyhedron
- face
- edge
- vertex
- prism
- pyramid
- cylinder
- cone
- sphere
- net

Materials
- $\frac{1}{4}$-in. grid paper
- scissors
- tape
- ruler or straightedge

Solid Figures

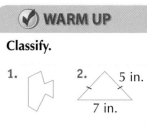 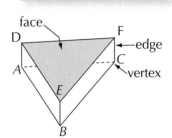
LEARN

What is a polyhedron?

A **polyhedron** is a three-dimensional figure made of flat surfaces called **faces.** The line segment where two faces intersect is called an **edge.** The point where several edges come together is a **vertex.**

face
D   F
          edge
A   C
          vertex
   E
      B

> **Example A**
>
> For the polyhedron shown above, count and name the vertices, edges, and faces.
>
> There are 6 vertices: *A, B, C, D, E,* and *F.*
>
> There are 9 edges: $\overline{AB}, \overline{AC}, \overline{BC}, \overline{DE}, \overline{DF}, \overline{EF}, \overline{AD}, \overline{CF},$ and $\overline{BE}.$
>
> There are 5 faces: $\triangle ABC, \triangle DEF,$ and quadrilaterals *ADEB, ADFC,* and *BEFC.*

A **prism** is a polyhedron with two parallel polygon-shaped bases. A prism is named by the shape of its bases. The faces are parallelograms.

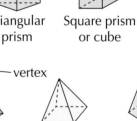

Triangular prism   Square prism or cube   Pentagonal prism

A **pyramid** is a polyhedron with one base. The edges of the base are joined to one point outside the base. A *vertex* can also be used to refer to this point.

vertex

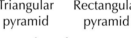

Triangular pyramid   Rectangular pyramid   Hexagonal pyramid

Three-dimensional figures with curved surfaces are not polyhedrons.

A **cylinder** has two circular bases which are parallel and congruent.

A **cone** has one circular base. The points on this circle are joined to one point outside the base.

A **sphere** has no base. Every point on a sphere is the same distance from its center.

✔ Talk About It

1. In any pyramid, what is the shape of the faces that are not bases?

How can you represent a solid?

A **net** is a plane figure which, when folded, gives the original 3-dimensional shape. Think about unfolding a box to make a net for a rectangular solid.

a. On grid paper, draw a net for the box of dog biscuits. Use the dimensions below to draw the net so it is like the diagram at the right.

front and back:	16 blocks by 20 blocks
top and bottom:	16 blocks by 6 blocks
left and right:	6 blocks by 20 blocks

b. Draw dotted lines where rectangles meet. Draw a solid outline around the outside of the figure made by the six rectangles. Using scissors, cut along this solid outline.

c. Fold along the dotted lines you drew to make a box. Use tape to hold the faces in place.

How can you identify a solid from a net?

Identify the solid from the net.

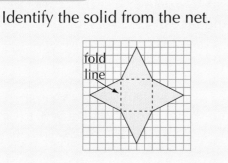

fold line

The net has 5 faces—1 square face and 4 triangular faces. The net represents a square pyramid.

Example C

Identify the solid from the net.

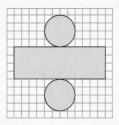

The net has 2 circular faces that appear to be parallel and congruent. The net represents a cylinder.

✔ Talk About It

2. A solid may have several different nets. Both nets at the right consist of congruent squares and can be folded to make the same solid. Identify the solid they form.

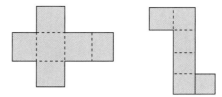

Classify each polyhedron. Name all vertices, edges, and faces.

1.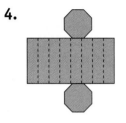

2.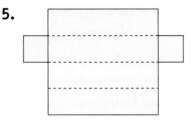

3.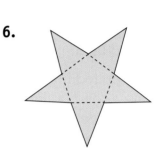

Identify the solid represented by each net.

4.

5.

6.

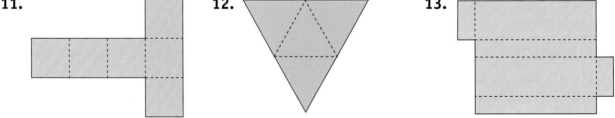

7. Reasoning How is the number of faces of a prism related to the number of sides of its base?

A **Skills and Understanding**

Classify each polyhedron. Name all vertices, edges, and faces.

8.

9.

10.

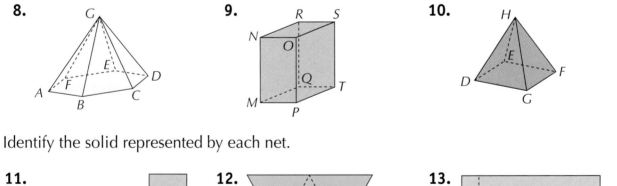

Identify the solid represented by each net.

11.

12.

13.

14. Reasoning Can you classify a polyhedron if you know the number of vertices, edges, and faces it has? Explain.

B Reasoning and Problem Solving

Math and Art

15. What is the total number of faces, edges, and vertices for the cubes in the *Cluster of Four Cubes* sculpture?

16. The dimensions of the sculpture are 541 cm by 312.4 cm by 281.9 cm. Convert each dimension to meters.

17. **Writing in Math** Describe the similarities and differences between pyramids and prisms.

C Extensions

The solid pictured at the right is made of unit cubes. Sketches of the front view, the side view, and the top view are shown below.

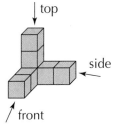

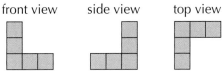

18. Draw front, side, and top views of the solid at the right, which is made from unit cubes.

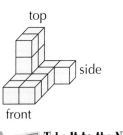

Mixed Review and Test Prep

Take It to the NET
Test Prep
www.scottforesman.com

Identify extra or missing information. Solve if you have enough information.

19. Dale bought 3 quarts of juice. She will serve the juice in 6-ounce glasses. About how many liters of juice did Dale buy?

20. Which of the following equals 115% of 300?

A. 345　　　　**B.** 315　　　　**C.** 325.5　　　　**D.** 255

Enrichment

Euler's Formula

Leonhard Euler (pronounced OY-ler) discovered a pattern involving the number of faces, vertices, and edges of a polyhedron.

1. Copy and complete the chart at the right.

Polyhedron	Faces (F)	Vertices (V)	F + V	Edges (E)
Cube	6	8	14	12
Triangular prism				
Rectangular pyramid				

2. Describe any pattern you see. Does your pattern work for a pentagonal pyramid? a hexagonal prism?

Algebra

Key Idea
You can use what you know about finding areas of polygons to find surface area of solids.

Vocabulary
• surface area (SA)

Think It Through
I can **make an organized list** of the dimensions of each face of a prism.

Surface Area

LEARN

How can you find the surface area of a prism?

To catch the consumer's eye, cereal manufacturers devote the majority of a boxes' surface area to advertising. The **surface area (SA)** of a prism is the sum of the areas of each face.

Example A

Find the surface area of a cereal box that is 12 inches high, 10 inches long, and 3 inches wide.

One Way
Use a net of a rectangular prism to find the surface area.

Find the area of each face.

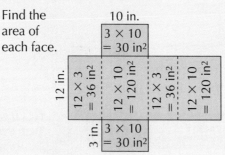

10 in.
$3 \times 10 = 30$ in²

12 in.

$12 \times 3 = 36$ in² $12 \times 10 = 120$ in² $12 \times 3 = 36$ in² $12 \times 10 = 120$ in²

3 in. $3 \times 10 = 30$ in²

Total the areas.
$36 + 120 + 36 + 120 + 30 + 30 = 372$

Another Way
Use a formula.

Opposite pairs of faces have the same area. There are 3 sets of opposite pairs.

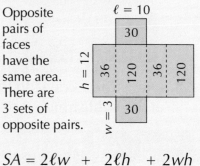

$\ell = 10$
30
$h = 12$ 36 120 36 120
$w = 3$ 30

$$SA = 2\ell w + 2\ell h + 2wh$$
$$= 2(30) + 2(120) + 2(36)$$
$$= 60 + 240 + 72$$
$$= 372$$

The surface area of the cereal box is 372 square inches.

Example B

Find the surface area of the triangular prism.

$$SA = 2(\tfrac{1}{2} \times 3 \times 4) + (4 \times 8) + (3 \times 8) + (5 \times 8)$$
$$= 12 + 32 + 24 + 40$$
$$= 108$$

The surface area is 108 ft².

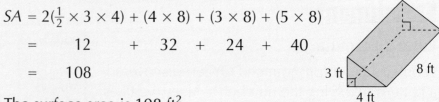

3 ft
4 ft
8 ft

✓ Talk About It

1. Write the formula for the surface area of a cube with edge *s*.

How can you use a formula to find the surface area of a pyramid?

Find the surface area of the square pyramid.

The net for the pyramid shows the base as a square 10 m on each side. Each face is a triangle with base 10 m and height 7 m.

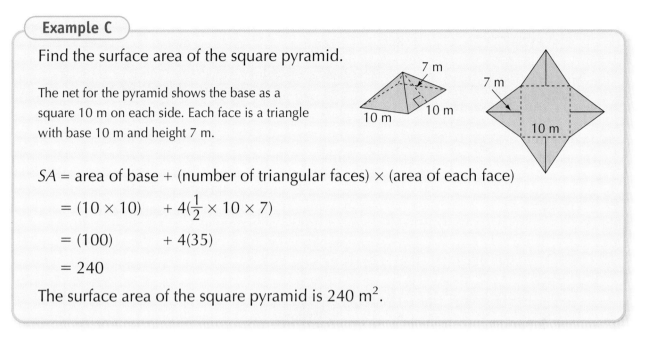

SA = area of base + (number of triangular faces) × (area of each face)

$= (10 \times 10)\quad + 4(\frac{1}{2} \times 10 \times 7)$

$= (100)\qquad\ + 4(35)$

$= 240$

The surface area of the square pyramid is 240 m².

✔ Talk About It

2. How does the base of the pyramid determine the number of triangular faces in Example C?

How can you find the surface area of a cylinder?

Find the surface area of the cylinder.

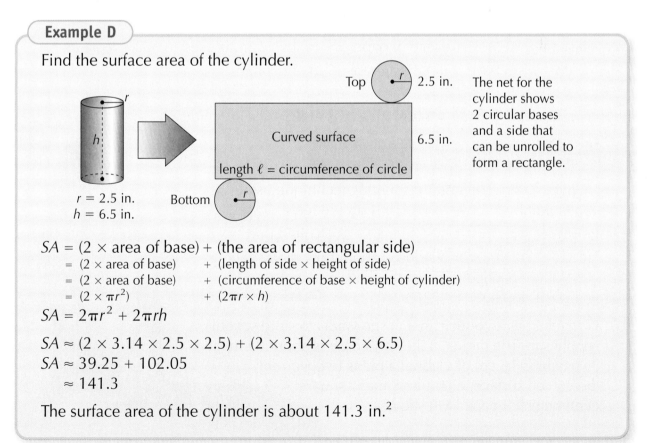

The net for the cylinder shows 2 circular bases and a side that can be unrolled to form a rectangle.

r = 2.5 in.
h = 6.5 in.

length ℓ = circumference of circle

SA = (2 × area of base) + (the area of rectangular side)

$\quad$ = (2 × area of base) $\quad$ + (length of side × height of side)

$\quad$ = (2 × area of base) $\quad$ + (circumference of base × height of cylinder)

$\quad$ = $(2 \times \pi r^2)$ $\qquad$ + $(2\pi r \times h)$

$SA = 2\pi r^2 + 2\pi rh$

$SA \approx (2 \times 3.14 \times 2.5 \times 2.5) + (2 \times 3.14 \times 2.5 \times 6.5)$

$SA \approx 39.25 + 102.05$

$\quad \approx 141.3$

The surface area of the cylinder is about 141.3 in.²

Find the surface area of each solid.

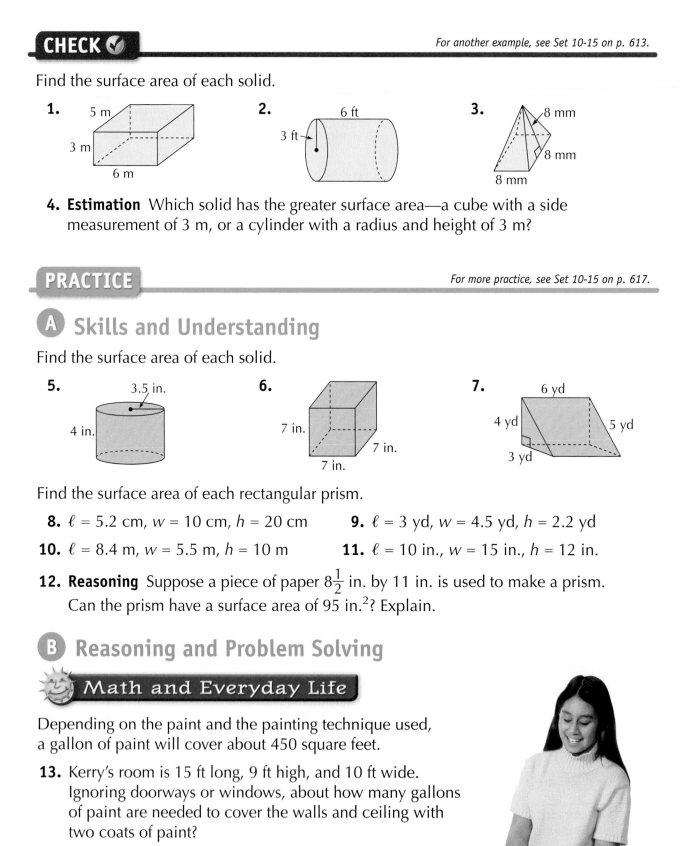

1. 5 m, 3 m, 6 m

2. 6 ft, 3 ft

3. 8 mm, 8 mm, 8 mm

4. Estimation Which solid has the greater surface area—a cube with a side measurement of 3 m, or a cylinder with a radius and height of 3 m?

PRACTICE

For more practice, see Set 10-15 on p. 617.

Ⓐ Skills and Understanding

Find the surface area of each solid.

5. 3.5 in., 4 in.

6. 7 in., 7 in., 7 in.

7. 6 yd, 4 yd, 5 yd, 3 yd

Find the surface area of each rectangular prism.

8. $\ell = 5.2$ cm, $w = 10$ cm, $h = 20$ cm

9. $\ell = 3$ yd, $w = 4.5$ yd, $h = 2.2$ yd

10. $\ell = 8.4$ m, $w = 5.5$ m, $h = 10$ m

11. $\ell = 10$ in., $w = 15$ in., $h = 12$ in.

12. Reasoning Suppose a piece of paper $8\frac{1}{2}$ in. by 11 in. is used to make a prism. Can the prism have a surface area of 95 in.²? Explain.

Ⓑ Reasoning and Problem Solving

Math and Everyday Life

Depending on the paint and the painting technique used, a gallon of paint will cover about 450 square feet.

13. Kerry's room is 15 ft long, 9 ft high, and 10 ft wide. Ignoring doorways or windows, about how many gallons of paint are needed to cover the walls and ceiling with two coats of paint?

14. Gabriella has a coffee can that she wants to store school supplies in. The radius of the can's base is about 8 cm, and its height is 16 cm. If Gabriella plans to cover only the curved surface, about how many square centimeters of paper will she need?

15. **Writing in Math** Is the explanation below correct? If not, tell why and write a correct response.

> Explain how to find the surface area of a triangular pyramid.
>
> *Since a triangular pyramid has 4 triangular faces, find the area of the base and multiply it by 4.*

C Extensions

A net for a small rectangular box is shown along with a net for a box having dimensions that are twice those of the first box. The dimensions for each box appear below.

Box A: $\ell = 3$, $w = 1$, $h = 1$ Box B: $\ell = 6$, $w = 2$, $h = 2$

16. How does the surface area of Box B compare with that of Box A?

17. **Reasoning** The dimensions of Box A are tripled. How would the surface area of the larger box compare with that of Box A?

Mixed Review and Test Prep

Take It to the NET
Test Prep
www.scottforesman.com

18. How many faces, edges, and vertices does a rectangular prism have?

19. Which represents 34,500 in scientific notation?

A. 3.45   **B.** 3.45×10^2 **C.** 3.45×10^4 **D.** 0.345×10^5

Learning with Technology

The Geometry Drawing eTool and Solid Figures

Draw a triangle. Then, copy the triangle and move it below the first. Connect the corresponding vertices of the two triangles with line segments to form a solid.

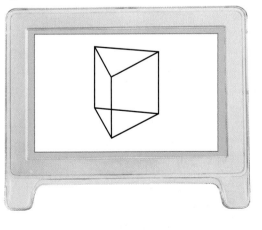

1. Is the solid a prism or pyramid? How can you tell?

2. Measure the edges of your solid and calculate the surface area.

3. Draw a rectangular prism. Then, find its surface area.

Algebra

Key Idea
What you know about area can help you find the volume of solid figures.

Vocabulary
• volume
• cubic units

Materials
• centimeter grid paper
• scissors
• tape
• centimeter or unit cubes
• ruler or straightedge

Volume

⊢ **LEARN**

Activity

How do you measure how much space a solid takes up?

Volume is a measure of the space inside a solid figure. You can measure the volume of a solid by counting the number of same-size **cubic units** that are needed to fill it. The cubic unit used to fill the boxes in this activity measures 1 cm on each edge and equals 1 cm³.

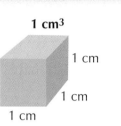

1 cm³

1 cm
1 cm
1 cm

a. Using centimeter grid paper, draw the partial nets of a cube and rectangular prism with the dimensions below.

   Cube: $s = 5$ cm
   Prism: $\ell = 5$ cm, $w = 4$ cm, $h = 3$ cm

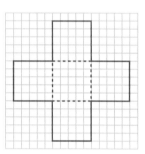

b. For both nets, find the area of the base (B) and record it on the net.

c. Cut out each net. Fold along the edges and tape the four sides.

d. Copy the table at the right.

Box	Area of base (B)	Number of layers	Total number of cubes
Cube			
Rectangular prism			

e. Fill each box by carefully layering rows of centimeter cubes. Count the number of layers and total number of cubes needed to fill each box. Record these results in the table.

f. Compare the area of the base and the number of layers with the total number of cubes. What pattern do you notice? How can you use this pattern to find the number of unit cubes that will fill a box with a 15 cm × 20 cm base and a height of 10 cm?

✓ **WARM UP**

Multiply.

1. $3(10 \times 12)$

2. $\frac{1}{3}(6 \times 27)$

3. $0.5(20 \times 6)$

4. 3^3

How can you use a formula to find the volume of prisms and cylinders?

Prisms and cylinders have two identical bases. The distance between the bases is the height (*h*). By thinking of a prism or cylinder as a base (*B*), layered *h* times, you can find the volume by multiplying the area of the base by the height.

> **Volume of a Prism or Cylinder**
>
> $V = Bh$

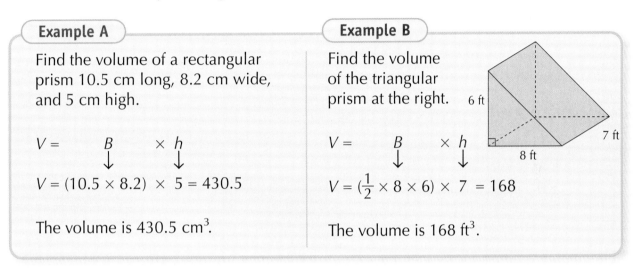

Example A

Find the volume of a rectangular prism 10.5 cm long, 8.2 cm wide, and 5 cm high.

$$V = \underset{\downarrow}{B} \times \underset{\downarrow}{h}$$

$V = (10.5 \times 8.2) \times 5 = 430.5$

The volume is 430.5 cm³.

Example B

Find the volume of the triangular prism at the right.

$$V = \underset{\downarrow}{B} \times \underset{\downarrow}{h}$$

$V = (\frac{1}{2} \times 8 \times 6) \times 7 = 168$

6 ft

7 ft

8 ft

The volume is 168 ft³.

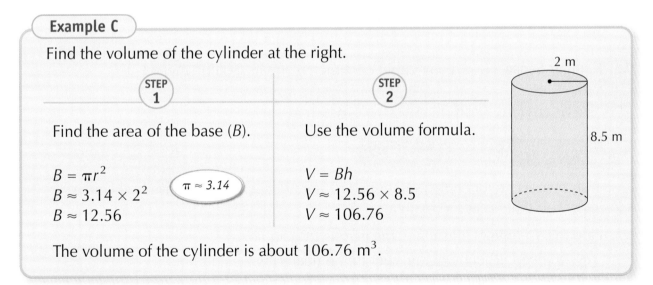

Example C

Find the volume of the cylinder at the right.

2 m

8.5 m

STEP 1

Find the area of the base (*B*).

$B = \pi r^2$

$B \approx 3.14 \times 2^2$ ($\pi \approx 3.14$)

$B \approx 12.56$

STEP 2

Use the volume formula.

$V = Bh$

$V \approx 12.56 \times 8.5$

$V \approx 106.76$

The volume of the cylinder is about 106.76 m³.

✔ Talk About It

1. All edges of a cube are the same length. How can you write a formula for the volume of a cube with edges of length *s*?

2. If you know the height of a cylinder and the circumference of one base, how can you find the volume?

3. Explain how you could use a roll of coins to show the formula for the volume of a cylinder.

Find the volume of each solid.

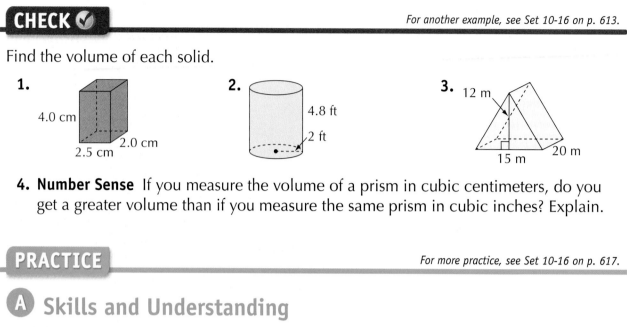

1. 4.0 cm 2.0 cm 2.5 cm

2. 4.8 ft 2 ft

3. 12 m 15 m 20 m

4. Number Sense If you measure the volume of a prism in cubic centimeters, do you get a greater volume than if you measure the same prism in cubic inches? Explain.

PRACTICE

For more practice, see Set 10-16 on p. 617.

A Skills and Understanding

Find the volume of each solid.

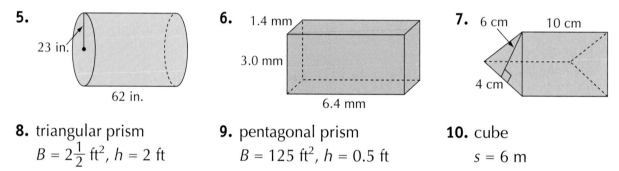

5. 23 in. 62 in.

6. 1.4 mm 3.0 mm 6.4 mm

7. 6 cm 10 cm 4 cm

8. triangular prism
$B = 2\frac{1}{2}$ ft^2, $h = 2$ ft

9. pentagonal prism
$B = 125$ ft^2, $h = 0.5$ ft

10. cube
$s = 6$ m

11. Number Sense How many cubic centimeters are in 1 cubic meter?

B Reasoning and Problem Solving

Math and Science

New fish owners are often recommended to start with a 10-gallon fish tank and a species of fish that is easy to maintain.

12. Find the volume of a fish tank measuring $20\frac{1}{4}$ in. long, $10\frac{1}{2}$ in. wide, and $12\frac{3}{4}$ in. deep. Round your answer to the nearest whole number.

13. Use the ratio $\frac{1\text{ft}^3}{1{,}728\text{ in.}^3}$ to find the volume of the tank in cubic feet.

14. Water weighs 62.4 pounds per cubic foot. What does the water in the tank weigh?

15. The recommended amount of water for a goldfish that is $\frac{3}{4}$-inch long is $\frac{3}{4}$ gallon. About how many $\frac{3}{4}$-inch goldfish can a 10-gallon tank hold?

16. An aquarium has a rectangular base 36 in. by 12 in. Its volume is 6912 in³. Find its height.

17. <u>Writing in Math</u> Describe the difference between surface area and volume.

C **Extensions**

Two rectangular solids are similar if the ratios of their corresponding edge lengths are equal.

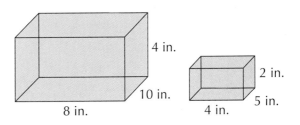

4 in.

10 in.

8 in.

2 in.

4 in.

5 in.

18. Are the solids above similar? Explain how you know.

19. How does the volume of the bigger solid compare to the volume of the smaller solid?

Mixed Review and Test Prep

Take It to the NET
Test Prep
www.scottforesman.com

20. Find the surface area of a cube with an edge measurement of 4 cm.

21. Find the amount of simple interest on a $1,500 deposit at 4% interest for $2\frac{1}{2}$ years.

A. $150   **B.** $156   **C.** $1,560   **D.** $1,656

Learning With Technology

Spreadsheet/Data/Grapher eTool: Finding the Surface Area and Volume of a Cylinder

You can create a spreadsheet that will calculate the surface area of a cylinder. Enter the information and formulas into a spreadsheet as shown below.

	A	B	C	D	E
1	Height	Radius	Base area	Area of Curved Surface	Total SA
2	5	2	= 3.14 * (B2 * B2)	= 2 * 3.14 * A2 * B2	= 2 * C2 + D2
3	13.8	9.6			

Copy the formulas from cells C2–E2 to cells C3–E3.

1. Use your spreadsheet to find which has more surface area, a cylinder with a height of 3 cm and a radius of 4 cm, or a cylinder with a height of 4 cm and a radius of 3 cm.

2. Add a column to calculate the volume of a cylinder. What formula will generate the volume of a cylinder? What is the volume of the cylinder in Row 2?

DK Problem-Solving Applications

Underground The most important parts of a city often lie beneath its streets. Cables supply electricity. Pipes carry gas, sewage, and water. Trains snake through tunnels. These features make up an entirely different kind of city beneath the streets.

Trivia To inspect underground pipes, engineers use tools nicknamed *pigs*. A computer and sensors built into the pig record information about the condition of the pipe as the pig travels through the pipe.

1 The Chicago Department of Sewers is responsible for maintaining more than 4,300 miles of sewer pipes, 230,000 catch basins, and 148,000 manholes. On average, about how many manholes are there for each mile of sewer pipe? Round your answer to the nearest whole number.

2 Some electrical wires are buried 3 feet below ground in PVC pipes which are 4 to 5 inches in diameter. Find the difference in the circumferences of a 4-inch pipe and a 5-inch pipe.

3 Compare the volume of a 1 foot-long section of pipe with a radius of 1 foot to the volume of a 1 meter-long section of pipe with a radius of 1 meter.

4 <u>Writing in Math</u> Water mains are large tunnels that may be in the deepest levels of the underground city. They may be as large as 24 feet in diameter. Does a 10-foot section of a round tunnel with a diameter of 24 feet hold twice the capacity of a tunnel with a diameter of 12 feet? Explain.

5 Rainwater is carried out of a city by various types of storm sewer pipes that are often 12 to 20 feet below ground. Which would hold more water, a 10 foot-long section of a round sewer pipe 8 feet in diameter, or a 10 foot-long section of a rectangular sewer pipe that measures 8 feet by 7 feet?

Using Key Facts

6 On weekdays in New York City, there is an average of about 615 people per subway run. Assuming that a round trip consists of 2 runs, estimate the total number of people that use the subway system each weekday.

Key Facts
New York City Subway

- 442 miles of tunnels with 468 stations
- 74,500 miles of cables
- 522 to 545 trains during rush hours
- 5,787 passenger cars
- 6,822 runs on average weekdays

7 **Decision Making** Cities often use underground storage tanks to hold rainwater during storms. If a tank is to hold between 2,000 and 2,200 cubic feet of water, determine one possible shape and the dimensions for the tank.

Good News/Bad News Before wires were buried, cities had unsightly webs of wires overhead. Storms sometimes broke these lines. Unfortunately, today's underground wires are more difficult to install, inspect and repair.

Do You Know How?

Do You Understand?

Solid Figures (10-14)

Classify each polyhedron. Name all vertices, edges, and faces.

1. **2.**

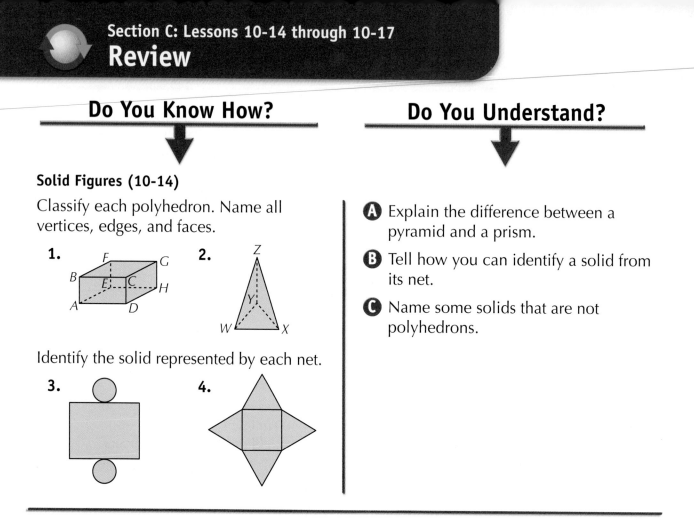

Identify the solid represented by each net.

3. **4.**

Ⓐ Explain the difference between a pyramid and a prism.

Ⓑ Tell how you can identify a solid from its net.

Ⓒ Name some solids that are not polyhedrons.

Surface Area (10-15)

Find the surface area of each solid.

5. **6.**

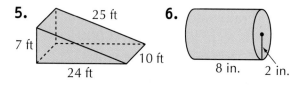

Find the surface area of the rectangular prism.

7. $\ell = 4$ m, $w = 2.3$ m, $h = 6.5$ m

Ⓓ Explain how you could find the surface area of a cube.

Ⓔ Tell how you found the surface area in Exercise 7.

Volume (10-16)

Find the volume of each solid.

8. **9.**

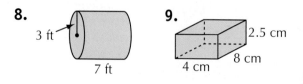

10. cube: $s = 6.5$ m

11. triangular prism: $B = 24$ ft^2, $h = 9$ ft

Ⓕ What formula did you use to find the volume of each solid?

Ⓖ A rectangular prism with a square base has a volume of 360 cm^3. The sides of the base are 6 cm long. Explain how to find the height of the prism.

Think It Through

You can **work backward** from each answer choice to solve the problem.

MULTIPLE CHOICE

1. The volume of a cube is 64 cubic feet. What is the length of each side of the cube? (10-16)

   A. $s = 4$ ft   **B.** $s = 5$ ft   **C.** $s = 6$ ft   **D.** $s = 8$ ft

2. Which solid figure has 4 vertices, 6 edges, and 4 faces? (10-14)

   A. rectangular prism   **B.** square pyramid

   C. triangular prism   **D.** triangular pyramid

FREE RESPONSE

Classify each polyhedron. Name all vertices, edges, and faces. (10-14)

3.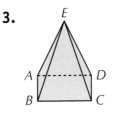

4.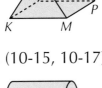

5.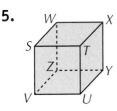

Find the surface area of each solid. (10-15, 10-17)

6.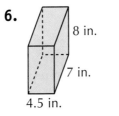

7.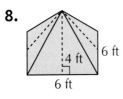

8. 6 ft / 4 ft / 6 ft / 6 ft

Find the volume of each solid. (10-16, 10-17)

9. 3 cm / 6.5 cm

10. 61 yd / 11 yd / 60 yd / 9 yd

11. 7 m / 5 m / 4.8 m

For Exercises 12–13, use the nets at right. (10-14, 10-15)

12. What solid is represented by each net?

13. What is the surface area of each net's solid?

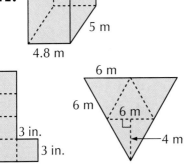

Net A   Net B

Writing in Math

14. Describe an everyday situation for which you would need to calculate the surface area of a solid. (10-15)

15. What polygons are always part of a prism? Explain. (10-14)

Test-Taking Strategies

Understand the question.

Get information for the answer.

Plan how to find the answer.

Make smart choices.

Use writing in math.

Improve written answers.

Make Smart Choices

To answer a multiple-choice test question, you need to choose an answer from answer choices. The steps below will help you make a smart choice.

1. The volume of this rectangular prism is 210 cubic inches. What is the height of the prism?

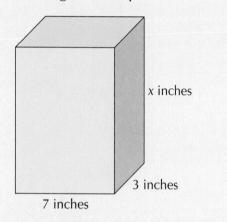

x inches

3 inches

7 inches

A. 100 inches

B. 21 inches

C. 10 inches

D. 8.4 inches

Understand the question.

• Look for important words. Finish the statement "I need to find ... ."

   I need to find the height of the prism.

Gather information for the answer.

*Both the **text** and the **picture** give numbers I need.*

Plan how to find the answer.

*I need to remember the **formula** $V = Bh$. I can use mental math to find B, the area of the base. Then I can see which answer choice works for h, the height.*

Make Smart Choices.

• Eliminate wrong answers.

• Check answers for reasonableness; estimate.

• Try working backward from an answer.

*The area of the base, 21 square inches, times the height must equal the volume, 210 cubic inches. Which height will work? I'll **use multiplication to work backward** and find out.*

Try answer choice A.
$21 \times 100 = 2,100$, so answer choice A is wrong.

Try answer choice B.
$21 \times 21 = 441$, so answer choice B is wrong.

Try answer choice C.
$21 \times 10 = 210$. That works.

The correct answer is C, 10 inches.

2. A rectangular park is split into two areas, one for picnics and one for the playground.

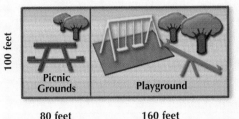

100 feet

Picnic Grounds | **Playground**

80 feet | 160 feet

If (80 + 160) × 100 is one expression for the area of the whole park, which of the following expressions is also correct?

A. 80 + (160 × 100)

B. (100 × 80) + 160

C. 100 × (160 − 80)

D. (100 × 80) + (100 × 160)

Think It Through

I need to find an expression for the area of the whole park. I can evaluate the expression given in the problem to find the area. (80 + 160) × 100 = 240 × 100 = 24,000. Now I can work backward from each answer to find another expression that's equal to 24,000. Try answer choice A. 80 + (160 × 100) = 80 + 16,000 = 16,080. So, A is wrong. Try B. (100 × 80) + 160 = 8,000 + 160 = 8,160. So, B is wrong. Try C. 100 × (160 − 80) = 100 × 80 = 8,000. It's not C. It must be D. I'll check. (100 × 80) + (100 × 160) = 8,000 + 16,000 = 24,000. It works.

Now it's your turn.

For each problem, give the answer and explain how you made your choice.

3. The area of this triangle is 48 square feet. What is its height?

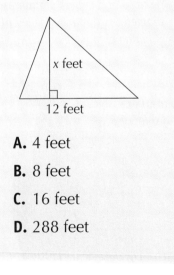

x feet

12 feet

A. 4 feet

B. 8 feet

C. 16 feet

D. 288 feet

4. One expression for the perimeter of this yard is (2 × 20) + (2 × 30).

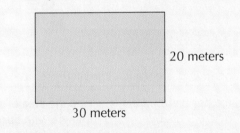

20 meters

30 meters

Which of the following expressions is also correct?

A. 20 + (30 × 2)

B. (2 × 20) + 30

C. 2 × (20 + 30)

D. (20 + 2) × (30 + 2)

Self Check

"Kilo-" means 1,000, "centi-" means $\frac{1}{100}$, and "milli-" means $\frac{1}{1,000}$.

Convert within and between systems of measurement. (Lessons 10-1, 10-2, 10-3, 10-4)

To change to a smaller unit, multiply. To change to a larger unit, divide.

5 yd 1 ft = ☐ in.

1 yd = 36 in.; 1 ft = 12 in.

$(5 \times 36) + (1 \times 12) = 192$

5 yd 1 ft = 192 in.

2,411 mL = ☐ L

1 L = 1,000 mL

$2,411 \div 1,000 = 2.411$

2,411 mL = 2.411 L

7 kg ≈ ☐ lb

$7 \times 2.2 = 15.4$

7 kg ≈ 15.4 lb

Which measurement is more **precise,** inches or centimeters?

The smaller the unit, the greater the precision.

Centimeters are more precise.

Customary and Metric Unit Equivalents

Length
1 in. = 2.54 cm
1 m ≈ 39.37 in.
1 mi ≈ 1.61 km

Weight/Mass
1 oz ≈ 28.35 g
1 kg ≈ 2.2 lb
1 metric ton ≈ 1.102 T

Capacity
1 L ≈ 1.06 qt
1 gal ≈ 3.79 L

1. Copy and complete: 2.5 pt = ☐ fl oz, 0.56 kg = ☐ g, and 44 in. = ☐ cm.

Self Check

A pie is shaped like a circle.

The ratio of a circle's **circumference** to its diameter is a number called **pi** (π). The value of π is about 3.14. (p. 576)

Find perimeter, area, and circumference. (Lessons 10-7, 10-8, 10-9, 10-10, 10-11, 10-12)

Find the **perimeter** of a rectangle 6.5 cm by 1.8 cm.

$P = 2\ell + 2w$

$P = 2(6.5) + 2(1.8)$

$P = 16.6$ cm

Find the **area** of a triangle with **base** 25 in. and **height** 13 in.

$A = \frac{1}{2}bh$

$A = \frac{1}{2} \times 25 \times 13$

$A = 162.5$ in^2

Find the **circumference** of a circle with diameter 6 ft. Use 3.14 for **pi.**

$C = \pi d$

$C \approx 3.14 \times 6$

$C \approx 18.84$ ft

2. Find the area of the rectangle and circle described above.

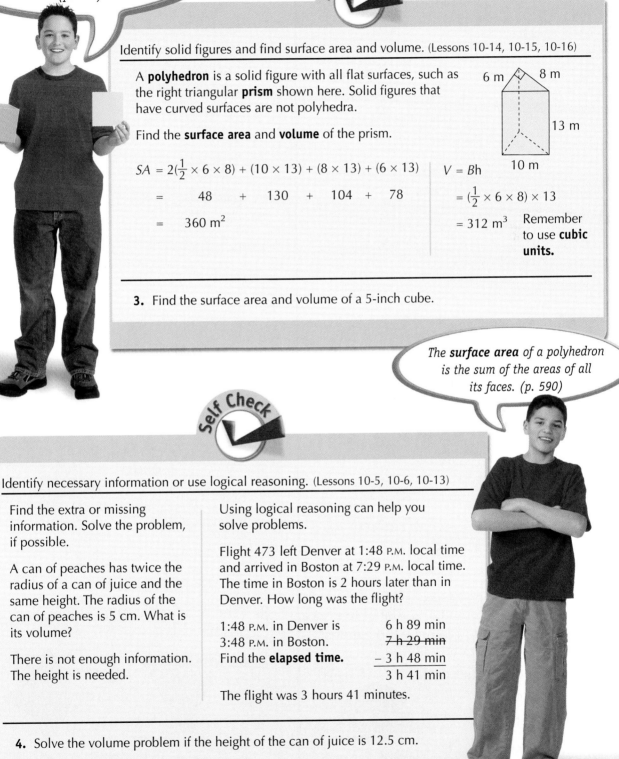

We use square units to measure the area of a square or other flat figures.

We use **cubic units** to measure the volume of a cube or other solid figure. (p. 594)

Self Check

Identify solid figures and find surface area and volume. (Lessons 10-14, 10-15, 10-16)

A **polyhedron** is a solid figure with all flat surfaces, such as the right triangular **prism** shown here. Solid figures that have curved surfaces are not polyhedra.

Find the **surface area** and **volume** of the prism.

6 m   8 m

13 m

10 m

$SA = 2(\frac{1}{2} \times 6 \times 8) + (10 \times 13) + (8 \times 13) + (6 \times 13)$

$\quad = \quad\quad 48 \quad + \quad 130 \quad + \quad 104 \quad + \quad 78$

$\quad = \quad\quad 360 \text{ m}^2$

$V = Bh$

$\quad = (\frac{1}{2} \times 6 \times 8) \times 13$

$\quad = 312 \text{ m}^3$ Remember to use **cubic units.**

3. Find the surface area and volume of a 5-inch cube.

The **surface area** of a polyhedron is the sum of the areas of all its faces. (p. 590)

Self Check

Identify necessary information or use logical reasoning. (Lessons 10-5, 10-6, 10-13)

Find the extra or missing information. Solve the problem, if possible.

A can of peaches has twice the radius of a can of juice and the same height. The radius of the can of peaches is 5 cm. What is its volume?

There is not enough information. The height is needed.

Using logical reasoning can help you solve problems.

Flight 473 left Denver at 1:48 P.M. local time and arrived in Boston at 7:29 P.M. local time. The time in Boston is 2 hours later than in Denver. How long was the flight?

1:48 P.M. in Denver is 3:48 P.M. in Boston.

Find the **elapsed time.**

       6 h 89 min
       ~~7 h 29 min~~
   − 3 h 48 min
       3 h 41 min

The flight was 3 hours 41 minutes.

4. Solve the volume problem if the height of the can of juice is 12.5 cm.

Answers: 1. 40; 560; 111.76 2. 11.7 cm²; 28.26 ft² 3. 150 in.²; 125 in.³ 4. 981.25 cm³

Chapter 10 Key Vocabulary and Concept Review   605

MULTIPLE CHOICE

Choose the correct letter for each answer.

1. Find the perimeter.

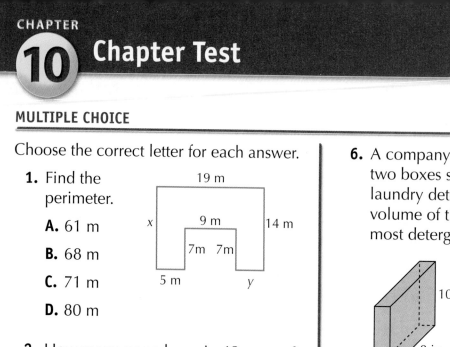

A. 61 m

B. 68 m

C. 71 m

D. 80 m

2. How many pounds are in 40 ounces?

A. 2.5 lb   **C.** 16 lb

B. 4 lb   **D.** 640 lb

3. Which solid figure has 8 vertices?

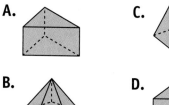

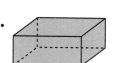

4. Tanya's piano recital started at 3:30 P.M. It ended at 5:15 P.M. How long was the recital?

A. 1 h 15 min   **C.** 2 h 15 min

B. 1 h 45 min   **D.** 2 h 45 min

5. Antoine has 30 feet of fencing to enclose a rectangular garden. He wants the garden to have the greatest area possible. In whole feet, what should be the dimensions of the garden?

A. 10 ft by 5 ft

B. 9 ft by 6 ft

C. 12 ft by 3 ft

D. 8 ft by 7 ft

Think It Through
I need to **watch for words like greatest.**

6. A company wants to use one of the two boxes shown below for its new laundry detergent. What is the volume of the box that will hold the most detergent when full?

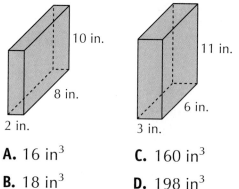

A. 16 in³   **C.** 160 in³

B. 18 in³   **D.** 198 in³

7. A hummingbird's egg has a mass of 0.75 gram. What is the egg's mass in milligrams?

A. 7.5 mg   **C.** 7,500 mg

B. 750 mg   **D.** 75,000 mg

8. Find the surface area of this solid.

A. 159 cm²

B. 318 cm²

C. 325 cm²

D. 378 cm²

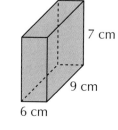

9. Which net represents a triangular prism?

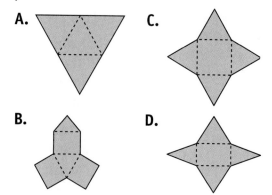

10. Which unit of measure is most precise?

A. gram   **C.** pound

B. milligram   **D.** ounce

FREE RESPONSE

Find the perimeter or circumference of each figure. Then find the area of each figure.

11.
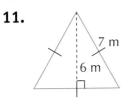
7 m
6 m

12.
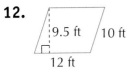
9.5 ft   10 ft
12 ft

13.
$2\frac{1}{2}$ yd
$2\frac{1}{2}$ yd

14.
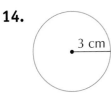
3 cm

Find each missing number.

15. 3.7 g = ☐ kg   **16.** 75 ft = ☐ yd

17. 0.5 m = ☐ mm   **18.** 36 oz = ☐ lb

19. 17.78 cm = ☐ in.   **20.** 5.3 qt ≈ ☐ L

Find the surface area and volume of each solid.

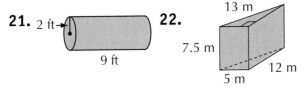
21. 2 ft
9 ft
22. 13 m
7.5 m
5 m
12 m

23. Explain how to use logical reasoning and a time zone map to solve the problem.

Think It Through
I will **write my steps in order.**

A flight from San Francisco to Chicago took 3 hours 25 minutes. If the plane landed in Chicago at 5:30 P.M. local time, at what time did it leave San Francisco?

24. Explain if the problem has extra or missing information. Solve if you have enough information.

Darius used two congruent triangles to make a kite. Each was an equilateral triangle with a perimeter of 45 inches. What was the area of the entire kite?

25. Each edge of a cube is 5 m long. Explain how to find the surface area and volume of the cube.

Number and Operation

MULTIPLE CHOICE

1. A six-pack of juice boxes is on sale for $2.70. What is the cost of one juice box?

   A. $0.27   **C.** $0.45

   B. $0.35   **D.** $2.70

2. Which of the following numbers does NOT name point X on the number line below?

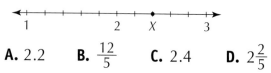

   A. 2.2   **B.** $\frac{12}{5}$ **C.** 2.4   **D.** $2\frac{2}{5}$

3. Which of the following shows the numbers in order from least to greatest?

   A. 0.4, 45%, $\frac{4}{5}$, 4.5

   B. 0.4, 45%, 4.5, $\frac{4}{5}$

   C. $\frac{4}{5}$, 45%, 0.4, 4.5

   D. 4.5, $\frac{4}{5}$, 45%, 0.4

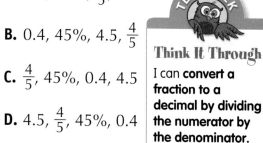

Think It Through

I can **convert a fraction to a decimal** by dividing the numerator by the denominator.

FREE RESPONSE

4. A city recycling program picks up glass items every 5 days, plastic items every 9 days, and paper products every 6 days. How often are all 3 items picked up on the same day?

5. What is the product of 79 and 326?

Writing in Math

6. There are 30 days in June. Corina's birthday is in June. Is it more likely that her birthday date is a prime number or a composite number? Explain your choice.

Geometry and Measurement

MULTIPLE CHOICE

7. Find the surface area of the rectangular prism with dimensions $\ell = 6.4$ cm, $w = 5$ cm, and $h = 3$ cm.

   A. 28.8 cm^2 **C.** 97.5 cm^2

   B. 66.2 cm^2 **D.** 132.4 cm^2

8. Bryant's train departed at 11:45 A.M. and arrived at 2:10 P.M. Find the elapsed time.

   A. 2 h 25 min   **C.** 3 h 35 min

   B. 2 h 55 min   **D.** 9 hr 35 min

9. Rhonda has 34 inches of wood to make a frame. What are the whole number dimensions of the rectangular picture with the greatest area that she can frame?

   A. 15 in. by 2 in.   **C.** 5 in. by 12 in.

   B. 8 in. by 9 in.   **D.** 10 in. by 7 in.

FREE RESPONSE

10. A circle has a circumference of 25.12 m. Find its area.

11. Toby bought 3 lb 4 oz of nuts. He used 1 lb 12 oz of them. Find the weight of the remaining nuts.

Writing in Math

12. Use geometric terms to describe one characteristic of the solids in each group.

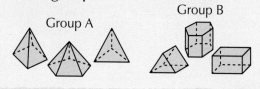

Group A   Group B

Data Analysis and Probability

MULTIPLE CHOICE

13. The heights of 5 basketball players are 1.7 m, 182 cm, 1.77 m, 177 cm, and 1,740 mm. Find the mean height.

A. 0.12 m   **C.** 1.77 m

B. 1.76 m   **D.** 1.82 m

14. Between 275 and 425 pounds of recycled cans were collected over 5 weeks. Which of the following intervals would be best for a bar graph of this data?

A. 1-lb intervals   **C.** 25-lb intervals

B. 20-lb intervals   **D.** 200-lb intervals

FREE RESPONSE

For 15–17, use the spinners below.

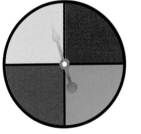 

Spinner A   Spinner B

15. You spin both spinners at the same time. How many possible outcomes are there?

16. If you spin Spinner A 60 times, how many times can you expect it to NOT land on blue?

Writing in Math

17. In a game for 2 players, each player chooses odd or even numbers. A player scores a point when the spinner lands on one of his or her numbers. Is this game fair using Spinner B? Explain your answer.

Algebra

MULTIPLE CHOICE

18. A phone company charges $0.50 for each long-distance call plus $1.25 per minute. Let m represent the number of minutes you talk on the phone. Which expression shows the total cost of your call?

A. $1.25 + 0.5 + m$ **C.** $0.5 + 1.25m$

B. $0.5 \times m \times 1.25$ **D.** $1.25 + 0.5m$

19. Which of the following equations does NOT have the solution of $n = 1.5$?

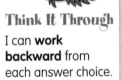

Think It Through

I can **work backward** from each answer choice.

A. $1 - n = -0.5$

B. $3n = 4.5$

C. $n^2 = 2.25$

D. $n + 3.75 = 5$

20. Which of the following rules describes the function below?

x	0	2	4	6	8
y	−1	3	7	11	15

A. $y = x - 1$ **C.** $y = x + 1$

B. $y = 2x - 1$ **D.** $y = 2x + 1$

FREE RESPONSE

21. What order of operations should you use to evaluate the expression $2 + m \div 3^2$, for $m = 7$?

Writing in Math

22. The area of a triangle is 12 cm². If its base is 4 cm long, what is its height? Explain how you used an equation to find your answer.

Set 10-1 (pages 542–545)

Copy and complete.

38 qt = ▧ gal
38 ÷ 4 = 9.5
38 qt = 9.5 gal

Think: 4 qt = 1 gal. To change from smaller units to larger units, divide.

6.25 ft = ▧ in.
6.25 × 12 = 75
6.25 ft = 75 in.

Think: 1 ft = 12 in. To change from larger units to smaller units, multiply.

Remember when you change from larger to smaller units, multiply. To change from smaller units to larger units, divide.

1. 7 lb = ▧ oz   **2.** 15 c = ▧ pt

3. 144 in. = ▧ yd   **4.** 1.5 T = ▧ lb

5. The school hallway is 5 yd 2 ft 8 in. long. What is the length of the hallway in feet? in inches?

Set 10-2 (pages 546–549)

Copy and complete.

0.6 km = ▧ m
0.6 × 1,000 = 600
0.6 km = 600 m

Think: 1 km = 1,000 m. A kilometer is larger than a meter, so multiply.

25 mg = ▧ g
25 ÷ 1,000 = 0.025
25 mg = 0.025 g

Think: 1,000 mg = 1 g. A milligram is smaller than a gram, so divide.

Remember that *kilo-* means 1,000, *centi-* means $\frac{1}{100}$, and *milli-* means $\frac{1}{1000}$.

1. 0.5 L = ▧ mL   **2.** 12 g = ▧ kg

3. 0.6 cm = ▧ mm   **4.** 17.9 L = ▧ kL

5. A bottle holds 2 liters of water. Find the capacity of the bottle in milliliters. in kiloliters.

Set 10-3 (pages 550–551)

Measure to the nearest sixteenth inch and nearest millimeter.

Nearest sixteenth inch:
$1\frac{13}{16}$ inches

INCHES

Nearest millimeter:
45 millimeters

CENTIMETERS

Remember to line up the zero mark of your ruler with one end of the object being measured.

1. ⊢————————⊣

2. ⊢——————————⊣

3. Which measurement is more precise, inches or millimeters? Explain.

Set 10-4 (pages 552–553)

Copy and complete. Round to the nearest tenth.

40 cm = ▧ in.
40 ÷ 2.54 = 15.7
40 cm = 15.7 in.

Think: 2.54 cm = I in. Since a centimeter is smaller than an inch, divide. Round to the nearest tenth.

7 kg ≈ ▧ lb
7 × 2.2 = 15.4
7 kg ≈ 15.4 lb

Think: 1 kg ≈ 2.2 lb. Since a pound is larger than a kilogram, multiply. Round to the nearest tenth.

Remember to look at the digit in the hundredths place when you round to the nearest tenth.

1. 8 km ≈ ▧ mi   **2.** 12 gal ≈ ▧ L

3. Which customary unit of capacity is closest to 1 liter? Which customary unit of length is closest to 1 meter?

Find the elapsed time.

6:15 P.M. to 9:08 P.M.

$$
\begin{array}{ll}
8 \text{ h } 68 \text{ min} \leftarrow \\
\cancel{9 \text{ h} \quad 8 \text{ min}} \leftarrow \text{End Time} \\
- 6 \text{ h } 15 \text{ min} \leftarrow \text{Start Time} \\
\hline
2 \text{ h } 53 \text{ min} \leftarrow \text{Elapsed Time}
\end{array}
$$

Think: 8 < 15.
1 h = 60 min.
Rename 9 h 8 min
as 8 h 68 min.

Remember you can count on from the starting time or count back from the ending time.

1. 7:19 A.M. to 11:03 A.M.

2. The school play lasted 1 hour and 50 minutes. It ended at 9:20 P.M. At what time did the play start?

When you use logical reasoning and time zones to solve a problem, follow these steps.

Step 1: Find a U.S. Time Zones map.

Step 2: Use the map to find the time zone difference.

Step 3: Use the time zone difference and local times to find the elapsed time.

Remember as you travel from west to east, time is later.

1. A plane left Los Angeles at 1:20 P.M. California time and arrived in Miami at 9:09 P.M. Florida time. How long did the flight take?

Find the perimeter.

One Way:

Add the side lengths.

$P = 25 + 37 + 25 + 37$
$P = 124$ ft

Another Way:

Use a formula.

$P = 2\ell + 2w$
$P = 2(25) + 2(37)$
$P = 50 + 74 = 124$ ft

37 ft

25 ft

Remember you can use the formula $P = 4s$ to find the perimeter of a square.

1.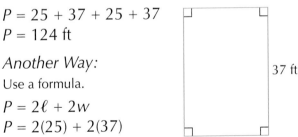

2.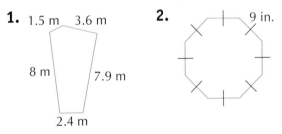

3. The perimeter of a square is 25.6 cm. What is the length of each side?

Find the area.

Use a formula.

$A = \ell \times w$
$A = 7.9 \times 3.8$
$A = 30.02$ m^2

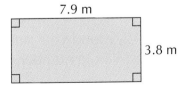

7.9 m

3.8 m

Remember area is always measured in square units, such as m^2, ft^2, or cm^2.

1. rectangle
$\ell = 19$ ft
$w = 12$ ft

2. square
$s = 2.5$ cm

3. If the area of a rectangle is 75 cm^2 and its length is 15 cm, what is its width?

Set 10-9 (pages 570–571)

Using whole units and an area of 36 units^2, find the dimensions of a rectangle with the shortest perimeter.

Find all the possible dimensions of a rectangle with an area of 36 units^2. Then find the perimeter of each.

Width	Length	Area	Perimeter
36	1	36	74
18	2	36	40
12	3	36	30
9	4	36	26
6	6	36	24

$\ell = 6; w = 6.$

Remember you can factor the given area of a rectangle to find all the possible whole unit dimensions.

Using whole units, find the dimensions of a rectangle with the shortest perimeter.

1. $A = 20$ **2.** $A = 196$

3. Using whole units, what are the dimensions of a rectangle with the greatest area if $P = 106$?

Set 10-10 (pages 572–575)

Find the area.

Use a formula.

$A = \frac{1}{2}bh$

$A = \frac{1}{2} \times 16 \times 15$

$A = 8 \times 15 = 120$ in.^{2}

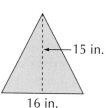
15 in.
16 in.

Remember the formula for the area of a parallelogram is $A = bh$.

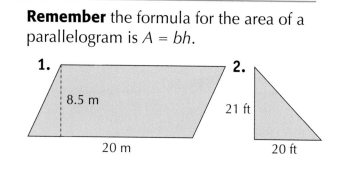

1. 8.5 m 20 m

2. 21 ft 20 ft

Set 10-11 (pages 576–579)

Find the circumference.

Use a formula.

$C = \pi d$

$C \approx 3.14 \times 20$

$C \approx 62.8$ yd

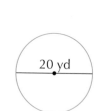
20 yd

Remember the diameter of a circle equals 2 times the radius.

1. $r = 7$ ft, $C =$ ▢

2. $C = 25.12$m, $d =$ ▢

Set 10-12 (pages 580–581)

Find the area.
Use a formula. Use 3.14 or $\frac{22}{7}$ for π.

$A = \pi r^2$
$A \approx 3.14 \times 4^2$
$A \approx 3.14 \times 16$
$A \approx 50.24$ cm^2

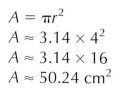
4 cm

Remember that $r^2 = r \times r$.

For 1–2, round your answer to the nearest whole number.

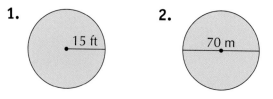

1. 15 ft **2.** 70 m

Decide if the problem has extra or missing information. Solve if you have enough information.

Joan made a rectangular quilt 8 feet long and 6 feet wide. She used 64 cloth squares to make the quilt. The perimeter of each square was 12 inches. Find the area of the quilt.

Think: I need to know the area of the quilt. The information about the square is extra.

Since I know $A = 8 \times 6 = 48$, Joan used 48 ft^2 of cloth to make the quilt.

Remember to identify what you know and what you want to know.

1. A rectangle has a length of 27 meters. Find its area.

2. A bicycle wheel has 30 spokes. Each 25-inch spoke is a radius of the wheel. How far will the bike travel in 10 rotations of its wheel?

Classify the polyhedron.

Since it has one base, and the edges are joined to one point outside the base, it is a pyramid. The base is triangular, so it is a triangular pyramid.

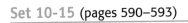

Vertices: A, B, C, D
Edges: $\overline{AB}$, $\overline{AC}$, $\overline{AD}$, $\overline{BC}$, $\overline{BD}$, $\overline{CD}$
Faces: $\triangle ABC$, $\triangle ADC$, $\triangle ABD$, $\triangle BDC$

Remember, solid figures with curved surfaces are NOT polyhedrons.

1.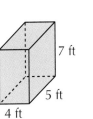

2.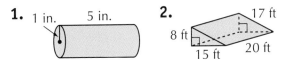

Find the surface area.

Use a formula.

$SA = 2\ell w + 2\ell h + 2wh$
$SA = 2(20) + 2(35) + 2(28)$
$SA = 40 + 70 + 56$
$SA = 166 \text{ ft}^2$

7 ft
5 ft
4 ft

Remember, surface area of a solid is the sum of the areas of each face.

1. 1 in.   5 in.

2.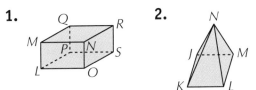
17 ft
8 ft
15 ft   20 ft

Find the volume.

Use a formula. Use 3.14 or $\frac{22}{7}$ for π.

$V = Bh$
$V = \pi r^2 \times h$
$V \approx 3.14 \times 9 \times 6$
$V \approx 169.56 \text{ cm}^3$

3 cm
6 cm

Remember that volume is always measured in cubic units, such as in.^{3}, ft^3, or m^3.

1. triangular prism: $B = 30$ in.^{2}, $h = 10$ in.

2. rectangular prism:
$\ell = 9.2$ m, $w = 7$ m, $h = 1.5$ m

3. If the volume of a cube is 125 ft^3, what is the length of each edge?

Set 10-1 (pages 542–545)

Copy and complete.

1. 51 in. = ▢ ft   **2.** 88 oz = ▢ lb   **3.** 24 qt = ▢ gal   **4.** 38 ft = ▢ yd

5. $2\frac{1}{2}$ lb = ▢ oz   **6.** 7 c = ▢ pt   **7.** 4 mi = ▢ yd   **8.** 5 gal = ▢ c

9. 4 pt = ▢ qt   **10.** 7 tons = ▢ lb   **11.** 6 lb = ▢ oz   **12.** 3 qt = ▢ fl oz

13. After the soccer game, Toby drank 24 fluid ounces of water. Alex drank 2 pints of water. and Ryan drank 5 cups of water. Who drank the most water?

Set 10-2 (pages 546–549)

Name the most appropriate metric unit for each measurement.

1. mass of a postage stamp   **2.** capacity of a drinking cup

3. length of a new pencil   **4.** distance from Tampa to New York

Copy and complete.

5. 14.5 km = ▢ m   **6.** 2.5 m = ▢ mm   **7.** 1,760 g = ▢ kg   **8.** 0.9 kL = ▢ L

9. 4.7 g = ▢ mg   **10.** 82.6 m = ▢ cm   **11.** 35 mL = ▢ L   **12.** 4 kg = ▢ mg

13. 180 mm = ▢ cm   **14.** 380 L = ▢ kL   **15.** 675 mg = ▢ g   **16.** 4.5 L = ▢ mL

17. A tree is 7.73 m tall. What is the height of the tree in cm? in mm?

Set 10-3 (pages 550–551)

Measure each segment to the nearest eighth inch and nearest centimeter.

1. ├────────┤   **2.** ├──────────────┤   **3.** ├──────────────────┤

Measure each segment to the nearest sixteenth inch and nearest millimeter.

4. ├──────────────┤

5. ├────────────────┤

6. Which measurement is less precise, millimeters or inches?

Set 10-4 (pages 552–553)

Copy and complete. Round to the nearest tenth.

1. 20 in. = ▢ cm   **2.** 16 L ≈ ▢ gal   **3.** 65 lb ≈ ▢ kg   **4.** 100 yd ≈ ▢ m

5. 7.5 mi ≈ ▢ km   **6.** 10 oz ≈ ▢ g   **7.** 12.75 L ≈ ▢ qt   **8.** 9 m ≈ ▢ in.

9. 14.2 g ≈ ▢ oz   **10.** 15 km ≈ ▢ mi   **11.** 75 kg ≈ ▢ lb   **12.** 18 qt ≈ ▢ L

13. Last weekend, Paula ran a 10-km race. Estimate the race distance in mi.

14. An eyelash is 11.3 mm long. About what fraction of an inch is this?

Take It to the NET
More Practice
www.scottforesman.com

Set 10-5 (pages 554–557)

Find each elapsed time.

1. 4:17 A.M. to 8:05 A.M.   **2.** 11:20 A.M. to 3:15 P.M.   **3.** 7:45 P.M. to 1:06 A.M.

Find each starting time or ending time using the given elapsed time.

4. End Time: 2:07 P.M.
Elapsed Time: 2 h 26 min

5. Start Time: 9:50 P.M.
Elapsed Time: 6 h 32 min

6. End Time: 10:18 A.M.
Elapsed Time: 8 h 40 min

7. Shawn finished the marathon race in 4 hours 21 minutes 45 seconds. Brent finished the race in 4 hours 30 minutes 57 seconds. How much longer did it take Brent to finish the race?

Set 10-6 (pages 560–561)

Use logical reasoning to solve each problem.

1. Alejandre's flight left Boston at 12 noon and arrived in Denver at 2:20 P.M. local time. Use a time zone map to find how long the flight took.

2. Allen practiced piano for 1 hour 25 minutes. Carolyn practiced from 11:15 A.M. to 12:30 P.M. John practiced longer than Allen. Shaneeka practiced less time than Carolyn did. Who practiced piano the longest?

Set 10-7 (pages 564–567)

Find the perimeter of each figure.

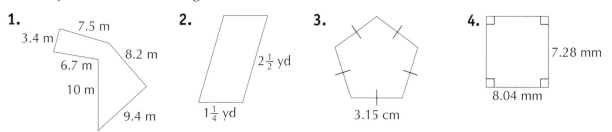

1. 7.5 m, 3.4 m, 8.2 m, 6.7 m, 10 m, 9.4 m   **2.** $2\frac{1}{2}$ yd, $1\frac{1}{4}$ yd   **3.** 3.15 cm   **4.** 7.28 mm, 8.04 mm

5. A square has a perimeter of 16.8 inches. Find the length of each side.

6. A regular dodecagon has a perimeter of 116.4 m. Find the length of each side.

Set 10-8 (pages 568–569)

Find the area of each figure.

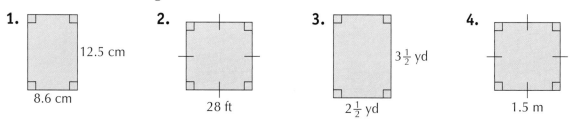

1. 12.5 cm, 8.6 cm   **2.** 28 ft   **3.** $3\frac{1}{2}$ yd, $2\frac{1}{2}$ yd   **4.** 1.5 m

5. A rectangle with a length of 16 cm has an area of 432 cm². Find its width.

6. A soccer field has an area of 8,800 yd² and is 80 yd wide. Find its length.

Set 10-9 (pages 570–571)

Using whole units and the perimeter given, find the dimensions of the rectangle with the greatest area.

1. *P* = 4   **2.** *P* = 10   **3.** *P* = 78   **4.** *P* = 66

Using whole units and the area given, find the dimensions of the rectangle with the shortest perimeter.

5. *A* = 56   **6.** *A* = 81   **7.** *A* = 132   **8.** *A* = 342

9. A rectangle has a length of 12.5 in. and a width of $\frac{3}{4}$ ft. What is its area?

10. A rectangle has a length of 25 cm and a perimeter of 70 cm. Find its area.

Set 10-10 (pages 572–575)

Find the area of each parallelogram or triangle.

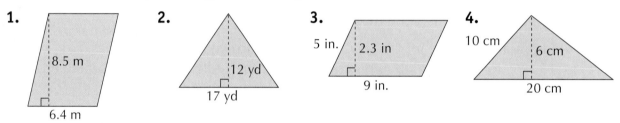

1. 8.5 m, 6.4 m   **2.** 12 yd, 17 yd   **3.** 5 in., 2.3 in, 9 in.   **4.** 10 cm, 6 cm, 20 cm

5. A triangle with a base of 11 m has an area of 33 m². Find its height.

Set 10-11 (pages 576–579)

Find each circumference to the nearest hundredth. Use 3.14 or $\frac{22}{7}$ for π.

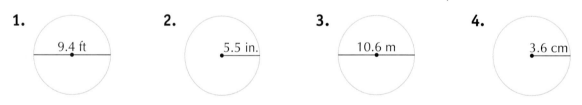

1. 9.4 ft   **2.** 5.5 in.   **3.** 10.6 m   **4.** 3.6 cm

5. A circle has a circumference of 12.56 ft. Find its radius.

Set 10-12 (pages 580–581)

Find the area of each circle to the nearest whole number. Use 3.14 or $\frac{22}{7}$ for π.

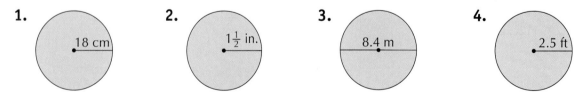

1. 18 cm   **2.** $1\frac{1}{2}$ in.   **3.** 8.4 m   **4.** 2.5 ft

5. A round game table has a diameter of 1 m. Will 1 square meter of plastic laminate cover the top of this table? Explain.

Take It to the NET
More Practice
www.scottforesman.com

Set 10-13 (pages 582–583)

Decide if the problem has extra or missing information. Solve if you have enough information.

1. The floor of a storage closet is a rectangle, 5 feet long and 6 feet wide. If 120 square tiles are used to cover the entire floor and each tile has a perimeter of 24 inches, what is the area of the closet floor?

2. Calvin is making a house front for the school play. The bottom of the house front is a 7 ft by 6 ft rectangle. The roof is an equilateral triangle with 7-foot long sides. How many square feet of wood does Calvin need to make the house front?

Set 10-14 (pages 586–589)

Classify each polyhedron. Name all vertices, edges, and faces.

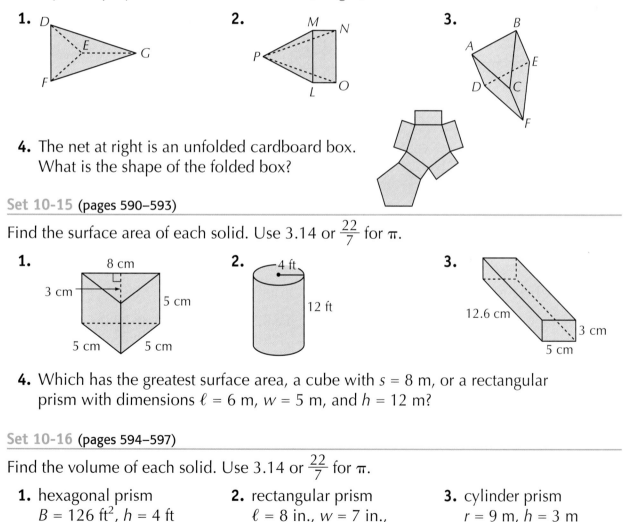

1.

2.

3.

4. The net at right is an unfolded cardboard box. What is the shape of the folded box?

Set 10-15 (pages 590–593)

Find the surface area of each solid. Use 3.14 or $\frac{22}{7}$ for π.

1.

8 cm
3 cm
5 cm
5 cm   5 cm

2.

4 ft
12 ft

3.

12.6 cm
3 cm
5 cm

4. Which has the greatest surface area, a cube with $s = 8$ m, or a rectangular prism with dimensions $\ell = 6$ m, $w = 5$ m, and $h = 12$ m?

Set 10-16 (pages 594–597)

Find the volume of each solid. Use 3.14 or $\frac{22}{7}$ for π.

1. hexagonal prism
$B = 126$ ft^2, $h = 4$ ft

2. rectangular prism
$\ell = 8$ in., $w = 7$ in.,
$h = 2.5$ in.

3. cylinder prism
$r = 9$ m, $h = 3$ m

4. The volume of a cube is 729 m^3. Find the length of each side.

DIAGNOSING READINESS

A Vocabulary
(Gr. 5 and pages 146, 316, 354, 448)

Choose the best term from the box.

1. In a fraction, the dividend is the numerator, and the __?__ is the denominator.

2. A __?__ is a ratio where the first term is compared to 100.

3. Numbers that have only two factors are __?__.

4. A __?__ states that two ratios are equal.

Vocabulary

- **percent** *(p. 354)*
- **T-table** *(p. 448)*
- **prime numbers** *(p. 146)*
- **proportion** *(p. 316)*
- **divisor** *(Gr. 5)*

B Ordering Numbers
(pages 78, 176, 412)

Order from least to greatest.

5. 9.7, 8.2, 9, 71, 8.35, 9.06, 8.4

6. −3, 4, −2, 0, 5, −1, 6, −7

7. 4.25, $\frac{69}{16}$, $\frac{8}{2}$, $4\frac{3}{16}$

8. 10.3, 11.04, 10.82, 10.90, 10.41, 11.1

9. 1.2, −7.5, 0, −3.9, −4.2, 2.7, 1.5

10. At a track meet, Chris, Jack, Michelle, and Adam ran a mile. The table shows their times. Who ran the fastest? the slowest?

Student	Chris	Jack	Michelle	Adam
Time	8 min 12 s	8.5 min	$8\frac{2}{5}$ min	$8\frac{1}{4}$ min

Do You Know...

How many times as tall is a giraffe than a 5-foot student?

You will find out in Lesson 11-17.

RUSSELL ASH
INCREDIBLE COMPARISONS

C Proportions and Percent

(pages 318, 370)

Solve each proportion.

11. $\frac{\$3}{4 \text{ lb}} = \frac{x}{5 \text{ lb}}$ **12.** $\frac{70 \text{ mi}}{2 \text{ hr}} = \frac{245 \text{ mi}}{y}$

13. $\frac{b}{18} = \frac{20}{3}$ **14.** $\frac{12}{t} = \frac{4}{32}$

Find the percent of each number.

15. 25% of 400 **16.** 16% of 92

17. 12% of 56 **18.** 45% of 70

19. 32% of 68 **20.** 78% of 135

21. A shirt is priced at $14.50. Josie receives a 15% store discount. How much will the shirt cost Josie?

D Fractions

(pages 204, 206, 252, 256)

Add. Simplify your answer.

22. $\frac{2}{3} + \frac{3}{5}$ **23.** $\frac{3}{8} + \frac{1}{8}$

24. $\frac{4}{5} + \frac{3}{4}$ **25.** $\frac{7}{12} + \frac{1}{2}$

26. $\frac{5}{6} + \frac{8}{9}$ **27.** $\frac{6}{7} + \frac{3}{4}$

Multiply. Simplify your answer.

28. $\frac{1}{5} \times \frac{1}{4}$ **29.** $\frac{2}{3} \times \frac{3}{5}$

30. $\frac{3}{8} \times \frac{2}{7}$ **31.** $\frac{1}{4} \times \frac{2}{3}$

32. $\frac{3}{10} \times \frac{4}{9}$ **33.** $\frac{5}{12} \times \frac{1}{12}$

619

Key Idea
A sample from
a population
can help you
learn about
the population.

Vocabulary
• data
• population
• sample
• survey
• representative
  sample
• biased sample
• statistics
• random sampling

Think It Through
I can **picture the
relationship**
between the
sample and
the population.

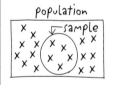

620

Samples and Surveys

LEARN

How are samples used?

Data, or information, about an entire **population** of people or things
is often collected and analyzed. Sometimes only a **sample,** or part,
of the population is studied.

Example A

Mandy sells trail mix by the ounce. She wondered what
percent of the weight is made up of raisins. She scooped
out a sample from the large bin that contains the trail mix.
The sample weighed 20 ounces. After she sorted the mix
into peanuts and raisins, Mandy found that the raisins
weighed 9 ounces.

$$\frac{\text{weight of raisins} \longrightarrow 9}{\text{weight of sample} \longrightarrow 20} = 0.45 = 45\%$$

Since 45% of the sample weight is made up of raisins,
about 45% of the total trail mix weight is probably
made up of raisins.

Surveys are often used to gather data from a sample of people.

Example B

Researchers **polled,** or asked, 1,400
of a newspaper's 800,000 subscribers:
"Which is the first section of the
newspaper that you read?" The
results are shown in the table.

Section	Subscribers
News	560
Want Ads	84
Entertainment	181
Sports	367
Business	208

Find the number of subscribers out of 800,000 who read
the news section first.

Write and solve a proportion.

news readers in sample $\searrow$ $\nearrow$ news readers in population

$$\frac{560}{1,400} = \frac{n}{800,000}$$

number in sample $\nearrow$ $\nwarrow$ number in population

$$560 \times 800,000 = 1,400n$$

$$320,000 = n$$

About 320,000 subscribers probably read the news section first.

✔ Talk About It

1. In Example A, what is the entire population?

2. What is another way to solve Example B using $\frac{560}{1,400} = 40\%$?

When are samples used?

The data from a sample only approximates the data from the entire population. Samples are used when it is unreasonable or impossible to study every member of the population, as illustrated in the following situations.

- In a truckload of apples, what percent have worms?

  → Study a sample because cutting open every apple in the population would destroy the population.

- In a town of 14,000 voters, how many are likely to vote for Candidate A?

  → Study a sample because polling every voter would be difficult and time consuming.

- What percent of cars on Florida highways have out-of-state license plates?

  → Study a sample because the actual data would vary from minute to minute.

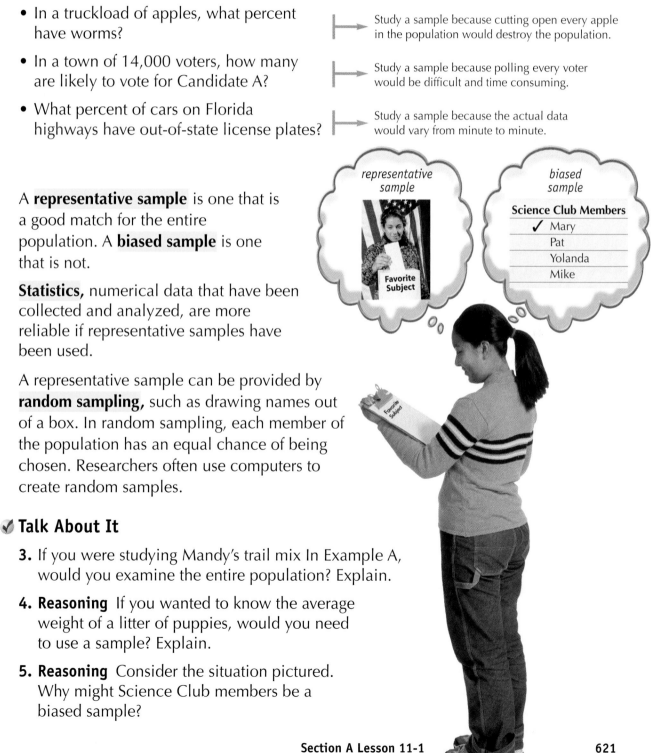

A **representative sample** is one that is a good match for the entire population. A **biased sample** is one that is not.

Statistics, numerical data that have been collected and analyzed, are more reliable if representative samples have been used.

A representative sample can be provided by **random sampling,** such as drawing names out of a box. In random sampling, each member of the population has an equal chance of being chosen. Researchers often use computers to create random samples.

✔ Talk About It

3. If you were studying Mandy's trail mix In Example A, would you examine the entire population? Explain.

4. Reasoning If you wanted to know the average weight of a litter of puppies, would you need to use a sample? Explain.

5. Reasoning Consider the situation pictured. Why might Science Club members be a biased sample?

For another example, see Set 11-1 on p. 688.

In Exercises 1 and 2, identify the population studied. Then tell whether you think the statistics are drawn from a sample or from the entire population. Explain your thinking.

1. Hallie read that the average life span of a grasshopper is about 50 days.

2. Mr. Cragin reported that the average height of his basketball team is 5 ft 11 in.

3. A manufacturer randomly tested 300 radios of the 400,000 produced. Four were defective. What percent of the 400,000 radios are probably defective?

4. Refer to the table in Example B. Estimate the number of subscribers out of 800,000 who read the *want ads* first.

5. Reasoning A company surveyed teenagers using the Internet to determine how many hours per week the typical teenager watches television. Do you think this was a representative sample or a biased sample? Explain.

For more practice, see Set 11-1 on p. 692.

A Skills and Understanding

In Exercises 6 and 7, identify the population studied. Then tell whether you think the statistics are drawn from a sample or from the entire population. Explain your thinking.

6. At River Bluff Middle School, 62% of the students are enrolled in a foreign language course.

7. Morgan determined that 22% of the fortunes in the fortune cookies served at his restaurant contain predictions about wealth.

8. Alex removed 16 ounces of the nut mix stored in a barrel. He found that 4 ounces were cashews. About what percent of the nut mix weight in the barrel is cashews?

9. A survey of 500 people with library cards revealed that 120 of those people are retired. Out of 12,400 card holders, how many are probably retired?

10. Reasoning Every student whose locker number ends in 8 was questioned in order to gather student input about plans for the new playground. Do you think this was a representative sample or a biased sample? Explain.

B Reasoning and Problem Solving

Math and Social Studies

An **exit poll** is a survey taken of voters as they leave a polling place. It is used to predict the final outcome of an election.

11. Use the exit-poll data at the right to predict the percent of votes each candidate will get.

Exit-poll Results		
Cortez	**Lake**	**Shriner**
74	121	55

12. <u>Writing in Math</u> Refer to Exercise 11. If 10,000 people vote, predict how many votes each candidate will get. Explain how you found the answer.

C Extensions

13. How could you use the spinner at the right to select a random sample of 30 students from a population of 460 students?

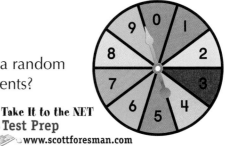

Mixed Review and Test Prep

Take It to the NET
Test Prep
www.scottforesman.com

14. Find the area and circumference of a circle with a diameter of 12 ft.

15. Which Property of Addition is used in $5 + 4 = 4 + 5$?

   A. Associative   **B.** Commutative   **C.** Inverse   **D.** Distributive

Enrichment

Other Sampling Methods

Researchers do not always use random sampling. Here are some examples of other sampling methods.

Convenience sampling uses any convenient method for forming the sample. For example, the first 50 customers to arrive at a shopping center are polled.	**Systematic sampling** uses a pattern to identify members of the sample. For example, every 100th person to arrive at a shopping center is polled.	**Responses to a survey** can be gathered from an oral interview or written questionnaire. For example, some shoppers might complete survey forms and mail them to the researcher.

Each specific situation needs to be examined to determine whether a sample is representative or biased. For example, polling every 500th person who arrives at a shopping center about his or her favorite store may give responses representative of all of the shoppers at that shopping center. But inspecting the workmanship of every 500th pair of jeans produced at a factory might not be representative. The jeans checked might all be produced during just one of several shifts.

For each situation below, tell which sampling method is used and whether you think it is a representative or biased sample.

1. A state legislator examines questionnaires about literacy issues that were completed and mailed to her office.

2. A pollster wants to know how voters feel about a tax increase to build a new stadium. The pollster talks to the first 100 people in line at a baseball game.

3. A restaurant owner interviews every 25th customer about customer satisfaction.

Key Idea
The mean, median, mode, and range are statistical measures that help describe a set of data.

Vocabulary
• range
• mean
• median
• mode
• minimum
• maximum

Mean, Median, Mode, and Range

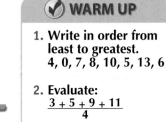

✓ **WARM UP**

1. Write in order from least to greatest.
   4, 0, 7, 8, 10, 5, 13, 6

2. Evaluate:
   $\dfrac{3 + 5 + 9 + 11}{4}$

LEARN

How can you describe a set of data?

Carey recorded the number of points she scored in each of 10 volleyball tournaments.

Tournament	1	2	3	4	5	6	7	8	9	10
Points Scored	9	6	10	9	15	9	12	12	20	13

The **range** tells you how spread out the data is, while the **mean**, **median**, and **mode** describe what is typical for a set of data.

Example A

Find the range, mean, median, and mode of Carey's scores.

Range: Subtract the **minimum,** the least number, from the **maximum,** the greatest number, in the set of data.

$$20 - 6 = 14 \qquad \text{The range is 14.}$$

Mean: Add all the data and divide the sum by the number of data values in the set. The mean is sometimes called the **average.**

$$9 + 6 + 10 + 9 + 15 + 9 + 12 + 12 + 20 + 13 = 115$$

$$\frac{115}{10} = 11.5 \qquad \text{The mean is 11.5.}$$

Median: Arrange the data in order. If there are an odd number of data values, select the middle number. If there are an even number of data values, find the mean of the two middle numbers.

6   9   9   9   **10   12**   12   13   15   20

$$\frac{10 + 12}{2} = 11 \qquad \text{The median is 11.}$$

Mode: Choose the number that occurs most often. Sometimes there is no mode, and sometimes there is more than one mode.

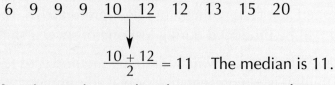

6 ⑨ ⑨ ⑨ 10   12   12   13   15   20

The mode is 9.

✔ Talk About It

1. Would you get the same number for the median if you arranged Carey's scores in order from greatest to least? Explain.

2. **Number Sense** What is the mean of a set of data that contains numbers that are all the same?

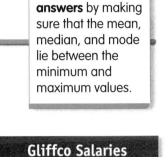

Think It Through
I can **check my answers** by making sure that the mean, median, and mode lie between the minimum and maximum values.

Should you use the mean, median, or mode?

The mean, median, and sometimes the mode are called **measures of center.** Often, they are close together, as in Example A, but that is not always the case.

Example B

Examine the statistics shown in the table. Does the mean, the median, or the mode best describe the typical salary at Gliffco?

Both the mean and the mode are greater than $100,000. But this does not seem to be a good representation of the salaries since six out of nine employees earn $50,000 or less.

In this case, the data are best described by the median, $48,000.

Gliffco Salaries	
Job	**Annual Salary**
President	$350,000
Vice-President	160,000
Vice-President	160,000
Sales	50,000
Sales	48,000
Sales	45,000
Sales	42,000
Sales	39,000
Secretary	32,000
Mean:	$103,000
Median:	48,000
Mode:	160,000

✔ Talk About It

3. Does this newspaper headline seem misleading? Is it accurate? Explain.

4. **Number Sense** Find the range of Gliffco salaries.

Average Gliffco Salary Tops $100,000

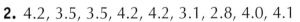

CHECK ✔✔

For another example, see Set 11-2 on p. 688.

Find the mean, median, mode, and range of each data set. Round decimal answers to the nearest hundredth.

1. 10, 4, 7, 4, 5, 6, 4, 7, 7, 8, 9, 3

2. 4.2, 3.5, 3.5, 4.2, 4.2, 3.1, 2.8, 4.0, 4.1

3. −6, 4, 6, −5, −5, 0

4. 100, 102, 105, 103, 106, 110, 110

5. 85, 78, 65, 77, 91, 88, 80, 93, 90

6. 10, 4, 11, 33, 6, 12, 9, 4, 7

7. **Number Sense** Does the mean, the median, or the mode best describe the typical size of art classes at Morissey Academy?

Morrissey Academy Art Classes

Class	Art 110	Art 140	**Art 205**	Art 220	Art 306	Art 330
Size	180	18	16	23	19	28

For more practice, see Set 11-2 on p. 692.

A Skills and Understanding

Find the mean, median, mode, and range of each data set. Round decimal answers to the nearest hundredth.

8. 6, 6, 7, 10, 12, 11, 7, 7, 7

9. 0.5, 0.6, 0.3, 0.5, 0.2, 0.9, 0.5, 0.5

10. 1.8, 1.95, 1.85, 1.8, 1.6

11. 12, 14, 10, 19, 10, 7, 16, 10, 5

12. $0.79, $2.47, $1.86, $1.92, $2.00

13. $240, $260, $280, $300, $400, $240

14. −9°F, −6°F, 0°F, 7°F, 4°F, −2°F, −7°F

15. −14, 12, 8, −6, 6, 6, 7, 3, 3, 3, −5, −5

16. Number Sense Does the mean, the median, or the mode best describe the math test scores listed below?

22, 67, 67, 70, 71, 69, 94, 88, 98, 94, 92, 95, 97, 99, 68, 67, 71

B Reasoning and Problem Solving

17. Algebra Marcy's mean score on four tests was 84. Three of the scores were 84, 88, and 80. What was the fourth score?

18. Refer to Carey's scores on page 624. How many points would she need to score in the eleventh game to raise the mean to 12?

19. Suppose the average salary at the Perling Company is $103,000, with a range of $22,000. Do you think the president of the Perling Company earns as great a salary as the president of Gliffco in Example B on page 625? Explain.

Math and Social Studies

The table shows the ages at the time of their inauguration of the ten most recent United States presidents.

President	Age
Eisenhower	62
Kennedy	43
Johnson	55
Nixon	56
Ford	61
Carter	52
Reagan	69
G. H. W. Bush	64
Clinton	46
G. W. Bush	54

20. To the nearest whole number, find the mean age.

21. What are the median, mode, and range of the ages?

22. If the next president is 60 years old when inaugurated, will the mean age of the eleven most recent presidents be greater than, less than, or the same as the mean age of the ten most recent presidents?

23. Writing in Math On the weekdays of last week, Mr. Jansen drove 240, 240, 250, 250, and 300 miles. To find the average distance traveled each day, he evaluated the expression at the right. Is his work correct? Explain.

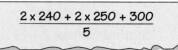

$$\frac{2 \times 240 + 2 \times 250 + 300}{5}$$

C Extensions

Write a set of data that fits the description.

24. The median is 8.　　**25.** The mean is 5.　　**26.** The mean and median are equal.

27. The mode is 13.　　**28.** The range is 0.　　**29.** The mean is 0, and the range is 4.

Mixed Review and Test Prep

Take It to the NET
Test Prep
www.scottforesman.com

30. In a survey, 54 out of 100 people favored the construction of a new bridge. How many people out of 24,000 would you expect to be in favor of its construction?

31. Which is the correct solution for $n + 432 = 845$?

　　A. 1,277　　　**B.** 1,250　　　**C.** 450　　　**D.** 413

Learning with Technology

Spreadsheet/Data/Grapher eTool:
Finding the Median and Mean

A spreadsheet can help you find the median, especially when there are large amounts of data.

The scores students received on a test in one class are shown below. Enter the 24 test scores into Column A of your spreadsheet. Use the Sort command to arrange the data from least to greatest.

Test Scores

78	95	83	75	78	50	88	78	93	43	93	48
90	80	88	58	78	93	93	93	75	88	90	70

	A	B
1	Test Scores	
2	78	
3	95	
4	83	
5	75	
6	78	
7	50	
8	88	

Locate the middle number in the data to find the median.

1. What is the median test score?

2. Four students were absent on the day of the test. Their scores on the make-up test were 77, 89, 80, and 92. Find the new median of the 28 scores.

A spreadsheet can also help you find the mean of a data set. Use a formula to find the sum of the test scores in Column A.

3. How can you use the test score sum to find the mean score?

4. Add a test score of 71 to make 29 scores in all. How can knowing a formula to find the mean help you to calculate the median of the 29 scores?

Key Idea
Making a frequency table or a line plot helps to organize and display data.

Vocabulary
• frequency table
• interval
• line plot
• outlier

Frequency Tables and Line Plots

LEARN

Activity

How can you make a frequency table and a line plot?

The manager of a shoe store recorded the ages of customers who purchased athletic shoes recently.

a. Copy the **frequency table** at the right. Then follow the steps below to complete the table.

Step 1 List age groups, or **intervals.**

Step 2 Make a **tally mark** for each data value.
Use ~~卌~~ for every five.

Step 3 In the far right column, show the frequency by writing the number of tally marks for that age group.

b. How many people 50 years of age or older bought shoes?

A **line plot** is another way to display data. Instead of tally marks, a line plot uses Xs.

c. Copy and complete the line plot of the shoe data.

d. How are the frequency table and line plot alike? How are they different?

e. What does the tallest column of Xs signify?

f. Could you have used different intervals for the frequency table or line plot? Do you think you would always need to use intervals? Explain.

WARM UP
Use the set of data below.
3, 7, 9, 2, 10, 5, 12, 8, 4, 18

1. Find the minimum, maximum, and range

2. Find the mean, median, and mode.

Ages of Customers		
14	37	30
25	19	31
8	20	
10	47	
12	61	
35	26	
26	38	
67	21	
23	20	
6	52	
55	11	
13	23	
34	41	
29	42	
9	62	
54	56	
43	34	
27	50	

Age Group	Tally	Frequency
0-9	III	3
10-19	卌 I	6
20-29	卌 卌	10
30-39		
40-49		
50-59		
60-69		

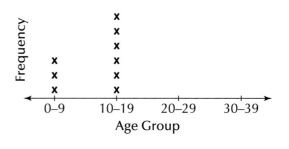

TEST TALK

Think It Through
I can **make a table** to show the frequency of various data values.

Take It to the NET
More Examples
www.scottforesman.com

How can you describe how data is distributed?

You can see in the line plots below that some sets of data are more spread out than others.

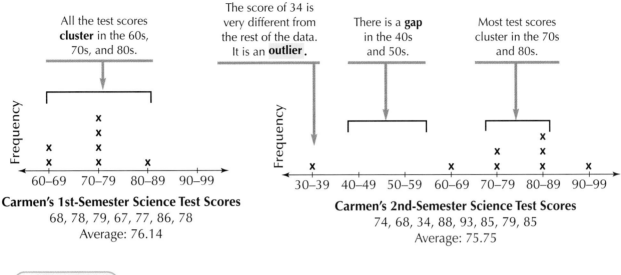

Carmen's 1st-Semester Science Test Scores
68, 78, 79, 67, 77, 86, 78
Average: 76.14

Carmen's 2nd-Semester Science Test Scores
74, 68, 34, 88, 93, 85, 79, 85
Average: 75.75

Example

Carmen complained, "If I just hadn't scored a 34 on that one test, my 2nd-semester average would have been better than my 1st-semester average." Is she right?

Find the mean of Carmen's 2nd-semester test score *without* the outlier.

$$74 + 68 + 88 + 93 + 85 + 79 + 85 = 572$$

$$\frac{572}{7} \approx 81.7$$

Carmen is right. Without the score of 34, her 2nd-semester average is about 81.7, which is more than 5 points higher than her 1st-semester average.

Sometimes outliers have a significant effect on the mean, but not always. The effect of an outlier depends on how many data values are in the set and how large the gap is between the outlier and the other data values.

✔ Talk About It

1. Find Carmen's median test score for the 2nd semester. What is it without the outlier?

2. **Number Sense** If Carmen's lowest test score had been 54 instead of 34, would her 2nd-semester average have been better or worse?

3. **Number Sense** Would one low test score have hurt Carmen's average as much if there had been 16, not 8, tests? Explain.

4. **Reasoning** Is the mode of a set of data affected by whether or not you include the outlier(s)? Explain.

Members of Mr. Handley's class recorded the outside temperatures at noon over a 10-day period.

Noon Temperatures				
75°F	72°F	73°F	71°F	71°F
84°F	74°F	73°F	74°F	73°F

1. Represent this data with a frequency table and a line plot. Identify any clusters, gaps, and outliers.

2. **Number Sense** Compute the mean with and without the outlier(s) and compare them.

PRACTICE

For more practice, see Set 11-3 on p. 692.

(A) Skills and Understanding

Heights in Inches of Middle School Basketball Team				
70	73	59	71	68
67	66	67	71	74
68	69	70	70	82

Follow these directions for each set of data at the right.

3. Represent the first set of data with a frequency table and the second set with a line plot.

4. Identify any clusters, gaps, and outliers.

5. **Number Sense** Compute the mean. If there are any outliers, compute the mean again without the outlier(s) and compare the means.

Ages of Swimmers at Community Pool					
8	12	21	35	6	12
13	44	9	10	13	43
64	71	15	35	24	17
15	48	69	17	8	20

(B) Reasoning and Problem Solving

Math and Science

Did you know that the tallest recorded sunflower was 25 feet tall? These line plots show the heights of sunflowers grown using two different plant foods.

6. Identify outliers, gaps, and clusters in each line plot.

7. Find the range, median, and mode of each set of data.

8. Based on just the appearance of the line plots, which data do you think has the greater mean? Why? Calculate each mean to check your prediction.

9. To grow taller sunflowers, which fertilizer would you use? Why?

10. **Writing in Math** Louis checked the cost to rent a video tape at 20 stores and displayed his findings in the table at the right. What is the mean of the data in this frequency table? Explain how you found the answer.

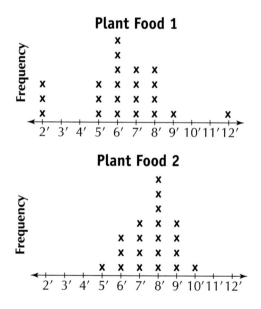

Plant Food 1

Plant Food 2

Video-Rental Cost	
Cost	Frequency
$2.50	4
$3.00	10
$3.50	6

C Extensions

A **histogram** is similar to a line plot. The Xs are replaced by bars that touch and have the same width. A scale is written along the vertical axis.

11. How many pumpkins weighed less than 15 pounds?

12. Do any pumpkins weigh 26 pounds? How do you know?

13. Make a histogram of the data in the activity on page 628.

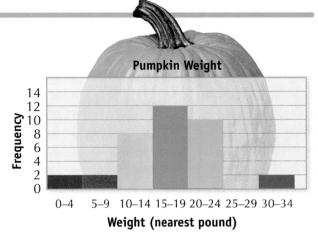

Pumpkin Weight

Frequency: 14, 12, 10, 8, 6, 4, 2, 0

Weight (nearest pound): 0–4, 5–9, 10–14, 15–19, 20–24, 25–29, 30–34

Mixed Review and Test Prep

Take It to the NET
Test Prep
www.scottforesman.com

14. Find the mean, median, mode, and range of these football scores.
28, 13, 21, 20, 6, 12, 7, 34, 19, 32, 26, 21

15. Which is 235.3 in scientific notation?

A. 2.353×10^1 **B.** 2.353×10^2 **C.** 23.53×10^1 **D.** 23.53×10^2

Enrichment

Box-and-Whisker Plots

The test score data below has been divided into four **quartiles.**

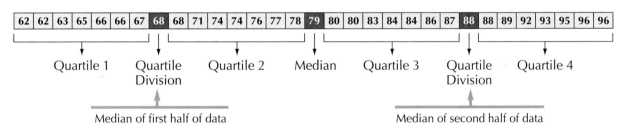

| 62 | 62 | 63 | 65 | 66 | 66 | 67 | **68** | 68 | 71 | 74 | 74 | 76 | 77 | 78 | **79** | 80 | 80 | 83 | 84 | 84 | 86 | 87 | **88** | 88 | 89 | 92 | 93 | 95 | 96 | 96 |

Quartile 1   Quartile Division   Quartile 2   Median   Quartile 3   Quartile Division   Quartile 4

Median of first half of data   Median of second half of data

A **box-and-whisker plot** includes a number line that shows the minimum and maximum, the median, and the quartile divisions. A *box* is drawn on top of the second and third quartiles. The part of the number line showing the first and fourth quartiles are the *whiskers*.

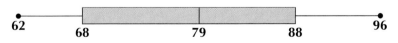

62   68   79   88   96

1. Make a box-and-whisker plot of the test scores below.

72, 77, 65, 60, 84, 89, 98, 75, 63, 69, 71, 72, 92, 80, 70, 78, 85, 88, 83, 74, 78, 90, 81

Key Idea
A stem-and-leaf plot shows numerical data in an organized chart.

Vocabulary
• stem-and-leaf plot

Think It Through
I need to **use place value** when I read or create a stem-and-leaf plot.

Stem-and-Leaf Plots

LEARN

What does a stem-and-leaf plot show?

A **stem-and-leaf plot** is a convenient way to display individual values in a set of numerical data.

The data shown in the stem-and-leaf plot below are the same data given in the table.

Number of Participants in Library Programs						
45	34	38	39	21	20	46
53	40	29	37	33	39	40

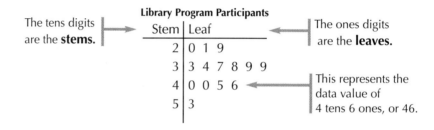

The tens digits are the **stems.**

Library Program Participants

Stem	Leaf
2	0 1 9
3	3 4 7 8 9 9
4	0 0 5 6
5	3

The ones digits are the **leaves.**

This represents the data value of 4 tens 6 ones, or 46.

✔ Talk About It

1. What data value is represented by 7 in the second row?

2. Explain how to find the median and mode in the stem-and-leaf plot.

Activity

How can you make a stem-and-leaf plot?

a. Arrange the numerical data in the table at the right in order from least to greatest.

b. Follow the steps below to make a stem-and-leaf plot.

Step 1 Write a title.
Step 2 Draw two columns and label them *Stem* and *Leaf.*
Step 3 Write the tens digits from the data in order from least to greatest in the *Stem* column.
Step 4 Next to each tens digit, in the *Leaf* column, write the ones digit for each data value from least to greatest.

March Computer Sales	
Salesperson	**No. Sold**
Harris	66
D'Aurea	37
Kline	40
Cortez	61
Lurvey	18
Stanley	40
McKenna	32
Chung	55
Grace	51
Whitewater	48
Petrillo	37
Casado	40

c. Describe any outliers.

This data shows the number of residents on each floor of a large apartment building.

Number of Apartment Building Residents											
Floor	1	2	3	4	5	6	7	8	9	10	11
Residents	31	20	34	26	31	38	29	30	22	34	28

1. Represent the data in a stem-and-leaf plot.

2. Find the median, mode, and range of the data.

3. Reasoning A stem-and-leaf plot has 28 leaves. How many values are in the set of data?

A Skills and Understanding

The table at the right shows the prices in dollars that customers paid for a model of scooter at various stores.

Scooter Prices ($)					
90	73	80	77	78	82
82	84	92	86	86	88
88	72	81	79	94	98

4. Represent the data in a stem-and-leaf plot.

5. Find the median, mode, and range of the data.

6. Reasoning Which leaf in a stem-and-leaf plot corresponds to the minimum? the maximum?

B Reasoning and Problem Solving

The class grades for two history tests are displayed at the right.

7. What was the range of the scores for each test?

8. Which set of scores has the greater median?

9. The passing grade is 65. How many students passed each test? How many students did not pass each test?

10. Writing in Math Can you tell, just by looking at these stem-and-leaf plots, which set of scores is better? Explain.

History Test 1

Stem	Leaf
6	0 1 2 2 4 5 6 8 8
7	2 2 3 6 7 8
8	1 1 1 3 5 6
9	0 2 2 3

History Test 2

Stem	Leaf
5	7
6	3 4 8
7	0 0 5 5 5 6 7 8
8	2 4 5 7 7 8 8 9 9
9	2 5 6 9

Mixed Review and Test Prep

Take It to the NET
Test Prep
www.scottforesman.com

11. Make a frequency table for the data in the activity on page 632.

12. Find 76.8×0.013.

A. 0.09984 **B.** 0.9984 **C.** 9.984 **D.** 99.84

All text pages available online and on CD-ROM.

Do You Know How?

Do You Understand?

Samples and Surveys (11-1)

1. In science class, Brenda recorded the eye-color of 25 fruit flies. She noted that 6 flies had white eyes. In a population of 1,200 flies, about how many flies will have white eyes?

A Identify the population studied in Exercise 1. Explain how you used the sample to predict the number of flies with white eyes.

Mean, Median, Mode, and Range (11-2)

Find the mean, median, mode, and range of each data set. Round decimal answers to the nearest hundredth.

2. 6.5, 7.0, 8.3, 4.7, 6.5, 5.8, 6.2

3. 12, 15, 16, 11, 19, 20, 25, 11, 16

4. −3, −1, 2, 2, −4, −6, −1, −1, 3, 4, 2, −3

B Explain how to find the mean, median, mode, and range of a data set.

Frequency Tables and Line Plots (11-3)

Math Test Scores for Mr. Riley's Class							
98	90	82	72	80	92	72	50
88	74	70	68	94	86	82	92

5. Make a line plot of the data.

6. Identify any clusters, gaps, and outliers.

C Describe how the frequency table and the line plot are alike and how they are different.

D Explain how an outlier can affect a data set. What does the effect of an outlier depend on?

Stem-and-Leaf Plots (11-4)

Ages of Chorus Members								
12	15	15	28	30	44	12	14	35
37	16	20	22	18	13	10	25	32

7. Make a stem-and-leaf plot of the data.

E Describe how data is organized in a stem-and-leaf plot.

MULTIPLE CHOICE

1. Which statistical measure tells you how spread out the data are? (11-2)

   A. mean   **B.** median   **C.** range   **D.** mode

2. What is the median of the data in the stem-and-leaf plot at the right? (11-4)

   A. 34   **B.** 35.5   **C.** 37.75   **D.** 48

Jean Prices

Stem	Leaf
2	0 1 2 5 8
3	2 2 4 4 5 6 9
4	5 8 8 8
5	0 0 4 4

FREE RESPONSE

Identify the population studied. Then tell whether you think the statistics are drawn from a sample or from the entire population. Explain your thinking. (11-1)

3. On the swim team, 32% of the swimmers are 12 years old.

4. A survey of 200 students showed that 96 play a team sport. Out of 1,500 students, how many probably play a team sport?

Find the mean, median, mode, and range of each data set. Round decimal answers to the nearest hundredth. (11-2)

Think It Through

I need to make sure I **understand vocabulary.** What is meant by mean, median, mode, and range?

5. $2.50, $1.20, $3.05, $4.25, $1.80

6. 6, 6, 9, 10, 12, 4, 6, 15,

7. −3, −5, −2, −5, 0, 2, 1, −1, 3, −6

8. 98, 95, 88, 95, 72, 46, 90, 80, 78

For Exercises 9–12, use the data about temperatures. (11-2, 11-3, 11-4)

9. Represent the data in a frequency table, a line plot, and a stem-and-leaf plot.

10. Identify any clusters, gaps, and outliers.

11. Find the mean, median, mode, and range of the data.

12. How can you quickly find the minimum and maximum value in your stem-and-leaf plot?

Monthly High Temperatures (°F)

25°	36°	38°	56°
60°	78°	84°	84°
76°	60°	42°	22°

Writing in Math

13. Explain the difference between a line plot and a stem-and-leaf plot. On which plot would it be easier to identify clusters, gaps, and outliers? Explain your thinking. (11-3, 11-4)

14. Use the frequency table of TV prices. Does the mean, median, or mode best describe the typical cost of a TV? Explain your answer. (11-2, 11-3)

TV Prices

Price	Frequency
$150	10
$200	8
$325	4
$520	12

Key Idea
Bar graphs show comparisons of numerical data. Two sets of similar data can be shown in a double-bar graph.

Vocabulary
• double-bar graph
• axis (pl. axes)

Materials
• $\frac{1}{4}$-in. grid paper
or tools

TEST TALK

Think It Through

I can **make a graph** to show comparisons between data values.

Bar Graphs

LEARN

Activity

How can you read and create a double-bar graph?

The **double-bar graph** shows the number of video tapes and DVDs rented from five movie rental stores.

a. At which store were more DVDs rented than video tapes?

b. Which store had the greatest number of video tape rentals?

July Movie Rentals

Legend: ■ video tapes ■ DVDs

(Bar graph: Number of Rentals (thousands) on vertical axis, 0 to 10; Store on horizontal axis: Dees Movies, Video Valley, Vans Video, Metro Movies, Movies Tonight)

c. At which store were there about twice as many video tape rentals as DVD rentals?

d. Would you be able to make these comparisons as quickly if the data were presented in a table? Explain.

e. Does the graph show precise or approximate data?

f. Using the data in the table at the right, copy and complete the double-bar graph below.

Art Fair Sales (number sold)

Type of Art	Saturday	Sunday
Paintings	110	121
Photographs	76	62
Ceramics	50	55
Jewelry	70	84

Step 1 Write a title.
Step 2 Label the horizontal and vertical **axes.**
Step 3 On one axis, mark equal intervals beginning with 0. Draw a line across the graph at each interval.
Step 4 On the other axis, write the categories.
Step 5 Choose your colors and make a key to show what each color represents.
Step 6 Draw a bar for each value of data.

Art Fair Sales

Legend: ■ Saturday ■ Sunday

(Bar graph: Number Sold on vertical axis, 0 to 125; Type of Art on horizontal axis: Paintings, Photographs, Ceramics, Jewelry)

WARM UP
Draw a number line. Locate and label each point.
1. *A* at 32   2. *B* at 38
3. *C* at 46   4. *D* at 41
5. *E* at 40   6. *F* at 35

For 1–3, use the double-bar graph at the right.

Average High and Low Temperatures in January (°F)

Legend: Average High, Average Low

City: Rome, London, Tokyo, Moscow, Mexico City

1. Which city has the coldest temperatures?

2. How many cities have an average high temperature greater than 50°F?

3. **Representations** Would a scale of 0 to 100 in intervals of 25 be as good a choice for the graph?

A Skills and Understanding

Number of Fish Sold (thousands)

Legend: Freshwater fish, Saltwater fish

Store: Fins and Feathers, Friendly Pets, Murphys Pet Shop

For 4–6, use the double-bar graph at the right.

4. Which pet shop sold the fewest number of freshwater fish? saltwater fish?

5. Which pet shop sold the greatest total number of fish?

6. **Representations** Would your answers to Exercises 4 and 5 change if the graph were drawn with horizontal bars?

B Reasoning and Problem Solving

7. Make a double-bar graph of the data in the Summer Ticket Sales table at the right.

8. **Writing in Math** Which values in a set of data correspond to the longest and shortest bars of a double-bar graph?

Summer-Ticket Sales (thousands)

Amusement Park	Adults	Children
River Heights	45	56
Silver Birch	22	40
Family Fair	16	25
Galaxy Land	49	62

C Extensions

9. Make a pictograph of the data on Library Books at the right.

Library Books

Library	Number of Books
Central	60,000
Newton	40,000
Jackson	35,000

Mixed Review and Test Prep

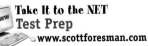

Take It to the NET
Test Prep
www.scottforesman.com

10. In a stem-and-leaf plot, what data values are represented by 7|3 5 7 9 9?

11. Which list gives all the factors of 28?

    A. 2, 4, 7, 14, 28   **B.** 1, 2, 4, 7, 14, 28   **C.** 1, 4, 7, 14   **D.** 1, 4, 8, 14, 28

Key Idea
Line graphs are
useful for
examining trends
in data.

Vocabulary
• line graph
• trend
• double-line graph
• axis (p. 636)

Materials
• $\frac{1}{4}$-in. grid paper
or  **tools**

Line Graphs

LEARN

Activity

How are data represented in a line graph?

Data collected over time are often represented in a **line graph.** A line graph shows data points connected with line segments. In some line graphs there is a **trend** in the data. This can be used to make predictions about how the data might behave in the future.

The table shows the annual circulation (number of issues sold) of two magazines.

a. Copy and complete the **double-line graph** below.

Magazine Circulation (thousands of issues)		
Year	Modern Teen Times	Contempo Teens
1996	120	87
1997	152	104
1998	141	119
1999	133	121
2000	160	131
2001	156	170
2002	159	222
2003	150	240

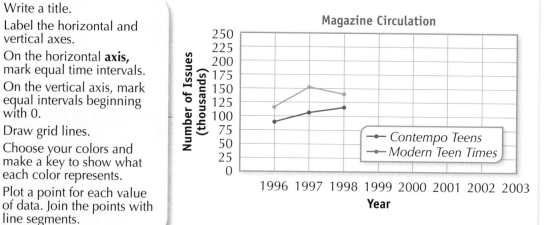

Step 1 Write a title.
Step 2 Label the horizontal and vertical axes.
Step 3 On the horizontal **axis,** mark equal time intervals.
Step 4 On the vertical axis, mark equal intervals beginning with 0.
Step 5 Draw grid lines.
Step 6 Choose your colors and make a key to show what each color represents.
Step 7 Plot a point for each value of data. Join the points with line segments.

Think It Through
• I can **make a graph** to show changes in data over time.

• I can **look at the way the graph rises or falls** to determine trends and make predictions.

b. During which years did *Contempo Teens* sell fewer issues than *Modern Teen Times?* How is this shown in the graph?

c. How can you tell from the graph when the circulation of a magazine increased? decreased? stayed about the same?

d. When did *Contempo Teens* surpass *Modern Teen Times?* How is this shown in the graph?

e. Predict the circulation of each magazine for the year 2004.

WARM UP

Plot each ordered pair on a coordinate plane.

1. *Q* (0, 2)   2. *R* (1, 3)

3. *S* (2, −4) 4. *T* (−3, −1)

5. Graph *y* = 2*x* and *y* = *x* + 4 on the same coordinate grid.

1. The table shows the temperatures in degrees Fahrenheit of two hospital patients. Show the data in a double-line graph. (Hint: Mark the vertical axis as shown at the far right.)

Time	Hastings	Morelli
12:00 A.M.	101.4°	101.1°
3:00 A.M.	101.5°	102.0°
6:00 A.M.	101.5°	102.2°
9:00 A.M.	102.6°	101.3°
12:00 P.M.	102.8°	99.9°
3:00 P.M.	102.9°	99.8°
6:00 P.M.	102.8°	99.9°
9:00 P.M.	103.4°	99.4°
12:00 A.M.	103.6°	98.8°

104.0
103.0
102.0
101.0
100.0
99.0
98.0
0

The jagged line indicates that the values between 0 and 98.0 are not being shown.

2. Describe the general trend you see in each patient's temperature.

3. **Reasoning** Normal body temperature is 98.6°F. Which patient do you think is more likely to have a normal temperature in the next 24 hours? Explain.

PRACTICE

For more practice, see Set 11-6 on p. 693.

Ⓐ Skills and Understanding

4. The Díaz family heats their home and water with natural gas. Everything else runs on electricity. This table shows their gas and electricity bills for a year. Show the data in a double-line graph.

	Jan.	Feb.	Mar.	Apr.	May	June	July	Aug.	Sept.	Oct.	Nov.	Dec.
Gas	$193	$176	$122	$60	$52	$40	$38	$41	$58	$86	$160	$186
Electricity	$61	$53	$50	$52	$58	$144	$162	$171	$70	$60	$52	$64

5. During which season are the gas bills highest? the electric bills?

6. **Reasoning** Do you think it is more likely that the Díaz family lives in Wisconsin or Alabama? Explain.

Ⓑ Reasoning and Problem Solving

Refer to the graph at the right.

7. What type of data is shown in the graph?

8. Do you see any trends? If so, describe them.

9. The next national census is in the year 2010. Predict the population for each state. How did you make your prediction?

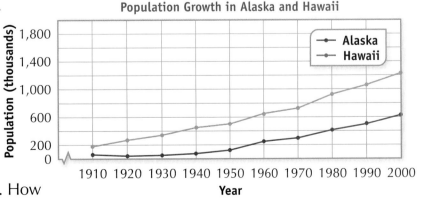

Population Growth in Alaska and Hawaii

— Alaska
— Hawaii

Math and Science

A science class heated samples of soil, sand, and water for 10 minutes. They recorded the temperatures in degrees Fahrenheit every 2 minutes. Then they turned off the heat source and continued to record the temperatures for another 10 minutes. Make a triple-line graph of their data, which is shown below.

Minutes	0	2	4	6	8	10	12	14	16	18	20
Soil	68°	73°	79°	84°	89°	90°	86°	82°	80°	77°	75°
Sand	68°	75°	82°	90°	93°	94°	93°	90°	86°	84°	81°
Water	68°	71°	73°	77°	78°	80°	77°	75°	73°	73°	72°

10. Rank the samples in order from the one showing the greatest change in temperature to the one showing the smallest change.

11. **Writing in Math** Explain how you can tell from the graph when the heat source was turned off.

C Extensions

A **scatterplot** is a graph that shows paired data. The scatterplot at the right shows how the number of monthly visits to a shopping mall is related to the shopper's distance from the mall.

A scatterplot may reveal a trend if the points lie in a pattern. The points in this scatterplot at the right have a rough pattern similar to Pattern B below. The scatterplot suggests that the greater the distance a shopper lives from the mall, the fewer trips the shopper makes.

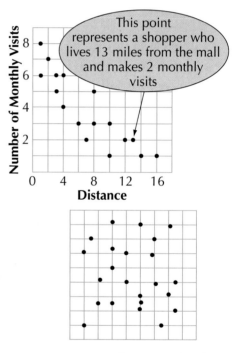

This point represents a shopper who lives 13 miles from the mall and makes 2 monthly visits

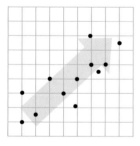

Pattern A As the value along one axis increases, the value along the other axis also increases.

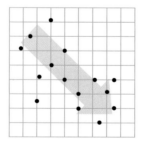

Pattern B As the value along one axis increases, the value along the other axis decreases.

No Pattern The scatterplot does not suggest a general trend.

12. The table below shows the number of pints of water consumed by various hikers. Make a scatterplot of the data. Do the points lie in a rough pattern? If so, what trend is suggested by the scatterplot?

Hours of Hiking	3	2	5	4	1	6	8	4	6	7	3	3	2	4	5
Pints of Water	2	1	2	4	1	4	5	3	5	6	1	3	2	2	4

Mixed Review and Test Prep

Take It to the NET
Test Prep
www.scottforesman.com

13. Make a double-bar graph of the data at the right.

14. Which quadrilateral has exactly two parallel sides?

    A. parallelogram   **C.** rectangle

    B. rhombus   **D.** trapezoid

Granville Factory Workers		
Facility	Day Shift	Night Shift
North Riverbanks	155	86
Park Haven	122	60
Dell Estates	97	55
Covington	130	66

Learning with Technology

Spreadsheet/Data/Grapher eTool: Creating Graphs

There are many ways to visually display data in order to make it easier to analyze. A big part of showing data clearly is choosing which kind of display to use. You can use a spreadsheet to organize data and display it in various forms.

The data set below shows population, life expectancy, and literacy rates for several of the world's countries.

Country	People (per square mile)	Percent Living in Cities	Life Expectancy M	F	Literacy Rate
Australia	7	85	77.02	82.87	100%
Austria	255	65	74.88	81.15	100%
Brazil	53	81	58.96	67.73	85%
Egypt	181	45	61.62	65.85	51%
Greece	211	60	76.03	81.32	95%
Japan	867	79	77.62	84.15	100%
Madagascar	71	29	53.08	57.68	80%
United States	79	76	74.37	80.05	97%

Enter the life expectancy data from the table above into a spreadsheet.

1. Select all cells containing life expectancy data. Using the graph option in your spreadsheet software, choose one of the graphs to display this data. Which graph do you think is best for displaying the life expectancy data? Explain.

2. Using your graph, what general statement can you make about the life expectancies of males and females?

	A	B	C	D	E	F
1	77.02	82.87				
2	74.88	81.15				
3	58.96	67.73				
4						

Key Idea
A circle graph shows how parts of a set of data compare to the whole set.

Vocabulary
• circle graph
• central angle (p. 502)
• sector (p. 502)

Materials
• compass
• protractor
• colored pencils
• circles or

 tools

Circle Graphs

LEARN

How are data represented in a circle graph?

A **circle graph** shows how different parts of a set of data compare to the whole set. Many circle graphs display the percent that corresponds to each part of the whole.

A township planned, or budgeted, $940,000 for expenses. The circle graph at the right shows how the expenses for different departments compare to the total.

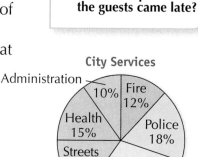

City Services

Example

How much money is budgeted for education?

The graph shows that 30% of the township's budget is spent on education.

Find 30% of 940,000.

Estimate: 30% of 940,000 is about $\frac{1}{3}$ of 900,000, or 300,000.

$0.3 \times 940,000 = 282,000$

The township budgeted $282,000 for education.

✔ Talk About It

1. Which two departments together are budgeted to receive the same amount of money as education? How can you tell that from the graph?

2. **Mental Math** How much money is budgeted for Administration?

Activity

How can you construct a circle graph?

A pollster asked 200 people what time they normally wake up on a weekday. The table of results is shown at the right.

a. Copy and complete the work on the next page. Then construct a circle graph to represent the data.

Wake-up Times	
Before 6:00 A.M.	81
6:00 A.M.–6:59 A.M.	53
7:00 A.M.–8:00 A.M.	40
After 8:00 A.M.	26

	Step 1 Find the percent for each category. Round to the nearest tenth of a percent.	Step 2 Use the percents to calculate the measure of each **central angle.** Round to the nearest whole degree. Remember, there are 360° in a circle.
Before 6:00 A.M.	$\frac{81}{200} = 0.405 = 40.5\%$	40.5% of 360 = 0.405 × 360 ≈ 146°
6:00 A.M.–6:59 A.M.	$\frac{53}{200}$	
7:00 A.M.–8:00 A.M.		
After 8:00 A.M.		

Step 3 Draw a circle. Using a protractor, draw a central angle whose measure is 146°. Color the **sector** and label it with the category name and the percent. Then draw the other central angles and color and label the sectors.

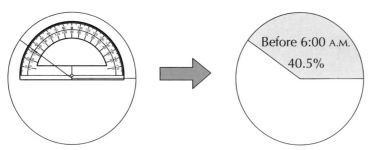

Think It Through

I can **check the angles I drew** by remembering these benchmarks:

25% of 360° ≈ 90°
50% of 360° = 180°

Step 4 Write a title above the circle.

b. Reasoning If you represent the survey data in a bar graph, which category would have the tallest bar and which category would have the shortest bar?

c. Number Sense In a sample of 1,000 people, how many people can you expect to wake up between 7:00 A.M. and 8:00 A.M.?

CHECK ✓

For another example, see Set 11-7 on p. 689.

The Smiths budgeted $3,800 for monthly expenses.

1. How much is budgeted for utilities?

2. **Mental Math** How much money do the Smiths budget for maintenance?

3. Use a benchmark fraction to estimate the total amount of money the Smith family budgets for maintenance and taxes.

4. **Estimation** Estimate the amount of money the Smith family budgets for rent.

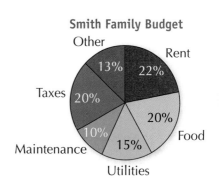

Smith Family Budget

Other 13%
Rent 22%
Taxes 20%
Food 20%
Utilities 15%
Maintenance 10%

A Skills and Understanding

Sam read that in the United States, the average person creates about 32 pounds of garbage per week.

What's in Our Garbage?

Other 14%
Food 7%
Glass 7%
Plastic 8%
Metals 8%
Yard Waste 18%
Paper 38%

5. Which material makes up most of the garbage?

6. How much paper does the average person throw away each week?

7. About how many pounds of yard waste does the average person throw away each week?

8. **Estimation** Estimate the amount of plastic discarded each year by the average person.

9. **Reasoning** What do you think "average person" means?

B Reasoning and Problem Solving

🎵 Math and Music

The Music Oasis sold 14,619 CDs in August.

10. In a circle graph of the data, which sector will be largest? smallest?

11. Which sectors should look about the same in size?

12. Make a circle graph of the data given in the table.

13. **Writing in Math** Explain how you found the measure of the sector for Jazz in the circle graph in Exercises 10–12.

AUGUST CD SALES	
Music Category	**Number of CDs sold**
Country	4,080
Rock	6,150
Jazz	1,251
Classical	1,306
Broadway/Film	1,189
Other	643

C Extensions

If a single piece of data in a circle graph represents more than 50%, the sector will have an angle greater than 180°. At the right are directions for drawing a sector with a 210° angle.

14. A researcher conducted a survey to find out people's favorite source for news. Make a circle graph of the results shown below.

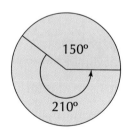

150°
210°

Primary Source of News	
Television	55%
Newspapers	20%
Radio	16%
Internet	5%
Magazines	4%

How to Draw a Sector with an Angle of 210°

Draw a central angle that measures 360° − 210° = 150°. The sector you want includes the sides of this angle and the region of the circle in the *exterior* of the angle.

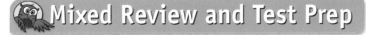 Mixed Review and Test Prep

 Take It to the NET
Test Prep
www.scottforesman.com

15. Algebra A customer has $86 and wants to buy a bicycle for $260. If the bicycle is on sale at 20% off, how much more money does the customer need?

16. Construct and label a double-line graph to represent these data. What trends are exhibited?

Utzinger Family Water Usage (thousands of gallons)

Year	Jan.	Feb.	Mar.	Apr.	May	June	July	Aug.	Sept.	Oct.	Nov.	Dec.
2002	16	13	14	15	18	20	21	21	18	15	16	16
2003	17	17	15	16	19	22	24	25	23	18	19	18

17. A motorist drove 280 miles in 5 hours. At this rate, how long would it take to drive 400 miles? Round to the nearest hour.

A. 4 hours   **B.** 5 hours   **C.** 7 hours   **D.** 8 hours

Discover Math in Your World

 Take It to the NET
Video and Activities
www.scottforesman.com

Mummies Age C-14

All living things contain radiocarbon, or carbon-14 (C-14). The amount of carbon-14 in an organism's tissue stays the same while the organism is alive. When an organism dies, the carbon-14 within its tissues decays at an exact and uniform rate. By measuring the radioactive decay in tissue samples, scientists can closely estimate the age of a mummy.

1. Every 5,700 years, the same fraction of carbon-14 decays. Based on the graph below, what would you estimate this fraction to be?

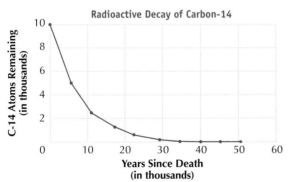

Radioactive Decay of Carbon-14

C-14 Atoms Remaining (in thousands)

Years Since Death (in thousands)

2. The oldest known complete Egyptian mummy is of Wati, a court musician who is estimated to be 4,400 years old. In what year did Wati die?

Understand Graphic Sources: Graphs

Understanding graphic sources such as graphs when you read in math can help you use the **problem-solving strategy, Make a Graph,** in the next lesson.

In reading, understanding graphs can help you understand what you read. In math, understanding graphs can help you solve problems.

Average High and Low Temperatures in Washington, D.C.

● average high
● average low

The labels along the axes of the graph describe the data that are in the graph.

This point indicates that the average high temperature in Washington, D.C. in November is 50°F.

The key tells what data set each color represents.

Each point on the graph corresponds to a month and either a high or low temperature.

1. What is the average high temperature in Washington, D.C., in May? the average low temperature in March?

2. Describe the trend you see in the temperatures in Washington, D.C., from January to July.

For 3–6, use the bar graph at the right.

3. What is the graph about? How do you know?

4. What does each bar represent?

5. Which parks have an area greater than 70,000 acres?

6. **Writing in Math** Write a sentence that gives some specific information displayed in the graph.

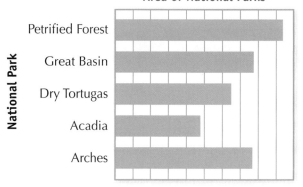

Area of National Parks

For 7–9, use the circle graph at the right.

7. What does the graph show?

8. What percent of the pets are dogs?

9. **Writing in Math** If 6 reptiles are owned by the students, how many fish do they own? Explain how you found your answer.

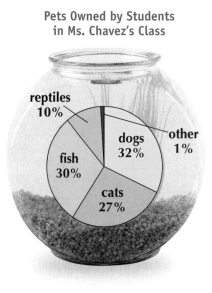

Pets Owned by Students in Ms. Chavez's Class

reptiles 10%
dogs 32%
other 1%
fish 30%
cats 27%

For 10–12, use the double-bar graph at the right.

10. Why are there two bars that correspond to each park?

11. At which park was the adults' attendance the greatest? the least?

12. **Writing in Math** Which park had the greatest total attendance? How do you know?

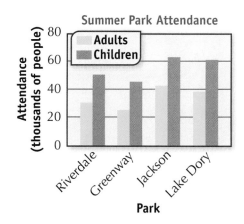

Summer Park Attendance

Problem-Solving Strategy

Reading Helps!

Understanding graphic sources such as graphs

can help you with...

the problem-solving strategy, *Make a Graph.*

Make a Graph

LEARN

Which graph is most appropriate?

The Slater Corporation is planning to build a new shopping mall. It will be located in either Floreen or Kyerville, whichever city has the faster growing population. Make the most appropriate graph to show the population data.

Population Data		
Year	Floreen	Kyerville
1997	7,020	4,208
1998	7,116	4,814
1999	7,259	5,350
2000	7,435	5,990
2001	7,580	6,222
2002	7,680	6,884
2003	8,027	7,510

Read and Understand

What do you know?   A new shopping mall will be built. The population data for the two possible sites are given.

What are you trying to do?   Make the best display of the data.

Plan and Solve

What strategy will you use?

Strategy: Make a Graph

Make a line graph to show changes in data over time. Since there are two sets of data, make it a double-line graph.

How to Make a Graph

Step 1   Decide on the type of graph appropriate for the data.

Step 2   Make the graph. Be sure to include a title, labels, accurate representation of data, and any required scales and key.

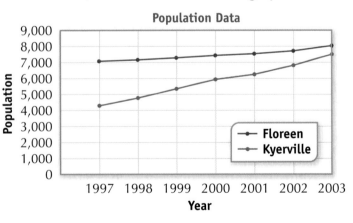

Look Back and Check

Is your answer reasonable?   Yes. A circle graph would not be appropriate because it shows how parts are related to the whole, and a bar graph does not as clearly show how data change over time.

✔ Talk About It

1. Which city has the faster-growing population? How can you tell?

2. In 2005, which city do you predict will have a greater population?

3. Where should the mall be built? Explain.

CHECK ✓

For another example, see Set 11-8 on p. 689.

Solve each problem.

1. The table at the right lists the summer tours conducted by Sunrise Travel.

   a. Make the most appropriate graph to show the data.

   b. Do the tours to England and France together represent more or less than half of all the tours?

Summer Tours

England	37%
France	17%
Germany	7%
Italy	26%
Japan	5%
Spain	8%

PRACTICE

For more practice, see Set 11-8 on p. 693.

Solve each problem.

2. The table at the right shows last year's car sales at Hurling Motors.

   a. Make the most appropriate graph to show the data.

   b. In which categories were more new vehicles sold than used?

Vehicle Sales
(thousands sold)

Vehicle	New	Used
Cars	6.1	3.4
SUVs	4.4	2.9
Vans	1.3	1.6
Minivans	3.4	2.2

3. Mrs. Ortega sliced a cake into equal-size pieces. Max ate 2 slices. Then Liz ate 1 slice, which was $\frac{1}{4}$ of what Max left on the cake plate. How many slices were there in the whole cake?

4. The table below gives the bank balances of two sisters.

	Mar.	Apr.	May	June	July	Aug.
Agnes	$332	$282	$257	$257	$257	$257
Linda	$195	$245	$270	$305	$330	$360

   a. Make the most appropriate graph to show the data.

   b. Which sister seems to be the better saver?

5. **Writing in Math** Eight teams are playing in a basketball tournament. If a team loses, it is out of the tournament. How many games are needed to determine the winner? Explain your solution.

STRATEGIES

- **Show What You Know**
  Draw a Picture
  Make an Organized List
  Make a Table
  Make a Graph
  Act It Out or Use Objects
- **Look for a Pattern**
- **Try, Check, and Revise**
- **Write an Equation**
- **Use Logical Reasoning**
- **Solve a Simpler Problem**
- **Work Backward**

Choose a tool

Mental Math

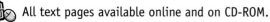

Key Idea
Data can be
presented in
such a way as
to misrepresent
a situation.

Materials
• $\frac{1}{4}$-in. grid paper
  or  tools

Think It Through
When I **use a
graph,** I should
analyze how it
was constructed
so I can decide if
the data are fairly
represented.

Misleading Graphs

LEARN

How can data-reporting
be misleading?

The way a graph is constructed affects how
fairly the data are represented.

WARM UP

Give reasonable
intervals for the
vertical axis of a line
graph that shows each
range of data.

1. 218 to 1,874

2. 6,709 to 28,661

Example A

In the Middle School election, Marcy
claimed that Nadya got about twice
as many votes as Lois. Is her claim
correct? Explain.

The bar for Nadya is about twice as
tall as that for Lois. But Nadya received
about 63 votes and Lois about 40.
Since 63 ≠ 2 × 40, Marcy's claim is not correct.

Middle School Election

Number of Votes: 70, 60, 50, 40, 30, 20

Lois Nadya Jon
Student

The graph in Example A is misleading because the vertical scale
does not start at zero and there is no indication that some
numbers have been skipped.

Example B

Which graph indicates that TekkCo profits have "skyrocketed"?

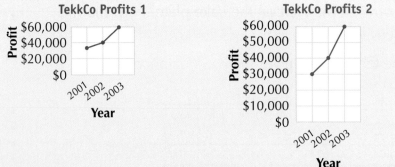

TekkCo Profits 1
Profit: $60,000 / $40,000 / $20,000 / $0
Year: 2001 2002 2003

TekkCo Profits 2
Profit: $60,000 / $50,000 / $40,000 / $30,000 / $20,000 / $10,000 / $0
Year: 2001 2002 2003

Since the second line graph appears to rise faster, it indicates
a sharper increase in profits.

✔ **Talk About It**

1. In Example B, do both graphs show the same data? Explain.

For 1–2, use the bar graph at the right.

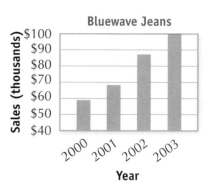

Bluewave Jeans

1. Explain why the claim is misleading. Sales tripled from 2000 to 2003.

2. **Reasoning** What would the sales in 2003 have to be to make the claim true?

PRACTICE

For more practice, see Set 11-9 on p. 694.

A Skills and Understanding

For 3–4, use the line graph at the right.

West Valley County Population

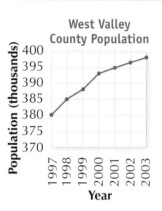

3. Explain why the claim is misleading. Population doubles.

4. **Reasoning** What would the population in 2003 have to be to make the claim true?

B Reasoning and Problem Solving

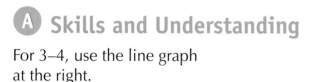

Math and Everyday Life

5. Refer to the table of bus fares at the right. Without skipping any numbers on the vertical scale, make an accurate line graph to suggest each claim.

   a. There were small yearly increases in bus fares.

   b. Bus fares increased sharply.

6. **Writing in Math** Explain one method graph makers use to affect the visual impact of a graph.

City Town Bus Fares

Year	Fares
1998	$1.25
1999	$1.30
2000	$1.50
2001	$1.60
2002	$1.75
2003	$2.00

Mixed Review and Test Prep

Take It to the NET
Test Prep
www.scottforesman.com

7. The table shows the makeup of the student body at Polk High School. Make the most appropriate graph of the data.

Freshmen	Sophomores	Juniors	Seniors
21%	23%	30%	26%

8. Which degree measure in a circle graph corresponds to a sector showing 25%?

   A. 0.25°   **B.** 25°   **C.** 45°   **D.** 90°

Do You Know How?

Do You Understand?

Bar Graphs (11-5)

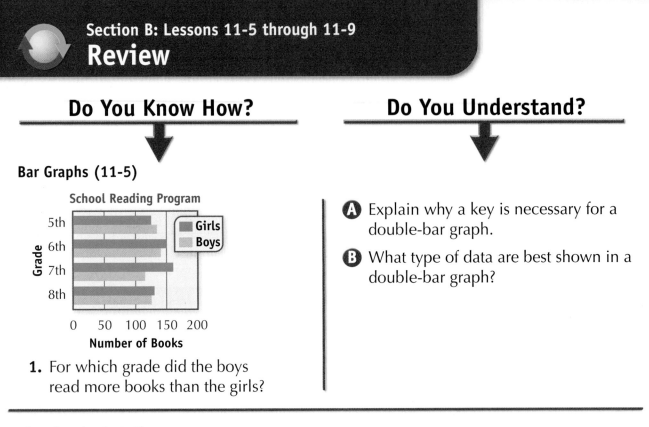

School Reading Program

Number of Books

1. For which grade did the boys read more books than the girls?

A Explain why a key is necessary for a double-bar graph.

B What type of data are best shown in a double-bar graph?

Line Graphs (11-6)

Toy Sales						
	Jan.	Mar.	May	July	Sept.	Nov.
2001	$2,000	$3,500	$4,000	$4,200	$3,700	$5,200
2002	$1,800	$2,200	$3,300	$5,000	$4,000	$6,300

2. Show the data in a double-line graph.

3. Describe the general trend you see in the sales for each year.

C Describe what type of data are best shown in a double-line graph.

D Explain how to use the data in the line graph to predict future toy sales.

Circle Graphs (11-7)

Josh has 80 books.

4. Find the number of comic books.

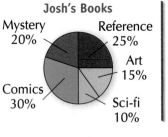

Josh's Books

Mystery 20%
Reference 25%
Art 15%
Sci-fi 10%
Comics 30%

E Explain how you determine the size of each sector of a circle graph given the percentage.

Problem-Solving Strategy: Make a Graph (11-8), Misleading Graphs (11-9)

Camp Enrollment				
Year	1999	2000	2001	2002
Campers	345	415	405	455

5. Make the most appropriate graph to show the data above.

F Explain the type of data that are most appropriate for a bar graph, a line graph, and a circle graph.

G Describe what is meant by a misleading graph.

MULTIPLE CHOICE

1. Which type of graph is most appropriate to compare the population increase of two cities? (11-8)

   A. double-line graph   **B.** double-bar graph

   C. circle graph   **D.** line plot

2. Who grew the most tomato and green pepper plants combined? (11-5)

   A. Julie   **B.** Mary   **C.** Mike   **D.** Oscar

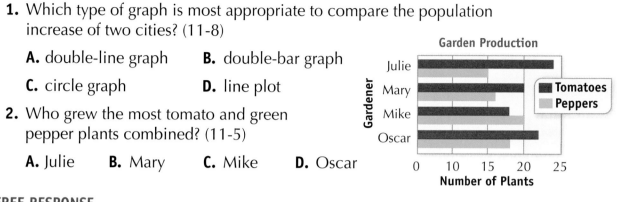

Garden Production

FREE RESPONSE

The table at the right shows book and movie sales for Movies & Books Plus. (11-6)

Book and Movie Sales (thousands)					
Year	1998	1999	2000	2001	2002
Books	48	65	80	75	95
Movies	40	68	90	70	65

3. Show the data in a double-line graph.

4. In which year(s) were movie sales greater than book sales?

5. Describe the trend you see in the sales of books and movies.

Melissa spent $250 on vacation. (11-7)

6. On which item did Melissa spend the most money?

7. How much money did Melissa spend on food?

Vacation Budget
Other 10%
Games 13%
Amusement park 17%
Food 36%
Souvenirs 24%

Think It Through
To answer the questions, I can **get information from graphics, tables, and text.**

Solve each problem. (11-8)

The table at the right lists Fred's and Danny's summer earnings.

8. Make the most appropriate graph to show the data.

Summer Earnings				
	May	**June**	**July**	**August**
Fred	$1,350	$1,275	$1,375	$1,425
Danny	$1,200	$1,300	$1,400	$1,500

Writing in Math

9. Explain why the claim below and the graph are misleading. (11-9)

   Sales have plummeted!

10. Make a bar graph that is misleading but visually supports the claim that twice as many households have dogs as cats. (11-9)

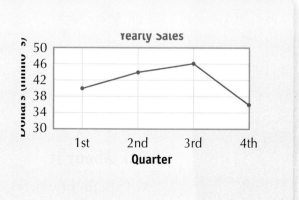

Yearly Sales

Counting Methods

LEARN

How can you show all possibilities?

Band members are served a breakfast bag whenever they play a Saturday morning concert. Students use the form at the right to place their order.

Breakfast Bag

Beverage
☐ Milk   ☐ Orange juice
Muffin
☐ Blueberry ☐ Cranberry ☐ Bran
Fruit
☐ Apple   ☐ Pear   ☐ Banana

Example A

Show all the different kinds of breakfast bags.

One Way   Draw a **tree diagram.**

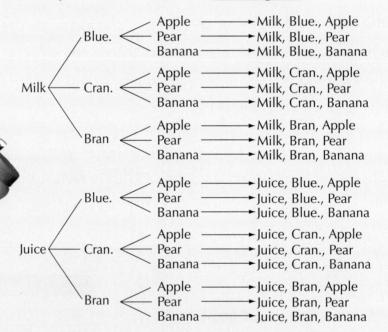

Another Way   Make an organized list.

Milk, Blue., Apple	Milk, Cran., Apple	Milk, Bran, Apple
Milk, Blue., Pear	Milk, Cran., Pear	Milk, Bran, Pear
Milk, Blue., Banana	Milk, Cran., Banana	Milk, Bran, Banana
Juice, Blue., Apple	Juice, Cran., Apple	Juice, Bran, Apple
Juice, Blue., Pear	Juice, Cran., Pear	Juice, Bran, Pear
Juice, Blue., Banana	Juice, Cran., Banana	Juice, Bran, Banana

Think It Through
The **different possibilities** are shown at the far right in the tree diagram.

✓ **Talk About It**

1. Explain how to count the different breakfast bags in the tree diagram.

How can you count possibilities using multiplication?

Both the tree diagram and the list show that there are 18 possible choices for breakfast bags. Instead of counting all the possible choices, you can use multiplication.

Choices for beverage		Choices for muffin		Choices for fruit		Total number of choices
2	×	3	×	3	=	18

When you multiply to find the total number of choices, you are using the **Counting Principle.**

✔ Talk About It

2. Suppose hot chocolate is added as a beverage option. Now how many different breakfast bags are there to choose from?

How can you count possible outcomes?

An **event** is the result, or **outcome,** of a single experiment. For example, you might toss a number cube and get a 4. The set of all possible outcomes of an experiment is the **sample space.**

A **compound event** is a combination of two or more single events. You can use any of the counting methods in this lesson to count the number of possible outcomes of a compound event.

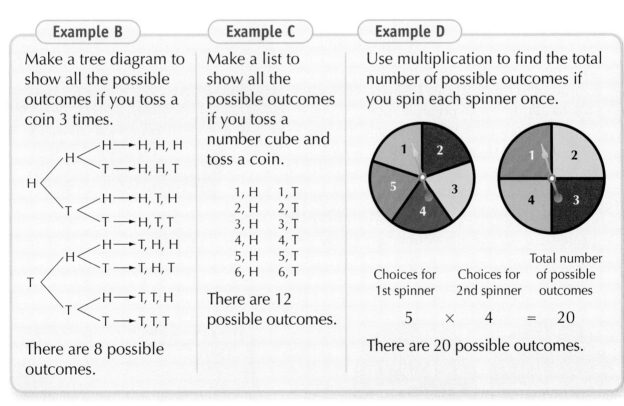

Example B

Make a tree diagram to show all the possible outcomes if you toss a coin 3 times.

H
- H
  - H → H, H, H
  - T → H, H, T
- T
  - H → H, T, H
  - T → H, T, T

T
- H
  - H → T, H, H
  - T → T, H, T
- T
  - H → T, T, H
  - T → T, T, T

There are 8 possible outcomes.

Example C

Make a list to show all the possible outcomes if you toss a number cube and toss a coin.

1, H	1, T
2, H	2, T
3, H	3, T
4, H	4, T
5, H	5, T
6, H	6, T

There are 12 possible outcomes.

Example D

Use multiplication to find the total number of possible outcomes if you spin each spinner once.

Choices for 1st spinner		Choices for 2nd spinner		Total number of possible outcomes
5	×	4	=	20

There are 20 possible outcomes.

✔ Talk About It

Take It to the NET
www **More Examples**
www.scottforesman.com

3. If you toss a number cube, what is the sample space?

4. If you toss two number cubes, how many possible outcomes are there?

1. For a vacation Carl packed a white and a gray shirt. He also packed blue, black, and tan pants. Make a tree diagram to show all of Carl's possible outfits.

2. Suppose you spin each spinner once. Make a list to show the sample space.

3. **Number Sense** In Leonard's state, the license plates are any two letters except O and I, followed by any three digits from 0 to 9. Find the total number of possible license plates if the letters and digits may repeat.

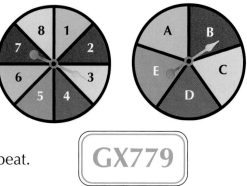

GX779

PRACTICE

For more practice, see Set 11-10 on p. 694.

A Skills and Understanding

4. Make a list to show all the possible choices of school sweatshirts.

5. Suppose you toss two number cubes. Make a tree diagram to show the sample space.

6. **Number Sense** Val's gym lock has a 3-number combination, 13-6-13. Estimate the total number of possible lock combinations if each number may be any number from 0 to 19, and the numbers may not repeat.

Sizes	Colors	Collar
Extra Small	Blue	Plain
Small	Gold	Hood
Medium		
Large		

B Reasoning and Problem Solving

In Exercises 7–8, use any counting method you like.

7. How many possible outcomes are there if you spin each spinner once?

8. Find the number of possible outfits if you wear each type of clothing.

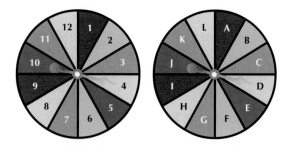

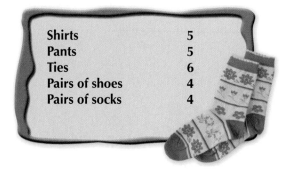

Shirts	5
Pants	5
Ties	6
Pairs of shoes	4
Pairs of socks	4

Math and Social Studies

A PIN (personal identification number) is a password that helps keep people's personal records, such as their bank accounts or computer files, private and secure. Access to these records is restricted to the person who knows the PIN (and sometimes other authorities such as certain bank employees). PINs are usually made up of numbers and letters. Here are some sample PINs.

4 6 8 6   H O W D Y 2   0 0 2 6 1 9 9   8 8 J Q R S 1 9

9. Nina needs to pick a 5-digit PIN. Each digit may be any number from 0 to 9. How many PINs are possible if the digits may repeat?

10. Katrina wants to choose a 3-digit PIN, all numbers, that has only odd digits. How many PINs are possible

  a. if the digits may repeat?

  b. if the digits may not repeat? (Hint: After each digit is chosen, there is one less choice for the next digit.)

11. Calculator Randy's bank uses PINs that have 4 characters. (A character is a letter or single-digit number.) How many PINs are possible if the characters may repeat and

  a. each character can be any letter?

  b. each character can be any letter except I and O?

  c. each character can be any letter or digit?

12. Writing in Math Elaine said that the number of possible outcomes if you toss a number cube three times is 6^3. Is she right? Explain.

Ⓒ Extensions

13. Algebra How many possible outcomes are there if you toss a coin 2 times? 3 times? 4 times? 5 times? 6 times? n times?

Mixed Review and Test Prep

Take It to the NET
Test Prep
www.scottforesman.com

14. $\frac{7}{8} + 2\frac{5}{6}$ **15.** $\frac{3}{4} \times \frac{5}{12}$ **16.** $4\frac{1}{2} \div \frac{9}{10}$ **17.** $12 - 6\frac{3}{7}$

18. What is suggested by the graph at the right? Is it misleading? Explain.

19. How many pints are in 3 gallons of water?

  A. 1.5   **B.** 3   **C.** 12   **D.** 24

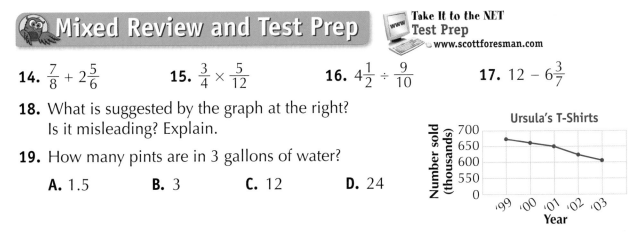

Ursula's T-Shirts

Number sold (thousands)

Key Idea
When you count the total number of possibilities, you have to decide whether order matters.

Vocabulary
• permutations
• combinations

Permutations and Combinations

LEARN

✓ **WARM UP**

1. How many different outfits can be made from 4 shirts, 3 pairs of pants, and 6 pairs of socks?

2. How many 2-digit codes can be made using even digits that may repeat?

How do you count arrangements?

Sometimes you need to count the number of ways you can choose some of the objects in a set. You must be careful to decide whether the order of the objects matters.

Alice has three favorite snapshots.

Volleyball

Recital

Friends

Example A

In how many ways can Alice choose 2 of her 3 snapshots for this double frame?

One snapshot goes on the left and one on the right, so the order of the snapshots chosen is important.

One Way

Use the counting principle.

Choices for left side	Choices for right side	Number of ways to choose
3	× 2	= 6

Another Way

Make a list.

VR	RV	FV
VF	RF	FR

There are 6 ways to choose.

Example B

In how many ways can Alice choose 2 of her 3 snapshots to mail to her grandmother?

The order of the snapshots mailed to Alice's grandmother doesn't matter. VR represents the same pair as RV.

One Way

Since the list in Example A shows each pair twice, divide that result by 2.

$6 \div 2 = 3$

There are 3 ways to choose.

Another Way

Make a list.

VR   VF   RF

There are 3 ways to choose.

When order is important, as in Example A, you are counting **permutations,** or arrangements. When order is not important, as in Example B, you are counting **combinations**.

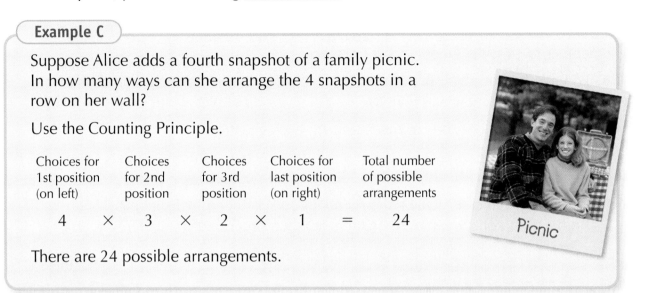

> **Example C**
>
> Suppose Alice adds a fourth snapshot of a family picnic. In how many ways can she arrange the 4 snapshots in a row on her wall?
>
> Use the Counting Principle.
>
> | Choices for 1st position (on left) | | Choices for 2nd position | | Choices for 3rd position | | Choices for last position (on right) | | Total number of possible arrangements |
> |---|---|---|---|---|---|---|---|---|
> | 4 | × | 3 | × | 2 | × | 1 | = | 24 |
>
> Picnic
>
> There are 24 possible arrangements.

✔ Talk About It

1. Suppose your class has 25 students. If your teacher wants to know how many ways she can choose 3 students for a team project, would the order matter? If your teacher wants to know how many ways she can choose 3 students to serve as president, secretary, and treasurer of the class, would order matter? Explain your thinking.

2. Is Example C an example of a permutation or combination? Why?

3. Use V, R, F, and P to represent Alice's four snapshots. Make a list of all the arrangements that start with V.

CHECK ✓

For another example, see Set 11-11 on p. 690.

Find the number of ways to choose the objects in each situation. Remember to consider whether order matters.

1. Inez is choosing 2 pizza toppings from a choice of 5 toppings.

2. Ethan is picking 2 of the 4 microwave dinners in the freezer to have for lunch and supper.

Find the number of possible arrangements for each situation.

3. Eight children line up at the water fountain.

4. Trent places 6 books on a shelf.

5. **Reasoning** What numbers would you multiply to find the number of arrangements of 5 snapshots in a row? (You do not need to find the answer.) 6 snapshots? Do you see a pattern? If so, describe it.

Ⓐ Skills and Understanding

Find the number of ways to choose the objects in each situation.
Remember to consider whether order matters.

6. Lorenzo is choosing 2 of his 7 shirts to wear on Saturday and Sunday.

7. Gloria is choosing 2 friends from a group of 6 to invite for a sleepover.

Find the number of possible arrangements for each situation.

8. Seven birds are sitting on a wire.

9. Jody has 9 stuffed animals lined up on her bed.

10. Reasoning Which is greater, the number of ways to choose 2 people from a group of 7 when order matters or when order doesn't matter?

Ⓑ Reasoning and Problem Solving

🖌 Math and Art

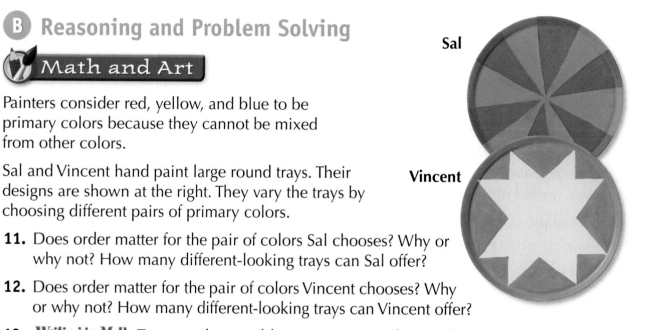

Sal

Vincent

Painters consider red, yellow, and blue to be primary colors because they cannot be mixed from other colors.

Sal and Vincent hand paint large round trays. Their designs are shown at the right. They vary the trays by choosing different pairs of primary colors.

11. Does order matter for the pair of colors Sal chooses? Why or why not? How many different-looking trays can Sal offer?

12. Does order matter for the pair of colors Vincent chooses? Why or why not? How many different-looking trays can Vincent offer?

13. **Writing in Math** To count the possible arrangements of 5 people lined up at the deli counter, Marcia evaluated 5^5. Is this correct? Explain.

Ⓒ Extensions

You have found that the number of ways that 4 objects can be arranged in a row is $4 \times 3 \times 2 \times 1$. This can be written 4!, which is read "four **factorial**." Here are some other uses of the symbol !.

$5! = 5 \times 4 \times 3 \times 2 \times 1$ $7! = 7 \times 6 \times 5 \times 4 \times 3 \times 2 \times 1$

$13! = 13 \times 12 \times 11 \times 10 \times 9 \times 8 \times 7 \times 6 \times 5 \times 4 \times 3 \times 2 \times 1$

14. Evaluate 4!, 5!, 6!, 7!, and 11!

15. How would you use the factorial symbol to express the number of ways that 6 objects can be arranged in a row? 7 objects? 8 objects? *n* objects?

Mixed Review and Test Prep

Take It to the NET
Test Prep
www.scottforesman.com

Copy and complete.

16. 1.2 km = ▢ m   **17.** 325 cm = ▢ m   **18.** 168 m = ▢ km

19. Listed below are the class sizes of history classes at a state university.

21, 21, 35, 42, 45, 46, 48, 214, 341, 519

Does the mean, median, or mode best represent the data? Explain.

20. How many ways are there to pick a three-digit PIN (personal identification number) if the second digit is odd and the digits can repeat?

A. 25   **B.** 500   **C.** 900   **D.** 1,000

Learning with Technology

The Probability eTool: Random-Number Generation

Suppose you want to find out the number of times you will get a sum of 8 if you spin each of 2 spinners 50 times. You can use the Probability eTool to create two spinners. Divide one spinner into 4 equal sections, the other into 6 equal sections. Spin 50 times. There are several ways to get a sum of 8. Using the table of results, count the number of times a sum of 8 occurs.

1. Use a counting method to find the total number of possible outcomes when each spinner is spun.

2. How many of the 50 trials resulted in a sum of 8? Will this number double if you perform 100 trials with the two spinners? Explain.

3. Would a sum of 8 occur more often if both spinners were divided into the same number of equal sections? Into how many equal sections should each spinner be divided? Create spinners to test your predictions.

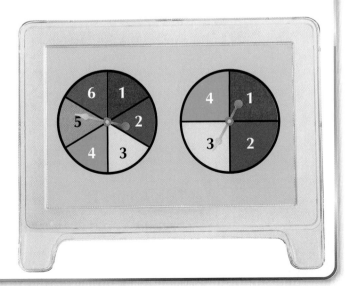

Key Idea
You can express the likelihood of something happening as a number.

Vocabulary
• probability
• impossible event
• certain event

Think It Through

I can **visualize** the likelihood of an event.

certain — 1

more likely

equally likely — $\frac{1}{2}$

less likely

impossible — 0

Probability

LEARN

How do you express a probability?

The **probability** of an event is a number that describes the likelihood that an event will occur. It ranges from 0 for an **impossible event** to 1 for a **certain event**.

$$P(\text{event}) = \frac{\text{number of favorable outcomes}}{\text{number of possible outcomes}}$$

7 3 6 2 8 8
7 6 6 4

✓ **WARM UP**

Write as a percent.

1. 0.4   2. 0.65

3. $\frac{13}{25}$ 4. $\frac{3}{20}$

5. 13 out of 50

Example A

A bag contains the number cards shown above. José draws one from the bag without looking. Find the probability of getting a prime number.

P(prime) means the probability of getting a prime number.

$P(\text{prime}) = \frac{4}{10}$ ← There are 4 favorable outcomes: 7, 3, 2, 7.
← There are 10 cards, so there are 10 possible outcomes.

The probability of getting a prime number is $\frac{4}{10}$, or $\frac{2}{5}$.

This can also be expressed as a decimal, 0.4, or a percent, 40%.

Example B

Mia tosses a number cube. What is the probability that she does *not* toss a 4? Not tossing a 4 is the **complement** of tossing a 4.

One Way

There are 5 favorable outcomes: 1, 2, 3, 5, 6.
There are 6 possible outcomes.

$P(\text{not } 4) = \frac{5}{6}$

The probability of not tossing a 4 is $\frac{5}{6}$.

Another Way

Use the fact that $P(\text{event}) + P(\text{not event}) = 1$.

First, find $P(4)$. Then subtract it from 1.

$P(4) = \frac{1}{6}$

$P(\text{not } 4) = 1 - \frac{1}{6} = \frac{5}{6}$

✓ Talk About It

1. In Example A, what is the probability that José draws a 5?

2. Give the probability in Example B as a decimal and as a percent rounded to the nearest tenth of a percent.

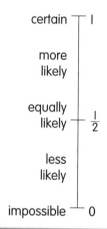

For another example, see Set 11-12 on p. 690.

Cards numbered from 1 to 50 are placed in a box. Sumi picks one without looking. Find each probability as a fraction, decimal, and percent.

1. *P*(number less than 25) **2.** *P*(two-digit number) **3.** *P*(not a multiple of 10)

4. Reasoning Is drawing an odd number more likely than, less likely than, or as equally likely as drawing an even number? Explain.

PRACTICE

For more practice, see Set 11-12 on p. 694.

Ⓐ Skills and Understanding

Doris gets one spin on the spinner. Find each probability as a fraction, decimal, and percent rounded to the nearest whole percent.

5. *P*(A) **6.** *P*(a letter in *DORIS*) **7.** *P*(not a vowel)

8. Reasoning Is spinning a letter in *ALEX* more likely than, less likely than, or as equally likely as drawing a letter in *HANK*? Explain.

Ⓑ Reasoning and Problem Solving

In Exercises 9–12, draw a set of 8 number cards that could yield each probability.

9. $P(3) = \frac{5}{8}$ **10.** $P(5) = 0$ **11.** $P(\text{prime}) = 1$ **12.** $P(\text{even number}) = \frac{3}{4}$

13. **Writing in Math** The probability of an event is $\frac{8}{15}$. Which is greater, the probability that the event will occur or the probability that it will not occur? Explain.

Ⓒ Extensions

The ratio that compares the number of favorable outcomes to the number of unfavorable outcomes gives the **odds** for an event. For example, the odds for tossing a 2 on a number cube are 1 to 5. The **odds against** tossing a 2 are 5 to 1. Give the odds for each event. Then give the odds against each event.

14. drawing an even number from the cards in Example A

15. spinning Z on the spinner above

Mixed Review and Test Prep

Take It to the NET
Test Prep
www.scottforesman.com

16. Find $4^3 + 7(5 - 2)$.

17. Draw a dodecagon.

18. In how many different ways can you stack 6 CDs?

A. 21 **B.** 36 **C.** 720 **D.** 46,656

All text pages available online and on CD-ROM.

Key Idea
You can use probability to make predictions.

Vocabulary
• theoretical probability
• experimental probability
• trial

Materials
• number cube or
 **tools**

TEST TALK

Think It Through
To **convert a fraction to a percent,** first I should divide to convert the fraction to a decimal.
$33 \div 60 =$
$0.55 = 55\%$

Predictions and Probability

LEARN

How can you use probability to make predictions?

At the fun fair, Ms. Clearwater has every student spin the spinner once.

Example A

If there are 260 students, how many stuffed animals might Ms. Clearwater expect to give away?

Multiply the probability by the number of spins.

$$\frac{1}{5} \times 260 = \frac{1}{\underset{1}{\cancel{5}}} \times \frac{\overset{52}{\cancel{260}}}{1} = \frac{52}{1} = 52$$

$P(\text{stuffed animal}) = \frac{1}{5}$

Ms. Clearwater might expect to give away about 52 stuffed animals.

What is experimental probability?

You learned how to calculate the **theoretical probability** in the last lesson. Sometimes you need to estimate the probability from experimental data. You can determine the **experimental probability** by comparing the number of **successes,** or favorable outcomes, to the number of **trials,** or experiments.

$$P(\text{event}) \approx \frac{\text{number of successes}}{\text{number of trials}}$$

Example B

In the basketball games so far this season, Hal has attempted 60 free throws and has made 33 of them. Estimate the probability, expressed as a percent, that he will make the next free throw.

$P(\text{make the next free throw}) \approx \dfrac{33}{60} \begin{matrix} \leftarrow \text{free throws made} \\ \leftarrow \text{free throws taken} \end{matrix}$

$\frac{33}{60} = 55\%$, so the probability that Hal will make the next free throw is 55%.

How many free throws might Hal expect to make out of the next 25?

Find 55% of 25.

$0.55 \times 25 = 13.75$.

Hal might be expected to make about 14 of the next 25 free throws.

✔ Talk About It

1. In Example C, why should Hal expect to make 14, not 13.75, free throws?

2. Why is ≈ used instead of = with experimental probability?

How do theoretical and experimental probabilities compare?

Sometimes an experimental probability is determined because it is difficult, or even impossible, to calculate the theoretical probability. In other situations, you can determine the probability both ways and see how they compare.

Activity

a. What is the theoretical probability, to the nearest percent, of tossing a 1 on a number cube?

b. Toss the number cube 30 times. Tally the number of times each outcome in the sample space occurs.

Total number of tosses	Number of 1s	Experimental probability
30		

c. How many times did you toss a 1? Determine the experimental probability, to the nearest percent, of tossing a 1. Record your answers in a table like the one started at the right. Is the theoretical probability the same as the experimental probability?

d. Repeat steps b and c. Did you get the same results?

e. Combine the results of your first 30 tosses and your second 30 tosses. Compute the experimental probability based on the 60 tosses. What changes do you see from the results based on 30 tosses?

f. Combine the results of your 60 tosses with those of several other students. Compute the experimental probability based on the combined data. What changes do you see from the results based on 30 tosses and 60 tosses?

g. Which do you think would give an experimental probability that is closer to the theoretical probability, 60 tosses or 6,000 tosses? Explain.

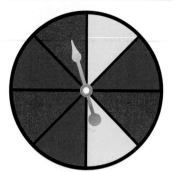

1. If you spin the spinner 400 times, how many times might you expect to get red? Do you think it will happen exactly that many times?

2. Sean dropped his buttered bread 200 times. It landed buttered-side-up 62 times.

   a. Estimate the probability, given as a percent, that next time Sean drops the bread, it will land buttered-side-up.

   b. How many times might Sean expect the bread to land buttered-side-up the next 350 times he drops it?

3. **Reasoning** Corinne said that if you scramble these lettered tiles and pick one without looking, the probability of drawing an E is $\frac{3}{10}$. Do you think this probability is theoretical or experimental? Explain.

PRACTICE

For more practice, see Set 11-13 on p. 695.

A Skills and Understanding

4. If you flip a coin 5,000 times, how many times might you expect to get heads? Do you think it will happen exactly that many times?

5. How many times might you expect to get a number less than 5 when you toss a number cube 360 times?

6. Clara dropped a spoon 350 times. It landed right-side-up 238 times.

   a. Estimate the probability, given as a percent, that next time Clara drops the spoon, it will land right-side-up.

   b. How many times might Clara expect the spoon to land right-side-up the next 150 times she drops it?

7. The manufacturer of Krunchy Klusters puts a prize in 80 out of every 500 boxes.

   a. What is the probability, expressed as a fraction, that a shopper will find a prize in a box of Krunchy Klusters?

   b. In a shipment of 7,000 boxes of Krunchy Klusters, how many boxes might be expected to contain prizes?

8. **Reasoning** Patty said that the probability of her dropping a clothespin in a bottle is $\frac{9}{20}$. Do you think this probability is theoretical or experimental? Explain.

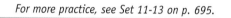

B Reasoning and Problem Solving

Math and Science

The United States Food and Drug Administration (FDA) must approve new medicines before they can be sold. Pharmaceutical companies conduct clinical trials, or experiments, with volunteers to test whether the new medicine produces the desired results and is safe.

9. Based on clinical trials, a pharmaceutical company concluded that the probability of someone experiencing a serious side effect from a new medicine is $\frac{11}{10,000}$. If 2,000,000 people take this medicine, about how many might be expected to experience serious side effects?

10. **Writing in Math** Chelsea flipped a coin 200 times and got heads 84 times. She said, "This coin isn't fair. I should have gotten heads 100 times." Do you agree with Chelsea? Explain.

C Extensions

Geometry is sometimes used to determine a theoretical probability. The probability of the spinner landing on pink can be found by comparing the central angle of the pink sector to the number of degrees in the whole circle.

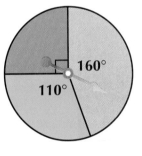

$$P(\text{pink}) = \frac{160}{360} = \frac{4}{9} \approx 44.4\%$$

11. Find $P(\text{blue})$ 12. Find $P(\text{green})$

13. **Calculator** At a carnival, a coin is tossed at random onto the carnival game board pictured. What is the probability, to the nearest percent, that it will land in the circle? (Hint: Compare the area of the circle to the area of the entire game board.)

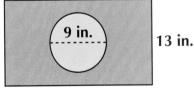

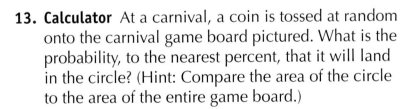
Mixed Review and Test Prep

Take It to the NET
www **Test Prep**
www.scottforesman.com

Algebra Solve each equation.

14. $\frac{n}{3} = 15$ 15. $\frac{a}{7} = -4$ 16. $\frac{30a}{17} = 45$ 17. $\frac{w}{5} = \frac{13}{5}$

18. If you toss a number cube, what is the probability that you do not get a number less than 3?

A. $\frac{1}{6}$ B. $\frac{1}{3}$ C. $\frac{1}{2}$ D. $\frac{2}{3}$

All text pages available online and on CD-ROM.

Key Idea
There are different types of compound events. To find probabilities involving compound events, you need to understand what type they are.

Vocabulary
• compound event (p. 654)
• mutually exclusive
• disjoint

Adding Probabilities

✔ **WARM UP**

1. $\frac{1}{2} + \frac{3}{5}$ 2. $\frac{1}{3} + \frac{1}{12}$

3. $\frac{1}{10} + \frac{1}{3}$ 4. $\frac{1}{9} + \frac{1}{8}$

LEARN

How do you find the probability that either of two events will occur?

Jodi and Sean want to find the probability of getting a sum of 5 or a sum of 7 when two number cubes are tossed.

They started by making this list to show all the possible outcomes of tossing the two number cubes. Then they identified the favorable outcomes, those with a sum of 5 or a sum of 7.

1, 1	1, 2	1, 3	1, 4	1, 5	1, 6
2, 1	2, 2	2, 3	2, 4	2, 5	2, 6
3, 1	3, 2	3, 3	3, 4	3, 5	3, 6
4, 1	4, 2	4, 3	4, 4	4, 5	4, 6
5, 1	5, 2	5, 3	5, 4	5, 5	5, 6
6, 1	6, 2	6, 3	6, 4	6, 5	6, 6

Jodi found P(sum of 5 or sum of 7).

P(sum of 5 or sum of 7) $= \frac{10}{36}$

There are 10 favorable outcomes, shown in the shaded boxes above.

There are 36 possible outcomes.

The probability of getting a sum of 5 or a sum of 7 is $\frac{10}{36}$, or $\frac{5}{18}$.

Sean found P(sum of 5) and P(sum of 7) and then added.

P(sum of 5) $= \frac{4}{36}$

There are 4 favorable outcomes, shown in the purple boxes.

There are 36 possible outcomes.

P(sum of 7) $= \frac{6}{36}$

There are 6 favorable outcomes, shown in the green boxes.

There are 36 possible outcomes.

$\frac{4}{36} + \frac{6}{36} = \frac{10}{36}$

The probability of getting a sum of 5 or a sum of 7 is $\frac{10}{36}$, or $\frac{5}{18}$.

✔ **Talk About It**

1. What is P(sum of 3)? P(sum of 12)? P(sum of 3 or sum of 12)?

What are mutually exclusive events?

The compound events getting a sum of 5 or a sum of 7 are **mutually exclusive**, or **disjoint**, events because both events cannot happen at the same time. Here are some other examples.

Toss a number cube, get a number less than 3 or a number greater than 5.	←	These are mutually exclusive because you cannot get a number less than 3 and a number greater than 5 at the same time.
Toss a number cube, get an even number or a prime number.	←	These are NOT mutually exclusive because if you toss 2, you can get an even number and a prime number at the same time.

Think It Through

I can **draw a Venn diagram** to picture compound events.

mutually exclusive

(1 2) (6)
less   greater
than 3   than 5

not mutually exclusive

(4 6 (2) 3 5)
even   prime
numbers numbers

Adding probabilities works *only* if the events are mutually exclusive. When computing the probability of compound events that are NOT mutually exclusive, you will need to add and subtract probabilities. Consider the example above. There are 6 outcomes when tossing a number cube. The second Venn diagram at the right shows that 2 is both even and prime. It is an outcome for both events, so it has been used twice, once when calculating P(even number) and once when calculating P(prime number). Therefore, P(even number or prime number) = P(even number) + P(prime number) − P(2) = $\frac{3}{6} + \frac{3}{6} - \frac{1}{6}$, or $\frac{5}{6}$.

✔ Talk About It

2. Suppose you toss a number cube. Give an example of an event that is mutually exclusive to tossing an odd number. Give an example of an event that is *not* mutually exclusive to tossing an odd number.

3. Reasoning Suppose two events are *not* mutually exclusive. To find the probability that one event or the other occurs, which method on page 668 would you use, Jodi's or Sean's? Explain.

CHECK ✓

For another example, see Set 11-14 on p. 691.

The twelve marbles shown are placed into a bag and one is drawn at random. Decide if the events are mutually exclusive. Then find each probability expressed as a fraction.

1. P(gray or white)

2. P(multiple of 3 or multiple of 4)

3. P(prime number or multiple of 4)

4. P(even number or number less than 5)

5. Reasoning Suppose two events are mutually exclusive. If the probability that one event will occur is $\frac{1}{2}$ and the probability that the other will occur is $\frac{1}{3}$, what is the probability that one event or the other will occur?

Skills and Understanding

Two number cubes are tossed. Decide if the events are mutually exclusive. Then find each probability expressed as a fraction.

6. *P*(sum of 4 or sum of 8)

7. *P*(sum of 6 or "doubles")

8. *P*(even sum or odd sum)

9. *P*(sum less than 5 or both numbers are 4)

10. *P*("doubles" or odd sum)

11. *P*(even sum or sum greater than 10)

12. Reasoning Are an event and its complement mutually exclusive? What is the sum of the probabilities that the event will occur or its complement will occur?

B **Reasoning and Problem Solving**

Math and Social Studies

It is believed that tops came to Japan from China over a thousand years ago. Through the centuries they have been enjoyed by children the world over. While most tops are circular, some have flat sides and are used in games. The top pictured at the right has six flat sides that show these pictures.

Find the probability that when the top is spun, it will land with the top side showing

13. an animal.

14. a child.

15. a flower or a child.

16. an animal or a 4-legged creature.

17. <u>Writing in Math</u> Suppose the probability that one event will occur is $\frac{1}{2}$ and the probability that the other will occur is $\frac{2}{3}$. Explain why these events cannot be mutually exclusive.

C **Extensions**

18. Algebra A bag contains *n* cards with counting numbers from 1 to *n*. The probability of choosing a card whose number is 10 or less is 0.4. How many cards are in the bag?

Mixed Review and Test Prep

Take It to the NET
Test Prep
www.scottforesman.com

Algebra Solve each equation.

19. $a - \frac{3}{4} = 2$　　**20.** $1\frac{1}{3}c = 2\frac{2}{3}$　　**21.** $x + 4\frac{5}{7} = 10$　　**22.** $\frac{m}{18} = \frac{5}{2}$

23. Wila tossed a paper cup 75 times and made the table at the right to record how it landed. How many times might Wila expect it to land on its side in 800 trials?

52	16	7

24. Algebra Which expression represents 2 times the sum of x and 5?

　　A. $2(x + 5)$　　**B.** $2x + 5$　　**C.** $2 + x + 5$　　**D.** $2(5x)$

Enrichment

Fair Games

A game is **fair** if every player has the same probability of winning.
If any player has a greater probability of winning, the game is **unfair.**

Are these coin-tossing games fair?

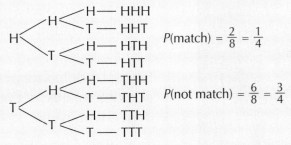

Two coins are tossed. If the coins match, Player A wins. Otherwise, Player B wins.

$P(\text{match}) = \frac{2}{4} = \frac{1}{2}$

$P(\text{not match}) = \frac{2}{4} = \frac{1}{2}$

The game is fair.

Three coins are tossed. If all the coins match, Player A wins. Otherwise, Player B wins.

$P(\text{match}) = \frac{2}{8} = \frac{1}{4}$

$P(\text{not match}) = \frac{6}{8} = \frac{3}{4}$

The game is not fair.

Use the spinner and determine if each game is fair.

1. If the spinner lands on orange or yellow, Player A wins. Otherwise, Player B wins.

2. If the spinner lands on orange or an odd number, Player A wins. Otherwise, Player B wins.

3. If the spinner lands on a factor of 10, Player A wins. Otherwise, Player B wins.

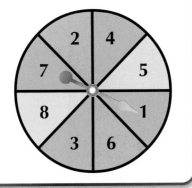

All text pages available online and on CD-ROM.

Vocabulary
• independent events
• dependent events

Think It Through
I need to **remember vocabulary terms.** Mutually exclusive events cannot happen at the same time. Independent and dependent events can happen at the same time.

Multiplying Probabilities

LEARN

✓ **WARM UP**
1. $\frac{3}{10} \times \frac{1}{9}$ 2. $\frac{7}{12} \times \frac{6}{11}$
3. $\frac{3}{25} \times \frac{5}{24}$ 4. $\frac{1}{8} \times \frac{1}{8}$

How do you find the probability that two events will occur?

Roxanne draws one marble from this bag without looking. Then she draws a second marble.

Example A

What is the probability that Roxanne will get a red marble each time if she replaces the first marble before she draws the second one?

Since she replaces the first marble before the second draw, the outcome of the first draw has no effect on the outcome of the second draw. The two draws are **independent events.**

To find P(red, red), find the probability of each event and multiply.

P(red, red) = P(red on 1st draw) × P(red on 2nd draw)

$$= \frac{3}{5} \times \frac{3}{5} = \frac{9}{25} = 36\%$$

1st draw

P(red) = $\frac{3}{5}$

2nd draw

P(red) = $\frac{3}{5}$

Example B

What is the probability that Roxanne will get a red marble each time if she does not replace the first marble before she draws second one?

Since the outcome of the first draw affects the outcome of the second draw, the two draws are **dependent events.**

To find P(red, red), find the probability of each event and multiply.

P(red, red) = P(red on 1st draw) × P(red on 2nd draw)

$$= \frac{3}{5} \times \frac{1}{2} = \frac{3}{10} = 30\%$$

1st draw

P(red) = $\frac{3}{5}$

2nd draw

P(red) = $\frac{1}{2}$

✓ **Talk About It**

1. In Example B, why is the probability of the first draw different from the second draw?

Take It to the NET
More Examples
www.scottforesman.com

For another example, see Set 11-15 on p. 691.

CHECK ✓

For 1–5, give each probability as a fraction and a percent rounded to the nearest tenth of a percent.

You select one letter without looking, replace it, and then select another.

1. Find P(A, G).　　**2.** Find P(vowel, M).

5. Reasoning Suppose you toss a coin 3 times. Find P(H, H, H).

You select one letter without looking, do not replace it, and then select another.

3. Find P(A, G).　　**4.** Find P(vowel, M).

PRACTICE

For more practice, see Set 11-15 on p. 695.

A Skills and Understanding

For Exercises 6–15, use the balls at the right. Give each probability as a fraction and a percent rounded to the nearest tenth of a percent.

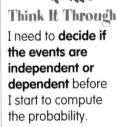

You select a ball without looking, replace it, and then select another.

6. Find P(1, 8).　　**7.** Find P(5, 9).　　**8.** Find P(prime, even).

You select a ball without looking, do not replace it, and then select another.

9. Find P(1, 8).　　**10.** Find P(5, 9).　　**11.** Find P(prime, 9).

Suppose you toss a number cube twice.

12. Find P(2, 5).　　**13.** Find P(even, 3).　　**14.** Find P(even, 2).

15. Reasoning Suppose you toss a coin 4 times. Find P(T, T, T, T).

TEST TALK

Think It Through
I need to **decide if the events are independent or dependent** before I start to compute the probability.

B Reasoning and Problem Solving

16. There are 6 gray socks and 14 white socks thrown loosely into Ted's sock drawer. If Ted pulls out a sock without looking, sets it on the bed, and pulls out another sock, does he have at least a 50% chance of choosing a pair of white socks?

17. **Writing in Math** Your teacher draws 2 names at random to pick the two co-captains of a team. Are these independent or dependent events? Explain.

🦉 Mixed Review and Test Prep

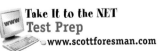

Take It to the NET
Test Prep
www.scottforesman.com

18. Suppose you toss 2 number cubes. Find P(sum of 3 or sum of 10).

19. Find the area of a triangle with base 5 cm and height 12 cm.

　　A. 17 cm^2　　　**B.** 30 cm^2　　　**C.** 34 cm^2　　　**D.** 60 cm^2

All text pages available online and on CD-ROM.

Problem-Solving Skill

Reading Helps!
Creating graphic organizers or brainstorming
can help you with...
writing to describe.

Key Idea
There are specific things you can do to write a good description in math.

Materials
- $\frac{1}{4}$-in. grid paper
- circles
- protractor

TEST TALK

Think It Through
I know that:
- In a **bar graph**, **data values** can be **compared** to one another.
- In a **line graph**, **changes in data values over time** are shown.
- In a **circle graph**, the **comparison of data values to the whole set of data** is shown.

Writing to Describe

LEARN

How do you write a good description?

When you **write to describe,** you can use pictures, tables, or graphs to help you organize your work.

Favorite Season The table at the right shows the results of a survey about favorite seasons. Jason made the bar graph below to show the number of students who prefer each season. Therese made the circle graph below to show the percent of students who prefer each season.

Favorite Season	
Season	**Number of Students**
Winter	130
Spring	300
Summer	320
Fall	250

Describe which graph more clearly shows that more than half the students prefer spring or summer. Describe the characteristics of the graph that justify your decision.

Writing a Math Comparison

- Analyze the data to decide what kind of graph is most appropriate.

- Write the reasons for selecting the graph in clear, concise sentences.

I think the circle graph shows more clearly that more than half of the students prefer spring and summer, because in a circle graph you can see how these numbers compare to the whole. It is easy to see that the sectors for spring and summer fill more than half of the circle.

Talk About It

1. In which graph, Jason's or Therese's, can you more quickly determine which seasons were chosen by at least 250 students? Describe the graph to justify your decision.

For another example, see Set 11-16 on p. 691.

CHECK ✓

1. Enrico made two graphs of the same set of data. Decide which graph more clearly shows there are 13 brass players. Describe the characteristics of the graph that justify your decision.

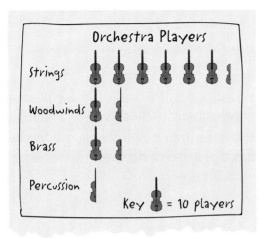

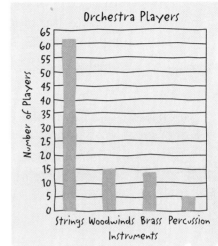

PRACTICE

For more practice, see Set 11-16 on p. 695.

2. Here are the class scores on a recent English test.

English Test Scores						
65	73	70	84	72	91	66
68	75	78	76	92	74	80
91	85	81	73	80	73	71

   a. Construct a line plot and a stem-and-leaf plot of the data.

   b. Decide which plot more clearly shows the mode. Describe the characteristics of the plot that justify your decision.

3. Ms. Kim recorded the number of yearly business trips that she has taken.

Business Trips	
Year	Number of Trips
1999	8
2000	13
2001	20
2002	27
2003	32

   a. Construct a line graph to show the number of trips taken each year.

   b. Make a circle graph showing the percent of the total number of trips taken each year.

   c. Decide which graph more clearly shows how the data has increased over the years. Describe the characteristics of the graph that justify your decision.

4. Wes wants to win the game at the right.

   a. Design a set of 7 number cards that could be used for the game.

   b. Which Player should Wes be? Describe how the rules work with your cards to justify your choice.

> **GAME RULES**
>
> If Player A draws a prime number, Player A wins. Otherwise, Player B wins.

Problem-Solving Applications

Age and Growth Mice can live to be 6 years old and are quite small. Elephants can live to be 77 years old and are enormous. Why do some plants and animals live longer or grow larger than others? The answer lies in the genetics of the organisms.

Trivia One of the largest living organisms in the world is known as the Humongous Fungus. This underground fungus covers 2,200 acres and has been growing for an estimated 2,400 years.

1 The base of one of the largest trees is about 11.1 meters across. The tallest giraffe was almost 6.09 meters tall. How much greater is the diameter of the tree than the height of the giraffe?

2 Record five of your classmates' ages in months. Find the mean, median, and mode of their ages.

3 **Writing in Math** An adult blue whale may weigh 143 tons. A one-year-old whale calf may weigh about 29 tons. About what fraction of the adult's weight does the calf weigh? Explain how you made your estimate.

4 An average lifespan of a rhinoceros is 50 years. The average lifespan of an elephant is 77 years. What benchmark fraction of an elephant's lifetime does a rhinoceros live?

Good News/Bad News The Titan Arum, one of the largest flowers in the world, is an amazing sight. It can grow to be over 170 pounds, 10 feet tall, and 4 feet in diameter. But you may not want to get too close when it is in full bloom. It gives off an odor reminiscent of rotting fish!

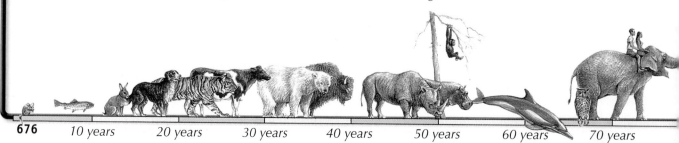

10 years   *20 years*   *30 years*   *40 years*   *50 years*   *60 years*   *70 years*

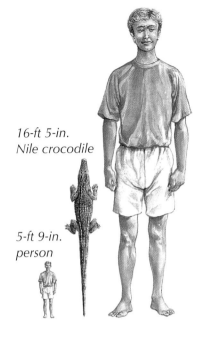

16-ft 5-in.
Nile crocodile

5-ft 9-in.
person

5 A baby Nile crocodile is about 10 inches long when it hatches. It can grow to be over 19 times this length. If humans grew to this extent, how tall would a 20-inch baby grow? Round your answer to the nearest foot.

Key Facts
Giant Growth

Organism	Size
• Coast redwood	363 ft
• Giant kelp	197 ft
• Blue whale	110 ft
• Giraffe	20 ft

Using Key Facts

6 About how many times as tall is a giraffe as a five-foot-tall student? About how many times as tall is the coast redwood as a five-foot-tall student?

7 **Decision Making** What type of graph would be best to show the human baby lengths given in the chart below? Make that graph and use it to predict the median lengths of 30-month-old males and females.

Age (months)	Median Female Length	Median Male Length
Birth	49 cm	50 cm
6	65 cm	67 cm
12	74 cm	75 cm
18	80 cm	82 cm
24	86 cm	87 cm

Do You Know How?

Do You Understand?

Counting Methods (11-10) Permutations and Combinations (11-11)

Meat	Vegetable	Side
Turkey	Carrots	Soup
Beef	Corn	Salad
	Broccoli	

1. How many possible dinner combinations can be made from the selections above?

A Explain two ways to find the number of dinner combinations.

B Describe the difference between a permutation and a combination. Give an example of each.

Probability (11-12) Predictions and Probability (11-13), (11-17)

2. What is the probability of choosing a red marble?

3. Out of 80 picks, how many times might you expect to pick a blue marble?

C Explain how you found the answer to Exercise 3.

D Describe the difference between theoretical probability and experimental probability.

Adding Probabilities (11-14) Multiplying Probabilities (11-15)

Find each probability.

4. *P*(red or white)   5. *P*(purple or yellow)

You select a card, do not replace it, and then select another.

6. Find *P*(yellow, blue)

7. Find *P*(red, not blue)

E Explain how you found the answer to Exercise 4.

F Describe the difference between independent and dependent events.

Problem-Solving Skill: Writing to Describe (11-16)

8. Construct a bar graph and a circle graph of the data at the right.

9. Which graph more clearly shows the favorite sport?

Favorite Sport	
Sport	Votes
Football	95
Soccer	70
Baseball	105
Tennis	30

G Describe some characteristics of each type of graph in Exercise 8.

H Explain how you would organize the data if you wanted to find the mean, median, and mode of a data set.

MULTIPLE CHOICE

1. How many possible outfits are there if you have 4 different shirts, 3 different pairs of pants, and 2 different pairs of shoes? (11-10)

   A. 9　　　　**B.** 12　　　　**C.** 14　　　　**D.** 24

2. What is the probability of spinning a number greater than 6 on the spinner? (11-12)

   A. $\frac{1}{4}$　　**B.** $\frac{5}{8}$　　**C.** $\frac{3}{8}$　　**D.** $\frac{3}{5}$

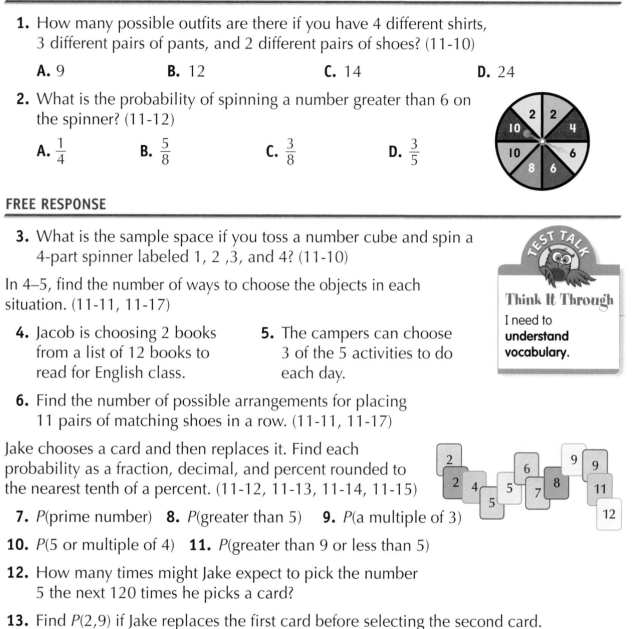

FREE RESPONSE

3. What is the sample space if you toss a number cube and spin a 4-part spinner labeled 1, 2 ,3, and 4? (11-10)

In 4–5, find the number of ways to choose the objects in each situation. (11-11, 11-17)

4. Jacob is choosing 2 books from a list of 12 books to read for English class.

5. The campers can choose 3 of the 5 activities to do each day.

Think It Through
I need to **understand vocabulary.**

6. Find the number of possible arrangements for placing 11 pairs of matching shoes in a row. (11-11, 11-17)

Jake chooses a card and then replaces it. Find each probability as a fraction, decimal, and percent rounded to the nearest tenth of a percent. (11-12, 11-13, 11-14, 11-15)

7. *P*(prime number)　**8.** *P*(greater than 5)　**9.** *P*(a multiple of 3)

10. *P*(5 or multiple of 4)　**11.** *P*(greater than 9 or less than 5)

12. How many times might Jake expect to pick the number 5 the next 120 times he picks a card?

13. Find *P*(2,9) if Jake replaces the first card before selecting the second card.

14. Find *P*(even, 5) if Jake does NOT replace the first card before selecting the second card.

Writing in Math

15. Harvey is studying the record high and low temperatures in his hometown. The table shows his findings. Decide which type of graph more clearly shows the trend in the data. Describe the characteristics of the graph that justify your decision. (11-16)

Record Temperatures		
Month	High	Low
July	104° F	48° F
Aug.	103° F	44° F
Sept.	101° F	30° F
Oct.	91° F	24° F
Nov.	86° F	9° F
Dec.	76° F	-4° F

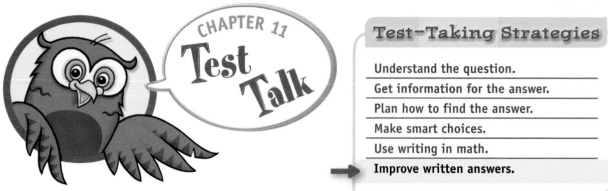

Improve Written Answers

You can follow the tips below to learn how to improve written answers on a test. It is important to write a clear answer and include only information needed to answer the question.

1. Stuart recorded the results of 40 spins of this spinner.

Spinner Results

Color	Red	White	Green	Blue
Number of Spins	15	7	5	13

Do Stuart's results agree with what you might expect? Explain your conclusion by comparing Stuart's results to those you might expect based on theoretical probability. Be sure to include at least one example from Stuart's results to support your conclusion.

Improve Written Answers

- Check if your answer is complete.

    In order to get as many points as possible, first I must determine if the results agree with my expectations. Then I must explain why by comparing the results with what I'd expect based on theoretical probability. I must include at least one example.

- Check if your answer makes sense.

    I should check that my explanation makes sense for all four colors even though I only need to discuss one of them.

- Check if your explanation is clear and easy to follow.

    I should reread my explanation to be sure it is accurate and clear. I shouldn't include any unnecessary information.

The rubric below is a scoring guide for Test Questions 1 and 2.

Scoring Rubric

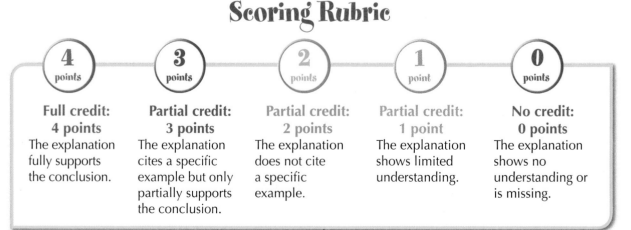

4 points	**3 points**	**2 points**	**1 point**	**0 points**
Full credit: 4 points	Partial credit: 3 points	Partial credit: 2 points	Partial credit: 1 point	No credit: 0 points
The explanation fully supports the conclusion.	The explanation cites a specific example but only partially supports the conclusion.	The explanation does not cite a specific example.	The explanation shows limited understanding.	The explanation shows no understanding or is missing.

Arlene used the scoring rubric on page 680 to score a student's answer to Test Question 1. The student's paper is shown below.

> Stuart's results do not agree with what I would expect. For example, the probability that the spinner will land on red is $\frac{1}{4}$.

Think It Through

The student cites an example to support his or her conclusion, but needs to say more. So I'd give the answer 3 points. Here's what I'd add: Since the probability is $\frac{1}{4}$, then I can expect the spinner to land on red about 10 times because $\frac{1}{4} \times 40 = 10$. But it landed on red 15 times.

Now it's your turn.

Score the student's paper. If it does not get 4 points, rewrite it so that it does.

2. Melinda rolled a number cube 60 times and recorded the results.

Outcome	1	2	3	4	5	6
Number of tosses	9	11	10	12	7	11

Do Melinda's results agree with what you might expect? Explain your conclusion by comparing Melinda's results to those you might expect based on theoretical probability. Be sure to include at least one example from Melinda's results to support your conclusion.

> Melinda's results agree with my expectations because they match the probability.

Outside and outlier both begin with out.

An **outlier** is a piece of data that lies outside, or away from, the rest of the data. (p. 629)

Organize and describe data. (Lessons 11-1, 11-2, 11-3, 11-4, 11-5)

The **data** in the **line plot** below was collected from a **sample** of 24 of the 320 people attending Cartoon Fest. Identify **outliers**, **gaps**, and **clusters**.

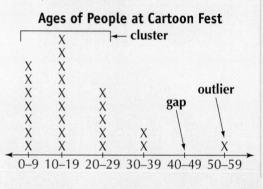

Ages of People at Cartoon Fest

Test Scores

Stem	Leaf
3	8
6	4
7	0 2 2 2 8
8	0 2 4 6
9	0 2 2 6 6

Measures of center and other measures help describe the **statistics** in this **stem-and-leaf plot.**

Minimum: 38   **Maximum:** 96

Range: 96 − 38 = 58

Mean (average): (38 + 64 + ... + 96) ÷ 16
= 1,264 ÷ 16 = 79

Median: (80 + 82) ÷ 2 = 81

Mode: = 72

1. Estimate the number of people at Cartoon Fest younger than 30.

2. Identify any outliers in the test score data.

Sometimes I follow the latest fashion trend.

A **trend** in data tells the direction the data is following. (p. 638)

Analyze and describe graphs. (Lessons 11-6, 11-7, 11-8, 11-16)

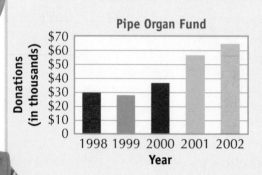

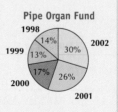

Which graph more clearly shows how the donations to the pipe organ fund changed over the years? Describe those changes.

The bar graph is better at showing **trends** over time. You can see right away that the amount of the yearly donations decreased slightly during 1999 and then sharply increased every year after that.

3. In which year were the donations equal to those of 1999 and 2000 combined? Which graph shows this more clearly?

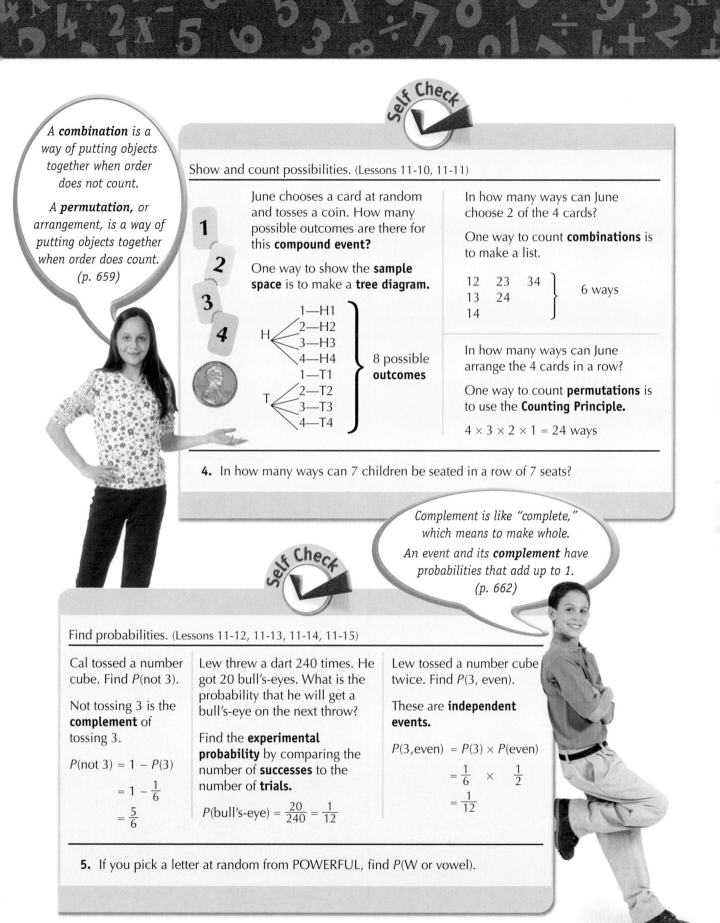

*A **combination** is a way of putting objects together when order does not count.*

*A **permutation**, or arrangement, is a way of putting objects together when order does count.*
(p. 659)

Self Check

Show and count possibilities. (Lessons 11-10, 11-11)

June chooses a card at random and tosses a coin. How many possible outcomes are there for this **compound event?**

One way to show the **sample space** is to make a **tree diagram.**

$$
H \begin{cases} 1\text{—}H1 \\ 2\text{—}H2 \\ 3\text{—}H3 \\ 4\text{—}H4 \end{cases} \Bigg\}
$$
$$
T \begin{cases} 1\text{—}T1 \\ 2\text{—}T2 \\ 3\text{—}T3 \\ 4\text{—}T4 \end{cases}
$$
8 possible **outcomes**

In how many ways can June choose 2 of the 4 cards?

One way to count **combinations** is to make a list.

$$
\left. \begin{array}{lll} 12 & 23 & 34 \\ 13 & 24 & \\ 14 & & \end{array} \right\} \text{6 ways}
$$

In how many ways can June arrange the 4 cards in a row?

One way to count **permutations** is to use the **Counting Principle.**

$4 \times 3 \times 2 \times 1 = 24$ ways

4. In how many ways can 7 children be seated in a row of 7 seats?

Complement is like "complete," which means to make whole.
*An event and its **complement** have probabilities that add up to 1.*
(p. 662)

Self Check

Find probabilities. (Lessons 11-12, 11-13, 11-14, 11-15)

Cal tossed a number cube. Find $P(\text{not }3)$.

Not tossing 3 is the **complement** of tossing 3.

$P(\text{not }3) = 1 - P(3)$
$= 1 - \dfrac{1}{6}$
$= \dfrac{5}{6}$

Lew threw a dart 240 times. He got 20 bull's-eyes. What is the probability that he will get a bull's-eye on the next throw?

Find the **experimental probability** by comparing the number of **successes** to the number of **trials.**

$P(\text{bull's-eye}) = \dfrac{20}{240} = \dfrac{1}{12}$

Lew tossed a number cube twice. Find $P(3, \text{even})$.

These are **independent events.**

$P(3, \text{even}) = P(3) \times P(\text{even})$
$= \dfrac{1}{6} \times \dfrac{1}{2}$
$= \dfrac{1}{12}$

5. If you pick a letter at random from POWERFUL, find $P(\text{W or vowel})$.

Answers: 1. 280 2. 38 3. 2002; circle graph 4. 5,040 ways 5. $\dfrac{1}{2}$

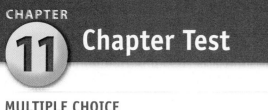
MULTIPLE CHOICE

Choose the correct letter for each answer.

At a crayon factory, a worker randomly selected 200 crayons. He noticed that 5 crayons were broken.

1. What percent of the crayons produced that day were probably broken?

A. 25% **B.** 5%   **C.** 2.5% **D.** 0.5%

2. If the factory produced 600 crayons, how many crayons might a worker expect to be broken?

A. 150 **B.** 30   **C.** 15   **D.** 3

3. Find the mean of the data set.
16, 16, 22, 20, 24, 28, 14, 18

A. 14   **C.** 19

B. 18.5   **D.** 19.75

For 4–5, use the line plot.

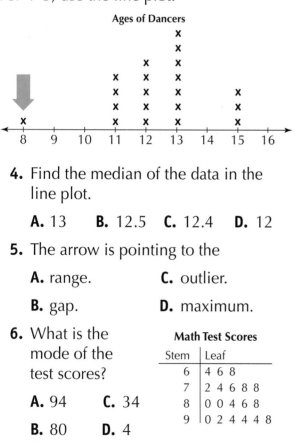

4. Find the median of the data in the line plot.

A. 13   **B.** 12.5 **C.** 12.4 **D.** 12

5. The arrow is pointing to the

A. range.   **C.** outlier.

B. gap.   **D.** maximum.

6. What is the mode of the test scores?

Stem	Leaf
6	4 6 8
7	2 4 6 8 8
8	0 0 4 6 8
9	0 2 4 4 4 8

Math Test Scores

A. 94   **C.** 34

B. 80   **D.** 4

7. Which city received the most precipitation in January and April combined?

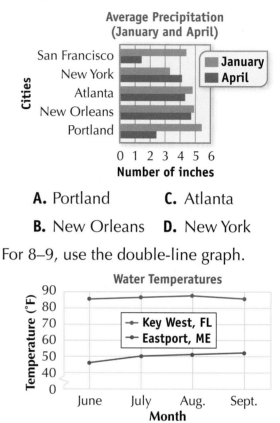

A. Portland   **C.** Atlanta

B. New Orleans   **D.** New York

For 8–9, use the double-line graph.

8. During which month is the water temperature in Eastport the highest?

A. June   **C.** August

B. July   **D.** September

9. Which statement is TRUE?

A. The water temperature is higher in Maine than in Florida.

B. The water temperature in both cities increases from June to September.

C. In the summer, the water temperature in Eastport is greater than 50°F.

D. The water temperature in Key West decreases from August to September.

10. Margie sold 450 ornaments. How many did she sell at craft fairs?

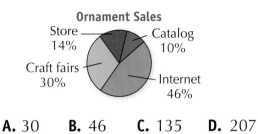

Ornament Sales
Store 14%
Catalog 10%
Craft fairs 30%
Internet 46%

A. 30   **B.** 46   **C.** 135   **D.** 207

11. For lunch Kathy can choose between a salad or soup, an apple, banana, or orange, and chicken, beef, or fish. How many possible combinations are there?

A. 8   **B.** 9   **C.** 12   **D.** 18

12. How many different ways can Patty seat 6 friends in a row?

A. 6   **B.** 30   **C.** 36   **D.** 720

FREE RESPONSE

Find the mean, median, mode, and range of the data. Round decimal answers to the nearest hundredth.

13. 6, 7, 8, 6, 6, 9, 11

14. Represent the data below in a frequency table and a line plot.

High Temperatures				
88°F	78°F	82°F	86°F	78°F
87°F	88°F	76°F	80°F	66°F
78°F	84°F	86°F	85°F	80°F

15. Jackie can choose to paint her room purple, pink, or white. She can use satin, gloss, or semi-gloss paint. She can use a flower, checkered, or striped border. Make a tree diagram to show all of Jackie's possible decorating choices.

16. Chris has 6 trophies. He can only display 2 of the trophies on a shelf. In how many ways can Chris choose 2 of the 6 trophies to display?

For 17–22 use the cards below. Find each probability.

1 2 2 3 1 M A T H 1

17. P(1)   **18.** P(odd number)

19. P(2 or A)   **20.** P(M or a number)

21. Find P(2, a letter) if the first card is replaced before the second is picked.

22. Find P(T,1) if the first card is NOT replaced before the second is picked.

Writing in Math

23. The table shows the results of a survey about favorite color.

Favorite Color			
Red	78	Yellow	38
Blue	86	Green	28
Purple	58	Orange	12

Make and describe the most appropriate graph to show the data.

24. Explain how to make a graph of the Favorite Color data using 3 colors that received the most votes, so it seems like red got twice as many votes as purple.

25. Explain the difference between a permutation and a combination.

Number and Operation

MULTIPLE CHOICE

1. What is 35% of 245?

   A. 35   **C.** 85.75

   B. 70   **D.** 210

2. What is the LCM for 4, 12, and 8?

   A. 4   **C.** 24

   B. 12   **D.** 48

3. Find $3\frac{3}{8} + 2\frac{3}{4}$.

   A. $5\frac{1}{2}$ **C.** $5\frac{1}{8}$

   B. $5\frac{3}{4}$ **D.** $6\frac{1}{8}$

FREE RESPONSE

4. Find $4\frac{1}{3} \div 1\frac{5}{6}$.

5. Find $8 \div \frac{4}{5}$.

6. In a bowl, there are 6 strawberries, 2 apples, and 4 bananas. Write the ratio of the number of strawberries to the number of bananas in three ways.

7. Find $(-6) - (-2)$.

8. Vince's account was $8 overdrawn. The bank charged $5 for being overdrawn. Then Vince made a $40 deposit. How much is in his account?

Writing in Math

9. Explain how to multiply a mixed number by a mixed number. Give an example.

10. A 2.5-lb package of beef is on sale for $8.95. A 3.0-lb package of beef is on sale for $10.56. Explain how to find which is the better deal.

Geometry and Measurement

MULTIPLE CHOICE

11. Which is the greatest capacity?

   A. 5 pints   **C.** $\frac{1}{2}$ gallon

   B. 4 quarts   **D.** 8 quarts

12. If $\overrightarrow{SB}$ is the bisector of $\angle RST$, which of the following is true?

   A. $m\angle RST = 90°$ **C.** $\angle RSB \cong \angle BST$

   B. $m\angle RSB = 90°$ **D.** $\overline{RS} \cong \overline{ST}$

13. How many lines of symmetry does the figure below have?

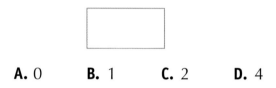

   A. 0   **B.** 1   **C.** 2   **D.** 4

FREE RESPONSE

14. Find the circumference of a circle with a radius of 4 cm.

15. Alan must replace the glass in a circular porthole that has a diameter of 16 in. He will cut the glass from a 16-in square. How much glass will be wasted?

16. Draw this figure after it is flipped over the y-axis and rotated 90° clockwise.

Writing in Math

17. Describe how to find the area of a triangle with a base of 5 inches and a height of 8 inches.

18. Explain the difference between complementary and supplementary angles.

Data Analysis and Probability

MULTIPLE CHOICE

19. What is the mean of the data in the stem-and-leaf plot?

Test Scores

Stem	Leaf
5	6
6	0 0 4 8
7	2 2 6 6 6
8	0 0 2 2 4 8 8
9	2 6 6

A. 40   **C.** 78

B. 77.4   **D.** 81.9

20. Using the spinner below, what is the probability of spinning red 2 times in a row?

A. $\frac{3}{10}$ **C.** $\frac{3}{5}$

B. $\frac{1}{5}$ **D.** $\frac{9}{100}$

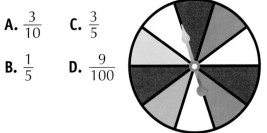

FREE RESPONSE

21. Natasha took a handful of beads from a bag. She noted that of the 16 beads in her hand 5 were white. About what percent of the beads in the bag are white?

22. A sandwich can be made with white, wheat, or rye bread. The filling can be ham or chicken. The bread can be toasted or untoasted. How many choices are there?

Writing in Math

23. Describe the difference between a double-bar graph, a double-line graph, and a circle graph. Explain what type of data each best shows.

Algebra

MULTIPLE CHOICE

24. Solve for the variable.
$$b - 5 = -3.$$

A. $b = 8$ **C.** $b = 2$

B. $b = -8$ **D.** $b = -2$

25. Find the value of y to make this proportion true.
$$\frac{y}{12} = \frac{2}{8}$$

A. $y = 3$ **C.** $y = 6$

B. $y = 4$ **D.** $y = 8$

FREE RESPONSE

Solve.

26. $4c = 56$ **27.** $\frac{-3}{5}b = 3\frac{3}{10}$

28. $3 - x = 21$ **29.** $\frac{-y}{11} = 13$

30. The mean of Janet's four test scores was 84.5. If three of her scores were 78, 82, and 92, what was her score on the fourth test?

31. Kenji and Paco shared the cost of a new television equally. The television cost $278.95 plus $6\frac{1}{2}\%$ sales tax. How much did each boy spend?

32. Tell whether the relation is a function.

x	-2	-3	6	-2
y	-1	0	3	1

Writing in Math

33. Explain how to find the actual dimensions of a room with a scale of 2 inches = 3 feet.

Set 11-1 (pages 620–623)

Sharita found that an 8-ounce sample from a container of mixed nuts contained 3 ounces of peanuts. What percent of the weight of mixed nuts in the container is probably peanuts?

$$\frac{\text{weight of peanuts} \rightarrow 3}{\text{weight of sample} \rightarrow 8} = 0.375 = 37.5\%$$

Because 37.5% of the sample weight is peanuts, about 37.5% of the entire container of mixed nuts is peanuts.

Remember to set up a ratio to compare the sample with the population.

1. A survey of 600 people revealed that 350 preferred the beach to the mountains. Out of 15,000 people, about how many prefer the beach?

Set 11-2 (pages 624–627)

Find the range, mean, median, and mode of this data set: 5, 5, 2, 3, 9, 6, 10, 8

Range: $10 - 2 = 8$.   The range is 8.

Mean: $5 + 5 + 2 + 3 + 9 + 6 + 10 + 8 = 48$

$\frac{48}{8} = 6$ The mean is 6.

Median: 2 3 5 5̲ 6̲ 8 9 10

$\frac{5 + 6}{2} = 5.5$ The median is 5.5.

Mode: 5 occurs most often.   The mode is 5.

Remember that the median is the middle number. Round decimal answers to the nearest tenth.

1. 2.8, 3.2, 4.5, 2.1, 3.2, 7.8, 9.5

2. 78, 80, 90, 94, 72, 80, 96, 78, 80

3. 110, 105, 104, 112, 110, 105, 105

Set 11-3 (pages 628–631)

Represent the data in a line plot.

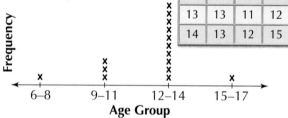

Age of Campers				
12	12	14	10	11
13	13	11	12	7
14	13	12	15	13

Remember to identify any clusters, gaps, and outliers.

1.

Number of Pages in the Reading List						
125	112	120	108	95	132	122
142	178	118	124	134	98	115

Set 11-4 (pages 632–633)

Represent the data in a stem-and-leaf plot.

Test Scores							
72	74	80	82	90	78	72	84
92	90	70	54	96	78	80	88

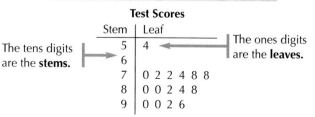

Test Scores

The tens digits are the **stems**.

Stem	Leaf
5	4
6	
7	0 2 2 4 8 8
8	0 0 2 4 8
9	0 0 2 6

The ones digits are the **leaves**.

Remember that a stem-and-leaf plot organizes data by place value.

1. Represent the data in a stem-and-leaf plot.

Number of Sit-ups Completed								
35	36	28	44	46	48	52	32	35
48	56	60	29	30	36	40	50	52

2. Find the median, mode, and range of the data above.

In which month were more blueberry
bagels sold?

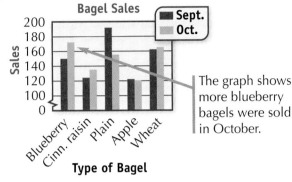

The graph shows
more blueberry
bagels were sold
in October.

Remember to look at the key to determine
what each bar in the graph represents.

1. Which type of bagel was sold the
   least in September?

2. Which type of bagel or bagels had a
   greater number sold in October than
   in September?

The data of high and low temperatures is
shown in the double-line graph.

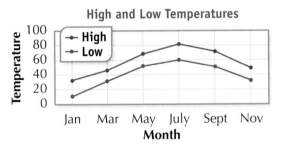

Remember that a double-line graph is
used to show data collected over time.

1. Show the data in a double-line
   graph. Describe the general trend.

Ticket Sales (thousands)					
	1998	**1999**	**2000**	**2001**	**2002**
Adult	400	360	425	515	625
Children	520	480	650	720	875

Maria budgets $1,500 for monthly
expenses. How
much is her rent?

Find 34% of $1,500.

$0.34 \times 1,500 = 510$

Maria spends
$510 on rent.

Maria's Budget

Miscellaneous
6%

Entertainment
22%

Rent
34%

Utilities
18%

Food
20%

Remember to use percents to find the
measure of each central angle.

1. How much did Maria budget for
   food and entertainment?

2. What is the measure of the central
   angle for the sector labeled utilities?

Make the most appropriate graph to
show the survey data.

Dog and Cat Owners		
Grade	Dogs	Cats
6th	88	92
7th	105	98
8th	107	105

Dog and Cat Owners

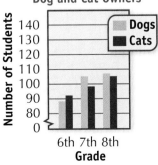

The data is best shown in a double-bar graph.

Remember to include a title and labels.

1. Make the most
   appropriate graph
   to show the data.

2. Do red and silver
   represent more or
   less than half of
   all the colors sold?

Jake's 2002 Car Sales

Car Colors	
Red	26%
Black	18%
White	9%
Tan	8%
Silver	32%
Green	7%

Set 11-9 (pages 650–651)

Explain why the claim, "Sales doubled from 2001 to 2002," is misleading.

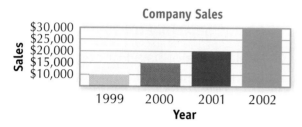

Company Sales

While the 2002 bar looks twice the size, the increase is less than double.

Remember to check the first number on the vertical scale.

1. "Attendance greatly decreased in 2003."

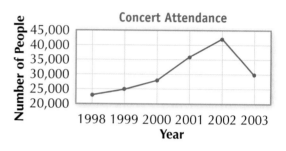

Concert Attendance

Set 11-10 (pages 654–657)

You toss the number cube and spin the spinner. Show all the possible outcomes.

Make a List

1, R	2, R	3, R	4, R	5, R	6, R
1, B	2, B	3, B	4, B	5, B	6, B
1, Y	2, Y	3, Y	4, Y	5, Y	6, Y
1, G	2, G	3, G	4, G	5, G	6, G

There are 6 × 4, or 24 possible outcomes.

Remember you can draw a tree diagram, or use multiplication to find the number of possible outcomes.

1. How many possible outcomes are there if you spin each spinner once?

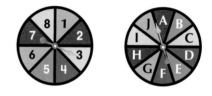

Set 11-11 (pages 658–661)

In how many ways can Eric arrange 5 books on a shelf?

5 × 4 × 3 × 2 × 1 = 120

There are 120 possible arrangements.

Remember to decide whether the order of the objects matter.

1. In how many ways can you choose 3 shirts from an assortment of 7 shirts?

Set 11-12 (pages 662–663)

Find the probability of choosing the letter M from a bag containing the letters:

$P(M) = \dfrac{2}{11}$ ← There are 2 favorable outcomes.

There are 11 letters, so there are 11 possible outcomes.

The probability of choosing the letter M is $\dfrac{2}{11}$.

Remember the probability of an event ranges from 0 to 1.

1. $P(3)$

2. $P(\text{less than } 6)$

3. $P(\text{even number})$

4. $P(\text{not } 1)$

Set 11-13 (pages 664–667)

How many times might you expect to get a number greater than 4 when you toss a number cube 240 times?

$P(\text{greater than 4}) = \frac{2}{6} \text{ or } \frac{1}{3}$

$\frac{1}{3} \times 240 = 80$ Multiply the probability by the number of tosses.

You would expect to get a number greater than 4 about 80 times.

Remember that experimental probability is an estimate.

1. In baseball games this season, Barry was up to bat 24 times and hit the ball 18 times. Estimate the probability that he will get a hit the next time at bat.

Set 11-14 (pages 668–671)

Find the probability of picking a yellow or a smiley-face card.

$P(\text{yellow}) + P(\text{smiley face}) = \frac{2}{15} + \frac{3}{15} = \frac{5}{15}$

The probability of picking a card that is yellow or has a smiley face is $\frac{5}{15}$, or $\frac{1}{3}$.

Remember to add the probabilities if the events are mutually exclusive.

1. $P(\text{red or heart})$
2. $P(\text{blue or smiley face})$
3. $P(\text{heart or not purple})$
4. $P(\text{heart or smiley face})$

Set 11-15 (pages 672–673)

Find $P(\text{red, blue})$

If the marble is replaced after the first pick:

$\frac{6}{16} \times \frac{5}{16} = \frac{30}{256}, \text{ or } \frac{15}{128}$

If the marble is NOT replaced after the first pick: $\frac{6}{16} \times \frac{5}{15} = \frac{30}{240}, \text{ or } \frac{1}{8}$

Remember that if an object is not replaced, the possible outcomes decrease by 1.

1. You select a marble, do not replace it, and then select another. Find $P(\text{white, white})$.

Set 11-16 (pages 674–675)

When you analyze the data, think:

Data values can be easily compared to one another in a bar graph.

Changes in data values over time are shown in a line graph.

The comparison of different data values to the whole set of data is shown in a circle graph.

Remember to write your reasons in clear, concise sentences.

Monthly Precipitation (in.)				
Feb.	Apr.	June	Aug.	Oct.
2.4	4.6	3.2	2.0	4.8

1. Construct the most appropriate graph. Describe the characteristics of the graph that justify your decision.

Set 11-1 (pages 620–623)

In Exercises 1 and 2, identify the population studied. Then tell whether you think the statistics are drawn from a sample or from the entire population. Explain your thinking.

1. Josh reported that the average age of his classmates is 12.3 years.

2. Lori determined that 22% of the population has green eyes.

3. In a bag of 30 lollipops, 5 were grape-flavored. Estimate the number of grape-flavored lollipops in a bag with 100 lollipops.

4. Benji surveyed 120 people in his town. He found that 45 people exercised everyday. What percent of the town population probably exercises everyday?

Set 11-2 (pages 624–627)

Find the mean, median, mode, and range of each data set. Round decimal answers to the nearest hundredth.

1. 18, 20, 16, 20, 19, 13, 17, 22   2. 5.5, 3.4, 8.2, 3.5, 7.6, 6.0, 4.2

3. $350, $420, $350, $425, $370, $430   4. −3°C, −2°C, 1°C, 2°C, −3°C, 2°C

Set 11-3 (pages 628–631)

Follow these directions for the set of data at the right.

1. Represent the set of data in a frequency table and a line plot.

2. Identify any clusters, gaps, and outliers.

3. Compute the mean with and without the outlier(s) and compare them.

Number of Push Ups

17	26	28	26	34
36	18	22	52	41
44	21	3	23	34

Set 11-4 (pages 632–633)

The table at the right shows prices for DVDs.

1. Represent the data in a stem-and-leaf plot.

2. Find the median, mode, and range of the data.

DVD Prices

$25	$32	$32	$45
$45	$39	$50	$45
$22	$24	$30	$40

The heights of students in the 6th-grade class are displayed in the stem-and-leaf plot below.

3. What is the range of heights? What is the mean, rounded to the nearest tenth?

Students' Heights (inches)

Stem	Leaf
4	6 8
5	2 3 5 5 8 8
6	0 0 1 2 3 4 4 6

Take It to the NET
www More Practice
www.scottforesman.com

Set 11-5 (pages 636–637)

The double-bar graph at the right shows the number of boys and girls that participate in each sport.

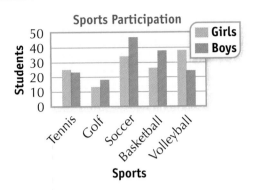

Sports Participation

1. In which sport do the greatest number of girls participate?

2. Make a double-bar graph of the data below.

Stuffed Animal Sales					
	July	Aug.	Sept.	Oct.	Nov.
Store A	$800	$750	$520	$810	$900
Store B	$700	$625	$650	$790	$910

Set 11-6 (pages 638–641)

1. The table shows the high and low temperatures for 6 days. Show the data in a double-line graph.

2. Describe the general trend you see in temperatures.

3. Tara wants to know what the temperature will be on Sunday. Predict what the temperature will be on Sunday. How did you make your prediction?

Weekly High and Low Temperatures		
Day	High	Low
Monday	83°F	62°F
Tuesday	78°F	60°F
Wednesday	78°F	56°F
Thursday	72°F	52°F
Friday	76°F	52°F
Saturday	78°F	54°F

Set 11-7 (pages 642–645)

The Biology Club earned $4,600.

1. What percent of the earnings came from club dues?

2. How much money was made with the T-shirt sales?

3. How much money did the club earn with the car wash and the recycling combined?

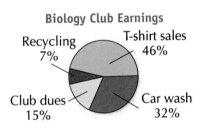

Biology Club Earnings

Recycling 7%
T-shirt sales 46%
Club dues 15%
Car wash 32%

Set 11-8 (pages 648–649)

The table at the right shows the balloons sold at a party shop last year.

1. Make the most appropriate graph to show the data at the right.

2. In which category were more flat than metallic balloons sold?

3. Based on last year's sales, of which color and type of balloon should the shop order the most? Explain.

Balloon Sales (thousands)		
Color	Flat	Metallic
Red	45	52
Blue	50	42
White	80	84
Purple	20	42
Green	25	30

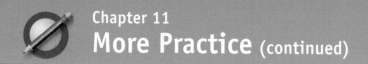
Set 11-9 (pages 650–651)

Explain why each claim is misleading.

1. Team A scored twice as many points as Team B.

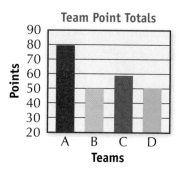

Team Point Totals

2. Sales have greatly increased.

Totally Toys Profits

Set 11-10 (pages 654–657)

1. Make a list to show all the possible choices for breakfast.

2. Veronica knows that the last four digits of her friend's phone number are 8, 5, and 0 with one of the digits repeating. How many different numbers are possible?

3. Suppose you toss a number cube and spin the spinner. Make a tree diagram to show the sample space. How many possible outcomes are there?

Breakfast		
Main	**Beverage**	**Fruit**
Eggs	Milk	Apple
Cereal	Juice	Banana
Pancakes		Strawberries
Waffles		

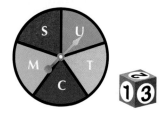

Set 11-11 (pages 658–661)

Find the number of ways to choose the objects in each situation.

1. Samantha is choosing 3 colors from a choice of 7 colors.

2. Greg is picking 2 of the 5 activities to do at camp.

Find the number of possible arrangements for each situation.

3. Nine players on the baseball team line up to bat.

4. Mrs. Yurri decides in which order to run her 4 errands.

Set 11-12 (pages 662–663)

Using the spinner, find each probability as a fraction, decimal, and percent rounded to the nearest whole percent.

1. $P(6)$

2. P(an odd number)

3. P(not 1)

4. P(a prime number)

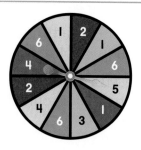

Take It to the NET
More Practice
www.scottforesman.com

Set 11-13 (pages 664–667)

1. Terence threw a dart at a dart board 25 times. He hit the bull's-eye two times.

   a. Estimate the probability, given as a percent, that the next dart Terence throws will hit the bull's-eye.

   b. How many times might Terence expect to hit the bull's-eye if he throws a dart 320 times?

2. How many times might you expect to get a 3 or a 6 when you toss a number cube 120 times?

Set 11-14 (pages 668–671)

Decide if the events are mutually exclusive. Then find each probability expressed as a fraction.

1. P(red or blue)

2. P(3 or 4)

3. P(2 or yellow)

4. P(blue or 1)

5. P(even number or green)

6. P(red or even)

Set 11-15 (pages 672–673)

In Exercises 1–8, give each probability as a fraction and a percent rounded to the nearest tenth of a percent.

A D D I T I O N 2 + 2 = 4

You select a card without looking, replace it, and then select another.

1. P(D, 2)   2. P(vowel, number)   3. P(symbol, letter)   4. P(+, I)

You select a card without looking, do not replace it, and then select another.

5. P(D, 2)   6. P(vowel, number)   7. P(symbol, letter)   8. P(+, I)

Set 11-16 (pages 674–675)

1. The table at the right shows the number of wins each baseball team had last year. Construct a bar graph showing the number of wins for each team and a circle graph showing the percent of the total number of wins for each team. Explain which graph more clearly shows which team had the most wins.

Number of Team Wins	
Team A	9
Team B	11
Team C	8
Team D	12
Team E	10

A Vocabulary

(pages 44, 45, 440, 448)

Choose the best term from the box.

1. Multiplication and division are __?__.

2. A __?__ is formed by the intersection of two number lines.

3. To keep an equation balanced, you do the same operation to both sides by using __?__.

4. The graph of a __?__ is a straight line.

Vocabulary

- **coordinate plane** (p. 440)
- **inverse operations** (p. 45)
- **linear equation** (p. 448)
- **ordered pair** (p. 440)
- **properties of equality** (p. 44)

B Comparing Numbers

(pages 12–13, 78–79, 176–179, 410–411)

Use <, >, or = to compare.

5. 9,842 ● 9,482

6. 4.75 ● 5

7. 3.05 ● 3.5

8. 0.176 ● 0.18

9. $2\frac{1}{5}$ ● 2

10. 1.5 ● $1\frac{1}{2}$

11. −4 ● 2

12. −6 ● 0

13. Letti's time in the 50-meter freestyle was clocked to the thousandths place, but rounded to 25.69 seconds. What is a possible slower time that would round to 25.69? a possible faster time?

14. Write a number that has a thousandths place and is between 8.75 and 8.739.

Do You Know...

How many athletes competed in the 2000 Summer Olympics?

You will find out in Lesson 12-9.

C Coordinate Graphing
(pages 440–443)

For 15–20, give the ordered pair for each point graphed below and name the quadrant or axis on which it lies.

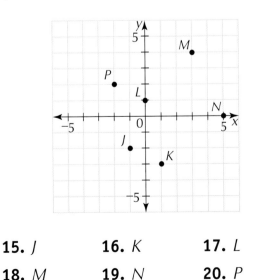

15. *J* **16.** *K* **17.** *L*

18. *M* **19.** *N* **20.** *P*

D Solving Equations
(pages 48–51, 112–119, 276–277, 430–431)

Solve each equation and check your answer.

21. $x - 15 = 25$ **22.** $y + 7 = 24$

23. $3n = 30$ **24.** $\frac{d}{8} = 9$

25. $4.8 = y + 1.4$ **26.** $4.5m = 1.8$

27. $\frac{2}{3} + k = 4$ **28.** $-54 = 6x$

29. Write and solve an equation to find the side length of a square with a perimeter of 58.4 meters.

30. The two congruent angles of an isosceles triangle each measure 25°. Write and solve an equation to find the measure of the third angle.

Algebra

Key Idea
You can use a number line to represent all the values that make an inequality true.

Vocabulary
• inequality

Materials
• number lines

LEARN

Activity

How can you graph an inequality?

An **inequality** is a mathematical sentence that contains >, <, ≥, or ≤. Any number that makes an inequality true is a **solution of the inequality.** Some solutions of $x > 6$ are $x = 6.5$, $x = 7$, and $x = 7.5$.

> Read ≥ as "is greater than or equal to."
>
> Read ≤ as "is less than or equal to."

You can graph the solutions of $x > 6$, on a number line.

Step 1: On the number line, draw an open circle at 6. An open circle shows that 6 is *not* a solution, but numbers close to 6 are.

<-----+---+---+---+---+---+---+---⊕---+---+--->
      −2 −1 0   1   2   3   4   5   6   7   8

Step 2: Locate 3 solutions of $x > 6$ on the number line. Start at the open circle and draw a thick line over the solutions. Draw an arrow to show that there are infinitely many solutions.

6.5   7.5

To graph an inequality like $y \le -1$, draw a closed circle at −1 to show that −1 is a solution. Then repeat Step 2.

<-----+---+---+---+---+---●---+---+---+---+---+--->
      −5 −4 −3 −2 −1 0   1   2   3   4   5

a. Name 3 solutions of each inequality. Then graph each inequality on a number line.

   $z < -2$ $a \le -5$ $c \ge 4$ $-3 < d$

b. Write an inequality for the graph below.

<-----+---+---+---+---+---●---+---+---+---+---+--->
      −5 −4 −3 −2 −1 0   1   2   3   4   5

c. Is it possible to list all solutions of $x \ge -5$? Explain.

Take It to the NET
More Examples
www.scottforesman.com

Name 3 solutions of each inequality. Then graph the inequality on a number line.

1. $m > 7$ **2.** $x \le 5$ **3.** $k \ge 30$ **4.** $p < 15$

5. Number Sense Is 2 a solution of the inequality graphed at the right? Is 24.5? Is −4? Explain how you know.

PRACTICE

For more practice, see Set 12-1 on p. 739.

Ⓐ Skills and Understanding

Name 3 solutions of each inequality. Then graph the inequality on a number line.

6. $a < 3$ **7.** $t \ge 12$ **8.** $r \le 20$ **9.** $k > 40$

10. $b \ge 9$ **11.** $n < 4$ **12.** $c \le 45$ **13.** $h > 16$

14. $p < 17$ **15.** $m \le 92$ **16.** $f > 10$ **17.** $u \ge 27$

18. Number Sense Is $x = 0.5$ a solution of $x > 11$? Explain how you know.

Ⓑ Reasoning and Problem Solving

19. The hot air balloon at the right was 25 feet above the ground before it began to lose altitude. Use $t < 25$ to name three possible altitudes of the balloon's descent.

20. Carter needed to earn at least $25.00 to buy a scooter. Use the inequality $m \ge 25$ to find three possible amounts that Carter needed to earn.

21. Reasoning Name three possible solutions of $x < 0$.

22. Writing in Math Explain why the graphs $x < 8$ and $x \le 8$ are not exactly the same.

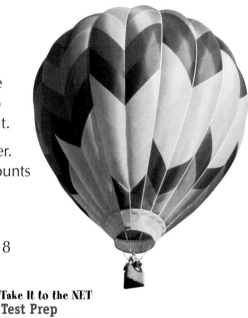

🦉 Mixed Review and Test Prep

Take It to the NET
Test Prep
www.scottforesman.com

The letter tiles at the right are put in a bag. You select one at random, replace it, and then select another one. Find each probability.

P R E
A L G E B R A

23. $P(E, B)$ **24.** $P(G, \text{vowel})$ **25.** $P(\text{vowel, vowel})$

26. Solve $x + 4.5 = 5.7$.

A. $x = 1.2$ **B.** $x = 1.3$ **C.** $x = 9.2$ **D.** $x = 10.2$

Algebra

Solving Inequalities

Key Idea
As with solving equations, there are operations and properties you can use to solve inequalities.

Vocabulary
• inverse operations (p. 45)
• properties of inequality

Think It Through
• I can **check my answer** by using a test point.
• I can **use inverse operations** to solve an inequality.

LEARN

How can you solve addition and subtraction inequalities?

Trisha has $3 to spend on lunch. She also has a coupon for $2 off any meal at Joe's Cafeteria. Which meals can she afford to buy?

Let c represent the cost of a meal. Use the inequality $c - 2 \leq 3$ to find the meal Trisha can afford.

To solve an addition or subtraction inequality, use **inverse operations** and **properties of inequality**.

Joe's Cafeteria

Hamburger Meal	$4.50
Chicken Strips Meal	$5.25
Chicken Salad Meal	$6.50
Veggie Burger Meal	$3.95

All meals include fruit and a medium beverage.

Properties of Inequality

Addition Property of Inequality Adding the same number to both sides of an inequality does not change the inequality.	You know: $4 < 6$ Therefore: $4 + 5 < 6 + 5$ $9 < 11$
Subtraction Property of Inequality Subtracting the same number from both sides of an inequality does not change the inequality.	You know: $4 < 6$ Therefore: $4 - 3 < 6 - 3$ $1 < 3$

Example A

Solve $c - 2 \leq 3$. Then graph the solution.

$c - 2 \leq 3$ Undo subtraction by adding 2 to both sides.

$c - 2 + 2 \leq 3 + 2$ Simplify.

$c \leq 5$

The solution is $c \leq 5$.

$$0 \quad 1 \quad 2 \quad 3 \quad 4 \quad 5$$

Check:
Test a point on the graph, like $c = 4$.

$c - 2 \leq 3$
$4 - 2 \leq 3$
$2 \leq 3$ The inequality is true, so $c \leq 5$.

Trisha can afford to buy any meal that costs $5 or less. She can buy the Hamburger Meal or the Veggie Burger Meal.

✔ Talk About It

1. In Example A, why is 2 added to both sides of the inequality instead of another number?

2. Which property of inequality would you use to solve $h - 5 \geq 7$?

How can you solve multiplication and division inequalities?

Another day, Trisha and two friends had a total of $18 to spend at Joe's Cafeteria. If they each ordered the same thing, which meals could they afford to buy?

Let c represent the cost of each meal. Use the inequality $3c \leq 18$ to find which meals the friends can afford.

To solve a multiplication or division inequality, use inverse operations and the following properties of inequality.

Properties of Inequality	
Multiplication Property of Inequality Multiplying each side of an inequality by the same positive number does not change the inequality.	You know: $\quad 4 \leq 6$ Therefore: $\quad 3(4) \leq 3(6)$ $\qquad\qquad 12 \leq 18$
Division Property of Inequality Dividing each side of an inequality by the same positive number does not change the inequality.	You know: $\quad 4 \leq 6$ Therefore: $\quad \dfrac{4}{2} \leq \dfrac{6}{2}$ $\qquad\qquad 2 \leq 3$

Example B

Solve $3c \leq 18$. Then graph the solution.

$$3c \leq 18$$
$$\frac{3c}{3} \leq \frac{18}{3} \qquad \text{Undo multiplication by dividing both sides by 3.}$$
$$c \leq 6 \qquad \text{Simplify.}$$

The solution is $c \leq 6$.

0 1 2 3 4 5 6 7 8 9 10

Check:
Test a point on the graph, like $c = 5$.

$$3c \leq 18$$
$$3(5) \leq 18$$
$$15 \leq 18 \qquad \text{The inequality is true, so } c \leq 6.$$

Trisha and her friends can afford to buy any meal that costs $6 or less. They each can buy any meal, except chicken salad.

✔ Talk About It

3. Which property of inequality would you use to solve $\dfrac{h}{4} \leq 1$?

Solve each inequality. Graph and check the solution.

1. $x + 3 \le 2$ **2.** $b - 5 < 0$ **3.** $5y \le 10$ **4.** $\frac{x}{4} \ge 25$ **5.** $a + 4 > 7$

6. Number Sense How can you tell that $x = 99$ is not a solution of $0.5x > 60$, without multiplying $0.5(99)$?

PRACTICE

For more practice, see Set 12-2 on p. 739.

Ⓐ Skills and Understanding

Solve each inequality. Graph and check the solution.

7. $w + 4 < 43$ **8.** $n + 3 < 10$ **9.** $b - 5 > 1$ **10.** $x - 3 \le 23$ **11.** $4v \ge 12$

12. $4t \ge 48$ **13.** $\frac{x}{9} \le 11$ **14.** $\frac{a}{2} < 10$ **15.** $5y < 0$ **16.** $h + 5 \ge 5$

17. Number Sense Without adding, how can you tell $x = 26.5$ is not a solution of $x + 4.29 < 26.5$?

Ⓑ Reasoning and Problem Solving

18. Together, Todd and a friend have a total of $11 to spend at Joe's Cafeteria. If they buy the same meal, which meals can they buy? Use the sign on page 700.

Think It Through
I can **use what I know.** There are 2,000 lb in a ton.

Math and Science

For 19–21, use the table at the right.

19. How many hippopotamuses can the zoo feed for a 30-day month with 2 tons of hay? Use the inequality $1,200h \le 4,000$ to solve. (Note: $1,200 = 30$ days $\times 40$ lbs.)

20. How many African elephants can the zoo feed for a 30-day month with 4 tons of hay?

21. If 205 pounds of hay is enough to feed an African elephant and a rhinoceros for a day, how much could a bale of hay weigh?

22. Suppose the average weight of a rhinoceros is 5,000 pounds. How many rhinoceroses could the zoo transport with a 8-ton capacity truck?

Large Land Mammals at the National Zoo	
Animal	**Pounds of Hay Eaten Daily by Each Animal**
African Elephant	125
Rhinoceros	one bale
Hippopotamus	40

C Extensions

23. <u>Writing in Math</u> Explain why Devon's work is correct.

Check that $x < 4$ is the solution of $3x < 12$.

0 is a
solution of $x < 4$

5 is not a
solution of $x < 4$

Solve each inequality. Graph and check the solution.

24. $4.7x > 14.1$ **25.** $x - \frac{1}{4} \le 3\frac{1}{2}$ **26.** $y + 9 \ge 3$ **27.** $\frac{2}{3}n < \frac{8}{9}$

Mixed Review and Test Prep

Take It to the NET
Test Prep
www.scottforesman.com

For 28–30, make a T-table. Then graph each equation.

28. $y = x + 2$ **29.** $y = -4 + x$ **30.** $y = -2x$

31. Which inequality is graphed at the right?

A. $a \ge 2$ **B.** $a \le 2$ **C.** $a > 2$ **D.** $a < 2$

32. Steven paid \$8 for 5 used books. Write this as a unit rate.

A. \$0.62 per book   **B.** \$0.63 per book   **C.** \$0.85 per book   **D.** \$1.60 per book

Enrichment

Translating Words to Inequalities

Translating words to inequalities is like translating words to equations, except for deciding which inequality sign to use.

Words	Inequality
5 more than n is **less than** 8	$n + 5 < 8$
3 less than n is **at most** 12	$n - 3 \le 12$
7 times n is **greater than** 18	$7n > 18$
2 less than n is **at least** 10	$n - 2 \ge 10$

For 1–5, write and solve each inequality.

1. 3 times n is at most 12

2. n divided by 2 is greater than 10

3. 7 less than n is at least 5

4. 20 more than n is less than 35

Predict and Verify

Predicting and verifying when you read in math can help you use the **problem-solving strategy, *Try, Check, and Revise*,** in the next lesson.

In reading, predicting and verifying can help you think about what comes next in a story. In math, predicting and verifying can help you try different answers and check if they are correct.

There are 270 yards of fencing around a rectangular play lot. The play lot is twice as long as it is wide. What are the dimensions of the play lot?

Predict	Verify		
Predict the width.	Multiply to find the length.	Find the perimeter. $2\ell + 2w = P$	Compare the perimeter to 270.
100	$100 \times 2 = 200$	$400 + 200 = 600$	too high
50	$50 \times 2 = 100$	$200 + 100 = 300$	too high
40	$40 \times 2 = 80$	$160 + 80 = 240$	too low
45	$45 \times 2 = 90$	$180 + 90 = 270$	correct

Predict a reasonable answer to try out.

To verify your first prediction, use information in the problem and check if it works.

Use the results of your first prediction to revise your prediction. Continue predicting and verifying until you find an answer that works.

1. Why should the first prediction be less than 270 yards?

2. Why was the prediction of 40 yards for the play lot's width too low?

For 3–6, use the problem below and the picture at the right.

Penny paid for a binder with nickels and quarters. She used 3 times as many nickels as quarters. How many of each coin did she use?

3. Make a prediction about the number of quarters.

4. If your prediction was not the correct solution, make a second prediction and check if it works.

5. How many of each coin did Penny use?

6. **Writing in Math** Explain how you can verify your prediction.

For 7–9, use the problem below and the schedule at the right.

Twelve minutes of commercials were aired during the *Law and Liberty* time slot. Each one was half a minute or one minute long. There were 3 more half-minute commercials than one-minute commercials. How many of each type of commercial were aired?

Channel 8 Shows, Tuesday

Southern Dreams 7:00 to 8:00 P.M.

The O'donovans 8:00 to 8:30 P.M.

High-Stake Risks 8:30 to 9:00 P.M.

Law and Liberty 9:00 to 10:00 P.M.

7. Make a prediction about the number of half-minute commercials.

8. How many half-minute commercials and one-minute commercials were aired?

9. **Writing in Math** Do you need to revise your prediction? Explain why or why not.

For 10–12, use the problem below.

Michael Jordan was born 5 years before Sammy Sosa. The sum of their birth years is 3,931. In what year was Sammy Sosa born?

10. Predict when Sammy Sosa was born and verify your prediction.

11. If necessary, make another prediction and verify it.

12. **Writing in Math** When was Sammy Sosa born? Explain how you knew you had solved the problem.

Problem-Solving Strategy

Reading Helps!

Predicting and verifying

can help you with...

the problem-solving strategy, *Try, Check, and Revise.*

Key Idea
The strategy Try, Check, and Revise can help you solve problems.

Try, Check, and Revise

LEARN

How do you try, check, and revise?

Final Exam Kyle needs an average score of 85 (without rounding) on three exams. His scores on the first two exams were 82 and 86. What score must he get on the last exam?

How to Try, Check, and Revise

Step 1: Think to make a reasonable first try.

Step 2: Check using information given in the problem.

Step 3: Revise. Use your first try to make a reasonable second try. Check.

Step 4: Use previous tries to continue trying and checking until you get the answer.

Read and Understand

What do you know?   Kyle needs an average score of 85. He scored 82 and 86 on two of the exams.

What are you trying to find?   Find the score on the last exam that will give him an average greater than or equal to 85.

Plan and Solve

Try 90: $82 + 86 + 90 = 258$, $258 \div 3 = 86$; 90 works. Since any score greater than or equal to 90 works, $s \geq 90$.

Try 85: $82 + 86 + 85 = 253$, $253 \div 3 \approx 84.3$; 84 is too low.

Try 86: $82 + 86 + 86 = 254$, $254 \div 3 \approx 84.7$; This rounds to 85 but Kyle's teacher does not round grades.

Try 87: $82 + 86 + 87 = 255$, $255 \div 3 = 85$; $s \geq 87$.

Answer: A score of 87 or greater on the last exam will give Kyle an average of 85 or greater.

Think It Through
I may need to **predict and verify** the exam score several times before I find the right one.

Look Back and Check

Is your work correct?   Yes. It makes sense that the third score must be greater than 85.

✔ Talk About It

1. After trying 90, how do you know any score greater than 90 works?

2. Why would 84 not be a good first try for solving this problem?

Solve. Write your answer in a complete sentence.

1. Ethan had $10 when he went shopping. He spent $2.85 on a notebook and $1.89 on pens. Assuming there is no sales tax, what can he afford to spend on a novel?

2. Stacey needs at least 8 gallons of punch for the party. She plans to mix 5 gallons of lemonade, 2 quarts of carbonated lemon-lime drink, 1 gallon of lime sherbet, and pineapple juice. How much pineapple juice must she use?

PRACTICE

For more practice, see Set 12-3 on p. 739.

Ⓐ Mixed Strategy Practice

Solve. Write your answer in a complete sentence.

3. Katie has 180 chairs to put in 15 rows. Write and solve an equation to find how many chairs she should put in each row.

4. The sum of the lengths of any two sides of a triangle is greater than the length of the third side. Between what two values is the length of the unknown side in the triangle below?

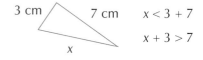

$x < 3 + 7$

$x + 3 > 7$

STRATEGIES

- **Show What You Know**
  Draw a Picture
  Make an Organized List
  Make a Table
  Make a Graph
  Act It Out or Use Objects
- **Look for a Pattern**
- **Try, Check, and Revise**
- **Write an Equation**
- **Use Logical Reasoning**
- **Solve a Simpler Problem**
- **Work Backward**

Choose a tool

Mental Math

5. There are 24 balls in a large bin. Two out of every three are basketballs. The rest are footballs. How many basketballs are in the bin?

6. Find three consecutive even integers whose sum is between 48 and 60.

7. A submarine began maneuvers by diving 75 feet. It then rose 100 feet, dove 125 feet, and rose 80 feet. If the submarine ended up 200 feet below sea level, where did the submarine start maneuvers?

8. **Writing in Math** The length of a rectangular picture frame must be at least 18 inches. The width must be at least 10 inches. You have only 60 inches of wood to use to make the frame. What whole number dimensions are possible for the picture frame? What problem-solving strategy did you use to find the dimensions?

Do You Know How?

Do You Understand?

Graphing Inequalities (12-1)

Name 3 solutions of each inequality. Then graph the inequality on a number line.

1. $x \geq 5$ **2.** $n < 18$

3. $y \leq 30$ **4.** $k > 23$

5. $g < 14$ **6.** $b \geq 32$

7. $n > 40$ **8.** $p \leq 47$

A Tell how you decided whether to use an open or closed circle when you graphed Exercise 1.

B Show that 8 is a solution of $x \geq 2$.

Solving Inequalities (12-2)

Solve each inequality. Graph the solution and check your answer.

9. $x - 7 < 11$ **10.** $y + 9 \geq 38$

11. $4n > 32$ **12.** $\frac{m}{6} \leq 12$

13. $k + 12 \leq 48$ **14.** $10g > 70$

15. $\frac{x}{15} > 5$ **16.** $\frac{n}{7} < 104$

C Describe how you solved the inequalities in Exercises 9 and 12. Tell what properties of inequality you used.

D Explain how to check your solution to Exercise 11.

Problem-Solving Strategy: Try, Check, and Revise (12-3)

Use the strategy Try, Check, and Revise to solve each problem. Write your answer in a complete sentence.

17. Calculator Including tax, Roberto can spend at most $35.45 for a calculator. What prices of calculator can he buy if the sales tax is 5%?

18. Golf Stacey and Leah were practicing their putting at the golf course. Stacey sank 35 putts. Leah said she sank at least $\frac{3}{4}$ as many as Stacey. How many putts could Leah have sunk?

E Tell the steps you used to try, check and revise to solve the Calculator problem.

F Is there only one correct number of putts that Leah could have sunk in the Golf problem? Explain.

MULTIPLE CHOICE

1. Which of the following is NOT a solution of $x \leq 4$? (12-1)

   A. 2   **B.** 3   **C.** 4   **D.** 5

2. Solve $x + 6 > 42$. (12-2)

   A. $x > 7$ **B.** $x > 35$ **C.** $x > 36$ **D.** $x > 48$

> **Think It Through**
> I should **look for key words** like NOT.

FREE RESPONSE

Name three solutions of each inequality and graph the inequality on a number line. (12-1)

3. $m < 9$ 4. $x \geq 5$ 5. $y \leq 24$ 6. $k > 30$

7. $n > 12$ 8. $p \leq 27$ 9. $c < 60$ 10. $b \geq 36$

Solve each inequality. Graph the solution and check your answer. (12-2)

11. $x + 7 \geq 42$ 12. $y - 14 > 39$ 13. $4a < 80$ 14. $\frac{n}{10} \leq 16$

15. $c - 6 < 35$ 16. $k + 19 \leq 46$ 17. $\frac{m}{15} \geq 4$ 18. $6p > 54$

19. Carly is expected to swim at least 15 laps during practice on Monday and Tuesday. She swam 8 laps on Monday. Write and solve an inequality to show how many laps she had to swim on Tuesday. (12-2)

Try, Check, and Revise to solve the problem. Write your answer in a complete sentence. (12-3)

20. **Hats** Trent has $7. He wants to buy a bottle of shampoo and a hat. The shampoo costs $1.87. Sales tax is 5%. Which of the hats at the right can he afford to buy?

$3.99

$4.89

$4.79

Writing in Math

21. In the Hats problem, if you found that Trent could afford the $4.79 hat, did you need to try the $3.99 hat? Explain. (12-3)

22. Explain how to graph $x \geq 2$. Describe how to decide whether to use an open or a closed circle and which direction to draw the arrow. (12-1)

23. Explain the Multiplication Property of Inequality with an example. (12-2)

Problem-Solving Skill

Algebra

Key Idea
Translating words to numerical expressions can help you solve problems.

Translating Words to Expressions

LEARN

How can you write an algebraic expression?

Sometimes, you need to translate phrases into algebraic expressions involving two operations.

Example A

Kayla's overtime hourly wage is $1 more than twice her regular hourly wage.

STEP 1 Use a variable.

Let n represent the amount of Kayla's regular wage.

STEP 2 Show the main idea.

n	n	$1

STEP 3 Write an algebraic expression.

$2n + 1$

Example B

Bryan's hourly wage is $2 less than half his overtime hourly wage.

Use a variable.

Let x represent the amount of Bryan's overtime wage.

Show the main idea.

x
$\frac{1}{2}x$
$2

Write an algebraic expression.

$\frac{1}{2}x - 2$

✔ Talk About It

1. In Example A, how do you know to add 1? To multiply n by 2?

2. In Example B, how do you know to subtract 2? To multiply x by $\frac{1}{2}$?

3. Explain why $\frac{1}{2}x = \frac{x}{2}$.

Write an algebraic expression for each.

1. The number of cars Nick has is 3 less than twice the number of trucks he has.

Let *t* = the number of trucks.

t	t
	3

2. Misty has one more than half as many compact disks as her brother.

Let *c* = the number of compact disks Misty's brother has.

c		
	$\frac{1}{2}c$	1

PRACTICE

For more practice, see Set 12-4 on p. 740.

Write an algebraic expression for each.

3. Mandy ran 2 miles more than two thirds as far as Chrissy ran.

Let *m* = the number of miles Chrissy ran.

4. The total cost to bowl if Chen paid $4.00 a game to bowl, plus $3.50 for shoes.

Let *x* = the number games Chen bowled.

5. 20 more than 4 times a number

6. 2 less than the quotient of a number and 5

7. 7 times a number minus 8

8. 15 less than the product of a number and 2

9. One third the sum of a number and 24 (Hint: Use parentheses.)

10. Eleven increased by 3 times a number

11. One magazine costs $0.30 more than twice as much as another one.

12. One pair of jeans cost $5 less than three times as much as another pair.

13. Suppose Kayla's overtime pay in Example A is $22 an hour. Use the problem-solving strategy Try, Check, and Revise to find Kayla's regular pay. Find a value for *n* so that $2n + 1 = 22$. Give the answer in a complete sentence.

14. Suppose Bryan's regular pay in Example B is $10 an hour. Use Try, Check, and Revise to find Bryan's overtime pay. Find a value for *x* that makes the expression $\frac{1}{2}x - 2$ equal 10. Give the answer in a complete sentence.

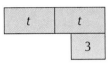

Algebra

Key Idea

You can use inverse operations and properties of equality to solve equations with more than one step.

Vocabulary

• inverse operations (p. 45)
• solve (p. 48)

Think It Through

I can solve two-step equations by **solving simpler problems.**

Solving Two-Step Equations

LEARN

Which is the first operation you undo?

Charles has saved $160 for his trip to Paris. He is leaving in 8 weeks. How much does he need to save each week to have $400 spending money?

Let m represent the money Charles needs to save each week.

Amount Charles can save in 8 weeks   Amount Charles has now   Amount Charles needs

$$8m \quad + \quad 160 \quad = \quad 400$$

When you solve a two-step equation, you should undo operations in the following order:

• First, undo addition or subtraction.

• Then, undo multiplication or division.

Example A

Solve $8m + 160 = 400$.

$$8m + 160 = 400.$$

$$8m + 160 - \mathbf{160} = 400 - \mathbf{160}$$ Undo addition by subtracting 160 from both sides.

$$8m = 240$$ Simplify. Undo multiplication by

$$\frac{8m}{8} = \frac{240}{8}$$ dividing both sides by 8.

Simplify.

$$m = 30$$

The solution is $m = 30$.

Check: $8m + 160 = 400$

$$8(\mathbf{30}) + 160 \overset{?}{=} 400$$

$$240 + 160 \overset{?}{=} 400$$

$$400 = 400 \quad \text{It checks.}$$

Charles needs to save $30 each week.

1. In Example A, which operation do you undo first?

2. After subtracting 160 from both sides, what simpler equation is left?

How can you solve an equation with more than one operation?

Example B

Solve $4x - 5 = 19$.

$$4x - 5 = 19$$

$4x - 5 + 5 = 19 + 5$ Undo subtraction by adding 5 to both sides.

$$4x = 24$$

$\dfrac{4x}{4} = \dfrac{24}{4}$ Undo multiplication by dividing both sides by 4.

$$x = 6 \qquad \text{Simplify.}$$

Check:

$$4x - 5 = 19$$

$$4(6) - 5 \overset{?}{=} 19$$

$$24 - 5 \overset{?}{=} 19$$

$$19 = 19 \qquad \text{It checks.}$$

The solution is $x = 6$.

Example C

Solve $16 = \dfrac{k}{9} + 6$.

$$16 = \dfrac{k}{9} + 6$$

$16 - 6 = \dfrac{k}{9} + 6 - 6$ Undo addition by subtracting 6 from both sides.

$$10 = \dfrac{k}{9}$$

$10 \times 9 = \dfrac{k}{9} \times 9$ Undo division by multiplying both sides by 9.

$$90 = k \qquad \text{Simplify.}$$

Check:

$$16 = \dfrac{k}{9} + 6$$

$$16 \overset{?}{=} \dfrac{90}{9} + 6$$

$$16 \overset{?}{=} 10 + 6$$

$$16 = 16 \qquad \text{It checks.}$$

The solution is $k = 90$.

✔ **Talk About It**

3. In Example B, how do you know to add 5 to both sides of the equation?

Take It to the NET
More Examples
www.scottforesman.com

CHECK ✔

For another example, see Set 12-5 on p. 737.

Solve each equation and check your solution.

1. $3x + 4 = 7$ 2. $2x - 38 = 32$ 3. $5d - 10 = 10$ 4. $\dfrac{n}{5} - 10 = 30$

5. **Reasoning** Use the picture at the right. Find w and check your solution. Tell what you did.

Ⓐ Skills and Understanding

Solve each equation and check your solution.

6. $15t + 15 = 45$　　**7.** $8w - 50 = 6$　　**8.** $\dfrac{x}{6} - 3 = 5$　　**9.** $\dfrac{k}{15} + 1 = 3$

10. $4a - 11 = 5$　　**11.** $7n - 8 = 27$　　**12.** $\dfrac{m}{11} + 8 = 12$　　**13.** $\dfrac{n}{3} - 5 = 7$

14. $11n - 1 = 10$　　**15.** $4h - 11 = 33$　　**16.** $\dfrac{y}{4} + 15 = 18$　　**17.** $\dfrac{x}{7} - 3 = 4$

18. Number Sense Without solving, how can you tell that $x = 8$ is NOT a solution of $2x + 5 = 10$?

Ⓑ Reasoning and Problem Solving

19. Suppose on page 712, Charles has $211 saved seven weeks before his trip to Paris. How much should he save each week to have $400 spending money?

🦉 Math and Art

The ancient Greeks and Romans thought golden rectangles were pleasing to the eye. In a golden rectangle, the ratio of the length to the width is close to 1.62:1.

For 20–22, use the equation to find the length. Then, determine whether or not the rectangle is in the shape of a golden rectangle.

Golden rectangles are often found in classical Greek and Roman art and architecture.

20.

x in.

21 in.

$P = 110$ in.

$2x + 42 = 110$

21.

x cm

55 cm

$P = 466$ cm

$2x + 110 = 466$

22.

x cm

89 cm

$P = 466$ cm

$2x + 178 = 466$

23. <u>**Writing in Math**</u> Is the explanation below correct? If not, tell why and write a correct response.

Solve $2x - 4 = 18$.

$2x - 4 = 18$

$\dfrac{2x}{2} - 4 = \dfrac{18}{2}$

$x - 4 = 9$

$x - 4 + 4 = 9 + 4$

$x = 13$

Think It Through
I need to identify **the steps in the process** of solving two-step equations.

C Extensions

Solve each equation and check your solution.

24. $55 = 15 - 10s$

25. $12 - 2g = 6$

26. $105 - 5t = 5$

27. $-4 = 2 - 9x$

28. $-25n + 7 = 17$

One way to solve $12 - 3x = 27$ is shown below.

$$12 - 3x = 27$$

$$12 + (-3x) = 27 \qquad \text{Rewrite } 12 - 3x \text{ as } 12 + (-3x).$$

$$12 + (-3x) - 12 = 27 - 12 \qquad \text{Subtract 12 from both sides.}$$

$$-3x = 15 \qquad \text{Simplify.}$$

$$\frac{-3x}{-3} = \frac{15}{-3} \qquad \text{Divide both sides by } -3.$$

$$x = -5 \qquad \text{Simplify.}$$

Mixed Review and Test Prep

Take It to the NET
Test Prep
www.scottforesman.com

Write an algebraic expression for each. Let n represent the number.

29. 18 less than twice a number

30. 5 more than a number divided by 8

31. Which best describes a quadrilateral whose sides all have the same length?

    A. trapezoid   **B.** isosceles triangle   **C.** rhombus   **D.** equilateral triangle

Practice Game

Coordinate Tic-1-Toe

Players: 2
Materials: Integer cards −5 to 5 (2 sets)
                Coordinate grid paper, Paper bag

1. After placing all cards in the bag, the first player randomly draws 2 cards.

2. The player uses the integers in either order to form an ordered pair. The player marks this ordered pair on the grid with an X, and returns the cards to the bag.

3. The second player repeats the procedure, marking his/her ordered pair with an O. If the point has already been marked, the player forfeits the turn.

4. The winner is the first player to get 5 Xs or 5 Os in a row, column, or diagonal.

All text pages available online and on CD-ROM.

Algebra

Key Idea

You can use a table to write an equation that represents a pattern of change.

Materials

- light cardboard or construction paper
- scissors

TEST TALK

Think It Through

- I can **use objects** to find the pattern.
- I can **write an equation** to describe the pattern.

Patterns and Equations

WARM UP

Write an equation to describe each function.

1.
x	0	1	2	3
y	10	11	12	13

2.
x	0	1	2	3
y	0	10	20	30

LEARN

Activity

How do you write an equation to describe a pattern?

Garret is designing a walkway using a row of octagonal tiles that measure one foot on each side. He wants to put garden edging around his walkway.

a. Cut out at least 5 octagons. Use these to create a model of Garret's walkway with 4 and 5 tiles. Copy and complete the table below.

Number of octagonal tiles used	1	2	3	4	5
Perimeter of walkway (ft)	8	14	20		
Pattern	2+6	2+6(2)	2+6(3)		

b. Cut out as many octagons as you need to help you extend the table and find a pattern. Write an equation for the perimeter (P) when Garret uses t tiles.

c. Use your equation to find how many feet of garden edging Garret needs to buy if he uses each number of tiles.

$t = 10$ $t = 20$ $t = 25$ $t = 32$

d. Suppose Garret uses square tiles that measure one foot on each side. Copy and complete the table below.

Number of square tiles used	1	2	3	4	5
Perimeter of walkway (ft)	2	6	8		
Pattern	2+2	2+2(2)	2+2(3)		

e. Write an equation to find the perimeter (P), if Garret uses t square tiles. Then, use your equation to find how many feet of garden edging Garret needs to buy if he uses 25 tiles.

Copy and complete each table.

1. $y = 4x + 3$

x	2	3	5	25
y				

2. $y = 8x - 2$

x	2	3	5	25
y				

3. Number Sense In the equation $y = 5x + 1$, by what value will y increase as x increases by 1?

PRACTICE

For more practice, see Set 12-6 on p. 741.

Ⓐ Skills and Understanding

Copy and complete each table.

4. $y = 6x - 2$

x	1	2	5	20
y				

5. $y = \frac{1}{2}x + 3$

x	2	8	10	60
y				

6. Number Sense In the equation $y = 3 - 2x$, by what value will y decrease as x increases by 1?

Ⓑ Reasoning and Problem Solving

7. Rafiq is designing a walkway with a row of regular decagonal tiles that measure one foot on each side. Write an equation for the perimeter (P) when Rafiq uses t tiles. Then, find the amount of garden edging Rafiq needs to use for 20 tiles.

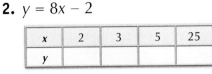

In 8–9, copy and complete the table. Write an equation for the total number of shapes y in the nth figure. Then find the number of shapes in the 20th figure.

8.

x	1	2	3	4
y	3	5		

9.

x	1	2	3	4
y	3	8		

10. Writing in Math Use the table at the right. Explain how to find the x values.

x				
$y = 5x - 4$	1	6	16	31

🦉 Mixed Review and Test Prep

Take It to the NET
www **Test Prep**
www.scottforesman.com

Solve each equation and check your solution.

11. $2x - 38 = 2$ **12.** $5d + 10 = 30$ **13.** $\frac{n}{8} + 3 = 7$ **14.** $\frac{m}{2} - 5 = 3$

15. Estimate the area of a circle when $d = 8$ cm.

    A. 192 cm²   **B.** 48 cm²   **C.** 27 cm²   **D.** 24 cm²

All text pages available online and on CD-ROM.

Algebra

Key Idea
You can use a T-table to graph equations that have two operations.

Vocabulary
• linear equation (p. 448)

Materials
• coordinate grid paper

TICKETS

Think It Through
I can **make an analogy.** Graphing equations with two operations is similar to graphing equations with one operation.

Equations and Graphs

LEARN

Activity

How do you graph an equation with two operations?

a. Copy and complete the T-table below for $y = 2x - 1$.

$y = 2x - 1$

x	y
−1	−3
0	
1	

$y = 2(-1) - 1 = -2 - 1 = -3$

b. Graph each ordered pair from the T-table onto a coordinate plane. Draw a line to connect the points.

c. Is the equation $y = 2x - 1$ a function? Why or why not?

d. Is $y = 2x - 1$ a **linear equation?** Explain.

e. At what point does the line $y = 2x - 1$ cross the y-axis? Is this point a solution of $y = 2x - 1$? Explain.

f. Is $(-2, -6)$ a solution of $y = 2x - 1$? Why or why not?

g. Copy and complete the T-tables for each of the equations below. Then graph each equation.

$y = 3x - 1$ $y = 2x + 3$ $y = 3 - 2x$

x	y
−1	
0	
1	

x	y
−1	
0	
1	

x	y
−1	
0	
1	

$y = \frac{1}{3}x + 2$ $y = 4 - \frac{1}{2}x$ $y = \frac{1}{4}x - 3$

x	y
−3	
0	
3	

x	y
−2	
0	
2	

x	y
−4	
0	
4	

h. Explain why x-values other than −1, 0, 1 were used in some of the T-tables above.

WARM UP
Draw a coordinate plane. Plot and label the points.

1. A (0,2)   2. B (2,5)

3. C (−1,4) 4. D (3,−4)

What can you tell from the graph of an equation?

Kara went to the county fair. Admission was $3. It also cost $0.75 for each ride ticket.

The equation $y = 3 + 0.75x$ gives the total money Kara spent for admission and x tickets.

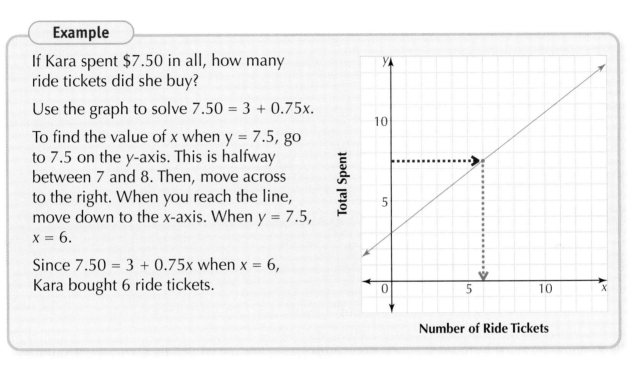

Example

If Kara spent $7.50 in all, how many ride tickets did she buy?

Use the graph to solve $7.50 = 3 + 0.75x$.

To find the value of x when $y = 7.5$, go to 7.5 on the y-axis. This is halfway between 7 and 8. Then, move across to the right. When you reach the line, move down to the x-axis. When $y = 7.5$, $x = 6$.

Since $7.50 = 3 + 0.75x$ when $x = 6$, Kara bought 6 ride tickets.

✔ Talk About It

1. How does the graph of $y = 3 + 0.75x$ show the solution of the equation $7.50 = 3 + 0.75x$?

2. Justin spent $12 in all. Explain how you can use the graph to find how many ride tickets he bought.

CHECK ✔

For another example, see Set 12-7 on p. 738.

For 1–2, make a T-table and graph each equation.

1. $y = 3x + 1$　　　　**2.** $y = \frac{1}{2}x - 1$

For 3–6, use the graph of $y = 0.5x - 1$ at the right to solve each equation.

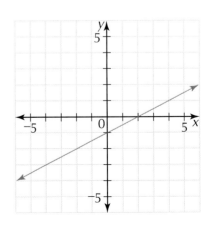

3. $-3 = 0.5x - 1$　　　　**4.** $-2 = 0.5x - 1$

5. $1 = 0.5x - 1$　　　　**6.** $0 = 0.5x - 1$

7. Number Sense Explain how you can tell from the graph at the right that $x = -3$ is not a reasonable solution of $10 = 0.5x - 1$.

Ⓐ Skills and Understanding

For 8–11, make a T-table and graph each equation.

8. $y = 2x - 2$

9. $y = 5 - x$

10. $y = \frac{1}{5}x - 3$

11. $y = 2 + \frac{1}{2}x$

For 12–14, use the graph of $y = 4 - 2x$ at the right to solve each equation.

12. $2 = 4 - 2x$ **13.** $-2 = 4 - 2x$ **14.** $4 = 4 - 2x$

15. Number Sense Explain how you can tell from the graph at the right that the solution of $-3 = 4 - 2x$ is positive.

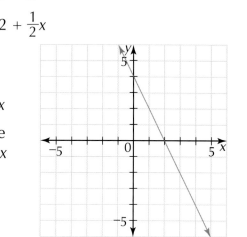

Ⓑ Reasoning and Problem Solving

As an object falls in a vacuum, its speed has a linear relationship with time. If you throw a ball downward with an initial speed of 15 feet per second, you can determine its speed s after t seconds with the equation $s = 15 + 32t$.

For 16–19, use the graph at the right to solve each equation. Then tell how many seconds it takes for the ball to reach the indicated speed.

16. $79 = 15 + 32t$; 79 feet per second

17. $175 = 15 + 32t$; 175 feet per second

18. $47 = 15 + 32t$; 47 feet per second

19. Explain why negative values are not included on the graph of the equation $s = 15 + 32t$.

20. <u>Writing in Math</u> Are the values in the T-table below correct? Explain why or why not.

Make a T-table for $y = 4 - \frac{2}{3}x$.

x	y
0	4
-3	6
3	2
6	0
9	-2

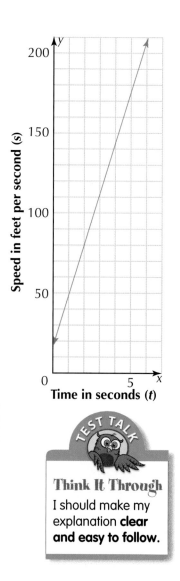

Think It Through
I should make my explanation **clear** and **easy to follow.**

C Extensions

Graph each of the following equations. Then tell whether the value of y increases or decreases as the value of x increases.

21. $y = 2x - 3$　　　**22.** $y = 3 - 2x$　　　**23.** $y = 2 - \frac{1}{4}x$　　　**24.** $y = \frac{1}{4}x - 2$

25. A **coefficient** is a number that multiplies a variable. The coefficient of x in Exercise 21 is 2. Use your graphs of Exercises 21–24 to explain how the coefficient of x affects the value of y.

 **Mixed Review and Test Prep**

 **Take It to the NET**
Test Prep
www.scottforesman.com

26. Copy and complete the table below for $y = 2x - 8$.

x	1	5	6	20
y				

27. Find the area of the parallelogram at the right.

A. 20 m^2　　**B.** 24 m　　**C.** 24 m^2　　**D.** 30 m^2

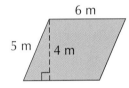

DIscovery CHANNEL SCHOOL　　Discover Math in Your World

Heart Line

There is a linear relationship between heart rate (HR), oxygen consumption, and workload during aerobic exercise. When monitoring exercise intensity, aerobic instructors rely on the following formula:

> Target HR = HR reserve × exercise intensity (%)
> + resting HR.

Using this formula, the target heart rate for a 50-year-old woman, having a heart rate reserve of 90, and resting heart rate of 80, is $y = 90x + 80$. The graph of this equation is at the right.

1. Describe the relationship between exercise intensity and target heart rate.

2. If the woman's target heart rate is 125 bpm, at what exercise intensity is she working?

 **Take It to the NET**
Video and Activities
www.scottforesman.com

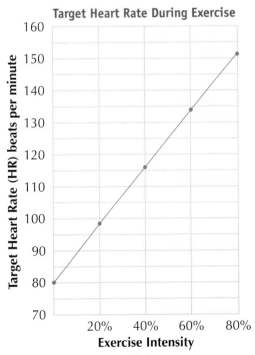

Target Heart Rate During Exercise

Target Heart Rate (HR) beats per minute

Exercise Intensity

Algebra

Key Idea

The metric and standard units for measuring temperature are related.

Vocabulary
• degrees Fahrenheit (°F)
• degrees Celsius (°C)

Temperature

LEARN

How do you convert between Fahrenheit and Celsius temperatures?

A thermometer is used to measure temperature in **degrees Fahrenheit (°F)**, or in **degrees Celsius (°C)**. The thermometer below shows the benchmark temperatures in both the customary and metric scales.

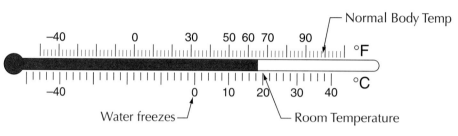

You can use the following two-step equations to convert between Fahrenheit and Celsius temperature scales.

Fahrenheit/Celsius Conversion Formulas	
Celsius (C) to Fahrenheit (F)	Fahrenheit (F) to Celsius (C)
$F = \frac{9}{5}C + 32$	$C = \frac{5}{9}(F - 32)$

Example A

Water in a dishwasher might be 50°C. What is this temperature in degrees Fahrenheit?

Use $F = \frac{9}{5}C + 32$.

$F = \frac{9}{5}(50) + 32$

$F = 90 + 32$

$F = 122$

The temperature is 122°F.

Example B

The temperature on a warm day might be 75°F. What is this temperature in degrees Celsius?

Use $C = \frac{5}{9}(F - 32)$.

$C = \frac{5}{9}(75 - 32)$

$C = \frac{5}{9}(43)$

$C = \frac{215}{9} = 23\frac{8}{9}$

$C \approx 24$

The temperature is about 24°C.

✔ Talk About It

1. The boiling point of water is 100°C. What is this temperature in degrees Fahrenheit?

Find each temperature in degrees Fahrenheit, to the nearest whole degree.

Find each temperature in degrees Celsius, to the nearest whole degree.

1. 70°C   **2.** −2°C   **3.** 180°F   **4.** −5°F

5. Number Sense If it is a very hot day, is the outside temperature 38°F or 38°C?

Ⓐ Skills and Understanding

Find each temperature in degrees Fahrenheit, to the nearest whole degree.

Find each temperature in degrees Celsius, to the nearest whole degree.

6. 55°C   **7.** −4°C   **8.** 18°F   **9.** −9°F

10. Reasoning Which seems like the greater temperature change, 15°C to 30°C or 15°F to 30°F?

Ⓑ Reasoning and Problem Solving

Math and Science

The wind chill temperature is the temperature a person feels because of the wind. For example, when the outside temperature is 5°F and the wind is blowing at a rate of 15 mph, it feels like it is −13°F. Use the table at the right to find the wind chill temperature for each of the following outside temperatures and wind speeds. Then change the wind chill temperatures to degrees Celsius.

Wind Chill Chart						
Wind Speed (mph)	Temperature (°F)					
	20	15	10	5	0	−5
5	13	7	1	−5	−11	−16
10	9	3	−4	−10	−16	−22
15	6	0	−7	−13	−19	−26
20	4	−2	−9	−15	−22	−29
25	3	−4	−11	−17	−24	−31
30	1	−5	−12	−19	−26	−33

11. 15°F, 5 mph   **12.** 0°F, 20 mph

13. 5°F, 15 mph   **14.** −5°F, 10 mph

15. **Writing in Math** Delta says she can estimate a Fahrenheit temperature by doubling the Celsius temperature and then adding 30. Is her method of estimation reasonable? Explain.

Mixed Review and Test Prep

Take It to the NET
Test Prep
www.scottforesman.com

In 16–19, make a T-table. Then graph each equation.

16. $y = 4x + 1$ **17.** $y = \frac{2}{3}x - 4$ **18.** $y = 2 - 3x$ **19.** $y = 1 - \frac{1}{4}x$

20. Which of the following is NOT a solution of $x < 23$?

     A. 23   **B.** 8   **C.** 5   **D.** −24

All text pages available online and on CD-ROM.

DK Problem-Solving Applications

Olympics The ancient Olympics grew from foot races to include other events. Modern Olympics have also evolved with the modification, addition, or elimination of events. For instance, the marathon distance has been increased, table tennis is now included as an event, and the rope climb has been eliminated. What has not changed is the spirit of competition that attracts athletes from all over the world.

Trivia At the 1904 Olympics, George Eyser won 6 medals, including the gold in the parallel bars, vault, and rope climb competitions. He won these medals despite the fact that he had a wooden leg!

1 During the 2000 Olympics, the average high temperature was 25.4°C. The average high temperature during the 1996 Olympics was 89°F. Find the difference between these temperatures in degrees Celsius.

Using Key Facts

2 In the 2000 Olympics, about 37.372 times as many athletes competed as in 1896. How many athletes competed in 2000?

Key Facts
First Modern Olympics

- It was held in Athens in 1896.
- 285 athletes from 13 countries competed.
- 43 events were held in 10 disciplines.

3 In a cycling event, the top finishers had times of 4 minutes 20.893 seconds, and 4 minutes 20.714 seconds. What is the difference between the two times? Write the word name for the difference.

4 The canoeing competition in the 2000 Summer Olympics took place on a 320-meter-long artificial river. How many kilometers long was this river?

⑤ Writing in Math Write your own word problem involving the Olympics. Write the answer in a complete sentence.

Good News/Bad News
The Olympics bring tourists, business and prestige to a city, but they also come at a great cost. It costs billions of dollars to host the games, and profits often are not large enough to pay the costs. The taxpayers usually have had to make up the difference.

⑥ In rhythmic gymnastics, final scores are found using the equation

$$S = \frac{(D + A + E)}{2}.$$

Let S represent the final score,
    D represent the routine-difficulty rating,
    A represent the artistic score, and
    E represent the routine-execution rating.

Find the final score when the difficulty rating is 4.2, artistic score is 3.9, and execution score is 8.3.

⑦ While no runner can maintain exactly the same pace during a race, the distance a sprinter has run during the 100-meter race might be estimated using the equation $D = 11T - 10$, where D represents the number of meters covered, and T represents the number of seconds into the race. Use the formula to find the number of meters remaining after 8 seconds.

⑧ Decision Making Suppose you are the judge for the 100-meter race at a school's Olympics. The top 2 finalists tied in the final race. One top finalist ran the first 3 heats with times of 15.5, 15.5, and 15.7 seconds. The second top finalist ran the first 3 heats with times of 15.2, 16.0, and 15.9 seconds. Who should get the gold medal? Explain.

Do You Know How?

Do You Understand?

Problem-Solving Skill: Translating Words to Expressions (12-4)
Patterns and Equations (12-6)

Write an algebraic expression for each.

1. 8 less than 4 times a number

2. 6 more than the quotient of a number and 5

Copy and complete the table.

3. $y = 3x + 4$

x	1	2	5	30
y				

(A) Draw a picture to show the main idea in Exercise 1.

(B) Explain how you found the pattern in Exercise 3.

Solving Two-Step Equations (12-5)

Solve each equation and check.

4. $5x + 9 = 24$ **5.** $3n - 7 = 11$

6. $\frac{m}{6} - 7 = 2$ **7.** $\frac{a}{4} + 2 = 12$

8. $2y - 15 = 3$ **9.** $\frac{x}{8} + 5 = 11$

(C) Describe how you used inverse operations to solve the equation in Exercise 7.

(D) Explain which operation you did first in Exercise 8.

Equations and Graphs (12-7)

Make a T-table. Then graph the equation.

10. $y = 1 + 5x$ **11.** $y = \frac{1}{3}x - 2$

12. $y = -2x - 2$ **13.** $y = 1 - 3x$

(E) Tell which values of x are easiest to use for Exercise 11.

(F) Explain why $y = 4 - 5x$ is a linear equation.

Temperature (12-8)

Find each temperature in degrees Fahrenheit, to the nearest whole degree.

14. 48°C   **15.** −16°C

Find each temperature in degrees Celsius, to the nearest whole degree.

16. 85°F   **17.** −8°F

(G) Tell how you decided which formula to use in Exercise 14.

(H) Explain why a person could have a body temperature of 38°C, but not 38°F.

Chapter 12 Section B
Diagnostic Checkpoint

MULTIPLE CHOICE

1. Write an algebraic expression for 8 less than 12 times a number. (12-4)

A. $12 - 8n$ **B.** $8n - 12$ **C.** $12n - 8$ **D.** $8 - 12n$

2. Find $-4°C$ in degrees Fahrenheit. (12-8)

A. $21°F$ **B.** $25°F$ **C.** $48°F$ **D.** $70°F$

> **Think It Through**
> I can **eliminate unreasonable answers.** I know $-4°C$ is much colder than $48°F$ or $70°F$.

FREE RESPONSE

For 3–6, solve the equation and check your solution. (12-5)

3. $5t + 6 = 41$ **4.** $4w - 25 = 75$ **5.** $\frac{x}{6} - 7 = 4$ **6.** $\frac{k}{15} + 14 = 16$

For 7–8, copy and complete each table. (12-6)

7. $y = 30 - 4x$

x	1	2	5	20
y				

8. $y = 7x + 2$

x	1	2	6	30
y				

For 9–11, make a T-table. Then graph the equation. (12-7)

9. $y = -3 - 2x$ **10.** $y = \frac{1}{2}x + 3$ **11.** $y = 3 - 3x$

12. Find $-5°C$ in degrees Fahrenheit. (12-8, 12-9)

13. Find $57°F$ in degrees Celsius. (12-8, 12-9)

14. Copy and complete the table at the right. Write an equation for the total number of stars y if x is the figure number. Then, find the number of stars in the 25th figure. (12-6)

x	1	2	3	4
y				

15. Pizza Slices Trevor ate one slice of pizza less than half the slices in the whole pizza. Write an algebraic expression for the number of slices of pizza Trevor ate. Let s represent the number of slices in the pizza. (12-4)

Writing in Math

16. In the Pizza Slices problem, suppose Trevor ate 3 slices of pizza. Tell how you can find how many slices were in the pizza. (12-5)

17. Explain how to use the graph of $y = 3 - 2x$ at the right to solve $-1 = 3 - 2x$. (12-7)

18. To cool a room, would you set the thermostat to $19°F$ or $19°C$? Explain. (12-8)

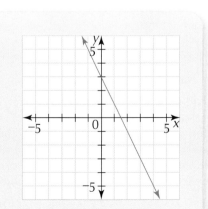

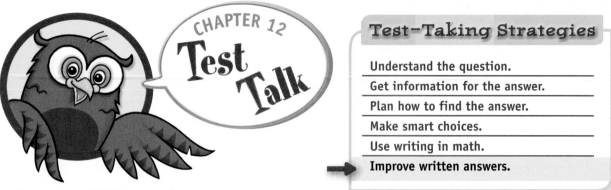

CHAPTER 12
Test Talk

Test-Taking Strategies

| Understand the question. |
| Get information for the answer. |
| Plan how to find the answer. |
| Make smart choices. |
| Use writing in math. |
| **Improve written answers.** |

Improve Written Answers

You can follow the tips below to learn how to improve written answers on a test. It is important to write a clear answer and include only information needed to answer the question.

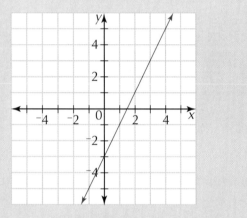

1 The graph of $y = 2x - 3$ is shown on the coordinate plane below.

Is (4, 5) a solution of $y = 2x - 3$? ___

On the lines below, explain how you decided the answer to the question.

_____

Improve Written Answers

• Check if your answer is complete.

*In order to **get as many points as possible,** first I must decide if (4, 5) is a solution of $y = 2x - 3$. Then I must explain how I figured out my answer.*

• Check if your answer makes sense.

*I should be sure that my explanation works for (4, 5). Is my **use of mathematical terms** correct?*

• Check if your explanation is clear and easy to follow.

*I should reread my explanation to be sure it is **accurate and clear.** I shouldn't include any unnecessary information.*

The rubric below is a scoring guide for Test Questions 1 and 2.

Scoring Rubric

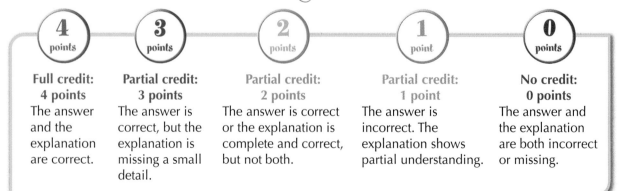

4 points	**3** points	**2** points	**1** point	**0** points
Full credit: 4 points The answer and the explanation are correct.	**Partial credit: 3 points** The answer is correct, but the explanation is missing a small detail.	**Partial credit: 2 points** The answer is correct or the explanation is complete and correct, but not both.	**Partial credit: 1 point** The answer is incorrect. The explanation shows partial understanding.	**No credit: 0 points** The answer and the explanation are both incorrect or missing.

Jeffrey used the scoring rubric on page 728 to score a student's answer to Test Question 1. The student's paper is shown below.

Is (4, 5) a solution to $y = 2x - 3$? __No__

On the lines below, explain how you decided the answer to the question.

The point located by the ordered

pair (4, 5) is not on the line.

_____

Think It Through

The student's answer and explanation are wrong. Maybe he or she plotted the point incorrectly. The point located by (4, 5) is on the line, so (4, 5) is a solution of $y = 2x - 3$. The explanation shows partial understanding, though, because the student seems to know that the point has to be on the line to be a solution. So this student scores 1 point.

Now it's your turn.

Score the student's paper. If it does not get 4 points, rewrite it so that it does.

2. The graph of $y = \frac{1}{2}x + 4$ is shown on the grid below.

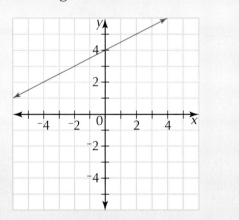

When $x = 2$, what is the value of y? Explain how you found the answer to the question.

When x = 2, y = 5. I could tell from

the graph.

_____

_____

"In-" means not, as in incomplete.

An **inequality** uses >, <, ≥, or ≤ to relate quantities that are not equal. (p. 698)

Graph inequalities and equations. (Lessons 12-1, 12-6, 12-7)

Graph the **inequality** $x \geq 2$.

≥ means **greater than or equal to.**
≤ means **less than or equal to.**

Use a closed circle when graphing sentences that have ≥ and ≤, and use an open circle for those with > and <.

$x \geq 2$

Graph the **linear equation** $y = 2x + 1$.

Make a T-table. Then graph each ordered pair from the T-table. Draw a line to connect the points.

x	y
−2	−3
−1	−1
0	1
1	3

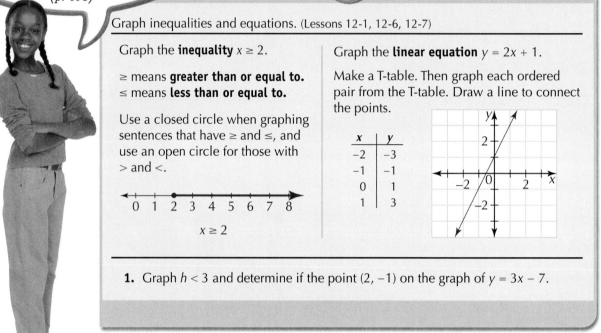

1. Graph $h < 3$ and determine if the point $(2, -1)$ on the graph of $y = 3x - 7$.

Linear equation contains the word "line."

Remember, the graph of a **linear equation** is a straight line. (p. 718)

Solve inequalities and linear equations. (Lessons 12-2, 12-5)

To solve inequalities, use inverse operations and **properties of inequality.**

$9m < 45$

$\dfrac{9m}{9} < \dfrac{45}{9}$ Undo multiplication by dividing.

$m < 5$

To solve equations, use inverse operations and properties of equality.

$9 = \dfrac{k}{2} + 5$

$9 - 5 = \dfrac{k}{2} + 5 - 5$ Undo addition by subtracting.

$4 = \dfrac{k}{2}$

$4(2) = \dfrac{k}{2}(2)$ Undo division by multiplying.

$8 = k$

2. Solve $4y \geq 84$ and $8w + 5 = 61$.

Self Check

Write expressions and convert between Fahrenheit and Celsius. (Lessons 12-4, 12-8)

Write an **algebraic expression.**	Convert temperatures.	

Write an **algebraic expression.**

At noon the **thermometer** showed a temperature 4°F more than half the temperature at midnight.

Let t be the temperature at midnight.

4 more than   half the temperature

$4 + \frac{1}{2}t$

Convert temperatures.

$25°C = \boxed{}°F$

$F = \frac{9}{5}C + 32$

$F = \frac{9}{5}(25) + 32$

$F = 45 + 32$

$F = 77$

$25°C = 77°F$

$12°F = \boxed{}°C$

$C = \frac{5}{9}(F - 32)$

$C = \frac{5}{9}(12 - 32)$

$C = \frac{5}{9}(-20)$

$C \approx -11$

$12°F \approx -11°C$

3. Copy and complete: $84°F = \boxed{}°C$ and $-15°C = \boxed{}°F$

Expressions
x
$4(10 - m)$
$6 + y$
$9a^2$
$2b + 3$

Self Check

Try, check, and revise to solve problems. (Lesson 12-3)

Try and check one answer. Then revise and try again until you solve the problem.

Maya's bowling average for 3 games was 132. She scored 135 and 119 on the first two games. What was her score on the third game?

Try 148: $135 + 119 + 148 = 402$, $402 \div 3 = 134$; too high

Try 140: $135 + 119 + 140 = 394$, $394 \div 3 = 131.\overline{3}$; too low

Try 142: $135 + 119 + 142 = 396$, $396 \div 3 = 132$; correct

Maya's score on the third game was 142.

4. What was Maya's score on the fourth game if her 4-game average was 130?

Answers: 1. [number line from 0 to 5, point at 2] ; yes 2. $y \geq 21$; $w = 7$ 3. about 29°C; 5°F 4. 124

Chapter 12 Vocabulary and Concept Review   **731**

MULTIPLE CHOICE

Choose the correct letter for each answer.

1. Which of the following is NOT a solution of $m \geq 9$?

A. $m = -11$ **C.** $m = 10.5$

B. $m = 9$ **D.** $m = 99$

2. Which inequality is graphed on the number line below?

A. $x \geq 8$ **C.** $x > 8$

B. $x < 8$ **D.** $x \leq 8$

3. Which property of inequality should you use to solve $4c \leq 28$?

A. Addition Property of Inequality

B. Subtraction Property of Inequality

C. Multiplication Property of Inequality

D. Division Property of Inequality

4. What is the solution of the inequality $w - 16 > 14$?

A. $w > 30$ **C.** $w < 30$

B. $w \geq 30$ **D.** $w \leq 30$

5. Let x represent the number of miles Gina ran. Paul ran 3 more than $\frac{1}{2}$ as many miles as Gina. Which expression represents the distance Paul ran?

A. $\frac{1}{2}(x + 3)$

B. $\frac{1}{2}x + 3$

C. $3x + \frac{1}{2}$

D. $2(x + 3)$

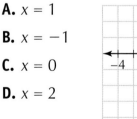

Think It Through

- I need to **translate phrases into algebraic expressions.**
- I will **read each part of the question carefully.**

6. Which tells the correct order of steps to follow to solve the equation $7n + 20 = 41$?

A. Subtract 20 from both sides of the equation. Then multiply both sides by 7.

B. Add 20 to both sides of the equation. Then divide both sides by 7.

C. Divide both sides of the equation by 7. Then subtract 20 from both sides.

D. Subtract 20 from both sides of the equation. Then divide both sides by 7.

7. Which of the following equations does NOT have the solution of $x = 4$?

A. $5x - 12 = 8$ **C.** $\frac{x}{2} + 15 = 17$

B. $\frac{1}{2}x + 2 = 2$ **D.** $2x + 7 = 15$

8. Which of the following is the solution of $7x - 8 = 6$?

A. $x = 0$ **C.** $x = 2$

B. $x = \frac{2}{7}$ **D.** $x = 14$

9. The graph of the equation $y = 4x - 2$ is shown below. Which of the following is the correct solution of $2 = 4x - 2$?

A. $x = 1$

B. $x = -1$

C. $x = 0$

D. $x = 2$

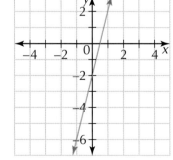

10. Anita wants to set the thermostat in her home at a comfortable room temperature. Which of the following temperatures would she most likely choose?

   A. 20°F   **C.** 53°C

   B. 20°C   **D.** 53°F

11. Chen's canteen has a capacity of 20 ounces. How many 6-ounce paper cups of water can he drink from the canteen? Use the inequality $6w \leq 20$ to solve.

   A. 3 cups   **C.** 6 cups

   B. 5 cups   **D.** 18 cups

12. Find −10°C in degrees Fahrenheit. Use the formula $F = \frac{9}{5}C + 32$.

   A. −10°F   **C.** 14°F

   B. −14°F   **D.** 18°F

FREE RESPONSE

Solve each inequality or equation.

13. $\frac{1}{2}x - 6 = 10$

14. $7x \leq 42$

15. $3x - 12 = 9$

Name three solutions for each inequality, and graph each inequality on a number line.

16. $x > 5$ **17.** $x \leq 11$

18. What inequality is graphed on the number line below?

$$\xleftarrow{\quad} \begin{array}{ccccccccccccc} & & & & & & & & \bullet & & & & \\ -1 & 0 & 1 & 2 & 3 & 4 & 5 & 6 & 7 & 8 & 9 & 10 \end{array} \xrightarrow{\quad}$$

For 19–20, make a T-table. Then graph each equation on a coordinate plane.

19. $y = 3x - 2$ **20.** $y = 2 - \frac{1}{2}x$

21. Use Try, Check, and Revise to solve this problem.

Larry needs an average score of 82 (without rounding) on his three quizzes. His scores on the first two quizzes were 79 and 80. What score must he get on the last quiz?

Writing in Math

22. Write an equation to find the perimeter (P), of a chain of 50 equilateral triangles that are joined side by side. Each side is 1 cm long.

Think It Through
• I can **draw pictures** to show my thinking.
• I will **use math terms** in my explanation.

Copy and complete the table. Use the pattern in the table to help you write the equation.

Number of triangles	1	2	3	4	5	10	50
Perimeter (cm)	3	4	5	6			

23. Explain how you can use inverse operations and the properties of inequality to solve $14w \leq 672$.

24. Explain the steps you would follow to graph the equation $y = 4x - 3$.

Number and Operation

MULTIPLE CHOICE

1. Which of the following numbers represents a value greater than 1?

   A. 10%   **C.** $\frac{2}{3}$

   B. $\frac{3}{2}$ **D.** 0.90

2. Which of the following is NOT represented by the array below?

   A. 6×6

   B. $6 + 6$

   C. $36 \div 6$

   D. 6^2

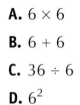

3. Which is the correct order of operations to evaluate the expression $5 + 9 \times \frac{1}{2}$?

   A. Add 5 and 9, then multiply by $\frac{1}{2}$.

   B. Add 5 and 9, then divide by 2.

   C. Multiply 9 by 2, then add 5.

   D. Multiply 9 by $\frac{1}{2}$, then add 5.

FREE RESPONSE

4. Brent purchased a football at a 25%-off sale. The original price was $48.00. What was the sale price of the football?

5. A factory can make 87 yo-yos every 30 minutes. What is a reasonable estimate for the number of yo-yos the factory can make in an 8-hour shift?

Writing in Math

6. Explain how to find the sum $\frac{3}{7} + 1\frac{1}{2}$. Give the sum and tell how you can check your answer.

Geometry and Measurement

MULTIPLE CHOICE

7. Jamal's school photo is 4.5 in. long and 3 in. wide. He ordered an enlargement of the photo, which will double its dimensions. What is the perimeter of the enlarged photo?

   A. 13.5 inches

   B. 15 inches

   C. 30 inches

   D. 54 inches

Think It Through
I can **use estimation** to eliminate wrong answer choices.

8. Find the Fahrenheit equivalent of 50°C.

   A. 10°F   **C.** 122°F

   B. 58°F   **D.** 147.6°F

9. A professional basketball hoop has an 18-inch diameter. What is the area of the hoop? Use $\pi = 3.14$.

   A. 28.26 in^2 **C.** 56.52 in^2

   B. 254.34 in^2 **D.** 1,017.36 in^2

FREE RESPONSE

10. Two angles of a triangle measure 35° and 117°. Find the third angle.

11. A map's scale is 1 cm = 25 mi. On the map, the distance between two cities is 3.5 cm. What is the actual distance between the two cities?

Writing in Math

12. A solid figure has 8 vertices, 12 edges, and 6 faces. What other information would be needed to help you make a definite distinction in classification?

Data Analysis and Probability

MULTIPLE CHOICE

13. From the letters in the bag below, what is the probability that you will pick a vowel?

A. $\frac{2}{9}$ C. $\frac{2}{3}$

B. $\frac{1}{3}$ D. $\frac{4}{9}$

14. If a letter from the bag above is picked and then replaced 30 times, how many times will the letter be a consonant?

A. 5 times   C. 15 times

B. 10 times   D. 20 times

FREE RESPONSE

For 15–17, use the circle graph below.

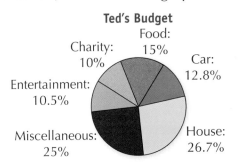

Ted's Budget
Food: 15%
Charity: 10%
Car: 12.8%
Entertainment: 10.5%
Miscellaneous: 25%
House: 26.7%

15. For which two categories combined does Ted spend $\frac{1}{4}$ of his budget?

16. If Ted earns $1,399 a month, about how much does he budget for entertainment each month?

Writing in Math

17. Do you think a circle graph is the best way to display Ted's budget data? Explain.

Algebra

MULTIPLE CHOICE

18. In order to be labeled "low calorie," a food must contain 40 calories or less per serving. If c = the number of calories per serving, which expression represents all foods that can be labeled "low calorie?"

A. $c = 40$ C. $c > 40$

B. $c \geq 40$ D. $c \leq 40$

19. Solve $7n + 6 = 90$.

A. $n = 12$ C. $n = 15$

B. $n = 13$ D. $n = 16$

20. Which of the following is the rule for the function below?

x	-2	-1	0	1	2
y	-5	-2	1	4	7

A. $y = x - 3$ C. $y = x + 1$

B. $y = 3x + 1$ D. $y = 3x - 1$

FREE RESPONSE

21. Write an algebraic expression for "3 less than the quotient of a number and 2."

22. Solve and graph the inequality $\frac{d}{4} \leq 9$. Is 36 a solution of the inequality? is 24? is 41.5?

Writing in Math

23. Graph the equation $y = 4 - 2x$. Explain how you can use your graph to solve the equation $-2 = 4 - 2x$.

Think It Through
- I need to **write my steps in order.**
- I will make my explanation **brief, but complete.**

TEST TALK

Set 12-1 (pages 698–699)

Name three solutions of each inequality. Then graph the inequality on a number line.

$x < 7$ Read as "x is less than 7."

Step 1: Draw an open circle at 7.

Step 2: Locate 3 solutions of $x < 7$ on the number line.

Step 3: Start at the open circle and draw a thick line over the solutions. Draw an arrow in the direction of the inequality.

$$-1\ 0\ 1\ 2\ 3\ 4\ 5\ 6\ 7\ 8\ 9\ 10$$

Remember when an inequality has the symbols ≤ or ≥, draw a closed circle on the number line.

1. $m < 8$

2. $p \geq 10$

3. $t \leq 19$

4. $x > 5$

5. Is $x = 0.5$ a solution of the inequality $x \geq 10$? Explain.

6. The number line below shows the solutions of an inequality. Is -3 a solution? is 10?

$$-1\ 0\ 1\ 2\ 3\ 4\ 5\ 6\ 7\ 8\ 9\ 10$$

Set 12-2 (pages 700–703)

Solve each inequality and check your answer.

$3x \leq 24$ Use inverse operations and properties of inequality.

$3x \leq 24$

$\dfrac{3x}{3} \leq \dfrac{24}{3}$ Undo multiplication by dividing both sides by 3. Simplify.

$x \leq 8$

Test a point on the graph, like $x = 5$.
$3(5) \leq 24$
$15 \leq 24$. The inequality is true, so $x \leq 8$.

Remember that you must add, subtract, multiply, or divide the same number from each side of the inequality to solve.

1. $m - 4 < 10$

2. $2p \geq 16$

3. $\dfrac{t}{3} \leq 5$

4. $x + 7 > 8$

5. Without multiplying, how can you tell that $x = 48$ is NOT a solution of $0.5x > 30$?

Set 12-3 (pages 706–707)

When you Try, Check, and Revise to solve problems, follow these steps.

Step 1: Think to make a reasonable first try.

Step 2: Check using information given in the problem.

Step 3: Revise. Use your first try to make a reasonable second try. Check.

Step 4: Use previous tries to continue trying and checking until you get the answer.

Remember to first decide what you know and what you want to know.

1. Ralph bought baseball cards for $10 each. When the price increased to $17 per card, he sold all of his cards except one. His profit was $46. How many baseball cards did Ralph buy?

2. Carla needs an average score of 75 (without rounding) on 3 tests. Her first 2 scores were 73 and 70. What score must she get on the third test?

Write an algebraic expression for each.

Six more than 3 times a number.

Step 1: Use a variable. Let n represent a number.

Step 2: Show the main idea.

n	n	n	6

Step 3: Write an algebraic expression.
$3n + 6$

Remember to state what your variable represents in each expression.

1. 2 more miles than half the distance Parker jogged

2. 15 more than the quotient of a number and 5

3. 3 less than one-third a number

4. The length of a rectangle is 4 feet more than twice the width. Explain how the expression $6w + 8$ represents the perimeter of that rectangle.

Solve each equation and check your solution.

$\frac{n}{3} + 2 = 6$

$\frac{n}{3} + 2 - 2 = 6 - 2$ Undo addition by subtracting 2 from both sides. Simplify.

$\frac{n}{3} = 4$

$\frac{n}{3} \times 3 = 4 \times 3$ Undo division by multiplying both sides by 3. Simplify.

$n = 12$

Check: $\frac{n}{3} + 2 = 6$

$\frac{12}{3} + 2 \stackrel{?}{=} 6$

$4 + 2 \stackrel{?}{=} 6$

$6 = 6$ It checks.

Remember to solve a two-step equation, undo addition or subtraction first. Then undo multiplication or division.

1. $4x - 8 = 12$ 2. $5p + 4 = 19$

3. $\frac{b}{6} - 10 = 26$ 4. $9 + 2w = 33$

5. $12d + 1 = 97$ 6. $\frac{s}{2} + 15 = 45$

7. Without solving or evaluating the expression $4x + 5$, how can you tell that $x = 2$ is NOT a solution of $4x + 5 = -3$?

Copy and complete the table.

$y = 2x + 1$

x	1	$\frac{5}{2}$	5	16
y	3	6	11	33

$y = 3$, so
$3 = 2x + 1$
$3 - 1 = 2x + 1 - 1$
$2 = 2x$
$1 = x$

For missing x values, substitute the related y-value into the equation and solve for x.

Remember to use substitution to check your solution.

1. $y = 3x - 4$

x				
y	0	11	20	23

2. $y = \frac{x}{2} - 2$

x	18	16	12	2
y				

Chapter 12
Reteaching (continued)

Set 12-7 (pages 718–721)

Make a T-table. Then graph the equation.
$y = 3x - 1$

x	y
-1	-4
0	-1
1	2

Choose 3 values for x. Use them to find the related values of y.

Use each row in the T-table as an ordered pair (x, y). Plot the ordered pairs. Then draw a line to connect the plotted points.

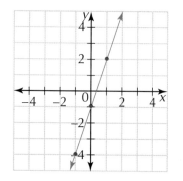

Remember the x-coordinate tells how many units to move left or right, and the y-coordinate tells how many units to move up or down.

1. $y = 2x + 1$ **2.** $y = 1 - 2x$

3. $y = \frac{1}{2}x + 1$ **4.** $y = -3 + 3x$

5. $y = 2 - 4x$ **6.** $y = \frac{3}{4}x - 2$

7. How can you tell from the graph below that the solution of $-8 = -4x - 1$ is positive?

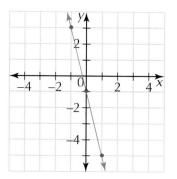

Set 12-8 (pages 722–723)

Find 30°C in degrees Fahrenheit.

Use the equation $F = \frac{9}{5}C + 32$.

$F = \frac{9}{5}(30) + 32$

$F = 54 + 32$

$F = 86$

30°C = 86°F

Find 20°F in degrees Celsius, to the nearest whole degree.

Use the equation $C = \frac{5}{9}(F - 32)$.

$C = \frac{5}{9}(20 - 32)$

$C = \frac{5}{9}(-12)$

$C = -\frac{60}{9} = -6\frac{6}{9} = -6\frac{2}{3}$

$C \approx -7$

20°F ≈ −7°C

Remember to use the correct order of operations when evaluating expressions.

Find each temperature in degrees Fahrenheit, to the nearest whole degree.

1. −4°C   **2.** 25°C   **3.** 0°C

4. 70°C   **5.** 30°C   **6.** −5°C

Find each temperature in degrees Celsius, to the nearest whole degree.

7. 78°F   **8.** 40°F   **9.** −10°F

10. 0°F   **11.** −12°F   **12.** 95°F

13. The Clarks spent the day swimming at the beach. Was the temperature outside 40°F or 40°C? Explain your choice.

Chapter 12
More Practice

Take It to the NET
www **More Practice**
www.scottforesman.com

Set 12-1 (pages 698–699)

Name three solutions to each inequality and graph each inequality
on a number line.

1. $m > 15$ **2.** $x \leq 4$ **3.** $k \geq 76$

4. $b < -7$ **5.** $f > 105$ **6.** $s \leq 3$

7. $y \geq 12$ **8.** $c < 9$ **9.** $n > -1$

10. $p < 20$ **11.** $q > 6$ **12.** $d \leq 13$

13. The graph of an inequality is shown
at the right. Is 5 a solution? is -5?
Explain how you know.

Set 12-2 (pages 700–703)

Solve each inequality. Graph and check the solution.

1. $m + 3 > 7$ **2.** $2x \leq 18$ **3.** $3 + k \geq 12$

4. $9b < 72$ **5.** $\frac{r}{5} \geq 12$ **6.** $6 + s \leq 20$

7. $y - 8 \geq 10$ **8.** $c + 12 < 30$ **9.** $\frac{d}{8} \leq 6$

10. $\frac{p}{7} < 5$ **11.** $4q > 28$ **12.** $12d \leq 60$

13. Without multiplying, how can you tell that $x = 23$ is NOT a solution
of $2x < 23$?

Set 12-3 (pages 706–707)

Try, check, and revise to solve each problem. Write each answer in
a complete sentence.

1. To get an A in math class, Tony needs an average score of at least 90
(without rounding) on three exams. His scores on the first two exams
were 93 and 85. What score must he get on the last exam?

2. Bryce spent $17.53 on pet food for his cats and dogs. The cat food cost
$0.89 per can and the dog food cost $1.19 per can. How many cans of
each type of pet food did he buy?

3. Sarah charges $7 per minivan and $4 per car to wash her neighbors'
vehicles. She earned $41 last weekend. How many vehicles of each
type did she wash?

4. Two trains are 225 miles apart and traveling toward each other
on parallel and adjacent tracks. If the eastbound train averages
50 miles per hour and the west bound train averages 40 miles
per hour, how long will it take before they meet?

Set 12-4 (pages 710–711)

Write an algebraic expression for each.

1. Carla's age if Carla is three years younger than twice Bill's age.

Let b = Bill's age.

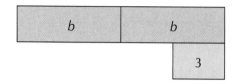

2. The number of hours Andrew worked if Andrew worked two more than half as many hours as Tim worked.

Let t = the hours Tim worked.

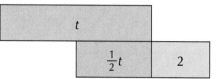

3. The total cost to ice skate if Ricky paid $3.00 an hour for rink time, plus $4.50 to rent skates. Let h = the number of rink time hours.

4. The distance Dawn lives from school if Dawn lives $1\frac{1}{2}$ miles closer to her school than her teacher does. Let m = the number of miles Dawn's teacher lives from school.

5. 15 more than 3 times a number

6. 9 less than half a number

7. three more than the quotient of a number and 12

8. 10 less than the product of a number and 2

Write an expression for each situation.

9. Juan bought supplies for his new gecko. He bought four plants for p dollars each. He also bought a 10-gallon tank for $10 and a water dish for $3.

10. Jaleesa bought juice for $3.25 and some fruit for $5.25. She also bought five beach passes for x dollars each.

Set 12-5 (pages 712–715)

Solve each equation and check your solution.

1. $4x + 2 = 10$

2. $2c - 15 = 20$

3. $\frac{n}{7} + 3 = 9$

4. $7t + 7 = 21$

5. $8n - 5 = 27$

6. $12 + 3q = 30$

7. $\frac{v}{4} - 2 = 6$

8. $11p + 9 = 53$

9. $\frac{s}{5} + 15 = 18$

10. $20 + 9b = 38$

11. $\frac{t}{8} - 7 = 1$

12. $6y - 2 = 46$

13. $\frac{x}{3} + 2 = 0$

14. $-35 = 4h + 1$

15. $-75 - k = -95$

16. $4 - \frac{y}{3} = -17$

17. $\frac{-d}{7} + 14 = 0$

18. $9 - 3p = -27$

19. $4a - 1 = 27$

20. $\frac{b}{6} + 3 = 6$

21. $12y + -6 = 138$

22. Use the picture at the right to find w and check your solution. Explain what you did.

Take It to the NET
More Practice
www.scottforesman.com

Set 12-6 (pages 716–717)

Copy and complete each table.

1. $y = 2x + 1$

x	1	2	3	8
y	3			

2. $y = 9x + 3$

x	0	$\frac{1}{3}$	$\frac{2}{3}$	1
y				

3. $y = 4x - 5$

x	1	3	5	13
y				

4. $y = 7x - 10$

x				
y	4	11	18	25

5. Without finding a pattern, explain how you can tell that the missing value for the function at the right is NOT −3.

x	1	2	3	4
y	−3	−1	1	

Set 12-7 (pages 718–721)

Make a T-table and graph each equation.

1. $y = 2x - 5$ **2.** $y = \frac{1}{2}x + 1$ **3.** $y = 7 - 3x$ **4.** $y = -1x + 2$

5. $y = \frac{1}{3}x - 3$ **6.** $y = 8 - x$ **7.** $y = 4 - \frac{2}{5}x$ **8.** $y = 3x - 4$

Use the graph of $y = 3 - 2x$ at the right to solve each equation.

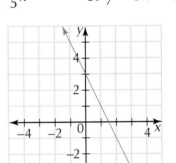

9. $5 = 3 - 2x$ **10.** $3 = 3 - 2x$

11. $-1 = 3 - 2x$ **12.** $1 = 3 - 2x$

13. How can you tell from the graph at the right that the solution of $-3 = 3 - 2x$ is positive?

Set 12-8 (pages 722–723)

Find each temperature in degrees Fahrenheit, to the nearest whole degree.

1. 20°C   **2.** 105°C   **3.** −10°C   **4.** 60°C

5. 100°C   **6.** −1°C   **7.** 5°C   **8.** 21°C

Find each temperature in degrees Celsius, to the nearest whole degree.

9. 14°F   **10.** 11°F   **11.** −22°F   **12.** 86°F

13. 100°F   **14.** 50°F   **15.** 79°F   **16.** −15°F

17. The lake water is frozen today. Is the outside temperature 20°F or 20°C? Explain.

A

absolute value The distance that a number is from zero on the number line. (p. 408)

acute angle An angle with a measure between 0° and 90°. (p. 477)

acute triangle A triangle with three acute angles. (p. 497)

adjacent angles A pair of angles with a common vertex and a common side but no common interior points. (p. 480)
Example:

angle Two rays with the same endpoint. (p. 476)

angle bisector A ray that divides an angle into two adjacent angles that are congruent. (p. 485)

arc A part of a circle connecting two points on the circle. (p. 484) *Example:*

area The number of unit squares of the same size needed to cover a region. (p. 568)

associative properties Properties that state the way in which addends or factors are grouped does not affect the sum or product. (p. 28)

axis (pl. axes) Either of two lines drawn perpendicular to each other in a graph. (p. 636)

B

base (in geometry) A designated side of a polygon to which the height is drawn perpendicular (p. 572); one of the two parallel and congruent faces on a prism (p. 586); a particular flat surface of a solid, such as a cylinder or cone. (p. 586)

base (in numeration) A number multiplied by itself the number of times shown by an exponent. (p. 8) *Example:* $4 \times 4 \times 4 = 4^3$, where 4 is the base.

benchmark fraction Common fractions used for estimating, such as $\frac{1}{4}, \frac{1}{3}, \frac{1}{2}, \frac{2}{3}$, and $\frac{3}{4}$. (p. 170)

biased sample A sample which is not representative of the population from which it is drawn. (p. 621)

break apart Using the Distributive Property to compute mentally. (p. 30)

C

capacity The amount a container can hold. (p. 543)

Celsius (°C) A metric unit for measuring temperature. (p. 722)

center The interior point from which all points of a circle are equally distant. (p. 502)

centi- Prefix meaning $\frac{1}{100}$. (p. 546)

central angle An angle with its vertex at the center of a circle. (p. 502)
Example:

certain event An event that is sure to occur and has a probability of 1. (p. 662)

chord A line segment with both endpoints on a circle. (p. 502)

circle A closed plane figure with all points the same distance from a given point called the center. (p. 502)

circle graph A graph that represents a total divided into parts. (p. 642)

circumference The distance around a circle. (p. 576)

clustering An estimation method where numbers that are approximately equal are treated as if they were equal. (p. 16) *Example:* 26 + 24 + 23 is about 25 + 25 + 25, or 3 × 25.

combination Each possible arrangement of the outcomes of an event where order is not important. (p. 659)

common denominator A denominator that is the same in two or more fractions. (p. 204)

common factor A factor that is the same for two or more numbers. (p. 150)

common multiple A multiple that is the same for two or more numbers. (p. 152)

commutative properties The properties that state the order of the addends or factors does not affect the sum or product. (p. 28)

compatible numbers Numbers that are easy to compute mentally. (p. 18)

compensation Choosing numbers close to the numbers in a problem, and then adjusting the answer to compensate for the numbers chosen. (p. 33)

complementary angles Two angles with measures that add up to 90°. (p. 480)

composite number A natural number greater than 2 that has more than two factors. (p. 147)

compound event A combination of two or more single events. (p. 655)

cone A three-dimensional figure that has one circular base. The points on this circle are joined to one point outside the base, sometimes called the vertex. (p. 586) *Example:*

congruent Having the same size and shape. (p. 472)

construction A geometric drawing that uses a limited set of tools, usually a compass and a straightedge. (p. 484)

coordinate plane A two-dimensional system in which a location is described by its distances from two perpendicular number lines called the *x*-axis and the *y*-axis. (p. 440)

Counting Principle If one choice can be made in *m* ways and a second choice can be made in *n* ways, then the two choices can be made together in *m* × *n* ways. (p. 655)

cross products The product of the first term of the first ratio and the second term of the second ratio, and the product of the second term of the first ratio and the first term of the second ratio. (p. 316)

cubed A number that is multiplied by itself three times. (p. 9) *Example:* 2 cubed = 2^3 = 8

cubic unit A unit measuring volume, consisting of a cube with edges one unit long. (p. 594)

cylinder A three-dimensional figure that has two circular bases which are parallel and congruent. (p. 586) *Example:*

D

data Information that is gathered. (p. 620)

decagon A polygon with ten sides. (p. 494)

decimal A number with one or more numbers to the right of the decimal point. (p. 76)

degree (°) A unit for measuring angles. (p. 476)

denominator The number below the fraction bar in a fraction; the total number of equal parts in all. (p. 160)

dependent events Events for which the outcome of one affects the probability of the other. (p. 672)

diagonal A line segment that connects two vertices of a polygon and is not a side. (p. 494) *Example:*

diameter A line segment that passes through the center of a circle and has both endpoints on the circle. (p. 502) *Example:*

discount The amount by which the regular price of an item is reduced. (p. 380)

disjoint Two or more events with no outcomes in common. (p. 669)

Distributive Property Multiplying a sum by a number produces the same result as multiplying each addend by the number and adding the products. (p. 30)
Example: 2 × (3 + 4) = (2 × 3) + (2 × 4)

dividend The number being divided by another number. (pp. 95,100) *Example:* In 12 ÷ 3, 12 is the dividend.

divisible A number is divisible by another number if its quotient is a whole number and the remainder is zero. (p. 142)

divisor The number used to divide another number. (pp. 100, 142) *Example:* In 12 ÷ 3, 3 is the divisor.

dodecagon A polygon with 12 sides. (p. 494)

double-bar graph A graph that uses pairs of bars to compare information. (p. 636)

double-line graph A graph that uses pairs of lines to compare information. (p. 638)

E

edge The line segment where two faces of a polyhedron meet. (p. 586)

elapsed time Total amount of time that passes from the beginning time to the ending time. (p. 555)

equal additions Adding the same number to two numbers in a subtraction problem does not affect the difference. (p. 33)

equation A mathematical sentence stating that two expressions are equal. (p. 44)

equilateral triangle A triangle with three sides of the same length. (p. 497)

equivalent fractions Fractions that name the same amount. (p. 164)

estimate To find a number that is close to an exact answer. (p. 16)

evaluate To find the number that an algebraic expression names by replacing a variable with a given number. (p. 41) *Example:* Evaluate $2n + 5$ when $n = 3$; $2(3) + 5 = 11$.

event An outcome or set of outcomes of an experiment or situation. (p. 655)

expanded form A number written as the sum of the place values of its digits. (p. 5)

expanded form using exponents A number written in expanded form with the place values written in exponential form. (p. 9) *Example:* $3,246 = (3 \times 10^3) + (2 \times 10^2) + (4 \times 10^1) + (6 \times 10^0)$

experimental probability A probability based on the statistical results of an experiment. (p. 664)

exponent The number that tells how many times the base is being multiplied by itself. (p. 8) *Example:* $8^3 = 8 \times 8 \times 8$, where 3 is the exponent and 8 is the base.

exponential form A way of writing repeated multiplication of a number using exponents. (p. 8) *Example:* 2^5.

expression A mathematical phrase containing variables, constants, and operation symbols. (p. 40) *Example:* $12 - x$.

F

face A flat surface of a polyhedron. (p. 586)

factor A number that divides another number without a remainder. (p. 142)

Fahrenheit (°F) A standard unit for measuring temperature. (p. 722)

flip (reflection) A mirror image of a figure. (p. 510)

formula A rule that uses symbols to relate two or more quantities. (p. 328)

fraction A number that can be used to describe a part of a whole, a part of a set, a location on a number line, or a division of whole numbers. (p. 160)

frequency table A table to organize data by showing the number of values that fall in particular groups. (p. 628)

front-end estimation A method of estimation using the first digits of each addend that have the same place value. (p. 16)

front-end estimation with adjusting A method of front-end estimation that adjusts the result based on the remaining digits of each addend. (p. 16)

function A relation in which each *x*-value is paired with exactly one *y*-value. (p. 444)

G

glide reflection Moving a figure by a slide (translation) followed by a flip (reflection). (p. 510)

gram (g) Metric unit of mass. (p. 546)

greatest common factor (GCF) The largest number that is a factor of two or more numbers. (p. 150)

H

height The segment from a vertex perpendicular to the line containing the opposite side (p. 572); the perpendicular distance between the bases of a solid. (p. 595)

heptagon A polygon with seven sides. (p. 494)

hexagon A polygon with six sides. (p. 494)

I

identity properties The properties that state the sum of any number and zero is that number and the product of any number and one is that number. (p. 28)

impossible event An event that will never occur and has a probability of 0. (p. 662)

improper fraction A fraction in which the numerator is greater than or equal to its denominator. (p. 168)

independent events Events for which the outcome of one does not affect the probability of the other. (p. 672)

inequality A statement that uses the symbols > (greater than), < (less than), ≥ (greater than or equal to), or ≤ (less than or equal to) to compare two expressions. (p. 698)

integers The set of positive whole numbers, their opposites, and zero. (p. 408)

interest A charge for the use of money, paid by the borrower to the lender. (p. 386)

intersecting lines Lines that have exactly one point in common. (p. 473)
Example:

interval Sets of numbers with the same range to represent data. (p. 628)

inverse operations Operations that "undo" each other, such as addition and subtraction, or multiplication and division (except multiplication by 0). (p. 45)

isosceles triangle A triangle with at least two congruent sides. (p. 497)

kilo- Prefix meaning 1,000. (p. 546)

L

least common denominator (LCD) The least common multiple of the denominators of two or more fractions. (p. 164)
Example: 12 is the LCD of $\frac{1}{4}$ and $\frac{1}{6}$.

least common multiple (LCM) The smallest number, other than zero, that is a multiple of two or more numbers. (p. 152)

like denominators Denominators in two or more fractions that are the same. (p. 204)

line A straight path of points that goes on forever in two directions. (p. 472)

line graph A graph used to show changes over a period of time. (p. 638)

line plot A plot that shows the shape of a data set by stacking Xs above each value or interval on a number line. (p. 628)

line segment Part of a line that has two endpoints. (p. 472)

line of symmetry A line on which a figure can be folded into two congruent parts. (p. 514)

linear equation An equation whose graph is a straight line. (p. 448)

liter (L) Metric unit of capacity. (p. 546)

M

mass Measure of the amount of matter in an object. (p. 546)

maximum (in a data set) The greatest value in a set of numbers. (p. 624)

mean The sum of the values in a data set divided by the number of values. (p. 624)

median The middle value when a set of numbers is listed from least to greatest. (p. 624)

meter (m) Metric unit of length. (p. 546)

metric system (of measurement) A system using decimals and powers of 10 to measure length, mass, and capacity. (p. 546)

midpoint The point that divides the segment into two segments of equal length. (p. 472)

milli- Prefix meaning $\frac{1}{1,000}$. (p. 546)

minimum (in a data set) The least value in a set of numbers. (p. 624)

mixed number A number that combines a whole number and a fraction. (p. 168)

mode The number or numbers that occur most often in a set of data. (p. 624)

multiple The product of a number and a whole number greater than zero. (p. 142)

Multiplication Property of Zero Property that states the product of any number and zero is zero. (p. 28)

multiplicative inverse (reciprocal) Two numbers whose product is one. (p. 267) *Example:* The multiplicative inverse of $\frac{3}{4}$ is $\frac{4}{3}$ because $\frac{3}{4} \times \frac{4}{3} = 1$.

mutually exclusive Events that cannot occur at the same time. (p. 669)

negative power of ten A number in exponential form where the base is ten and the exponent is a negative integer. (p. 106)

net A plane figure pattern, which when folded, makes a solid. (p. 587)

nonagon A polygon with nine sides. (p. 494)

numerator The number above the fraction bar in a fraction; the number of objects or equal parts being considered. (p. 160)

O

obtuse angle An angle with a measure between 90° and 180°. (p. 477)

obtuse triangle A triangle with an obtuse angle. (p. 497)

octagon A polygon with eight sides. (p. 494)

opposite The integer on the opposite side of zero from a given number, but at the same distance from zero. (p. 408) *Example:* 7 and −7 are opposites.

order of operations A set of rules mathematicians use to determine the order in which operations are performed. (p. 24)

ordered pair A pair of numbers (x,y) used to locate a point on a coordinate plane. (p. 440)

origin The point (0,0), where the x- and y-axes of a coordinate plane intersect. (p. 440)

outcome The result in a probability experiment. (p. 655)

outlier A number very different from the other numbers in a data set. (p. 629)

P

parallel lines Lines in the same plane that do not intersect. (p. 473)

parallelogram A quadrilateral with both pairs of opposite sides parallel. (p. 500)

pentagon A polygon with five sides. (p. 494)

percent A ratio where the first term is compared to 100. (p. 354)

perimeter Distance around a figure. (p. 564)

permutation An arrangement of a group of things in a particular order. (p. 659)

perpendicular bisector A line, ray, or segment that intersects a segment at its midpoint and is perpendicular to it. (p. 484)
Example:

perpendicular lines Intersecting lines that form right angles. (p. 473)

pi (π) The ratio of the circumference of a circle to its diameter. Pi is approximately 3.14 or $\frac{22}{7}$. (p. 576)

plane A flat surface that extends forever in all directions. (p. 472)

point An exact location in space. (p. 472)

polygon A closed plane figure made up of three or more line segments. (p. 494)

polyhedron A three-dimensional figure made of flat surfaces that are polygons. (p. 586)

population The entire group of people or things that are being analyzed. (p. 620)

power The number of times a number is multiplied by itself. (p. 8)

prime factorization The set of primes whose product is a given composite. (p. 147) *Example:* $60 = 2^2 \times 3 \times 5$

prime number A whole number greater than 1 with exactly two whole positive factors, 1 and itself. (p. 147)

principal An amount of money borrowed or loaned. (p. 386)

prism A polyhedron with two congruent and parallel polygon-shaped faces. (p. 586)
Examples:

probability A ratio of the number of ways an event can happen to the total number of possible outcomes. (p. 662)

proper fraction A fraction less than 1; its numerator is less than its denominator. (p. 168)

properties of equality Properties that state performing the same operation to both sides of an equation keeps the equation balanced. (p. 44)

properties of inequality Properties that state adding or subtracting the same quantity or multiplying or dividing by the same positive quantity does not change the inequality. (p. 700)

proportion A statement that two ratios are equal. (p. 316)

pyramid A polyhedron whose base can be any polygon and whose faces are triangles. (p. 586)
Examples:

Q

quadrant One of the four regions into which the x- and y-axes divide the coordinate plane. The axes are not parts of the quadrant. (p. 440)

quadrilateral A polygon with four sides. (p. 494)

quotient The answer in a division problem. (p. 100) *Example:* In 45 ÷ 9 = 5, 5 is the quotient.

R

radius Any line segment that connects the center of the circle to a point on the circle. (p. 502)
Example:

random sampling Means of providing a representative sample, where each member of the population has an equal chance of being chosen. (p. 621)

range The difference between the greatest and least numbers in a set of data. (pp. 18, 624)

rate A ratio that compares two quantities with different units of measure. (p. 306)

ratio A pair of numbers that shows a comparison of two quantities and can be written as 9:4, $\frac{9}{4}$, or 9 to 4. (p. 300)

rational number Any number that can be written as a quotient $\frac{a}{b}$, where a and b are integers and $b \neq 0$. (p. 412)

ray Part of a line with one endpoint, extending forever in only one direction. (p. 472)

reciprocal Two numbers whose product is one. (p. 267) *Example:* The reciprocal of $\frac{3}{4}$ is $\frac{4}{3}$ because $\frac{3}{4} \times \frac{4}{3} = 1$.

rectangle A parallelogram with four right angles. (p. 500)

reflection (flip) The mirror image of a figure about a line of symmetry. (p. 510)

reflection symmetry Property of a figure that can be reflected onto itself. (p. 514)

regular polygon A polygon that has sides of equal length and angles of equal measure. (p. 494)

relation A set of ordered pairs (x,y). (p. 444)

repeating decimal A decimal in which a digit or digits repeat endlessly. (p. 173)

representative sample A sample which is representative of the population from which it is drawn. (p. 621)

rhombus A parallelogram with all four sides the same length. (p. 500)

right angle An angle which measures 90°. (p. 477)

right triangle A triangle with one right angle. (p. 497)

rotational symmetry Property of a figure that rotates onto itself in less than a full turn. (p. 514)

round To give an approximation for a number to the nearest one, ten, hundred, thousand, and so on. (p. 14)

S

sample Part of the population upon which an experiment or survey is conducted. (p. 620)

sample space The set of all possible outcomes of an experiment. (p. 655)

scale The ratio of the measurements in a drawing to the actual measurements of the object. (p. 330)

scale drawing A drawing made so that distances in the drawing are proportional to actual distances. (p. 330)

scalene triangle A triangle with no congruent sides. (p. 497)

scientific notation A number expressed as a product of a number greater than or equal to 1, but less than 10 and a power of 10. (p. 110) *Example:* $350 = 3.50 \times 10^2$

sector A region bounded by two radii and an arc. (p. 502) *Example:*

semicircle An arc that connects the endpoints of a diameter. (p. 502)

side A segment used to form a polygon (p. 494); a ray used to form an angle. (p. 476)

similar figures Figures that have the same shape, but not necessarily the same size. (p. 506)

simple interest Interest paid only on the principal, found by taking the product of the principal, rate, and time. (p. 386)

simplest form A fraction for which the greatest common factor of the numerator and denominator is 1; also, *lowest terms.* (p. 165)

skew lines Lines that lie in different planes that do not intersect and are not parallel. (p. 473)

slide (translation) The image of a figure that has been moved to a new position without flipping (reflecting) or turning (rotating). (p. 510)

sphere A three-dimensional figure such that every point is the same distance from the center. (p. 586) *Example:*

square A rectangle with all sides congruent. (p. 500)

squared A number that is multiplied by itself two times. (p. 9) *Example:* 5 squared = $5^2 = 25$.

statistics Numerical data that have been collected and analyzed. (p. 621)

stem-and-leaf plot A frequency distribution that arranges data in order of place value. The leaves are the last digits of the numbers; the stems are the digits to the left of the leaves. (p. 632)

straight angle An angle which measures 180°. (p. 477)

supplementary angles Two angles with measures that add up to 180°. (p. 480)

surface area (SA) The sum of the areas of each face of a polyhedron. (p. 590)

survey Method to collect data from a sample to study some characteristic of the group. (p. 620)

T

T-table A table of *x*- and *y*-values used to graph an equation. (p. 448)

terminating decimal A decimal with a finite number of digits. (p. 173)
Example: 0.375

tessellation A pattern of congruent shapes covering a surface without gaps or overlaps. (p. 516)

theoretical probability Ratio of the favorable outcomes to the possible outcomes of an event. (p. 664)

translation (slide) The image of a figure that has been moved to a new position without flipping (reflecting) or turning (rotating). (p. 510)

trapezoid A quadrilateral with only one pair of opposite sides parallel. (p. 500)

tree diagram A diagram used to organize all the possible outcomes in a sample space. (p. 654)

trend A clear direction in a line graph suggesting how the data will behave in the future. (p. 638)

trial One of the instances of an experiment. (p. 664)

triangle A polygon with three sides. (p. 494)

turn (rotation) A transformation that turns a figure around a given point. (p. 510)

U

unit rate A rate in which the second number in the comparison is one unit. (p. 306)
Example: 25 feet per second

unlike denominators Denominators in two or more fractions that are different. (p. 206)

V

variable A quantity that can change or vary, often represented with a letter. (p. 40)

vertex (in an angle) The common endpoint of two rays that form an angle. (p. 476)

vertex (in a polygon) The point of intersection of two sides of a polygon. (p. 495)

vertex (in a polyhedron) The point of intersection of the edges of a polyhedron. (p. 586)

vertical angles A pair of angles formed by intersecting lines, the angles have no side in common. Vertical angles are congruent. (p. 480)
Example:

volume The number of cubic units that fit inside a space figure. (p. 594)

X

x-axis The horizontal line on a coordinate plane. (p. 440)

x-coordinate The first number in an ordered pair that tells the position left or right of the *y*-axis. (p. 440)

Y

y-axis The vertical line on a coordinate plane. (p. 440)

y-coordinate The second number in an ordered pair that tells the position above or below the *x*-axis. (p. 440)

Measures–Customary

Length
1 foot (ft) = 12 inches (in.)
1 yard (yd) = 36 inches
1 yard = 3 feet
1 mile (mi) = 5,280 feet
1 mile = 1,760 yards

Weight
1 pound (lb) = 16 ounces (oz)
1 ton (T) = 2,000 pounds

Capacity
1 cup (c) = 8 fluid ounces (fl oz)
1 pint (pt) = 2 cups
1 quart (qt) = 2 pints
1 gallon (gal) = 4 quarts

Area

1 square foot (ft^2) = 144 square inches (in.^{2})
1 square yard (yd^2) = 9 square feet

1 acre = 43,560 square feet
1 square mile (mi^2) = 640 acres

Measures–Metric

Length
1 millimeter (mm) = 0.001 meter (m)
1 centimeter (cm) = 0.01 meter
1 kilometer (km) = 1,000 meters

Mass/Weight
1 milligram (mg) = 0.001 gram (g)
1 centigram (cg) = 0.01 gram
1 kilogram (kg) = 1,000 grams
1 metric ton (t) = 1,000 kilograms

Capacity
1 milliliter (mL) = 0.001 liter (L)
1 centiliter (cL) = 0.01 liter
1 kiloliter (kL) = 1,000 liters

Area

1 square centimeter (cm^2) = 100 square millimeters (mm^2)
1 square meter (m^2) = 10,000 square centimeters

1 hectare (ha) = 10,000 square meters
1 square kilometer (km^2) = 1,000,000 square meters

Measures–Customary and Metric Unit Equivalents

Length
1 in. = 2.54 cm
1 m ≈ 39.37 in.
1 m ≈ 1.09 yd
1 mi ≈ 1.61 km

Weight and Mass
1 oz ≈ 28.35 g
1 kg ≈ 2.2 lb
1 metric ton (t) ≈ 1.102 tons (T)

Capacity
1 L ≈ 1.06 qt
1 gal ≈ 3.79 L

Symbols

=	is equal to
≠	is not equal to
>	is greater than
<	is less than
≥	is greater than or equal to
≤	is less than or equal to
≈	is approximately equal to
≅	is congruent to
~	is similar to
%	percent

π	pi (approximately 3.14)
°	degree
°C	degree Celsius
°F	degree Fahrenheit
$\overleftrightarrow{AB}$	line AB
$\overline{AB}$	line segment AB
$\overrightarrow{AB}$	ray AB
∠ABC	angle ABC
△ABC	triangle ABC

∥	is parallel to
2:5	ratio of 2 to 5
10^2	ten to the second power
+4	positive 4
−4	negative 4
(3, 4)	ordered pair 3, 4
$P(E)$	probability of event E
⊥	is perpendicular to

Formulas

$P = 2\ell + 2w$	Perimeter of a rectangle
$A = \ell \times w$	Area of a rectangle
$A = b \times h$	Area of a parallelogram
$A = \frac{1}{2} \times b \times h$	Area of a triangle

$C = \pi \times d$	Circumference of a circle
$A = \pi \times r^2$	Area of a circle
$V = \ell \times w \times h$	Volume of a rectangular prism
$I = p \times r \times t$	Simple interest